A Biographical Index to

California & Western Artists

A handbook providing reference to over 50 books
and exhibition catalogs as biographical sources

Edward L. Korb

Old Master Gallery Press
LAWNDALE CALIFORNIA

I have known the author for a number of years, as an art collector, customer, and friend. Through the years, I have watched
him accumulate a wealth of biographical reference material for
his personal pocket-sized handbook. He has summarized many of
the major reference books, along with many rare books, and major
exhibitions of California and Western artists from the turn-of-
the-century. I, along with other friends, have urged him to al-
low publication of his handbook as a convenience to those in-
terested in California and Western art. When he finally agreed,
I decided to undertake publishing myself.

This biographical index is designed as a true pocket handbook;
to be at hand at all times for the collector and dealer. It
answers your first question, "Is the artist listed?", and tells
you what references to go to for further data.

Norman Davies
Old Master Gallery
15438 Hawthorne Blvd.
Lawndale, CA 90260

FOREWORD

This handbook is very simple in concept. Through listing the
artists included in over 50 biographical directories or sig-
nicicant exhibitions, it provides means for you to answer the
questions, "Is the artist listed?" and "Where can I go to find
biographical or other data on the artist?". It was initiated as
a pocket abstract of my library, with the major emphasis being
on the California and Western artists before 1960. As the Publisher stated in his preface, I was persuaded to have this
published as an aid to other collectors. Hopefully, it will
simplify the location of biographical data, provide a road map
to some of the more important publications, and generally spur
interest in the area of art that I so admire.

When I started collecting, I encountered many difficulties
in researching artists. Many of the basic reference books
were out-of-print and only available in libraries, and some
could be found only in a few specialized art libraries. Also
not one of the books was all-inclusive. They either covered
a restricted time period, a restricted location (such as Laguna Beach or Southern California), or often both. For the
reseacher to gather a reasonable perspective, the use of many
publications was required.

Because of this situation, I started assembling data on the
location of artist's biographies into a pocket handbook that
I could have with me on visits to flea markets, antique shops,
and galleries. This permitted me to establish swiftly where
I could find biographical data on a particuliar artist, and
whether he had shown in major exhibitions. In effect, I had
developed a biographical index of California and Western artists, but by book, rather than in a single matrixed alphabetical list. Although it takes longer to research an artist
in my format, one can usually develop more references than
in the more conventional index, and can more easily establish
the nature of a particuliar exhibition, for instance, through
a scan of the artists included. I hope to be able, when time
permits, to develop an unified alphabetical index.

You will find much valuable data herein. The Panama-Pacific
International Exposition of 1915 in San Francisco featured an
outstanding exhibition of California art, but the specifics
can only be found in some rare books which can only be located in
specialized art libraries. The Cowboy in Art, while not quite
as rare, is difficult to purchase and can only be found in
larger libraries. Many of the exhibition catalogs can only be
found on collectors' shelves or in the good art libraries.

In addition to the California and Western listings, I have
included a USA category. First, within that category we
have two very significant national _elective_ art organizations; the National Academy of Design (NAD) and the American Watercolor Society (AWS). Checking these lists will
establish whether your artists have achieved that degree
of national recognition.

Frequently in my search for new art, I would encounter
paintings of obvious quality, but painted too recently to
expect the artist to be included in some of the general
purpose reference books. For this reason I added the USA
Modern category.

Inclusion of an artist on any of these lists does not de-
fine a painting's value. The real value of a piece of art
is determined by demand. And demand can only be demonstra-
ted through sales or auction records. Mayer, Sotheby, Phillips, and Leonard are some of the compilers of current auction prices. You will find these volumes in university and
the larger city libraries.

Please remember that this handbook was designed for personal, not consumer, use. By printing directly from my
hand-typed orginals, the Publisher can offer the handbook for much less than if it were typeset. But this
means more errors because I'm far from an accomplished
typist. I have corrected all that I could find. I apo-
logize for those I missed.

In assembling my pocket guide, I was primarily concerned
with developing a list of the included artists. Infre-
quently, I found ready-made lists that I could use intact.
More often, I was forced to laboriously assemble and type
the list of names. Often I tried to provide additional
data such as writeup length for Moure's _Dictionary_. Where
possible, I combined the data from several publications as
in _Artists USA_.

In using this handbook, one should attempt to locate the
publications referred to in the libraries available to
you. You might also want to purchase a biographical index
with international coverage such as Havlice or Mallett.
With the index and handbook in the field, and the other
publications located, you should be able to operate ef-
fectively. As to sources, I have found the Pasadena, Long
Beach, and Los Angeles central libraries to be excellent.
The university libraries are also good; I've used CSU Fullerton, and Claremont. But the best source is the special
art library, such as those at UCLA and the LA County Museum
of Art. I've been told that both the main city libraries
and the museum libraries of Oakland and San Francisco have
excellent art references, as do UC Berkley and Davis.

Edward L. Korb

DEDICATION

I dedicate this book to my understanding wife, Patricia, who
graciously allows me to decorate the walls of our home----
while retaining, in exchange, exclusive rights as to what
goes on the floors and ceilings.

ACKNOWLEDGMENTS

I should like to acknowledge my considerable debt to Nancy
Dustin Wall Moure for assembling the Southern California,
Artist Exhibition in 1979 which initially sparked my interest, for developing the basic reference books necessary
to the collection of the traditional Southern California
art, and especially for her personal help in locating many
of the rare reference works included herein.

I should also like to express special thanks to:
  - Dr. J. A Baird, assembler of the Baird Archive at UC,
    Davis and a major force in Northern California art cir-
    cles as an art educator, historian, collector, and moti-
    vator, for his kind encouragement and suggestions.
  - Dr. Russell Ludwick, collector and rescuer of lost art,
    for sharing his knowledge, enthusiasm, and pleasant com-
    panionship on our art forays.
  - DeWitt McCall, for gently nurturing my interest in Cali-
    fornia art, and for sharing his knowledge.
  - Ken Roberts and Norman Davies, for their counsel and for
    allowing the use of hard-to-locate books from their libra-
    ries.

Table of Contents Including type document and location

B= BOOK, C= EXHIBITION CATALOG, L= LIST/INDEX, &O= OTHER

Tab/Title	B	C	L	O	Page No.	Buy	Local Lib.	Main Lib.	Art Lib.
SF Hospital Medical Collection'77			X		87				X
Calif. Painters/Sculptors-Modern		X			88			X	X
A Century of Calif. Painting '70		X			89			X	X
Baird Archive of Calif. Art. '79				X	90		(index only		X
Sacramento Valley Landscapes 1979		X			100				X
Impressionism Calif. 1890-1930		X			100		X	X	X
Plein Air Painters of Calif. 1982	X				101	X	X	X	X
Virginia Steele Scott Coll. 1980		X			101			X	X
WESTERN - SAMUELS									
Artists of the American West	X				103	X	X	X	X
WESTERN - DAWDY									
Artists of the American West V.1	X				113	X	X	X	X
Artists of the American West V.2	X				121	X	X	X	X
WESTERN - OTHER									
Western Americana, Harmsen	X				129	X	X	X	X
American Western Art, Harmsen	X				129	X	X	X	X
The West Remembered		X			130			X	X
Cumulative Index, Southwest Art			X		131		X	X	X
The Cowboy in Art, Ed Ainsworth	X				136		X	X	X
The West as Art		X			139			X	X
Artists of the Canyons & Caminos	X				140	X	X	X	X
Fifty Great Western Illustrators	X				141	X	X	X	X
Woman Artist in the Amer. West		X			141			X	X
7th Ann. Exhib. Cowboy Artists		X			141			X	X
USA - NAD									
National Academy Membership			X		143			X	X
USA - AWS									
Amer. Watercolor Soc. Membership			X		149			X	X
USA - OTHER									
Prize-Winning Painters 1960-1967	X-7 volumes				157				X
Artists/USA 1970-1975	X-3 volumes				162			X	X
Dictionary of Contemporary American Artists-Cummings	X				168	X	X	X	X

Principal REFERENCE BOOKS

TITLE	VOLS.	AUTHOR	PUBLISHER	DESCRIPTION
BIOGRAPHICAL INDICIES				Direct reader to the principal sources of biographical data.
Index to Artistic Biography	2+1 vol. supp.	Patrice Havlice	Scarecrow Press	Guide to 64 Biographical Directories. Covers USA and principal int'l. artists.
Mallett's Index of Artists	1+1v. supp.	Daniel T. Mallett	R. R. Bowker Co. orginal; Peter Smith reprint.	Includes 27,000 artists. Refers to 24 main reference books and 957 catalogs/monographs.
A Biographical Index of American Artists	1	Ralph C. Smith	Williams & Wilkens org.; Gale Research for reprint.	Covers 4700 artists and refers to 42 books & catalogs.
BIOGRAPHICAL DIRECTORIES -CALIF				Provides biographical data on artists.
Dictionary of Art & Artists in So. Calif. Before 1930	1 ⬢	Nancy Dustin Wall Moure	Dustin Publications	Contains biographic data culled from many sources. Extensive research of local media.
Plein Air Painters of Calif.- The Southland	1' ⬢	Ruth Lilly Westphal	Westphal Publishing	In depth coverage of 30 top painters from LA, SD, & Laguna Bch. --biography & paintings
OTHER CALIFORNIA				
The Calif. Watercolor Society, Prize Winners 1931-1954	1 ⬢	Nancy Dustin Wall Moure	Dustin Publications	Lists all exhibitors by year w/picture title + all prize winners.
Artist Clubs & Exhibitions in So. Calif. Before 1930	1 ⬢	Nancy Dustin Wall Moure	Dustin Publications	Lists all exhibitors by show, year, and picture title + all prize winners.
California Artists, 1935-1956	1 ⬢	Dewitt Clinton McCall	DeRu's Fine Art Books	Covers California artists listed in Who's Who in American Art Vols. 1-6. Provides dates & specialities.
BIOGRAPHICAL DIRECTORIES WESTERN				Provides biographical data on artists.
Artists of the American West	1 ⬢	Peggy & Harold Samuels	Doubleday	Well researched biographical data inc. work sample, signature location, & sometimes price data.

TITLE	VOLS.	AUTHOR	PUBLISHER	DESCRIPTION
<u>Artists of the American West</u>	1v + 1v Supp. ⬡	Doris Ostrander Dawdy	Sage Books Chicago	Volume 1 provides biographical data on 1350 artists born before 1900. Vol. 2 inc. additional & new names.
<u>The Cowboy in Art</u>	1 ⬤	Ed Ainsworth	World Publishing	Covers over 400 artists. Includes biographical data, artist picture, & sample of art.
<u>BIOGRAPHICAL DIRECTORIES - USA</u>				
<u>Who's Who in American Art</u>	About 15	Edited by Jaques Cattell Press	Bowker Company	Published since 1936 at 2-4 year intervals. Contains biographical data on over 6000 artists per issue. Lists awards & exhibitions
<u>Dictionary of American Painters Sculptors & Engravers.</u>	1	Mantle Fielding	2 versions in updated form. Modern Books & Crafts, & Jas. F. Carr	Contains biographical data on Amer. **artists active prior** to 1900.
<u>A Dictionary of Contemporary American Artists</u> (Many editions & sizes)	1 ⬡	Paul Cummings	St. Martin's Press	Biographical data on the modern(concept, not age) artists. Covers about 900 artists.
<u>BIOGRAPHICAL DIRECTORIES - WORLD</u>				
<u>Dictionaire critique et documentaire des peintres sculpteurs, dessinateurs, et graveurs.</u>	10	Edited by Libräirie Gründ E. Bénézit originator	Libräirie Gründ	Biographical data on 300,000 world artists. Gives location of works, and sometimes, price.
<u>Allgemeines Lexikon der bildenden Künstler von der Antike bis zur Gegenwart.</u>	37	Thieme, Ulrich & Becker, Felix	Reprint by F. Allmann, Leipzig	The most complete & scholarly of the biographical directories. Covers 19th Century & before artists
<u>Allgemeines Lexikon der bildenden Künstler des XX. Jahrhunderts.</u>	6	Hans Vollmer	E. A. Seemann	Supplement to the Thieme-Becker volumes. Covers the 20th Century artists.

CALIFORNIA - MOURE

Nancy Moure is, without question, the pre-
eminent authority on our Southern California art heritage (in more modern terms,
"Guru" would be a more apt title). She has
led the revival of interest by providing
both the tools and inspiration. Her four
books have become the basic reference books
of the field. Her three major shows have
created the excitement and set the stan-
dards.

Three of the Moure books (the 4th is a bib-
liographic reference) and her three major
exhibitions are included in this section.
Her Dictionary, containing approximately
3000 artists, comes first and includes an
indication of writeup size. Her two books
on art club exhibitions have been combined
onto one list. This is followed by a combined listing of the 1979 Laguna Beach and
the 1980 LACMA exhibitions. Finally we
have a listing of those included in her
Drawing and Illustration show, which also
includes those discussed in the show catalog.

Southern California Artists—Before 1930

= tenths of a full column devoted to the artist's write-up

A

Abascal, Mary	1
Abbott, Jacob B.	3
Abbott, Marguerite E.	2
Abel, Christine Jeanette	2
Abelmann, August	2
Abelmann, Kate	2
Abels, E. A.	1
Acker, Herbert Van B.	4
Adams, J.	1
Adams, Burres Dorothy	1
Adams, Charles Partridge	4
Adams, Edward A.	1
Adams, Frances E.	1
Adams, Lulu J.	1
Adams, Marian	2
Adams, Velma	2
Af Ekenstam, Marta	2
Ahlroth, Arthur	1
Ainslie, Frank	2
Ainsworth, Kathryn C.	1
Akins, Rheta M.	1
Alburtus, John	1
Aldeman, Josephine	1
Alderson, E. M. Mrs.	1
Aldrich, Clarence N.	1
Aldrin, Andrew Gustave	4
Alexander, Georgia E.	1
Alexander, H. R. Mrs.	1
Alexander, Ruth	2
Alexander, Sara Dora B.	2
Allen, George E.	2
Allen, Gregory Seymour	2
Allen, Mary Coleman	4
Allen, Richard H.	1
Allen, Winthrop	1
Allers, Gladys	1
Alliott, Hector	6
Allis, Harry C.	4
Allison, J. S.	1
Allison, L. C. Mrs.	1
Allman, Richard	1
Alter, Harry R.	1
Althouse, Lillian	1
Alvarez, Mabel (Armen)	6
Aly, Marie A.	1
Ames, Arthur	1
Ames, Edwin I.	2
Ames, Florence	1
Amlauer, Herman	3
Anderson, Anthony	6
Anderson, Dorothy Visju	3
Anderson, Ida May	1
Anderson, Milo L.	1
Anderson, Paul	1
Andres, Adela	1
Andrews, Charles J.	1
Anhorn, E.	2
Annis, Verle L.	1
Anthony, Lucile L.	1
Apache, Antonio	3
Archer, J. Miss	1
Arklin, Haig	2
Armstrong, Adelaide D.	1
Armstrong, Edna L.	1
Armstrong, Samuel	1
Arnold, B. C.	1
Arnold, Edwin C.	2
Arthurs, G. W.	1
Artique, Pierre	1

Asanger, Jacob	2
Ashbrook, R. M.	1
Ashley, Hammond	1
Ashmead, Margaret	2
Askenazy, Maurice	3
Atkinson, William O.	1
Atwood, Mary Hall	2
Aulmann, Theodora	2
Austin, Charles Percy	10
Austin, Erma Fisk	2
Avery, Kenneth	1
Ayers, Martha Oathout	3

B

Babcock, Ida Dobson	2
Bachman, P. J.	1
Backus, E. M. Elizabeth	2
Bacon, Aroline E.	1
Baden, Frank	1
Badger, Stanwood	1
Baer, Burt	1
Baer, C. A.	1
Bagdatopoulos, William S.	5
Bagnel, E. W.	1
Baguez, Salvadore	1
Bailey, Bernice M.	1
Bailey, Mrs. Chapman	2
Bailey, Harry Lewis	4
Bailey, Henry Lewis	1
Bailey, Laura Miller	1
Baines, S. C.	1
Baird, M. A. Mrs.	1
Baker, F. A.	1
Baker, Jean Jessie	3
Baker, Leonard E.	1
Baker, Minnie	1
Baker-Smith, Francis	1
Baldaugh, Anni Westrum	2
Baldwin, Clifford P.	1
Baldwin, Clayton M.	1
Baldwin, E. C.	1
Baldwin, H. P.	1
Balfour, Helen	5
Ball, Ruth Norton	2
Ballagh, Blanche M.	1
Ballbusch, Peter	1
Ballin, Hugo	9
Balobopre, Alfred	2
Bancroft, Ashley L.	2
Barber, A. V.	2
Barbier, Maurice	1
Barclay, H. A. Lily A.	1
Barcony, Leopold	3
Barienbrock, Fred C.	1
Baright, S. W. Mrs	1
Barker, Edna C.	1
Barker, George Jr.	3
Barker, Olive	1
Barkley, R. H.	1
Barndollar, H.	1
Barney, Alice Pike	7
Barney, Ester Stevens	1
Barry, John Joseph	3
Barry, William J.	2
Barrymore, Lionel	3
Bartholowsky, John V.	1
Bartlett, Dana	15
Barton, Loren Babcock	18
Baskerville, Elizabeth	3
Bassett, Truman	1

Batchelder, Ernest A.	6
Bates, Lorita Frances	1
Batz, Jose D.	2
Baughman, D. A.	1
Bauman, E. F.	1
Baxter, Martha Wheeler	5
Beaumont, Arthur	6
Beckman, Jessie Mary	4
Bedford, G.	1
Behne, Z. Miss	1
Behre, Frederick John	2
Bemus, Mary B.	2
Benjamin, Charles Henry	3
Benjamin, Fannie	1
Benke, A. A.	1
Bennett, Flora B.	1
Bennett, Ruth Manerva	3
Bensinger, Anna M.	2
Benton, Arthur Burnett	3
Bergesen, O. W.	2
Berlin, Ben F.	3
Berra, Romero	1
Berra, Robert T.	2
Bessinger, Frederick Herb.	2
Bethell, Worden	2
Billings, Lucy	2
Bingley, R. C.	1
Bintliff, Martha B.	2
Biorci, A.	1
Birch, Geraldine	3
Bird, Bessie	1
Bisant, L. M. Miss	2
Bischoff, Franz A.	11
Bishop, Helene	2
Bissiri, Adriano	2
Bissiri, Augusto	3
Bixby, David W.	1
Bixby, E. Miss	1
Bjurman, Andrew	3
Black, Agnes	1
Black, Mae	1
Black, Mary, C. W.	2
Blackburn, Mary	1
Blackman, C. B. Mrs.	1
Blackman, Vance	1
Blackton, J. Stuart	2
Blair, Lee	1
Blaize, Lewis Elbert	2
Blake, Althea Arlen	1
Blanchard, Francis	1
Blanchard, Frederick W.	4
Blanchard, H. S.	1
Blanchard, Porter	3
Blanchard, Richard	1
Blank, Pauline	1
Blethen, Grace	3
Blodgett, A. E. Miss	1
Bloser, Florence Parker	3
Blue, Benjamin	10
Blum, Helen	3
Blumue, Edna	1
Bodero, James S.	1
Bogert, A. S. Mrs.	1
Bohan, E. B. Mrs.	1
Bohnen, Aloys	2
Boldsen, Thyra	1
Bolles, Ira Randell	2
Bolton, Molly	1
Bonar, Lester M.	1

Bond, Ella Tyler	1
Bond, Gertrude	1
Bond, J. Dalton Mrs	3
Bond, Mary E.	1
Bone, J. D.	1
Bone, K. D.	1
Bonnet, Leon Durand	3
Boney, Ena Westcott	1
Bonnot, Lola B.	1
Booth, James Scripps	3
Borein, John Edward	8
Boovier, Essie M.	1
Borg, Carl Oscar	27
Borglum, Elizabeth Collins	7
Borglum, John Gutzon	6
Borman, Leonard	3
Borough, Randal William	3
Borsa, P. V.	1
Boswell, Norman Gould	1
Bosworth, Hobart vZandt	5
Bothwell, Dorr Hodgson	1
Botke, Cornelis	5
Botke, Jessie Arms	8
Bourdieu, Aimee F.	1
Bowen, Irene	2
Bowles, Caroline Hutchin.	4
Boyd, Everett	2
Braasch, Minna	1
Brackenridge, Marian	1
Braden, Coral A.	1
Bradfield, C. P. Mrs.	3
Bradley, Elliott	1
Bradley, Lucy H.	1
Bradley, M. W. Mrs.	1
Bradshaw, Beatrice P.	1
Bradshaw, N. Mrs.	2
Braggins, Alma J. I.	1
Brainard, Grace M.	1
Brammer, William G.	1
Brandon, H. C.	2
Brandon, John A.	1
Brandriff, George Kennedy	8
Brasz, Arnold Franz	2
Braun, Maurice	14
Breckenfield, Bertha A.	1
Breuer, Henry Joseph	4
Brewer, Ethel V.	1
Brewster, Eugene V.	1
Brice, Catherine	1
Bridge, J. Dwight	3
Brigante, Nick	4
Brodbeck, J. Miss	1
Bromley, L. R.	1
Brooks, Anna P.	1
Brooks, Gertrude F.	1
Brooks, Mildred Bryant	1
Brooks, Walter	1
Brothers, Hal J.	1
Brotze, Edward F.	3
Brougier, Adolph M.	2
Brougier, Rudolph, W.	2
Brower, George	1
Brown, Austin Cullen	1
Brown, Benjamin Chambers	23
Brown, Dayton	1
Brown, Fannie E.	1
Brown, Grace Marion	3
Brown, Howell C.	5
Brown, John Wallace	1
Brown, Lucille Rosemary	3
Brown, Margaret	1
Brown, Nina	1
Brown, Van Dyke	2
Brown, William J.	2
Brown, Willie Elice	1
Browne, Belmore	1
Browne, Carl Albert	3
Browne, Estella Mary	1
Browne, Frederick L.	1
Bruce, Fannie B.	2
Bruce, H. M. Miss	1
Bruer, H. A.	1
Brunner, E. Lucille	2
Bryan, Catherine	1
Bryant, Alice D.	2
Bryant, Everett L.	1
Bryson, Hope Mcereau	2
Buchanan, Albyn	1
Buchanan, D. R.	1
Buchanan, Ella	5
Buchanan, Luvena	1
Buckley, Dorothy E.	1
Budlong, L. A.	1
Buff, Conrad II	15
Bulmer, Evelyn	1
Bunting, Lily M.	1
Burbank, Elbridge Ayer	13
Burdick, Ruth	1
Burgher, Jessie R.	1
Burgher, Juana	1
Burk, William E.	1
Burke, Howard	1
Burkland, August P.	3
Burn, W. L.	1
Burnham, J. Paul	2
Burnham, Roger Noble	5
Burns, F. E.	1
Burns, M. J.	2
Burns, M. S. Mrs.	2
Burrell, Lou	3
Burton, Elizabeth Eaton	5
Bush, Charles H.	1
Bush, Ella Shepard	5
Bush, Gladys Lewis	1
Butler, Anna May	1
Butler, Edward Burgess	4
Butler, H. B.	1
Butler, Howard Russell	3
Byrne, Jno. J.	2

C

Cadorin, Ettore	6
Cahill, Arthur James	4
Cahill, Katherine K.	2
Cahill, William Vincent	7
Calder, Alexander Stirl.	13
Calder, Nanette	4
Caldwell, Eleanor B.	1
Caldwell, Vernon	1
Califano,	1
Call, Mary E.	2
Cam, Billy	1
Cambensy, Ant.	1
Campbell, Byram C.	1
Campbell, Isabelle Frowe	3
Campbell, William S.	2
Cane, Arthur	1
Cannom(n), Alzada K.	2
Cannon, Henry W.	4
Cannon, Lawrence H.	2
Canright, Bess Hadden	1
Cantello, Frank	2
Cantello, Joseph	2
Cantu, Federico	5
Canright, B. Hadden	1
Cappel	2
Carbines, Jean	1
Carew, Berta	2
Carey, Helen V.	1
Carl, James	3
Carlin, Mary	1
Carling, Rose S.	1
Carlisle, Dacotah	1
Carlisle, Mary Helen	4
Carpenter, Dudley	1
Carpenter, George Mulford	3
Carpenter, L. R.	1
Carpenter, Lewis	1
Carpenter, Robert B.	1
Carr, Lulu	1
Carre, Ben	1
Carson, Gladys M.	2
Carson, Roth Butts	1
Carter, Gorden Knowles	3
Carter, Justice	1
Carter, Pruette	5
Cartmel, Daniel	1
Carvalho, Solomon Nune	3
Carveny, Gladys Hadley	1
Casey, Katherine M.	2
Cashman, Rhea	1
Caskey, Mary K.	1
Casoli, Constance E.	1
Cassell, Helen Lewis	2
Cassidy, Dorothea L.	1
Cassidy, Ira D. Gerald	8
Cassidy, Mary Daniels	1
Castruccio, Romilda	1
Cavanaugh, L. E. Mrs.	1
Chabot, John T.	1
Chaffin, George Duclos	3
Chalker, Dorothy	1
Chalmers, Helen August	2
Chamberlain, Katherine P.	2
Chamberlain, Mellin	1
Chamberlain, Norman S.	4
Chamberlin, Adelaide	2
Chamberlin, Frank Tolles	7
Chamberlin, Mary Potteng.	1
Chambers, Josephine	1
Champ, Alfred	2
Champlin, Ada Belle	3
Chandler, Helen Clark	4
Chang, Wah Ming	1
Chapella, Edward P	2
Chapin, William Emerson	5
Chaplin, Prescott	3
Chapman, Abby W.	1
Charle, J.	1
Charles, Shirley N.	1
Chase, Ada M.	1
Chase, Anna Webber	2
Cheever, Walter L.	4
Cheney, Russell	4
Chess, Edna Anita	3
Chisholm, Stuart	1
Choate, Christian	1

Name	No.
Chopin, Oscar Charles	1
Chouinard, Nelbert Murph.	3
Christie, Mary	1
Chubb, E. R. Mrs.	1
Cicero, Antonino	1
Clampitt, Barbara Hallan	2
Clark, Alson Skinner	15
Clark(e), Emilia Gold.	3
Clark, Frances	2
Clark, Hattie Mrs	1
Clark, J. G. Mrs.	1
Clark, Mabel B. Smith	3
Clark, Marian Hughes	1
Clark, Seldon	1
Clarke, Harrison	1
Classen, Otto A.	1
Clawson, John Willard	7
Clay, W. P.	1
Claysen, Eddie	1
Clayton, Gladys Sherwood	1
Cleaver, Lorita Bates	1
Cleaves, Gail	1
Clements, Grace	2
Clements, Judith M.	1
Clements, Lydia	1
Clendenin, Flora	2
Clendenin, Louis K.	1
Clewett, Ruth	1
Cliff, Doris	1
Cloud, Teresa	3
Clovell, Johanna	1
Clunie, Robert	3
Clyne, Evelyn	2
Coan, Helen B.	5
Coast, Oscar Regan	3
Coblentz, George W.	2
Coburn, Frank	3
Cochrane, N. W.	1
Cody, D. E.	1
Coffing, Le Clair	1
Coffman, Harold	3
Cole, Addie L.	1
Cole, Blanche Dugan	3
Cole, E. Miss	1
Cole, George Townsend	5
Cole, Helen	1
Cole, William Henry	3
Coleman, George Sumner	1
Coleman, Harvey B.	2
Coleman, Mary Dartes	1
Coler, Bertha T.	1
Coles, Wilson	1
Colgrove, J.	1
Collin, Martin	1
Colyer, Vincent	2
Colman, Roi Clarkson	7
Colman, Samuel	2
Colyer, Clifford C.	1
Comfort, Tyrone	1
Comings, E. S.	1
Comins, Eben F.	3
Compera, Alexis	4
Comstock, John	1
Concannon, Winifred B.	1
Conchman, Victoria Mrs.	1
Condit, J. L.	1
Condra, Catherine L.	1
Cone, Blanche Murdock	1
Conger, Nann	1
Conlan, J. Harry	1
Conner, Albert Clinton	4
Conner, John Anthony	1
Conner, Paul	2
Conner, Rose	1
Conner, Tanner	1
Connor, Clinton B.	1
Connor, Isabel	1
Cook, Alma May	1
Cook, Edna Rogerson	1
Cook, Estelle	2
Cook, George	1
Cook, George L.	1
Cook, Katherine L.	1
Cook-Smith, Jean Beman	2
Cooke, Dorothea	3
Cooke, Edwin	2
Cooke, Helen	1
Coolidge, John Earle	6
Cooper, Colin Campbell	8
Cooper, Maggie	1
Cooper, Mario Ruben	3
Cooper, Virginia S.	2
Coover, Nell	2
Corbaley, R. L.	2
Corbit, George C.	1
Cordrey, Earl S.	3
Cordy, N.	1
Cornejo, Francisco	8
Cornelius, Mildred	1
Cornell, A. D.	1
Cornell, Albert	1
Cornwell, Dean	9
Corrieri, Ferdinand	2
Corrin, Phillip	1
Corsi, Antonio	8
Cortright, C. M.	1
Corwin, Margaret	1
Cosgrove, Jack	1
Costello, Valentine J.	3
Cotton, John Wesley	9
Cotton, R. Leo	1
Couchman, Victoria	1
Coultas, Jim	1
Coulter, Lillian	2
Coulter, Mary J.	5
Courvoisier, Marian	1
Coutts, Gordon	6
Coventry, Stanley H.	1
Covey, Verna	1
Cowan, Elsie	1
Cowdrey, Dick	1
Cowles, Clifford	2
Cox, George J.	1
Cox, Merle T.	2
Craft, Elsworth	1
Craise, Alice L.	1
Cram, Allan Gilbert	3
Cramer, Harriet T.	1
Crandall, Esther	1
Crandall, Marion	2
Crane, Douglas	1
Cranz, Theo	1
Crawford, Esther Mabel	5
Creal, James Pirtle Jr.	3
Creaser, G. W.	1
Crespo, Jorge Juan	4
Cressey, Herbert C.	4
Cressey, Meta	3
Crez, Maria Marcella	1
Cristadoro, Charles C.	2
Crocker, Charles Matthew	6
Croft, M. E. Mrs.	1
Cromwell, Joan Christian	3
Cronenwett, Clare	1
Crosby, Wade	1
Crosnell, Mary E.	1
Cross, Alta Mrs.	1
Cross, Lee H.	2
Croswell, E. T. Mrs.	1
Crow, Marie Francis	3
Crowe, Wm. Francis	1
Crowther, Richard Layton	1
Crundall, Becheley	1
Cruze, Charles	1
Cugat, Francesic	5
Culbertson, Mabel F.	1
Cummings, Charles Atherton	2
Cummings, E. L.	1
Cummings, Hiel	1
Cuoco, Camillo	1
Cuprien, Frank W.	8
Curran, Mary E.	3
Currier, Cyrus Bates	2
Currier, William Barron	3
Curtis, Leland	10
Curtis, Truman	1
Curtiss, F. W. Mrs.	1
Cushman, Henry	3

D

Name	No.
Daggett, Maude	7
Dahl, Joris	2
Dahl, Olga	1
Dakin, Tilden	1
Dampair, William	2
Dana, Esther G.	1
Danar, Ellen	2
Dando, Susie May Berry	9
Daniell, William Swift	12
Daniels, Mark Roy	4
Daniels, Z. A. Miss	1
Dann, Anna See Skeele	1
Dann, Frode N.	1
Danner, Sara Kolb	3
Daraio, Innocenzo	2
Darby, Louise	1
Davey, M. R. S.	1
Davis. Cecil Clark Mrs.	1
Davis, Harry	1
Davis, Leonard M.	1
Davis, Lurah C.	1
Davis, Maud	1
Davis, Warren	2
Davison, R. Isabelle	1
Dawes, Edwin	4
Dawson, Richard T. Mrs.	1
Day, Harold	1
Day, Richard W.	4
Day, Robert	1
Dayton Lillian	2
Dean, Eva Ellen	3
Dean, Lillian Reubina	2
Deardorf, Carlotta	1
DeBouthillier, Guy	1
Deethman, Edwin C. F.	1
DeForest, Lockwood	4
DeHaafe, M.	1
DeHaven, C. H.	1
DeHospodar, Stephen	4
DeKruif, Henri Gilbert	10

Name	No.
DeKruif, Muriel Earle	1
DeLaBarre, Agnes	1
DeLaBaere, C. Miss	2
Delano, Annita	5
DeLaTorre, Francis M.	3
Delbey, Desire	1
DeLongpre, Paul	20
DeMey, Charles F. Dr.	3
Dennis, Morgan	2
Denublia, N. L.	1
Denman, Lucien	1
DePaizthery, Arpad	2
DeQuelin, Rene T.	5
Derby, J. Frank	1
DeRibcowsky, Dey	3
Dethloff, Peter Hans	2
Deutsch, Boris	10
DeVerley, Ivy	4
DeVol, Eugene	2
DeVol, Howard	1
DeVol, Pauline Hamill	3
DeVos, Gleb	1
DeVriendt, Stefan vR	3
DeWolf, E.	1
DeWolf, Wallace Leroy	3
Dickinson, Daisy	1
Dickinson, Edward	1
Dickinson, Ross Edward	4
Dieppe, Ferdinand	2
Dietrickson, D. N.	1
Dike, Philip Latimer	6
Diller, Alfred C.	1
Dillman, Louis	1
Dionysius, Dooly	2
Dixon, Francis Stillwell	2
Dixon, Layfayette Maynard	27
Dobbs, Winifred	1
Dodge, Arthur Burnside	5
Dodge, D. Frank	1
Doering, Eric	1
Doering, Paul	2
Domela, Jan Marinus	4
Dominguez, Martin	1
Dominique, John A.	1
Donaldson, Douglas	8
Donaldson, Ethel A.	1
Donaldson, Louise Towle	1
Donaldson, Margaret	1
Donnell, Mary E.	1
Donovan, John Ambrose	8
Doolittle, Harold Lukens	4
Dooner, Clara	2
Dore, Calla Miss	1
Doss, W. Galen	2
Douglas, E. Graham	1
Douglas, Haldane	6
Douglas, R. H.	1
Dowd, Helen C.	1
Dowiatt, Dorothy	2
Downard, M. W.	1
Drain, Lillian	6
Dreyfus, Isadora C.	2
Driscoll,	1
Duffie, Jane	1
Dukes, Katherine	1
Dukwitz, Helen	1
Dumond, Frederick Melville	8
Duncan, Geraldine Birch	2
Duncan, R. G.	1
Duncan, W. M.	1
Dunham, Theodore Jr. Mrs.	1
Dunlap, Helena Adele	14
Dunlap, Mary Stewart	6
Dunn, Charles A.	1
Dunn, David	2
Dupre, J. F.	1
Durenceau, Andre	2
Durston, Arthur	1
Dustin, Silas	3
Duvall, Fanny Eliza	10
Dwiggins, Clare E.	1

E

Name	No.
Eadie, May Helen	1
Eager,	1
Earle, Ferdinand Piney	9
Earle, Muriel	3
Earnest, Florence R.	1
Eaton, Lois Lee	2
Eddy, G. A.	1
Edelman, Abram E.	1
Edmond, Elizabeth	4
Edmunds, Flora	2
Edstrom, Peter David	17
Edwards, Howard Arden	3
Edwards, Lionel	1
Edwards, Norman	3
EdwardsWilliam M.	2
Egen, Max	1
Eickert, W. C.	1
Elliott, A. B.	1
Elliott, Don	1
Elliott, H. B.	2
Elliott, L. C.	1
Elliott, Ruth Cass	1
Ellis, Clyde Garfield	3
Ellis, Fremont	4
Ellis, Genevieve, R.	1
Ellis, Howard	1
Ellison, J. Milford	1
Elwell, Myrna	1
Emory, William Hemsley	3
Engelman, William F.	1
Englander, E.	1
Englehardt, Walter J.	1
English, Harold M.	3
Entler, Kathryn Estelle	2
Erickson, Ernest C.	2
Ernest, Aleta	2
Ernst, F. J.	2
Escherick, Elsa Falk	2
Eskey, W. A.	2
Eskridge, Robert Lee	4
Esner, Arthur L.	1
Espey, Josie S.	1
Espino, Ricardi	1
Espoy, Angel	1
Esse, Earl J.	1
Estabrook, Gertrude	2
Esterwold, Isabel	1
Estes, Ruth	1
Estill, Ella Howard	1
Estill, J. W.	1
Estill, John Wilmott Mrs.	2
Etheridge, Edith G.	1
Evans, Dick	1
Evans, E	1
Evans, Frank Elwin	2
Evans, Gertrude	1
Evans, M. Eleanor Mrs.	4
Evans, Nela H.	1
Everett, Louise	4
Everett, Mary Orwig	3
Everts, Harvey Clay	3
Ewing, Athol L.	2
Ewing, E. A. Mrs.	1
Ewing, Robert S.	4
Eyler, Shirley	1
Eytel, Carl A.	3

F

Name	No.
Fages, Alphonse, B.	1
Fagin, Ella Woodward	2
Faille, C. A.	1
Fairall, Alice Frances	1
Fairbanks, Alice	1
Farber, C. I.	1
Farish, Jane	1
Farmer, Albert E.	1
Farnell, Margaret T. C.	1
Farnsworth, Ethel Newcomb	2
Faron, C. A.	1
Farr, Ellen B.	3
Farris, Constance	1
Faust, Eleanor Challis	2
Favretto, E. E.	1
Fay, Horace, T.	1
Featherstone, J. P. Miss	1
Fechin, Nickoli Ivanowich	9
Feinblatt, Rose	1
Feinstein, Mary	1
Feitelson, Lorser	1
Feldman, Dorothy	1
Feltham, Will	1
Fenn, Walter J.	1
Fenyes, Eva Scott	1
Ferenz, F. K.	1
Ferguson, George D	1
Furguson, Lillian Prest	6
Fickessen, Bertha	1
Fidaroff, Simon	1
Fiedler, Charles Kern	1
Field, Charlotte S.	1
Field, Thyrsis	1
Finley, C. L. Miss	1
Finley, Halleck J.	3
Fish, Mary L. S.	2
Fisher, David	1
Fisher, E. S.	1
Fisher, George Harold	2
Fisher, Howard	1
Fiske, Stella A.	1
Fitch, Adela Russell	1
Fitch, Wm. Russell Mrs.	1
Fitzhenry, George O.	1
Flaherty, Lillian Emily	1
Flammer, C.	1
Flanders, C. J.	1
Fleming, Margaret Eddy	1
Fletcher, S. L.	1
Fletcher, Frank Morely	4
Fletcher, J. T.	1
Fletcher, L. P. Miss	1
Fletcher, Robert Mrs.	2
Fletcher, S. L.	1
Floie, Mrs Arthur Bull	2
Flournoy, Jeanette	2
Flower, George	1
Flynn, Hazel L.	1
Foerster, Arnold	1
Forbes, L. C. O.	1
Force, Clara G.	3

Name	
Ford, Henry Chapman	6
Foresman, Alice Carter	3
Forestal, Ernest	2
Fordman, Ruth	1
Formhals, Henry	1
Forsell, John	1
Forsythe, Victor Clyde	9
Forsythe, J. H.	1
Fort, Jean	2
Forward, Martha	1
Foster, Arthur Gilbert	1
Foster, Arthur Turner	3
Foster, Bertha Knox	1
Foster, Walter T.	3
Foster, Wm. Frederick	4
Foster, Willett S.	1
Fountan, M. E. Mrs.	1
Fox, F. Dobson	1
Fox, Mary L.	1
Fracker, Ruth Miller	1
Francisco, Enid	1
Francisco, John Bond	18
Frank, Eugene C.	8
Frank, Marie G.	1
Franklin, Elizabeth W.	1
Franquinet, Eugene	2
Fraser, A. W. C.	1
Frazzee, Isaac, Jenkinson	2
Frechette, Marie Marguer.	2
Fredericks, Remy	1
Free, Mable	1
Freeman, Earl	2
Freeman, Robert	2
French, Park	1
French Viola	1
Frey, Joseph	3
Friedrichsen, Peter	1
Fries, Charles Arthur	5
Frolich, Finn Haakon	5
Frost, H. C.	1
Frost, J. Ernest	1
Frost, John Jack	6
Frost, Mabelle G.	2
Fuetsch, Charles	1
Fullerton, Alice V.	2
Fullerton, Fannie L.	1
Fullonton, Evelyn Mrs.	2
Fullonton, Robert	3
Fulop, Karoly	1
Fulton, Bernice	1
Fulton, Fitch B.	2
Fyfe, Gilbert G.	1

G

Name	
Gabellieri, Alessandro	3
Gabriel, Michael	1
Gaensslen, Robert Carl	3
Gaffney, Claribel H.	1
Gaffney, Louis E.	1
Gage, Robert Merrell	8
Gagne, Jules	1
Gale, Edmund W.	1
Gamble, Dora	2
Gamble, Edna	3
Gamble, John Marshall	6
Gammon, Stella M.	1
Ganson, Eve	1
Garbutt, Bernard	5
Gardelle, Carlton	4
Garden, Miss	2
Gardner, J. P.	2
Gardner, William H. Jr.	2
Garey, K. E. Miss	1
Garner, Archibald	1
Garnsey, Julian Ellsworth	6
Garrett, Clara Pfeifer	3
Garret, Louise	1
Garrigues, Edith H.	2
Gasell, Marion F.	1
Gates, Emily E.	1
Gavaza,	3
Gay, Mary	2
Gaydon, C. O.	1
Gaylord, Helen	1
Gaze, Harold	3
Gearhart, Edna	3
Gearhart, Frances Hamm.	9
Gearhart, May	7
Geddes, Norman Bel	8
Gentry, Thurston	1
Genung, Robert	1
George, Gladys	1
Gerard, Edgar	1
Gere, Nellie Huntington	5
Geritz, Frank (Franz)	21
Gervais, A. E.	1
Getty, A. W. Mrs.	1
Gibbons, Cedric	1
Gibbs, Roy A.	1
Giff, J. L.	1
Giffen, Elizabeth Helene	1
Gifford, May C.	1
Gigas, Virginia	1
Gilbert, Arthur Hill	12
Gilbert, Bess	1
Gilbert, Robert	1
Gilchrist, Jack	2
Gilchrist, Meda	2
Gillespie, Manda E.	1
Gillies, Jessie	1
Gilmore, Doris	1
Giorgi, Federico	1
Girardin, Frank J.	5
Glass, Roy	1
Gleason, Elizabeth	1
Gleason, Joe Duncan	14
Gleich, George Frederick	1
Glenn, E. Elston	1
Glick, Hayrold Russ	1
Glover, Edwin S.	2
Goddard, Florence M.	2
Godfrey, Mildred	1
Goebe, William J.	1
Goethals, Victor	2
Goforth, Marguerite M.	1
Goldner, Dorothy Thompson	1
Goldner, Orville	1
Goldschlager, Belle	1
Golitzin, Alex	1
Good, Iris	1
Goodan, John A.	1
Goodan, Tilman P.	2
Goodchild, Cecil Wray	1
Goode, Henry	1
Goodenow, Rolf Julian	1
Gooding, H. I. Miss	1
Goodman, Frances D.	1
Goodrich, E. H. Mrs.	2
Goodwin, Ella S.	1
Goodwin, Emma Frances	2
Goodwin, Guy Parker	3
Goodwin, Jean	3
Gorney, J.	1
Graham, C. M.	1
Graham, Donald Wilkinson	1
Graham, Douglass	2
Grahn, Zella Ong	1
Gramatky, Hardie	3
Grandjean, Arthur Mrs.	1
Grant, G. A.	2
Grant, George Albert	2
Grant, H.	1
Grant, Joe	1
Grant, Lee	1
Grausman, Roy	2
Gray, Alice	1
Gray, Claude	1
Gray, Marion M.	1
Gray, Ruth	1
Green, Alice Gorden	1
Green, Caroline A.	1
Green, J. C.	1
Green, Mary Amory	1
Greenbaum, Joseph	20
Greene, Alice Goodrich	1
Greene, Frank F.	3
Greene, Lucille Brown	1
Greenlee, Herbert C.	2
Greegg, Genevieve G.	2
Gregory, Florence	1
Grey, Elmer	2
Grievenow, Margaret	1
Griesbach, David	2
Griffith, Conway	3
Griffith, Evelyn	1
Griffith, Kate B.	1
Griffith, Katherine Patton	1
Griffith, Lillian	2
Griffith, William Alexand.	5
Grisdale, Arthur	1
Griswold, Gilbert	1
Griswold, Mary F.	2
Groesbeck, Dan Sayre	8
Groshon, E. L. Mrs.	1
Gross, Mathilda L.	1
Grosser, Lenora M.	1
Grossman, Roy	2
Grosvenor, Frederika	2
Grot, Anton	1
Groton, Dorothy	1
Grubb, Agnes M.	1
Gruenfeld, Johan Casper L.	4
Gruhler, Beatrice	1
Guenot, Maurice	1
Gunderson, Stanley H.	1
Gunn, A. S.	1
Gunn, Florence	1
Gunn, Lois F.	1
Gunther, Raphael Y.	1
Gunther, Yela	2
Guptill, Ada A.	2
Gurnee, Marion B.	2
Gwinn, John	2

H

Name	
Haas, Lotta L.	2
Haddock, Jerelyn O.	1
Haeckel, Ernest	1
Haeckel, Maria	1
Haenel, Theodore	1
Hagberg, Rudolph F.	1
Hage, W. B. Mrs.	1

Name	Count
Hague, Josephine B.	1
Hahne, Thelyn	1
Haig, Mabel George	2
Haines, Curry W.	2
Hale, Florence Chenett	1
Hale, Girard	1
Hale, J. B.	1
Hall, Albert Lawrence	2
Hall, J. A. Mrs.	1
Hall, John Belmar	1
Hall, Shirley M.	1
Hall, Wayne	1
Haller, Constance Reed	1
Haller, Nellie Ward	2
Hallett, Herbert H.	2
Halliday, Mary Hughitt	2
Halpin, Mary A.	1
Halseth, Edna Scofield	2
Halstead, Maud	1
Halstead, Muriel	1
Halsted, Robert G.	1
Hamblett, Junie	1
Hamer, H. A.	2
Hamilton, Hamilton	3
Hamilton, J. B.	1
Hamilton, William	1
Hamlin, Doris	1
Hammack, Edward	1
Hammond, W. P. Mrs.	1
Hanscom, Trude	1
Hansen, Daisy	1
Hansen, Ejnar	6
Hantman, Murray	1
Harbeson, Pearl W.	1
Harcoff, Lyla M.	1
Harkness, Edwin Keith	2
Harland, Mary	4
Harper, Effie	1
Harriman, Marjorie B.	1
Harris, Edward N.	1
Harris, Greta	1
Harris, Harwell	2
Harris, Jessica	1
Harris, May	2
Harris, S. G. Mrs.	2
Harris, Sam Hyde	3
Harrison, Florence	1
Harrison, Grace Earle	1
Harrison, Tom C.	1
Harrison, William Preston	8
Hart, L. M.	2
Hartlet, Clair H.	1
Harty, Louise	1
Hartzig, Mildred Viola	3
Harvey, Eli	4
Harvey, J. Allen	2
Harvey, Paul	3
Hashimoto, Michi	3
Haskell, W. L.	1
Haskell, William	2
Hastings, H. S.	1
Hastings, M. V. Mrs.	1
Hatch, Marie Louise	1
Hatch, Minnie L.	2
Hatch, Velma	1
Hatfield, Dalzell	3
Hauck, Fred	1
Hauverman, Laura	1
Hawthorne, Connie	2
Hawxhurst, Henry Ivins	1
Hay, Eleanor	2
Hayden, Mary Dodge	1
Hayes, Alice V.	1
Hayes, Gayl	2
Hayes, J. E.	2
Hayes, O. P.	1
Hayfold, L. A.	1
Haynes, Elsie H.	2
Haynes, Grace C.	2
Hayward, Roger C.	3
Hazard, Arthur Merton	8
Hazen, Bessie Ella	6
Heald, W. F. Mrs.	1
Healy, Grace	1
Heaney, A. T.	1
Heap, A. M. Miss	1
Heaslip, A. H. Mrs.	1
Heckman, A. F.	2
Heckman, Frederick R.	2
Hed, Eva	1
Hedges, Warren T.	2
Hefferman, Lawrence	1
Heflinger, Grace Katherine	2
Heil, Francis J.	1
Heisley, George	2
Helms, Addison, D.	1
Hels, Louis	1
Hemphill, Ethel	2
Henderson, L. R. Miss	1
Hendrix, Hail	2
Henke, Bernard	2
Henners, H. H.	1
Henry, Harry Raymond	5
Hentch, John	1
Hentel, F. G. Mrs.	1
Herbert, Myrta Estelle	2
Herding, Franz	1
Herlihy, H. W.	1
Herman, Lydia Jean	1
Herrick, Hugh M.	2
Herron, Jason Mrs.	4
Herter, Adel	4
Herter, Albert	8
Herwig, William	2
Herzog, Herman	3
Heslet, Desmond	2
Hess, Beatrice	1
Hesse, Henry M.	1
Hesse, Hugo C.	1
Hessova, Boza	3
Hester, Orrel	1
Hewitt, Ernest W.	1
Hewson, H. L.	1
Hider, Russel John	1
Higgens, E. J. Mrs.	1
Hild, Georgia Marion	1
Hill, Jessie F.	2
Hill, W. E.	4
Hiller, Helen Craig	1
Hiller, William	1
Hillman, Rosana	1
Hills, Anna Althea	11
Hilstad, John Roy	1
Hilty, Bernadine	1
Hinchman, John Herbert	3
Hiney, F. S.	2
Hinkle, Clarence Keiser	11
Hinkle, Lucile Bernice	3
Hinman, Helen	1
Hiraga, Kamesuke	3
Hise, Ura Mrs.	1
Hoagland, W. M. Mrs.	1
Hobson, Ed. B.	1
Hobush, Wilhelmina	1
Hocks, Ferdinand	2
Hodges, Catherine M.	1
Hodges, Marjorie	2
Hoeffer, Louis C.	1
Hoer, Elizabeth	1
Hoff, Helen Lu Marie	2
Hoffman, Emma G.	1
Holladay, Ben Campbell	1
Holland, Beryl S.	1
Hollen, L. P.	1
Holliday, Ben C.	1
Hollowell, Beulah	1
Holman, Ida	1
Holmes, C. H.	2
Holmes, Ralph William	6
Holmes, Stuart	1
Holmwood, Loren C.	2
Holt, Geoffery	1
Holt, Mary L.	1
Homola, A. J.	1
Hon, Billy	1
Honeywell, Annette	1
Hong, Anna Helga	4
Hood, E. Socoleano	2
Hood, Jane	1
Hooker, Kate Putham	1
Hooper, Rosa	1
Hooper, Samuel G.	1
Hooper, Z. V. Miss	1
Hope, Thelma Paddock	3
Hopkins, Grace F.	1
Hopkins, Una Nixson Mrs.	3
Hord, Donal	7
Horlocker, Lets	8
Hornsby, Alice Gibson	2
Horne, Nellie M.	1
Horning, Benjamin	3
Horton, Lester	1
Hough, Francis R.	2
Houghton, H. E.	1
Houghton, J. Dunbar	2
Hounsell, C. Lillian	2
House, Sada	1
Hough, Henrietta	2
Houssier, Julia	1
Houston, Oliver	1
Howard, Chester	1
Howard, Hazel F.	1
Howard, R. V.	1
Howell, Helen	2
Howell, Youldon, C.	1
Howes, Miss	1
Hubbard, W. C.	1
Hubbert, E. L. Mrs.	2
Hudson, Elladora	1
Hughes, Daisy Marguerite	4
Hughes, West Dr.	2
Hugunin, Grace	1
Hulbert, Mary A.	2
Hume, C. M. Miss	1
Humphrey, E. A.	2
Hunley, Katherine Jones	3
Hunt, Esther	3
Hunt, George	1
Hunt, Myra B.	1
Hunt, Thomas L.	5

Name	No.
Kranth, Charles P.	1
Krasnow, Peter	13
Krauss, Elfrieda S.	2
Krauth, Charles Philip	2
Krayer, Arnold D.	1
Kromer, Adelaide	2
Kruger, Pauline	2
Kruger, Richard	4
Kruse, Alice	1
Kubic, J. C.	1
Kuehne, Esther	1
Kuhnle, Paul	1
Kurtzworth, Harry Muir	1
Kutcher, Ben	5
Kyes, Vern L.	1

L

Name	No.
La Cava, G. Mrs.	1
Laidlaw, Cora M.	1
Laird, Marshall	1
L'Allemand, Gordon Lynn	4
Landacre, Paul Hambleton	7
Landers, Alice M.	1
Lane, Martella Chase	1
Lang, George	1
Langley, Edward M.	3
Langley, Sarah G.	2
Langston, Birgit	2
Langworthy, L. R.	1
Lanoe, J. Jicquel	1
Lanphear, James	1
Lanz, Ernest E.	1
Lapius, Blanche	1
Lapworth, A. J.	1
Larimer, Barbara	1
Larimer, Ruth M.	2
Larrinaga, Mario	1
Larson, Adele	1
Larson, Robert	1
Larter, Anne	1
Lasky, Bessie Mona	5
Lathrop, Ada Frances	3
Lattig, Ada G.	1
Laton. Helen E.	1
Lauderbach, Frances	1
Laudermilk, Helen Gaylord	2
Laudermilk, Jerome Douglas	4
Lauman, Hester	1
Laurence, Sydney	5
Lauritz, Paul	16
Lauter, H. E.	1
Lavrillier, Gaston Albert	2
Law, Harry V.	2
Lawrie, Lee	4
Lawson, P. J.	1
Lawton, Almira C. Mrs.	1
Leavers, William W.	2
Leavy, Katherine	1
Ledeboer, Hans	1
Ledgerwood, Helen J.	1
Lee, Elva	1
Lee, Leslie W.	3
Lee, R. B. Miss	1
Lee, Selma	1
Lee, Sylvia	1
Lee, Walt	1
Leekney, Frederick A.	2
Legler, Flora	1
Lehmann, Marian	2
Leighton, Kathryn Woodman	25
Lemley, George,	1
Lemley, Jack	1
Lenggenhager, Warner	1
Lenhardt, Walmsley	2
Lenour, Laura	1
Leonard, Ide C.	1
Leonard, Jack	1
Leonard, Phil	1
Leslie, Jean G.	1
Lester, Leonard	3
Lethen, Alex T.	2
Lettelier, P. E. Miss	1
Leverenz, Carol M.	1
Levine, Francis	1
Lewerenz, Carol M.	1
Lewerenz, Margaret G.	1
Lewis, Arley	1
Lewis, Arthur M.	2
Lewis, H. Emerson	1
Lewis, Jessie Miles	1
Lewis, Lola C.	1
Lewis, Tom E.	1
Lewis, Vera B.	1
Libby, Frank	1
Lichty, Eugene Mrs.	1
Liddell, Frank R.	2
Liechty, Vivian L.	1
Lierd, Hallie W.	1
Lillian, E. Christine	1
Lincoln, Alice R.	1
Linderman, Winifred	1
Linder, Harry	2
Lindhe, Ivan	2
Lindsay, Ruth Andrews	3
Lion, Henry	8
Lippincott, Rose	2
Lippincott, Josephine	1
Litchfield, M. B.	1
Little, Charlotte F.	1
Little, Gertrude E.	1
Little, Gertrude L.	3
LLoyd, Eleanor	1
Lloyd, Lucile	4
Lloyd, Lucy	1
Lloyd, R. D.	1
Lockhart, Marcelite	1
Lockwood, Robert A.	4
Long, Eula	1
Long, H. A.	1
Loomis, A. L.	1
Loomis, M. M.	1
Loop, Edith H.	1
Loring, Margaret	1
Loucks, B. W.	1
Lovatelli, Ephy	1
Lovell, Duke	1
Lovins, Henry	7
Lowd, Edna B.	1
Lowe, Frances	2
Lowe, S. V. Miss	1
Lowry, H. J.	1
Lowry, Lorraine	1
Ludlow, Margery N.	1
Ludovici, Alice Emily	3
Ludovici, Frieda	1
Ludovici, Julius	3
Luke, Keye	1
Lukene, Anna M.	1
Lukens, Glen	1
Lukits, Theodore Nikolai	4
Lum, Bertha Boynton	7
Lundberg, Helen	1
Lungren, Fernand	9
Lutz, Gladys M.	1
Lutz, Paul Henry	1
Lux, Catherine C.	1
Lyman, Elizabeth	1
Lyon, Charles	1
Lyon, Duane Evans	3
Lyon, Kathryn R.	1
Lyon, Rose Hooper	1

M

Name	No.
McArthur, A. F. Mrs.	1
McArthur, J. B.	1
McBride, Eva Ackley	3
McBurney, James Edwin	8
McCaig, Flora Thomas	2
MacCarthy, Susie L.	1
McCartney, Marion C.	1
McCartney, Norma	1
McCauley, George Edward	1
McClelland, Amy Woller	1
McClelland, Lela	1
McCleave, Valencia Raff.	1
McCloskey, Alberta Bin.	4
McCloskey, Wm. Joseph	4
McClung, M. Miss	1
McCollum, Dora	1
McCormack, Blanche	1
McCrabbe, Inez	1
McCrary, Miriam T.	1
McDermid, Amy B.	1
McDermid, W. H.	1
MacDonald, Joseph Farre.	4
McDonald, Katherine H.	1
MacDonald-Wright, Stant.	1
MacDowell, Edward Emer.	3
McDuffie, Jane Lee	1
McFetridge, Blanche E.	1
McGarry, Amadeo	1
McGowan, V. Carroll	1
MacGuire, Ray M.	1
Machado, Alonzo	1
Mack, Florence	1
MacKay, Clifton C.	1
McKay, T. H.	2
McKay, Thomas	2
MacKeever, Ed J.	2
MacKenzie, G. J.	1
MacKenzie, H. B. Mrs.	1
MacKinnon, Annabelle	1
McLane, Jean	1
McLean, Grace	1
McLean, Irene	1
McLellan, Kenneth L.	2
MacLennan, Eunice	1
MacLeod, Louise E. G.	8
MacLeod, Malcolm	3
McLoughlin, Gregory	1
McLouth, Farley D.	1
McManaman, Kath. Hern.	3
McNaughton, Elizabeth B.	1
McNeeley, Irene	1
McNeeley, Perry	4
McPhail, Annie	2
MacQuoid, Clarence	1
McWhirter, Emma	1
Madsen, Thorwald	2
Magnussen, G. A.	3
Maier-Krieg, Eugene	5
Maison, Mary Edith	5
Mako, B.	1

Name	#
Manbert, Barton	2
Mann, Aimee	1
Mannheim, Jean	20
Manoir, Irving	6
Manship, Luther F.	2
Manuelli, Pasquale	1
Many, Alexis B.	2
March, Dorothy	1
Marchese, V. A.	1
Marcheski, James	1
Mardeld, Jean	1
Marks, Ida Lee	1
Marks, Janet E.	1
Marks, Lucie E.	2
Marrolta, Silva	1
Marsh, Charles Howard	3
Marsh, Mary E.	3
Marsh, S, James	1
Marten, Althea	1
Martens, Bertha H.	1
Martin, A. C.	1
Martin, Earl	1
Martin, Fletcher	1
Martin, Hazel S.	1
Martin, Margaret	1
Martin, Robert	2
Martinez, Alfredo Ramos	4
Maslenikoff, Margarita	1
Mason, Elizabeth	2
Masson, Kalma C.	2
Maston, J. Kendall	1
Masuda, Sojiro	1
Mathews, Alfred Edward	3
Mathieson, Laura Way	2
Matson, Nathalie	1
Matsubara,	2
Mattias, Martha	1
Maxwell, Everett Carroll	5
Maxwell, J. R.	1
Maxwell, Mary Margaret	1
May, Beulah	3
Mayhew, Nell Danely B.	8
Mayo, S. I. Mrs.	2
Mays, B. B.	1
Mazy, Leon	2
Mead, Leon	2
Mead, Ida	1
Meadows, Cora Dell	4
Means, Elliott Anderson	3
Mears, Margaret	1
Medlock, O.	1
Meeker, Chris Marie	1
Megargee, Lon Alonzo	5
Meier, Barton,	1
Melcher, Bertha Corbett	2
Melcher, George Henry	2
Melcher, Virginia I.	1
Melchor, A. P. Miss	1
Melville, Antonia	6
Melzer, William	1
Menhennick, Ellen E.	1
Mennig, Lucy P.	1
Meripol, Abraham A.	5
Merriam, James A.	1
Merrild, Knud	6
Merrill, S. C.	1
Merwin, Antoinette dF.	3
Messenger, Ivan	3
Messick, Benjamin Newton	5
Messinger, Marcus	1
Meyer, E. G. Miss	1
Meyer, Zel	1
Michelson, Eric Gust.	2
Milburn, Oliver	3
Miles, Harold Whitney	5
Miles, Ruth	1
Miller, Barse	13
Miller, Charles M.	1
Miller, Edith Maude	1
Miller, Evylena Nunn	10
Miller, Lorenzo C.	1
Miller, Maude Alvera	2
Miller, Minnie R.	1
Miller, Ralph Davison	8
Miller, Richard	3
Miller, Ruth	4
Millier, Arthur Henry T.	19
Miner, Frederick Roland	6
Minishian, Harry	1
Minor, L. E. Miss	1
Mistume Kawe	1
Mitchell, Alfred R.	4
Mitchell, Estelle	1
Mitchell, Laura M. D.	7
Mitchell, John	2
Mitchell, I. W. Miss	2
Mitchell, Margaret	1
Mitton, A. E. Miss	1
Miyagi, Yotoku	3
Mocine, Emily Rutherford	1
Mocine, Ralph Fullerton	6
Modesti, Angelina S.	1
Modie, Edna	1
Modra, Theodore	7
Moeller, Ruth	1
Moffatt, Edna C.	1
Mohler, R. Hamilton	2
Moir, L. M. Miss	1
Molkenboer, Antoon	5
Mondon, Evelyn	1
Monhoff, Frederick	5
Monroe, Milton	2
Monroe, Ruth	1
Monsen, Courtney	1
Montalboddi, Ida Mellish	3
Montalboddi, Raffaello	4
Montgomery, Alfred	3
Montgomery, William Cum.	2
Montrichard, R. D.	1
Moody, Vinnie R.	1
Moon, Carl	1
Moore, A. C. Mrs	1
Moore, C. M.	2
Moore, Dorothea Dr.	3
Moore, E. Andrews	1
Moore, E. J. Mrs.	1
Moore, E. S.	2
Moore, Frank Montague	4
Moore, S. W. Miss	1
Moorman, Lewis Jr.	1
Morahan, Eugene	1
Moran, Paul Nimmo	4
Moran, Thomas	4
Morel, P. E.	1
Morgan, Barbara Brooks	1
Morgan, Barbara J.	4
Morgan, Lois Waag	1
Morimoto, Charles	2
Morin, G. E. Miss	2
Morin, S. W. Mrs.	1
Morley, A. M. Mrs.	1
Morris, Adelaide Miss	3
Morrison, Katherine	1
Morrison-Kahle, Katherine	1
Morse, Esther B.	1
Morse, Mary S.	1
Morse, Vernon J.	2
Mortensen, Helen Hollister	1
Mott-Smith, May	4
Mottram, Grace V.	1
Moses, Walter Farrington	1
Mountfort, Arnold C.	4
Mow, Albert R.	1
Muckley, Louis Fairfax	3
Mudd, W. Seeley Mrs	1
Mueller, Alexander	2
Mueller, F. B.	1
Mueller, Martin	1
Mullen, Carrie S.	1
Mumma, Mary C.	1
Munsell, Wm. A. O.	2
Munson, M. J.	1
Murillo, Raoul	2
Murphy, Bernardine	1
Murphy, Lawrence	2
Murphey, Marjorie C.	2
Murray, F. S.	3
Muschi, John	1
Muski, John	1
Mutton, Hilda	2
Myers, Datus B.	3

N

Name	#
Nafe, Marie P.	1
Nakanisi, Kinichi	1
Napolitano, Pasquale G.	3
Neff, Andrew	1
Negulesco, Jean	1
Neilson, C. P.	3
Nelli, Guido	1
Nemoy, Maurice	1
Nettleton, George P. Jr.	1
Neubauer, F. LaFay	1
Neville-Smith, H.	1
Newcomb, Olive	1
Newcombe, Warren	3
Newell, Gordon	1
Newking, Nathalie	4
Newman, Maude	1
Newman, Wanda	1
Nichols, Caroline	1
Nichols, Harley DeWitt	3
Nichols, Peggy Martin	2
Nichols, Wilbur Diehl	1
Nicholson, Charles W.	1
Nicholson, Grace	6
Nicoll, John W.	5
Nielsen, Harry A.	2
Nielsen, Niels	2
Nielsen, Peter	2
Nieuwenhuis, Celeste W.	2
Nightingale, Wesley	1
Nimmo, Louise Evertt	3
Noble, Miriam	1
Nolan, H. J.	1
Nopobtani, P. G.	1
Nordin, Oscar	2
Nordstrom, Algot	1

Name	No.
Noren, Carl	2
Northridge, Ed	1
Norton, Helen Gaylord	2
Nott, Raymond	2
Nottage, Grace	1
Nowell, Dora May	1
Nubila, N. L.	1
Nugent, Frances Roberts	1
Nunn, Evylena	1
Nye, Myra	2

O

Name	No.
Obninsky, Peter V.	1
OBrien, Eugene	1
Obzina, Martin	1
Odgard, Marie R.	1
Off, Louisa A.	1
OHagen, John L.	3
Okey, Jack C.	3
OKane, Regina	5
Okubo, Benji	3
Olesen, Julie Haskell	1
Oliver, Annie	1
Oliver, Dorothy Welsh	1
Oliver, Louise	1
Oliver, T. P.	1
OLoughlin,	1
Olson, A. S.	1
Olson, George	1
Olson, H.	1
OMalley, Power	5
ONeill, Lee	2
Ong, Zella	1
Ooley, Orpha Klinker	1
Orbe, Helen Ruth	1
Orchardson, Chas. M. Q.	3
Orcutt, Eunice	1
Ordayne, Neale	6
Orland, Edith	2
Orr, Alfred Everett	3
Orselli, Alfredo	1
Ortlieb, Ruth Powers	1
Osborn, Twyla	1
Osborne, Edith Helen	2
Osgood, Virginia Mae	3
Oshanna, John S.	2
OShea, John	6
Osthaus, Edmund Henry	9
Oswald, Emilie L.	2
Otis, George Demont	8
Otte, William Louis	3
Outcalt, Adele M.	1
Outwater, Ethel H.	1
Overton, Katherine F.	1
Owen, AA. Mrs.	1
Owen, Bertha	1
Owen, C. H. Mrs.	1
Owen, Jessie	1
Owen, Marie	1
Owens, Charles Hamilton	13
Owens, E. Merrill	2

P

Name	No.
Paap, Hans	3
Packard, J. Creighton	1
Packard, Mabel	4
Packer, Fred Little	4
Paddock, Ruth	1
Paddock, Thelma	2
Padelford, Morgan C.	1
Pafflin, Roberta	1
Page, Maxine	1
Paine, Robert	6
Paliza, Flavio L.	1
Palmer, Amelia	1
Palmer, Edith	3
Palmer, Samuel Morrow	1
Paradise, Phil	1
Parfianowicz, John	1
Park, Charles	1
Park, David	1
Parker, Jessie D.	2
Parker, Walter H.	1
Parkinson, Donald Berthold	3
Parkinson, Grace Wells	2
Parmeter, G. E.	2
Parrish, Alice	1
Parshall, DeWitt	7
Parshall, Douglass Ewell	10
Parshall, Lesette Miss	2
Paton, Clara M.	1
Patrick, James	1
Patterson, I. M. Mrs.	2
Patterson, Patti	1
Paul, Andrew G.	2
Pauling, Adeline Coombs	1
Paulus, Daniel Christopher	2
Paulus, Gertrude	2
Pavesigh, P.	1
Pawla, Frederick Alexand.	2
Paxton, William A.	2
Payne, Aurella de Walt	2
Payne, Edgar Alwyn	18
Payne, Elsie Palmer	3
Payne, Pauline	1
Payzant, Charles	2
Peabody, L. L. Mrs.	2
Peabody, Ruth Eaton	3
Peachy, Elizabeth A.	1
Peacock, Jon	1
Peano, Felix Achilles	5
Pearce, Franklin	1
Peck, Frances E.	1
Peck, M. L. Mrs.	1
Pedretti, Humberto J.	4
Pedretti, Raphael	1
Peet, J. S. Mrs.	1
Pelton, S. K. Miss	1
Pelz, J. F.	1
Pember, Ada H.	1
Penelon, Henri	3
Penfield, Georgw Wallace	3
Penfield, Katherine C.	1
Penney, Frederick Doyle	2
Penney, Janice Dolorws	1
Penny, Laura Annette	1
Percival, Olive	2
Perine, Eva G.	2
Perl, Margaret Anneke	1
Perrine, Edith E.	1
Perry, Annette	1
Perry, Emilie Stearns	4
Perry, Evadna Kraus	1
Perry, Lotta D.	1
Perry, Ollie Montgomery	1
Peters, Jock D.	4
Peters, Ruth	1
Petersen, Einer	3
Peterson, Clarence	1
Petricolas, Sherry	3
Pettit, Grace G.	1
Pettit, J.	1
Pfafflin, Roberta	2
Phelan, Alice M.	1
Phelps, Adele C.	1
Philippe, Felicien	2
Phillipi, Charles	1
Phillips, C. B.	2
Phillips, Carlotta V.	3
Phillips, Florence	1
Phillips, Lois A. B.	1
Philp, Mary	1
Pierce, Annie	1
Pierce, E. C. Mrs.	1
Pierce, W. H. C.	1
Pierce, Mildred	1
Pierre, Anton	1
Pierri, Antonio	1
Pijoan Y Soteras, Jose	4
Pilkington, W. H.	1
Pingree, E. A. Miss	1
Piper, Natt	1
Plank, Ester	2
Platt, C. S.	1
Platt, Juliette P.	1
Plau, Eleanor	1
Plawitz	1
Pletsch, Ethel E.	1
Plummer, Elmer	1
Pociecha, Stan	1
Podchernikoff, Alexis M.	2
Pogany, Willy	1
Pogson, Annie L.	2
Polk, Catherine G.	1
Polkinghorn, George	3
Pomeroy, Elsie Lower	1
Poore, Shirley	1
Ponet, M. V.	1
Pope, Marion Holden	7
Poppe, John	1
Poray, Stan Pociecha	8
Porter, James Tank	1
Porter, Julia S G.	1
Porter, Katherine Page	1
Porter, Lenore B.	1
Possner, Hugo A.	3
Pottenger, Mary L.	1
Potter, B. Mrs.	1
Potter, Blanche	1
Potter, F McRae	1
Potter, V. G	1
Pottinger, Roy	1
Powell, C L. Mrs.	1
Powell, H. M T	3
Powell, J. S.	1
Powelson, Doris,	1
Powers, Lyman W	1
Pratt, H C.	2
Pratt, Katharine	1
Pratt, Ruth	1
Prentice, Helen M.	1
Prest, Martha	1
Preston, Alice Hulick	1
Price, Lida S.	4
Price, William Henry	4
Priger, Nelita Hain	1
Pritchard, Walter Howli.	7
Probst, Rasmine Matilda	2
Probst, Thorwald	5
Proctor, Alexander Phim.	6
Proctor, Burt,	4
Prunier, Arthur H.	1

Pulsifer, Mina Schutz	1	
Punsch, Henry O.	3	
Purcell, Joseph	1	
Purcell, Norah	3	
Purdy, Evelyn G.	1	
Purrier, Evelyn Mondon	1	
Purviance, John David	1	
Pushman, Hovsep	13	
Puthuff, Hanson Duvall	24	
Putnam, Arion	2	
Putnam, Claude George	6	
Putnam, L. Jaynes Mrs.	2	
Putnam, Rose	1	

Q

Quigley, Helen	1
Quijano, Leopoldo	1
Quincy, Henrietta S.	1
Quivey, C. E.	1

R

Rabino, S.	1
Rackintor, Peter	1
Rackwitsz, Piet Peter	2
Raffaelli, Gino	1
Ragan, Nannie	1
Rall, Mrs.	1
Rambeau, J. C.	1
Ramsey, N. Miss	1
Randall, Daisy F.	1
Ramon, A.A.	1
Rapp, George	1
Rappaport, Dario	1
Rasche, Herbert	1
Raulston, Marion Church.	M3
Rauschwald, M. B.	1
Ravell, Henry	2
Ray, Joseph Johnson	3
Raymond, Julie E.	3
Raynor, Lois	1
Razalle, Emma	1
Razelle, Tess S.	1
Reaburn, Maude Lightfoot	2
Ream, Wm. Reginald	1
Reckless, Stanley Z.	1
Reddick, Ruth Dresslar	1
Redmond, Granville	10
Redmond, James MaKay	2
Reed, Charlotte	2
Reed, Dorothy H.	1
Reed, I. L. Miss	1
Reeder, Emelyn	1
Reeder, W. H.	1
Rees, Frances Truman	1
Reese, Ada L. E.	1
Reeves, George	4
Regli, Alver	2
Regnas, A. E.	1
Reid, Aurelia Wheeler	3
Reid, Velma	1
Reid, Victor E.	2
Reiffel, Charles	8
Reinhard, Lulu M.	1
Reinhart, E. T. Mrs.	1
Reiterman, Ethel	1
Remfree, Helen F.	1
Rendon, Ignatus	1
Renick, Claribel H.	1
Renner, Katherine	1
Reno, Louis H.	2
Reno, Max	2
Renshaw, Robert	1
Renwick, Julien	1

Reuter, Herman	2
Reveles, Antonio	2
Reynolds, George W.	2
Rhead, Frederick Hurten	4
Rhead, Lois Whitcomb	2
Rhine, Leonora B.	1
Ribcowski, Dey de	1
Rice, Maude A.	1
Rich, John Hubbard	20
Richards, Mabel C.	1
Richardson, Alice	1
Richardson, Roberta	1
Richardson, Z. B. Mrs.	1
Richmond, Evelyn K.	1
Richter, Henry L.	4
Riddell, Annette Irwin	2
Riddell, William Wallace	3
Ridder, Caroline	1
Rider, Charles Joseph	4
Ridgway, John Linzey	3
Rieber, Winifred,	3
Riediger, George A.	1
Riegelmaier, C.	1
Riethmuller, Aloise D.	2
Rilliet, Vivian Faure	1
Ring, Alice Blair	3
Rintelman, C. D.	1
Ripley, Thomas E.	1
Ristelhueber, Joseph	1
Rittenhouse, Jean	1
Ritter, E. W.	1
Roan-Horse, Ralph	1
Robbins, Thea	1
Roberts, A. J.	1
Roberts, A. L. Miss	1
Roberts, Frances	1
Roberts, John E.	1
Roberts, Josephine Seaman	1
Roberts, Ruth Goodwin	1
Roberts, W. A.	1
Robertson, Alexander W.	4
Robertson, Eilen	1
Robertson, Fred H.	2
Robertson, Maude	1
Robertson, Stewart	3
Robinson, Ada Chalfant	2
Robinson, Ann	1
Robinson, Delia Mary	2
Robinson, Elsie	2
Robinson, Ione	5
Robinson, Irene Bowen	5
Robinson, P. B.	1
Robison, Ann	1
Robson, J. W.	1
Rochard, Pierre	3
Roche, John D.	2
Rocle, Margaret King	2
Rocle, Marius Romain	2
Rodman, Lillian M.	1
Rodman, Peter	1
Roe, E.	1
Roessler, Pauline	1
Rogers, Paul A.	6
Rogers, E. E. Mrs.	1
Rogers, Eleanor Gale	1
Rogers, O. A.	1
Rohrbough, Herbert L.	1
Rokkaku, Shuja	1
Rollins, Warren B.	14

Romanelli, Carlo	3
Rorabeck, Edson	1
Rose, Ethel Boardman	4
Rose, Guy	17
Rosenhause, Beatrice C.	1
Rosenthal, Doris	7
Rossart, Michael	1
Roth, Edward A.	1
Rouse, Charles G.	1
Rouse, S. Estelle	1
Rowland, A. M. Miss	1
Rowland, W. Earl	4
Royar, N. C.	1
Rozaire, Arthur D.	4
Rubens, S. L.	1
Rudesill, Betty	1
Ruegg, Versena	1
Rugar, Jennie S.	1
Rushton, Desmond	2
Russell, Charles Marion	4
Russell, Adele	1
Russell, Bruce	1
Russell, E. B.	1
Russell, Hilda	1
Russell, Morgan	7
Russell, Sigurd	5
Ruth, Clara L.	1
Ruth, Esther A.	2
Rutherford, Emily	3
Ruthrauff, Frederick Gray	2
Rutt, Anna Hong	1
Ruttan, C. E.	1
Ryan, F. L. Miss	1
Ryan, William Redmond	2
Ryerson, Beulah, H.	1

S

Sachs, Herman	6
Sacks, Joseph	4
Sackman, Marie	1
St. Clair, Charles	2
St. Clair, Norman	10
St. John, S. H. Mrs.	2
Salveson, Alpha Knox	1
Samman, Detlef	6
Sample, Leslie	1
Sample, Paul Starrett	8
Sampson,	1
Sanders, Margaret	1
Sanders, Spencer E.	1
Sandham, Harry	4
Sargent, Paul Turner	3
Sauer, Wanda	2
Sauerwein, Frank Paul	7
Saunders, J. M. Mrs.	1
Sauter, Mary C.	1
Savage, G. R.	1
Sawtelle, Essie G.	1
Sayre, Fred Grayson	8
Scarpitta, Salvatore C.	5
Schaefer, Frank R.	1
Schaetzel, May Conly	2
Schaible, Frederick J.	2
Scheck, Helen N.	1
Schem, Henrietta	1
Schlesinger, Alfred	1
Schloat, G. Warren	1
Schmidt, Karl	3
Schmierer, Martha	1
Schneider, C. W.	1
Schneider, Esther	1

Stoner, Betty S.	1	
Storm, Cecile E.	1	
Storm, Floyd	2	
Stoton, E. W. Arnold	3	
Stover, Allan	1	
Strain, G. Willis	1	
Stratton, Mattie E.	1	
Stratton, Zelma	1	
Streator, Harold Arthur	3	
Stringfield, Vivian F.	4	
Stroebel, Oscar	1	
Strobridge, Idah Meachum	4	
Strode, Catherine	2	
Strom, William	1	
Stuber, Dana	1	
Stuber, Dedrick Brandes	5	
Stubergh, Katherine	1	
Sturge, Adolphus	1	
Sturgeon, Ruth B.	1	
Sturgis, F. E.	1	
Sturgis, George	1	
Sturtevant, L. V. Mrs.	1	
Suib, Joseph	2	
Sullivan, Mary O.	1	
Suman, Alvin L.	2	
Sumerlin, Mable	1	
Sutter, Joseph	1	
Sutton, A. M. N.	1	
Swan, Paul	5	
Swansee, Hans	1	
Swartz, Harold	7	
Sweet, Gertrude, M.	1	
Sweet, Ralph	1	
Swenning, R. T. Miss	1	
Swing, Mr.	1	
Swinnerton, James Guil.	12	
Switzer, Patty	2	
Symmonds, Albert	1	
Symons, Geo. Gardner	7	
Sype, Ioma B.	1	
Sysol, Geneva A.	1	
Szukalski, Stanislaw	1	

T

Taber, P. C.	2	
Taggart, Richard	1	
Tait, B. M.	1	
Talbert, Zel E.	1	
Talbot, Hattie Crippen	2	
Taliaferro, Lucene Good.	1	
Tamburini, A. C.	1	
Tanaka, T.	1	
Tanberg, Ella Hotelling	3	
Tanburg, Lillian Ferg.	1	
Tange, Herman	1	
Tanino, C. K.	1	
Tanner, Charles	2	
Tanner, William Charles	2	
Tasca, Fausto	4	
Tasche, Herbert	1	
Tauszky, David Anthony	5	
Taylor, Frank Johnson	1	
Taylor, Ida Lillie	2	
Taylor, Kathleen	1	
Taylor, Minnie M.	2	
Taylor, Margaret	4	
Taylor, Virginia	1	
Taylor, Wycliffe	1	
Teasdale, Mary H.	3	
Tefft, Iona	1	
Tench, Allen	1	

Terhell, Herman	2	
Terry, Marion	1	
Tew, Marguerite R.	3	
Thackento, John	1	
Thatcher, S. B. Mrs.	2	
Thayer, George C.	1	
Theiss, John William	5	
Thomas, Alice Blair	4	
Thomas, D. F.	2	
Thomas, Elizabeth	1	
Thomas, Ella	2	
Thomas, Georgia Seaver	1	
Thomas, Kathryn	1	
Thomas, Stephen Seymour	8	
Thomas, W. V.	1	
Thomason, Rosemary	1	
Thompson, Francis	2	
Thompson, G. N.	1	
Thompson, Hannah	2	
Thompson, Louise G.	1	
Thompson, M. A. Mrs.	1	
Thornburg, Florence V.	1	
Thorndike, Willis H.	3	
Thorne, J. Frederick	1	
Thurber, Lucile	1	
Thurston, Jane McDuffie	4	
Tiffany, Helen Carter	1	
Tillcock, Harry N.	1	
Tilman, C. B.	1	
Tingle, Minnie	6	
Titus, Aime Baxter	3	
Titus, Lela J.	1	
Titus, W. C.	1	
Tobiasson, Mary E.	1	
Todd, Ethel M.	1	
Tolman, Pauline Gediman	1	
Tompkins, Florence	1	
Tonge, Gilbert R.	1	
Toole, Charlotte O.	1	
Torrey, Elliot Bouton	4	
Torrey, Eugene	5	
Torrey, Frederick C.	1	
Totten, Don	1	
Tottenham, Arley G. Miss	2	
Towner, Xarifa Hamilton	4	
Townsley, Channel Pick.	8	
Tracy, Lucile Snow	1	
Trafford, Martha	1	
Trafton, G. G.	1	
Tralle, Earle	1	
Traver, C. W.	1	
Traxler, H.	1	
Trease, Sherman	2	
Trefry, Harold E.	1	
Trepanier, F. L.	1	
Trine, Robert	1	
Trout, James F.	1	
Truax, Sarah Elizabeth	3	
True, E. G. Mrs.	1	
Truesdell, Edith Park	4	
Truesdell, Fannie	1	
Tubbs, C. D. Miss	1	
Tuck, Douglas	1	
Tuckerman, Lilia McCauley	3	
Turnbull, Ruth	2	
Turner, C. K.	1	
Turner, Charles Louis	4	
Turner, Ernest	1	
Turner, Mary M.	1	
Tuxen, Laurits	2	

Tydeman, Edith L.	1	
Tyler, May Belle	1	
Tyrrell, C.	1	

U

Uehling, Teodorovna	1	
Ueyama, Tokio	2	
Ueland, Emma M.	1	
Ulber, Althea	3	
Ulber, J. E.	2	
Ulianoff, Vsevolod	3	
Unsworth, Edna Ganzhorn	2	
Usher, Esther Grace	1	
Uyeno, Sikishun M.	1	

V

Vaillancourt, A. A.	2	
Valentien, Albert R.	4	
Valentien, Anna Marie	3	
Valero, Maroussia	1	
Valk, Ella S.	1	
Van Cina, Theodore	2	
Vanderbosch, E. J.	1	
Vandercook, W. A.	1	
Vanderflier, Hendricka	1	
Vandeveer, Mamie W.	1	
Van Dyke, Theodore Strong	5	
Van Eppe, Cora A.	1	
Van Evera, Caroline	1	
Van Halle, F. J.	2	
Van Kessel, Herman	1	
Van Norden, Virginia	2	
Van Noy	1	
Van Renselaer, R. Schuy.	3	
Van Veen, Pieter J. L.	4	
Van Vranken, Garrett	1	
Van Wagner, Clayton	1	
Van Winkle, Oliver G.	1	
Van Zandt, Hilda	3	
Vaughan, R. W.	1	
Velasco, F. C.	1	
Vernon, Arthur G.	2	
Vernon, Cora L.	1	
Vernon, Mildred S.	1	
Vester, Louise A.	1	
Vickland, Marie	1	
Villa, Hernando Gonzallo	7	
Vinette, Barbara I.	1	
Vittur(Vitter), Robert	1	
Volkmer, Bernard	3	
Vollmer, Grace Libby	2	
Von Briesen, Alice S.	1	
Von Keith, J. H.	3	
Von Palm, Herr	2	
Von, Pribosic, Victor	1	
Von Rohan, Arthur	1	
Von Rosenberg, Mr.	2	
Von Schneidau, Christian	10	
Von Trutschler, Wolo	1	
Vorkapick, Slavko	1	
Vosburg, Lillian	2	
Vreeland, Francis Wm.	5	
Vuchinich, Vuk	2	
Vysekal, Edouard Antonin	14	
Vysekal, Luvena Buchanan	6	

W

Wachtel, Elmer	20	
Wachtel, Marion Kavanaugh	15	
Wackenreuder, Vitus	2	
Wade, J. Ralph	1	
Wadler, R. C.	4	
Wadsworth, Phoebe Ray	1	
Wagenhals, Katherine W.	3	

Name	No.	Name	No.	Name	No.
Waggoner, Elizabeth	4	Wenzlick, Winona	1	Williamson, F. G.	1
Wagner, A. M. Miss	3	Werner, Fritz	1	Willis, Hazel	1
Wagner, Blanche Collet	1	Wenzell, Albert Beck	4	Willis, Ralph T.	1
Wagner, E. C. Mrs.	1	Wesselhoeft, Mary Fraser	2	Wills, Charles	1
Wagner, Robert Leicester	11	West, Nella A.	1	Willson, Leon	1
Wagoner, Harry B.	6	Westcott, Rowena	1	Wilson, Ellena T.	1
Waite, Eric	1	Westervelt, R. D.	1	Wilson, Ernest M.	1
Waite, Margaret A.	1	Weston, Carol Caskey	2	Wilson, Estol	2
Walden, Howard	2	Weston, M. L. Mrs.	1	Wilson, Harold F.	1
Waldo, Edith H.	1	Westwater, Eunice	1	Wilson, Melba Z.	2
Walker, John	1	Westwood, H. G. Miss	1	Wilson, Nevada	1
Wallace, Amy S.	1	Wheeler, Fern Gordon	3	Wilson, Stella	1
Wallace, Les	2	Wheeler, L. A.	1	Wilson, William J.	1
Walp, M. Vignes Mrs.	2	Wheeler, Lyle Reynolds	1	Winchell, Fannie	2
Walsh, Florence	1	Whelan, Blanche	3	Winchell, Ward	2
Walsh, Frank	1	Whelan, Mary E.	1	Winebrenner, Harry Field.	5
Walter, Albert Eugene	2	Whipple, Louise C.	1	Winn, James H.	1
Walter, Olivia B.	1	Whisman, C. A.	1	Winter, Alice Beach	2
Walters, Grace	1	Whitaker, Ruth Townsend	1	Winterburn. George T.	3
Waltz, Edith	1	White, A. C. Mrs.	1	Wintermote, M. W. Mrs.	1
Wamsley, Frank C.	4	White, Dorothy	1	Winters, Raymond T.	3
Wanley, Grace Utt	1	White, Edith	4	Wirth, Anna M.	1
Ward, Beatrice	3	White, Eleanor W.	1	Wise, Helen Peck	1
Ward, Charles S.	3	White, Emily H.	4	Withers, Celeste	1
Ward, Irene	2	White, L. E. Miss	1	Witherspoon, F. V. Mrs.	1
Ward, Jean S.	1	White, Lillian	1	Witt(e), I.. O.	3
Ward, J. Stephen	2	White Lucretia W.	1	Witte, E. L. Mrs.	2
Ward, Lily A.	2	White, Natalie	1	Wittstein, Helen	1
Wardrop, Ethel F.	1	White, Nona L.	4	Wolf, Hamilton Achille	12
Ware, Florence	1	White, Orrin	11	Wolfskill, Jose	2
Warne, Alice Schaeffer	1	White, Will	1	Wolhaupter, Helen P.	2
Warner, Nell Walker	5	Whitford, Alice M.	1	Wood, Caroline S.	1
Warren, Allene	1	Whitice, Belle	1	Wood, Eva Adeline	1
Washburn, Jessie M.	2	Whiting, Lillian V.	1	Wood, Katheryn Leone	2
Watanabe, Torajiro	2	Whitlock, Frances Jeanette	2	Wood, Leona P.	1
Waters, Mildred	1	Whitney, Erminia C.	1	Woodbridge, Virginia	1
Watkins, Catherine W.	2	Whitson, C. F. Miss	1	Woodford, Sylva	1
Watrin, Fred	1	Whyte, C. Evers	1	Woodhull, Carolyn	1
Watrous, Mary E.	2	Wiboltt, A. C.	1	Woodruff, G. M. Leonard	3
Watson, Adele	4	Wiboltt, Barbara	1	Woods, E. F.	1
Watson, Jesse N.	1	Widman, Berthold	1	Woods, Frances M.	1
Watson, Mabel	2	Wieczorek, Max	20	Woods, L. E.	1
Wattles, Gurdon H.	1	Wieland, Fred	3	Woodward, Norah	1
Wauters, David S.	1	Wilbur, C. E.	1	Woodward, Robert S.	2
Weary, Stella	1	Wilbur, Ruth Ann	2	Wooky, Harold W.	1
Weatherbee, F. I.	1	Wilcox, Cora H.	2	Woollett, William Lee	4
Weatherhead, Arthur C.	2	Wilcox, N. W.	1	Woolley, Virginia	3
Weaver, Harold	2	Wilde, Fred H.	3	Wooster, George	1
Weaver, R. B.	1	Wildhaber, Paul	3	Worcester, Mildred	1
Webb, Edith Buckland	2	Wildhack, Robert J.	3	Workman, Emmagene T.	1
Webb, Herbert C.	1	Wiles, Gorden W.	1	Worrell, Agnes	1
Webb, Margaret Ely	3	Wilfort, Mary Eliz.	1	Worth, M. F.	1
Webber, H. J. Mrs.	1	Wilhelm, Arthur L.	1	Wostrey, Carl(o)	4
Weber, Kem	7	Wilkin, Mildred Pierce	2	Woy, Leota	2
Webster, Erle	1	Wilkinson, C. E.	1	Wright, C. K. Mrs.	1
Webster, Frederick	2	Wilkinson, Donald R.	1	Wright, Doris E.	1
Webster, Ida J.	1	Wilkinson, Melroy	1	Wright, H. E. Mrs.	1
Wedemeyer, Archibald M.	1	Willard, Howard	4	Wright, Henry	2
Weidler, Alfred	1	Williams, Althea B.	1	Wright, James Couper	5
Weigel, C. A.	1	Williams, Caryl	1	Wright, Josephine M.	1
Weil, Aldolphe	2	Williams, Dorothy	1	Wright, Jud	3
Weingarten, Clemens	1	Williams, H. R.	1	Wright, Kenneth	2
Weisman, Joseph	1	Williams, Katharine Foote	1	Wright, N. H. Mrs.	1
Welch, Thaddeus	4	Williams, Lorena B.	1	Wright, Otey	1
Welcome, Virginia D.	1	Williams, Mary Belle	2	Wright, Stanton, MacD.	15
Wellington, Charles H.	3	Williams, O. L. Miss	1	Wurtele, Isobel Keil	2
Wendling, Abbie R.	1	Williams, Otis	4	Wyckoff, Anna Brooks	1
Wendt, Julia Bracken	21	Williams, Paul R.	1	Wylie, Marion E.	1
Wendt, William	31	Williams, Reed	3	**Y**	
Wennberg, Evelyn O. Mrs	1	Williamson, A. C.	1	Yager, Ydress	1

Yens(Jens), Karl   11
Yerbysmith, Ernest A.   1
Yerks, Colonel   2
Yoakum, Q. L. Miss   1
Yohn, C. H.   1
Yost, Ross   2
Young, E. H.   1
Young, Ella B.   1
Young, Eunice E.   2
Young, Florence   1
Young, Florence Upson   1
Young, H. M.   1
Young, L. C. Mrs.   1
Young, L. deWolf   1
Youngblood, Janet   1
Younglove, Ruth Ann   1
Youngstrom, Eleanor M.   1

Z

Zellner, L.   1
Zeran, William   1
Ziegler, Nellie Evelyn   1
Zillig, Fritz   1
Zim, Marco   5
Zimmerer, Frank J.   2
Zimmerman, Beatrice   1
Zimmerman, Carl   1
Zimmerman, Frederick A.   3
Zins, Alexander   1
Ziskind, A. K.   1
Ziskind, Frank   1
Zoline, Esther N.   2
Zucker, Anna   3

Moure's Club Shows

1st column- inclusion in **Artist Clubs & Exhib**.......
2nd column- inclusion in **Calif. Watercolor Society**..

Name	Artist Clubs & Exhib	Calif. Watercolor Society
Abascal, Mary	x	
Abdy, Rowena Meeks	x	x
Abramovich, Ida	x	
Ackerman, Frank	x	
Adams, Clinton	x	
Adams, Velma	x	
Addams, Clifford	x	
Ahlberg, Florence M	x	
Ahring, Jaine	x	
Albright, Gertrude P.	x	
Albright, H. Oliver	x	x
Albro, Maxine	x	
Aldrich, Clarence N.		
Aldrin, Anders G.	x	x
Aldritt, Cyril		x
Alexander, Dora B.	x	
Alexander, Margo	x	
Aller, Gladys	x	x
Alvarez, Mabel	x	
Amato, Sam		x
Ames, Arthur	x	
Ames, Florence	x	
Amos, Arthur C.	x	
Amyx, Leon		x
Anderson, Dorothy V.	x	
Anderson, Edward A.		x
Andres, Adele	x	
Andrus, Zoray		x
Archambault, A. Marg.	x	
Archer, Edmund	x	
Arledge, Sara Kathryn	x	
Arnold, Edwin C.		x
Arnold, Richard		x
Arouni, Lynette		x
Asanger, Jacob	x	
Ashlock, Rex		x
Askinazy, M.	x	
Atkinson, William O.	x	
Attridge, Irma		x
Atwood, Mary Hall		x
Ault, George	x	
Austin, Charles P.	x	x
Avery, Kenneth Newell	x	
Ayars, Margaret C.	x	
Ayres, John		x
Ayres, Martha Oathout	x	
B		
Backus, Standish Jr		x
Badger, Stanwood	x	
Bagdatopoulos, W. S.	x	x
Bailey, Harry L.	x	
Bailey, Henry Lewis	x	
Bailey, Laura Miller	x	
Bains, James H.		x
Baird, Theodore A.		x
Baker, George	x	
Baker, Leonard E.	x	
Bakos, Joseph G.	x	
Baldaugh, Anni	x	x
Baldwin, C. Park	x	
Baldwin, Clark	x	
Baldwin, Henriette B.	x	
Balfour, Helen	x	x
Ballin, Hugo	x	
Baltekal-Goodman, M.		x

Name	Artist Clubs & Exhib	Calif. Watercolor Society
Barker, George	x	
Barker, George Jr.	x	
Barker, Olive	x	x
Barlow, Jarvis	x	
Barnes, Mathew R.	x	
Barney, Ester Steven	x	
Barr, Roger		x
Barres, M. Des	x	
Barrett, Lisbeth Stone	x	
Bartlett, Dana	x	x
Bartlett, Grace L.	x	
Bartlett, Ivan	x	
Barton, Loren R.	x	
Barton, Macena	x	
Bartram, Clara	x	
Baskerville, Eliz.	x	x
Bates, Kenneth	x	
Bauman, E. F.	x	
Baxter, Martha W.	x	
Beaumont, Arthur	x	x
Becker, Edwin W.		x
Beckman, Jessie Mary	x	
Beck-Meyer, Rick	x	
Beecher, Florence	x	
Beecher, Genevieve T.	x	
Beetz, Carl		x
Behn, Harry	x	
Behr, Betty	x	
Bell, Sidney	x	
Bemus, Hazel Nell	x	
Benjamin, C. H.		x
Benkkerti, Margot	x	
Bennett, Jewel		x
Bennet, Raney		x
Bennett, Ruth	x	x
Bensco, Charles J.	x	
Bensinger, Anne M.	x	x
Bentherti, Margot	x	
Benton, Janet		x
Benton, Thomas Hart	x	
Bentz, John	x	
Berend, Charlotte		x
Bergman, Carl		x
Berman, Eugene		x
Bernie, J. P.	x	
Berninghaus, J. Chas.	x	
Berninghaus, Oscar E.	x	
Berry, Cyril		x
Bessinger, Frederick	x	
Bester, Donald		x
Bethell, Worden	x	
Betts, Edward		x
Beynon, William		x
Biberman, Edward	x	
Biddle, George	x	
Biles, Ellsworth	x	
Bill, Sally Cross	x	
Billings, Lucie		x
Billington, Jules	x	x
Binford, Julien		x
Birch, Geraldine	x	
Bischoff, Franz A.	x	
Bisttram, E.	x	
Bjurman, Andrew J.	x	
Black, Helen Harris		x

Name	Artist Clubs & Exhib	Calif. Watercolor Society
Black, Mary C. W.	x	
Black, William	x	
Blair, Lee	x	x
Blair, Lynette	x	
Blair, Mary Robinson	x	x
Blair, Preston		x
Blanchett, Jean		x
Blank, Pauline	x	x
Blaustein, Joseph H.		x
Blazek, Anton	x	
Bliss, Alma Hirsig	x	
Bliss, John A.		x
Bloser, Florence P.	x	
Blower, David H.	x	
Blum, Helen	x	
Blumberg, Ron		x
Blumve, Edna	x	
Boag, Robert	x	
Boardman, Rosina Cox	x	
Bode, Burnaby	x	
Bode, Catherine B.	x	
Bode, Margaret		x
Bodero, James S.	x	
Boehme, Hazel	x	x
Boericke, Joanna M.	x	
Bohan, Ruth Harris	x	
Bohrod, Aaron	x	
Boldsen, Thyra	x	
Bolles, Ida Randall	x	
Bond, Ella Tyler	x	
Bonsall, Mary W.	x	
Boone, Cora M.	x	
Booth, George W.		x
Booth, James S.	x	
Borg, Carl Oscar	x	x
Borowsky, Marvin		x
Bosche, W. R.		x
Bosserman, Lyman W.		
Bothwell, Dorr	x	
Botke, Cornelis	x	x
Botke, Jessie Arms	x	x
Botz, Donald		x
Bourdieu, Aimee F.	x	
Bowen, Irene	x	
Bowles, Caroline H.	x	
Bowne, William		x
Boyd, Doris	x	
Boyle, Sarah Y. M.	x	
Boynton, Constance	x	
Boynton, Ray	x	x
Bradley, Elliott R.	x	
Bradshaw, Alexandra	x	x
Bradshaw, Glenn R.		x
Bradshaw, William		x
Brandriff, George K.	x	
Brandt, Joan Irving		x
Brandt, Rex	x	x
Brash, Viola	x	
Brasz, A. Franz	x	x
Braun, Maurice		
Breckenridge, Hugh H.	x	
Breckman, Mary		x
Bremer, Anne M.	x	
Breuer, H. J.	x	
Brewer, Nicholas	x	

Name	1	2
Brigante, Nicholas	x	x
Bristol, Tanci	x	x
Brooks, Alexander	x	
Brooks, Anna P.	x	
Brooks, Leonard		x
Brooks, Mildred Bryant	x	
Brossard, Raymond	x	
Brough, Richard		x
Brown, Austin C.	x	
Brown, Benjamin C.	x	
Brown, Dorothy		x
Brown, Lucille Rose.	x	
Brown, Pamela Vinton	x	
Brown, Roy	x	
Brown, William J.	x	
Bruce, Edward	x	
Brunswig, Marguerite	x	
Bruton, Margaret	x	
Bryant, Everett L.	x	x
Bryson, Hope Mercereau	x	x
Bubeshko, Emilia	x	
Buchanan, Albyn	x	
Buchanan, Ella	x	
Buchanan, Luvena	x	
Buck, Helen	x	
Buckley, Jean		x
Buel, Hubert	x	x
Buff, Conrad	x	
Buller, Jewell B.		x
Bumstead, Henry		x
Burbank, E. A.	x	
Burchfield, Charles		x
Burdick, Ruth	x	
Burgdorff, F.	x	
Burgeson, Genevieve	x	
Burgher, Juana		x
Burk, W. E. Jr.	x	
Burkhard, Verona Lor.	x	
Burkhardt, Hans		x
Burkland, August P.	x	
Burlin, Paul	x	
Burner, Adella S.	x	
Burnett, Ted		x
Burnham, John	x	
Burnham, Roger Noble	x	
Burrell, Louie	x	
Burton, Elizabeth E.		x
Bush, Ella Shepard	x	
Bush, Gladys Lewis	x	
Butler, Edward B.	x	
Butler, H. B.	x	
Butler, John	x	
Butler, Leonard C.		x
Byrne, William	x	

C

Name	1	2
Cabral, Flavio		x
Cadmus, Paul		x
Cady, Fred A.	x	
Cahero, E. G.	x	
Cahill, Katherine K.	x	
Cahill, William V.	x	
Cailliet, Helen Amoy		x
Cailliet, Marcel	x	x
Cain, Joseph		x
Cain, Joy		x

Name	1	2
Caldwell, Frances	x	
Call, Mary E.	x	
Callahan, Frances	x	
Campanello, Vincent	x	
Campbell, Charles M.		x
Campbell, Floy	x	
Campbell, Isabella F.	x	
Campbell, Myrtle H.	x	
Cannon, Dorothy	x	x
Cannon, J. Vedderstm.	x	
Carew, Berta	x	
Carey, Paul T.		x
Carmichael, Joe		x
Carlson, Margaret	x	
Carpenter, Ellen		x
Carroll, John	x	
Carter, C. H.		x
Carter, Gordon K.	x	x
Carter, Jane Downs		x
Carter, Pruett	x	
Casebier, Cecil Lang		x
Casello, Alfred	x	
Cassell, Helen Lewis	x	
Cassidy, Gerald	x	
Cassidy, Harold		x
Casterton, Eda Nemode	x	
Castruccio, Rominlda	x	
Chamberlain, Norman S	x	
Chamberlin, F. Tolles	x	x
Champlin, Ada Belle	x	
Chandler, Helen Clark	x	x
Chapin, Francis	x	x
Chapman, Minerva J.	x	
Chase, Ada M.	x	
Chase, Anna Webber	x	
Cheever, Walter L.	x	
Cheney, Warren	x	
Cherry, Herman J.	x	
Chess, Edna	x	
Chevy, Herman J.	x	
Chi, Chen		x
Chiapella, Edward E.	x	
Chino, Thomas Fort.		x
Chouinard, Nelbert	x	
Christensen, Ethel	x	
Christenson, John		x
Christo, T. John		x
Churchill	x	
Cikovsky, Nicolai	x	x
Clapp, Charlotte I.	x	
Clapp, Howard C.	x	x
Clapp, William H.	x	
Clark, Alson Skinner	x	x
Clark, Emelia G.	x	
Clark, Frances	x	
Clark, M. Beatrice	x	
Clark, Marie S.	x	
Clark, Seldon	x	
Clarke, Arthur G.	x	
Clarke, Kim	x	x
Claus, May Austin	x	
Clayberger, Samuel R		x
Cleaves, Gail	x	
Clement, Judith M.	x	
Clements, Grace	x	

Name	1	2
Clements, Lydia Brooks		x
Cley, Alfred		x
Clkubo, Benji	x	
Clunie, Robert	x	
Coakley, John		x
Coan, Helen E.	x	
Coats, Claude	x	x
Coburn, Frank	x	
Codman, Ruth		x
Cogswell, Kathleen	x	
Cohen, Lois Green		x
Cohn, Max	x	
Colburn, Eleanor	x	x
Colby, Horace F.	x	
Cole, Gail		x
Cole, Geo. Townsend	x	x
Cole, Geo. I.		x
Cole, Helen	x	
Coleman, Glenn A.	x	
Coleman, Harvey B.	x	
Coles, Wilson	x	x
Colman, R. Clarkson	x	
Colescott, Warrington		x
Colton, Harriett		x
Comfort, Tyrone	x	
Comins, Eben F.	x	
Conchman, Victoria	x	
Cook, Howard N.		x
Cooke, Dorthea		x
Coolidge, Bertha	x	
Coolidge, John E.	x	
Cooper, Calvin C.	x	
Cooper, Collin Camp.	x	
Cooper, George A.		x
Cooper, Mario		x
Cooper, Virginia S.	x	
Coover, Nell	x	
Corbino, Jon		x
Corbit, George C.	x	
Corich, George		x
Cornell, Allela	x	
Cornin, Jon		x
Costello, Valentine	x	x
Costigan, John		x
Cotton, John	x	x
Cotton, William		x
Coulter, Lillian	x	
Coulter, Mary J.	x	
Couse, E. Irving	x	x
Coventry, Stanley	x	
Cowan, Cora	x	
Cowan, Elsie		x
Cowles, Russell		x
Cox, Lyda M.	x	
Craig, Tomas	x	x
Craise, Alice L.	x	
Cram, Allan G.	x	
Cramer, Harriet T.	x	
Crandall, Marian	x	
Crane, Douglas	x	
Crawford, Esther M.	x	
Crawford, Lanson H.		x
Creal, Jim Jr.	x	
Cressey, Bert C.	x	
Cressey, David B.		x

Name		
Cressey, Meta	x	
Cron, Nina Nash	x	
Cronenwett, Clare	x	
Cross, Jay Lee	x	
Cross, Watson		x
Crow, Louise	x	
Crown, Keith		x
Cuneo, Rinaldo	x	
Cunningham, Benj. F.	x	
Cunningham, May M. S.	x	
Cuprien, Frank W.	x	
Currier, Walter B.	x	
Curry, John Steuart	x	
Curtis, Ida M.	x	
Curtis, I. Maynard	x	
Curtis, Leland S.	x	
Curtis, Marion	x	x
Cushman, Henry	x	
Cutrow, Leonard		x
Cytron, David S.		x
Cytron, Lois B.		x

D

Name		
Daggett, Grace E.	x	
Daggett, Maud	x	
Dagradi, Don		x
Dahl, Olga	x	
Dahlgreen, Charles W.	x	
Dalrymple, Lucile S.	x	
Daly, Emily R.	x	
Dana, Esther G.	x	
Dando, Susie M. B.	x	
Daniell, Wm. Swift	x	
Daniels, E. H.	x	
Dann, Frode N.	x	x
Danner, Sarah Kolb	x	x
Darr, William	x	
Darrow, Paul		x
Date, Hideo	x	
Davey, Randall	x	
David, Donald		x
Davies, Elton Morrow		x
Davis, Charles Hulbert	x	
Davis, E. Flannigan	x	
Davis, Gladys Rockmore	x	
Davis, Harry	x	
Davis, Lew E.	x	x
Dawes, Edwin M.	x	
Day, Adele	x	
Day, Martha B. Willson	x	
Dayton, Lillian	x	
Dean, Eva		x
Dean, Free		x
DeCarlo, Charles		x
Deckert, L. Hutton	x	
Dedeaux, Helen		x
DeDiego, Julio		x
DeErderly, Francis		x
DeGavere, Cora	x	
Dehn, Adolph		x
Dehner, Walter		x
DeJoiner, L. E.	x	
DeKruif, Henri G.	x	x
Delano, Annita	x	x
Delbridge, W. C.	x	
DeMers, Joseph	x	x

Name		
Denman, Lucien	x	
Dethloff, P. H.	x	
Deutsch, Boris	x	x
Devol, Eugene	x	
Devriendt, Stefan V.	x	
DeWilde, Victor		x
DeWitt, Robert	x	x
DeWolf, Wallace L.	x	
Dickey, Dan	x	x
Dickinson, Daisy	x	
Dickinson, Edward	x	
Dickinson, Edwin	x	
Dickinson, Ross	x	
Dickstein, Eva		x
Dike, Phil	x	x
Diller, Alfred	x	
Dillmann, Louis C.	x	
Dionysius, Dooley		x
Dixon, Louis Carlton		x
Dixon, Maynard	x	
Djey, Djey El	x	
Doak, Jeanette		x
Dobson, Margaret A.	x	
Dodd, Lamar		x
Dodge, Arthur B.	x	
Dole, William		x
Domela, Jan	x	
Donaldson, Douglas	x	
Donaldson, Elise		x
Donaldson, Margaret	x	
Dooner, Clara	x	
Doro		x
Douglas, Haldane	x	x
Douglas, Harry	x	
Dowiatt, Dorothy	x	x
Dranko, Robert L.		x
Driscoll, Harold		x
DuBois, Guy Pene	x	
Duffie, Jane S.	x	
Dumond, F. Melville	x	
Duncan, Charles S.	x	
Duncan, Geraldine R.	x	
Duncan, John	x	
Dunham, Francis V.		x
Dunlap, Helena	x	x
Dunn, Marjorie Cline	x	
Dunton, W. Herbert	x	
Durston, Arthur	x	
Dustin, Silas S.	x	
Duvall, Fannie E.	x	
Dyer, Briggs	s	
Dyer, Carlos	x	

E

Name		
Eaton, Catherine		x
Edmond, Elizabeth	x	
Edmondson, Leonard		x
Edstrom, David	x	
Edwards, H. Arden	x	
Edwards, Norman	x	
Edwards, Stanley	x	
Egen, Max	x	
Eilshemius, Louis M.	x	
Eliot, Don	x	
Elliott, Hannah	x	
Elliott, Ruth	x	

Name		
Ellis, Fremont	x	
Engard, Robert O.		x
Engel, Jules		x
Engelberg, Sydney		x
Ennis, George P.		x
Erickson, Clifford	x	
Erickson, Roy D.		x
Ernest, Aleta		x
Erwin, John B.		x
Escherich, Elsa Falk	x	
Eskridge, Robert Lee		x
Estes, Ruth	x	
Estill, Ella Howard	x	
Etheridge, Edith G.		x
Eudey, Dora Higgens		x
Evans, E.	x	
Evans, Elinor		x
Evans, Ivor Gordon		x
Everett, Eugenia	x	
Everett, Louise	x	
Everett, Mary O.	x	
Everritt, William R.	x	
Ewing, Edgar		x

F

Name		
Faille, C. A.	x	
Fairbanks, J. B.	x	
Fairbanks, J. Leo	x	
Farmer, Brigitta Moran	x	
Farnsworth, Ethel N.	x	
Farnsworth, Jerry	x	
Farrington, Walter	x	
Farrington, Wesley	x	
Faucett, Lionel		x
Fechin, Nicholai	x	
Fee, Fred Carver	x	
Feininger, Lionel		x
Feinstein, Mary	x	
Feitelson, Lorser	x	
Feldman, Dorothy		x
Ferguson, George D.		x
Ferguson, Lillian P.	x	
Ferguson, Mabel B.	x	
Fernow, Bernice P. A.	x	
Ferrell, Lucille E.		x
Ferren, John Millard	x	
Fidaroff, Simon	x	
Fiedler, Charles K.	x	
Fiene, Ernest	x	
Finch, Keith		x
Fink, Jackson Rader	x	
Finley, Mary Louise	x	x
Firth, Karl		x
Fisher, George H.	x	
Fiske, Gertrude	x	
Fitch, Adele Russell		x
Fitzgerald, James		x
Fitz-Gibbon, Frank	x	
Fitzhenry, Geo. O.	x	
Flack, John		x
Fleck, Joseph A.	x	
Fleck, Robert J.		x
Fletcher, Frank M.	x	
Fletcher, S. L.	x	
Flower, George J.	x	
Foley, Cornelia Mac.	x	

Name		
Fon, Jade	x	x
Forbes, L. C. O.		x
Force, Clara G.	x	
Foresman, Alice Cart.	x	
Forker, Edwin L.	x	
Forkner, Edgar	x	
Forsythe, Clyde	x	
Fortune, E. Charlton	x	
Fossum, Syd		x
Foster, Arthur Gilbert	x	
Foster, Arthur Turner	x	x
Foster, Ben	x	
Foster, Bertha Knox	x	
Foster, Willet	x	x
Fowler, Helen	x	
Fox, Mary L.	x	
Fracker, Ruth Miller	x	
Francisco, J. Bond	x	
Franquinet, Eugene	x	
Frary, Michael		x
Fraser, Hap		x
Fraser, Harold T.		x
Fraser, Juliette May		x
Frazer, Priscilla J.		x
French, John		x
French, Park		x
Frendenthal, David		x
Friedman, Alethea	x	
Friel, Patricia		x
Fries, Charles Art.	x	
Frolich, Finn Haakon	x	
Frost, John	x	
Fry, D. H.	x	
Fry, Jack	x	
Fry, Mary L. Finley	x	x
Frye, Pearl		x
Fujita, Sadamitsu		x
Fullonton, Robert D.	x	
Fulop, Karoly	x	x
Fulton, D. Kines	x	
Fulton, Dorothy	x	
Fulton, Fitch	x	x
Funk, Joe	x	
Fyfe, Gilbert G.		x

G

Name		
Gaal, Steven	x	
Gabel, Robert W.		x
Gaffney, Claribel H.	x	
Gage, Merrill	x	
Gale, Jane G.		x
Gambee, Martha		x
Ganine, Pierre	x	
Ganso, Emil		x
Gardelle, Carlton	x	
Gardner, Maurice		x
Garner, Archibald	x	
Garnsey, Julian E.	x	x
Garrigue, Edith H.	x	
Garson, Ann		x
Garth, John	x	
Gary, Fanchon	x	
Gasser, Henry		x
Gavere, Cor De	x	
Gaw, William A.	x	x
Gay, August F.	x	

Name		
Gaylord, Helen	x	
Gearhart, May	x	
Gela	x	
Gellert, Emery	x	
George, Dorothy	x	
Gerard, Edgar	x	
Gere, Nellie Hunt.	x	
Geritz, Franz	x	
Gerrity, J. M.	x	
Gershjoren, Milton		x
Gibson, George	x	x
Giffen, Eliz. Helene	x	
Gilberg, Robert G.		x
Gilbert, Arthur Hill	x	
Gilbert, Robert	x	x
Gilchrist, Meda	x	
Gile, Seldon Connor	x	
Gilien, Ted		x
Gillette, Henry S.		x
Gilmore, Pricilla A.	x	
Girardin, Frank	x	
Gist, Salome	x	
Gjertson, Roy		x
Glackens, William J.	x	
Gladding, Hope		x
Glassell, Joan		x
Gleason, Joe Duncan	x	
Glenn, Sally		x
Godwin, Iris		x
Goff, Harper	x	x
Goldschlager, Belle	x	
Goldstein, Phil	x	
Goldthwaite, Anne	x	
Good, Marje		x
Goodhue, Alice Fuller	x	
Goodman, Michael B.	x	x
Goodwin, Jean	x	x
Gordon, Allyn		x
Gould, Allan	x	
Grabach, John R.	x	
Graham, Donald Wilk.	x	
Graham, Eliz. Suther.		x
Graham, Harold	x	
Graham, Robert A.	x	
Gramatky, Hardie	x	x
Grant, Blanche	x	
Grant, Campbell	x	
Grant, Gordon K	x	
Grant, James Edward		x
Grant, Lee	x	
Grath, Bruno	x	
Graves, Ed		x
Gray, Alice C.	x	
Green, Florence Topp.	x	
Green, James L.		x
Green, Lucille Brown		x
Greenbaum, Joseph	x	
Greenwell, Julian	x	
Griebenow, Margaret		x
Greiser, Howard A.	x	
Gren, Neil A.	x	
Greutert, Henry	x	
Griesbach, David	x	
Griffen, Davenport	x	
Griffith, Elsa C.	x	

Name		
Griffith, Katherine P	x	
Griffith, Lillian	x	
Griffith, William A.	x	
Gropper, William		x
Grossman, Roy	x	
Grosz, George		x
Groth, Bruno	x	
Grovcock, Alice R.	x	
Grube, Vara		x
Gruenfeld, Casper	x	
Guerin, Jean	x	
Guptil, Ada A.	x	
Gustin, Paul Morgan	x	
Guttridge, Eleanor N.		x

H

Name		
Haaff, Cornelia De	x	
Haase, Madeline		x
Hahn, Blanche		x
Haig, Mabel George	x	x
Haines, Angela M.		x
Haines, Kenneth		x
Haines, Richard		x
Haley, John		x
Hall, Clem		x
Hall, Jean Gates		x
Haller, Constance R.	x	
Haller, Nellie Ward	x	
Halliday, Hughitt	x	
Halpert, Samuel	x	
Halseth, Edna Scofield	x	
Halstead, Muriel		x
Hamilton, Herbert	x	
Hand, Jo Hale	x	
Hansen, Armin	x	x
Hansen, Ejnar	x	x
Hansen, Gaylen		x
Hansen, James	x	
Harby, Thornton	x	
Harcoff, Lyla Marshall	x	
Harding, G. Powell	x	x
Harding, Herrica		x
Hardy, Merlin	x	
Hargrave, Harry S.	x	
Harker, Lucille		x
Harkness, E. Keith	x	
Harmetz, Herrica H.		x
Harper, Marian Dunlap	x	
Harter, Thomas J.		x
Harris, Alexandrina	x	
Harris, George	x	
Harris, Harwell	x	
Harris, Robert	x	
Harris, Sam Hyde	x	
Harrison, William J.	x	
Hartley, Marsden	x	
Hartman, Isabel	x	
Hartzell, Molly Ayer		x
Hartzig, Mildred	x	x
Harvey, Eli	x	
Hashimoto, Michi	x	x
Haskell, William	x	
Hasslein, Geo. Johann		x
Hatfield, Harvey D.	x	
Haugaard, Kay		x
Hawkins, Robert E.		x

Name	1	2
Hawthorne, Charles W.	x	
Hawthorne, Connie	x	
Hayakawa, Miki	x	
Hayes, Gayl	x	
Hayes, Thomas	x	
Haynes, Grace	x	
Haynes, John W.	x	
Hays, Gertrude V.	x	
Hayward, Roger		x
Hazard, Arthur M.	x	
Hazen, Bessie Ella	x	x
Healy, Arthur K.		x
Hecht, Zoltan	x	
Heckman, A. F.	x	
Heflinger, Grace	x	
Heidel, Frederick II		x
Heilborn, Carl	x	x
Heinemann, Arthur M.	x	
Heitland, W. Emerson		x
Helder, Z. Vanessa		x
Helfensteller, Veronica		x
Heliker, John		x
Hemphill, Ethel		x
Henderson, William P.	x	
Hennesy, Dale		x
Hennings, E. Martin	x	
Henri, Robert	x	
Henry, Albert	x	
Henry, Coah	x	
Hentch, John	x	
Herbert, Myrta E.	x	
Hernandez, Caesar A.		x
Herrick, H. M.	x	
Herron, Jason	x	
Herron, Jessie E.	x	
Hersch, Lee	x	
Herwig, William	x	
Hess, Charles		x
Hesse, Henry Melton	x	x
Hessova, Bozena	x	
Heuermann, Magda	x	
Hewes, Dorothy		x
Hibberts, Forrest		x
Higgins, Eugene	x	
Hill, Herbert	x	
Hill, Jessie F.	x	
Hill, Montine		x
Hillinck, Henri		x
Hills, Anna Althea	x	
Hilstad, John Roy		
Hilton, John	x	
Hinchman, John H.	x	
Hinckley, Lawrence		x
Hinkle, Clarence K.	x	x
Hinkle, Lucile	x	x
Hinkley, Lawrence B.	x	
Hinrichs, Marie H.	x	
Hirsch, Joseph	x	
Hirsch, Stefan	x	
Hiss, John M.	x	
Hobart, Clark	x	
Hodges, Marjorie	x	
Hoerman, Carl	x	
Hoff, Helen Lu M.	x	x
Hoffman, Mabel		x

Name	1	2
Hogue, Alexandre	x	
Holderman, Robert L.		x
Holladay, Ben Camp.	x	
Holland, Leza		x
Holland, Mildred O.		x
Holman, Ida B.	x	
Holmes, Ethel Green.	x	
Holmes, Miles E.	x	
Holmes, Ralph	x	
Holmes, Stuart	x	
Holmquist, Robert		x
Hong, Anna Helga	x	
Hooper, Rosa	x	
Hoopes, Henrietta		x
Hope, Thelma Paddock	x	
Hopkins, Anna Mary	x	
Hopper, Edward		x
Hord, Donal A.	x	
Horter, Earl		x
Horton, Adrienne		x
Hoskins, Winfield S.	x	x
Houlahan, Kathleen	x	
Hounsell, C. Lillian	x	
Houston, Leta K.	x	
Howard, Charles H.	x	
Howard, Elizabeth		x
Howard, John L.	x	
Howard, Leon Jr.	x	
Howard, R. V.	x	
Howard, Robert B.	x	
Howell, Helen	x	
Howell, Phoebe	x	x
Howell, Youldon C.	x	
Hubley, John	x	
Huebner, Mentor	x	
Hueter, James		x
Huffine, Ray		x
Hugh, Kenneth Marcus		x
Hughes, Daisy M.	x	x
Hughes, Francis K.		x
Hugunin, Grace		x
Hulett, Ralph		x
Humphrey, Frances		x
Hunley, K. J.	x	
Hunley, Katherine	x	
Hunt, Thomas L.	x	
Hunter, R. Vernon	x	x
Hurd, Peter		x
Hutchinson, Mabel		x
Huttl, Robert Leon	x	
Hylen, Arnold	x	
Iliff, Cynthia	x	
Ingels, Frank L.	x	
Ingels, Kathleen Bev.	x	
Ingersoll, Emma Hess	x	
Inglis, Barbara		x
Ingraham, Rex	x	
Inukai, Kyohei	x	
Inverarity, Beryl	x	
Irvin, Va. Hendrickson	x	
Irving, Joan		x
Irwin, Kay		x
Irwin, William Hyde		x
Isaacs, Walter T.	x	

Name	1	2
Isnow, Irene		x
Ito, K.	x	

J

Name	1	2
Jack, Ella		x
Jack, Lucy Blair	x	
Jackson, Annie Hurl.	x	
Jackson, Everett Gee	x	
Jackson, Hazel Drake	x	
Jackson, Martin J.	x	
Jackson, Mims		x
Jackson, Nathalie L'H.	x	
Jackson, Pansy Mabel	x	x
Jackson, Robert		x
Jacoby, Ned		x
Jacques, Dorothy		x
Jahn, Helma Heynsen	x	
Jaho, Bert N.	x	
James, Austin	x	
James, George R.		x
Jankai, Tibor		x
Jarvaise, James		x
Jeakins, Dorothy	x	
Jenkins, H. J.	x	
Jenkins, Hannah T.	x	
Jenson, Frank A.		x
Jepson, Herbert		x
Johansen, Waldemar	x	
Johanson, Edward W.		x
Johns, Jeannette	x	x
Johnson, Arthur Monrod		x
Johnson, Barbara	x	x
Johnson, Burt W.	x	
Johnson, Clarence R.	x	
Johnson, Frank Tenney	x	
Johnson, Jeanne Payne		x
Johnson, John S.	x	
Johnson, Marie	x	
Johnson, Reginald	x	x
Johnson, S. Kenneth		x
Johnson, Stanley F.	x	x
Johnston, Frederic	x	x
Johnston, Lucile M.		x
Johnston, Ynez		x
Johnstone, Ralph W.		x
Johonnot, Ralph Helm	x	
Jones, E. S.	x	
Jones, Edna A.	x	
Jones, Elbert Mohler	x	
Jones, Essie Love	x	
Jones, Jessie Love	x	
Jones, Martha M.	x	
Jones, Prescott		x
Jordan, Dorothy		x
Jordan, Helen A.	x	
Josselyn, Christine S	x	x
Judson, William Lees	x	
Julian, Paul		x
Jurecka, Cyril	x	

K

Name	1	2
Kaher, Fritz	x	
Kamins, Boris		x
Kaminski, Edward	x	
Kamp, Lapchep	x	
Kanne, H. W. Jr.		x
Kantor, Morris	x	

Name	1	2
Karfiol, Bernard	x	
Karras, Spiros Jojn	x	
Kassler, Charles H.	x	
Katchmakoff, Atanas	x	
Katz, Leo	x	
Kaufman, Meyer	x	
Kaufman, Van		x
Kaufmann, Ferdinand	x	
Kavanaugh, Katherine	x	
Kay, Gertrude S.		x
Kaye, Arthur L.		x
Kayo, Arthur L.		x
Keck, Charles		x
Keeler, Katherine D	x	
Keller, Edgar	x	
Keller, Florence D.		x
Keller, George A.	x	
Keller, Henry G.		x
Kelley, Sue E.	x	
Kelly, Clyde		x
Kelly, Edna	x	
Kelly, Francis		x
Kelsey, Richmond I		x
Kendall, Marie Boening	x	
Kennedy, Louise		x
Kennicott, Robert H.	x	x
Kenward, Torki		x
Kenworthy, Mildred T.		x
Keplinger, Lona M.	x	
Kerns, Fannie M.	x	x
Kerns, Maude		x
Kerwin, Mary Catherine	x	
Kester, Lenard		x
Keszthelyi, A. S.	x	
Ketchum, Austin	x	
Kibbey, Ilah Marion	x	
Killingsworth, Edw.		x
Kilpatrick, Aaron E.	x	x
King, Albert Henry	x	x
King, John M.	x	
King, Mary Eliz.	x	
Kingman, Dong		x
Kirby, Emmett	x	
Kirk, Frances C.	x	
Kirkgaard, L. Maria	x	
Kirkgaard, W.	x	
Kirkland, Lance Hall	x	x
Kirsten, Richard		x
Klauber, Alice	x	x
Klauch, Edward		x
Kleidman, Rose		x
Klein, David Fedric		x
Kleitsch, Joseph	x	
Kley, Alfred J.		x
Klinker, Orpha	x	
Klitgaard, Georgina	x	
Klokke, Helen	x	
Klynn, Herbert		x
Knath, Karl	x	
Knee, Gina		x
Knop, Siegfried		x
Knott, A. H.	x	
Knowles, Elizabeth	x	
Knowles, F. McG.	x	
Knowles, Joseph	x	x
Kocher, Fritz	x	
Koester, William H.	x	
Kohler, Eleanor K.	x	
Kohler, Eleanore L.	x	
Kohlmeier, Helen L	x	
Kohn, Edmond	x	
Kollorsz, Richard	x	
Kooyman, Olga Seem		x
Kopenhaver, Josephine	x	x
Kopta, Emry	x	
Korb, Robert P.	x	x
Kosa, Emil J. Jr.	x	x
Kosa, Emil Sr.	x	
Kosa, Mimi	x	
Kosleck, Martin	x	
Kostellow, A. J.	x	
Kotoku, Shiyei	x	
Kraft, Emma	x	
Krakauer, Gustave H.	x	
Kramer, Albert John		x
Kramer, Harold M.		x
Krasnow, Peter	x	
Krauth, Charles P.	x	
Kreindler, Doris B.	x	
Kroll, Leon	x	
Kromer, Adelaide	x	x
Kubacki, Raymond		x
Kuehne, Max	x	
Kuhnle, Paul	x	
Kuniyoshi, Yasuo	x	x
Kurtzworth, Harry M.	x	
Kurutz, Joseph		x
Kushner, Dor. Browdy		x
Kwok, John J.		x

L

Name	1	2
Labaudt, Lucien	x	
LaCom, Wayne		x
Lacy, Ernest		x
Lagorio, Irene		x
Lahey, Richard	x	
L'Allemand, Gordon	x	
L'Amantia, James		x
Landacre, Paul	x	
Landy, Art		x
Lane, Frank A. Jr.		x
Langley, Edward	x	
Langston, Birgit		x
Lanpher, Helen F.	x	
Large, Philip M.		x
Larimer, Barbara	x	
Larimer, Ruth Myers	x	x
Larson, Robert	x	
Larsson, E. W.	x	
Larzelere, Charles L.	x	
Lasky, Bessie	x	
Lauderbach, Frances	x	
Lauritz, Paul	x	
Lauritzen, Dillon T.		x
Lavrillier, Gaston A	x	
Law, Harry		x
Lawler, Charles B.	x	
Lawrence, James A.		x
Lawrence, Josephine	x	
Lawson, Russell E.	x	
Leach, Frank H.	x	
Leake, Gerald	x	
Leale, Marion	x	
LeBarts, Al	x	
Lee, Lee	x	
Lee, Leslie	x	
Lee, Ming-Cho		x
Lee, Selma	x	
Leekney, Frederick A.		x
Leeper, John P.		x
Lehman, Harold	x	
Leigh, Lily	x	
Leighton, Kathryn W.	x	
Leonard, Elizabeth	x	
Leonard, Joe C.	x	
Leonard, Jack	x	
Leopold	x	
Levee, John		x
Leverenz, Carol M.	x	
Levine, David	x	x
Levine, Francis	x	
Levy, Hilda		x
Lewis, Alonzo Victor	x	
Lewis, H. Emerson	x	
Lewis, James A.		x
Lewis, Jeannette M.	x	
Lewis, Jessie M.	x	
Lewis, Lola C.		x
Lewis, Phillips F.	x	x
Lewis, Tom E.	x	x
Liddell, Frank P.	x	
Liebig, Carolyn		x
Liliano, Ada May	x	
Lincoln, Alice R.	x	
Linderman, Winifred	x	
Lindsay, Ruth Andrews	x	
Lingren, Paula		x
Linsey, Martin		x
Linus, Axel	x	
Lion, Henry	x	
Lippman, D. R.		x
Little, Gertrude L.		
Lloyd, Mary Jean		x
Lockhart, Marcelite	x	
Lockwood, Florence	x	
Lockwood, Robert	x	x
Lockwood, Ward		x
Loeffler, Gisella		x
Logan, Maurice	x	x
Long, Eula	x	
Loop, Edith H.	x	
Loop, Jack	x	
Lopez, Rene H.		x
Loran, Erle		x
Love, Paul		x
Lovins, Henry	x	
Lowd, Edna B.	x	
Lowden, Elsie Motz	x	
Loxley, Ruth Y.		x
Ludovici, Alice E.	x	
Ludovici, Frieda	x	
Lugano, Ines S.	x	
Lukens, Glen	x	
Lukits, Theodore N.	x	
Lundeberg, Helen	x	
Lundmark, Leon	x	

M

Name	1	2
Lungren, Fernand	x	
Lutz, Daniel	x	x
Lynch, Anna	x	
Lyon, Rosa Hooper	x	
McAfee, Ila	x	
McBeth, Mary		x
McBride, Eva A.	x	
McBride, Mrs. J. H.	x	
McCall, Wm. Sherrod	x	
McCallister, Va. Ann		x
McCartney, Marion C.	x	
McClelland, Douglas		x
McCloud, Howard	x	
McClung, Florence	x	
McClymont, J. I.	x	
McConaha, Lawrence	x	
McCutcheon, George	x	
MacDonald, St. Claire	x	
MacDonald, Susanne	x	
McDuffie, Jane Lee	x	
McElroy, Dixie		x
McGrew, Brownell	x	
MacGurrin, Buckley	x	
Mack, Robert	x	
McKay, T. H.	x	x
McKinley, Hazel		x
McKinney, Dale		x
MacKinnon, Anabel		x
MacKenzie, Claudia	x	
Macky, Constance	x	
Macky, E. Spencer	x	
McLane, Jean	x	
MacLaskey, Ellen	x	
McLean, Grace	x	
MacLennan, Eunice C.	x	x
McLoughlin, Gregory	x	
McLouth, Farley D.	x	
McMorris, Leroy D.	x	
McNaughton, Eliz. B.	x	x
McNee, John Jr.	x	
McNeely, Perry	x	
McPhail, Annie	x	x
MacSoud, Nicholas S.	x	
McVicker, J. Jay		x
Madsen, Ludwig	x	
Maggi, Cecil A.	x	x
Mahoney, William E.		x
Maier-Kreig, Eugene	x	
Maison, Mart	x	
Majors, Robert	x	x
Mako, Bartholome	x	
Mallet, Roma		
Mallon, Grace E.		x
Mansbert, Barton	x	
Mangravite, Peppino	x	x
Mannheim, Jean	x	
Manoir, Irving	x	
Marans, Moissaye	x	
March, Dorothy	x	
Marcin, Theo		x
Margules, De Hirsch		x
Marks, Stella Lewis	x	
Marootian, Dorothy		x
Marsh, Charles H.	x	x
Marsh, Reginald		x

Name	1	2
Marshall, Albert S.	x	
Martens, Arthur R.	x	
Martin, Fletcher	x	x
Martin, Robert	x	
Martin-Nichols, Pegus		x
Martinez, Alfredo R.	x	
Marulis, Athan	x	
Maslenikoff, Margarita	x	
Mason, Elizabeth	x	
Masuda, Sojiro	x	
Mathews, Marjorie		x
Matlick, Myrtle	x	
Mattias. Martha		x
Mattson, Henry	x	
Maxwell, Laura W.	x	
May, Beulah	x	
Mayhew, Nell Brooker	x	x
Mazzetti, Louis A.		x
Meadows, Dell	x	
Measham, Dajnah G.	x	
Medary, Aimie Hampton	x	
Megargee, Lon	x	
Meier, Barton	x	
Meiers, Fred		x
Melcher, Virginia I.	x	
Melnicoe, Ruth C.		x
Melvill, Antonia	x	
Melzian, Harlee		x
Mendelowitz, Daniel M.	x	
Merideth, John		x
Meripol, A. A.	x	
Merriam, Irma S.	x	
Merrild, Knud	x	x
Merwin, Antoinette D.	X	
Messenger, Ivan	x	x
Messick, Ben	x	
Methven, Ella		x
Metzgar, David		x
Meyer, Zel	x	
Milburn, Oliver	x	x
Miles, Harold W.	x	x
Miller, Barse	x	x
Miller, Davis T.		x
Miller, Delie	x	
Miller, Dorothy E.		x
Miller, Edith Maude	x	
Miller, Evylena Nunn	x	
Miller, John B.		x
Miller, Kenneth Hayes	x	
Miller, Richard	x	
Miller, Ruth B.	x	
Miller, Susan Barse	x	
Millier, Arthur	x	x
Mills, Elisabeth Ann	x	
Miner, Frederick R.	x	
Mintz, Harry	x	
Mishelevich, Alex		x
Mitchell, Alfred R.	x	
Mitchell, Fred	x	
Mitchell, Laura M. D.	x	
Mitchell, Mary		x
Modra, Theodore B.	x	x
Moffett, Ross	x	
Monhoff, Fred	x	x
Montgomery, W. N.		x
Montrichard, Raymond	x	

Name	1	2
Moodey, Joe		x
Moon, Carl	x	
Moore, Frank M.		x
Morahan, Eugene	x	
Morgan, Barbara J.	x	x
Morgan, David J,		x
Morgan, M. DeNeale		x
Morgan, Theodore J.	x	
Morimoto, Charles	x	
Morony, Margaret		x
Morris, Adelaide	x	x
Morris, Alice		x
Morris. Patricia		x
Morse, Marjorie	x	
Morse, Mary S.	x	
Morse, Vernon Jay	x	x
Morton, Burdette		x
Moser, Julon	x	x
Moses, Walter Farr.	x	
Mottram, Grace V.	x	
Mountfort, Arnold	x	
Mow, Albert R.	x	
Moylan, Lloyd	x	
Mozley, Loren		
Mueller, Martin	x	
Munsell, Richard	x	
Munson, William		x
Murphy, Bernardine	x	
Murphy, Earl Vincent		x
Murphy, Lawrence M.	x	
Murphy, Marjorie C.	x	
Murray, Grace H.	x	
Murry, Jerre	x	
Musselman, Darwin		x
Mutton, Hilda	x	
Myers, Datus	x	
Myers, Jerome	x	
Myers, Ruth Larimer	x	

N

Name	1	2
Nagelvoort, Betty		x
Nahl, Perham W.	x	
Nakanisi, Kinichi	x	
Naohara, Kay		x
Naomi, L. B.	x	x
Napolitano, P. Giovanni		x
Nash, Willard	x	
Neilson, Dorothy		x
Nelson, Bruce	x	
Nepote, Alexander		x
Nesbit, Florence H.		x
Neuhaus, Eugen	x	
Nevill-Smith, H.	x	x
Newcomb, Olive	x	
Newcombe, W. J. B.		x
Newcombe, Warren, A.	x	
Newell, Gordon	x	
Newking, Nathalie	x	
Newton, Ruth	x	
Nichols, Carlisa		x
Nichols, Hobart	x	
Nichols, Peggy	x	x
Nichols, Pegus Martin	x	
Nichols, Wilbur Diehl	x	
Nicholson, John		x
Nielsen, Harry A.	x	
Nielsen, Josephine V.		x

Name		
Nielsen, Peter	x	
Nieuwenhuis, Celeste	x	
Nieuwenhuis, John D.	x	
Nightingale, Walter	x	
Nightingale, Wesley W.	x	
Nimmo, Louise Everett	x	
Nolde, Karl Erich		x
Nopobtani, P. G.	x	
Nordfeldt, B. J. O.	x	
Nordstrom, Algot	x	
Norling, Ernest R.	x	
Norris, Ben	x	x
Norton, Helen G.	x	
Nowell, Dora May		x
Nugent, Francis R.		x
Nunes, Gordon		x
Nunn, Evylena	x	
Nutting, Myron C.		x
O		
Obata, Chiura		x
Oberteuffer, Karl	x	
O'Gorman, Jacqui		x
O'Hara, Eliot		x
Okubo, Benji	x	
Oldfield, Oyis	x	
Olds, Marion		
Oleson, Julie Haskell		x
Oliver, Louise	x	x
Oliver, Myron A.	x	
Oliver, Steff	x	
Olson, Albert B.	x	
Olson, John		x
Omalev, Zuka		x
O'Malley, J. M.		x
Onaitis, Stanley		x
Orbe, Helen Ruth	x	
Orde, Gertrude C.	x	
Ortlieb, Ruth Powers	x	x
Osgood, V. M.	x	
Oskiow, Belle		x
Otis, George Demont	x	
Owens, Dale		x
Owens, E. Merrill	x	
P		
Pabian, James Anthony	x	x
Packard, Mabel	x	
Paddock, Thelma	x	x
Padelford, Morgan	x	
Page, Marie D.	x	
Page, Maxine		x
Pajaud, Wm. E. Jr.		x
Palansky, Abraham		x
Palmer, Arthur W.	x	
Palmer, Wilson		x
Panesis, Nicholas	x	
Paradise, Phil	x	x
Park, Charles	x	
Parker, Viola Wolfe		x
Parkinson, Grace Wells	x	
Parshall, DeWitt	x	
Parshall, Douglas	x	x
Parshall, G.	x	
Parsons, Sheldon	x	
Parsons, Virginia		x
Patrick, James H.	x	x
Patrick, Marcia A.	x	
Pattee, Elsie Dodge	x	
Patterson, Ambrose	x	
Patterson, Rebecca B.		x
Paul, Clem		x
Pauling, Adeline	x	
Pavel, Phillip	x	
Paxton, William A.	x	
Payne, Edgar A.	x	
Payne, Elsie Palmer	x	x
Payne, Janet Benton		x
Peabody, L. L.	x	
Peabody, Ruth	x	
Peano, Felix	x	
Pearce, Eliz. Jones		x
Peavy, Paulina	x	
Pedretti, Humberto	x	
Peirce, Waldo		x
Pell, Gene	x	
Pell, Genevieve	x	
Penny, Aubrey J. R.		x
Penny, Frederick Doyle	x	x
Penney, Janice Delores	x	x
Perine, Robert		
Perl, Margaret Anneke	x	
Perrine, Edith	x	
Perrine, Van Derring	x	
Persson, Fritiof	x	
Peters, Jock D.	x	
Peters, Ruth	x	
Peterson, Einar C.	x	
Peticolas, Sherry	x	
Phelps, Edith Catlin	x	
Phillips, Bert G.	x	
Phillips, Josephine N.	x	
Piazzoni, Gottardo	x	
Pickford, Rollin Jr.		x
Pierce, Mildred		x
Pintner, Dora	x	
Pittman, Shirley		x
Pitz, Henry C.		x
Place, Vera Clark	x	
Pleshette, Donald		x
Penney, Frederic D.		x
Penney, Janice Dolores		x
Perine, Robert		x
Perrine, Edith E.		x
Pickford, Rollin Jr.		x
Pierce, Mildred		x
Pittman, Shirley		x
Pitz, Henry C.		x
Pleshette, Donald		x
Pletsch, Ethel E.	x	
Pluff, Frank N.	x	
Plummer, Elmer	x	x
Pogany, Willy	x	
Pohl, Hugo D.	x	
Polifka, B.	x	
Polisher, Regina K.	x	
Politi, Leo	x	
Polk, Pauline		x
Polkinghorn, George	x	x
Pollet, Joseph	x	
Polousky, Julie		x
Pomeroy, Elsie Lower		x
Poole, Abram	x	
Poor, Henry Varnum	x	
Poray, Stan Pociecha	x	
Portanova, Joseph D.	x	
Porter, Mardi	x	
Post, Alan		x
Post, George		x
Pottenger, Mary L.	x	
Potter, Frederick	x	
Potter, William J.	x	
Pottinger, Roy	x	
Power, Ruk	x	
Preeman, Louise		x
Prellwitz, Edith	x	
Prendergast, James D.		x
Prescott, Preston L.	x	
Pressoir, E.		x
Preston, Alice Hurlick	x	
Pribosic, Viktor Von	x	
Price, C. S.	x	
Price, Harold F.	x	x
Price, Rosalie Pettus		x
Price, William Henry	x	
Probst, Thorwald A.	x	
Proctor, Burt	x	
Proctor, N. Bailey	x	
Provins, Clark M.		x
Puccinelli, Raymond	x	
Pumphrey, Bert		x
Purcell, Joseph Wm.	x	
Purdie, Evelyn	x	
Purdum, M. Bertha	x	
Pushman, Hovsep	x	
Putthuff, Hanson	x	x
Putnam, Arion	x	
Putnam, Thor		x
Q		
Quinn, Noel		x
Quispez, Carlos	x	
R		
Rabin, Jack	x	
Rackintor, Peter	x	
Randolph, Lee F.	x	
Raphael, Joseph	x	
Rathborne, Eleanor	x	
Raulston, Marion C.	x	
Ravenel, Pamela V.	x	
Raymond, Julie E.	x	x
Read, Henry	x	
Reagh, William	x	
Reckless, Stanley	x	
Redmond, James	x	
Reed, Rosemary		x
Reep, Edward A.		x
Reeves, J. Mason	x	
Reid, Aurelia Wheeler	x	
Reid, Robert	x	
Reid, V. E.	x	
Reiffel, Charles	x	
Reiss, Roland		x
Reitherman, Wolfgang		x
Renick, Claribel	x	
Ret, Etienne		x
Reynolds, George W.	x	
Rhome, Lily B. P.	x	
Rice, William S.		x
Rich, John Hubbard	x	x
Richey, Georgia A.	x	

Name		
Richmond, Evelyn K.		x
Richmond, G. D.	x	
Richter, Henry L.	x	x
Rider, Arthur G.	x	
Riley, Arthur Irwin		x
Ring, Alice Blair	x	
Ritchie, Ward	x	
Ritschel, William	x	x
Ritter, Anne Gregory	x	
Rizzo, Anthony		x
Roberts, Georgina		x
Roberts, John E.	x	
Roberts, Josephine S.		x
Robertson, Stewart	x	
Robinson, Ada Chalfant	x	
Robinson, Charles		x
Robinson, Delia	x	
Robinson, Ione	x	
Robinson, Irene Bowen	x	x
Robison, Jessie Howe	x	
Rocle, Margaret King	x	
Rocle, Margot	x	
Rocle, Marius	x	
Roeding, Frances	x	
Rogers, Frank V.	x	
Roland, Edward	x	x
Romanelli, Carlo	x	
Romano, Umberto	x	
Ronnebeck, Louise E.	x	
Rookus, Faith	x	
Rose, Ethel	x	x
Rose, Guy	x	
Rosen, Charles	x	
Rosenhouse, Beatrice	x	
Rosenthal, Charles	x	
Rosenthal, Doris	x	x
Rossart, Michael	x	
Rottenberg, Joseph	x	
Rowland, W. Earl	x	
Rozaire, Arthur D.	x	
Ruben, Richards		x
Rubino, Arnoldo B.	x	
Ruegg, Verena	x	
Ruffner, Kenneth		x
Rungius, Carl	x	
Rush, Olive	x	
Rushton, Desmond V.	x	
Russell, Morgan	x	
Russell, Shirley	x	
Ruthorauff, F. G.	x	
Ryan, Helen M.	x	
Ryan, Lewis C.		x
Rydell, Roy	x	
Ryman, Herbert D.	x	

S

Name		
Sacks, Joseph	x	
Saemundsson, Nina	x	
Safford, Charles	x	
Saltzman, Florence		x
Samerjan, George	x	x
Samman, Detlef	x	
Sample, Paul Starrett	x	x
Samuelson, Fred B.		x
Sanders, Spencer E.		x
Sandona, Matteo	x	
Sandzen, Birger	x	x
Sargeant, Geneve Rix.	x	x
Saulter, Leon	x	
Sawyer, Clifton H.	x	
Sawyer, Edith	x	
Sawyer, Myra	x	
Sayre, F. Grayson	x	x
Scarpitta, Castaino	x	
Scarpitta, Salvatore	x	
Schaible, Frederick J.	x	
Schaikjer, J. A.	x	
Schatz, Zahara		x
Scheu, Leonard		x
Schiewetz, Edward		x
Schiff, E. Madeline	x	
Schifrin, Arnold		x
Schlein, Charles	x	
Schloat, G. Warren	x	
Schnakenberg, Henry	x	
Schnaufer, Gertrude		x
Schneider, Otto H.	x	
Schnier, Jacques	x	
Schofield, W. Elmer	x	
Scholl, Edward	x	
Schoneberg, Sheldon		x
Schoppe, Palmer		x
Schram, Charles H.	x	
Schreiber, Georges		x
Schubert, Agnes	x	
Schuster, Donna	x	x
Schuster, Will	x	
Schutzenberger, Jac.	x	
Schwacka, George		x
Schwankovsky, Fred.	x	
Schwartz, William S.	x	
Schworm, Melvina C.		x
Scofield, Edna M.	x	
Scott, Clyde	x	
Scott, David		x
Scott, Edith		x
Scott, Jonathan		x
Scott, Marie T.	x	x
Seeley, Walter Fred.	x	
Seletz, Emil	x	
Sellew, Paul K.	x	
Seloc, Ned	x	
Sepesky, Zoltan		x
Serisawa, Sueo		x
Sersen, Fred M.	x	x
Sewall, Edward	x	
Sexton, Fred R.	x	
Seyffert, Leopold	x	
Shaffer, Myer	x	
Sharp, Joseph Henry	x	
Sharp, Louis Hovey	x	
Sharpless, Ada May	x	
Shaw, Ben C.		x
Shaw, Sydney Dale	x	
Sheeler, Charles	x	
Sheets, Millard	x	x
Sheppard, Margaret W.		x
Sheridan, Clare	x	
Sheridan, Mary B.		x
Sherman, Elizabeth	x	
Sherman, John W.	x	
Sherman, Leslie	x	x
Sherriff, George R.	x	
Shields, Phyllis	x	
Shisler, Clare S.	x	
Shively, Douglas	x	
Shock, Catherine S.	x	x
Shore, Henrietta M.	x	x
Shortreed, L. Q.	x	
Shoven, Hazel Brayton	x	
Shrader, E. Roscoe	x	
Shreve, Catherine S.	x	x
Shuster, Will	x	
Siboni, Emma	x	
Sides, Dorothy Smith	x	
Siegriest, Louis	x	
Silsby, Clifford	x	
Silva, William P.	x	
Silverman, Miles M.		x
Silvius, Paul T.	x	
Simms, Freeland		x
Simpson, Margaret B.		x
Sims, Florence	x	
Singer, Burr		x
Singer, Clyde	x	
Singer, William Earl		x
Siporin, Mitchell		x
Skeele, A. Katherine	x	x
Skelton, Phillis H.		x
Skinner, C. B.	x	
Sklar, Dorothy		x
Smith, Beryl Kirk		x
Smith, Charles L. A.		x
Smith, F. Carl		x
Smith, Francis Drexel	x	
Smith, George Wash.	x	
Smith, Jack Wilkinson	x	
Smith, Jessie Sherwd.	x	
Smith, Lillian Wilhelm		x
Smith, Margery Hoffman	x	
Smith, Marie Vaughn		x
Smith, May Mott	x	
Smith, Ralph L.		x
Smith, Tessie		x
Smith, Violet Thompson	x	
Smith, William Arthur		x
Snavely, Dick	x	
Sogioka, Gene		x
Soldini, Fran		x
Solotaroff, Moi		x
Sooy, Louise	x	x
Soper, J. H. Gardner	x	
Sorensen, Katherine		x
Sorensen, Rex	x	
Sosin, Dorothy	x	
Spalding, Elizabeth	x	
Spalding, James M.	x	
Speight, Francis	x	
Spencer, Edward Sanders	x	
Spencer, Niles	x	
Spencer, Robert	x	
Spenner, E. E.	x	
Spicer, Catherine		x
Spidell, Ruth Campbell		x
Spille, Dean		x
Spohn, Stanley	x	
Sprenkle, Arthur Geo.	x	x

Name		
Springer, Eva	x	
Sprunck, Marian Leaver	x	x
Sprunck, P. G.	x	
Squires, Warren	x	
Stacey, Anna Lee	x	
Stackpole, Ralph	x	
Stacy, John F.	x	
Stahl, Edith Osborne	x	
Stahmer, E.	x	
Stalter, Marcile		x
Stanfield, Mary	x	
Stanley, George	x	
Stanley, Maitland C.		x
Stanson, George C.	x	
Stapleton, Robert D.		x
Stark, Jack Gage	x	
Starkweather, R. E.	x	
Starr, Ed		x
Starr, Katherine	x	
Starr, Maxwell		x
Steele, Gile	x	
Steere, Lora Woodhead	x	
Steinlauf, Saul		x
Steinmetz, S. R.	x	
Steketer, Mrs. P. V.	x	
Sten, Anna		x
Stengel, Constance		x
Stephens, Clara J.	x	
Stephens, Richard		x
Stephey, Eva	x	
Stern, Maurice	x	
Sternfield, Edith A.		x
Sterrett, Virginia F.	x	
Stetson, Katherine B.	x	
Stevens, Dwight		x
Stevens, W. Lester	x	
Stevenson, Barbara	x	
Stevenson, Tom		x
Stewart, LeConte	x	
Still, Constance	x	
Stirrett, Wylie		x
Stoddard, Alice Kent	x	
Stoddard, Edna		x
Stoever, Kenneth B.		x
Stojana, Gjura	x	
Stone, Frank F.	x	
Storm, Alfrida A.	x	
Stover, Allan		x
Strean, Maria J.	x	
Stringfield, Vivian F.		x
Stroebel, Ken		x
Stuber, Dedrick B.	x	
Stussy, Jan Frederic		x
Sugimoto, Henry		x
Surendorf, Charles	x	
Sutter, Joseph	x	
Swan, Paul	x	
Swartz, Harold C.	x	
Swift, Florence A.	x	
Swiggett, Jean	x	
Swinnerton, James	x	
Syminton, Emily	x	x
Symmonds, Albert		x
Symon, Gail S.		x
Symons, Gardner	x	
Szukalski, Stanislaw	x	

T

Name		
Tack, Augustus Vincent	x	x
Tadama, F.	x	
Taggart, Richard	x	
Talbot, Hattie C.	x	
Tanaka, T.	x	
Tanberg, Ella Hot.	x	
Tanino, C. K.	x	
Tarbell, E. C.	x	
Tauszky, David Ant.	x	
Taylor, Emily Drayton	x	
Taylor, Ethel Bonney		x
Teasdale, Mary		x
Teel, Raymond		x
Tennent, Madge	x	
Teplitzky, Joseph	x	
Tew, Marguerite R.	x	
Thieme, Anthony	x	
Thomas, D. F.	x	
Thomas, George	x	
Thomas, Georgia Seaver		x
Thomas, Lillian M.	x	
Thomas, S. Seymour	x	
Thomason, Rosemary		x
Thompson, Hannah	x	
Thompson, John	x	
Thompson, Louise G.		x
Thorne, J. Frederic	x	
Thurston, Jane McD.	x	x
Thurtle, Mrs. C. P.	x	
Tiessen, Natasha	x	
Tillcock, Harry N.	x	
Tingle, Minnie	x	
Tinker, Glen	x	
Titus, A. B.	x	
Tobey, Mark	x	
Toerring, Helene	x	
Tolson, Norman	x	
Tomkins, Margaret	x	x
Tomkins, Florence J.	x	
Toor, Nishan	x	
Torrey, Elliot	x	
Totten, Don	x	
Towner, Xarifa	x	
Townsley, C. P.	x	
Tracy, Charles		x
Trebilcock, Paul	x	
Truax, Sarah E.	x	
True, Allen	x	
Truesdell, Edith P.	x	
Trueworthy, J.	x	
Tuckerman, Lilia	x	
Tumelty, Ruth A.		x
Turle, Sarah A.	x	
Turnbull, Ruth	x	
Turner, Helen	x	
Turner, Janet E.		x
Turner, Matilda H.	x	
Tuttle, Adrianna	x	
Twigg-Smith, G.	x	
Tyler, Maryellen	x	

U

Name		
Uecker, Robert		x
Uetsugi, Kitaro	x	
Ueyama, Tokio	x	

Name		
Ufer, Walter	x	
Ulber, Althea	x	
Ulianoff, Vsevolod	x	x
Ullman, Jane F.	x	
Ullrich, B. P.		x
Unsworthy, Edna G.	x	
Usher, Ruby Walker	x	
Uyeno, Sekishun M.	x	
Uzzell, Onestus	x	

V

Name		
Vaca, Salvatore		
Valenta, Jara H.	x	
Valentine, Josephine D.	x	
Valiant, Tom		x
Vance, James		x
Van Evera, Caroline		
Vann, Loli		x
Van Norden, Virginia	x	x
Van Norman, Evelyn	x	
VanOttenfeld, A	x	
Van Sloun, Frank	x	
Van Soelen, Theodore	x	
Van Young, Oscar		x
Van Zandt, Hilda		x
Vaughan, S. Edson	x	
Vawter, John T.		x
Vergara, George R.	x	
Vernon, Arthur G.	x	
Villa, Hernando G.	x	
Vitovsek, Juanita		x
Vivian, Calthea	x	
Vollmer, Grace L.	x	
Vonnoh, Robert	x	
Von Schneidau, Christ	x	x
Vysekal, Edouard A		x
Vysekal, Luvena B.		x

W

Name		
Wachtel, Elmer	x	
Wachtel, Marion K.	x	x
Wagenhals, Katherine	x	
Wagner, B. Collet		
Wagner, Rob	x	
Wakefield, James	x	
Waldo, Edith	x	
Walker, Helen E.	x	
Walker, John Law	x	x
Walker, Zippora Adina	x	
Walkinshaw, Jeanie W.	x	
Wallace, Amy	x	
Wallace, Brooks	x	
Wallett, William	x	x
Walter, Jeanie	x	
Walty, Nancy D.		x
Wamsley, Frank C.	x	
Wands, Alfred J.	x	
Ward, J. Stephen	x	
Warhanik, Elizabeth Q.		x
Waring, Brooke	x	
Warner, Elsie F.		x
Warner, Everett L.	x	
Warner, Nell Walker	x	x
Warshawsky, Alexander	x	
Washington, Elizabeth	x	
Watanabe, Torajiro	x	
Waterbury, Mrs. G. W.	x	

Name		
Watson, Adele	x	
Watson, Dudley Crafts		x
Watson, Jessie N.	x	x
Wattis, Ruth	x	
Watts, William C.	x	x
Weaver, Harold Buck	x	
Weber, Kem	x	
Weber, Max	x	
Webster, Erle	x	x
Weinberg, E. Sievert	x	
Weindorf, Paul F,	x	
Weiner, D. S.		x
Weisman, Joseph,	x	x
Welch, Mabel R.	x	
Wells, Cady		x
Wendt, Julia Bracken	x	
Wendt, William	x	
Werbe, Anna Tavick	x	
Wesselhoeft, Mary F,	x	x
Wessels, Glenn		x
Westerlund, Stirling	x	
Westfall, S. H.		
Weston, Brett	x	
Weston, Carol Caskey	x	x
Weston, Edward	x	
Westfahl, Katherine		x
Wetherill, E.	x	
Wheatland, Ruth		x
Whedon, Harriet	x	
Whelan, Blanche	x	
Whetsel, Gertrude P.	x	
Whitaker, Frederic		x
Whitaker, R. Townsend		x
White, Dorothy	x	
White, Nona L.	x	
White, Orrin A.	x	
Whitice, Belle	x	
Whiting, Lillian V.	x	
Whitlock, Frances J.	x	
Whitlock, Ursula	x	
Whitney, Erminia C.	x	
Whorf, John		x
Wiboltt, Jack	x	
Wickson, Guest	x	
Wideman, Florice		x
Widfoss, Gunnar		x
Wieczorek, Max	x	x
Wilcox, Cora H.	x	x
Wilde, Ida M.	x	
Wildhaber, Paul Jr.	x	x
Wiley, Fred		x
Wilford, Loran F.		x
Wilimovsky, Charles	x	
Wilke, Ulfert		x
Wilkin, Mildred P.		x
Williams, Carleton	x	
Williams, Chester R.		x
Williams, Dorothy		x
Williams, Howes	x	
Williams, Julian	x	
Williams, Mary Belle	x	
Williams, Otis	x	
Williams, Patricia		x
Williams, Pauline B.	x	
Williamson, Ada C.	x	
Willis, Brooks		x

Name		
Wilson, Anna	x	
Wilson, Betty Palmer		x
Wilson, Dorothy G.	x	
Wilson, John		x
Wilson, Melba Z.	x	
Wilson, Minetta		x
Wilson, William	x	
Windas, Cedric W.	x	
Winebrenner, Harry F.	x	
Winterburn, George P.	x	
Wintermote, M. W.	x	
Winters, Denny		x
Wiser, Guy Brown	x	
Withers, Celeste	x	
Witsel, Theo.		x
Wolf, Hamilton Ach.	x	
Wolf, Pegot	x	
Wolhaupter, Helen		x
Wong, Cyrus	x	
Wong, Tyrus	x	x
Wood, Grant	x	
Wood, Kathryn Leone	x	
Wood, Robert E.		x
Wood, Stanley	x	x
Woolley, Virginia	x	
Woolsey, Robert	x	
Worrell, Agnes	x	
Wright, A. H.		x
Wright, James Cooper	x	x
Wright, Josephine M.	x	
Wright, Otey	x	x
Wright, Richard D.		x
Wright, Stanton McD.		x
Wuermer, Carl	x	
Wurtele, Isobel Keil	x	
Wyeth, Andrew		x
Wylde, Henry Anson	x	
Wynne, Bernard		x
Ybarra, Alfred	x	
Yens, Karl	x	x
Yoreska, Marian	x	
Young, Harold V.	x	
Young, John C.		x
Young, Mahonri	x	
Young, Myrtle M.	x	
Younglove, Ruth Ann	x	x
Zach, Louis	x	
Zann, Lillian A.	x	
Zeigler, Nellie	x	
Zen, Paula	x	
Zenor, Virgil	x	
Zeran, William	x	
Ziegler, Nellie E.	x	
Zillig, Fritz	x	
Zim, Marco	x	
Zimmerer, Frank J.	x	
Zimmerman, Frederic A.	x	
Zimmerman, Lowell A.		x
Zink, Eugenia	x	
Zorach, William	x	x
Zornes, Milford	x	x
Zoro, Ettore De	x	
Zorthian, Jirayr H.		x

Moure's 1969 & 1970 Exhibitions

1979 — Southern California Artists 1890–1940

1980 — Painting and Sculpture in Los Angeles 1900–1945

	National Academy	Amer. W/C Society	'79 1979 Laguna Show	'80 1980 LACMA Show
Charles Partridge Adams			X	
Ivan Lorraine Albright	X	X	X	
Mischa (Maurice) Askenazy			X	
Carroll Barnes				X
Dana Bartlett			X	
Loren Barton (Babcock) (Miller)		X	X	
Charles Bensco			X	
Louis Betts	X		X	
Franz Bischoff			X	X
John Edward Borein			X	
Carl Oscar Borg	X		X	
Jessie Arms Botke		X	X	X
George Kennedy Brandriff			X	X
Rex Brandt	X	X		X
Maurice Braun			X	
Nick Brigante				X
Mildred Bryant Brooks			X	
Benjamin Chambers Brown			X	
Conrad Buff			X	X
William Vincent Cahill			X	
Norman Stiles Chamberlain			X	
Frank Tolles Chamberlin			X	X
Elanor Colburn			X	
Roi Clarkson Colman			X	
Colin Campbell Cooper	X	X	X	
Dean Cornwell	X		X	
Frank William Cuprien			X	
William Swift Daniell			X	
William S. Darling	3 Oscars		X	
Boris Deutsch			X	X
Philip Latimer Dike	X	X	X	X
Lafayette Maynard Dixon			X	
Eugenia Everett				X
Edgar Louis Ewing			X	
Nicolai Ivanovich Fechin			X	X
Lorser Feitelson				X
Lillian Prest Ferguson			X	
John Bond Francisco			X	
Karoly Fulop				X
John Marshall Gamble			X	
Gertrude Gazelle Gardner			X	
Cedric Gibbons				X
Joe Duncan Gleason			X	
William Alexander Griffith			X	
Richard Haines			X	
Armin Carl Hansen	X		X	
Ejnar Hansen		X	X	X
Alexander Harmer			X	
Sam Hyde Harris			X	
Harry Richmond Henry			X	
Adele Herter				
Albert Herter	X	X	X	
Anna Althea Hills			X	
Clarence Keiser Hinkle			X	
Donal Hord			X	
Thomas L. Hunt			X	

	NAD	AWS	'79 Show	'80 Show
George Edward Hurrell			X	
Oscar Theodore Jackman			X	
Frank Tenney Johnson	X	X	X	X
William Keith			X	
Joseph Kleitsch			X	
Orpha Klinker			X	
Emil Jean Kosa	X	X	X	X
Peter Krasnow				X
Eugen Maier-Krieg			X	
Paul Lauritz			X	
Kathryn Woodman Leighton			X	
Helen Lundeberg				X
Stanton Macdonald-Wright				X
Jean Mannheim			X	X
Fletcher Martin	X		X	
Arthur Frank Mathews			X	
Knud Merrild				X
Barse Miller	X	X		X
Arthur Henry Millier			X	
Laura M. D. Mitchell (Tennyson)			X	
George Demont Otis			X	
Peterpaul Ott			X	
Paul Outerbridge			X	
Douglass Parshall	X		X	
Edgar Alwyn Payne			X	X
Ruth Eaton Peabody			X	
Charles Rollo Peters			X	
Housep Pushman			X	
Hanson Duvall Puthuff			X	
Granville Seymour Redmond			X	X
Henry L. Richter			X	
William Ritschel	X	X	X	
Warren Rollins				X
Guy Rose			X	X
Paul Sample	X	X		X
Donna Norine Schuster			X	
Millard Sheets	X	X	X	X
Rex Slinkard				X
Jack Wilkinson Smith			X	
H. T. Spaller			X	
Will Sparks			X	
Norman St. Clair			X	
Albert Stewart				X
James Guilford Swinnerton			X	
George Gardner Symons	X		X	
Manuel Valencia			X	
Hernando Gonzallo Villa			X	
Grace Libby Vollmer			X	
Edouard Antonin Vysekal			X	X
Elmer Wachtel			X	
Marion Kavanaugh Wachtel			X	X
Julia Bracken Wendt			X	X
William Wendt	X		X	
Orrin Augustine White			X	
Max Wieczorek		X	X	X
Virginia Woolley			X	
James Couper Wright			X	
Raymond Dabb Yelland			X	
Karl Yens			X	
James Milford Zornes	X	X	X	

Mabel Aaron
Martin Absena
Ivan Albright
Zissley Albright
James Madison Alden
Anders Aldrin
Gene Allen
Arthur Ames
Alexander Archipenko
Frederich Avey

B
Hugo Ballin
Hanna-Barbera
Joseph Barberi
Carl Barks
Hugo Barndollar
Carl Beetz
Ben Berlin
Eugene Berman
Edward Biberman
James Stuart Blackton
Lee Blair
Preston Blair
William Phipps Blake
Irving Block
John Edward Borein
Carl Oskar Borg
Stephen Bosustow
Hobart Bosworth
Dorr Bothwell
Henry Botkin
Mrs C. P. Bradfield
Will Bradley
Paul Branson
Maurice Braun
William Brice
Nick Brigante
Morris Broderson
Reynold Brown
Conrad Buff
Hans Gustav Burkhardt
Peter Burness
John Byers

C
William V. Cahill
John Canavier
Robert Cannon
Federico Cantu
Edward Carfagno
George M. Carpenter
Katherine Casey
F. Tolles Chamberlin
Will Chaplin
Jean Charlot
Nelbert Chouinard
C. Christoffels

Josephine Chuey
Robert Chuey
Robert Clampett
Grace Clements
Robert Clunie
Sam Colbean
George Cole
Dave Constable
Dean Cornwall
Val Costello
Russel Cowles
Chase Craig
Charles Cristadoro
Watson Cross

D
Inocenza Daraio
William Darling
Richard Day
Edwin Deakin
John Decker
John DeCuir
Francis de Erdely
Gene Deitch
Francis De La Torre
Ferdinand Deppe
Boris Deutsch
Harry Diamond
Phil Dike
Walt Disney
Maynard Dixon
Hans Dreier
Eugene Duflot de Mofras
Auguste Duhaut-Cilly
Andre Durenceau
Arthur Durston

E
Eyvand Earle
Ferdinand P. Earle
Susan Ehrlich
Jules Engel

F
Nicolai Fechin
Lorser Feitelson
Keith Finch
Giovanni Fischetti
Oscar Fischinger
David Fleischer
Ruth Fletcher
Emil Flohri
Henry Chapman Ford
Victor Clyde Forsythe
Arthur Turner Foster
Harlan Frazer
Isadore Freleng
Park French
Finn Froelich

G
Edmund W. Gale
Bernard Garbrett
Archibald Garner
Harold Gaze
Norman Bel Geddes
Franz Geritz
Cedric Gibbons
George Gibson
Joe Duncan Gleason
Alexander Golitzen
Donald Graham
Hardie Gramatky
Charles Greene
Dan Sayre Groesbeck
Anton Grot
Eric Gurney
Philip Guston

H
Richard Haines
Dannt Hall
Dave Hall
Ejnar Hansen
Frederick Hammersley
William D. Hanna
Hugh Harman
Alexander Harmer
Ted Haworth
Carl Heilborn
Joseph Henninger
George Herriman
Albert Herter
Henry Hesse
William Hayes Hilton
Clarence Hinkle
Hans Hoffmann
Ralph Holmes
Ferdinand Horvath
Olin Howland
John Hubley
Mentor Huebner
Richard Huemer
Jane Hunt
Richard Hunt
William M. Hunt
Earl Hurd
Justine Hurd
Albert Hurter
William Rich Hutton

I
Robert Irwin
Estelle Ishigo
Rudolph Ising
Ubbe Iwerks

J
Helen Hunt Jackson
H. C. Jacobsmeyer
George W. James
Dorothy Jeakins
Herbert Jepson

Frank Tenney Johnson
Harold Johnson
MacDonald Johnson
Stan Johnson
Charles Jones
Seth C. Jones
William L. Judson
Martin Justice

K

Fred Kann
Elena Karina
Atanas Katchmakoff
Leo Katz
Edgar M. Keller
Dorothy Kent
Rockwell Kent
Margaret Kidder
Ernest G. Klein
Isadore Klein
Edmund Kohn
Charles Koppel
Emil Kosa JR.
Hal Kraemer
Peter Kusnaw
Benjamin Kutcher

L

Paul Landacre
Walter Lantz
Bessie Lasky
Tom Laursen
Rico Lebrun
John Lincoln
Robert Lockwood
Al Londraville
Wright Ludington
Charles Lummis
Helen Lundeberg
Fernand Lundgren
Dan Lutz

M

Guy MacCoy
Joseph F. MacDonald
Charles Mackelmarry
Fletcher Martin
S. I. Mayo
Clifford McBride
Evelyn McCormick
Edward E. McDowell
Henry Lee McFee
Robert McIntosh
George McManus
William B. McMurtie
Wm. Cameron Menzies
Benjamin N. Messicks
Harold Miles
Randolph Miller
Charles Mintz
Heinrich B. Mollhausen
Fred Monhoff

Carl Moon
Richard A. Moores
William Moore
Joseph Mugnaini
Lawrence Murphy

N

Richard Neutra
Warren Newcomb
John Nicoll
Kay Nielsen
Myron Nutting

P

James Patrick
Edgar Payne
A. Sheldon Pennoyer
Pablo Peyri
Willy Pogany
Van Ness Polglase
H. M. T. Powell
Vincent Price
Clark Province
Wm. Ptaszynski
Hansen Puthuff

Q

Leopoldo Quijano
Fred Quimby

R

Man Ray
Granville Redmond
Mason Reeves
Nicolai Remisoff
Etienne Ret
Joseph W. Revere
John Hubbard Rich
Arthur Rider
Stewart Robertson
Alfred Robinson
Gladys Lloyd Robinson
Irene Bowen Robinson
Milli Rocque
Ginger Rogers
Doris Rosenthal
Morgan Russell
Herbert Ryman

S

Sai
Ludwig Salvator
George Samerjan
Paul Sample
Emmanuel Sandelius
J. Henry Sandham
Rudolph M. Schindler
Leon Schlesinger
Elise Seeds
Fred Serson
Millard Sheets
Marsha Shlaudeman
Clifford Silsby
Wilson Silsby

David A. Siqueriros
Rex Slinkard
J. Frances Smith
Jack Martin Smith
Langdon Smith
Lutah Maria Smith
William Smart
Teresa Sorce
Sergei Soudeikin
Duncan A. Spencer
Charles H. Spenner
Robert B. Stacy-Judd
John Mix Stanley
Norman St. Clair
Josef V. Sternberg
George Stojana
James Guilford
        Swinnerton
John Sykes
Stanislaw Szukalski

T

Alfred Taliaferro
Frank Tashlin
Ignatius Tirsch
Lorenzo Todesco
Arley G. Tottingham
Vladimir Tytla

U

Robert Usher

V

Karin Van Leyden
Mary Vartikian
Hernando Villa
Edward Vischer
Josef Von Sternberg
F. W. Vreeland
Edouard Vysekal

W

Charles S. Ward
Lily A. Ward
Howard Warshaw
Lyle Weaver
Kem Weber
J. A. M. Whistler
Bert Whitman
Richard Whorf
Olaf Wieghorst
Max Wieczorek
Tyrus Wong
William Woollett
Frank Lloyd Wright
Stanton MacDonald
        Wright

Y

Alfred Ybarra

CALIFORNIA - McCALL

DeWitt McCall's book, <u>California Artists 1935-1956</u>, picks up the California artists approximately where Moure's Dictionary ends,1935, and carries on to 1956. Although it contains only elemental biographical data, it is derived from the California artists listed in <u>Who's Who in American Art</u>, Volumes 1-6, where biographical data can be found. It covers <u>all</u> California artists listed during that period. The book contains many excellent illustrations of Calif. art, with a number in color.

A

Abbott, Edith A.
Abdy, Rowena Meeks
Abel, Jean
Abro, Maxine
Acker, Herbert VanB.
Ackerman, Frank E.
Adair, Ruby Prior
Adams, Charles Partridge
Adams, Clinton
Adams, Velma
Ahlberg, Florence M.
Albright, Gertrude Part.
Albright, Hedwig E. G.
Albright, Herman Oliver
Aldrich, Clarence Nelson
Aldrin, Anders Gustave
Alexander, Sara D. Block
Allen, Gregory Seymour
Aller, Gladys
Allman, Richard M.
Altman, Aaron
Alvarez, Mabel
Ames, Jean Goodwin
Amyx, Leon Kirkman
Anderson, Charles Webster
Anderson, Dorothy Visju
Anderson, Heath
Anderson, Milo Elvyn
Andrus, James R.
Andrus, Zoray
Antonia, Ta'mara
Argall, Charles G.
Arledge, Sara Kate
Armer, Ruth
Armitage, Elise
Armstrong, Roger Joseph
Armstrong, Samuel John
Arnautoff, Victor Michael
Asanger, Jacob
Askensky, Mischa
Atkins, Alan
Atkins, Florence Eliz.
Atkinson, William Osborn
Attridge, Irma Gertrude
Atwood, Mary Hall
Aurner, Kathryn Dayton
Austin, Charles Percy
Avery, Kenneth Newell
Ayres, Martha Oakhout

B

Babcock, Ida Dobson
Baca, Catherine Eaton
Bach, Robert Otto
Backus, Standish Jr.
Baer, Martin
Bagdatopoulos, Wm. Spencer
Bailey, Evelyn
Bailhache, Anne Dodge
Baker, Doris Winchell
Baker, Jean Jessie
Baker, Lloyd Theron
Baldaugh, Anni (Ami)
Baldwin, Clifford Park

Baldwin, Frances
Balfour, Roberta
Ball, Ruth Norton
Ballard, Louise Elizabeth
Ballin, Hugo
Baltekal, (Goodwin) Mich.
Band, Max
Baranceanu, Belle
Barker, George
Barker, Olive Ruth
Barlow, Walter Jarvis Jr.
Barnes, Matthew Rackham
Barr, Roger Terry
Barron, Dorothy L. Hatch
Bartlett, Dana
Bartlett, Ivan
Barton, Loren Roberta
Basinet, Victor Hugo
Batchelder, Alix
Baugh, Dorothy Geraldine
Baum, Franz
Baumann, Karl Herman
Baxter, Martha Wheeler
Bay, Howard
Beach, Warren
Beall, Leah
Bear, Donald
Beaumont, Arthur Edwaine
Beaumont, Arthur J.
Beck, Dunbar
Beck, (Meyer), Richard C.
Becker, Frederick W.
Beecher, Genevieve Thom.
Beeck, Kisa
Beetz, Carl Hugo
Beggs, Thomas Montague
Bellis, Daisy Maud
Belt, A. Elmer
Benepe, Katherine Buzzell
Bennett, Franklin
Bennett, Isabelle Jewel
Bennett, Joseph Hastings
Bennett, Lyle Hatcher
Bennett, Ruth Manerva
Bensco, Charles J.
Bensinger, Anne Mosejiere
Berg, George Louis
Bergman, Karola
Bergman(n), Franz Walter
Berlandina, Jane Clara
Berman, Eugene
Bernat, Martha Miligan
Bertoia, Harry
Bertrand, Raymond C.
Bessinger, Frederick Herb.
Best, Harry Cassie
Best, Jane Hayden
Best, Nellie Geraldine
Bethers, Ray
Bewley, Murray Percival
Beynon, William P.
Biberman, Edward
Billington, John J.
Billington, John Jules

Bintliff, Martha Bradshaw
Birch, Geraldine Rose
Bird, Harry
Bischoff, Elmer Nelson
Bjerregaard(Poulson) Jacob
Bjurman, Andrew
Black, Mary C. W.
Blackburn, William Thomas
Blair, Lee Everett
Blair, Mary Robinson
Blair, Preston Erwin
Blair, Streeter
Blanchard, Porter
Blazek, Anton
Bliel, Charles George
Block, Maurice
Bloodworth, Alvin Hale
Blos, May
Blos, Peter
Bloser, Florence Parker
Blower, David Harrison
Blumberg, Ron
Blumert, Johanna Marie
Boak, Milvia W.
Bode, Catherine Burnaby
Boehme, Hazel Fetterley
Boething, Majory Adele
Bohnenblust, Eleanor
Bolinger, Ethel King
Bonnet, Leon Durand
Booth, Eunice Ellenetta
Booth, George Warren
Boratko, Andre
Borein, Edward
Borg, Carl Oscar
Born, Ernest Alexander
Boru, Sorcha
Bosserman, Lyman Webber
Boswell, Normen Gould
Bothwell, Dorr Hodgson
Botke, Cornelius
Botke, Jessie Arms
Boundey, Burton Shepard
Bowden, Harry
Boyd, Doris Paulin
Boynton, Raymond Sceptre
Braddock, Katherine
Bradley, Will
Bradshaw, Alexandra Chris.
Braghetta, Lulu H.
Brandon, John A.
Brandriff, Geo. Kennedy
Brandt, Rexford Elson
Brannan, Sophie Marston
Braun, Maurice
Breasted, James Henry Jr.
Breneiser, Elizabeth Day
Breneiser, John Day
Breneiser, Stanley G.
Brezee, Evelyn
Brice, William
Brigante, Nicholas P.
Bristol, Tancie
Brodie, Howard Joseph

Brodie, Philip B.
Brooks, Mildred Bryant
Brown, Benjamin Chambers
Brown, Dorothy
Brown, Howell Chambers
Brown, Lucille Rosemary
Browne, Belmore
Browne, Lewis
Bruton, Esther
Bruton, Helen
Bruton, Margaret
Bryant, Everett Lloyd
Buchanan, Ella S.
Buck, Claude
Buck, Leslie Binner
Buckley, Jean
Bufano, Beniamino B.
Buff, Conrad
Burgdorff, Ferdinand
Burnham, Roger Noble
Burrell, Alfred Ray
Bush, Ella Shepard

C

Cadorin, Ettore S.
Cadwalader, Louise
Cain, Robert Sterling
Calkins, Loring Gary
Callaway, Eliz. R. Jordan
Cameron, William Ross
Campbell, Isabella Frowe
Campbell, John Garden
Campbell, Richard
Campbell, William Addison
Canfield, Lillian Caroline
Cannon, Dorothy
Cannon, Jennie Vennerst.
Cantley, Maurine
Capehart, Eliz. Scudder
Cappeller, Ettore dZ D.
Carew, Berta
Carlberg, Wolfgang
Carlton, Brents
Carmichael, Joe
Carr, Alice Robertson
Carroll, Maud Clifton
Carter, Dudley C.
Carter, Pruett A.
Castaing, Camille K.
Cavana, Elise
Center, Bill
Chaffee, Olive H.
Chalmers, Helen Augusta
Chamberlain, Norman Stiles
Chamberlin, Frank Tolles
Champlin, Ada Belle
Champlin, Prescott
Chapman, Minerva J.
Chase, Marion Monks
Cheese, Ralph
Cheever, Walter L.
Cheney, Warren
Chepourkoff, Michael G.
Chiapella, Edouard Emile
Chittenden, Alice Brown

Chodorow, Eugene
Chouinard, Nelbert Murphy
Christensen, Ethel Lenora
Christenson, John Leonard
Chun, David P.
Church, Robert M.
Churchman, Isabelle Sch.
Clapp, William Henry
Clark, Alson Skinner
Clark, Arthur Bridgman
Clark, Claude
Clark, Emelia M. Goldswhy.
Clark, Mabel Beach
Clark, (Mabel) Bee Smith
Cleland, Thomas M.
Clemens, Paul Lewis
Clement, Helen Barbara
Clements, Grace
Clover-Bew, Mattie May
Clunie, Robert
Coan, Helen E.
Coates, Palgrave Holmes
Coats, Claud
Codman, Ruth
Colburn, Elanor Rush
Coldwell, Ardath
Cole, Gail Shepardson
Colman, Roi Clarkson
Colton, Harriett
Comfort, Tom Tyrone
Conner, John Anthony
Conner, Paul
Cooch, Marian Clark
Cook, Alma May
Cook, John
Cooke, Dorothea
Coolidge, John Earle
Cooper, Colin Campbell
Cooper, Virginia S.
Cooper, William Leonard
Coover, Nell B.
Cordrey, Earl Somers
Cornin, Jon (Corka)
Corka, Jon Cornin
Cotton, Leo
Coughlin, Mildred M.
Coulter, Mary J.
Coutts, Gordon
Cox, J. Halley
Coze, Paul Jean
Craig, Thomas
Cram, Allan Gilbert
Cravath, Dorothy P.
Cravath, Ruth
Crawford, Bernetta Herrmn.
Crawford, Esther Mabel
Cromwell, Joan Christian
Cross, Waltson, Jr.
Crowder, Conrad Wms.
Crown, Keith Jr.
Cruess Marie Gleason
Cruze, Charles
Culbertson, Josephine M
Cummings, Harold W.

Cuneo, Rinaldo
Cunningham, Ben Frazier
Cunningham, Fern Frances
Cunningham, John
Cunningham, Marion
Cunningham, Patricia
Cuprien, Frank W.
Currier, Cyrus Bates
Curtis, Ida Maynard
Curtis, Leland
Curtis, Marian
Cushman, Henry
Cutrow, Leonard A.

D

D'Agostino, Vincent
Daggett, Maud
Da Gradi, Donald
Dakin, Sidney Tilden
Dampier, William
Dando, Susie M. Berry
D'Andrea, Italo
Danes, Gibson
Daniels, Earl I.
Daniels, Elmer Harland
Dann, Frode Nielson
Danner, Sara Kolb
Daraio, Innocenzo
Darling, William S.
Daroux, Leonora
Darrow, Paul Gardner
David, Don Raymond
Davidson, John
Davies, Elton Morrow
Davis, Emma Lu
Davis, E. M.
Davis, Goode Paschall
Davis, Leonard Moore
Davy, James Banjamin
Dean, Eva Ellen
Dean, Mallette
De Barkow, Broness Ilona
De Boronda, Tulita
DeDeaux, Helen
Dedini, Eldon
DeErdely, Francis
Defenbacher, Daniel S.
Defini, Eldon
DeGavere, Cornelia
Degen, Ida Day
Degenhart, Pearl C.
DeHospodar, Stephen
DeJoiner, Luther E.
DeKruif, Henri Gilbert
Delacour, Jean T.
Delano, Annita
DeLaTorre, William
DelCastillo. Mary Virgin.
DeLemos, Pedro J.
DelMue, Maurice August
DelPino, Jose Moya
Dennis, Charles H.
Dentzel, Carl Schaefer
Dethloff, Peter Hans
Deutsch, Boris

Devol, Pauline Hamill
DeWilde, Victor
DeWitt, Jessie R.
DeYong, Joe
DeZoro DeiCappeller, Ettor
Dibblee, Anita L.
Dickey, Dan
Dickinson, Daisy Oliva
Dickman, Charles John
Dike, Philip Latimer
Dinning, Robert James
Dionysius, Dooley
Disney, Walt E.
Dixon, Harry St.John
Dixon, Layfayette Maynard
DoBos, Andrew
Dobson, Margaret A.
Doggett, Jean
Dole, William
Dominique, John Augustus
Donaldson, Douglas
Donaldson, Elise
Dooley, Helen Bertha
Doolittle, Harold Lukens
Dorgeloh, Marg. Redman
Dougherty, Paul
Dowiatt, Dorothy
Dripps, Clara Reinicke
Drogkamp, Charles
Drudis, Jose
Duer, Bene
Duncan, Charles Stafford
Duncan, Dorothy
Dunlap, Helena Adele
Dunn, Majorie Cline
Dunphy, Nicholas
Dupont, Kedma
Duquette, Mae
D'usseau, Leon
Dustin, Silas S.
Dye, Clarkson
Dye, Olive Bagg
Dyer, Carlos

E

Earnist, Florence Reinhold
Eaton, Catherine
Edmiston, HenryEdmondson,
Edstrom, David
Edwards, Lionel L.
Elarth, Herschel
Elarth, Wilhelmina V.Ingen
Elliott, Ethel M.
Elliott, Ruth Cass
Ellis, Clyde Garfield
Ellison, J. Milford
Ellsworth, Clarence Arth.
Emery, Margaret Rose
Engel-Leisinger, Irma
English, Harold M.
Eric-Alt,Lenore
Espoy, Angel
Evans, Naomi
Everett, Eugenia
Everett, Mary Orwig
Ewing, Edgar

F

Falkenstein, Claire
Farmer, Edward McNeil
Farmer, Mabel McKibbin
Farrington, Walter
Faulkner, Ray
Fay, Jean Bradford
Fechin, Nicolai Ivanovich
Feitelson, Lorser
Fels, Catherine Phillips
Ferguson, Lillian Prest
Ferren, John
Finch, Keith
Finley, Mary L.
Finney, Betty
Finta, Alexander
Fisher, Anya
Fitzgerald, James
Fleck, Robert John
Flemming, Amy Dewing
Fletcher, Frank Morley
Forbes, Helen Katherine
Force, Clara G.
Fordham, Elwood James
Foresman, Alice Carter
Forsythe, Victor Clyde
Fortune, Ms. E. Charlton
Foster, Bertha Knox
Foster, Enid
Foster, Wm. Frederick
Fox, Milton S.
Fracker, Ruth Miller
Frances, Gene Mrs.
Frankenstein, Al. Victor
Frankl, Paul Theodore
Franklin, Arla
Frantz, Sam. Marshall
Fraser, Douglass
Freed, Ernest Bradford
Freeman, Don
Frey, Joseph
Fries, Charles Arthur
Frolich, Finn Haakon
Fry, Finley (Mary L.)
Fuller, Alfred
Fulop, Karoly
Fulton, Dorothy E.
Fulton, Fitch B.

G

Gaffney, Claribel Honor
Gage, Merrell
Gale, Edmund W.
Gale, Jane Greene
Galgiani, Oscar
Gambee, Martin
Gambel, John Marshall
Gammon, Stella
Ganine, Peter (Pierre)
Garner, Archibald
Garnsey, Julian Ellsworth
Garrett, Clara Pfeifer
Garth, John
Gavencky, Frank J.
Gaw, William A.
Gearhart, Frances Hammel

Gearhart, May
Gebhardt, Harold
Gellert, Emery
Geogetti, Wedo
Gere,Nellie Huntington
Geritz, Franz
Gerritty, John Emmett
Gershoy, Eugene
Gerstle, William Lewis
Gerth, Ruth
Gilberg, Robert George
Gilbert, Arthur Hill
Gile, Selden Conner
Gillam, Wm. Chas. F.
Gillette, Frances W.
Ginno, Eliz. DeGebele
Girardin, Frank J.
Glass, Bertha Walker
Gleason, Joe Duncan
Glenn, Sally
Gluckmann, Grigory
Goeller-Wood, Shotwell
Goethe, Joseph Alex.
Goodchild, Cecil Wray
Goodell, William Newport
Goodenow, Lucene
Goodenow, Rolf Julian
Graf, Gladys H.
Graham, Harold E.
Gramatky, Hardie
Grant, Charles Henry
Gray, Percy
Green, David Oliver Jr.
Greene, J. Barry
Greene, Lucille Brown
Greenwood, George Arthur
Gren, Nils
Griffith, Lillian
Griffith, Wm. Alexander
Gruenfeld, Casper
Guenther, Pearl Harder
Gurrey, Mrs. Hartley F.
Gutmann, John
Guttridge, Eleanor N.

H

Haase, Madeline Frances
Hagen, Ethel Hall
Haig, Mabel George
Haines, Richard
Haley, John Charles
Hall, Parker L.
Hamilton, Cenevieve Bart.
Hamilton, Leah Rinne
Hamilton, May Stewart
Hamlin, Edith A.
Hammargren, Frederick E.
Hand, Jo Hale
Hankins, Vina S.
Hanscom, Trude
Hansen, Armin Carl
Hansen, Ejnar
Hansen, Florence Froney
Hansen, James L.
Harcoff, Lyla Marshall
Harding, Goldie Powell

Harris, George Albert
Harris, Laurence W.
Harris, Samuel Hyde
Hartman, Hazel
Hartmann, Sadikichi
Hartmetz, Herrica H.
Harvey, Eli
Hastings, Marion Keith
Hatfield, Dalzell
Hatlo, Jimmy
Hawkins, Grace Milner
Hayakawa, Niki
Hayden, Mary Dodge
Hayes, Thomas
Hazen, Bessie Ella
Hazen, Fannie Wilhelmina
Heath, Edda Maxwell
Herbert, Marian
Heil, Dr. Walter
Hekking, William M.
Helder, Z. Vanessa
Heller, Bessie Peirce
Hendersin, Evelyn
Hendrickson, David
Henninger, Joseph
Henry, Charles Trumbo
Heron, Edith Harvey
Herrick, Hugh M.
Herrmann, Fernande Luise
Herron, Jason (Jessie)
Herter, Albert
Hess, Sara
Hesse, Henry Melton
Hesthal, William
Hickey, Rose Van Franken
Hilton, John W.
Hinckley, Lawrence Brad.
Hinkle, Clarence Keiser
Hinkle, Lucile Bernice
Hobby, Carl Frederick
Holden, James Albert
Hollingshead, Clive
Holmes, Ralph Edward
Holmes, Stuart
Hoowij, Jan P.
Hope, Thelma Paddock
Hopkins, Charles Benj.
Hord, Donal
Horton, Charles Orson
Horvath, Ferd. Huszti
Hoskins, Winfield S.
Hough, Halley
Houser, Allan C.
Houser, Victor Carl
Howard, John Langley
Howard, Robert Boardman
Howe, Thomas Carr Jr.
Howen, Ellis Alexander
Howen, Lillian Harris
Hrdy, Olinka
Hudson, Charles Bradford
Huff, William Gordon
Hueter, James W.
Hughes, Daisy M.
Hulett, Ralph P.

Hume, Samuel James
Hunley, Katherine J.
Hurd, Angela M.
Hurtt, Arthur R.
Hustead, Elvera C.
Hyde, Josephine E.
Hyde, Marie A.
Hynes, Edith

I

Ilyin, Peter A.
Imrie. Herbert David
Ingels, Frank Lee
Ingels, Kathleen Bev.
Iredell, Russell
Ireland, Beryl
Irving, Joan P.
Irwin, Susan Benteen
Irwin, William Hyde
Ivanoff, Eugene

J

Jackman, Oscar Theodore
Jackson, Ann
Jackson, Everett Gee
Jackson, Gordena Parker
Jackson, Howard Merritt
Jackson, Martin Jacob
Jacoby, Ned
Jalanivich, Manuel E.
James, Frances K.
James, Roy Walter
Janson, Andrew R.
Jenkins, Hanna Tempest
Jester, Ralph
Joff, Edward E. Mathew
Johanson, Edward W.
Johnson, Clinton
Johnson, Mrs. Danny S.
Johnson, Doris Miller
Johnson, Frank Tenney
Johnson, Fred
Johnson, J. Theodore
Johnson, M. Martin
Johnson, Reginald
Johnson, Sargent Claude
Johnston, Frederick
Johnston, Margaret Isabell
Johnston, Mary Virginia
Johnston, Ynez
Jones, Elberta Mohler
Jones, Glen
Jones, Harry Donald
Jones, John Paul
Jones, Martha Miles
Jordan, Elizabeth R.
Jordan, Helen Adelia
Julian, Paul Hull
Jurecka, Cyril

K

Kadish, Reuben
Kaiser, Estelle Elizabeth
Kaiser, Rueben
Kaminski, Edward B.
Kangoony, Gregory
Kann, Frederic L.
Kapousouz, Vasileos

Kasimir, Luigi
Karl, Mabel Fairfax Smith
Karnes, Harley
Karpf, Fay B.
Kassler, Charles Moffat II
Katchamakoff, Atanas
Katz, Leo
Kaufmann, Ferdinand
Kayser, Louise Darmstaeder
Kayser, Stephen S.
Keeler, Charles Butler
Kees, Weldon
Keffer, Frances
Kegg, George W.
Keller, Clyde Leon
Kelley, Sue E.
Kelly, Edna
Kelly, Francis Robert Jr.
Kelsey, Richmond (Dick) I.
Kempster, Ruth
Kendall, Marie Boening
Kendall, Viona Ann
Kende, Geza
Kennicott, Robert H.
Kent, Adaline
Kerwin, Mary Catherine
Kester, Lenard
Keszthelyi, Alex. Samuel
Kilpatrick, Aaron Edward
Kingman, Dong (Don) M.
Kirby, Glo
Kirkgaard, L. Maria
Kitts, Jasmine (Jessie) D.
Klapp, Freda Leslie
Klauber, Alice E.
Kleidman, Rose
Kleiser, Lorentz
Kleitsch, Mrs. Joseph
Kley, Alfred J.
Klinker, Orpha
Kloss, Gene
Klumpke, Anna Elizabeth
Klynn, Herbert David
Knight, Julia Murray
Koch, Gerd
Koch, Irene Skiffington
Kohlmeier, Helen Louise
Kopenhaver, Josephine Y.
Korybut, Kasimir
Korybut, Wanda
Kosa, Emil Jean Jr.
Krauth, Charles Philip
Krehm, William P.
Kromer, Carol Adelaide
Kubacki, Raymond
Kurtzworth, Harry Muir
Kushner, Dorothy Browdy
Kutcher, Ben

L

Labaudt, Lucien
LaCom, Wayne Carl
Lagorio, Irene R.
L'Allemand, Gordon Lynn
Landacre, Paul Hambleton
Landy Art

Lane Martella Cone
Lanfair, Harold Edward
Lanfair, Harriet Keese
Langdon, Gordon
Lanz, Emil
LaRiar, Lawrence
Lasky, Bessie Mona
Laurence, Sydney
Lauritz, Jack
Lauritz, Paul
Lauterer, Arch
Lawyer, Jean
LeBrun, Frederico
Lee, Bertha Stringer
Lee, Leslie W.
Leeper, John P.
Leeper, Vera
Leighton, Kathryn Woodman
Lesaar, Charles M.
Levin, Alexander
Levine, David Phillip
Levine, Gilbert
Levy, Beatrice S.
Levy, Hilda
Lewis, Elizabeth
Lewis, H. Emerson
Lewis, Jeannette Maxfield
Lewis, Jennie M.
Lewis, Monty
Lewis, Tom E.
Leyden, Louise Hannon
Lidow, Leza
Lieberman, Frances Beat.
Liebes, Dorothy Wright
Lindsay, Ruth Andrews
Link, Carl
Linn, Orson
Lion, Henry
Little, Gertrude L.
Littlejohn, Hugh Warwick
Lloyd, Lucile
Lockwood, John Ward
Logan, Maurice
Longstreet, Stephen
Loomis, Andrew
Loran, Erle
Louden, Orren R.
Lovins, Henry
Lowe, Peter
Loxley, Ruthann Youngglove
Ludenkens, Fred
Ludovici, Alice Emilie
Lukens, Edward Glen
Lukits, Theodore N.
Lum, Bertha Boynton
Lundy, Fred Ralph
Lutz, Dan S.

M

MacAgy, Douglas
MacCoy, Guy
MacCuiston, Jacques
MacDonald, Katherine H.
MacDonald-Wright, Stanton
MacHefert, Adrian Claude
MacKenzie, Florence Bryant

MacKnight, Ninon
Macky, Eric Spencer
MacLennan, Eunice Cashion
Magnussen, Erik
Maier-Krieg, Eugene
Maison, Mary Edith
Majors, Robert J.
Mallary, Robert Wenley
Mallet, Roma
Mallon, Grace Elizabeth
Malmquist, Olof Carl
Mannheim, Jean
Manoir, Irving K.
Manuel, Donaldo
Mark, Bendor
Marsh, Charles Howard
Marshall, Frank Howard
Martin, Caroline Louise
Martin, Fletcher
Martin, Keith
Martinez, Xavier
Mason, Roy Martell
Mathews, Arthur Frank
Matthew, John Britton
Matthews, Lester Nathan
Matzinger, Phillip Fred.
May, Beulah
Mayhew, Nell Booker
Mays, Paul Kirkland
McBride, Clifford
McCall, Hester Arnetta
McClelland, Douglas Eugene
McClelland, Amy Woller
McClure, Caroline S.
McCluskey, Grace Dickover
McComas, Francis
McComas, Gene Frances
McCormick, Robert James
McCoy, Wilton
McCullough, Alice M.
McDermitt, William Thomas
McFee, Henry Lee
McGlynn, Thomas A.
McKee, Katherine Louise
McLean, Grace
McNeely, Perry
Meador, Joshua Lawrence
Melcher, George Henry
Melvill, Antonia
Melzian, Harley
Mendelowitz, Daniel Marc.
Merideth, John Gray
Merrild, Knud
Merwin, Antoinette D'F.
Mesic, Ms. Julian C.
Messick, Benjamin Newton
Meyer, Frederick H.
Milam, Elizabeth, Coffman
Miles, Harold W.
Miller, Barse
Miller, Doris Louise
Miller, Dorothy Elizabeth
Miller, Evylena Nunn
Miller, Lola Sleeth
Miller, Marie Clark

Miller, Mildred Bunting
Miller, Ralph Davison
Miller, Reeva
Miller, Suzanne
Millier, Arthur
Mills, Paul Chadbourne
Milsk, Mark
Mitchell, Alfred R.
Mitchell, Laura M.D.
Mocine, Emily Rutherford
Monhoff, Frederick
Moody, Helen Wills
Moon, Carl
Moore, Frank Montague
Mora, Joseph Jacinto
Morahan, Eugene
Moran, Earl
Morgan, Charlotte E. Bodwl.
Morgan, Mary DeNeale
Morley, Grace L. McCann
Morris, Adelaide
Morris, Alice
Morris, Patricia
Morse, Vernon Jay
Moser, Julon Modjeska
Moses, Walter Farrington
Motts, Alice Sundt
Moxon, Jack
Mullett, Suzanne
Mulroney, Regina Winifred
Mundt, Ernest Karl
Munsell, Richard
Munsell, William A. O.
Murphy, Harry Daniel
Murry, Jerre
Musselman, Darwin B.
Myers, Charles Stowe
Myers, Frank Harmon
Myers, Lloyd Burton

N

Nagelvoort, Betty
Napolitano, Pasquale Giov.
Nash, Willard Ayer
Natzler, Gertrude
Natzler, Otto
Nelson, Lucretia
Nepote, Alexander
Nesemann, Enno
Neuhaus, Eugen
Neumeyer, Alfred
Neutra, Richard Joseph
Newcomb, Rexford
Newcombe, Warren
Newell, Gordon
Newman, Azadia Herman
Newton, Helen F.
Nichols, Harley DeWitt
Nichols, Pegus (Peggy M.)
Nicholson, Douglas Cornw.
Nicholson, Edward H.
Nicholson, Emrich
Nicholson, Isabel Leder.
Nicolosi, Joseph
Nieto, Grace
Nimmo, Louise Evertt

Saemondsson, Nina
Safford, Charles Putnam
Sage, Cornelia Bentley
Salz, Helen
Samerjan, George E.
Sample, Paul Starrett
Sandefur, John Courtney
Sanford, Frank Leslie
Sandona, Matteo
Sandow, Franz
Sands, Gertrude Louis
Sanford, Isobel Burgess
Sargeant, Geneve Rixford
Saul,(Saul Kovner)
Saulter, Leon
Savage, Marguerite Down.
Savery, Helen H. Brewster
Sayer, Edmund S.
Sayre, Fred Grayson
Scarpitta, G. Salvatore C
Schaeffer, Rudolph
Schaffer, Myer
Scheu, Leonard
Scheuer, Suzanne
Schevill, W. V.
Schmidt, Carl
Schmitt, Paul A.
Schneider, Elsbeth
Schneider, Isobel
Schneider, Otto H.
Schnier, Jacques
Schoener, Jason
Schrack, Joseph Earl
Schultz, Isabelle
Schuster, Donna Norine
Schwankovsky, Frederick
Schweigardt, Frederick Wm.
Scott, Benton F.
Scott, Clyde Eugene
Scott, David Winfield
Scott, Jonathan
Seeberger, Pauline Bridge
Seeds, Elise
Seely, W. Frederick
Seielstad, Benjamin Good.
Seigle, Ralph Cornell
Sekido, Yoshida
Seletz, Emil
Selinger, Armand
Sentovic, John M.
Serbaroli, Hector
Serisawa, Sueo
Severance, Julia Gridley
Shackelford, Kath. Buzzel
Shafer, Burr
Sharp, Joseph Henry
Sharp, William Alexander
Sharpless, Ada May
Shaw, Thomas B.
Shear, Fera Webber
Sheets, Millard Owen
Shepard, Isabel B.
Sheridan, Joseph Marsh
Shively, Douglas
Shoemaker, Vaughn

Shore, Henrietta M.
Shoven, Hazel Brayton
Shrader, Edwin Roscoe
Shrock, John Granville
Sichel, Harold
Sider, Deno
Sieberns, Caroline Lenore
Siegiest, Louis B.
Siegiest, Lundy
Siemer, Chris
Silsby, Clifford F.
Silsby, Wilson
Silva, William Posey
Simms, T. Freeland
Simons, Amory Coffin
Simons, Elvera, H.
Simpson, Marion
Simpson, Martha
Singer, Burr (Mrs.)
Singer, William Earl
Skeele, Anna Katherine
Skelton, Phillis Hepler
Skinner, Charlotte B.
Sklar, Dorothy
Slivka, David
Sloan, James Blanding
Smiley, Ralph J.
Smith, Dorman Henry
Smith, Ernest Browning
Smith, F. Carl
Smith, Hassel Wendell Jr.
Smith, Howard Everrett
Smith, Howard Ross
Smith, Isabel E.
Smith, Jack Wilkinson
Smith, J. Francis
Smith, Jessie Sherwood
Smith, John Francis
Smith, Margery Hoffman
Smith, Maria Vaughan
Smith, Walt Allen
Smyth, Edmund R.
Snaer, Seymour W.
Snowden. George Holburn
Sooy, Louise Pinkney
Sopher, Bernhard D.
Sotomayor, Antonio
Sparks, Will
Spohn, Clay Edgar
Spratt, Alberte'
Sprenkle, Arthur George
Stacey, Anna L.
Stacey, John F.
Stackpole, Ralph
Stanley, George M.
Stark, Jack Gage
Starkey, Jo-Anita
Starr, Katherine Payne
Steele, Juliette
Steere, Lora Woodhead
Steinitz, Kate Trauman
Stensen, Matthew Christ.
Stephens, Richard
Stetson, Katherine Beecher
Stewart, Albert T.

Stirling, Glen
Stirnaman, Marilou
Stirrett, Wylie
Stoddart, Edna
Stoll, John Ted. Edw.
Stone, Fern Cunningham
Stone, Frank Frederick
Stone, Viola Pratt
Stoner, John Lawrence
Story, Ala
Stout, Virginia Hollinger
Stowitts, Hubert J.
Strain, Oma
Strawbridge, Edward R.
Strawn, Mel
Streat, Thelma Johnson
Strickland, Phyllis Alba
Strong, Elizabeth
Strong, Ray Stanford
Struck, Herman
Stuart, James Everett
Stuber, Dedrick B.
Sugimoto, Henry Yuzuru
Suman, Lawrence
Surendorf, Charles Freder.
Sussman, Robert N.
Swain, Ruth Newton
Swartz, Harold
Swift, Dick
Swift, Florence Alston
Swiggert, Jean Donald
Swinnerton, James
Symmonds, Albert

T

Tabb, Gladys Clark
Taggart, Richard T.
Talbott, Katherine
Tauszky, David Anthony
Taylor, Edgar Dorsey
Taylor, Edward DeWitt
Taylor, Farwell M.
Taylor, Jean
Taylor, John C. E.
Teague, Donald
Templeton. Albin Fredrick
Terada, Edward Takeo
Tew, Marguerite R.
Thomas, Grace Thornton
Thomas, Stephen Seymour
Thorpe, Dorothy Carpenter
Thurston, Jane McDuffie
Timmins, Harry L.
Todhunter, Francis
Tolegian, Manual J.
Tompkins, Florence W. Lusk
Tonge, Gilbert
Toor, Nishau
Torrey, Elliot Bouton
Toth, Steven Jr.
Tranquillitsky, Vasily G.
Travis, Kathryne H.
Trease, Sherman
Truax, Sara Elizabeth
Truesdell, Edith Park
Trueworthy, Jay (Jessie)

Tuckerman, Lilia McCauley
Tufts, Florence Ingalsbe
Turnbull, Gale
Turner, Jean Leavitt

U

Ulber, Althea
Ullman, Jane F.
Ullrich, Beatrice
Ulreich, Edward Buk
Usher, Ruby Walker

V

Vaganov, Benjamin G.
Valentia, Manuel W. Jr.
Valentien, Anna Marie
Valentiner, Wm. Reinhold
VanAlstine, Mary J.
VanCleve, Helen Mann
VanDeVelde, Alfred E. R.
VanLeyden, Ernst Oscar
VanLeyden, Karin Eliz.
VanValkenburgh, Peter
VanWolf, Henry
VanYoung, Oscar
VanZandt, Hilda
Vann, Loli
Vaughan, David Alfred
Vaught, Larken G.
Verhaeren, Carolus
Vickery, Frederick P.
Vidar, Frede
Villa, Hernando G.
Volkmar, Leon
Vollmer, Grace Libbey
Volz, Herman
VonBelfort, Charles
VonFalkenstein, Clair
VonMeyer, Michael
VonSchneidau, Christian
Vreeland, Francis William
Vysekal, Edouard Antonin
Vysekal, Luvena Buchanan

W

Waano-Gano, Joe
Wachtel, Marion Kavanaugh
Wack, Henry Wellington
Wagner, Blanche Collet
Wagner, Robert Leicester
Walcott, Anabel H.
Waldvogel, Emma
Walker, John Law
Wall, Bernhardt T
Wall, Gertrude Rupel
Waller, Robert
Walton
Ward, Louisa Cooke
Wardman, John William
Warner, Nell Walker
Warren, Harold Edmond
Washburn, Kenneth
Watkins, Catherine W.
Watkins, Frances Emma
Watson, Adele
Watson, Jesse Nelson
Watson, Robert
Watts, Wm. Clothier

Weaver, Harold Buck
Webb, James Elwood
Webb, Margaret Ely
Wedo, Georgette
Wein, Albert W.
Weinberg, Emilie Sievert
Weiner, Abraham S.
Weisman, Joseph
Wendt, Julia M. Bracken
Wendt, William
Wesselhoeft, Mary Fraser
Wessels, Glenn Anthony
Westfall, Gertrude Benn.
Westfall, Tulita Bennett
Wheeler, Janet D.
Whelan, Blanche
White, Nona
White, Orrin Augustine
Whitlock, Mary Ursula
Whitman, Paul
Wiboltt, Aage Christian
Wideman, Florence P.
Wieczorek, Max
Weighorst, Olaf
Wilcocks, Edna Marrett
Wildman, Mary Frances
Wilmovsky, Charles A.
Wilke, William Hancock
Wilkevich, Eleanor
Wilkin, Mildred Pierce
Wilkinson, Jack
Williams, Howe
Williams, Milton Franklin
Williams, Patricia Gert
Williamson, Paul Broadwell
Williamson, Shirley
Williamson, Wm. Harvey
Willis, Ralph Troth
Wilmer, George
Wilmeth, Hal Turner
Wilson, Ernest M.
Wilson, Frederick Francis
Wilson, Nevada
Wilson, William J.
Wiman, Vern
Winebrenner, Harry Field.
Winkler, John W.
Winn, James H.
Winterburn, Phyllis
Wintermote, Mamie W.
Wirth, Anna Maria Barbara
Wiser, Guy Brown
Wolf, Hamilton Achille
Wolfe, Natalie
Wong, Tyrus Y.
Wood, Beatrice (Beato)
Wood, E. Shotwell
Wood, Kathryn Leone
Wood, Stanley
Woolley, Virginia
Works, Katherine S.
Wright, James Couper
Wright, Redmond Stephens
Wulf, Lloyd William
Wylie, Marion E.

Wynne, Leslie Bernard Jr.

Y

Yacoe, Donald Edward
Yardley, Ralph O.
Yens, Karl   also Jens
Yip, Richard D.
Yoakum, Delmer J.
Young, Clara Huntington
Young, Florence Upson
Young, J. Donald
Young, Joseph Louis
Younglove, Ruth Ann
Yphantis, George

Z

Zakheim, Bernard Baruch
Zeidler, Avis
Zilzer, Gyula
Zimmerman, Frederick Alm.
Zornes, James Milford
Zorthian, Jirayr Hamparz.

CALIFORNIA - OTHER

This section covers major and 'example'
exhibitions, and those books with more
limited coverage than Moure's or McCall's.
For instance, Ruth Westphal's book, <u>Plein
Air Painters of California - The South-
land</u> is one of the most beautiful and in-
depth book on California art, but it
covers only 30 top artists.

Two especially important inclusions in
this section are the 1932 CA&A list of
California artists (a WPA financed project) and the biographical files of the
Baird Archive. The Southern California
portion of the CA&A list was the basis
for Moure's Dictionary, but the Northern
Calif. group have not been systematically
covered elsewhere. Dr. Baird's biographical files, diligently assembled over a
period of many years, provide especially
good coverage of the Northern Calif. artists.

This material is arranged approximately in
chronological order.

California Design 1910

From book of same name by Anderson, Moore, and Winter, Peregrine Smith Inc. 1980

Franz A. Bischoff	Arthur Frank Mathews
Edward Borein	Lucia Kleinhans Mathews
Carl Oscar Borg	Francis John McComas
John Gutzon Borglum	Thomas Moran
Maurice Braun	Eugen Neuhaus
Benjamin Chambers Brown	Jules Francois Pages Jr.
Alexander S. Calder	Edgar Alwin Payne
Charles Mathew Crocker	Charles Rollo Peters
Edwin Deakin	Gottardo Piazzoni
Paul de Longpre	Hanson Duvall Puthuff
L. Maynard Dixon	Arthur Putnam
Harold Doolittle	Granville Redmond
John Bond Francisco	Guy Rose
John Marshall Gamble	Jack Wilkenson Smith
Henry Percy Gray	Will Sparks
Armin Hanson	James G. Swinnerton
Sam Hyde Harris	Manuel Valencia Jr.
Thomas Hill	Albert R. Valentien
Anna Althea Hills	Hernando Villa
Grace Carpenter Hudson	Elmer Wachtel
Christian Jorgenson	Marion Kavanagh Wachtel
William Lees Judson	Thaddeus Welch
William Keith	William Wendt
Fernand Harvey Lungren	
Jean Mannheim	
Xavier Martinez	

Painters of the Exposition

1915 Pan-Pacific Exposition

From the book, <u>ART IN CALIFORNIA</u>, R. L. Bernier Co. 1916

A
Arthur Atkins

B
Cora Boone
Carl Oscar Borg
Lester D. Boronda
Maurice Braun
Anne M. Bremer
Henry Joseph Breuer
Benjamin Chambers Brown
Ferdinand Burgdorff

C
Guiseppe Cadenasso
William Vincent Cahill
Emil Carlsen
Rinaldo Cuneo

D
Maurice Del Mue
P. Betty DeJong
John Dickman
Maynard Dixon
Helena Dunlap

F
E. Charlton Fortune
Maren M. Froelich

G
John Gamble
Percy Gray
Joseph Greenbaum

H
Armin Hansen
Herman G. Herkomer
K. Hinkle
Clark Hobart
Isabel Hunter

J
Rixford Johnson
Amadee Joullin
G. Chapel Judson

K
William Keith
William Keith   (4 pain-
William Keith   tings)
William Keith

L
Lorenzo P. Latimer
Florence Lundborg
Fernand Lungren

M
E. Spencer Macky
Jean Mannheim
Xavier Martinez

Arthur F. Mathews
Lucia K. Mathews
Francis McComas
M. Evwlyn McCormick
Jules Mersfelder
M. DeNeale Morgan

N
Perham Nahl
Eugen Neuhaus
Bruce Nelson

P
Jules Pages
Orrin Peck
Ernest Peixotto
A. Sheldon Pennoyer
Charles Rollo Peters
Henry Varnum Poor
Bruce Porter
C. S. Price
Hansen Puthuff

R
Lee F. Randolph
Joseph Raphael
Granville Redmond
John Hubbard Rich
Mary Curtis Richardson
Winifred Rieber
William Ritschel
Guy Rose
Toby Rosenthal

S
Matteo Sandona
Geneve Rixford Sargeant
Donna Schuster
Henrietta M. Shore
Will Sparks
John A. Stanton

T
C. P. Townsley

V
Frank J. Van Sloun
Calthea Vivian

W
Elmer Wachtel
Marion Kavanagh Wachtel
Rob Wagner
William Wendt
Orrin White
Theodore Wores

<u>SCULPTURE</u>

Robert Aitken
Chester Beach
Earl Cummings
Maud Daggett
Elizabeth Edmond
J. McQuarrie
Joseph J. Mora
Arthur Putnam
Douglas Tilden
Edgar Walter
Julia Bracken Wendt

<u>DRAWINGS</u>

Carl Oscar Borg
Armin Hansen
Clark Hobart
Pedro J. Lemos
Louis C. Mullgardt
Gertrude Partington
Isobelle C. Percy
Gottardo F. Piazzoni
L. F. Randolph
Joseph Raphael
Worth Ryder
William H. Wilke

WPA Murals in California

From <u>New Deal Art: California</u>

Exhibition developed by the University of Santa Clara based upon WPA records, and shown at DeSaisset Galleries in 1976. (Mural photos) Number = separate murals by artist.

Artist	No.	Artist	No.	Artist	No.
Ahring, Jaine	1	Dean, Mallette	2	Hiler, Hilaire	2
Albee, Maia	1	de Kruif, Henri	1	Hirst, Pauline	1
Albro, Maxine	3	del Mue, Maurice	2	Hogg, Zack	2
Ames, Arthur	4+	del Pino, Moya	4	Holden, James A.	1
Ariss, Brucw	1	De Mers, Joseph	1	Holmes, Stuart	4
Arnautoff, Victor	6	Deutsch, Boris	2	Hord, Donal	5
Atkinson, William O.	1	De Vriendt, Stefan	2	Howard, Charles	1
Ayres. Martha O.	1	Dickey, Dan	1	Howard, John L.	1
		Dickinson, Ross	4	Howard, Robert B.	2
Ballin, Hugo	1	Dixon, Maynard	5	Hrdy, Olinka	4
Baranceanu, Belle	4	Djey, Djey el	2		
Barnett, Earl	1	Douglas, Haldane	1	Jackson, Howard	1
Barney, Esther S.	1	Duchow, Casper	4	Johnson, Sargent	1
Bartlett, Ivan	3	Dyer, Carlos	1	Julian, Paul	5
Bergman, Franz W.	3				
Bertrand, Ray	1	Edstrom, David	2	Kassler, Charles II	2
Berlandina, Jane	1	Elwell, Myrna	1	Katchamakoff, Atanas	1
Best, Nellie	1	Etcheverry, Lousia	1	Katz, Leo	2
Biberman, Edward	2	Everett, Eugenia	3	King, Albert H.	1
Blazek, Anton	1			Keller, Lew	1
Boag, Robert	1	Feitelson, Lorser	5	Kendall, Marian	1
Bothwell, Dorr	4	Fitzgerald, James	2		
Boundey, Burton S.	3	Foerster, Arnold	2	Labaudt, Lucien	2
Bowers, Frank K.	1	Forbes, Helen K.	5	Laman, Thomas	3
Boynton, Ray	2			Leigh, Lily	1
Braghetta, Lulu H.	2	Gattney, Claribel	1	Leitner, Arthur J.	1
Brandt, Rex	3	Gage, Merrell	1	Lewis, Tom E.	2
Brasz, A. F.	3	Galgiano, Oscar	1	Lion, Henry	4
Bruton, Helen	3	Gano, Wanno	1	Lloyd, Lucile	1
Buckhard, Verona	1	Garner, Archibald	7	Lundeberg, Helen	5
Bufano, Benjamino	6	Garth, John	1		
Buff, Conrad	3	Gaskin, William	1	Macdonald-Wright, S.	4
Burnham, Roger N.	2	Gay, August	3	MacGurrin, Buckley	6
		Gerrity, John	1	Machefert, Adrien	3
Calfee, William	1	Gile, Seldon G.	1	MacRitchie, Lewis	1
Cane, Arthur	2	Goodwin, Jean	3	Maier-Krieg, Eugene	1
Caredio, Primo	1	Goff, Harper	1	Mako, Bartholume	2
Catrer, Dudley	1	Goldstein(Guston),Phill		Marsh, Jesse	1
Chamberlain, Norman S.	4	Graham, Harold	1	Martin, Fletcher	2
Chamberlin, Frank T.	1	Grant, Campbell	2	Mendelowitz, Daniel	1
Chepourkoff, Michael	1	Grant, Gordon K.	2	Messick, Ben	1
Chesse, Ralph	1	Gren, Nils	1	Miller, Barse	2
Cleaves, Gail	1			Miller, Suzanne	3
Clements, Grace	6	Haines, Richard	1	Monk, Lisa	1
Colburn, Eleanor	1	Hall, Parker	1	Morahan, Eugene	1
Colburn, Eleanor	1	Hamlin, Edith	3	Murry, Jerre	2
Comfort, Tyrone	4	Hanks, Rose	1		
Cornwell, Dean	2	Hansen, Armin	1	Napolitano, Giovanni	5
Cuneo, Rinaldo	2	Hansen, James	4	Nemkoff, Vladimir	2
Cunningham, Benjamin	3	Harcoff, Lyla M.	1	Newell, Gordon	4
		Harris, George	2	Nicholson, Emrich	1
Date, Hideo	2	Hartman, Murray	1	Noble, Raymond	1
Daum, Hebe	1	Heller, Bessie	2		
Davis, Charles H.	2	Herron, Jason	2	O'Hanlon, Richard	2
Davis, Lew E.	2	Hesthal, William	2		
				Palo-Kangas, John	7

WPA HISTORIES OF CALIF. ARTISTS

From *California Art Research* by WPA Writers Project-1930s

C. A. & A. Artist List 1932

(Biographical material is not located in this volume.)

From California Arts & Architecture, 1932 under Directory of California Artists.... A survey of all Calif. artists.

A

ABASCAL, Mary, *Painting*
523 S. Commonwealth Ave., Los Angeles
ABBOTT, Jacob B., *Painting*
P. O. Box 97, Altadena
ABDY, Rowena Meeks, *Watercolors*
1050 Lombard St., San Francisco
ABEEL, Ethel M., *Painting*
4286 Terrace St., Oakland
ABEL, Jean, *Crafts, Teacher*
1307 E. Wilson Ave., Glendale
ABBOTT, Mary Beth, *Painting, Teacher*
1440 E. Broadway, Glendale
ACKER, Herbert Van Blarcom, *Portraits*
1422 Wilson Ave., San Marino
ADAMS, Burres Dorothy, *Painting*
122 S. Westlake Ave., Los Angeles
ADAMS, Ansel Easton, *Photography*
131 24th Ave., San Francisco
ADAMS, Charles Partridge, *Painting*
Box 854, Laguna Beach
ADAMS, Edward A., *Advertising Illustrate, Teach*
2544 W. 7th St., Los Angeles
ADAMS, Frances E., *Teacher*
13720 Vanowen St., Van Nuys
ADAMS, Lulu J., *Painting*
648 San Juan Ave., Venice
ADAMS, Marian, *Crafts*
1409 Crenshaw Blvd., Los Angeles
ADAMS, Velma, *Sculpture, Etching*
714 S. Oxford Ave., Los Angeles
Af EKENSTAM, Marta, *Crafts*
765 E. Del Mar, Pasadena
AINSWORTH, Kathryn C., *Teacher*
939 S. Figueroa St., Los Angeles
AISENSTEIN, Antonia Tamara, *Painting*
2575 Le Conte Ave., Berkeley
AKERS, Len, *Commercial*
1053 Howard St., San Francisco
AKINS, Rheta M., *Teacher*
420 9th St., Huntington Beach
ALBEE, Maja, *Weaving, Teacher*
136 St. Anne St., San Francisco
ALBERTO, Iris, *Weaving*
Carmel
ALBRIGHT, Gertrude Partington, *Painting*
737 Buena Vista Ave., San Francisco
ALBRIGHT, H. Oliver, *Painting*
737 Buena Vista Ave., San Francisco
ALBRO, Maxine, *Painting, Fresco*
2046 Beach St., San Francisco
ALDEMAN, Josephine, *Teacher*
400 S. Rimpau Blvd., Los Angeles
ALDRICH, Clarence N., *Watercolors*
1834 Dawson Ave., Los Angeles
ALDRIN, Andrew G., *Painting, Sculpture*
2526 Riverside Dr., Los Angeles
ALEXANDER, Dora Block, *Painti*
4038 Euclid Ave., San Diego
ALEXANDER, Kenneth, *Photography*
8474½ Sunset Blvd., Hollywood
ALEXANDER, Ruth, *Painting*
Laguna Beach
ALLAN, Ted, *Commercial*
6380 Hollywood Blvd., Hollywood
ALLARDT, Marian, *Painting*
780 Kingston Ave., Piedmont
ALLEN, Emma, *Painting*
3440 Palm St., San Diego
ALLEN, Richard H., *Decoration, Teacher*
2315½ 4th Ave., Los Angeles
ALLEN, Ann H., *Painting*
418 9th St., Santa Monica
ALLEN, B. H., *Painting*
2628 Haste St., Berkeley
ALLEN, Winthrop, *Painting*
111 Chestnut St., Pasadena
ALLER, Gladys, *Painting*
2243 Cheswick Lane, Los Angeles
ALLISON, Mrs. L. C., *Crafts*
229 S. Carondelet St., Los Angeles
ALLISON, Vera, *Commercial*
728 Montgomery St., San Francisco
ALLMAN, Richard, *Painting, Etching, Sculpture, Teacher*
3743 Ramona Dr., Riverside
ALTER, Harry R., *Commercial*
232 E. 4th St., Los Angeles
ALTHOUSE, Lillian, *Painting*
235 S. Figueroa St., Los Angeles
ALTMANN, Aaron, *Teacher*
2944 Pierce St., San Francisco
ALVAREZ, Mabel, *Painting, Lithographs*
144 S. Plymouth Blvd., Los Angeles
AMES, Arthur, *Painting*
114½ E. 4th St., Santa Ana
AMES, Barbara, *Painting*
1360 Drake Ave., Burlingame
AMES, Earl, *Painting*
80 Boyce St., San Francisco
AMES, Florence, *Teacher*
1648 S. Van Ness Ave., Los Angeles

ANDERSON, Anna Maud, *Teacher*
1704 Beale Ave., Bakersfield
ANDERSON, Heath, *Commercial*
16 Beale St., San Francisco
ANDERSON, Ida May, *Teacher*
2837 W. 42nd St., Los Angeles
ANDERSON, Milo L., *Costume Design, Cinema*
822 N. Vista St., Hollywood
ANDERSON, Paul, *Painting*
630 Harvard Ave., Claremont
ANDRES, Adela, *Block Prints*
1456 S. Orange Drive, Los Angeles
ANDREWS, Charles J., *Oils*
1230 Meade Ave., San Diego
ANDREWS, Willard H., *Commercial*
Russ Bldg., San Francisco
ANGELO, Valenti, *Painting*
1941 Leavenworth St., San Francisco
ANNIS, Margaret, *Teacher*
Willowbrook
ANNIS, Verle L., *Teacher*
2338 Scarff St., Los Angeles
ANTHONY, Lucile L., *Crafts, Sculpture*
1236 Tremaine Ave., Los Angeles
ARCHER, Fred R., *Photography*
4061 S. Main St., Los Angeles
ARKATOV, Alexander, *Photography*
410 Lake St., San Francisco
ARMER, Laura Adams, *Painting*
1329 Arch Street, Berkeley
ARMER, Ruth, *Painting*
2368 Broadway, San Francisco
ARMER, Sidney, *Commercial*
417 Montgomery St., San Francisco
ARMSTRONG, Edna L., *Teacher*
2401 Channel Dr., Ventura
ARMSTRONG, Samuel, *Murals*
2759 Lauro Canyon Rd., Santa Barbara
ARNAUTOFF, Victor, *Sculpture*
47 White St., San Francisco
ARNOLD, Edwin C., *Painting, Pastels*
Route 1, Box 856-H, San Diego
ASANGER, Jacob, *Posters, Landscapes*
2062 Watsonia Terrace, Los Angeles
ASHBROOK, Mrs. R. M., *Woodcarving*
9225 Magnolia Ave., Riverside
ASHLEY, Hammond, *Woodcarving, Furniture*
1814 W. 7th St., Los Angeles
ASKINAZY, M., *Figures, Portraits*
4051 Clinton St., Los Angeles
ATKINS, Florence Elizabeth, *Painting*
1040 Bush St., San Francisco
ATKINSON, William O., *Watercolors*
789 Kensington Rd., Los Angeles
ATWOOD, Mary Hall, *Painting*
4175 W. 5th St., Los Angeles
AULMANN, Theodora, *Painting*
1541 N. Hobart Blvd., Los Angeles
AUSTIN, Charles P., *Painting*
1619 Hill St., Santa Monica
AVERY, Dean, *Commercial*
617 Montgomery St., San Francisco
AVERY, Kenneth, *Painting*
2020 San Pasqual Ave., Pasadena
AYRES, Martha Oathout, *Sculpture*
642 Nectarine St., Inglewood

B

BABCOCK, Ida D., *Painting*
919 College Ave., Redlands
BACON, Aroline E., *Painting*
344 S. Occidental Blvd., Los Angeles
BADDELEY, Frank, *Crafts, Teacher*
Lincoln High School, Los Angeles
BADEN, Frank, *Design, Furniture, Decoration*
235 S. Vermont Ave., Los Angeles
BADGER, Stanwood, *Etching, Drawing*
672 S. Lafayette Park Pl., Los Angeles
BAER, Burt, *Painting, Costume Design, Teach*
5164 Rockland Ave., Eagle Rock
BAGDATOPOULOS, W. S., *Painting*
"Bramcote," Laurel Canyon Rd., Sta. Barbara
BAGUEZ, Salvador, *Newspaper Art*
Care The Times, 100 N. Broadway, L. A.
BAILEY, Bernice M., *Painting*
738 E St., San Diego
BAILEY, Harry, *Painting*
175 N. Almont Dr., Beverly Hills
BAILHACHE, Anna Dodge, *Painting*
2519 Octavia St., San Francisco
BAINES, S. C., *Commercial*
Garnier Engr. Co., 407 E. Pico St., L. A.
BAKER, Jean, *Painting*
842 N. Sycamore Ave., Los Angeles
BAKER, Leonard E., *Sculpture*
609 N. Main St., Santa Ana
BAKER-SMITH, Francis, *Stage Design, Cinema*
5330 Loma Linda Ave., Hollywood
BALDAUGH, Anni, *Miniatures*
501 Robinson St., San Diego

BALDWIN, Cliff P., *Painting*
5030 Almaden Dr., Los Angeles
BALDWIN, Clayton M., *Teacher*
4577 Rosewood Ave., Los Angeles
BALDWIN, H. F., *Sculpture*
2039 N. Hobart Blvd., Los Angeles
BALFOUR, Roberta, *Painting*
Carmel
BALL, Ruth Norton, *Sculpture*
4135 Normal St., San Diego
BALLAGH, Blanche M., *Painting*
1012 N. Berendo St., Los Angeles
BALLBUSCH, Peter, *Sculpture*
368 N. Bronson Ave., Los Angeles
BALLIN, Hugo, *Painting, Murals*
567 Almoloya Dr., Pac. Palisades Sta. Moni
BALTEKAL-GOODMAN, Michael, *Woodbloc*
1780 Highland Pl., Berkeley
BANNISTER, Raymond, *Commercial*
318 Kearny St., San Francisco
BARBIER, Maurice, *Woodcarving*
2314 W. Santa Barbara Ave., Los Angeles
BARIENBROCK, Fred C., *Watercolors*
526 Palisades Ave., Santa Monica
BARKER, Edna C., *Painting*
3635 Villa Terrace, San Diego
BARKER, George, Jr., *Painting*
535 Alma Real Dr., Pac. Palisades, Sta. Moni
BARKER, Olive, *Watercolors*
535 Alma Real Dr., Pac. Palisades, Sta. Moni
BARNARD, Beatrice, *Teacher*
232 N. Van Ness Ave., Fresno
BARNDOLLAR, Harry, *Commercial, Cinema*
Paramount Studios, 5451 Marathon St., Hollywood
BARNES, Cornelia, *Painting*
21 Hillside Ct., Berkeley
BARNES, Matthew, *Painting*
123 Joice St., San Francisco
BARNHART, Robert B., *Sculpture*
1737 N. Highland Ave., Los Angeles
BAROS, Michael, *Leather Craft*
6715 Hollywood Blvd., Los Angeles
BARR, William, *Painting*
141 Broderick St., San Francisco
BARRETT, Elsie E., *Watercolors*
116 S. Berendo St., Los Angeles
BARROWS, Albert, *Painting*
217 14th Ave., San Francisco
BARTLETT, Dana, *Painting*
3358 W. 1st St., Los Angeles
BARTLETT, Emily C., *Painting*
32 Church St., Santa Cruz
BATCHELDER, E. A., *Painting*
625 Arroyo Dr., Pasadena
BATCHELDER, Ralph J., *Teacher*
392 S. Catalina St., Los Angeles
BATESON, Mildred M., *Teacher*
6131 Glen Tower Ave., Hollywood
BATTEN, McLeod, *Painting*
Mill Valley
BAUGHMAN, Douglas, *Commercial*
1663 Lafayette Rd., Los Angeles
BAUMAN, E. F., *Painting*
4173 McConnell Blvd., Venice
BAUMAN, John W., *Painting*
892 S. Euclid Ave., Pasadena
BAXLEY, Barbara E., *Painting*
1822 Virginia St., Berkeley
BAXTER, Blanche, *Weaving*
3010 First Ave., San Diego
BAXTER, Martha Wheeler, *Miniatures*
740 State St., Santa Barbara
BAZART, John A., *Painting*
1406 Linda Vista Ave., Eagle Rock
BEACH, I. E., Jr., *Painting*
4386 Campus Ave., San Diego
BEAUMONT, Arthur, *Painting, Etching*
1809 Oak St., Los Angeles
BECK, Violet, *Painting*
411 21st St., La Jolla
BECKHAM, J. H., *Crafts*
4062 Wilshire Blv., Los Angeles
BECKMAN, J. C., *Painting*
325 W. Lomidta Ave., Glendale
BEGGS, Thomas M., *Painting, Teacher*
Pomona College, Claremont
BEHME, Edward, *Block Prints*
5266 Mt. Royal Dr., Eagle Rock
BEHR, Betty, *Painting*
445 N. Alvarado St., Los Angeles
BELCHER, Gertrude, *Crafts*
5209 Hollywood Blvd., Los Angeles
BELEW, Jane, *Design*
1613 Highland Ave., Glendale
BELL, Marion, *Painting*
1040 Fir Ave., Inglewood
BELL, Trudie M., *Crafts*
4438 38th St., San Diego
BEMIS, Georgia E., *Painting, Etching, Sculpture*
5439 Edgeware Rd., San Diego
BEMUS, Hazel Nell, *Teacher*
725 S. Main St., Santa Ana

BENACK, Flora D., *Painting*
1458 Home Pl., Los Angeles
BENFIELD, Sallie, *Painting*
2432 S. Park Ave., Palo Alto
BENJAMIN, C. K., *Watercolors*
2215 Lewis Ave., Altadena
BENJAMIN, Charles Henry, *Crafts*
2215 Lewis Ave., Altadena
BENKE, August, *Commercial*
1943 Vine St., Hollywood
BENNETT, Ruth, *Painting, Woodcarving*
1746 McCadden Pl., Los Angeles
BENSCO, Charles J., *Painting*
8199 Ellenwood Dr., Eagle Rock
BENSINGER, Anne M., *Watercolors, Teach*
141 W. Santa Barbara Ave., Los Angeles
BENTOR, Mary, *Teacher*
2941 2nd St., San Diego
BERCOVITZ, Esther, *Costume Design, Teach*
1700 Octavia St., San Francisco
BERGESEN, Oscar W., *Commercial*
108 W. 6th St., Los Angeles
BERGMAN, Frank W., *Murals*
293 Corbett Ave., San Francisco
BERGMAN, Karola, *Painting*
58 Santa Barbara Ave., San Francisco
BERGVELT, Karl, *Decoration, Teacher*
741 S. Grandview St., Los Angeles
BERINGER, L. C., *Photography*
177 Post St., San Francisco
BERLAND, Israel, *Leather Craft*
1925 W. 10th St., Los Angeles
BERLAND, Nell de Waiet, *Leather Craft*
1925 W. 10th St., Los Angeles
BERLANDINA, Jane, *Painting*
1561 Willard St., San Francisco
BERNARDI, Theodore C., *Painting*
948 The Alameda, Berkeley
BERNE, Agnes da Fonte, *Ceramics, Teach*
Sacramento Jr. College, Sacramento
BERNSTEIN, Harry Marcus, *Painting*
2924 9th Ave., Los Angeles
BERRY, Cyril, *Painting*
318 Guarantee Bldg., Los Angeles
BERRY, Mary Lillian, *Watercolors, Prints*
580 A Ave., Coronado
BERSON, Adolphe, *Painting*
41 Hancock St., San Francisco
BERTRAND, Ray, *Painting*
554 6th Ave., San Francisco
BESSINGER, Frederick H., *Painting*
731 Ashland Ave., Santa Monica
BEST, H. C., *Painting*
Yosemite National Park
BEST, Jane H., *Painting*
4465 Fourth St., Riverside
BEST, Loretta, *Teacher*
2501 Vallejo St., San Francisco
BETHELL, Worden, *Painting*
2509 W. 7th St., Los Angeles
BETHERS, Ray, *Painting*
1242 Taylor St., San Francisco
BEW, May Clover, *Sculpture*
535 39th St., San Francisco
BICKFORD, Chester, *Painting*
1122-B Wilshire Blvd., Santa Moniac
BICKFORD, Mary, *Leather Craft*
6032 Monte Vista St., Los Angeles
BIERMAN, Daisy Kessler, *Painting*
El Cajon
BILGER, Mrs. Carl, *Crafts*
3840 W. 27th St., Los Angeles
BILLINGS, Lucie, *Watercolors*
1250 Mendocino St., Altadena
BILLS, Edison D., *Commercial*
510 Battery St., San Francisco
BINTLIFF, Mrs. Martha B., *Painting*
1522 Virginia Way, La Jolla
BIRCH, Geraldine Duncan, *Portraits, Etchin*
1550 N. Garfield Ave., Pasadena
BISCHOFF, Frank A., *Painting*
320 Pasadena Ave., South Pasadena
BISSINGER, Elizabeth, *Painting, Drawing*
2430 Broadway, San Francisco
BISSIRI, Adriano, *Commercial*
1206 S. Hill St., Los Angeles
BIXBY, David W., *Design*
21 Prospect Ave., Long Beach
BJURMAN, Andrew, *Sculpture*
834 S. Garfield Ave., Alhambra
BLACK, Agnes, *Sculpture*
1355 N. Sycamore Ave., Los Angeles
BLACK, Mae, *Painting, Woodcarving*
5758 Magnolia Ave., Riverside
BLACK, Mary C., *Painting*
Box H, Monterey
BLACKBURN, Herbert, *Jewelry*
1719 N. Gardner St., Broadway
BLACKMAN, J. Vance, *Commercial*
Mills Bldg., San Francisco
BLAIR, Lee, *Painting, Drawing*
1138 Elm Ave., Glendale
BLAKE, Aletha Arlen, *Miniatures*
c/o Barker Bros., Los Angeles
BLANCHARD, Porter, *Silver Craft*
3921 Magnolia Ave., Burbank
BLANCHARD, Richard, *Crafts*
11152 Riverside Dr., Los Angeles
BLANK, Pauline, *Teacher*
1211 N. Edgemont St., Los Angeles
BLEIL, Charles G., *Painting*
1484 Jackson St., San Francisco
BLOSER, Florence Parker, *Painting*
349 S. New Hampshire Ave., Los Angeles
BLUM, Helen, *Watercolors*
599 Prospect Blvd., Pasadena

BLUMERT, Johanna Marie, *Painting*
5125 Grove St., Oakland
BOEHME, Hazel, *Painting*
2658 Ivanhoe Dr., Los Angeles
BOHNEN, Aloys, *Painting*
Box 505, Point Loma
BOLDSEN, Thyra, *Sculpture*
446 E. 4th St., Long Beach
BODRERO, James S., *Watercolors*
541 N. Orange Grove Ave., Pasadena
BOLLES, Ida Randall, *Painting*
Laguna Beach
BOLTON, Molly, *Painting*
2163 Guy St., San Diego
BONAR, Lester M., *Commercial*
425 S. 6th St., Alhambra
BOND, Gertrude, *Teacher*
1310 S. Central Ave., Glendale
BOND, Mary E., *Decoration*
1155 S. Burlington St., Los Angeles
BONEY, Ena Westcott, *Painting*
1274 Upland Fla., Eagle Rock
BONNET, Leon, *Painting*
Bonita
BONNOT, Lola B., *Tapestries, China*
743 E. Ave. 43, Los Angeles
BOONE, Cora M., *Teacher*
1562 Jackson St., Oakland
BOOVIER, Essie M., *Painting*
707 W. 52nd Pl., Los Angeles
BOREIN, Ed, *Etching*
Paseo De La Guerra, Santa Barbara
BORG, Carl Oscar, *Painting, Etching*
1339 N. Hobart Blvd., Los Angeles
BOSWELL, Normen Gould, *Painting*
643 Juanita Ave., Los Angeles
BOTHWELL, Dorr, *Painting*
1024 Pasco St., San Diego
BOTKE, Cornelis, *Etching, Painting*
Wheeler Canyon, Santa Paula
BOTKE, Jessie Arms, *Painting*
Wheeler Canyon, Santa Paula
BOUNDEY, Burton S., *Painting*
Monterey
BOURDIEU, Aimée F., *Painting, Teacher*
576 Gerhart St., Los Angeles
BOWDEN, Henry, *Painting*
2613 Channing Way, Berkeley
BOWMAN, Carl, *Painting*
785 3rd Ave., San Francisco
BOYD, E. C., *Painting*
319 S. 5th St., San Jose
BOYD, Everett, *Painting*
1178 W. Madison Ave., Los Angeles
BOYE, Ruth, *Textiles*
298 Dorantes Ave., San Francisco
BOYNTON, Ray, *Painting, Murals*
750 Montgomery St., San Francisco
BOYNTON, Ruth, *Painting*
221 Cedar Court, Montebello
BRACE, Winfield E., *Commercial*
Pacific Bldg., San Francisco
BRADDOCK, Katherine, *Painting*
539 West Willow St., Stockton
BRADEN, Coral A., *Painting*
845 S. Manhattan Pl., Los Angeles
BRADLEY, Elliott, *Painting*
1707 Stanford St., Santa Monica
BRADLEY, Lucy H., *Teacher*
1549 Glenwood Rd., Glendale
BRADSHAW, Alexandra, *Painting, Teacher*
State College, Fresno
BRADSHAW, Beatrice P., *Teacher*
725 W. 107th St., Los Angeles
BRAGDON, William V., *Ceramics*
1335 Hearst Ave., Berkeley
BRAMMER, William G., *Watercolo*
1115 N. Central Ave., Glendale *Lithograp*
BRAND, Yvonne, *Illustration, Teachere*
1990 California St., San Francisco
BRANDELEIN, George, *Commercial*
693 Mission St., San Francisco
BRANDON, John A., *Drawing*
240 N. Myrtle Ave., Monrovia
BRANDON, John A., *Drawing*
240 N. Myrtle Ave., Monrovia
BRANDRIFF, George K., *Painting*
Laguna Beach
BRANDT, Franz D., *Painting*
2615 Parker St., Berkeley
BRANSTEN, Mrs. Joseph, *Painting*
49 Seacliff Ave., San Francisco
BRASZ, A. Franz, *Painting, Etching*
1250 S. Maryland Ave., Glendale
BRAUN, Maurice, *Painting*
507 Silvergate Ave., Point Loma
BRAY, Arnold, *Painting, Etching*
1155 Divisadero St., San Francisco
BRECKENFELD, Bertha H., *Teacher*
338 Chadbourne Ave., Los Angeles
BREHM, Cora, *Painting*
6044 Del Rey Ct., Riverside
BRENEISER, Elizabeth Day, *Crafts*
Box 547, Santa Maria
BRENEISER, John A., *Crafts*
Box 547, Santa Maria
BRENEISER, Stanley G., *Teacher*
Lower Orcutt Rd., Santa Maria
BREUER, Alice P., *Textiles*
1284 67th St., Emeryville
BREUER, Gustave, *Painting*
1284 W. 67th St., Emeryville
BREWER, Ethel L., *Leather Craft*
8460 San Gabriel Ave., Southgate, Los Angel

BREWSTER, Eugene V., *Painting*
1512 N. Beverly Dr., Beverly Hills
BRIGANTE, N. P., *Watercolors*
2620 Rutherford Dr., Los Angeles
BRIGMAN, Anne, *Photography*
65 Roswell Ave., Long Beach
BRINDLE, Ewart M., *Painting, Commerci*
16 Beale St., San Francisco
BRISSEY, Forrest L., *Painting*
5035 Trask St., Oakland
BRONSTRUP, Gus, *Cartoons*
c/o The Chronicle, San Francisco
BRODER, Steve, *Painting*
628 Montgomery St., San Francisco
BROOKS, Frances, *Painting*
345 O'Farrell St., San Francisco
BROOKS, Gertrude F., *Teacher*
1205 Green St., Glendale
BROOKS, Mildred Bryant, *Etching*
95 Monterey Rd., South Pasadena
BROOKS, Walter, *Commercial*
1206 S. Maple Ave., Los Angeles
BROTHERS, Hal J., *Etching*
Mission Hotel, Cahuenga Blvd., Hollywood
BROWN, Benjamin C., *Painting, Etching*
120 N. El Molino Ave., Pasadena
BROWN, Charles H., *Photography*
504 W. Victoria St., Santa Barbara
BROWN, Dayton, *Etching*
201 N. Ave. 66, South Pasadena
BROWN, De Marcus, *Stagecraft*
142 Knoles Way, Stockton
BROWN, Elfreda Nagel, *Painting*
2510 Funston Ave., San Francisco
BROWN, Fannie E., *Teacher*
719 N. Electric Ave., Alhambra
BROWN, Grace, *Design*
1231 Hilldale Ave., Los Angeles
BROWN, Helen Cheney, *Painting*
Carmel
BROWNING, Arnold, *Painting*
440 Jerome Ave., Piedmont
BROWN, Howell D., *Etching*
120 N. El Molino Ave., Pasadena
BROWN, John Wallace, *Painting*
2726 Questa Rd., Santa Barbara
BROWN, Grace Marion, *Costume Design*
4901 Lockhaven St., Los Angeles
BROWN, Lucille R., *Teacher*
Santa Monica High School, Santa Monica
BROWN, Margaret, *Teacher*
337 Pasadena Ave., Pasadena
BROWN, Nina, *Teacher*
1321 Edgecliffe Dr., Los Angeles
BROWN, William J., *Painting*
7923 Santa Fe Ave., Huntington Park
BROWN, Willie Elice, *Painting*
1207 W. 3rd St., Los Angeles
BROWNE, Belmore, *Painting*
914 Santa Barbara St., Santa Barbara
BROWNE, Estella Mary, *Teacher*
2510 Manhattan Ave., Hermosa Beach
BRUCE, Edward, *Painting*
Box 1375, Carmel
BRUCE, Fannie B., *Commercial*
424 S. Broadway, Los Angeles
BRUECK, Marian B., *Teacher*
Box 365, King City
BRUTON, Esther, *Woodblocks*
1240 St. Charles St., Alameda
BRUTON, Helen, *Woodblocks*
1240 St. Charles St., Alameda
BRUTON, Margaret, *Painting*
1240 St. Charles St., Alameda
BRYAN, Catherine, *Watercolors*
3702 Franklin Ave., Riverside
BRYANT, Ernestine, *Painting*
3121 West St., Oakland
BRYANT, Everett L., *Painting, Murals*
5070 Williams Pl., Los Angeles
BRYSON, Hope Mercereau, *Painting*
4291 Hermosa Way, San Diego
BUCHANAN, Bertha L., *Crafts*
842 25th St., San Diego
BUCHANAN, Ella, *Sculpture*
1539 N. Edgemont Ave., Los Angeles
BUCKLEY, Dorothy E., *Painting*
4156 Middlesex Dr., San Diego
BUFF, Conrad, *Painting, Murals, Lithograp*
1225 Linda Rosa Ave., Eagle Rock
BULKELEY, Mary, *Jewelry*
Carmel
BULMER, Evelyn, *Commercial*
1019 Bankers Bldg., Los Angeles
BUNTING, Lily M., *Textiles*
731 Harvard Ave., Menlo Park
BURDICK, Ruth, *Teacher*
1427 E. Ocean Ave., Long Beach
BURG, G. F., *Commercial*
163 Sutter St., San Francisco
BURGDORFF, Ferdinand, *Painting, Etching*
Pebble Beach
BURGHER, Jessie R., *Painting*
422 W. University Ave., San Diego
BURGHER, Juana, *Watercolors*
10807 Lindbrook St., West Los Angeles
BURK, William E., Jr., *Sculpture*
2317 Ewing St., Los Angeles
BURKE, Howard, *Newspaper Art*
Care The Examiner, Los Angeles
BURMISTER, Anne Porter, *Etching*
2210 Vallejo St., San Francisco
BURNER, Adella L., *Crafts*
Glendora

BURNHAM, J. Paul.
1007 S. Grand Ave., Los Angeles
BURNHAM, Roger Noble. *Sculpture*
3516 W. 3rd St., Los Angeles
BURRELL, Ray, *Etching*
2916 Clay St., San Francisco
BURT, Flo. *Commercial*
115 O'Farrell St., San Francisco
BUSH, Charles H., *Painting*
1446 Gordon St., Los Angeles
BUSH, Gladys Lewis, *Sculpture*
3706 W. 4th St., Los Angeles
BUSH, Ella Shepard, *Miniatures*
223 W. Laurel Ave., Sierra Madre
BUTLER, Anna May, *Painting*
5742 La Mirada Ave., Los Angeles
BUTLER, H. Russell, *Painting*
c/o Alson Clark, 1149 Wotkins Dr., Pasade
BYNON, Hannah C., *Teacher*
2831 Van Ness Blvd., Fresno
BYRNE, Susan L., *Painting, Teacher*
State College, San Jose
BYRON, Marguerite Redman, *Painting, Etchi*
Franciscan Hotel, San Francisco

C

CADORIN, Ettore, *Sculpture*
2645 Puesta del Sol Road, Santa Barbara
CAM, Billy, *Commercial*
1151 S. Broadway, Los Angeles
CALDWELL, Vernon, *Commercial, Teacher*
741 S. Grandview St., Los Angeles
CALL, Mary, *Painting, Teacher*
San Anselmo
CAM, Billy, *Commercial*
1151 S. Broadway, Los Angeles
CAMERON, W. R., *Commercial*
1123 Hearsrt Bldg., San Francisco
CAMPBELL, Byram C., *Painting*
705 N. Camden Dr., Beverly Hills
CAMPBELL, Isabella F., *Painting*
7021 Lanewood Ave., Los Angeles
CAMPBELL, Rose, *Painting*
Carmel
CANE, Arthur, *Painting*
902 Victoria Ave., Riverside
CANNOM, Alzada, *Painting*
3680 Sunset Ridge Rd., Altadena
CANNOM, Lawrence H., *Commercial*
1206 Maple Ave., Los Angeles
CANNON, Jennie V., *Painting, Drawing*
1633 La Vereda Rd., Berkeley
CANNON, Lawrence H., *Commercial*
1206 Maple Ave., Los Angeles
CANRIGHT, Bess Hadden, *Decoration*
1318 S. Figueroa St., Los Angeles
CANTU, Frederico, *Painting*
1113 W. Jefferson St., Los Angeles
CARBINES, Jean, *Watercolors*
3064 5th Ave, San Diego
CANWRIGHT, B. Hadden, *Commercial*
760 W. 6th St., Los Angeles
CAREY, Helen V., *Ceramics*
1203 N. Kenmore St., Los Angeles
CARLING, Rose S., *Painting*
2411 Budlong St., Los Angeles
CARLISLE, Dacotah, *Costume Design*
1546 N. Serrano Blvd., Los Angeles
CARLTON, Brents, *Sculpture*
2430 Polk St., San Francisco
CARPENTER, Dudley, *Painting*
322 E. Canon Perdido Ave., Santa Barbar
CARPENTER, George M., *Stained Glass*
Route 1, Box 702, La Canada
CARPENTER, Lewis, *Copper Craft*
Box 91, Chino
CARPENTER, Orpha Klinker   *Painti*
830 Capitola Pl., Los Angeles   *Commer.*
CARPENTER, Robert Bird, *Drawing*
1007 S. Grand Ave., Los Angeles
CARR, Lulu, *Woodcarving*
5437 Sierra Vista Ave., Los Angeles
CARRE, BEN, *Painting*
1660 N. Western Ave., Los Angeles
CARROLL, J. C., *Commercial*
Call Bldg., San Francisco
CARTER, Fred William, *Photography*
1019 California Ave., Santa Monica
CARTER, Gordon K., *Painting*
1236 W. 54th St., Los Angeles
CARTER, Justis, *Watercolors*
1303½ W. 24th St., Los Angeles
CARTER, Pruett, *Illustration*
2256 E. Live Oak Dr., Los Angeles
CARVENY, Gladys Hadley, *Portraits*
1611 Donaldson St., Los Angeles
CASELLA, Alfred, *Painting*
1384 Francisco St., San Francisco
CASKEY, Mary A., *Painting*
2461 E. Horseshoe Rd., Los Angeles
CASOLI, Constance E., *Painting*
1505 Colorado Blvd., Eagle Rock
CASSELL, Helen Lewis, *Painting*
722 N. Sycamore Ave., Los Angeles
CASSIDY, Dorothea L., *Teacher*
1240 W. 31st St., Los Angeles
CASSIDY, Mary Daniels, *Sculpture*
348 25th St., Santa Monica
CASTRUCCIOO, Romilda, *Painting*
P. O. Box 696, Laguna Beach
CATLIN, John, *Wrought Iron*
Carmel

CAVANAUGH, Mrs. L. E., *Leather Crafts*
507 S. Carondelet St., Los Angeles
CERF, Janet R., *Painting, Leather Craft*
2660 Greenwich St., San Francisco
CHALKER, Dorothy, *Teacher*
342 Daisy Ave., Long Beach
CHALMERS, James D. S., *Painting*
2953 Leeward Avee., Los Angeles
CHAMBERLAIN, Mrs. Mellen, *Painting*
1731 Micheltorena Avee., Los Angeles
CHAMBERLAIN, W. E., *Painting*
Los Gatos
CHAMBERLIN, F. Tolles, *Painting, Sculp*
223 S. Catalina St., Pasadena
CHAMBERLIN, Mary Pottenger, *Painting*
350 S. Harvard Blvd., Los Angeles
CHAMBERLIN, Norman, *Painting*
350 S. Harvard Blvd., Los Angeles
CHAMBERLIN, Winnie E., *Drawing, Tea*
46 San Jose Ave., Los Gatos
CHAMBERS, Josephine, *Teacher*
3980 Dalton Ave., Los Angeles
CHAMPLIN, Ada Belle, *Painting*
640 Prospect Blvd., Pasadena
CHAN, Eva Fong, *Painting*
866 Jackson St., San Francisco
CHANDLER, Helen C., *Teacher*
131 S. Carmelina Ave., Los Angeles
CHANG, Dai Song, *Block Prints*
628 Montgomery St., San Francisco
CHANG, Wah Ming, *Graphic Arts*
916½ Westbourne Dr., West Hollywood
CHANG, Wahso, *Painting*
44 8th St., Oakland
CHAPELLA, Edward E., *Painting*
755 Kings Rd., Los Angeles
CHAPIN, Will E.,   *Painting, Sculpt*
5347 Lexington Ave., Hollywood   *Carto*
CHAPLIN, Prescott, *Painting, Wood Block*
Box 24, Station M, Los Angeles
CHAPMAN, Abby W., *Teacher*
715 S. Van Ness Ave., Santa Ana
CHAPONOT, L. C., *Commercial*
693 Mission St., San Francisco
CHARLES, Shirley N., *Teacher*
5077 Cape May Ave., Ocean Beach
CHASE, Anna Webber, *Painting*
2455 Earl St., Los Angeles
CHEEVER, Walter L., *Painting, Teacher*
1514 Garden St., Santa Barbara
CHEFFINS, Florabelle M., *Painting, Draw*
6324 California St., San Francisco
CHENEY, Margaret, *Decoration*
33 Spruce St., San Francisco
CHENEY, Warren, *Sculpture, Teacher*
Mills College P. O.
CHESS, Edna A., *Teacher*
153 Highland Pl., Monrovia
CHESS, Martha, *Teacher*
940 N. Argonaut St., Stockton
CHESSEY, Ralph, *Painting, Puppets*
7 Blackstone Ct., San Francisco
CHILDS, E. Earle, *Commercial*
2518 Monticello Ave., Oakland
CHISHOLM, Stuart, *Painting*
2599 Glenn Green, Los Angeles
CHITTENDEN, Alice B., *Painting*
1301 Leavenworth St., San Francisco
CHOATE, Christian, *Sculpture*
4868 Eagle Rock Blvd., Eagle Rock
CHOPIN, Oscar Charles, *Cartoons*
c/o The Examiner, Los Angeles
CHOUINARD, Nelbert M., *Painting, Teac*
741 S. Grandview St., Los Angeles
CHURCHER, Agatha, *Painting*
1430 Sacramento St., San Francisco
CICERO, Antonino, *Commercial*
1248 W. 24th St., Los Angeles
CLAPP, William H., *Painting, Monotype Pr.*
Oakland Art Gallery, Oakland
CLARK, Alson, *Painting, Murals, Lithogra*
1149 Workyns Dr., Pasadena
CLARK, Alicia, *Painting*
Carmel Highlands
CLARK, Arthur B., *Prof. Emeritus Graphic*
767 Santa Ynez Ave., Stanford University
CLARK, Emelia M. G., *Decoration*
1114 W. 42nd St., Los Angeles
CLARK, Fletcher, *Painting*
81 Park Hill Ave., San Francisco
CLARK, Frances, *Painting*
22 Oak Knoll Gardens, Pasadena
CLARK, M. Beatrice Smith, *Miniatures*
1079 W. Kensington Rd., Los Angeles
CLARK, Marian Hughes, *Crafts*
182 S. Virgil St., Los Angeles
CLARK, Seldon, *Painting*
1317 De Long St., Los Angeles
CLARKE, Harrison, *Painting*
426 N. Hobart Blvd., Los Angeles
CLASSEN, Otto, *Painting*
272 Center St., Santa Monica
CLAYSEN, Eddie, *Commercial*
1624 N. Vine St., Hollywood
CLAYTON, Gladys Sherwood, *Prints*
4960 Genevieve Ave., Los Angeles
CLEAVER, Lorita Bates, *Commercial*
421 San Pasqual Ave., Los Angeles
CLEAVES, Gail, *Commercial*
672 S. Lafayette Park Pl., Los Angeles
CLEMENTS, Grace, *Painting*
300 N. Fremont Ave., Los Angeles
CLEMENTS, Judith M., *Block Prints*
2902 W. 43rd Pl., Los Angeles

CLEMENTS, Lydia, *Painting*
1308 N. Wilcox Ave., Los Angeles
CLEWETT, Ruth, *Teacher*
130 Linden Ave., Long Beach
CLIFF, Doris, *Jewelry*
4350 Beverly Blvd., Los Angeles
CLOVELL, Johanna, *Painting*
209 Palmetto Dr., Alhambra
CLUNIE, Robert, *Painting*
311 Palm Court, Santa Paula
COAN, Helen, *Painting*
204 N. Burlington St., Los Angeles
COBLENTZ, George W., *Commercial*
443 S. San Pedro St., Los Angeles
COBURN, Frank, *Painting*
Laguna Beach
COFFING, Le Claire, *Painting*
1207 W. 70th St., Los Angeles
COGSWELL, M. Kathleen, *Teacher*
217 S. Carondelet St., Los Angeles
COHEN, Rachel, *Teacher*
331 S. Rampart Blvd., Los Angeles
COHN, Max, *Painting*
1237 Rosecrans Ave., Gardena
COLBURN, Daisy Dunton, *Painting*
3638 28th St., San Diego
COLBURN, Elanor, *Painting*
Box 565, Laguna Beach
COLE, Addie L., *Painting*
2525 Alsace Ave., Los Angeles
COLE, Augusta M., *Painting*
Box 44, Seabright Sta., Santa Cruz
COLE, George Townsend, *Painting*
1103 N. El Centro Ave., Los Angeles
COLEMAN, Clarkson, *Painting*
Laguna Beach
COLEMAN, George Sumner, *Painting*
613 W. Central Ave., Balboa
COLEMAN, Harvey B., *Painting*
406 Ledoux Rd., Los Angeles
COLEMAN, Mary D., *Painting*
406 Ledoux Rd., Los Angeles
COLER, Bertha T., *Painting*
1342 5th St., Santa Monica
COLES, Wilson, *Painting*
P. O. Box 1264, Laguna Beach
COLGAN, Lenore De Liers, *Painting*
726 2nd Ave., San Francisco
COLLINGE, J Walter, *Photography*
8 E. Carrillo St., Santa Barbara
COLYER, Clifford C., *Pewter*
4930 Gramercy Pl., Los Angeles
COMFORT, Tyrone, *Painting*
1324 Hanscom Dr., Los Angeles
COMINS, Alice R., *Painting*
Carmel
CONDER, Kathleen, *Painting*
6139 Middleton St., Huntington Park
CONDIT, J. L., *Painting*
2114 Holly Dr., Los Angeles
CONE, Blanche Murdock, *Painting*
Box 1264, Laguna Beach
CONGER, Nann, *Painting*
6768 Magnolia Ave., Riverside
CONNELL, Will, *Photography*
423 S. Rampart Blvd., Los Angeles
CONNER, John Anthony, *Painting*
4975 Highland View Ave., Eagle Rock
CONNER, Paul, *Painting*
1718 E. Ocean Blvd., Long Beach
CONNER, Rose, *Crafts*
526 La Roma St., Pasadena
CONNER, Tanner, *Commercial*
203 Bendix Blvd., Los Angeles
CONNOR, A. Clinton, *Painting*
Manhattan Beach
CONNOR, Isabel, *Teacher*
54 Bennett Ave., Long Beach
COOK, Edna R., *Painting*
346 21st Pl., Santa Monica
COOK, George, *Block Prints*
2322½ Miramar St., Los Angeles
COOK, George L., *Batiks*
4129 Eighth St., Riverside
COOK, Mrs. Katharine L., *Painting*
3429 Descanso Dr., Los Angeles
COOKE, Dorothea, *Etching*
4534 Melbourne Ave., Los Angeles
COOKE, Gaylord, *Commercial*
473 Fourteenth St., Oakland
COOKE, Helen, *Block Prints*
4534 Melbourne Ave., Los Angeles
COOLIDGE, John, *Painting*
2132 Fargo St., Los Angeles
COOPER, Colin Campbell, N.A, *Painting*
1320 Anacapa St., Santa Barbara
COOPER, Elizabeth A., *Painting*
20 Broderick St., San Francisco
COOPER, F. G., *Cartoons*
Belvedere, Marin County
COOPER, Virginia, *Painting, Sculpture*
817 N. Kingsley Dr., Los Angeles
COOVER, Neil, *Painting*
601 S. Kenmore St., Los Angeles
CORBALEY, R. L., *Commercial*
1206 Maple Ave., Los Angeles
CORBETT, Eleanor Jane, *Painting*
3007 Benrenue Ave, Berkeley
CORBETT, Mario, *Painting*
2222 Leavenworth St., San Francisco
CORBIT, George C., *Painting*
3043 46th St., San Diego
CORDY, N., *Painting*
538 E. Ave. 39, Los Angeles

CORNEJO, Francisco, *Painting*
    644 Lucas Ave., Los Angeles
CORNELIUS, Mildred, *Weaving*
    364 Summit Ave., Pasadena
CORNELL, A. D., *Painting*
    209 N. Catalina St., Burbank
CORNELL, Albert, *Painting*
    3949 La Salle St., Los Angeles
CORNWELL, Dean, *Illustration, Murals*
    3006 Wilshire Blvd., Los Angeles
CORRIN, Phillip, *Commercial*
    Adv. Dept., Bullock's, 657 S. Broadway, L.
CORSON, Frederic W., *Etchings, Drawings*
    1024 Sierra St., Berkeley
CORWIN, Eleanor, *Watercolors*
    Chino
COSGROVE, Jack, *Painting*
    446 Bentley Ave., West Los Angeles
COSTELLO, Val, *Painting*
    518 W. 53rd St., Los Angeles
COTTON, R. Leo, *Newspaper Art*
    Care The Examiner, Los Angeles
COUCHMAN, Victoria, *Crafts, Teacher*
    717 W. 80th St., Los Angeles
COULTAS, Jim, *Painting*
    11328 Burbank Blvd., North Hollywood
COULTER, Lillian, *Painting*
    2838 N. Griffin Ave., Los Angeles
COULTER, Mary J., *Painting, Etching, Cra*
    11 Hermosillo Rd., Santa Barbara
COURVOISIER, Marian, *Crafts*
    6552 Yucca St., Los Angeles
COUTTS, Gordon, *Painting*
    Palm Springs
COVENTRY, J. N., *Painting*
    268 Post St., San Francisco
COVENTRY, Stanley H., *Painting*
    124 Miramar Ave., Santa Barbara
COVEY, Verna, *Teacher*
    1110 E. Main St., Alhambra
COWAN, Elsie, *Watercolors*
    676 S. Rampart Blvd., Los Angeles
COWDREY, Dick, *Painting*
    5321 Lankershim Blvd., North Hollywood
COWLES, J. C., *Painting*
    1203 Waterloo St., Los Angeles
COX, George J., *Teacher*
    University of California at Los Angel
    Westwood Village, Los Angeles
COX, J. H., *Commercial*
    1512 Santee St., Los Angeles
COX, Merle T., *Commercial*
    1007 S. Grand Ave., Los Angeles
CRAFT, Elsworth, *Painting*
    2206 Meade Pl., Venice
CRAM, Alan G., *Painting*
    Santa Barbara
CRANDALL, Leslie C., *Painting*
    628 Montgomery St., San Francisc
CRAMER, Harriet T., *Painting*
    410 E. Mesa Ave., Claremont
CRANDALL, Esther, *Painting*
    368 Wilson Ave., Glendale
CRANDALL, Marion, *Painting*
    119 S. Adams St., Glendale
CRAPUCHETTES, Emile Jean, *Painting*
    27 King St., Mill Valley
CRAVATH, Ruth, *Sculpture*
    2432 Leavenworth St., San Francisco
CRAVENS, Junius, *Stage Settings, Costum*
    2510 Leavenworth St., San Francisco
CRANFORD, Esther M., *Painting*
    716 N. Ave. 66, Los Angeles
CRESPO, Jorge Juan, *Painting, Murals*
    5653 La Mirada Ave., Los Angeles
CRESSEY, Bert, *Painting*
    1830 N. Sierra Bonita Ave., Hollywood
CRESSEY, Meta, *Painting*
    1830 N. Sierra Bonita Ave., Hollywood
CREZ, Maria Marcella, *Painting*
    735 E. 54th St., Los Angeles
CRISTADORO, Charles C., *Sculpture*
    2022 Griffith Park Blvd., Los Angeles
CRITES, Roy V., *Teacher*
    2001 Allston Way, Berkeley
CROMWELL, Joane, *Painting*
    1909 Weepah Way, Los Angeles
CRONENWETT, Clare, *Painting, Etching*
    Gold Hill Studio, Monrovia
CROOKS, Marjorie, *Teacher*
    Hughson Hotel, Modesto
CROSBY, Wade, *Commercial*
    Paramount Theater, 6th & Hill Sts., L. A.
CROSNELL, Mary E., *Teacher*
    1624 Olive St., Santa Barbara
CROSS, Lee H., *Commercial*
    1206 Maple Ave., Los Angeles
CROSWELL, Mrs. E. T., *Teacher*
    State Teachers College, Santa Barbara
CROWE, Marie, *Painting*
    821 S. Berendo St., Los Angeles
CROWE, William Francis, *Painting*
    5141 Lockhaven Ave., Eagle Rock
CROWTHER, Richard Layton, *Painting*
    1795 Titus St., San Diego
CRUESS, Marie Gleason, *Painting*
    1466 Scenic Ave., Berkeley
CRUNDALL, Becheley, *Commercial*
    412 W. 6th St., Los Angeles
CRUZE, Charles, *Commercial*
    629 S. Hill St., Los Angeles
CUGAT, Xavier, *Watercolors, Pastel*
    Ambassador Hotel, Los Angeles *Caricatur*

CULBERTSON, Josephine M., *Painting*
    Carmel
CULBERTSON, Mabel F., *Painting*
    4139 Palmetto Way, San Diego
CUMMINGS, G. J., *Painting*
    2001 Hoover Ave., Oakland
CUMMINGS, Hiel, *Commercial*
    1611 Argyle St., Hollywood
CUMMINGS, M. Earl, *Sculpture*
    3966 Clay St., San Francisco
CUNEO, Rinaldo, *Painting*
    722 Montgomery St., San Francisco
CUNNINGHAM, Ben, *Painting*
    20 Jessop Pl., San Francisco
CUNNINGHAM, Imogen, *Photography*
    4540 Harbor View Ave., Piedmont
CUPRIEN, Frank W., *Painting*
    Laguna Beach
CURRIER, Walter Barron, *Block prints, Book*
    binding, Bookplates
    432 15th St., Santa Monica
CURTIS, Ida Maynard, *Painting*
    Carmel
CURTIS, Leland, *Painting*
    1444½ La Veta Ter., Los Angeles
CURTIS, Truman, *Painting*
    327 N. Maryland Ave., Los Angeles
CUSHMAN, Henry, *Painting*
    4823 Genevieve Ave., Los Angeles
CUTTING, Frank H., *Painting*
    Box 693, Campbell

D

DABELSTEIN, William F., *Commercial*
    1569 Post St., San Francisco
DAGGETT, Maud, *Sculpture*
    725 S. Catalina Ave., Pasadena
DAKIN, Mary, *Painting, Etching*
    2811 Hillside Dr., Burlingame
DAKIN, Tilden, *Painting*
    3458 San Marino St., Los Angeles
DAMIANAKES, Cleo, *Painting*
    327 Lenox Ave., Oakland
DANDO, Susie M., *Painting*
    126 Brooks Ave., Venice
DANERI, Aurelia, *Painting*
    4244 Alta Mirano Way, San Diego
DANIELL, William Swift, *Painting*
    Laguna Beach
DANIELL, Earl, *Painting*
    129 12th Ave., San Francisco
DANN, Frode N., *Decoration*
    454 E. Green St., Pasadena
DANNER, Sara Kolb, *Painting*
    Las Tunas Rd., Santa Barbara
DAPPRICH, Fred R., *Photography*
    2430 Kent St., Los Angeles
DARAIO, Innocenzo, *Painting*
    1012 N. Sanborn Ave., Los Angeles
DARBY, Louise, *Painting*
    3582 Sidney Pl., San Diego
DARLING, H. Guilbert, *Commercial*
    265 Santa Rosa Ave., Sausalito
DAROUX, Leonora, *Paintings*
    2702 O St., Sacramento
DAUM, Max, *Painting*
    2546 Hyde St., San Francisco
DAVEY, M. R. S., *Painting*
    7001 Lanewood Ave., Los Angeles
DAVIDSON, L. Glenn, *Commercial*
    Hearst Bldg., San Francisco
DAVIES, Conway, *Painting, Lithographs*
    2511 Jones St., San Francisco
DAVIES, H. C., *Painting*
    5821 Beaumont Ave., Oakland
DAVIS, Mrs. Cecil Clark, *Painting*
    2155 Mission Ridge Rd., Santa Barbara
DAVIS, Evelene Flanagan, *Painting*
    1801 Highland Pl., Berkeley
DAVIS, H., *Sculpture*
    1058 Dundas St., Los Angeles
DAVIS, Leonard M., *Painting*
    2520 W. 7th St., Los Angeles
DAVIS, Maud, *Painting*
    328 Pasadena Ave., Los Angeles
DAVISON, Millah, *Painting*
    336 Aston Ave., San Francisco
DAWSON, Mrs. Richard T., *Crafts*
    4453 Hermosa Way, San Diego
DAY, Doris, *Decoration*
    64 Sacramento St., San Francisco
DAY, Edward, *Painting*
    202 Tamalpais Ave., San Rafael
DAY, Harold, *Commercial*
    216 Venice Blvd., Los Angeles
DAY, Richard, *Lithographs, Cinema*
    1041 N. Formosa St., Los Angeles
DAY, Robert, *Painting*
    641 N. Brand Blvd., Glendale
DEAN, Eva, *Painting*
    601 S. Rampart Blvd., Los Angeles
DEAN, Mailette, *Painting*
    722 Montgomery St., San Francisco
De BOUTHILLIER, Guy, *Watercolors*
    2037 N. Las Palmas Ave., Hollywood
DEBUC, Theil, *Painting*
    1767 Spruce St., Berkeley
DEETHMAN, Edwin C. F., *Commercial*
    121 E. 6th St., Los Angeles
DeFERRARI, Edmond, *Commercial*
    840 Market St., San Francisco

DeGASTEL, Maria, *Painting*
    1504 Garnet Ave., Pacific Beach
DeGASTON, Paul, *Photography*
    693 Sutter St., San Francisco
DeGAVERE, Cor, *Painting*
    Box 55, R. D. 3, Santa Cruz
DeHAVEN, C. H., *Painting*
    1540 N. Gower St., Los Angeles
DeHOSPODAR, Stephen, *Block Prints*
    1459 Silver Lake Blvd., Los Angeles
DeJOINER, L. E., *Painting*
    Box 33, Ben Lomond
DeKRUIF, Henri, *Painting, Etching*
    2324 Miramar Ave., Los Angeles
DeKRUIF, Muriel, *Crafts*
    2324 Miramar Ave., Los Angeles
De la BARRE, Agnes, *Leathercraft*
    119½ S. Reno St., Los Angeles
DELANO, Annita, *Painting*
    Univ. of Cal., Westwood Village, Los Angel
DeLAPFE, W. R., *Commercial*
    114 Sansome St., San Francisco
DELBEY, Désiré, *Painting*
    1310 E. Haley St., Santa Barbara
Del MUE, Maurice, *Painting*
    Box 45, Forest Knolls, Marin Co.
Del PINO, José Moya, *Painting*
    3820 Washington St., San Francisco
DeMARI, Valere, *Painting, Woodblocks*
    2211 Divisadero St., San Francisco
DeNUBLIA, N. L., *Painting*
    723 N. Hill St., Los Angeles
DENMAN, Lucien, *Painting*
    727 S. Figueroa St., Los Angeles
DENNETT, Mary H., *Painting*
    2317 Prospect St., Berkeley
DENNISON, George, *Crafts*
    "Cathedral Oaks," Alma, Santa Clara Co.
DePASZTHORY, Arpad, *Painting*
    335 E. Mountain St., Pasadena
De PERELMA, Ossip, *Painting, Etching*
    San Clemente
DERBY, J. Frank, *Painting*
    2405 Echo Park Ave., Los Angeles
DETHLOFF, Peter H., *Painting*
    349 W. 82nd St., Los Angeles
DeVERLEY, Ivy, *Painting*
    2049 N. Las Palmas Ave., Los Angeles
DEVERT, Frederic, *Painting*
    123 Steiner St., San Francisco
DeVOL, Howard, *Commercial*
    213 S. Broadway, Los Angeles
DeVOL, Pauline Hamill, *Painting, Teacher*
    4267 Ampudia St., San Diego
De VRIENDT, Stefan, *Sculpture*
    1862 N. Edgmont Ave., Los Angeles
DeWOLF, E., *Etching*
    2923 W. 6th St., Los Angeles
DIAMOND, Louise Thian, *Commercial*
    576 Sacramento St., San Francisco
DIBBLEE, Anita L., *Painting*
    Bolinas
DICKIESON, Marjorie H., *Painting, Drawi*
    617 Montgomery St., San Francisco
DICKINSON, Daisy, *Painting*
    3877 Seneca St., Los Angeles
DICKINSON, Ross, *Painting*
    3877 Seneca St., Los Angeles
DICKINSON, Susan, *Painting*
    3351 Fernside Blvd., Alameda
DICKMAN, Charles J., *Painting*
    Bohemian Club, San Francisco
DIETRICKSON, D. N., *Painting*
    800 Architects Bldg., Los Angeles
DIKE, Phil, *Painting*
    2025 W. 3rd St., Los Angeles
DILLER, Alfred C., *Painting*
    836 Elizabeth St., Pasadena
DILLMAN, Louis, *Painting*
    1129 Wotkyns Dr., Pasadena
DINSDALE, Aldice O., *Toys*
    730 26th Ave., San Francisco
DINWIDDIE, John E., *Etching*
    2815 Oak Knoll Ave., Berkeley
DISNEY, Walt, *Mickey Mouse Cartoons*
    2719 Hyperion Ave., Los Angeles
DIXON, Harry, *Metal Craft*
    1104 Sutter St., San Francisco
DIXON, Maynard, *Painting, Murals*
    728 Montgomery St., San Francisco
DOANE, H. W., *Painting*
    3025 Ellis St., Berkeley
DOBBS, Winifred, *Commercial*
    145 S. Westmoreland Ave., Los Angeles
DODGE, Arthur B., *Painting, Etching*
    329 S. Normandie St., Los Angeles
DODGE, D. Frank, *Painting*
    457 S. Hudson St., Pasadena
DOERING, Eric, *Painting*
    1143 W. 89th St., Los Angeles
DOMELA, Jan, *Painting*
    5824 Carlton Way, Los Angeles
DOMINGUEZ, Martin, *Design, Painting*
    1525 N. Van Ness Ave., Hollywood
DOMINIQUE, John A., *Painting*
    574 E. Valley Rd., Santa Barbara
DONALDSON, Douglas, *Crafts, Color, Desi*
    4960 Melrose Hill, Los Angeles
DONALDSON, Ethel A., *Crafts*
    820 N. Oxford St., Los Angeles
DONALDSON, Louise Towle, *Crafts*
    4960 Melrose Hill, Los Angeles
DONALDSON, Margaret, *Crafts*
    820 N. Oxford St., Los Angeles

DONDO, Mathurin M., *Painting*
  1321 Tamalpais Rd., Berkeley
DOOLEY, Dionysius, *Design*
  1106 S. St. Andrews Pl., Los Angeles
DOOLITTLE, H. L., *Etching*
  127 N. Catalina St., Pasadena
DOOLITTLE, James N., *Photography*
  1016 4th Ave., Los Angeles
DOSS, W. Galen, *Painting*
  Laguna Beach
DOUD, Ruth F., *Painting*
  1290 Portola Dr., San Francsico
DOUGHERTY, Elizabeth, *Painting*
  628 Montgomery St., Oakland
DOUGHERTY, Paul, *Painting*
  Carmel Highlands
DOUGLAS, E. Graham, *Painting*
  1836 Monterey Rd., S. Pasadena
DOUGLASS, Haldane, *Watercolors, Cinema*
  Fox Film Corp., Fox Hills, Los Angeles
DOUPNIK, Janet S., *Painting*
  117 Delmar St., San Francisco
DOW, Hazelle E., *Drawing*
  1412 Broadway, Alameda
DOWD, Helen C., *Painting*
  4027 32nd St., San Diego
DOWIATT, Dorothy, *Painting, Etching*
  421 N. Greenleaf Ave., Whittier
DOWNARD, M. W., *Painting*
  3440 Florida St., San Diego
DREIFUSS, Leopold, *Sculpture*
  45 Second St., San Francisco
DREIS, Edward, *Painting*
  628 Montgomery St., San Francisco
DREIS, Hazel, *Bookbinding*
  Santa Cruz
DRISCOLL, Harold Quinton, *Painting*
  7212 DeSoto St., Owensmouth
DROST, Gerard, *Painting*
  1439 Havenscourt Blvd., Oakland
DUINO, F. A., *Commercial*
  311 Turk St., San Francisco
DUKES, Katherine, *Prints*
  1467 Ridgeway St., Los Angeles
DUNCAN, Charles Stafford, *Painting*
  930 Chestnut St., San Francisco
DUNCAN, Dorothy J., *Painting*
  930 Chestnut St., San Francisco
DUNCAN, Gregor, *Painting*
  628 Montgomery St., San Francisco
DUNCAN, Preston, *Photography*
  1624 N. Vine St., Hollywood
DUNHAM, Mrs. Theodore, Jr., *Leather Cra*
  718 S. Los Robles Ave., Pasadena
DUNLAP, Helena K., *Painting*
  760 S. Windsor Blvd., Los Angeles
DUNN, Charles A., *Watercolors*
  Route 1, Box 23 F. Pacific Beach
DUNN, David, *Painting, Commercial*
  257 S. Spring St., Los Angeles
DUNPHY, Nicolas R., *Etching*
  617 Montgomery St., San Francisco
DUPONT, Kedma, *Painting*
  65 Buena Vista Ave., San Francisco
DURENCEAU, André, *Color, Cinema, Painti*
  Technicolor Studios,
   823 N. Seward St., Los Angeles
DURSTON, Arthur, *Painting*
  360 Mt. Washington Dr., Los Angeles
DUSTIN, Silas S., *Painting*
  172 N. La Brea Ave., Los Angeles
DUVALL, Fannie, *Painting*
  4547 Marmion Way, Los Angeles
DWIGGINS, Clare V., *Cartoons*
  1727 Nichols Canyon Rd., *Los Angeles*
DWORZEK, Pauline, *Painting*
  R. D. 2, Box 476, Santa Cruz
DWYER, James, *Painting*
  2502 E. 24th St., Oakland

E

EADIE, May Helen, *Teacher*
  530 4th St., San Bernardino
EARNIST, Florence R., *Painting*
  3939 E. 2nd St., Long Beach
EATON, Lois, *Painting*
  694 Monterey Blvd., San Francisco
EATON, Lois Lee, *Painting*
  328 Scenic Dr., Monrovia
EATON, Marjorie Lee, *Painting*
  1441 Van Ness Ave., San Francisco
EBY, Frances, *Painting*
  1449 Wellington Ave., Oakland
EDDY, G. A., *Commercial*
  308 E. 9th St., Los Angeles
EDGREN, Robert D., *Black and White*
  Del Monte
EDSTROM, David, *Sculpture*
  Hollywood Plaza Hotel,
   1637 N. Vine St., Los Angeles
EDWARDS, Eloise, *Painting*
  1261 Lombard St., San Francisco
EDWARDS, H. Arden, *Painting*
  1203 Kipling Ave., Eagle Rock
EDWARDS, John Paul, *Photography*
  1347 Trestle Glen Ave., Oakland
EDWARDS, Lionel, *Painting, Teacher*
  628 S. Norton Ave., Los Angeles
EDWARDS, Norman, *Fashion Design, Teach*
  136 St. Anne St., San Francisco
EGEN, Max, *Painting, Woodcuts*
  4139 Jackson Ave., Culver City

EHERT, Howell, *Painting*
  915 Woodland Ave., San Leandro
ELAM, Gladys, *Painting*
  2701 Durant Ave., Berkeley
ELLIOTT, Don, *Illustration, Commercial*
  41 E. Green St., Pasadena
ELLIOTT, Ruth Cass, *Painting*
  540 Mandeville Canyon Dr., W. Los Angel
ELLIS, Clyde G., *Painting*
  1218 N. Westmoreland Ave., Los Angeles
ELLIS, Howard, *Decoration*
  1731 S. Burlington Ave., Los Angeles
ELLISON, J. Milford, *Watercolors*
  4482 34th St., San Diego
ELWELL, Myrna, *Painting, Watercolors*
  4688 Jurupa Ave., Riverside
EMERSON, Sybil, *Painting*
  2519 Hill St., Berkeley
ENGELMAN, William F., *Painting*
  2901 Beverly Blvd., Los Angeles
ERNEST, Aleta, *Painting, Block Prints*
  216 W. 65th St., Los Angeles
ESCHERICH, Elsa F., *Painting*
  3333 N. Marengo Ave., Altadena
ESKEY, W. A., *Etching*
  319 N. Brand Blvd., San Fernando
ESNER, Arthur L., *Painting*
  1664 N. Bronson Ave., Los Angeles
ESPOY, Angel, *Painting*
  1316 Talmadge St., Los Angeles
ESTERWOLD, Isabel, *Teacher*
  803 N. Catalina Ave., Pasadena
ESTILL, J. W., *Sculpture*
  853 E. Kensington Rd., Los Angeles
EVANS, E., *Painting*
  962 S. Berendo St., Los Angeles
EVANS, Gertrude, *Teacher*
  1652 Upas St., San Diego
EVERETT, Eugenia, *Sculpture*
  13224 Rose Ave., Hawthorne
EVANS, Nela H., *Painting*
  8361 Magnolia Ave., Riverside
EVERETT, Mary, *Painting*
  980 S. Manhattan Pl., Los Angeles
EULALIE, *Illustration*
  672 S. Lafayette Park Pl., Los Angeles
EWING, A. L., *Newspaper Art*
  Care The Times, 100 N. Broadway, L. A.
EYLER, Shirley, *Teacher*
  Lancaster High School, Lancaster

F

FAGES, Alphonse B., *Design*
  538 W. 10th St., Pomona
FAILLE, C. A., *Painting*
  4651 Bermuda Ave., Ocean Beach
FAIRALL, Alice, *Teacher*
  1116 S. Mesa St., San Pedro
FAIRBANKS, Alice, *Teacher*
  407 12th St., Santa Monica
FANNON, Jack, *Commercial*
  507 Montgomery St., San Francisco
FARISH, Jane, *Teacher*
  443 21st St., Santa Monica
FARMER, Albert E., *Watercolors, Woodcarv*
  802 W. 6th St., Corona
FARMER, Edward M., *Painting, teacher*
  270 Fulton St., Palo Alto
FARMER, Mabel M., *Painting*
  240 Fulton St., Palo Alto
FARNELL, Margaret T. C., *Portraits*
  751 N. Marguerita Ave., Alhambra
FARNSWORTH, Ethel N., *Painting*
  484 Prospect Terrace, Los Angeles
FAUST, Challiss, *Painting, Portraits*
  730 S. Damask St., Inglewood
FAVRETTO, E. E., *Portraits*
  128 N. Main St., Los Angeles
FAY, George F., *Painting*
  Box 103, R. F. D. 1, Pasadena
FAY, Arthur E., *Commercial*
  576 Sacramento St., San Francisco
FAY, Horace T., *Commercial*
  536 S. Broadway, Los Angeles
FAYE, Ida C., *Painting*
  3122 Claremont Ave., Berkeley
FEATHERSTONHAUGH, Olive, *Painting*
  Belvedere, Marin County
FEE, Marcia, *Painting, Woodblock*
  2616 Buchanan St., San Francisco
FEINBLATT, Rose, *Painting*
  1174 Los Angeles Ave., Los Angeles
FEINSTEIN, Mary, *Teacher*
  314 N. Soto St., Los Angeles
FEITELSON, Lorser, *Teacher*
  4219 Cumberland Ave., Los Angeles
FELDMAN, Dorothy, *Watercolors, Blo*
  7110 Hawthorne Ave., Los Angeles *Pri*
FELTHAM, Will, *Painting*
  5167 Dahlia Dr., Eagle Rock
FENN, Walter J., *Drawing, Painting*
  Fredericka Home, Chula Vista
FERENZ, F. K., *Design*
  55 Olvera St., Los Angeles
FERGUSON, George D., *Painting*
  17 Golden Ave., Long Beach
FERREN, John Millard, *Sculpture*
  722 Montgomery St., San Francisco
FIEDLER, Charles Kern, *Painting*
  344 S. Holliston Ave., Pasadena
FIELD, Charlotte S., *Bas-reliefs*
  3490 Lime St., Riverside
FIELD, Thyrsis, *Painting, Copper Craft*
  3490 Lime St., Riverside

FIELD, Mary D., *Painting*
  2548 Hyde St., San Francisco
FINE, Telma, *Painting*
  226 Shasta St., Yuba City
FISHER, Howard, *Painting*
  367314 Motor Ave., Palms
FISHER, Leeana, *Painting*
  177 S. 8th St., San Jose
FISKE, Stella A., *Painting*
  5333 Hartwick Ave., Eagle Rock
FITCH, Adela Russell, *Painting*
  1750 E. 3rd St., Los Angeles
FITCH, Mrs. William Russell, *Watercolors*
  812 E. 15th St., Los Angeles
FITZGERALD, J. M., *Painting*
  20 Joice St., San Francisco
FITZGERALD, James, *Painting*
  Monterey
FITZHENRY, George O., *Block Prints*
  1416 N. Alvarado St., Los Angeles
FLAHERTY, Lillian E., *Leather Craft, Teach*
  7092 Owensmouth Ave., Canoga Park
FLECKENSTEIN, Louis, *Photography*
  1510 E. 3rd St., Long Beach
FLEMING, Margaret Eddy, *Drawing*
  Box 236, La Jolla
FLEMMING, Amy Dewing, *Painting, Drawi*
  572 Summit Ave., Mill Valley
FLETCHER, Frank Morley, *Woodcuts in Col*
  2626 Fuesta del Sol Rd., Santa Barbara
FLYNN, Hazel L., *Teacher*
  435 Patterson Ave., Glendale
FOERSTER, Arnold, *Sculpture*
  407 E. Chestnut St., Glendale
FONDA, Harry Stuart, *Painting*
  Bohemian Club, San Francisco
FONG, Sam, *Painting*
  828 Grant Ave., San Francisco
FORBES, Helen K., *Painting, Fresco*
  1405 Montgomery St., San Francisco
FORCE, Clara G., *Painting*
  1800 E. Mountain St., Pasadena
FORD, John Carter, *Painting*
  1533 Waverly St., Palo Alto
FORD, J. R., *Painting*
  1714 Everett St., Alameda
FORD, Ted, *Painting*
  1714 Everett St., Alameda
FORESMAN, Alice C., *Miniatures*
  6720 Franklin Pl., Los Angeles
FORESTAL, Ernest, *Commercial*
  2714 Clyde Ave., Los Angeles
FORDMAN, Ruth, *Teacher*
  4314 Kingswood Ave., Los Angeles
FORMHALS, Henry, *Commercial*
  Acme Engr. Co., 1220 Maple Ave., L. A.
FORSTER, Paul Quentin, *Commercial*
  544 Market St., San Francisco
FORSYTHE, Clyde, *Painting*
  1449 St. Albans Rd., San Marino
FORTUNE, E. Charlton, *Painting*
  Monterey
FORWARD, Martha, *Painting*
  4144 Lark St., San Diego
FOSTER, Bertha Knox, *Teacher*
  1437 Ardmore Ave., Glendale
FOSTER, Enid, *Painting*
  1770 Green St., San Francisco
FOSTER, Will, *Painting*
  1142 N. Seward St., Hollywood
FOSTER, Willett S., *Watercolors*
  3589 Beachwood Ave., Riverside
FOURTANE, Edward E., *Commercial*
  1139 Broadway, San Francisco
FOURTANE, Loyola L., *Watercolors*
  81 N. River St., San Jose
FOX, F. Dobson, *Painting*
  300 S. Camino St., Redondo Beach
FRANCISCO, Enid, *Painting*
  1402 29th St., San Diego
FRANK, Marie G., *Leather Craft*
  1714 S. Euclid Ave., Ontario
FRANKLIN, Elizabeth W., *Design*
  4452 W. 5th St., Los Angeles
FRANQUINET, Eugene, *Painting, Portraits*
  5100 Briggs Ave., La Crescenta
FRASER, A. W. C., *Watercolors, Pastels*
  1035 Meadowbrook Ave., Los Angeles
FRASER, Bernice, *Weaving*
  Carmel
FRASER, Douglass, *Painting*
  203 Sacramento St., Vallejo
FRATES, William, *Painting*
  50 Foothill Blvd., Hayward
FRECHETTE, Marie, *Painting*
  3231 Fourth Ave., San Diego
FREDERICKS, Remy, *Decoration*
  3475 W. 6th St., Los Angeles
FRENCH, Park, *Watercolors, Cinema*
  10106 Toluca Lake Ave., North Hollywo
FRENCH, Viola, *Fashion Art*
  629 S. Hill St., Los Angeles
FREY, Joseph P., *Painting*
  528 Pedregosa St., Santa Barbara
FRIEDRICHSEN, Peter, *Design, Col*
  2405 W. 6th St., Los Angeles *Stagecr*
FRIES, C. A., *Painting*
  2876 F St., San Diego
FROLICH, Finn H., *Sculpture*
  5152 La Vista Ct., Los Angeles
FROST, Annie S. R., *Painting*
  401 Haddon Rd., Oakland
FROST, H. C., *Watercolors*
  709 W. Patterson St., Glendale

FROST, J. Ernest, *Commercial*
Acme Engr. Co., 1220 Maple Ave., L. A.
FRUND, Delia Mannion, *Painting*
315 Glen Dr., Sausalito
FUETSCH, Charles, *Painting*
2245 Lake Shore Ave., Los Angeles
FULLERTON, Adolphine Sutro, *Painting*
2121 Sacramento St., San Francisco
FULLERTON Alice V., *Painting*
Laguna Beach
FULLONTON, Robert E., *Painting*
Laguna Beach
FULOP, Karoly, *Painting*
730 S. Catalina Ave., Los Angeles
FULTON, Bernice, *Teacher*
1545 Columbia Dr., Glendale
FULTON, Fitch B., *Painting*
1545 Columbia Dr., Glendale
FYFE, Gilbert, *Painting*
1601 S. Western Ave., Los Angeles

G

GABELLIERI, Alessandro, *Sculpture*
7058 Hollywood Blvd., Hollywood
GABRIEL, Ruth W., *Painting, Sculpture*
3637 Baker St., San Francisco
GABRIEL, Michael, *Painting*
Architects Bldg., Los Angeles
GAER, Fay, *Painting*
1199 Spruce St., Berkeley
GAFFNEY, Claribel H., *Sculpture*
2600 S. Hoover St., Los Angeles
GAFFNEY, Louis E., *Painting, Pastels*
1061 W. 54th St., Los Angeles
GAGE, Merrell, *Sculpture*
456 Mesa Rd., Santa Monica
GALE, Edmund W., *Cartoons*
c/o Times, 100 N. Broadway, Los Angeles
GAGNE, Jules, *Costume Design, Teacher*
741 S. Grandview St., Los Angeles
GALE, Goddard, *Painting*
2003, E. 29th St., Oakland
GALGIANI, Oscar, *Block Prints*
Rm. 7, County Court House, Stockton
GALLAGHER, Anna Addison, *Fashion Desi*
1290 Sutter St., San Francisco .... *Teac.*
GAMBLE, John M., *Painter*
813 State St., Santa Barbara
GAMMON, Stella M., *Crafts*
2085 Navarro St., Pasadena
GANSON, Eve, *Illustration*
1512 Gramercy Pl., Los Angeles
GARDNER, J. P., *Illustration*
222 California St., Santa Monica
GARNER, Archibald, *Sculpture*
6016 Eleanor Ave., Los Angeles
GARNSEY, Julian E., *Watercolors, Murals*
3305 Wilshire Blvd., Los Angeles
GARRETT, Louise, *Painting*
236 Mabery Rd., Santa Monica
GARRIGUES, Edith H., *Painting, Crafts*
849 Howard Pl., Pasadena
GARTH, John, *Painting*
535 Sacramento St., San Francisco
GARTHWAITE, W. B., *Painting*
644 Monadnock Bldg., San Francisco
GASKIN, William, *Painting*
1351 Sutter St., San Francisco
GATES, Emily E., *Painting, Ceramics*
1919 Cerro Gordo Ave., Los Angeles
GAW, William A., *Painting*
1409 Edith St., Berkeley
GAY, August, *Painting, Woodcarving*
Monterey
GAYDON, C. O., *Painting*
726 Stanford Ave., Los Angeles
GAZE, Harold, *Painting*
215 S. Euclid Ave., Pasadena
GEARHART, Edna, *Painting, Teacher*
595 S. Fair Oaks Ave., Pasadena
GEARHART, Frances, *Woodcuts in Color*
611 S. Fair Oaks Ave., Pasadena
GEARHART, May, *Painting, Design*
529 N. Alexandria Ave., Los Angeles
GENTRY, Thurston, *Commercial*
218 Oleson Bldg., Hollywood
GEORGE, Gladys, *Teacher*
1230 W. 8th St., Los Angeles
GERARD, Edgar, *Painting*
730 S. Bonnie Brae St., Los Angeles
GERARDIN, Frank, *Painting*
6308 Madden Ave., Los Angeles
GERE, Nellie Huntington, *Teacher*
529 N. Alexandria Ave., Los Angeles
GRING, J. H., *Painting*
1147 E. 88th Pl., Los Angeles
GERITZ, Franz, *Etching, Block Prints*
2058 W. 24th St., Los Angeles
GERRITY, John Emmett, *Painting*
66 Panoramic Way, Berkeley
GERSTLE, William L., *Painting*
310 Sansome St., San Francisco
GIBB, Charles L., *Painting*
5724 Broadway, Oakland
GIBBONS, Cedric, *Cinema*
M-G-M Studios, Culver City
GIFFEN, Elizabeth Helene, *Watercolors*
2062 W. Highland Ave., Los Angeles
GIFFORD, May C., *Leather Craft*
2046 Meridian Ave., South Pasadena
GIGAS, Virginia, *Painting*
2031 Milan Ave., South Pasadena

GILBERT, Arthur Hill, *Painting*
P. O. Box 164, Monterey
GILBERT, Bess, *Painting*
139 Fir St., San Diego
GILBERT, Robert, *Painting*
2407 French St., Santa Ana
GILCHRIST, Meda M., *Painting, Woodcarvi*
1152 W. 51st St., Los Angeles
GILE, Seldon Connor, *Painting*
Belvedere
GILLAM, W. C. F., *Etching*
1470 Broadway, Burlingame
GILLIES, Jessie, *Painting*
415 N. Curtis St., Alhambra
GILMORE, Doris, *Leather Craft*
3922 Tracy St., Los Angeles
GIORGI, Federico, *Sculpture, Painting*
2513 Wellington Rd., Los Angeles
GIRARDIN, Frank, *Painting*
6308 Madden Ave., Los Angeles
GLADDING, Hope, *Painting*
58 Tamalpais Ave., Berkeley
GLASS, Roy, *Painting*
550 Bradford Sr., Pasadena
GLEASON, J. Duncan, *Painting*
2411 Edgemont Glen, Los Angeles
GLEASON, Elizabeth, *Crafts, Teacher*
6332 S. Albany St., Huntington Park
GLEICH, George Frederick, *Painting*
Palm Springs
GLENN, E. Elston, *Painting, Teacher*
55 N. Meredith Ave., Pasadena
GLICK, Hayrold Russ, *Metal Craft*
1681 N. Foothill Blvd., Pasadena
GODDARD, Florence M., *Etching, Craft*
2870 Sunset Pl., Los Angeles   *Teach*
GODFREY, Mildred, *Commercial*
8 Terrace Villa, Pasadena
GOEBE, William J., *Portraits*
300½ S. Los Angeles St., Los Angeles
GOELLER, E. Shotwell, *Painting, Fresco*
727 Parnassus Ave., San Francisco
GOFORTH, Marguerite Morse, *Painting*
Box 156, La Mesa
GOLDMAN, Hal, *Painting*
1380 Washington St., San Francisco
GOLDNER, Dorothy Thompson, *Watercolor*
1916 Weepah Way, Hollywood   *Illustratic*
GOLDNER, Orville, *Painting, Block Prints*
1916 Weepah Way, Hollywood
GOLITZIN, Alex, *Design, Cinema*
1750 N. Wilton Pl., Los Angeles
GOOD, Iris, *Decoration*
2600 S. Hoover St., Los Angeles
GOODAN, John A., *Illustration*
412 W. 6th St., Los Angeles
GOODCHILD, Cecil Wray, *Painting, Woo*
641 N. Normandie Ave., Los Angeles   *bloc*
GOODE, Henry, *Illustration*
10581 Almayo Ave., Los Angeles
GOODENOW, Rolf Julian, *Silver Craft*
8027 Willow Glen Rd., Los Angeles
GOODLOE, Nellie Stearns, *Printing, Drawi*
2391 Filbert St., San Francisco
GOODMAN, Frances D., *Painting*
2275 Colorado Blvd., Eagle Rock
GOODRICH, M. Montgomery, *Painting*
111 Southampton Ave., Berkeley
GOODWIN, Jean, *Painting, Illustration, Cra*
606 E. Santa Clara Ave., Santa Ana
GOODWIN, Guy, *Commercial*
1618 Laurel St., South Pasadena
GOODYEAR, Grace E., *Painting*
2164 Hyde St., San Francisco
GORDON, Frank W., *Painting*
Box 662, Concord
GORES, Walter J., *Painting*
316 W. 59th Pl., Los Angeles
GORMY, Eilanor X., *Painting*
974 Plymouth Ave., San Francisco
GORNEY, J., *Sculpture*
c/o Gladding, McBean Co.,
2685 Los Feliz Dr., Glendale
GRAHAM, Cecilia, *Painting*
53 Plaza Dr., Berkeley
GRAHAM, Clyde D., *Commercial*
11 Stedman Bldg., San Francisco
GRAHAM, Donald Wilkinson, *Painting*
442 Mesa Rd., Santa Monica
GRAHN, Zella Ong, *Decoration*
6867 Camrose Dr., Los Angeles
GRAMATKY, Hardie, *Painting*
501 E. Whitmore St., Wilmar
GRANT, Charles Henry, *Painting*
Bohemian Club, San Francisco
GRANT, Joe, *Newspaper Art*
Care The Record, Los Angeles
GRANT, Lee, *Painting*
2600 S. Hoover St., Los Angeles
GRAVESON, Richard C., *Painting*
293 41st St., Oakland
GRAY, Alice, *Teacher*
3305 McClintock Ave., Los Angeles
GRAY, Claude, *Painting*
2752 Francis Ave., Los Angeles
GRAY, Marion M., *Watercolors*
667 W. Doran Ave., Glendale
GRAY, Percy, *Painting*
Monterey
GRAY, Ruth, *Painting*
5475 Elmwood Dr., Riverside
GREATHEAD, John, *Painting*
231 B St., Vallejo

GREBS, Emil, *Painting, Commercial*
1674 Eddy St., San Francisco
GREEN, Alice Gordon, *Painting*
5174 Hallwood Dr., Riverside
GREEN, Caroline A., *Painting*
1981 Addison Way, Eagle Rock
GREEN, J. C., *Painting*
278 Chamb. Com. Bldg., Los Angeles
GREEN, Mary Amory, *Watercolors*
1512 W. Walnut St., San Diego
GREENBAUM, Joseph, *Portraits*
3135 Hamilton Way, Los Angeles
GREENE, Alice Goodrich, *Painting*
3525 Albatross St., San Diego
GREENE, Frank F., *Commercial*
6365 Selma Ave., Hollywood
GREENLEE, H. C., *Commercial*
1556 Murrary Circle, Los Angeles
GREENWELL, Julian, *Painting*
Monterey
GREGORY, D. L., *Commercial*
417 Montgomery St., San Francisco
GREGORY, Florence, *Teacher*
121 S. Euclid Ave., Pasadena
GREMKE, H. D., *Painting*
544 38th St., Oakland
GREN, Nils, *Painting*
1482 Sutter St., San Francisco
GRIEBENOW, Margaret, *Watercolors*
616 Hilgard Ave., Westwood Village, L.
GRIESBACK, David, *Sculpture*
1347 Coronado Ter., Los Angeles
GRIFFETH, Lillian, *Painting*
Box 656, Azusa
GRIFFETH, T. R., *Painting*
3975 Halldale Ave., Los Angeles
GRIFFITH, Evelyn, *Silversmith*
4522 Aurora Dr., Riverside
GRIFFITH, Kate B., *Painting*
4179 Ibis St., San Diego
GRIFFITH, Katherine Patton, *Portraits*
5918 Echo St., Los Angeles
GRIFFITH, William A., *Painting*
Laguna Beach
GRISMORE, John Thomas, Jr., *Painting*
2210 23rd Ave., Oakland
GRISWOLD, Gilbert, *Sculpture*
6867 Franklin Ave., Hollywood
GROSS, Mathilda, L., *Crafts, Teacher*
130 S. Ave., 63, Los Angeles
GROT, Anton, *Cinema*
Warner Bros., Burbank
GROTON, Dorothy, *Design, Commercial*
53 Olvera St., Los Angeles
GRUBB, Agnes M., *Painting*
255 Columbia St., Pomona
CHUBB, Ethel McAllister, *Painting*
224 Presidio Ave., San Francisco
GRUENFELD, Caspar, *Sculpture*
209 E. 31st St., Los Angeles
GUENOT, Maurice, *Decoration*
606 W. 108th St., Los Angeles
GUNDERSON, Stanley H., *Etching, Ble*
5422 El Verano Ave., Eagle Rock   *Pri*
GUNN, Florence, *Paintnig*
4527 N. Griffin Ave., Los Angeles
GUNTHER, Raphael Y., *Painting*
6666 Selma Ave., Hollywood
GUPTILL, Ada A., *Crafts, Teacher*
1212 N. Hobart Blvd., Los Angeles
GURNEE, Marion, *Teacher*
1102 S. Tremaine Ave., Los Angeles
GUTTRIDGE, Eleanor, *Painting*
529 Coventry Rd., Berkeley

H

HACKWOOD, H. McKinley, *Painting*
633 Van Ness Ave., San Francisco
HADDOCK, Jerelyn O., *Monotypes, Weavin*
237 Spruce St., San Diego   *Leather, Potte*
HAECKEL, Ernest, *Weaving*
1773 Griffith Park Blvd., Los Angeles
HAECKEL, Maria, *Weaving, Design*
3553 Carnation Ave., Los Angeles
HAGE, Mrs. W. B., *Painting*
2570 Third St., San Diego
HAGEMEYER, Johan, *Photography*
Carmel
HAGUE, Josephine B., *Watercolors*
1045 S. Bronson Ave., Los Angeles
HAHNE, Thelyn, *Sculpture*
333 Columbia Ave., Los Angeles
HAIG, Mabel G., *Watercolors*
535 E. Hadley St., Whittier
HAINES, C. W., *Commercial*
1206 Maple Ave., Los Angeles
HALE, Florence Chenett, *Painting*
2525 Moreno Blvd., San Diego
HALE, Girard, *Painting*
Box 632, Santa Barbara
HALE, J. B., *Sculpture*
1117 N. Bronson Ave., Los Angeles
HALEY, John C., *Painting*
Art Dept., Univ. of Calif., Berkeley
HALL, Anna, *Weaving*
3855 Jackson St., San Francisco
HALL, John Belmar, *Painting, Woodcuts*
4026 Beverly Blvd., Los Angeles
HALL, Marian, *Painting*
1694 The Alameda, San Jose
HALL, Parker L., *Woodcarving, Sculpture*
716 Montgomery St., San Francisco

HALL, Shirley M., *Painting*
1300 Woodstock Dr., Pasadena
HALL, Wayne, *Commercial*
1240 S. Main St., Los Angeles
HALLER, Constance Reed, *Painting*
251 S. Berendo St., Los Angeles
HALLIDAY, Hughitt, *Painting*
316 Adelaide Dr., Santa Monica
HALSTEAD, Maud, *Illustration, Commerc*
938 S. Orange Ave., Los Angeles
HALSTEAD, Murial, *Watercolors*
201 N. Normandie Ave., Los Angeles
HAMBLETT, Junie, *Painting, Teacher*
1148 Shenandoah Ave., Los Angeles
HAMER, H. A., *Commercial*
108 W. 6th St., Los Angeles
HAMLIN, Doris, *Design*
535 Spencer Ave., Santa Rosa
HAMLIN, Edith Anne, *Painting, Woodbloc*
119 S. Branceforte Ave., Santa Cruz
HAMMACK, Edward, *Commercial*
1220 Maple Ave., Los Angeles
HANSEN, Armin, *Painting, Etching*
716 Pacific St., Monterey
HANSCOM, Trude, *Painting, Etching*
2466 W. 18th St., Los Angeles
HANSEN, Daisy, *Watercolors*
426 S. Burlington Ave., Los Angeles
HANSEN, Eijnar, *Painting*
238 Wyoming St., Pasadena
HANSEN, Norvie G., *Commercial*
165 Post St., San Francisco
HANTMAN, Murray, *Painting*
4438 W. Point Loma Blvd., Ocean Beach
HARCOFF, Lyla M., *Painting*
29 E. De la Guerra St., Santa Barbara
HARDING, Goldie Powell, *Painting*
551 Prince St., Oakland
HARKER, Katherine Van Dyke, *Painti*
44 Ralston Ave., Mill Valley *Block Pri*
HARKNESS, E. Keith, *Painting, Sculpture*
1217 S. Magnolia Ave., Los Angeles
HARLAND, Mary, *Miniatures*
1523 14th St., Santa Monica
HARMON, Charles, *Painting*
39 Azurias Bldg., San Jose
HARPE, Sophie, *Teacher*
4615 Manbert Ave., Los Angeles
HARPER, Effie, *Painting*
233 Marguerita St., Santa Monica
HARRIMAN, Marjorie B., *Painting, Teac*
637 S. Lucerne Blvd., Los Angeles
HARRIS, B. F., *Painting*
P. O. Box 356, Campbell
HARRIS, Edward N., *Sculpture*
430 N. Craig Ave., Pasadena
HARRIS, G. Albert, *Painting*
1395 Union St., San Francisco
HARRIS, Harwell, *Sculpture*
1128 W. 28th St., Los Angeles
HARRIS, Jessica, *Teacher*
623 S. Bonnie Brae St., Los Angeles
HARRIS, Sam Hyde, *Painting, Commercial*
631 S. Spring St., Los Angeles
HARRISON, Grace Earle, *Painting*
2421 5th Ave., San Diego
HARRISON, Florence, *Watercolors, Pastels*
2421 5th Ave., San Diego
HARRISON, Grace Earle, *Painting*
2421 5th Ave., San Diego
HARRISON, Tom C., *Watercolors*
7650 Denker Ave., Los Angeles
HARROLD, Alice A., *Painting*
1305 Weber St., Alameda
HARTLET, Claire H., *Painting*
1721 E. 68th St., Los Angeles
HARTMAN, Hazel, *Design, Textiles, Costum*
649 Brown St., Fresno
HARTWELL, Marian, *Design, Color*
800 Chestnut St., San Francisco
HARTY, Louise, *Painting*
Barcelona Hotel, San Diego
HARTZIG, Mildred, *Teacher*
8611 West Knoll Dr., Los Angeles
HARVEY, Eli, *Sculpture*
22 Champion Pl., Alhambra
HASHIMOTO, Michi, *Painting*
1947 Sawtelle Blvd., West Los Angeles
HASTINGS, H. S., *Commercial*
510 W. 6th St., Los Angeles
HATCH, Marie Louise, *Painting, Prints*
730½ S. Eastman St., Los Angeles
HATCH, Velma, *Teacher*
476 21st St., Santa Monica
HATFIELD, Dalzell, *Painting*
2509 W. 7th St., Los Angeles
HAUVERMAN, Laura, *Teacher*
2321½ N. New Hampshire Ave., Los Ange
HAWXHURST, Henry Ivins, *Painting*
115 Bonita Ave., Sierra Madre
HAYAKAWA, Miki, *Painting, Drawing*
628 Montgomery St., San Francisco
HAYDEN, Mary Dodge, *Painting, Portraits*
4411 Jurupa Ave., Riverside
HAYES, Alice V., *Painting*
1240 11th St., San Diego
HAYES, Gayl, *Teacher*
236 E. Palm Ave., Monrovia
HAYFELD, L. A., *Painting*
2203 W. 25th St., Los Angeles
HAYNES, Grace C., *Teacher*
1430 W. 37th Dr., Los Angeles
HAYWARD, Roger, *Watercolors*
365 S. Wilson Ave., Pasadena
HAZEN, Bessie Ella, *Painting, Teacher*
1042 W. 36th St., Los Angeles

HEALD, Mrs. W. F., *Leather Craft*
2660 Catherine Rd., Altadena
HEALY, Grace, *Painting*
940 Glorietta Blvd., Coronado
HEARD, Sidney, *Painting*
5540 Taft Ave., Oakland
HEATH, Edda Maxwell, *Painting*
Carmel
HEATH, Lillian, *Painting*
21 Third St., Santa Cruz
HECKMAN, Frederick R., *Commercial*
1007 S. Grand Ave., Los Angeles
HED, Eva, *Commercial*
1019 Bankers Bldg., Los Angeles
HEE, Hon Chew, *Painting*
933 Stockton St., San Francisco
HEFFLINGER, Grace, *Crafts, Teacher*
3968 Budlong Ave., Los Angeles
HEIL, Miss F. J., *Teacher*
530 N. Glassell St., Orange
HEISE, Bertha, *Crafts, Teacher*
238 Live Oak St., Walnut Park
HEISLEY, George, *Commercial*
1220 Maple Ave., Los Angeles
HELMS, Addison D., *Painting*
1030 W. 8th St., Los Angeles
HELS, Louis, *Prints*
423 W. Montecito St., Santa Barbara
HEMPHILL, Ethel, *Watercolors, Painting*
697 N. Michigan Ave., Pasadena
HENKE, Bernard, *Painting*
1176 E. Villa St., Pasadena
HENRY, H. Raymond, *Painting*
9216 Sunset Blvd., Beverly Hills
HENTEL, Mrs. F. G., *Etching*
557 Penn St., Pasadena
HERBERT, Barbara, *Sculpture*
800 Chestnut St., San Francisco
HERBERT, Myrta, *Teacher*
Lincoln High School, Los Angeles
HERDING, Franz, *Painting*
P. O. Box S-1, Hollywood
HERLIHY, H. W., *Painting*
1440 San Pasqual Ave., Los Angeles
HERKOMER, H. G., *Painting*
Auburn
HERMAN, Lydia, *Painting*
627 S. Lafayette Park Pl., Los Angeles
HERON, Edith, *Painting*
Pacific Grove
HERRING, Charles M., *Painting*
350 Upper Terrace, San Francisco
HERRON, Jason, *Sculpture*
1008 W. Kensington Rd., Los Angeles
HERSAVA, Boza, *Painting*
1120 Poinsettia Dr., Los Angeles
HERVEY, Wilna, *Painting*
Carmel
HESS, Radolph, *Painting*
360 Dorantes Ave., San Francisco
HESSE, Henry M., *Watercolors*
450 W. Dryden Ave., Glendale
HESTER, Orrel, *Teacher*
651 Glenwood Rd., Glendale
HESTHAL, William J., *Painting*
2004 Divisadero St., San Francisco
HEWITT, Ernest W., *Painting*
13803 Oxnard St., Van Nuys
HEWSON, H. L., *Crafts*
630 E. Colorado St., Pasadena
HEYN, Mary, *Painting*
707 Stratford Rd., Oakland
HEYNEMAN, Amy J., *Painting*
33 Jordan Ave., San Francisco
HEYNEMAN, Julie Helen, *Painting*
1770 Green St., San Francisco
HIDER, Russell John, *Paintng, Murals*
121 Roselawn Pl., Los Angeles
HILD, Georgia Marion, *Pottery*
500 S. Serrano St., Los Angeles
HILL, Susan Leland, *Jewelry*
3132 Eaton St., Berkeley
HILLER, Helen Craig, *Painting*
4288 Navajo St., North Hollywood
HILLER, William, *Painting*
4288 Navajo St., North Hollywood
HILLMAN, Rosana, *Teacher*
995 N. Figueroa St., Los Angeles
HILLS, Metta V., *Painting*
1570 Hawthorne Terrace, Berkeley
HINCHMAN, John H., *Painting*
571 Agate St., Laguna Beach
HINER, Charles L., *Commercial*
85 2nd St., San Francisco
HINKLE, Clarence K., *Painting*
Laguna Beach
HINMAN, Helen, *Painting*
2122½ Beachwood Ter., Los Angeles
HITCHCOCK, Mary Alexandra, *Painting*
2289 Shattuck Ave., Berkeley
HOAGLAND, Mrs. W. M., *Painting*
3450 Orange St., Riverside
HOBART, Clark, *Painting*
1372 Sutter St., San Francisco
HOBUSH, Wilhelmina, *Teacher*
1516 N. Hobart Blvd., Los Angeles
HODGES, Catherine M., *Teacher*
641 N. Mariposa St., Los Angeles
HODGES, K. C., *Commercial*
321 Bush St., San Francisco
HOEFFER, Louis C., *Leather Craft*
317 E. Lomita St., Glendale
HOER, Elizabeth, *Painting*
730 5th St., Santa Rosa
HOFF, Helen M., *Illustration, Teacher*
Polytechnic High School, Long Beach

HOLDEN, James A., *Painting*
3016 Bona St., Oakland
HOLDEN, Octavia, *Leather Craft*
2382 Jackson St., San Francisco
HOLL, Gertrude E., *Ceramics*
1350 Ulloa St., San Francisco
HOLLAND, Beryl S., *Painting*
2872 Juniper St., San Diego
HOLLEN, L. P., *Wrought Iron*
8845 Sunset Blvd., Los Angeles
HOLLIDAY, Ben C., *Painting*
1940 West Blvd., Los Angeles
HOLLINGSHEAD, Harold F., *Commercial*
617 Montgomery St., San Francisco
HOLMAN, Luella, *Painting*
1142 McKinley Ave., Oakland
HOLMES, Miles E., *Painting*
481 Collingwood Ave., San Francisco
HOLMES, Ralph, *Painting*
6553 Colgate Ave., Los Angeles
HOLMES, Stuart, *Painting*
6764 Fountain Ave., Hollywood
HOLT, Geoffrey, *Painting*
1414 Quintero St., Los Angeles
HOLT, Mary L., *Painting*
3504 Larchwood Ave., Riverside
HOMOLA, A. J., *Commercial*
811 W. 7th St., Los Angeles
HON, Billy, *Cartoons*
P. O. Box 486, Hollywood
HONEYWELL, Annette, *Commercial*
412 W. 6th St., Los Angeles
HOOD, Jane, *Teacher*
559 N. Alexandria St., Los Angeles
HOOK, Kenneth G., *Commercial*
16 Beale St., San Francisco
HOOPER, Samuel G., *Miniatures*
609 Elm Dr., Beverly Hills
HOPE, Thelma Paddock, *Portraits*
802 Laurel Ave., Los Angeles
HOPKINS, Grace F., *Painting*
1041 N. Ave. 49, Los Angeles
HORD, Donal, *Sculpture*
1024 Pasco St., San Diego
HORLOCKER, Leta, *Crafts*
1621½ W. 7th St., Los Angeles
HORNE, Nellie M., *Portraits*
85 N. Holliston Ave., Pasadena
HORTON, Charles Orson, *Painting*
2856 13th Ave., Oakland
HORTON, Lester, *Painting*
1805 Hill Dr., Eagle Rock
HOSS, Della T., *Linoleum Prints*
Yosemite National Park
HOUGHTON, H. E., *Commercial*
815 S. Hill St., Los Angeles
HOUNSELL, C. Lillian, *Painting*
512 E. Chestnut St., Glendale
HOUSE, Sada, *Teacher*
1822 W. 48th St., Los Angeles
HOUSSIER, Julia, *Painting*
State College, Santa Barbara
HOUSTON, Oliver, *Painting*
1249½ W. 31st St., Los Angeles
HOWARD, Chester, *Painting*
567 N. Johnston St., Los Angeles
HOWARD, Hazel F., *Painting*
3445 Texas St., San Diego
HOWARD, John Langley, *Painting*
Box 412, Monterey
HOWARD, Robert Boardman, *Painting, Mu*
20 Jessup Pl., San Francisco
HOWELL, Helen, *Teacher*
317 N. New Hampshire St., Los Angeles
HOWELL, Youldon C., *Painting*
1612 El Sereno Ave., Pasadena
HUDSON, Charles Bradford, *Painting*
Pacific Grove
HUDSON, Eiladora, *Teacher*
Beverly Hills High School, Beverly Hills
HUDSON, Muriel, *Block Prints*
774 Sausalito Blvd., Sausalito
HUFF, William, *Painting*
2706 Fulton St., Berkeley
HUGHES, Daisy M., *Painting*
614 S. Normandie Ave., Los Angeles
HUNLEY, Katherine J., *Painting*
437 Summit St., Redlands
HUNT, A. R., *Commercial*
580 Market St., San Francisco
HUNT, George, *Design, Furniture*
171 E. California St., Pasadena
HUNT, Myra B., *Painting*
527 N. Orange Ave., Glendale
HUNT, Paul, *Painting*
1261 Lombard St., San Francisco
HUNTER, Isabel, *Painting*
2050 Santa Clara Ave., Alameda
HUNTSMAN-TROUT, Helen, *Leather Cra*
1640 N. Hobart Blvd., Los Angeles
HURTT, Arthur, *Painting, Illustration*
1518 Mohawk St., Los Angeles
HUSING, R., *Commercial*
6328 Hollywood Blvd., Hollywood
HUSTON, Florence, *Commercial*
320 Market St., San Francisco
HUTTLE, Robert Leon, *Painting*
1212 W. 53rd St., Los Angeles
HYDE, Josephine, *Painting*
1505 Pine Ave., Long Beach
HYDE, Leland, *Painting*
105 Buena Vista Terrace, San Francisco
HYDE, O. E., *Painting*
Box 1, Campbell

HYLIA, Arnold, *Painting*
1304 W. 58th Pl., Los Angeles
HYMAN, Caroline Fenna, *Painting*
3421 Jackson St., San Francisco

I

IGNATIEFF, Alex, *Painting*
5370 La Mirada Ave., Los Angeles
INFIELD, J. Floyd, *Commercial*
2422⅓ S. Hope St., Los Angeles
INGELS, Frank L., *Sculpture*
1455 N. Lowell Ave., Los Angeles
INGELS, Kathleen B., *Sculpture*
1455 N. Lowell Ave., Los Angeles
INGER, Archie J., *Painting*
1110 Oak St., Alameda
INGERSON, Frank, *Painting, Crafts*
"Cathedral Oaks," Alma, Santa Clara Co.
INGHAM, Tedd, *Painting*
Box 283, Laguna Beach
INGRAM, Lenora, *Teacher*
1124 E. California St., Glendale
INGRAM, Robert, *Commercial*
337 Seventeenth St., Oakland
INNES, Andrew, *Woodcarving*
421 N. Euclid Ave., Pasadena
INNES, Robert B., *Woodcarving*
585 S. Marengo St., Pasadena
INOKUMA, Y., *Painting*
1822 Buchanan St., San Francisco
ILYIN, Gleb A., *Painting, Portraits*
1961 Green St., San Francisco
ILYIN, Peter, *Painting, Portraits*
1961 Green St., San Francisco
IMRIE, Herbert D., *Etching*
728 San Luis Rd., Berkeley
IRWIN, Beatrice, *Color, Illumination*
3715 W. 1st St., Los Angeles
IRWIN, Howard M., *Commercial*
Adv. Dept., The Broadway, Los Angeles
IRWIN, William Hyde, *Painting*
Brookdale
ITO, K., *Sculpture*
618 S. Coronado St., Los Angeles
IVANOFF, Eugene, *Painting*
2004 Divisadero St., Los Angeles
IZANT, C. S., *Painting*
5051 Ambrose Ave., Los Angeles

J

JACK, Lucy B., *Painting, Teacher*
1534 Calmar Ct., Palms Station, Los Ang
JACKMAN, Theo, *Painting*
10480 Troon Ave., Westwood Village, L.
JACKSON, Catherine, *Painting*
258 S. Alexandria St., Los Angeles
JACKSON, Enrique, *Painting*
101 S. Mariposa Ave., Los Angeles
JACKSON, Everett Gee, *Painting*
4671 Harvey Dr., San Diego
JACKSON, Howard M., *Painting*
1350 Fifth Ave., San Francisco
JACKSON, Ida M., *Painting*
1622 G St., Sacramento
JACKSON, Jessie Short, *Painting*
1334 Euclid Ave., Berkeley
JACKSON, Martin J., *Painting*
304 S. Broadway, Los Angeles
JACOB, Curt, *Painting*
1452 Poinsettia Pl., Los Angeles
JACOBY, Graziella, *Pastels, Portraits*
Maryland Hotel, Los Angeles
JALANIVICH, Manuel E., *Pottery*
2930 Baker St., San Francisco
JAMES, Austin, *Sculpture*
2282 Pepper Dr., Los Angeles
JAMES, Roy Walter, *Painting*
Covina
JAMESON, Kenneth, *Painting*
1516 The Strand, Manhattan Beach
JANMIE, Louis, *Painting*
2709 Dwight Way, Berkeley
JANEL, Emil, *Woodcarving*
Care G. T. Marsh & Co., 400 Post St., S.
JARVIS, Peggy, *Painting*
1862 N. Los Robles Ave., Pasadena
JAUCHEN, Hans, *Metal Craft*
969 Sutter St., San Francisco
JEHLE, Clara Antonia, *Painting*
Laguna Beach
JELINEK, Joseph, *Painting*
6767 Selma Ave., Hollywood
JENNINGS, Alita Corcoran, *Painting*
1013 Vallejo St., San Francisco
JENNINGS, Lee C., *Commercial*
110 W. 11th St., Los Angeles
JENSEN, Helen Webster, *Sculpture*
533 W. Rustic Rd., Santa Monica
JENSEN, Henry T., *Painting*
2026 Pasadena Ave., Los Angeles
JEPSON, Herbert, *Painting, Decoratio*
212 N. Verdugo Rd., Glendale
JEWELL, Foster, *Painting*
1627 8th Ave., San Diego
JOHNS, Jeannette, *Watercolrs*
2407 Ocean Ave., Los Angeles
JOHNSEN, John D., *Commercial*
108 W. 6th St., Los Angeles
JOHNSON, Addison, *Commercial*
Rives-Strong Bldg., Los Angeles
JOHNSON, Albert E., *Painting*
237 Downey St., San Francisco

JOHNSON, Arthur Monrad, *Painting, Paste*
10733 Wellworth Ave., Westwood Village,
Los Angeles
JOHNSON, Charles E., *Commercial*
1151 S. Broadway, Los Angeles
JOHNSON, Florence, *Painting*
766 N. Kenmore Ave., Los Angeles
JOHNSON, Frank Tenney, *Painting*
22 Champion Pl., Alhambra
JOHNSON, Harry, *Commercial*
3819 Wilshire Blvd., Los Angeles
JOHNSON, John Stanley, *Watercolors*
438 Parkman St., Los Angeles
JOHNSON, Marie, *Painting*
255 S. Fair Oaks Ave., Pasadena
JOHNSON, Richard C., *Commercial*
651 Twentieth St., Oakland
JOHNSON, Sargent, *Sculpture*
277 Park St., Berkeley
JOHNSON, Stanley, *Painting*
1432 Westerly Ter., Pasadena
JOHNSTON, Frederic, *Painting*
3694 Briscoe Ave., Riverside
JOHNSTON, F. Kirk, *Commercial*
617 Montgomery St., San Francisco
JOHONNOT, Ralph, *Painting, Design*
Pacific Grove
JONES, Bob, *Painting*
c/o Santa Cruz Art League, Santa Cruz
JONES, Anne B., *Teacher*
741 El Morado Ct., Ontario
JONES, Cecil, *Ceramics*
5843 Camerford Ave., Los Angeles
JONES, Edith F., *Crafts*
1007 Watts Bldg., San Diego
JONES, Edna A., *Teacher*
943 S. Burnside Ave., Los Angeles
JONES, Elberta Mohler, *Portraits*
1276 N. Sweetzer Ave., Los Angeles
JONES, Emma Floreace, *Watercolo*
2324 London St., Los Angeles *Decorati*
JONES, Genevieve, *Watercolors, Teacher*
131 E. Ave. 35, Los Angeles
JONES, Harold Hemenway, *Illustratio*
712 W. 47th St., Los Angeles *Posters, Teac*
JONES, Martha M., *Painting, Miniatures*
718 Forward St., La Jolla
JONES, William, *Painting*
1816 Wood St., Alameda
JONES, Winifred E. Harris, *Commercial*
Call Bldg., San Francisco
JONSSON, Stanley, *Sculpture*
1312 Carmelita Ave., Sawtelle
JORDAN, Elizabeth R., *Painting*
330 Serra Rd., Stanford University
JORDAN, Helen A., *Painting*
75 N. Auburn St., Sierra Madre
JORGENSEN, C. A., *Painting*
444 Mountain View Ave., Piedmont
JOSEPH, Sydney, *Painting*
1200 Washington St., San Francisco
JOSSELYN, Christine, *Painting*
Normandie Hotel, Los Angeles
JUDSON, Almira A., *Painting*
123 Edgewood Ave., San Francisco
JUDSON, C. Chapel, *Painting*
Pebble Beach
JUDSON, Walter H., *Stained Glass*
200 S. Ave. 66, Los Angeles
JUIN, Molli, *Painting*
1885 Golden Gate Ave., San Francisco
JULIAN, George Bennett, *Painting*
1079 Broadway, San Francisco
JURECKA, Cyril, *Sculpture, Teacher*
163 W. 11th St., Claremont

K

KAHN, Mathilde H., *Painting*
Hotel Normandie, San Francisco
KALMUS, Nathalie, *Color, Cinema*
Technicolor Studios, Hollywood
KAMINSKI, Edward B., *Painting*
1830 N. Orange Grove Ave., Hollywood
KAMPS, Norman, *Illustration, Commercial*
30 N. Raymond Ave., Pasadena
KAMPSCHROER, John J., Jr., *Painting*
115 Wellington St., Oakland
KARRAS, Spiros John, *Painting*
1819 Olive Dr., Pasadena
KATCHAMAKOFF, Atanas, *Sculpture*
1125 N. El Centro Ave., Los Angeles
KAUMEYER, George F., *Painting*
611 S. Corondelet St., Los Angeles
KAUN, Valerie, *Sculpture*
1429 Leroy Ave., Berkeley
KECK, Josephine Frances, *Painting*
c/o Santa Cruz Art League, Santa Cruz
KEELER, Katharine Dukes, *Teacher*
449 N. Alta Vista Ave., Los Angeles
KEITH, Ileen, *Textiles*
2956 Scott St., San Francisco
KELLER, Edgar, *Painting*
1439 N. Alta Vista Ave., Los Angeles
KELLER, W. R., *Commercial*
524 S. Spring St., Los Angeles
KELLETT, Medita H., *Sculpture*
1924 Walnut St., Berkeley
KELLEY, Katherine E., *Painting*
1356 Virginia Way, La Jolla
KELLEY, Sue E., *Painting*
3350 Redwood Dr., Riverside
KELLOGG, Ellen Scripps, *Watercolors, Prin*
145 Mariposa, Altadena

KELLY, Edna, *Sculpture*
112 E. Broadway, Long Beach
KELSEY, Richmond I., *Painting*
1831 Front St., San Diego
KENDALL, Marie B., *Painting*
Hollywood Riviera, Los Angeles
KENDALL, Marion, *Weaving*
4051 Bayview Ct., San Diego
KENDE, Geza, *Painting, Portraits*
1144 N. Hudson Ave., Los Angeles
KENNEDY, Martha, *Painting*
303 N. Vendome St., Los Angeles
KENNEDY, Norman M., *Crafts*
1232 Hilldale Ave., Los Angeles
KENNICOTT, Robert H., *Painting*
2410 4th Ave., Los Angeles
KENT, Adaline, *Sculpture*
1030 Vallejo St., San Francisco
KENYON, Haidee, *Painting*
2893 Nutmeg St., San Diego
KEPPLE, Evelyn, *Teacher*
553 W. 41st Pl., Los Angeles
KERN, Marie L., *Teacher*
141 S. Spruce St., Montebello
KERNS, Correa, *Design, Crafts*
2867 W. 7th St., Los Angeles
KERNS, Fannie M., *Teacher*
1210 N. Granada Ave., San Marino
KERWIN, Mary Catherine, *Miniatures*
3303 W. 23rd St., Los Angeles
KESSINGER, Thelma Rogers, *Painting, Wat.*
Pachappa Mt., Riverside *colors, Woodcarvi*
KESZTHELYI, A. S., *Painting, Portraits*
1147 N. Hudson Ave., Los Angeles
KIDDER, Margaret, *Painting*
237 Los Flores Ave., Pasadena
KIDDER, Zinnie, *Painting*
2712 Regent St., Berkeley
KIESTER, Lucille, *Crafts, Color, Design*
4351¾ Willowbrook Ave., Los Angeles
KILPATRICK, Aaron E., *Painting*
Morro Bay
KING, Albert Henry, *Painting, Sculpture*
3612 N. Griffith Ave., Los Angeles
KING, Edythe, *Commercial*
111 Ford Pl., Pasadena
KINNEY, Enid, *Painting*
455 Coleridge Ave., Palo Alto
KINZER, Gordon Neale, *Watercolors, Illu*
5314 Coringa Dr., Los Angeles *tratio*
KIRBY, Emmett, *Watercolors, Sculpture*
1179 Market St., San Francisco
KIRK, Frances, *Teacher*
920 S. Olive St., Los Angeles
KITTLE, John T., *Painting*
Ross, Marin County
KITTS, Jasmine de Lancey, *Painting*
1246 25th Ave., San Francisco
KLAUBER, Alice, *Painting*
3060 6th Ave., San Diego
KLAUBER, Leda, *Painting*
312 Gravilla St., La Jolla
KLFIN, Ernst, *Painting*
6101 Sunset Blvd., Los Angeles
KLEINE, Theodore I., *Commercial, Plastic*
1134 N. Westmoreland Ave., Hollywood
KLEIST, Addie L., *Painting*
87 Kenneth St., Santa Cruz
KLETZKER, C. Harry, *Commercial*
544 Market St., San Francisco
KLINGER, Katherine, *Teacher*
831 S. Westlake Ave., Los Angeles
KLIPPLE, Maude, *Painting*
921 Locust St., Long Beach
KLOSS, Gene, *Etching*
3420 Webster St., Oakland
KLUSSMAN, Freida, *Painting*
955 Clayton St., San Francisco
KNIGHT, Edward E., *Commercial*
1777 Neale St., San Diego
KNOTT, Harold M., *Painting*
Morro Bay
KNOWLES, Squire, *Painting*
Pittsburg
KOCHER, Fritz, *Painting*
1851 W. 37th Pl., Los Angeles
KOETHEN, Cora B., *Painting*
5098 Brockton Ave., Riverside
KOHLER, Elleanor, *Painting*
258 E. Greeley Ave., Tujunga
KOHLMEIER, Helen M., *Painting, Portra*
1054 Ingraham St., Los Angeles
KOLLORSZ, Richard, *Painting*
368 N. Bronson Ave., Los Angeles
KORFF, Baroness S. A., *Crafts*
1660 Loma Vista Ave., Pasadena
KORU, James, *Decoration*
6332 Warner Dr., Los Angeles
KOSA, Emil J., Jr., *Painting*
1279 Sunset Blvd., Los Angeles
KOTOKU, Shivei, *Watercolors*
417 S. San Pedro St., Los Angeles
KRANTH, Charles P., *Watercolors*
Laguna Beach
KRAYER, Arnold D., *Painting*
936 Venice Blvd., Los Angeles
KREKE, Eric E., *Commercial*
500 Sansome St., San Francisco
KRESS, E. W., *Painting*
1318 Bates Rd., Oakland
KROMER, Adelaide, *Watercolors*
124 N. Thomas St., Los Angeles
KRUMEL, Leopold, *Commercial*
24 California St., San Francisco

KRUSE, Alice, *Painting*
2012 7th Ave., National City
KUBIC, J. C., *Wrought Iron*
5212 Wilshire Blvd., Los Angeles
KUHNLE, Paul, *Sculpture*
3701 4th Ave., Los Angeles
KURMAN, O., *Painting*
903 Eddy St., San Francisco
KURTZWORTH, Harry Muir, *Painting,*
325 S. Ardmore St., *Sculpture, Graphic*
Los Angeles *Crafts*
KUTCHER, Ben, *Illustration*
3107 Barbara Ct., Hollywood
KYES, Vera L., *Painting*
3696 Franklin Ave., Riverside

L

LABADI, Luci, *Painting*
7 Moss Ave., Oakland
LABAUDT, Alvyne, *Painting*
528 Powell St., San Francisco
LABAUDT, Lucien, *Painting, Costumes*
528 Powell St., San Francisco
LABAUDT, Yliane, *Painting*
528 Powell St., San Francisco
La CAVA, Mrs. G., *Painting*
445 17th St., Santa Monica
LAIDLAW, Cora M., *Painting*
315 F Ave., Coronado
LAIRD, Marshall, *Design, Furniture*
2861 W. 7th St., Los Angeles
L'ALLEMAND, Gordon, *Painting, Etching*
1963 N. Alexandria St., Los Angeles
LAINHART, Grace L., *Crafts*
1307 E. Wilson St., Glendale
LAMAN, Thomas, *Painting*
767 N. Point St., San Francisco
LAMB, Mrs Frederick S., *Stained Glass*
1853 San Juan Ave., Berkeley
LANDACRE, Paul H., *Woodblock Prints*
1916 Walcott Way, Los Angeles
LANE, Martella Cone, *Painting, Teacher*
4245 Monroe St., Los Angeles
LANG, Lucien, *Commercial*
693 Mission St., San Francisco
LANGDON, Jane, *Painting*
2659 Green St., San Francisco
LANGE, Catherine Woolsey, *Teacher*
122 Woolsey St., San Francisco
LANGE, Dorothea, *Photography*
802 Montgomery St., San Francisco
LANGLEY, Edward, *Painting*
1201 Fuller Ave., Los Angeles
LANGTON, Birgit, *Teacher*
354-B N. Rodeo Dr., Beverly Hills
LANGWORTHY, L. R., *Watercolors*
834 Toledo Ave., Coronado
LANPHEAR, James, *Commercial*
1245 Trenton St., Los Angeles
LANZ, Ernest, *Painting, Portraits*
626 Echo Park Ave., Los Angeles
LAPIUS, Blanche, *Painting*
15921 S. Menlo Ave., Gardena
LARIMER, Barbara, *Painting*
751 S. Windsor Blvd., Los Angeles
LARIMER, Ruth, *Painting, Portraits*
751 S. Windsor Blvd., Los Angeles
LARSEN, Amy Farley, *Painting*
1701 Gough St., San Francisco
LARSON, Adele, *Portraits*
8601 West Knoll Dr., Los Angeles
LARSON, Robert, *Painting*
1950 S. Mariposa St., Los Angeles
LARTER, Anne, *Painting*
1957 Canyon Dr., Hollywood
LaSELLE, E. C., *Commercial*
143 2nd St., San Francisco
LATIMER, Lorenzo P., *Painting*
2514 Woolsey St., Berkeley
LATTIG, Ada G., *Teacher*
2212 5th Ave., Los Angeles
LATON, Helen E., *Leather Craft*
1925 W. 10th St., Los Angeles
LAUCK, Louis A., *Commercial*
405 Sansome St., San Francisco
LAUDERBACK, Frances, *Painting*
1519 N. Lake Ave., Pasadena
LAUDERMILK, Helen Gaylord, *Cartoon*
Batiks, Illustration
Forbes Ave., Claremont
LAUDERMILK, Jerome D., *Design, Color*
Forbes Ave., Claremont
LAUMAN, Hester, *Teacher*
830 Valley View Rd., South Pasadena
LAURITZ, Paul, *Painting*
3955 Clayton Ave., Los Angeles
LAUTER, H. E., *Painting*
1352 6th Ave., San Diego
LAVRILLIER, Gaston A., *Sculpture, Paint*
1237 N. Poinsettia Pl., L. A. *Portr*
LAW, Harry W., *Watercolors*
8441 S. Antonia Ave., South Gate, L.
LAW, Lila, *Painting*
1000 Arapahoe St., Los Angeles
LAWATCH, Rudolf, *Design, Furniture*
1500 Sanborn Ave., Los Angeles
LAWSON, F. J., Jr., *Painting*
4430 Rubidoux Ave., Riverside
LEAVY, Katherine, *Teacher*
1309 2nd Ave., Long Beach
LEDEBOER, Hans, *Painting*
5546 Bayer Ave., Los Angeles

LEDGERWOOD, Helen J., *Teacher*
1039 Stratford Ave., South Pasadena
LEE, Bertha Stringer, *Painting*
2744 Steiner St., San Francisco
LEE, Elva, *Teacher*
1501 Oxford Ave., Pasadena
LEE, Leslie W., *Painting, Etching*
1234 Franciscan Way, San Diego
LEE, Selma, *Painting*
2717 Fleur Dr., San Marino
LEE, Sylvia, *Painting*
Barcelona Apts., San Diego
LEE, Walt, *Newspaper Art*
Care Illustrated Daily News, Los Angeles
LEGLER, Flora, *Painting*
1214 Upas St., San Diego
LEIGHTON, Kathryn W., *Painting*
1633 W. 46th St., Los Angeles
LEMOS, Pedro J., *Painting, Teacher*
460 Churchill St., Palo Alto
LENGGENHAGER, Warner, *Painting*
2401 Wilshire Blvd., Los Angeles
LEONARD, Jack, *Painting*
Box 495, Laguna Beach
LEONARD, Phil, *Newspaper Art*
Care The Times, 100 N. Broadway, L. A.
LESLIE, Jean G., *Painting*
1629 Georgina Ave., Santa Monica
LEVINSON, Homer, *Painting*
Carmel
LEVY, Nat, *Commercial*
617 Montgomery St., San Francisco
LEVY, Wynette, *Textiles*
1851 Fulton St., San Francisco
LEWERENZ, Carol M., *Painting, Teacher*
1900 E. Ocean Blvd., Long Beach
LEWERENZ, Margaret G., *Crafts, Teache*
3926 Tracy St., Los Angeles
LEWIS, Arley, *Painting*
8217 Sunset Blvd., Los Angeles
LEWIS, H. Emerson, *Painting*
1091 S. Plymouth Blvd., Los Angeles
LEWIS, Jeannette, Maxfield, *Painting*
3136 Huntington Blvd., Fresno
LEWIS, Jessie Miles, *Teacher*
3917½ S. Flower St., Los Angeles
LEWIS, Lola C., *Painting*
2631 Westview St., Los Angeles
LEWIS, Tom E., *Painting*
Box 1264, Laguna Beach
LEWIS, Vera B., *Teacher*
233 E. Whitney Ave., Fullerton
LICHTY, Mrs. Eugene, *Painting, Prints*
3617 Monroe Ave., San Diego
LIEBERMAN, Frances, *Painting*
3949 Washington St., San Francisco
LIEBES, Dorothy W., *Weaving*
1001 California St., San Francisco
LIERD, Hallie W., *Teacher*
3076 Palm St., San Diego
LILJESTROM, G. F., *Painting*
895 38th Ave., San Francisco
LILLIAN, E. Christine, *Drawing*
Palm Springs
LINCOLN, Alice R., *Teacher*
1207 W. 3rd St., Los Angeles
LINCOLN, Edith J., *Painting, Drawing*
4356 California St., San Francisco
LINDEMAN, Winifred, *Miniatures*
2600 Wilshire Blvd., Los Angeles
LINFORTH, Edward, *Block Printi*
2465 Telegraph Ave., Berkeley *Woodcar*
LINKS, Julian A., *Commercial*
268 Market St., San Francisco
LION, Henry, *Sculpture*
761 McCarthy Vista, Los Angeles
LIPMAN, Rowena, *Commercial*
Hearst Bldg., San Francisco
LIPPINCOTT, Josephine, *Weaving*
1256 W. Adams St., Los Angeles
LITCHFIELD, M. B., *Painting*
1178 Victoria Ave., Los Angeles
LITCHFIELD, Roscoe R., *Painting*
687 Durant Ave., San Leandro
LITTLE, Charlotte F., *Teacher*
807 N. Terrace St., San Pedro
LITTLE, Gertrude, *Miniatures*
4417 Prospect Ave., Los Angeles
LITTLE, Philip, *Block Prints, Commercial*
507 Montgomery St., San Francisco
LITTLEJOHN, Hugh W., *Painting*
2701 Belrose Ave., Berkeley
LIVINGSTON, Alice Lord, *Watercolor Etchi*
2360 Filbert St., San Francisco
LLOYD, Eleanor, *Teacher*
910 N. Alpine Dr., Beverly Hills
LLOYD, Lucile, *Mural Painter a Decora*
4611 Melbourne Ave., Los Angeles
LLOYD, Lucy, *Crafts*
El Pueblo Rivera, La Jolla
LLOYD, R. D., *Painting*
912 S. Crenshaw Blvd., Los Angeles
LOCKHART, Marcelite, *Sculpture*
1004 N. La Jolla Ave., Hollywood
LOCKWOOD, Florence, *Painting*
41 Highland Ave., Burlingame
LOGAN, Maurice, *Painting, Commercial*
507 Montgomery St., San Francisco
LONG, Eula, *Painting*
6782 Milner Rd., Los Angeles
LONG, H. A., *Painting*
3604 Mississippi St., San Diego
LORING, Margaret, *Watercolors, Block Prin*
4613½ Park Blvd, San Diego
LORTSCH, Vara B., *Woodcarving, Textiles*
1367 3rd Ave., San Francisco

LOUCKS, B. W., *Painting*
2112½ Colorado Blvd., Eagle Rock
LOVATELLI, Ephy, *Weaving*
2923 Hope St., Los Angeles
LOVELL, Duke, *Watercolors, Pastels*
4382 Keeler St., San Diego
LOVINS, Henry, *Painting, Decoration*
1737 N. Highland Ave., Hollywood
LOWD, Edna B., *Crafts, Teacher*
122 S. Alexandria St., Los Angeles
LOWE, Frances, *Drawing, Watercolors*
Spreckels Theatre Bldg., San Diego
LOWRY, Lorraine, *Teacher*
922 Victoria St., Corona
LUDEKENS, Fred, *Commercial*
Lord & Thomas, Russ Bldg., San Francisco
LUDLOW, Margery N., *Metal Craft*
2720 Ganesha Ave., Altadena
LUDOVICI, Alice, *Miniature*
167 N. Orange Grove Ave., Pasadena
LUDOVICI, Frieda, *Miniatures*
167 N. Orange Grove Ave., Pasadena
LUKE, Keye, *Design, Illustration, Cinema*
842 N. Gardner St., Los Angeles
LUKENE, Anna M., *Painting, Portraits*
4457 Victoria Park Dr., Los Angeles
LUKENS, Glen, *Crafts, Teacher*
128 Ellis Pl., Fullerton
LUKITS, Theodore N., *Painting*
121 S. Normandie Ave., Los Angeles
LUNDBERG, Helen, *Painting*
854 N. Holliston Ave., Pasadena
LUNDY, Bernita, *Painting, Pastels, Drawi*
779 14th Ave., San Francisco *Woodbloc*
LUSCOMB, Mrs. R. E., *Painting*
2749 28th St., San Diego
LUTHE, Bernice, *Painting*
642 Clara St., Oakland
LUTZ, Gladys M., *Leather Craft*
11216 Iowa Ave., West Los Angeles
LUTZ, Paul Henry, *Leather Craft*
11216 Iowa Ave., West Hollywood
LUX, Catherine C., *Teacher*
6516 Lexington Ave., Los Angeles
LYON, Kathryn R., *Commercial*
111 Sutter St., San Francisco
153 S. Serrano Ave., Los Angeles
LYONS, Mary Elizabeth, *Teacher*

Mc

McCAIG, Flora Thomas, *Painting*
Foothill Blvd., La Canada
McCAN, Patterson, *Sculpture*
716 Pacific St., San Francisco
McALLISTER, Virginia Ann, *Watercolors*
1818 N. Kenmore St., Los Angeles
McARTHUR, Warren, *Design, Furniture*
810 E. 61st St., Los Angeles
McBRIDE, Clifford, *Painting*
1098 Palm Terrace, Pasadena
McCARTNEY, Marion C., *Painting*
2201 S. Figueroa St., Los Angeles
McCARTNEY, Norma, *Teacher*
3855½ S. Flower St., Los Angeles
McCAULEY, George Edward, *Painti*
1131 E. Maple Ave., Glendale *Teach*
McINTOSH, Rhea, *Bookplates, Commercial*
1842 S. Sycamore Ave., Los Angeles
McCLELLAND, Amy Woller, *Design, Teach*
3789 Menlo Ave., Los Angeles
McCLEAVE, Valencia Rafferty, *Painting*
Grossmont
McCLELLAND, Lela, *Leather Craft*
1258 N. Euclid Ave., Ontario
McCOMAS, Francis, *Painting*
Pebble Beach
McCOMAS, Jean, *Painting*
Pebble Beach
McCORMACK, Blanche, *Teacher*
325 W. 17th St., Los Angeles
McCRARY, Miriam T., *Teacher*
342 E. Walnut St., Huntington Park
McDANIEL, Helen I., *Painting*
Box 103, Colton
McDERMID, Amy B., *Batiks, Textiles*
660 N. El Molino Ave., Pasadena
McDERMID, W. H., *Commercial*
1155 Venice Blvd., Los Angeles
McDONALD, Katherine H., *Block Prints*
800 B Ave., Coronada
McEWEN, Katherine, *Painting, Murals*
410 S. Alvarado St., Los Angeles
McFARLAND, Lucille G., *Painting*
291 27th Ave., San Francisco
McFETRIDGE, Blanche E., *Sculpture*
1625 Plumosa Way, San Diego
McGAW, Blanche Baldwin, *Painting*
1020 Green St., San Francisco
McGOWAN, V. Carroll, *Teacher*
4140 N. Camellia Ave., North Hollywood
McINTOSH, Mabel D., *Metal Craft, Enam*
Bolinas *Potte*
McKANNAY, Ruth, *Painting, Drawin*
3466 21st St., San Francisco *Sculptu*
McKAY, T. H., *Watercolors*
4466 Maplewood Ave., Los Angeles
McLAREN, Matie, *Painting*
628 Montgomery St., San Francisco
McLEAN, Grace, *Painting*
4846 Glacier Dr., Eagle Rock
McLEAN, Irene, *Teacher*
24 N. Olive Ave., Los Angeles
McLEOD, Mrs. L. E. Gardner, *Painting*
403 S. Occidental Blvd., Los Angeles

McMANAMAN, Kathryn, *Painting*
705 White Oak Ave., Monrovia
McNAUGHTON, Elizabeth Baskerville, *Painti*
1156 W. 56th St., Los Angeles
McNEELEY, Irene, *Painting*
4257 W. 61st St., Los Angeles
McNEELY, Perry, *Painting*
4257 W. 61st St., Los Angeles
McPHAIL, Annie, *Painting, Teacher*
1730 W. 43rd Pl., Los Angeles
McWHIRTER, Emma, *Teacher*
2621 Magnolia Ave., Los Angeles

M

MAAS, Henry B., *Commercial*
354 Pine St., San Francisco
MacDONALD, S. Anne, *Commercial*
16 Beale St., San Francisco
MacGUIRE, Ray M., *Painting*
5327 Santa Monica Blvd., Los Angeles
MACKAY, Clifton C., *Painting*
1194 Avoca Ave., Pasadena
MacKINNON, Annabelle, *Painting*
1668 W. Jefferson Ave., Los Angeles
MACKY, Constance, *Painting*
3973 16th St., San Francisco
MACKY, E. Spencer, *Painting*
California School of Fine Arts, San Franci
MacLENNAN, Eunice, *Painting*
21 Mimosa Lane, Santa Barbara
MacQUOID, Clarence, *Commercial*
1007 S. Grand Ave., Los Angeles
MAHER, Kate Heath, *Painting*
11 Fair Oaks Ave., San Francisco
MAHR, Dr. August C., *Painting*
Stanford University
MAIER-KREIG, Eugene, *Sculpture*
517 Garfield Ave., South Pasadena
MAISON, Mary, *Painting*
2320 Highland Ave., Manhattan Beach
MAKO, B., *Painting*
3871 Edenhurst Ave., Los Angeles
MALLEN, Roy E., *Commercial*
2161 Shattuck Ave., Berkeley
MANHEIM, Erwin, *Painting*
91 Dufour Ave., Santa Cruz
MANNEL, George F., *Commercial*
85 2nd St., San Francisco
MANNHEIM, Jean, *Painting*
500 S. Arroyo Blvd., Pasadena
MANOR, Marian, *Painting*
6126 Harwood Ave., Oakland
MANUELLI, Fasquale, *Sculpture*
522 Fremont St., South Pasadena
MARCH, Dorothy, *Painting*
2714 Fluer Dr., San Marino
MARCHESE, V. A., *Commercial*
3605 N. Figueroa St., Los Angeles
MARCHESKI, *James, Commercial*
1240 S. Main St., Los Angeles
MARDFELD, Jean, *Watercolors*
767 N. Kenmore Ave., Los Angeles
MARKS, Ida Lee, *Teacher*
Whittier Union High School, Whittier
MARKS, Janet E., *Teacher*
117 S. Dolores St., Wilmington
MARROLTA, Silva, *Painting*
812 N. Edgemont Ave., Los Angeles
MARSH, S. James, *Commercial*
1240 S. Main St., Los Angeles
MARTEN, A. F., *Design, Furniture*
1501 Sutter St., San Francisco
MARTEN, Althea, *Leather Craft*
343 14th St., Santa Monica
MARTIN, A. C., *Commercial*
420 S. Broadway, Los Angeles
MARTIN, Earl, *Commercial*
430 S. Broadway, Los Angeles
MARTIN, Fletcher, *Painting*
4658 Lilycrest Ave., Los Angeles
MARTIN, Hazel S., *Teacher*
810 W. 40th Pl., Los Angeles
MARTIN, Margaret, *Painting*
626 W. 82nd St., Los Angeles
MARTINEZ, Alfredo Ramos, *Painting*
5057½ Sunset Blvd., Los Angeles
MARTINEZ, Xavier, *Painting*
816 Scenic Ave., Piedmont
MARVIN, Helen, *Painting*
964 Kensington Ave., Piedmont
MASON, Lolita D., *Painting*
2605 El Moran St., Los Angeles
MASON, Nan, *Painting*
Carmel
MASTON, J. Kendall, *Watercolors*
6809 Neptune Pl., La Jolla
MASUDA, Sojiro, *Watercolors*
429 N. Fremont Ave., Los Angeles
MATHEWS, Arthur F., *Painting, Murals*
670 Fell St., San Francisco
MATHEWS, Lucia K., *Painting*
670 Fell St., San Francisco
MATSON, Nathalie, *Design*
345 25th St., Santa Monica
MATSUBARA, K., *Painting*
430 Grant Ave., San Francisco
MATTHEWS, Lester, *Painting*
1087 66th St., Oakland
MATTHIAS, Martha, *Watercolors*
1236 S. Bonnie Brae St., Los Angeles
MATTOCKS, Gertrude E., *Painting*
509 Georgetown Ave., San Mateo

MAUER, Olga, *Painting*
2557 Hilgard Ave., Berkeley
MAXWELL, Mrs. J. R., *Crafts*
1227 No. Hayworth Ave., Los Angeles
MAXWELL, Mary Margaret, *Teacher*
1032 Coronado Terrace, Los Angeles
MAY, Beulah, *Sculpture*
R. F. D. 1, Box 4, Santa Ana
MAYEDA, Yasutada, *Painting*
2634 Sutter St., San Francisco
MAYER, Evelyn S., *Painting*
1900 Washington St., San Francisco
MAYHEW, Nell Brooker, *Painting, Etching*
5016 Aldama St., Los Angeles
MEAD, Ida B., *Teacher*
1416 Calumet Dr., Los Angeles
MEADOWS, Dell, *Painting, Etching*
1133 W. 36th Pl., Los Angeles
MEARS, Margaret, *Ceramics*
1432 N. Foothill Blvd., Pasadena
MEDINA, W. A., *Commercial*
576 Sacramento St., San Francisco
MEEKER, Chris Marie, *Painting, Illustra*
2522 N. Highland Ave., Hollywood
MEGARGEE, Lon, *Painting*
723 S. Figueroa St., Los Angeles
MEIER, Barton, *Painting*
730 W. 17th St., Los Angeles
MELLER, Reginald B., *Commercial*
417 Market St., San Francisco
MELLES, J. M., *Painting*
2532 Bancroft Way, Berkeley
MELVILLE, Antonia, *Painting, Portraits*
717 S. Alvarado St., Los Angeles
MELZER, William, *Etching*
437 S. Cummings St., Los Angeles
MENNIG, Lucy P., *Weaving, Crafts*
Casa del Adobe, Pasadena
MERRIAM, James, *Painting*
527 S. Kenmore Ave., Los Angeles
MERRILD, Knud, *Painting, Sculpture*
2610 S. Robertson Blvd., L. A.   *Desig*
MERRITT, Warren Chase, *Painting, Murals*
61 Carl St., San Francisco
MERVIN, Carol, *Painting*
612 16th St., Oakland
MERWIN, Antoinette de Forest, *Painting*
1064 Armada Dr., Pasadena
MESSENGER, Ivan, *Painting*
2470 B St., San Diego
MESIC, Julian C., *Architectural Models*
1140 E. 22nd St., Oakland
MEYER, Frederick H., *Teacher*
California School of Arts & Crafts, Oaklan
MEYER, George, *Painting*
c/o Art Center, 730 Montgomery St., S. F.
MEYER, Zel, *Painting, Portraits*
622 N. Detroit St., Los Angeles
MIHSFELDT, Gertrude Wiebe, *Painting*
Drawing, Sculpture, Woodcarving
2150 Seventh Ave., Sacramento
MILBURN, Oliver, *Painting*
536 N. Las Palmas Ave., Los Angeles
MILES, Harold, *Painting, Cinema*
6160 Glen Holly, Hollywood
MILLER, Barse, *Painting, Murals*
Box 366 H, Route 1, La Canada
MILLER, Charles M., *Painting*
1811 Woodrow Ave., Eagle Rock
MILLER, Evylena Nunn, *Painting*
2224 Reservoir St., Los Angeles
MILLER, Gertrude Herzberg, *Painting*
721 Quintara St., San Francisco
MILLER, Lorenzo C., *Crafts, Teacher*
1737 N. Highland Ave., Los Angeles
MILLER, Minnie R., *Painting*
5295 Mt. View Dr., San Diego
MILLER, Ralph Davisson, *Painting*
1221 N. Vermont Ave., Los Angeles
MINTER, Mary M., *Painting*
Naval Hospital, San Diego
MILLER, N. John, *Painting, Decoration*
4350 Beverly Blvd., Los Angeles
MILLER, Ruth, *Painting*
630 Prospect Blvd., Pasadena
MINER, Fred R., *Painting*
360 S. Westlake Ave., Los Angeles
MITCHELL, Alfred R., *Painting*
1035 29th St., San Diego
MITCHELL, Estelle, *Painting*
1838 Lucile Ave., Los Angeles
MITCHELL, Laura M. D., *Miniatures*
507 S. 4th St., Alhambra
MITCHELL, Margaret, *Teacher*
1209 E. 1st St., Long Beach
MOCINE, Emily Rutherford, *Woodcarving*
5226½ Santa Monica Blvd., Los Angeles
MOCINE, Ralph F., *Commercial*
112 W. 9th St., Los Angeles
MODESTI, Angelina S., *Painting*
2517 8th Ave., Los Angeles
MOELLER, Nora, *Painting*
2508 Ridge Rd., Berkeley
MOELLER, Ruth, *Teacher*
1379 N. Serrano Ave., Los Angeles
MOFFATT, Edna C., *Teacher*
1153 Oberlin Ave., Glendale
MOFFITT, Edward Raymond, *Woodcarving*
Monterey
MOHR, Art E., *Commercial*
361 Sutter St., San Francisco
MOIR, Miss L. M., *Portraits*
1819 S. St. Andrews St., Los Angeles
MONDON, Evelyn, *Teacher*
219 W. 38th St., Los Angeles

MONHOFF, Fred, *Painting, Design*
430 Marigold Ave., Altadena
MONROE, Ruth, *Leather Craft*
4329 Ponca Ave., North Hollywood
MONTAGUE, Ward, *Woodcarving*
1501 Leavenworth St., San Francisco
MONTRICHARD, R. D., *Painting*
1943 W. 29th St., Los Angeles
MOODY, Helen Wills, *Drawing*
1130 Sacramento St., San Francisco
MOODY, Vinnie R., *Crafts, Teacher*
5081 Montezuma Ave., Los Angeles
MOON, Carl, *Painting*
565 N. Mentor Ave., Pasadena
MOORE, E. Andrews, *Painting*
440 Westbourne Dr., West Hollywood
MOORE, Frank M., *Painting*
P. O. Box 57, Pasadena
MOORMAN, Lewis, Jr., *Painting*
2830 W. 8th St., Los Angeles
MORA, Jo, *Sculpture*
Pebble Beach
MORAHAN, Eugene, *Sculpture*
1017 3rd St., Santa Monica
MORGAN, Barbara Brooks, *Prints, Teacher*
2437 Echo Park Ave., Los Angeles
MORGAN, Catherine, *Painting*
408 Blair Ave., Piedmont
MORGAN, Charlotte E., *Painting*
Carmel
MORGAN, Lois Waag, *Teacher*
550½ S. New Hampshire St., Los Angeles
MORGAN, M. DeNeale, *Painting*
Box 67, Carmel
MORGAN, Mary R., *Painting*
1336 4th Ave., San Francisco
MORRIS, Adelaide, *Watercolors*
855 N. Vermont Ave., Los Angeles
MORRISON, Katherine, *Crayon Drawings*
3745 Grim Ave., San Diego
MORRISON-KAHLE, Katherine, *Painting*
3353 Albatross St., San Diego
MORRISON, Mary Black, *Painting*
Monterey
MORSE, Esther B., *Painting, Drawing*
Lemon Grove
MORSE, Mary S., *Crafts, Teacher*
310 S. Vendome St., Los Angeles
MORSE, Vernon Jay, *Painting*
965 Sinaloa Ave., Pasadena
MORTENSEN, Helen Hollister, *Teacher*
320 Market St., Venice
MORTENSEN, William, *Photography*
Laguna Beach
MORTIGIA, M. J., *Painting*
51 Priest St., San Francisco
MOTTRAM, Grace, *Teacher*
1122 Cloverdale Ave., Los Angeles
MOTT, Helen M., *Commercial*
Route 2, Box 17, Petaluma
MOTTRAM, John, *Painting*
1360 Drake Ave., Burlingame
MOSES, Walter Farrington, *Painting*
Egan Gallery, 1324 S. Figueroa St., L. A.
MOUNTFORT, Arnold, *Portraits*
701 S. Kingsley Dr., Los Angeles
MOW, Albert, *Painting*
819 E. 105th St., Los Angeles
MUDD, Mrs. W. Seeley, *Painting*
2232 S. Harvard Blvd., Los Angeles
MUELLER, F. B., *Commercial*
1411 Maple Ave., Los Angeles
MULLEN, Carrie S., *Teacher*
364 W. 41st Pl., Los Angeles
MUMMA, Mary G., *Leather Craft*
1645 Golden Gate Ave., Los Angeles
MUNSON, Harriet Sherrill, *Painting, Portra*
La Sierra Heights, Route 1, Arlington
MURPHY, Bernardine, *Sculpture*
2076 W. Adams St., Los Angeles
MURPHY, Lawrence, *Painting, Illustration*
741 S. Grandview St., Los Angeles
MURRAY, Alexander, *Painting, Teacher*
Pacific Beach
MUSKI, John, *Painting*
Bryson Bldg, Los Angeles
MYERS, Helen E., *Weaving Crafts*
3434 Jackson St., San Francisco

N

NAFE, Marie P., *Painting*
4933 Fifth Ave., Los Angeles
NAHL, Perham W., *Painting*
Art Dept., Univ. of Calif., Berkeley
NAPOLITANO, Pasquale, *Painting*
823 N. Figueroa St., Los Angeles
NARBUTT, Helen, *Painting*
1555 Plymouth Ave., San Francisco
NEFF, Andrew, *Pottery*
182 E. California St., Pasadena
NEGULESCO, Jean, *Painting*
1961 Glencoe Way, Hollywood
NEILY, R. M., *Painting*
Bohemian Club, San Francisco
NELLI, Guido, *Bronze Casting*
3132 Alosta St., Los Angeles
NELSON, Mrs. C., *Painting*
3360 Octavia St., San Francisco
NEMIYAMA, Koichi,
1745 Laguna St., San Francisco
NEMKOFF, Vladimir, *Painting*
1850 Pine St., San Francisco

NEMOY, Maurice, *Commercial*
  542 Florence Ave., Inglewood
NESBIT, Phil, *Painting*
  2308 Buchanan St., San Francisco
NETTLETON, George P., Jr., *Commercial*
  1512 Santee St., Los Angeles
NEUBAUER, Dr. F. LaFay, *Etching*
  520 Bradbury Bldg., Los Angeles
NEUHAUS, Eugen, *Painting*
  922 Derby St., Berkeley
NEVILL-SMITH, H., *Watercolors*
  2904 W. 7th St., Los Angeles
NEWCOMB, Olive, *Srafts, Teacher*
  224 N. Hoover St., Los Angeles
NEWCOMBE, Warren A., *Painting, Cinema*
  546 N. Cliffwood Dr., Brentwood Hts., L.
NEWELL, Bertha Stafford, *Prints*
  Women's City Club, San Francisco
NEWELL, Gordon, *Sculpture*
  6717 Milner Rd., Hollywood
NEWELL, Mildred, *Painting*
  2126 Pine St., San Francisco
NEWKING, Nathalie, *Painting*
  5612 Fountain Ave., Hollywood
NEWMAN, Maude, *Crafts*
  58 Atlantic Ave., Long Beach
NEWMAN, Wanda, *Painting*
  702 W. 49th St., Los Angeles
NICHOLL, John W., *Painting*
  595 Summit Ave., Pasadena
NICHOLS, Caroline C., *Sculpture*
  1735 N. Wilcox Ave., Hollywood
NICHOLS, Harley D., *Etching*
  San Juan Capistrano
NICHOLS, Pegus Martin, *Painting*
  517 S. Coronado St., Los Angeles
NICHOLSON, Charles W., *Painting*
  04 N. Bonnie Brae St., Los Angeles
NIELSEN, Harry A., *Painting*
  580 Woodward Blvd., Pasadena
NIELSEN, Peter, *Painting*
  5198 Ellenwood Dr., Eagle Rock
NIGHTINGALE, Wesley, *Sculpture*
  1964 Wagner St., Pasadena
NIMMO, Louise Everett, *Painting, Sculpture*
  910 S. Lucerne Bld., Los Angeles
NIMMO, Mida E., *Bookbinding, Leathercra*
  730 Easy St., Downey
NOBLE, Miriam, *Design. Screens*
  3644 Fourteenth St., Riverside
NOLAN, H. J., *Commercial*
  224 E. 11th St., Los Angeles
NORDIN, Oscar, *Commercial*
  1121 S. Hill St., Los Angeles
NORRIS, Mary Dixon, *Painting*
  5228 Miles Ave., Oakland
NORTHRIDGE, Ed., *Commercial*
  914 Bank of America Bldg., San Diego
NORTON, Elizabeth, *Watercolors, Block prin*
  353 Lowell Ave., Palo Alto
NORTON, Helen G., *Watercolors*
  7451 Magnolia Ave., Riverside
NOTTAGE, Grace, *Teacher*
  814½ N. Ardmore St., Los Angeles
NOWELL, Dora May, *Watercolors*
  217 Clubhouse Ave., Venice
NUBILA, N. L., *Painting*
  1129 Hyperion Ave., Los Angeles
NUGENT, Frances Roberts, *Teacher*
  11207 Cashmere St., West Hollywood

O

OBATA, Chiura, *Painting*
  1875 Sutter St., San Francisco
OBNINSKY, Peter V., *Design, Cinema*
  4622 Finley Ave., Hollywood
O'BRIEN, Eugene, *Sculpture*
  334 Los Colinas Ave., Eagle Rock
O'BRIEN, Smith, *Etching*
  2032 Baker St., San Francisco
OBZINA, Martin, *Design, Decoration, Mural.*
  3731 Fredonia Dr., Hollywood
O'CONNOR, Kendall, *Commercial*
  16 Beale St., San Francisco
ODGARD, Marie R., *Teacher*
  1251 Justin Ave., Glendale
OESTERMANN, Mildred, *Painting, Etchi*
  1462 Seventh Ave., San Francisco
OGASAWARA, Kensie K., *Painting*
  221 Scott St., San Francisco
O'HAGEN, John L., *Painting*
  Hotel Vista del Arroyo, Pasadena
O'HANLON, Dick F., *Painting*
  800 Chestnut St., San Francisco
OLDFIELD, Otis, *Painting, Crafts*
  1405 Montgomery St., San Francisco
OLESEN, Julie Haskell, *Watercolors*
  Park Manor Hotel, San Diego
OLIVER, Annie, *Watercolors*
  4613 Budlong Ave., Los Angeles
OLIVER, Dorothy Welsh, *Painting*
  2511 W. 1st St., Los Angeles
OLIVER, Louise, *Watercolors*
  2672 Glendower Ave., Hollywood
OLIVER, Myron A., *Painting*
  502 Pierce St., Monterey
OLMSTEAD, J. M. D., *Painting*
  2583 Buena Vista Way, Berkeley
OLSEN, Ingvardt, *Pottery*
  2930 Baker St., San Francisco
OLSON, Elizabeth M., *Teacher*
  R. F. D., Box 38, Lodi
OLSON, George, *Painting*
  4623 Willis Ave., Van Nuys

O'MALLEY, Helen A., *Painting. Teacher*
  1135 Filbert St., San Francisco
O'NEILL, Alice, *Painting*
  45 Armanino Court, Oakland
O'NEILL, Lee, *Decoration*
  8268 Gould Ave., Los Angeles
OPDAHL, Carl, *Painting*
  2909 Madison St., Alameda
ORCUTT, Eunice, *Sculpture*
  3250 El Cajon Blvd., San Diego
ORDE, Gertrude C., *Painting*
  202 N. Ridgewood Pl., Los Angeles
ORSELLI, Alfredo, *Painting*
  200 St. Albans St., South Pasadena
ORTLIEB, Ruth Powers, *Painting*
  4162 Fourth St., San Diego
OSGOOD, Virginia N., *Painting*
  1020 Annandale Blvd., Los Angeles
O'SHAUGHNESSY, Elizabeth, *Design*
  2732 Vallejo St., San Francisco
O'SHEA, John, *Painting*
  Carmel Highlands
OSGOOD, Virginia M., *Painting*
  7220 N. Figueroa St., Los Angeles
OSTENDORF, Marguerite, *Crafts*
  1600 Grove St., Berkeley
O'SULLIVAN, Michael, *Commercial*
  Hearst Bldg., San Francisco
OTIS, George DeMont, *Painting*
  304 Avon St., Burbank
OTTE, William Louis, *Painting*
  Las Alturas Rd., Santa Barbara
OUTCALT, Adele M., *Painting*
  925 Robinson St., San Diego
OUTWATER, Ethel H., *Teacher*
  4017 Country Club Dr., Los Angeles
OVERTON, Katherine F., *Painting*
  Laguna Beach
OWEN, Adelaide, Silva, *Watercolors, Cray*
  644 Lovell Ave., Mill Valley
OWEN, Jessie, *Teacher*
  4030 Monroe St., Los Angeles
OWEN, Marie, *Teacher*
  4030 Monroe St., Los Angeles
OWENS, Charles, *Newspaper Art*
  Care The Times. 100 N. Broadway, L. A.
OWENS, E. Merrill, *Painting*
  1307 W. 56th St., Los Angeles
OWENS, Ruth Lillian, *Teacher*
  7th and Coast Highway, Carpenteria

P

PAAP, Hans, *Painting*
  923 Harvard Blvd., Los Angeles
PACKARD, J. Creighton, *Commercial*
  1512 Santee St., Los Angeles
PACKARD, Mabel, *Miniatures*
  2031 Berkshire Ave., South Pasadena
PADELFORD, Morgan C., *Painting*
  Scripps College, Claremont
PAGE, Maxine, *Watercolors*
  1321 Amherst Ave., West Los Angeles
PAHL, Amy A., *Teacher*
  1726 N. San Joaquin St., Stockton
PALIZA, Flavio, *Commercial*
  210 Central Bldg., Los Angeles
PARADISE, Phil, *Painting*
  835 E. Anapamu St., Santa Barbara
PARK, David, *Painting*
  6310 Franklin Circle, Hollywood
PARKER, Arvilla, *Watercolors*
  1350 Pine St., San Francisco
PARKER, Charles Hadden, *Painting*
  47 Mora St., Santa Cruz
PARKER, Gordena B., *Painting*
  2451 Hearst Ave., Berkeley
PARKER, Walter H., *Painting*
  6363 Hollywood Blvd., Hollywood
PARKINSON, Grace Wells, *Sculpture*
  1605 San Vicente Blvd., Santa Monica
PARMENTER, George, *Newspaper Art*
  Care The Examiner, Los Angeles
PARSHALL, DeWitt, *Painting*
  78 Hot Springs Rd., Santa Barbara
PARSHALL, Douglass, *Painting*
  Olive Hill Rd., Santa Barbara
PARSONS, Nell Williams, *Painting*
  318 Alta Ave., Whittier
PARTRIDGE, Roi, *Etching, Teacher*
  Mills College P. O., Oakland
PATIGIAN, Haig, *Sculpture*
  898 Francisco St., San Francisco
PATRI, Giacomo G., *Commercial*
  628 Montgomery St., San Francisco
PATRICK, James, *Painting*
  20 N. Harvard Blvd., Los Angeles
PATTERSON, Laurence, *Painting*
  109 Baldwin Ave., San Mateo
PATTERSON, Mary F., *Teacher*
  Univ. of California, Berkeley
PATTERSON, Patti, *Design, Costumes, Stag*
  craft, Teacher
  741 S. Grandview St., Los Angeles
PAULING, Adeline Coombs, *Teacher*
  632 Sycamore Dr., San Gabriel
PAULUS, Gertrude, *Crafts*
  9518 Grape St., Los Angeles
PAUSON, Rose, *Textiles*
  2510 Jackson St., San Francisco
PAVILIA, J. R., *Painting*
  Box 622, Monterey
PAXTON, William A., *Painting, Etching*
  955 E. Edgeware Rd., Los Angeles

PAYNE, Edgar Alwyn, *Painting*
  3006 W. 7th St., Los Angeles
PAYNE, Elsie Palmer, *Watercolors*
  621 S. Virgil St., Los Angeles
PAYNE, Robert, *Sculpture*
  1011 Tamarind Ave., Los Angeles
PAYZANT, Charles, *Watercolors*
  1507 N. Detroit St., Los Angeles
PEABODY, Ruth, *Painting*
  2160 Coast Blvd., Laguna Beach
PEACHY, Elizabeth J., *Teacher*
  129 E. Avenue 40, Los Angeles
PEACOCK, Jon, *Block Prints*
  Palos Verdes Estates
PEANO, Felix, *Sculpture in Metal*
  484 N. Hawthorne Blvd., Hawthorne.
PEARCE, Franklin, *Painting*
  371 E. 9th St., Riverside
PEARL, Sol, *Commercial*
  15 Stockton St., San Francisco
PEARSE, Franklin, *Painting*
  2509 Ninth St., Riverside
PEARSON, Helen Maye, *Painting*
  1390 Broadway, San Francisco
PEBBLES, Frank M., *Painting*
  1160 Bay St., Alameda
PECK, Frances E., *Paintign, Textiles, Craft*
  4264 Commonwealth Ave., Flintridge
PECKHAM, Mary, *Painting. Etching*
  1668 Grove St., San Francisco
PEDRETTI, Humbert, *Sculpture*
  1825 N. Alexandria St., Los Angeles
PEDRETTI, Raphael, *Painter*
  2941 S. Brighton Ave., Los Angeles
PELENC, Siméon, *Painting, Fresco*
  728 Montgomery St., San Francisco
PEMBER, Ada H., *Painting*
  24 La Vereda Rd., Santa Barbara
PENFIELD, George W., *Commercial*
  1220 Maple St., Los Angeles
PENFIELD, Katharine C., *Watercolors*
  3157 Suncrest Dr., San Diego
PENNEY, Janice Dolores, *Watercolors*
  223 N. Coronado St., Los Angeles
PENNEY, Frederic Doyle, *Painting*
  142 N. Rampart Blvd., Los Angeles
PENNY, Laura Annette, *Teacher*
  687 Islay, San Luis Obispo
PENNIMAN, Leonora Naylor, *Painting*
  317 Water St., Santa Cruz
PERCIVAL, Olive, *Painting*
  906 Hibernian Bank Bldg., Los Angeles
PERKINS, Dorris E., *Painting*
  4710 Fair Ave., Oakland
PERL, Margaret Anneke, *Painting*
  120 W. Hellman Ave., Monterey Park, L.
PERLE, Emilie, *Painting, Charcoal*
  1901 Milvia St., Berkeley
PERRINE, Edith E., *Watercolors, Block Prin*
  3608 Larchwood Ave., Riverside
PERRY, Annette, *Painting, Teacher*
  238 S. Serrano Ave., Los Angeles
PERRY, Evadna Kraus, *Teacher*
  Court House Annex, Santa Ana
PERRY, Gene E., *Commercial*
  Pacific Bldg., San Francisco
PERRY, Lotta D., *Teacher*
  3696 First Ave., San Diego
PERRY, Ollie Montgomery, *Painting*
  1416 Myrtle Ave., San Diego
PETERS, Jock D., *Design, Cinema*
  1651 Hill Dr., Eagle Rock
PETERS, Ruth, *Painting*
  6132½ Buena Vista Ter., Los Angel
PETERS, Mrs. R. D., *Crafts*
  Devore Ranch, Devore
PETERSEN, Einar, *Painting. Decoration*
  4350 Beverly Blvd., Los Angeles
PETERSON, Clarence, *Commercial*
  524 S. Spring St., Los Angeles
PETERSON, Rubye Parsons, *Teacher*
  503 S. 8th St., San Jose
PETICOLAS, Sherry, *Sculpture, Teacher*
  837 N. Lafayette Park Pl., Los Angeles
PETTIT, J., *Commercial*
  2410 S. Bronson Ave., Los Angeles
PHELAN, Alice M., *Teacher*
  350½ N. Cornell Dr., Burbank
PHELPS, Adele C., *Painting*
  519 Cedar Ave., Long Beach
PHILLIPI, Charles, *Commercial*
  2719 Hyperion Ave., Los Angeles
PHISTER, Grace A., *Painting*
  5547 Kales Ave., Oakland
PIAZZONI, Gottardo, *Painting. Murals*
  712 Montgomery St., San Francisco
PIAZZONI, Mireille, *Painting*
  446 Lake St., San Francisco
PIELKE, Rolf, *Painting*
  Carmel
PIEPENBURG, Virgil Jean, *Commercial*
  414 Latham Sq., Oakland
PIERCE, Annie, *Watercolors*
  3836 First St., San Diego
PIERCE, Lucy, *Painting, Charcoal*
  2600 Ridge Rd., Berkeley
PIERCE, W. H. C., *Watercolors*
  406 Maple St., San Diego
PIERRI, Antonio, *Painting*
  1233 N. Mansfield Ave., Los Angeles
PIERSON, Pauline, *Design*
  Carmel
PINNER, Philip, *Painting*
  2844 Fulton St., San Francisco

PIPER, Natt, *Watercolors, Crafts*
1224 Linden St., Long Beach
PLAU, Eleanor, *Teacher*
3615 Fountain Ave., Long Beach
PLETSCH, Ethel E., *Painting*
521 N. Madison Ave., Pasadena
PLUMMER, Alice G., *Teacher*
2656 Etna St., Berkeley
PLUMMER, Elmer, *Painting*
R. F. D. 1, Redlands
PODCHERNIKOFF, Alexis, *Painting*
1044 E. Green St., Pasadena
POGANY, Willy, *Design, Illustration, Cines*
1901 N. Orchid Ave., Hollywood
POLKINGHORN, George, *Painting*
2651 Kenwood Ave., Los Angeles
POLOS, Theodore, *Painting*
229 Steiner St., San Francisco
POMEROY, Elsie Lower, *Watercolors*
4456 Fourth St., Riverside
POMMER, Julius, *Painting, Etching*
2126 Pine St., San Francisco
POOLE, H. Nelson, *Painting, Etching*
728 Montgomery St., San Francisco
POORE, Shirley, *Teacher*
School Department, Long Beach
POPPE, John, *Mural Decoration*
1633 W. 70th St., Los Angeles
PORAY, Stan Pociecha, *Painting*
2509 W. 7th St., Los Angeles
PORTER, James Tank, *Sculpture*
8470 El Cajon Ave., La Mesa
PORTER, Julia S. G., *Painting*
Box 158, Escandido
PORTER, Katherine Fage, *Teacher*
2213 N. 20th St., Los Angeles
PORTER, Lenora B., *Painting*
8470 El Cajon Blvd., La Mesa
PORTER, Mildred, *Commercial*
200 Bush St., San Francisco
PORTER, Will, *Commercial*
942 Market St., San Francisco
POSSNER, Hugo A., *Commercial*
304 S. Broadway, Los Angeles
POST, George, *Painting*
839-A N. Point St., San Francisco
POST, Lou MacLean, *Painting*
839-A N. Point St., San Francisco
POTTER, Elizabeth Jo, *Commercial*
576 Sacramento St., San Francisco
POTTER, F. McRae, *Drawing, Etching*
6136 Yucca Ave., Hollywood
POTTINGER, Roy, *Painting*
951 S. Euclid Ave., Los Angeles
POWELL, Mrs. C. L., *Crafts*
1959 Taft Ave., Los Angeles
POWELL, J. S., *Drawing, Design, Teacher*
2761 Beachwood Dr., Los Angeles
POWELSON, Doris, *Teacher*
3103 Balch Ave., Los Angeles
POWERS, Lyman W., *Painting*
939 S. Broadway, Los Angeles
PRATT, Ernest M., *Photography*
45 Olvera St., Los Angeles
PRATT, Ruth, *Leathercrafts, Bookbinding*
236 E. Cole St., Downey
PRESLEY, Florence, *Drypoint*
2435 Divisadero St., San Francisco
PREON, L. W., *Teacher*
95 Lucretia Ave., San Jose
PREST, Martha, *Painting*
208 Breeze Ave., Venice
PRESTON, Alice Hulick, *Painting*
2542 Front St., San Diego
PRICE, Lida S., *Painting*
1323 14th St., Los Angeles
PRICE, William Henry, *Painting*
1835 E. Mountain St., Pasadena
PRIGER, Nelita Hain, *Crafts, Teacher*
2131 3rd Ave., Los Angeles
PRIOR, Ruby Adair, *Painting*
Box 238, Belmont
PROBST, Thorwald, *Painting*
3445 W. 1st St., Los Angeles
PRUNIER, Arthur H., *Posters*
2328 Miramar St., Los Angeles
PUCCINELLI, Dorothy Wagner, *Painting, Pencil*
2506-A Leavenworth St., San Francisco
PUCCINELLI, Raymond W., *Sculpture*
2506-A Leavenworth St., San Francisco
PULSIFER, Mina Schutz, *Painting*
4166 Rochester Rd., San Diego
PURCELL, Joseph, *Design, Ceramics*
2501 Vista Laguna Ter., Pasadena
PURDY, Evelyn G., *China Painting*
1011 N. Harvard Ave., Fullerton
PURRIER, Evelyn Mondon, *Watercolors*
3937 Eighth St., Riverside
PURRINGTON, Lillian R., *Painting*
Santa Cruz
PURVIANCE, John David, *Painting*
2310 Farriel Ave., Westwood Hills, L. A. Angeles
PUTHUFF, Hanson, *Painting*
744 E. Alturas Ave., La Crescenta
PUTNAM, Arion, *Photography*
1935 Hill Dr., Eagle Rock
PUTNAM, Claude G., *Illustration, Commercial*
403 S. Hill St., Los Angeles
PUTNAM, Rose, *Painting*
1935 Hill Dr., Eagle Rock

Q

QUIGLEY, Helen, *Commercial*
346 S. Clay St., Los Angeles
QUINAN, Corinne, *Weaving*
2512 Washington St., San Francisco

R

RABINO, S., *Painting*
4029 Market St., Riverside
RAMBEAU, Gail, *Commercial*
576 Sacramento St., San Francisco
RAMBEAU, J. C., *Commercial*
1121 S. Hill St., Los Angeles
RANDALL, Daisy F., *Bookbinding, Leather*
20260 Sherman Way, Canoga Park
RAMON, A. A., *Etching*
6070 Hayes Ave., Los Angeles
RANDALL, Margaret L., *Commercial*
320 Market St., San Francisco
RANDOLPH, Lee, *Painting, Teacher*
Calif. School of Fine Arts, San Francisco
RAPP, George, *Commercial*
1021 S. Main St., Los Angeles
RAPFAPORT, Dario, *Painting*
8568 Lookout Mt. Dr., Hollywood
RASCHE, Herbert, *Commercial*
1512 Santee St., Los Angeles
RASMUSSEN, Just, *Painting*
2009 Shattuck Ave., Berkeley
RAULSTON, Marian Churchill, *Painting, P*
200 S. Hudson Ave., Los Angeles   tru
RAUSCHNABEL, W. F., *Commercial*
544 Market St., San Francisco
RAUSCHWALD, M. B., *Commercial*
1512 Santee St., Los Angeles
RAYMOND, Julie E., *Watercolors*
Laguna Beach
RAYNOR, Lois, *Leathercrafts, Bookbinding*
3859 Tracy St., Los Angeles
RAZELLE, Tess, *Sculpture*
1942 14th St., Santa Monica
RECKLESS, Stanley Z., *Painting, Teacher*
2416 Loma Vista Pl., Los Angeles
REDDICK, Ruth Dresslar, *Teacher*
825 Ojai Rd., Santa Paula
REDMOND, Granville, *Painting*
1515 W. 8th St., Los Angeles
REED, Charlotte, *Teacher*
540 East D St., Ontario
REEDER, Emelyn, *Teacher*
6409 Rita Ae., Huntington Park
REEDER, W. H., *Bookbinding, Leathercraft*
4031 Kansas Ave., Los Angeles
REES, Frances Truman, *Painting*
5130 Ellenwood Dr., Eagle Rock
REESE, Ada L. E., *Painting*
1533 Reid St., Los Angeles
REEVES, George, *Woodcarving*
8735 Melrose Ave., Los Angeles
REEVES, Joseph Mason, Jr., *Painting, P*
2008 W. 7th St., Los Angeles   tru
REGNAS, A. E., *Commercial*
930 Chapman Bldg., Los Angeles
REID, Aurelia Wheeler, *Miniatures*
252 W. 11th St., San Pedro
REID, Eloise, *Painting*
1908 Delaware St., Berkeley
REID, Velma, *Teacher*
1338 Woodruff St., Los Angeles
REIFFEL, Charles, *Painting*
5302 Orange Ave., San Diego
REIMERS, Marie A., *Painting*
2617 Rose St., Berkeley
REINHARD, Lulu M., *Commercial*
1521 S Harvard Blvd., Los Angeles
REINHART, Mrs. E. T., *Painting*
4262 Alta Mirano Way, San Diego
REITERMAN, Ethel, *Teacher*
216 N. Coronado St., Los Angeles
REMFREE, I. F., *Painting*
4768 Reno Dr., San Diego
RENDON, Ignatius, *Painting*
5036 E. Florence Ave., Bell
RENICK, Claribel H., *Painting*
817½ N. Coronado St., Los Angeles
RENNER, Katherine, *Commercial*
629 S. Hill St., Los Angeles
RENO, Louis H., *Commercial*
524 S. Spring St., Los Angeles
RENWICK, Julien, *Bookbinding, Leathercra*
315 N. Doheny Dr., Beverly Hills
REVALEON, Albert La Martine, *Painting*
2242 Larkin St., San Francisco
REXROTH, Andrée, *Paint ing*
1106 Gough St., San Francisco
REYNOLDS, Helen Baker, *Copper, Enamels*
154 Yerba Buena Ave., San Francisco
RHINE, Leora B., *Bookbinding, Leathercraf*
23 Owen Ave., Arcadia
RICE, Ann, *Painting*
1261 Lombard St., San Francisco
RICE, Maude A., *Painting*
4215 Stephens St., San Diego
RICE, William S., *Woodcuts in color*
2083 Rosedale Ave., Oakland
RICH, John Hubbard, *Painting, Portraits*
2262 San Marco Dr., Los Angeles
RICHARDS, Mabel C., *Teacher*
852 Monterey Rd., South Pasadena
RICHARDSON, Alice, *Teacher*
4081 Chestnut St., Riverside

RICHARDSON, Roberta, *Painting*
4799 Bandini Ave., Riverside
RICHMOND, Evelyn K., *Watercolors*
2025 Plaza Bonita, Santa Barbara
RICHTER, Catherine M., *Crafts*
2134 Olive Ave., Long Beach
RICHTER, Henry R., *Painting*
2134 Olive Ave., Long Beach
RIDEOUT, William E., *Painting*
617 Boulevard Way, Oakland
RIDER, Charles Joseph, *Watercolors*
Newport Beach
RIDDELL, William W., *Painting*
Laguna Beach
RIDDER, Caroline, *Weaving*
60 Atlantic Ave., Long Beach
RIEDIGER, George A., *Commercial*
124 W. 4th St., Los Angeles
RIEGELMAIER, C., *Sculpture*
726 W. 27th St., Los Angeles
RILLIET, Vivian Faure, *Teacher*
786 N. 9th St., Colton
RINEHART, Florence, *Teacher*
2800 Regent St., Berkeley
RING, Alice Blair, *Miniatures*
225 E. Pasadena St., Pomona
RINNE, Leah J., *Painting*
1810 Addison St., Berkeley
RIPLEY, Thomas E., *Painting*
Mission Canyon Rd., Santa Barbara
RISLING, Edloe J, *Painting, Commercial*
2515 Octavia St., San Francisco
RITSCHEL, William, *Painting*
Carmel Highlands
RITTENHOUSE, Jean, *Pastels, Drawing*
5000 Voltaire, Ocean Beach
ROAN-HORSE, Ralph, *Painting*
Care Otis Art Institute,
2401 Wilshire Blvd., Los Angeles
ROBBINS, Thea, *Painting*
185 S. Virgil St., Los Angeles
ROBERTS, Frances, *Painting, Pottery*
4472 Hortensia St., San Diego
ROBERTS, John E., *Commercial*
404 Braun Bldg., Los Angeles
ROBERTS, Josephine Seaman, *Watercolo*
2341 Scarff St., Los Angeles
ROBERTS, Ruth Goodwin, *Bookbinding,*
319 Date St., Brea
ROBERTSON, Eilen, *Teacher*
8632 Wonderland Ave, Laurel Canyon, L.
ROBERTSON, Fred H., *Pottery*
1700 Grandview St., Glendale
ROBERTSON, Maude, *Painting*
Laguna Beach
ROBERTSON, Stewart, *Portraits, Etching*
837 N. Lafayette Park Pl., Los Angeles
ROBINSON, Ione, *Painting*
133 N. Reno St., Los Angeles
ROBINSON, Irene Bowen, *Painting*
2310 S. Palm Grove Ave., Los Angeles
ROBINSON, P. B., *Commercial*
222 E. 4th St., Los Angeles
ROBISON, Ann, *Painting*
6253 Warner Dr., Los Angeles
ROCHARD, Pierre, *Painting*
647 St. Paul Ave., Los Angeles
ROCHE, John D., *Commercial*
739 So Hope St., Los Angeles
ROCKWOOD, Paul, *Commercial*
535 Sacramento St., San Francisco
ROCLE, Margaret King, *Painting*
899 Fourth Ave., Chula Vista
ROCLE, Marius R., *Painting*
899 Fourth St, Chula Vista
RODMAN, Leah Helen, *Painting*
1308 N. Vista St., Los Angeles
RODMAN, Lillian M., *Painting*
1233 Lodi Pl., Hollywood
RODMAN, Peter, *Painting*
2201 Ocean View Ave., Los Angeles
ROGERS, Julia, *Painting*
1678 Broadway, San Francisco
ROGERS, Louis J., *Illustration, Etching*
1045 Sansome St., San Francisco
ROGERS, Margaret, *Painting*
Box 122, Seabright
ROHRBOUGH, Herbert L., *Painting*
733 Pacific Ave., Long Beach
ROLLIN, Gerome, *Painting*
866 Green St., San Francisco
ROMANELLI, Carlo, *Sculpture*
970 N. Hoover St., Los Angeles
ROMER, Paul, *Painting*
Care Calif. Ins. Co., 315 Montgomery S.
San Francisco
RONCHI, Ottorino D., *Cariature*
2621 Divisadero St., San Francsico
RORABECK, Edson, *Commercial*
404 F W. Braun Bldg., Los Angeles
ROSE, Bert Miles, *Painting*
Santa Cruz
ROSE, Ethel, *Painting*
676 La Loma Rd., Pasadena
ROSENHAUSE, Beatrice C., *Sculpture*
1218 N. Mansfield Ave., Los Angeles
ROSENSHINE, Annette, *Sculpture*
131 Lyon St., San Francisco
ROSENTHAL, Mildred G., *Painting, Prints*
76 Sixth Ave., San Francisco
ROSHER, Frederick Woods, *Painting*
36 Ventura Ave., San Francisco
ROSS, Leighton, *Painting*
Box 769, San Jose
ROSS, Orrin C., *Commercial*
766 Pacific Bldg, San Francisco

ROSSART, Michael, *Painting*
352 S. Hill St., Los Angeles
ROTH, Edward A., *Painting*
222 N. Ave. 52, Los Angeles
ROUDEBUSH, Harriet W., *Painting, Etching*
273 Green St., San Francisco
ROUSE, Charles G., *Copper Craft*
Mt. Rubidoux, Riverside
ROUSE, S. Estelle, *Woodcarving, Metal*
Mt. Rubidoux, Riverside
ROWLAND, W. Earl, *Painting, Block Prints*
3448 Gardenside Lane, Los Angeles
ROWLANDS, Marvellen, *Teacher*
11 Pala Ave., Piedmont
RUDESILL, Betty, *Bookbinding, Leathercraft*
836 W. Huntington Dr., Arcadia
RUEGG, Verena, *Painting, Lithographs*
7733 Hampton St., Los Angeles
RUGAR, Jennie S., *Teacher*
716 Beacon Ave., Los Angeles
RUSK, Henry, *Crafts*
1356½ Tenth Ave., San Francisco
RUSSELL, Adele, *Painting*
3601 Cerritos Aev., Long Beach
RUSSELL, Bruce, *Newspaper Art*
Care The Times, 100 N. Broadway, L. A.
RUSSELL, E. B., *Painting*
Box 535, Station C, Los Angeles
RUTH, Clara L., *Painting*
3560 28th St., San Diego
RYAN, Helen M., *Teacher*
Hotel Glenmore, Compton
RYAN, Mrs. J. P., *Painting*
315 Hawes Ave., Fresno
RYDER, Worth, *Painting, Teacher*
2772 Hilgard Ave., Berkeley
RYNERSON, Beulah H., *Painting*
4088 First Ave., San Diego

S

SACHS, Herman, *Painting*
1811 Edgecliff Dr., Los Angeles
SACKMAN, Marie, *Watercolors, Drawing, Pr*
2454 Evergreen St., San Diego
SALMI, Hazel Gowan, *Painting, Sculpture*
1009 Barrett Ave., Richmond
SALVESON, Alpha Knox, *Teacher*
Box 36, R. D. 3, Anaheim
SALZ, Helen Arnstein, *Pastels*
3838 Clay St., San Francisco
SAMMONS, Carl, *Pastels*
2634 Peralta Ave., Oakland
SAMPLE, Leslie, *Ceramics*
1432 N. Foothill Blvd., Pasadena
SAMPLE, Paul Starrett, *Painting, Teacher*
676 La Loma Rd., Pasadena
SANDERS, Margaret, *Teacher*
1534 S. Wilton Pl., Los Angeles
SANDERS, Spencer E., *Watercolors*
3931 Boyle Ave., Los Angeles
SANDONA, Matteo, *Painting, Portraits*
471 Buena Vista Ave., San Francisco
SANDS, Gertrude, *Painting*
1521 Euclid Ave., Berkeley
SARGEANT, Geneve Rixford, *Painting, Water colors, Pastels, Lithographs*
628 Montgomery St., San Francisco
SARGEANT, Sidney F., *Painting*
2442 Piedmont Ave., Berkeley
SAUTER, Mary C., *Block Prints*
921 A Ave., Coronado
SAWYER, Ken, *Commercial*
163 Sutter St., San Francisco
SAYERS, C. M., *Woodcarving*
Carmel
SAYRE, F. Grayson, *Painting*
1150 N. Louise St., Glendale
SAZEVICH, Sigismund, *Sculpture*
1338-A Filbert St., San Francisco
SCAMMON, L. N., *Etching*
1892 Tiffin Rd., Oakland
SCARPITTA, S Cartaino, *Sculpture*
2684 N. Beachwood Dr., Los Angeles
SCHAEFER, Frank R., *Painting*
560 S. Main St., Los Angeles
SCHAEFFER, Rudolph, *Design, Color, Teac*
136 St. Anne St., San Francisco
SCHAIBLE, F. J., *Sculpture*
Box 1331, Station C, Los Angeles
SCHARY, Harry, *Painting*
624 Mariposa, Oakland
SCHECK, Helen N., *Crafts, Teacher*
2080 N. Vine St., Los Angeles
SCHEM, Henrietta, *Crafts*
1415 West Blvd., Los Angeles
SCHERBAKOFF, Sergev, *Painting*
1421 Hyde St., San Francisco
SCHEUER, Suzanne, *Painting*
1312 California St., San Francisco
SCHEVILL, Margaret Erwin, *Watercolors, Des*
77 Tamalpais Rd., Berkeley
SCHLESINGER, Alfred, *Teacher*
1669 W. 57th St., Los Angeles
SCHLOAT, G. Warren, *Painting*
1291 S. Highland Ave., Los Angeles
SCHMIDT, Elmer G., *Painting*
2521 Durant Ave., Berkeley
SCHMITT, Paul A., *Painting, Commercial*
1968 Thirty-sixth Ave., Oakland
SCHNEIDER, Esther, *Painting*
2981 Eighth St., Riverside
SCHNEIDER, Gertrude, *Watercolors*
943 Arapahoe St., Los Angeles

SCHNEIDER, Otto H., *Painting*
Ocean Beach
SCHNEIDER, Rose, *Painting*
3966 Falcon St., San Diego
SCHNIER, Jacques, *Sculpture, Woodcarving*
20 Jessop Pl., San Francisco
SCHOEPPE, Harry A., *Metal Craft, Jewelry*
599 Eldora Rd., Pasadena
SCHOLL, Edward, *Painting*
P. O. Box 1433, Hollywood
SCHREIBER, George L., *Painting*
230 Twenty-first Pl., Santa Monica
SCHROTH, Dorothy L., *Painting, Textiles*
725 Laguna Honda Blvd., San Francisco
SCHULTZ, Isabelle, *Sculpture, Prints, Batik*
312 Gravilla, La Jolla
SCHUSTER, Donna, *Painting*
2672 Glendower Ave., Los Angeles
SCHWANKOVSKY, Frederick J., *Teacher*
1231 W. 76th St., Los Angeles
SCOTT, Clyde, *Painting, Commercial*
574 Market St., San Francisco
SCOTT, Katherine, *Painting*
125 Nevada St., Long Beach
SCOTT, LeHilton, *Painting*
3012 Courtland Dr., Oakland
SCOTT, M., *Painting*
1615 Joaquin Miller Rd., Oakland
SCOTT, Marie, *Watercolors*
970 W. 105th St., Los Angeles
SCOTT, Walter G., *Painting*
3012 Courtland Dr., Oakland
SCUDDER, Alice R., *Painting*
508 La Loma Rd., Pasadena
SEABURY, Roxoli, *Painting*
1905 Laguna St., San Francisco
SEARS, Marylee, *Painting*
427 Presidio Ave., San Francisco
SEAWELL, Henry W., *Painting*
1617 California St., San Francisco
SEEBOLD, James G., *Jewelry*
F. O. Box 411, National City
SEELY, Walter F., *Painting*
8804 Sunset Blvd., Los Angeles
SEIDENECK, Catherine, *Painting, Crafts*
Carmel
SEIDENECK, George, *Painting*
Carmel
SELLON, Edward L., *Commercial*
544 Market St., San Francisco
SEWELL, Elizabeth, *Teacher*
136 E. Main St., Compton
SEXTON, Fred, *Painting*
408 S. Hope St., Los Angeles
SEYARTO, Judith C., *Painting*
3826 S. Hope St., Los Angeles
SEYDLITZ, Paul, *Painting*
1926 Kane Ave., Los Angeles
SEYMOUR, Celia B., *Painting*
333 Adams St., Oakland
SHAPER, Helen E., *Teacher*
Box 22, Rialto
SHARPLESS, Ada May, *Sculpture*
1142½ N. Seward St., Los Angeles
SHATTUCK, Ross, *Painting*
2320 Highland Ave., Hollywood
SHAWL, Louis, *Commercial*
544 Market St., San Francisco
SHEETS, Lurline E., *Teacher*
Box 194, Hanford
SHEETS, Millard, *Painting, Etching, Drawin*
2509 W. 7th St., Los Angeles
SHEPARD, Marguerite, *Painting*
Mills College, Mills College P. O.
SHERIDAN, Joseph, *Painting*
2419 Haste St., Berkeley
SHERMAN, Elizabeth E., *Painting*
708 A Ave., Coronado
SHERMAN, Emily, *Teacher*
Alameda
SHERMAN, Mrs. Gerry, *Bookbinding, Leath*
Route 1, Box 723, La Canada
SHERRIFF, George, *Painting*
230 N. El Molino Ave., Pasadena
SHERWOOD, F. P., *Watercolors*
Box 571, La Jolla
SHERWOOD, Lionel C., *Painting*
2317 Hickory St., San Diego
SHIELDS, Irion, *Painting*
3421 Polk Ave., San Diego
SHIELDS, Phyllis, *Painting*
3967 S. Hill St., Los Angeles
SHIMIZU, Mitsuzo, *Painting*
1631 A Post St., San Francisco
SHIRELY, Dorothy E., *Painting*
4607 E. Talmage Dr., San Diego
SHISLER, Clare Shepard, *Miniatures*
581 Mountain View St., Pasadena
SHIVELY, Douglas, *Painting*
106 S. Hill St., Santa Paula
SHORE, Henrietta M., *Painting, Lithographs*
Box 1884, Carmel
SHOUP, Agnes, *Teacher*
7135 Seville St., Huntington Park
SHROPSHIRE, Eileen, *Teacher*
1041 Eighteenth St., Santa Monica
SHOVEN, Hazel Brayton, *Painting*
2151 W. California St., San Diego
SHRADER, E. Roscoe, *Painting, Teacher*
4300 Oakwood Ave., La Canada
SHREVE, Catherine Shock, *Painting, Prints*
501 W. Lorraine St., Glendale
SHRIVER, George, *Painting, Portraits*
230 Twenty-first Pl., Los Angeles

SHULER, Herbert, *Watercolors*
5548 Elmer St., North Hollywood
SHUMADA, H., *Painting*
429 N. Westmoreland Ave., Los Angeles
SHUMAN, Ray, *Newspaper Art*
Care The Examiner, Los Angeles
SIBONI, Emma, *Miniatures*
1115 Maple St., South Pasadena
SIDES, Dorothy Smith, *Miniatures, Wood-carving*
4554 Beatty Dr., Riverside
SIEBE, Viola B., *Teacher*
424 Lyons Ave., Turlock
SIEMER, Chris, *Painting*
1166 S. Hill St., Los Angeles
SIEVWRIGHT, Carol, *Design, Decoration*
309 S. Coronado St., Los Angeles
SILSBEE, Bertha W., *Sculpture*
3019 Ibsen St., San Diego
SILSBY, Wilson, *Etching*
1748 N. Sycamore Ave., Hollywood
SILVA, Roberto, *Painting, Design, Commercia*
3142 S. Catalina St., Los Angeles
SILVA, William P., *Painting*
Carmel
SILVERTON, Bessie, *Painting*
Route 1, Box 28, Perris
SILVIUS, Paul T., *Painting*
2925 S. Hobart Blvd., Los Angeles
SIMMONS, Martha, *Etching*
49 San Rafael Ave., Pasadena
SIMMONS, Nell, *Painting*
1160 Page St., San Francisco
SIMON, Howard, *Painting, Woodcuts*
722 Montgomery St., San Francisco
SIMON, Natalie, *Commercial*
259 Geary St., San Francisco
SIMONS, Amory C., *Sculpture*
115 W. Anapamu St., Santa Barbara
SIMPSON, Charlotte A., *Teacher*
San Jose
SIMPSON, Ethel May, *Teacher*
1020 Avon Pl., South Pasadena
SIMPSON, Marian, *Painting, Graphic Arts*
976 Miller Ave., Berkeley
SIMS, John Morgan, *Commercial*
163 Sutter St., San Francisco
SINCLAIR, Irving, *Commercial*
125 Hyde St., San Francisco
SINDELAER, Charles, *Painting, Etching*
6200 Fountain Ave., Los Angeles
SISKA, Piko, *Painting, Decorative Illu ratio*
8014 Lewis Ter., Laurel Canyon, Los Angele
SISSON, Jane Giguette, *Teacher*
545 S Euclid Ave., Pasadena
SKEELE, A. Katharine, *Painting*
225 Monroe Pl., Monrovia
SKINNER, Charlotte, *Painting*
Lone Pine, Inyo County
SKINNER, Harold R., *Commercial*
2536 Clay St., San Francisco
SKINNER, William Lyle, *Painting*
Lone Pine, Inyo County
SKLAR, Dorothy, *Costume Design, Stagecraft*
1075 S. Plymouth Blvd., Los Angeles
SLANY, Paul P., *Sculpture*
2750 W. Marengo St., Altadena
SLATE, Marjorie, *Weaving*
303 B Filbert St., San Francsico
SLOAN, Blanding, *Painting, Prints, Wood-carving*
1605 N. Ivar St., Hollywood
SMALL, Margaret, *Watercolors*
4831 Rubidoux Ave., Riverside
SMART, E. Hodeson, *Painting, Portraits*
3305 Wilshire Blvd., Los Angeles
SMERALDI, John B., *Mural Painter and Decorator*
470 Blake St., Pasadena
SMITH, Mrs. A. B., *Crafts*
227 S. Lucerne Blvd., Los Angeles
SMITH, Beryl Kirk, *Painting, Teacher*
500 Central Bldg., Los Angeles
SMITH, Charles L. A., *Painting*
185 S Virgil St., Los Angeles
SMITH, Cora A., *Painting, Monotypes*
4119 Voltaire Ave., Ocean Beach
SMITH, Crea, *Commercial*
1521 Valencia St., San Francisco
SMITH, Doris Rose, *Teacher*
219 N. Soto St., Los Angeles
SMITH, Elizabeth Hay, *Painting, Drawing*
1355 Willard St., San Francisco
SMITH, Ernest Browning, *Painting*
2146 Loma Vista Pl., Los Angeles
SMITH, F. Carl, *Painting*
217 S. Oakland Ave., Pasadena
SMITH, Gordon E., *Commercial*
55 New Montgomery St., San Francisco
SMITH, H. Wilson, *Commercial*
1003 Roosevelt Ave., Richmond
SMITH, Hilda K., *Painting, Black and Whi*
309 North St., Sausalito
SMITH, Jack Wilkinson, *Painting*
16 Champion Pl., Alhambra
SMITH, Jessie Sherwood, *Crafts, Teacher*
523 S. Coronado St., Los Angeles
SMITH, John Christopher, *Painting*
1142 Kipling Ave., Eagle Rock
SMITH, L. Laurette, *Teacher*
Fillmore
SMITH, Lillian May, *Teacher*
1923 Micheltorena St., Los Angeles
SMITH, Madeline, *Teacher*
616 W. 6th St., Burbank
SMITH, Margaret D., *Pottery, Weaving*
2832 El Cajon Ave., San Diego

SMITH, Mary Vaughan, *Bookbinding, Leath-*
crafts, Teacher
1624 Huntington Dr., South Pasadena
SMITH, Maurice, *Commercial*
1121 So. Hill St., Los Angeles
SMITH, Miriam, *Painting, Pastels*
1417 Park Row, La Jolla
SMITH, N. Lincoln, *Painting*
523 Soleman Ave., Los Angeles
SMITH, Queen M., *Teacher*
Inglewood
SNYDER, Robert W., *Painting*
3634 Third St., San Diego
SODERSTROM, Clare E., *Painting*
1034 Seeley Ave., West Los Angeles
SOLER, Urbici, *Sculpture*
1351 Sutter St., San Francisco
SOMERBURY, L. E., *Painting*
643 Berger Ave., Belvedere Gardens, L. A.
SOMERVILLE, Marbury, *Etching*
539 S. Mariposa St., Los Angeles
SONDAG, Alphonse, *Painting*
417 Montgomery St., San Francisco
SONNESCHEIN, Lillian D., *Teacher*
1605 Tenth Ave., Oakland
SOOY, Louise Pinckney, *Teacher*
10737 Ashton Ave., Westwood Village, L.
SOPER, J. H. Gardner, *Painting, Portraits*
251 S. Mariposa St., Los Angeles
SORENSON, Katherine, *Painting*
325 Sorenson Ave., Whittier
SOSIN, Dorothy Sharpe, *Painting*
1630½ Cicero Dr., Los Angeles
SOTO, Silvano, *Painting*
3458 E. 3rd St., Los Angeles
SOTOMAYOR, Antonio, *Painting, Drawing*
2682 Union St., San Francisco
SOUTHWICK, Betty, *Painting*
4960 Glacier Dr., Eagle Rock
SOUTHWICK, Harriet, *Teacher*
5209 Benton Way, San Diego
SOWERS, Pauline B. S., *Painting, Etching*
495 Maylin St., Pasadena
SPALDING, James M., *Painting*
1810 Foothill St., South Pasadena
SPALTEHOLZ, Charlotte, *Teacher*
Washington School, Stockton
SPARKS, Will, *Painting*
163 Sutter St., San Francisco
SPAULDING, Cora Alice, *Painting*
1117 Douglas St., Los Angeles
SPAULDING, John Calvin, *Stained Glass*
552 S. Gramercy Pl., Los Angeles
SPENCER, Doris, *Teacher*
4844 Briggs Ave., La Crescenta
SPENCER, Jeannette Dyer, *Painting, Design*
Furniture, Stained Glass
960 Chestnut St., San Francisco
SPERRY, W. A., Jr., *Commercial*
709 Mission St., San Francisco
SPIESS, Florence Louise, *Teacher*
812½ Heber St., Calexico
SPOHN, Clay, *Painting*
2171 Pacific Ave., San Francisco
SPOTTS, Nell, *Commercial*
617 Montgomery St., San Francisco
SPRATT, Alberte, *Painting, Lithographs*
4523 Prospect Ave., Los Angeles
SPRINGSTEEN, Annette Joy, *Teacher*
3837 Woodruff, Oakland
SQUIRES, Warren L., *Painting*
3945 Beechwood Ave., Riverside
SRESOVICH, Joe, *Commercial*
1676 W. 12th St., Los Angeles
STACKPOLE, Adele, *Textiles*
16 Taurus Pl., Oakland
STACKPOLE, Ralph, *Sculpture*
27 Jessop Pl., San Francisco
STAFFORD, Katherine June, *Sculpture*
New Mexico Bldg., Balboa Park, San Diego
STAHL, Edith Osborne, *Painting*
5265 W. College Ave., Eagle Rock, L. A.
STAHMER, Ella, *Crafts, Teacher*
722 S. Lake St., Los Angeles
STANHOPE, William A., *Painting*
2859 Sunset Pl., Los Angeles
STANIFORD, Roy, *Commercial*
580 Market St., San Francisco
STANLEY, George M., *Sculpture*
2970 London St., Los Angeles
STANLEY, Rosamunde, *Watercolors*
Art Dept., Univ. of California, Berkeley
STANTON, Jess, *Watercolors, Sculpture*
Care Gladding, McBean & Co.,
2901 Los Feliz Blvd., Los Angeles
STARR, Judson L., *Block Prints, Commerc.*
726 Thirty-fourth Ave., San Francisco
STEARNS, Marion Booth, *Painting*
943 Maltman Ave., Los Angeles
STEBBINS, Mary Emma Flood, *Painting*
1940 Vallejo St., San Francisco
STEELE, Gile McLaury, *Painting*
619 S. Windsor Blvd., Los Angeles
STEERE, Lora Woodhead, *Sculpture*
2814 Glendower Ave., Hollywood
STEFFES, Ann McDonald, *Painting*
1795 Titus St., San Diego
STEINBRUNN, Hermann, *Metal Crafts*
1386 College Ave., Palo Alto
STEINER, Rose, *Painting*
8842 Rosewood Ave., West Hollywood
STELLMAN, Edith K., *Painting*
535 Sacramento St., San Francisco
STENBERG, W. T., *Painting*
2578 E. 27th St., Oakland

STEPHENS, Richard, *Commercial*
521 Grant Ave., San Francisco
STEPHENS, Walter H., *Painting*
804 Fell St., San Francisco
STEPHENSON, Madge E., *Teacher*
609 W. Doran St., Glendale
STEPHENSON, Sara Stark, *Crafts*
4305 S. Harvard Blvd., Los Angeles
STEPHY, Eva, *Painting*
1532 N. Ave. 56, Los Angeles
STERN, Alexander, *Commercial*
Chronicle Bldg., San Francisco
STERNER, Robert, *Fashion Illustration,*
742 S. Grandview St., *Commercial, Teach.*
Los Angeles
STERRETT, Roger John, *Teacher*
4612 Welch Pl., Los Angeles
STETSON, Katherine Beecher, *Sculpture*
223 S. Catalina Ave., Pasadena
STEVICK, Richenda, *Sculptor*
1335 Hearst Ave., Berkeley
STEWART, D. McLaren, *Painting*
628 Montgomery St., San Francisco
STEWART, Francis, *Watercolors*
3601 E. 59th Pl., Los Angeles
STEWART, Lawrence O., *Painting*
Box 126, Santa Monica
STIBOLT, Louisa, *Watercolors*
2880 Grape St., San Diego
STICH, Harry J., *Stained Glass*
7420 S. Broadway, Los Angeles
STIFFLER, Eugenie Pack, *Portrait,*
1124 Orange St., Redlands *Miniatu.*
STILSON, Jeannette E., *Crafts*
1724 Hillside Dr., Glendale
STIMSON, Thomas E., *Ceramics*
10555 Holman Ave., Los Angeles
STIVERS, Howard, *Commercial*
138 4th St., San Francisco
STOCKFLETH, Lucy Gray, *Painting*
159 Garfield St., Santa Cruz
STOCKTON, Marion Brown, *Teacher*
919 Gaffey St., San Pedro
STODDARD, Gayne, *Painting*
1532 N. Detroit St., Hollywood
STOJANA, Gjura, *Painting, Wood Sculpture*
3501 Dahlia Ave., Los Angeles
STOKES, Robert George, *Teacher*
1261 S. Central Ave., Glendale
STOLL, John T. E., *Etching, Commercial*
1310 Montgomery St., San Francisco
STONE, Anna B., *Watercolors*
5607 La Mirada Ave., Los Angeles
STONE, Frank F., *Sculpture*
1033 S. Bonnie Brae St., Los Angeles
STONE, Mimi, *Pastels, Etching*
1831 Balboa St., San Francisco
STONER, John L., *Painting*
Box 6, Point Loma
STONER, Betty S., *Painting*
Box 6, Point Loma
STORM, Cecil E., *Commercial*
122 E. 7th St., Los Angeles
STOTON, E. W. A. B., *Watercolors*
2619 Niagara Ave., Ocean Beach
STOVER, Allan, *Painting*
1141 Kipling Ave., Eagle Rock, Los Ange.
STOVER, Adele T. Closs, *Painting*
486 Funston Ave., San Francisco
STOY, Anna, *Painting*
2305 Scott St., San Francisco
STRAIN, G. Willis, *Drawing*
810 S. Spring St., Los Angeles
STRATTON, Zelma, *Commercial*
1019 Bankers Bldg., Los Angeles
STRINGFIELD, Vivian F., *Painter, Teacher*
229 S. Normandie Ave., Los Angeles
STROBEL, Oscar, *Painting*
1306 N. Harper Ave., Los Angeles
STROM, William, *Painting*
P. O. Box 122, Point Loma
STRONG, Elizabeth, *Painting*
Carmel
STRUCK, Herman, *Painting*
191 Ralston St., San Francisco
STRUSS, Karl, *Photography, Cinema*
1343 N. Orange Grove Ave., Hollywood
STUBER, Dana, *Painting*
2672 Glendower Ave., Hollywood
STUBER, Dedrick Brandes, *Painting*
2216 Kelton Ave., Los Angeles
STUBERGH, Katherine, *Sculpture*
1805 Hill Dr., Eagle Rock
STUMP, John, *Painting*
100 Harrison St., Sausalito
STURGEON, Ruth B., *Crafts, Teacher*
5411 Newtonia Dr., Los Angeles
STURTEVANT, Roger, *Photography*
730 Montgomery St., San Francisco
STURTEVANT, Mrs. L. V., *Teacher*
1442 Scott Ave., Los Angeles
STRYKER, Cecile F., *Crafts*
4549 Lincoln Ave., Oakland
SULLIVAN, Mary O., *Teacher*
Hotel Pasadena, Pasadena
SUMAN, A. L., *Commercial*
815 So. Hill St., Los Angeles
SUMERLIN, Mabel, *Painting*
4011 Ingalls St., San Diego
SUTTER, Joseph, *Woodcarving*
3338 W. 10th St., Los Angeles
SUTTER, Samuel, *Painting*
433 Waller St., San Francisco
SUZUKI, Sakari, *Painting*
1875 Sutter St., San Francisco

SWAN, Katharine, *Painting*
802 Montgomery St., San Francisco
SWANSEE, Hans, *Sculpture, Woodcarving*
1320 Oak Grove Dr., Eagle Rock
SYMMONDS, Albert, *Watercolors*
Fullerton
SWARTZ, Harold, *Sculpture*
3827 Ronda Vista Pl., Los Angeles
SWEENEY, Dan C., *Painting*
510 Montgomery St., San Francisco
SWEET, Gertrude M., *Teacher*
1426 S. Maple St., Los Angeles
SWEET, Ralph, *Etching*
Woodland Clinic, Woodland
SWIFT, Florence Alston, *Painting*
148 Tunnel Rd., Berkeley
SWINDELLE, J. L., *Commercial*
374 Brannan St., San Francisco
SWINNERTON, James G., *Painting*
Box 125, Palo Alto
SYPE, Ioma B., *Commercial*
7155 Hope St., Los Angeles
SYSOL, Geneva A., *Painting, Crafts*
404 Locust Ave., Long Beach
SZUKALSKI, Stanislaw, *Sculpture, Drawing*
2530 Outpost Dr., Hollywood

T

TAGGART, Richard, *Painting*
2516 N. El Molino Ave., Altadena
TAKEDA, Shiro, *Painting*
15 Darrell Pl., San Francisco
TALBERT, Zel E., *Miniatures*
600 Columbia Bldg., Los Angeles
TALBOT, Esther, *Teacher*
1078 Brace St., San Jose
TALBOT, Harriet A., *Painting*
3104 Freeman St., Loma Portal
TALBOT, Hattie C., *Painting*
442 El Camino Dr., Beverly Hills
TALIAFERRO, Lucene Goodenow, *Ivory Carv.*
802 Willow Glen Rd., Los Angeles
TAMBURINI, A. C., *Painting*
377 Arroyo Terrace, Pasadena
TANAKA, T., *Painting*
227 N. San Pedro St., Los Angeles
TANBERG, Lillian Ferguson, *Painting*
141 S. Beaudry Ave., Los Angeles
TANGE, Herman, *Painting*
1642 W. 46th St., Los Angeles
TANNER, William Charles, *Murals, Portra.*
425½ N. Ogden Dr., Los Angeles
TASCA, Fausto, *Painting*
617 Gillette St., Los Angeles
TASCHE, Herbert, *Commercial*
1512 Santee St., Los Angeles
TAUCH, Edgar, *Painting*
655 Third Ave., San Francisco
TAYLOR, Edgar D., *Painting*
2520 Ridge Rd., Berkeley
TAYLOR, Edward DeWitt, *Etching*
404 Mission St., San Francisco
TAYLOR, Farwell, *Painting*
800 Chestnut St., San Francisco
TAYLOR, Frank Johnson, *Painting*
401 N. Cañon Dr., Beverly Hills
TAYLOR, Kathleen, *Teacher*
549 Spencer Pl., Glendale
TAYLOR, Minnie C., *Painting*
1424 Gough St., San Francisco
TAYLOR, Virginia, *Teacher*
4308 Ninth Ave., Los Angeles
TAYLOR, Wyclife, *Painting*
3864 Ridge Rd., Riverside
TEAGUE, Emmett B., *Painting*
316 Taurus St., Oakland
TEASDALE, Mary, *Watercolors*
595 Mullen Ave., Los Angeles
TEFFT, Iona, *Pottery*
3882 Twelfth St., Riverside
TENCH, Allen, *Commercial*
213 S. Broadway, Los Angeles
TERADA, Edward, *Painting*
1605 Laguna St., San Francisco
TEREBOVA, Franciena, *Painting*
1150 Gough St., San Francisco
TERRY, Marion, *Teacher*
1102 S. Tremaine Ae., Los Angeles
THACKENTO, John, *Painting*
2207 Griffith Park Blvd., Los Angeles
THIENE, Paul G., *Painting*
Union Bank Bldg., Los Angeles
THEISS, John Williams, *Painting*
1308 E. 46th St., Los Angeles
THOMAS, Chauncy R., *Ceramics*
1335 Hearst Ave., Berkeley
THOMAS, Alice Blair, *Painting*
556 S. Hobart Blvd., Los Angeles
THOMAS, D. F., *Miniatures*
N. Merced Ave., Baldwin Park
THOMAS, Elizabeth, *Crafts*
518 N. Serrano St., Los Angeles
THOMAS, Ella, *Watercolors*
1445 Front St., San Diego
THOMAS, Georgia Seaver, *Painting*
523 Muirfield Rd., Los Angeles
THOMAS, Seymour, *Painting, Portraits*
4617 Rosemont Ae., La Crescenta
THOMAS, W. V., *Painting*
5141 Marlborough, San Diego
THOMASON, Rosemary, *Watercolors*
R. D. 1, Box 14, Garden Grove
THOMPSON, Agnes J., *Painting, Portraits*
7608 La Jolla Blvd., La Jolla

THOMPSON, G. N., *Commercial*
1007 S. Grand Ave., Los Angeles
THOMPSON, Louise G., *Teacher*
529 N. Alexandria, Los Angeles
THURBER, Lucile, *Painting*
6663 Neptune Pl., La Jolla
THURSTON, Jane McDuffie, *Painting, Etchi*
173 N. Pine Ave., Tujunga
THWING, J. F., *Commercial*
166 Geary St., San Francisco
TIFFANY, Helen Carter, *Painting*
Laguna Beach
TILDEN, Douglas, *Sculpture*
734 Channing Way, Berkeley
TITUS, Aimée B., *Painting*
Spreckels Bldg., San Diego
TITUS, Lela J., *Painting*
2924 Juniper St., San Diego
TITUS, W. C., *Painting*
3547 S. Flower St., Los Angeles
TJADER, Callen, *Stagecraft*
1229 B St., San Mateo
TOBIASSON, Mary E., *Painting*
4298 Maryland St., San Diego
TODD, Ethel M., *Teacher*
4227 Eighth Ave., Los Angeles
TODHUNTER, Alice C., *Painting*
2330 South Court, Los Angeles
TODHUNTER, Francis J., *Drawing, Etchi*
114 Sansome St., San Francisco *Commerc*
TOGNI, Marie, *Teacher*
2736 Haste St., Berkeley
TOLERTON, David, *Metalcraft*
Allied Arts Guild, Menlo Park
TOLMAN, Pauline Gediman, *Teacher*
2730 California St., Huntington Park
TOMPKINS, Florence, *Watercolors*
866 N. Chester Ave., Pasadena.
TONGE, Gilbert R., *Painting*
3125 Hamilton Way, Los Angeles
TONN, Dorothy, *Commercial*
631 O'Farrell St., San Francisco
TOOLE, Charlotte O., *Painting*
207 S. Granada Ave., Alhambra
TORREY, Elliot, *Painting*
4716 Panorama Way, San Diego
TOWNSEND, Geraldine, *Painting*
948 Taraal St., San Francisco
TRACY, Lucile Snow, *Woodcarving, Furnit*
825 Seagirt Court, Mission Beach
TRAFFORD, Martha, *Crafts, Teacher*
2113 Oak St., Los Angeles
TRALLE, Earle, *Commercial*
1206 S. Maple Ave., Los Angeles
TRAMONTI, Albert, *Commercial*
1233 Taylor St., San Francisco
TREASE, Sherman, *Prints*
3545 Bear Dr., San Diego
TREAT, Eleanor L., *Painting*
45 Parker Ave., San Francisco
TREFRY, Harold E., *Woodcuts in color*
5136 Windermere Ave., Eagle Rock, L. A.
TRESKOW, Millie, *Painting*
Kentfield
TREVETT, Mary, *Painting, Portraits*
Carmel
RIGG, Muriel V., *Weaving*
1442 N. Foothill Blvd., Pasadena
TRINE, Robert, *Pottery*
1944 Franklin Circle, Hollywood
TROUT, James F., *Commercial*
1304 Crenshaw Blvd., Los Angeles
TRUAX, Sarah E., *Painting, Miniatures*
3620 Fairmount Ave., San Diego
TRUESDELL, Edith, *Painting*
6310 Franklin Circle, Los Angeles
RUESDELL, Fannie, *Crafts*
117 South East Blvd., Corona
TUCKERMAN, Lilia J., *Painting*
Carpinteria
TUFT, Edward C., *Commercial*
74 New Montgomery St., San Francisco
TUFTS, Florence Ingalsbe, *Watercolors*
2733 Buena Vista Way, Berkeley
TUFTS, Dr. J. B., *Painting*
2733 Buena Vista Way, Berkeley
TURNBULL, Ruth, *Sculpture*
7229 Selma Ave., Hollywood
TURNER, Mrs. C. K., *Painting*
411 E. Pasadena Ave., Pomona
TURNER, Mary M., *Teacher*
1205 W. Pico St., Los Angeles
TURNER, Ruth Wooster, *Teacher*
San Jose
TYDEMAN, Edith L., *Teacher*
1410 E. Third St., Long Beach
TYLER, May Belle, *Painting*
4227 S. Vermont Ave., Long Beach
TYRRELL, C., *Commercial*
643 Bendix Bldg., Los Angeles

U

UEBELE, Eunice R., *Teacher*
Bakersfield
UEHLING, Teodorovna, *Painting, Portraits*
515 Crestline Dr., Brentwood Heights, L.
UEJAMA, Tokio, *Painting*
3708 Folsom St., San Francisco
UELAND, Emma M., *Leathercraft*
151 S. Jackson St., Glendale
ULBER, Althea, *Painting*
1053 S. New Hampshire Ave., Los Angeles
ULIANOFF, V., *Painting, Design, Decorat*
3622 Monon Ave., Los Angeles

ULMAN, Elinor E., *Painting*
321 Filbert St., San Francisco
UNSWORTH, Edna G., *Painting*
412 Dolores St., San Francisco
UNSWORTH, Robert B., *Painting, Etchi.*
320 Market St., San Francisco *Commerc*
USHER, Esther Grace, *Painting*
4542 Bandini St., Riverside

V

VAILLANCOURT, A. A., *Commercial*
822 W. 6th St., Los Angeles
VALENTIEN, Anna M., *Painting, Sculptu*
3903 Georgia St., San Diego *Cra*
VALENTINE, Dorothy Histon, *Watercolc*
2422 Prospect St., Berkeley *Fre*
VALERO, Maroussia, *Painting, Portraits*
5214 Melrose Ave., Los Angeles
VALK, Ella S., *Painting*
Golf Road, Santa Barbara
Van CINA, Theodore, *Decoration*
128 E. Ortega St., Santa Barbara
Van CLEVE, Helen Mann, *Watercolors*
Durant Hotel, Berkeley
VANDERBOSCH, E. J., *Painting*
250 N. Kenmore St., Los Angeles
Van Der FLIER, Hendricka, *Crafts, Weaving*
1954 N. Bronson Ave., Hollywood
Van DEVEER, Mamie W., *Teacher*
544 Patterson Ave., Glendale
Van Der VOORT, Pearl, *Commercial*
394 Twelfth St., Oakland
Van EPPE, Cora A., *Painting*
4125 S. Figueroa St., Los Angeles
Van ERP, Dirk, *Metalcraft*
1104 Sutter St., San Francisco
Van EVERA, Caroline, *Painting*
1030 Olive Ave., Coronado
Van HORN, Lucretia, *Watercolors, Pastels*
1825 Highland Pl., Berkeley
Van HORN, Margaret, *Lithographs*
1825 Highland Pl., Berkeley
Van HORN, Robert C., *Woodcarving*
1825 Highland Pl., Berkeley
Van KESSEL, Herman, *Commercial*
417 E. Pico St., Los Angeles
Van NORDEN, Virginia, *Teacher*
516 S. Carondelet St., Los Angeles
Van RENSSELAER, *Commercial*
100 S. Grand Ave., Los Angeles
Van SLOUN, Frank, *Painting, Murals, Etchi*
1617 California St., San Francisco *Monoty*
Van Valkenburgh, Peter, *Painting*
45 Armanino Court, Oakland
Van WAGNER, Clayton, *Etching, Watercol*
6100 Afton Pl., Hollywood
Van ZANDT, Hilda, *Painting, Teacher*
3740 Bluff Pl., San Pedro
VAUGHAN, R. W., *Etching*
316 Los Olivos St., Santa Barbara
VERNON, Mildred S., *Teacher*
1227 S. Central Ave., Glendale
VESTAL, Clara, *Crafts, Color, Design*
136 St. Anne St., San Francisco
VICKLUND, Marie, *Leathercraft, Bookbind*
3835 W. 59th Pl., Los Angeles
VILLA, Hernando, *Commercial*
1007 S. Grand Ave., Los Angeles
VIOLANTE, A. J., *Commercial*
Hearst Bldg., San Francisco
VIVIAN, Calthea, *Painting*
Hotel Claremont, Berkeley
VOLLMER, A. L., *Watercolors*
Box 12, Laguna Beach
VOLLMER, Grace L., *Painting*
2754 Woodshire Dr., Hollywood
Von BRIESEN, Alice S., *Painting*
2429 Brant St., San Diego
Von FALKENSTEIN, Claire, *Watercolors*
1681 Scenic Ave., Berkeley
Von PRIBOSIC, Victor, *Block prints*
115 W. Macy St., Los Angeles
Von RIDELSTEIN, Herbert, *Painting*
407 Castenada Ave., San Francisco
Von RIDELSTEIN, Maria, *Design, Textile*
407 Castenada Ave., San Francisco
Von SCHNEIDAU, Christian, *Portraits, Mur*
920 S. St. Andrews Pl., Los Angeles
Von TRUTSCHLER, Wolo, *Caricatures*
29 Olvera St., Los Angeles
VORKAPICH, Slavko, *Painting*
2100 Benedict Canyon Dr., Beverly Hills
VREELAND, Francis William, *Painting*
2206 Live Oak Dr., Hollywood
VULETICH, Dono, *Painting*
153 Hartwell St., Monterey
VYSEKAL, Edouard A., *Painting, Teacher*
1978 Lucile Ave., Los Angeles
VYSEKAL, Luvena B., *Painting, Drawing*
1978 Lucile Ave., Los Angeles

W

WACHTEL, Marian Kavanaugh, *Painting*
1155 Lida St., Pasadena
WADE, J. Ralph, *Commercial*
2901 Partridge Ave., Los Angeles
WADSWORTH, Phoebe Ray, *Teacher*
1304½ Fremont Ave., South Pasadena
WAGGONER, Elizabeth, *Sculpture, Teacher*
2041½ Pinehurst Rd., Hollywood
WAGNER, Blanche Collet, *Painting, Tapestr*
1135 Winston Ave., San Marino

WAGNER, Katherine, *Commercial*
21 Columbus Ave., San Francisco
WAGNER, Rob, *Painting*
608 N. Crescent Dr., Beverly Hills
WAGONER, Harry B., *Painting*
2737 Page Dr., Altadena
WAINWRIGHT, Florence, *Commercial*
510 Battery St., San Francisco
WAITE, Eric, *Coppeercraft*
4310 Merrill Ave., Riverside
WAITE, Margaret A., *Teacher*
845 Olive Ave., Long Beach
WAITE, Sarah Lenora, *Painting*
8 Park Way, Watsonville
WAKEFIELD, Ruth Cravath, *Sculpture*
2432 Leavenworth St., San Francisco
WALDEN, Howard, *Commercial*
1242 Santee St., Los Angeles
WALDO, Edith H., *Painting*
3972 Halldale Ave., Los Angeles
WALDVOGEL, Emma, *Weaving*
Monterey
WALKER, John, *Painting*
614 Vrovidencia Ave., Burbank
WALKER, Margaret C., *Painting*
2812 Washington St., San Francisco
WALL, Gertrude, *Pottery*
Carmel
WALLACE, A. R., *Commercial*
714 Santa Marina Bldg., San Francisco
WALLACE, Amy S., *Painting*
2427 N. Gower St., Los Angeles
WALLACE, Ethel M., *Painting, Fresco*
1635 Mason St., San Francisco
WALLACE, Ethel, *Painting, Fresco*
1635 Mason St., San Francisco
WALLACE, Frances Revett,
    Painting, Pen and Ink, Decoration
2700 Pacific Ave., San Francisco
WALLACE, Leontine, *Painting*
1340 Arch St., Berkeley
WALLACE, Moira, *Painting, Portraits, Mur*
Carmel
WALLER, Robert, *Painting*
468 Vallejo St., San Francisco
WALSH, Frank, *Commercial*
Detwiler Bldg., Los Angeles
WALTER, Edgar, *Drawing, Sculpture*
1940 Broadway, San Francisco
WALTER, Olivia B., *Teacher*
523 S. Westmoreland Ave., Los Angeles
WALTERS, Grace, *Teacher*
Ingelwood
WALTZ, Edith, *Painting*
Massachusetts Ave., Riverside
WANLEY, Grace Utt, *Teacher*
1263 First St., Norwalk
WARD, E. Grace, *Teacher*
Stockton
WARDE, Walter T., *Commercial*
1675 Eddy St., San Francisco
WARDROP, Ethel F., *Teacher*
428 S. Rexford Dr., Beverly Hills
WARE, Florence, *Painting*
Laguna Beach
WARNE, Alice Schaeffer, *Teacher*
1144 N. Normandie Ave., Los Angeles
WARNER, Nell Walker, *Painting*
2436 Orange Ave., La Crescenta
WASHBURN, Gertrude, *Painting*
428 El Centro Rd., Hillsborough
WASHBURN, Jessie M., *Painting*
Laguna Beach
WASZAK, Jack, *Commercial*
617 Montgomery St., San Francisco
WATANABE, Tojiro, *Painting*
117 N. San Pedro St., Los Angeles
WATERS, Mildred, *Watercolors*
3067 Walnut Ave., Riverside
WATRIN, Fred, *Painting*
3214 W. Avenue 32, Los Angeles
WATROUS, Hazel, *Design, Color*
Carmel
WATSON, Adele, *Painting*
283 S. Grand Ave., Pasadena
WATSON, Horace H., *Etching*
2527 Etna St., Berkeley
WATSON, Jesse N., *Watercolors*
704 N. Louise St., Glendale
WATTLES, Gurdon H., *Design, Commercial*
1653 Santa Barbara Ave., Glendale
WATTS, William Clothier, *Painting*
Carmel Highlands
WAUTERS, David S., *Wood Sculpture*
317½ S. Flower St., Los Angeles
WAYLAND, Adele, *Sculpture, Decoration*
42 Allston Way, San Francisco
WEARY, Stella, *Design*
1422 Amherst St., Glendale
WEATHERHEAD, Arthur C., *Teacher*
University of Southern California, Los Ange
WEAVER, Harold, *Painting*
2025 Ocean View Ave., Los Angeles
WEAVER, R. B., *Watercolors*
3206 Thirteenth St., Riverside
WEBB, Herbert C., *Painting*
8287 Santa Monica Blvd., Los Angeles
WEBBER, Mrs. H. J., *Painting*
University Knoll, Riverside
WEBB, Margaret Ely, *Bookplates*
26 W. Micheltorena St., Santa Barbara
WEBER, Kem, *Design, Cinema, Teacher*
1326 Palmer Ave., Glendale
WEBSTER, Anna Cutler, *Painting*
576 Gerona Rd., Stanford University

WEBSTER, Er'e, *Watercolors*
816 W. 5th St., Los Angeles
WEBSTER, Ida J., *Teacher*
115 Piedmont Ct., Pomona
WEDEMEYER, Archibald M., *Teacher*
373 S. Santa Anita Ave., Pasadena
WEEKS, Harold H., *Painting*
4445 Moraga Ave., Oakland
WEIDLER, Alfred, *Architectural Models*
1433 N. Normandie Ave., Los Angeles
WEIGEL, C. A., *Painting*
168 S. Berendo St., Los Angeles
WEIL, Adolph, *Painting*
168 S. Westgate Ave., Brentwood Hts., L.
WEINBERG, Emilie Sievert, *Painting*
International House, Berkeley
WEISMAN, Joseph, *Watercolors*
436½ St. Louis St., Los Angeles
WELCOME, Virginia D., *Teacher*
1988 Queensberry Rd., Pasadena
WELLER, Miss H. Z., *Teacher*
2455 Ashby Ave., Berkeley
WENDLING, Abbie R., *Crafts, Teacher*
1132 Fremont Ave., South Pasadena
WENDT, Julia Bracken, *Sculpture*
2814 N. Sichel St., Los Angeles
WENDT, William, *Painting*
Laguna Beach
WENNBERG, Mrs. Evelyn O., *Teacher*
920½ Belmont Ave., Long Beach
WENZLICK, Winona, *Teacher*
1224 Elden Ave., Los Angeles
WERNER, Fritz, *Painting, Portraits*
3006 Wilshire Blvd., Los Angeles
WESSELHOEFT, Mary F., *Painting, Stai*
914 Santa Barbara St., Santa Barbara *gl*
WESSELS, Glen, *Painting, Teacher*
20 Darrell Pl., San Francisco
WEST, Isabelle Percy, *Painting*
220 Spencer Ave., Sausalito
WEST, James, *Painting*
745 Fifth Ave., San Rafael
WEST, Nella A., *Teacher*
437 N. Oxford St., Los Angeles
WESTERVELT, R. D., *Painting, Commerc*
1389 Hill Dr., Eagle Rock
WESTFALL, Gertrude B., *Painting*
Box 43, Monterey
WESTON, Brett, *Photography*
2 City Hall Plaza, Santa Barbara
WESTON, Carol, *Watercolors*
701 Cogswell Rd., El Monte
WESTON, Edward, *Photography*
Carmel
WESTON, Mrs. M. L., *Painting*
Box 564, Carlsbad
WHEDON, Harriet F., *Painting*
795 Pine St., San Francisco
WHEELER, L. A., *Commercial*
1206 S. Maple Ave., Los Angeles
WHEELER, Lyle Raynolds, *Painting*
El Puebla Ribera, La Jolla
WHELAN, Blanche, *Painting*
147 N. Norton Ave., Los Angeles
WHELAN, Mary E., *Teacher*
521 Montana Ave., Santa Monica
WHIPPLE, Louise C., *Teacher*
1100 S. Los Robles, Pasadena
WHISMAN, C. A., *Sculpture*
4632 Santa Monica Blvd., Santa Monica
WHITAKER, Ruth Townsend,
Painting, Drawing
5063 Santa Monica Ave., Ocean Beach
WHITE, Alma Glasgow, *Painting*
660 Second Ave., San Francisco
WHITE, Eleanor W., *Teacher*
135½ N. La Brea Ave., Hollywood
WHITE, Fred J., *Commercial*
321 Bush St., San Francisco
WHITE, Natalie, *Teacher*
533 Mt. Holyoke Ave., Pacific Palisades
WHITE, Nona L., *Painting*
1134 Wabash St., Pasadena
WHITE, Orrin A., *Painting*
1025 Linda Vista Ave., Pasadena
WHITE, Ruth Taylor, *Commercial*
703 Market St., San Francisco
WHITE, Will, *Commercial*
130 S. Broadway, Los Angeles
WHITFORD, Alice M., *Painting*
143 Hollister Ave., Santa Monica
WHITICE, Belle, *Teacher*
602 Chestnut Ave., Los Angeles
WHITING, Lillian V., *Painting, Teacher*
1441 Avon Terrace, Los Angeles
WHITLOCK, Frances J., *Teacher*
Fresno
WHITMAN, Paul, *Painting, Etching*
Box 1122, Carmel
WHITNEY, Ermina C., *Painting, Teacher*
254 S. Vendome St., Los Angeles
WHYTE, C. Evers, *Commercial*
Grosse Bldg., 6th & Spring Sts., Los Angel
WIBOLTT, A. C., *Painting, Portraits*
360 N. Euclid Ave., Pasadena
WIBOLTT, Barbara, *Painting*
2631 Manhattan Ave., Los Angeles
WICKES, Ethel M., *Painting*
519 Webster St., San Francisco
WICKSON, Guest, *Painting*
2723 Bancroft Way, Berkeley
WIDEMAN, Florence, *Painting, Etching*
Los Altos
WIDEN, Carl, *Painting*
355 Huntley Dr., Sherman
WIDFORSS, Gunnar, *Painting*
1845 Gough St., San Francisco

WIECZOREK, Max, *Painting*
1007 S. Grand Ave., Los Angeles
WIELAND, Fred, *Stained glass*
3162 El Cajon Blvd., San Diego
WIGGINS, A. Z., *Painting*
2000 Shattuck Ave., Berkeley
WIGHT, Clifford, *Sculpture*
15 Jessop Pl., San Francisco
WILCOX, Evelyn, *Jewelry*
Kifer Road, Santa Clara
WILCOX, N. W., *Teacher*
386 S. Los Robles Ave., Pasadena
WILDMAN, Mary F., *Etching*
Stanford University
WILES, Gordon W., *Cinema*
1311 N. Sycamore Ave., Hollywood
WILFORT, Mary Elizabeth, *Sculpture*
Route 1, Box 246, Montebello
WILHELM, Arthur L., *Newspaper Art*
Care The Times, 100 N. Broadway, L. A.
WILKE, William H., *Etching, Illustration*
447 Sansome St., San Francisco
WILKINS, Mildred Pierce, *Watercolors*
Route 1, Chino
WILKINSON, Melroy, *Teacher*
819 Belmont Ave., Long Beach
WILLIAMS, Althea B., *Teacher*
4442 Main St., Riverside
WILLIAMS, Caryl, *Block prints, Design*
29 Olvera St., Los Angeles
WILLIAMS, Dorothy, *Painting*
4959 Melrose Ave., Los Angeles
WILLIAMS, Lorena B., *Watercolors*
3318 W. 27th St., Los Angeles
WILLIAMS, Mary Belle, *Painting, Miniatu*
1626 Seventh St., San Diego
WILLIAMS, Otis, *Children's Portraits*
227 S. Spring St., Los Angeles
WILLIAMS, Paul R., *Design, Furniture*
781 S. San Fernando Rd., Glendale
WILLIAMS, Reed, *Commercial*
1965 N. Cahuenga Blvd., Hollywood
WILLIAMSON, A. C., *Painting*
640 S. Grand Ave., Pasadena
WILLIAMSON, F. G., *Painting*
6716 Leland Way, Los Angeles
WILLIAMSON, Mayme E., *Painting*
628 Montgomery St., San Francisco
WILLIS, Hazel, *Teacher*
3345 Sanborn Ave., Lynwood
WILLIS, Ralph T., *Painting*
Encinitas
WILLIS, Reg, *Commercial*
617 Montgomery St., San Francisco
WILLS, Charles, *Painting*
2289 W. 27th St., Los Angeles
WILSON, Dorothy, *Painting*
37 Hazel Ave., Mill Valley
WILSON, Ellena T., *Illustration, Watercolors*
3441 W. First St., Los Angeles
WILSON, Ernest M., *Watercolors*
9811 S. Normandie Ave., Los Angeles
WILSON, Harold F., *Sculpture*
609 N. Alvarado St., Los Angeles
WILSON, Melba Z., *Sculpture*
115 N. Normandie Ave., Los Angeles
WILSON, Mildred Lewis, *Commercial*
200 Bush St., San Francisco
WILSON, Nevada, *Painting*
1337 Lucile Ave., Los Angeles
WILSON, William J., *Painting*
1628 Rose St., Long Beach
WINEBRENNER, Harry, *Sculpture, Teach*
1354 Ashland Ave., Ocean Park
WING, Marian C., *Painting*
345 Lincoln Ave., Palo Alto
WINKLER, Arthur J., *Etching*
Victorville
WINKLER, John W., *Etching*
3048 Benvenue Ave., Berkeley
WINN, Emilie W., *Painting, Drawi*
Ross, Marin County *Woodbloc*
WINN, James H., *Sculpture, Jewelry*
43 S. El Molino Ave., Pasadena
WINTER, Alice Beach, *Painting*
1330 Hillcrest Ave., Pasadena
WINTERBURN, George T., *Teacher*
Polytechnic High School, Los Angeles
WINTERBURN, Phyllis, *Block prints, Desi*
945 Sausalito Blvd., *Textiles, Teach.*
Sausalito
WINTERHALDER, Erwin, *Commercial*
1809 Lyon St., San Francisco
WINTERMOTE, Mrs. M. W., *Painting*
1916½ N. Highland Ave., Hollywood
WINTERS, Raymond, *Commercial*
939 S. Broadway, Los Angeles
WIRTH, Anna M., *Miniatures*
2025 Rubio Ct., Altadena
WISE, Helena Peck, *Crafts*
Box 545, Indio
WITTE, I. O., *Commercial*
257 S. Spring St., Los Angeles
WITTMAN, Irma L., *Teacher*
3318 Fernside Blvd., Alameda
WITTSTEIN, Helen, *Leathercraft*
2724 W. 15th St., Los Angeles
WOLF, Bayard, *Painting*
730 Montgomery St., San Francisco
WOLFE, Meyer R., *Painting*
154 Carmel St., San Francisco
WOLHAUPTER, Helen, *Painting*
918 Sixteenth St., Santa Monica

WONG, Suey, *Painting*
722 Montgomery St., San Francisco
WOOD, Caroline S., *Crafts, Teacher*
2255 W. 24th St., Los Angeles
WOOD, Eva Adeline, *Watercolors*
P. O. Box 329, Encinitas
WOOD, Grant, *Painting*
1219 Twelfth Ave., San Francisco
WOOD, Helen Snyder, *Painting*
1533 Posen Ave., Berkeley
WOOD, Irene, *Sculpture*
2340 Pacific Ave., San Francisco
WOOD, Helen Snyder, *Painting*
1533 Posen Ave., Berkeley
WOOD, Irene, *Sculpture*
2340 Pacific Ave., San Francisco
WOOD, Leona P., *Metalcraft, Woodcarving*
3701 Shannon Road, Los Angeles
WOOD, Stanley, *Watercolors, Lithographs*
Box 1082, Carmel
WOODBRIDGE, Virginia, *Teacher*
405 Hilgard, Los Angeles
WOODFORD, Salva, *Painting*
212 S. Grand Ave., Los Angeles
WOODHULL, Carolyn, *Teacher*
2830 Santa Anita Ave., Altadena
WOODS, E. F., *Painting*
1344 Thirty-third St., San Diego
WOODS, Frances M., *Leathercraft, Bookbindi.*
2303 Juliet St., Los Angeles
WOODS, Marcy, *Painting*
209½ W. Lodi Ave., Lodi
WOODWARD, Norah, *Painting*
Point Loma
WOOKY, Howard W., *Commercial*
1332 N. Sycamore St., Hollywood
WOOLDRIDGE, Margaret S., *Painting*
International House, Berkeley
WOOLLEY, Virginia, *Painting*
Laguna Beach
WORCESTER, Mildred, *Teacher*
1920 S. Western Ave., Los Angeles
WORES, Theodore, *Painting*
Bohemian Club, San Francisco
WORKMAN, Emmagene T., *Teacher*
2113 Oak St., Los Angeles
WORKS, Don, *Painting*
802 Montgomery St., San Francisco
WORKS, Katherine Swan, *Painting*
802 Montgomery St., San Francisco
WORTH, M. F., *Sculpture*
8001 Vista Dr., La Mesa
WOSNAK, Vernon, *Commercial*
617 Montgomery St., San Francisco
WOY, Leota, *Design, Bookplates*
533 S. Westmoreland Ave., Los Angeles
WRIGHT, Doris E., *Teacher*
635 E. 9th St., Long Beach
WRIGHT, Earnest M., *Painting*
Sherman Institute, Arlington
WRIGHT, Gerald D., *Commercial*
617 Montgomery St., San Francisco
WRIGHT, James Couper, *Watercolors, Stain*
740 State St., Santa Barbara *gla*
WRIGHT, John R., *Commercial*
114 Sansome St., San Francisco
WRIGHT, Josephine M., *Painting*
1010 Stoneman Ave., Alhambra
WRIGHT, Jud, *Commercial*
1221½ Wall St., Los Angeles
WRIGHT, Kenneth, *Commercial*
741 San Fernando Bldg., Los Angeles
WRIGHT, S. Macdonald, *Painting*
1544 Sixteenth St., Santa Monica
WULFF, Timothy M., *Painting*
2245 Turk St., San Francisco
WURTELE, Isobel K., *Painting*
6340 Maryland Dr., Los Angeles
WYCKOFF, Anna Brooks, *Painting*
1016 Tiverton St., West Los Angeles
WYCKOFF, Florence Richardson, *Sculpture*
1059 Broadway, San Francisco
WYLIE, Marion E., *Painting*
4539 Park Blvd., San Diego
WYNNYK, Beryl, *Painting*
628 Montgomery St., San Francisco

Y

YAGER, Ydress, *Painting*
4640 El Cerrito Dr., San Diego
YELLAND, W. R., *Drawing*
Financial Center Bldg., Oakland
YENS, Karl, *Painting*
2079 Coast Blvd., Laguna Beach
YERBYSMITH, Ernest A., *Sculpture*
1115 Hacienda Pl., West Los Angeles
YOHN, C. H., *Pottery*
1789 New York Ave., Altadena
YORESKA, *Miniatures*
1501 Leavenworth St., San Francisco
YOUNG, Ella B., *Crafts*
5149 Bakman Ave., North Hollywood
YOUNG, Florence, *Painting*
27 S. Granada Ave., Alhambra
YOUNG, Florence Upson, *Watercolors*
1800 N. Harvard Blvd., Los Angeles
YOUNG, L. de Wolf, *Painting*
128 N. Thomas St., Los Angeles
YOUNG, Pearl Bray, *Painting*
1302 W. Park St., Stockton
YOUNGBLOOD, Janet, *Crafts, Design*
1757 N. Las Palmas Ave., Hollywood

YOUNG-HUNTER, Mary, *Paitning, Gesso*
  Carmel
YOUNGLOVE, Ruth Ann, *Watercolors*
  616 Hilgard Ave.. Westwood Village. L.
YOUNGSTROM, Eleanor M., *Leathercra*
  4425 S. Figueroa St., Los Angeles *Teach*

Z

ZACHARIE, George, *Commercial*
  500 Sansome St , San Francisco
ZAKHEIM, Bernard, *Painting*
  851 Bryant St., San Francisco
ZERAN, William, *Painting*
  5315 Packard St., Los Angeles
ZIEGLER, Nellie Evelyn, *Painting*
  1086 Frospect Blvd., Pasadena
ZILLIG, Fritz, *Painting*
  1219 Maryland Ave.. Los Angeles
ZIMMERER, Frank, *Painting, Crafts*
  29 Olvera St., Los Angeles
ZIMMERMAN, Beatrice, *Teacher*
  1241 W. Santa Barbara St., Los Angeles
ZIMMERMAN, Carl, *Painting*
  1023 N. Rose Ave., Pasadena
ZIMMERMAN, Frederick A., *Painting, Sculptu*
  1180 Afton St., Pasadena
ZOELLEN, Ray, *Sculpture*
  767 North Point St., San Francisco

CALIF. ART—S.F. WORLD'S FAIR 1940

From the Official Catalog   Two Shows: <u>CALIFORNIA ART TODAY</u> and <u>CALIFORNIA ART IN RETROSPECT</u>

#=number of pictures shown

CALIFORNIA ART TODAY

A

Rowena Meeks Abdy	1
Ethel M. Abeel	2
Ida Abramivitch	1
Jaine Ahring	1
Maxine Albro	2
Andy Aldridge	1
Anders Aldrin	1
Mabel Alvarez	1
Llon K. Amyx	1
Sara-Kathryn Arledge	1
Victor Arnautoff	1
Irma Attridge	1
John Ayres	2

B

Robert Bach	1
Standish Backus Jr.	1
Anni Baldaugh	1
Belle Baranceanu	1
Matthew Barnes	1
Grace L. Bartlett	1
Ivan Bartlett	1
Loren Barton	1
Karl Baumann	1
Martha W. Baxter	1
Arthur Beaumont	1
Fred J. Behre	1
Charles Bensco	2
Franz Bergmann	1
Jane Berlandina	1
Ray Bethers	3
Edward Biberman	1
Jules Billington	1
Lee Blair	2
Mary Blair	1
Milvia W. Boak	1
Dorr Bothwell	1
Ray Boynton	2
Rex Brandt	1
Muriel M. Branegan	1
Maurice Braun	1
Otis L. Briar	1
N. Brigante	2
Tanci Bristol	2
Everett L. Bryant	1
A. Ray Burrell	1

C

Marcel E. Cailliet	1
Mary Cane	1
Margaret Cavaney	1
Janet Ruth Cerf	1
F. Tolles Chamberlin	2
David P. Chun	1
William H. Clapp	1
Alson S. Clark	2
Wm. Lewis Clarke	1
Arthur Clough	1
P. Holmes Coats	2
Grover Cole	1
Marian C. Cooch	1
George C. Corbit	1
C. C. Coyle	2
Thomas Craig	1
Carl Critz	1
Marie G. Cruess	1
Rinaldo Cuneo	1
Marian Cunningham	1
Marian Curtis	2

D

Italo D'Andrea	1
Charles C. Daniels	1
Frode N. Dann	2
Charles H. Davis	1
James B. Davy	2
Mallette Dean	2
Maurice Del Mue	1
Victor De Wilde	2
Dan Dickey	2
Phil Dike	1
Mary Dill	2
Maynard Dixon	1
James Budd Dixon	2
Amy Donaldson	1
Marguerite Dorgeloh	1
Charles Dornbach	1
Dorothy Duncan	2
Nicholas Dunphy	1
Briggs Dyer	1

E

Marjorie Eakin	1
Stanley Edwards	1
Thomas K. Elrick	1
Irma Engel-Leisinger	2
Helen Beth Ewing	2

F

Edward M. Farmer	2
Mabel McK. Farmer	2
Olive Fetherstonhaugh	1
Fong Yan-Ting	1
Helen Forbes	3
James H. Forman	1
Jane Foster	1
Will Foster	1
Ruth M. Fracker	1
Karoly Fulop	1

G

George Gaethke	2
John Garth	1
William A. Gaw	2
Arthur H. Gilbert	1
Elizabeth Ginno	1
Bertha W. Glass	1
Ellwood Graham	1
Nils Gren	2
Dorothy Grover	1

H

John Haley	3
Jean Gates Hall	1
Parker Hall	1
Ruth E. Halvorsen	2
Leah R. Hamilton	3
Einar Hansen	2
Merlin Hardy	3
Marian Hebert	1
William Hesthal	1
Hisako Hibi	1
Hilaire Hiler	1
Lawrence Hinckley	1
Clarence Hinkle	1
Fred Hocks	1
Miles E. Holmes	1
Carl W. Holt	1
John L. Howard	2
Louis J. Hughes	2
Helmut Hungerland	1
Mabel R. Hutchinson	2

I

Pauline Ivancovich	1
Eugene S. Ivanoff	2

J

Everett Gee Jackson	1
Edward Johanson	1
Doris M. Johnson	2
E. Holland Johnson	1
Reginald Johnson	1
Robert B. Johnson	1
Frederic Johnston	1
Josephine Joy	

K

Florence D. Keller	1
Ed Killingsworth	1
Dong Kingman	2
Dave Klein	1
Louis Klein	1
Orpha Klinker	1
Helen A. Klokke	1
Gene Kloss	2
Joseph Knowles	1

| Josephine Kopenhaver | 2 |
| Emil J. Kosa Jr. | 2 |

L

Lucien Labaude	2
George A. Laisuer	1
Paul Lauritz	3
Al Lebarts	1
Rico Lebrun	1
Chee Chin E. C. Lee	1
Carlton Lehman	2
Kathryn W. Leighton	1
Aurel J. Leitner	2
Leiulf	2
Lee Leonard	1
Nat Levy	1
Jeanette M. Lewis	1
Jennie Lewis	2
Tome E. Lewis	1
Seymour Locks	1
Erle Loran	2
Dan Lutz	2

M

Mary MacBeth	1
Spencer Macky	1
Eunice MacLennan	1
Clyde W. McGill	2
Jean Mannheim	1
Robert Maxfield	2
James McCray	2
Harley Melzian	2
Daniel M. Mendelowitz	1
Ivan Messenger	1
Stan Metz	1
Ester C. Meyer	1
Doris H. Michels	2
Gertrude W. Mihsfeldt	1
Barse Miller	2
Mark Milsk	2
Carl A. Morris	1
Jose Moya Del Pino	1
Richard Munsell	1
Jerre Murry	2

N

Peggy Nelson	1
Alexander Nepote	1
Eugen Neuhaus	2
Helen Neumann	1
Warren Newcombe	2
Harold H. Newsom	1
Peter Nielsen	1
Wesley Nightingale	1
Ken Nishi	1

O

Mine Okubo	1
Otis Oldfield	1
Marion Olds	1
Barbara Olmsted	1
Frederick Olmsted	2
Dale Owen	1

P

Phil Paradise	2
Douglas Parshall	1
Roi Partridge	2
James Patrick	1
Ethel Pearce	1
Fred D. Penney	1
Laura A. Penny	1
Fritiof Persson	1
DeWitt Peters	1
Margaret Peterson	2
Edith Catlin Phelps	1
Werner Philipp	1
Mireille Piazzoni	1
Philip Pinner	1
Max Pollak	1
Theodore C. Polos	2
Elsie L. Pomeroy	1
Julius Pommer	2
Mildred Pommer	2
Nelson Poole	2
Stan P. Poray	1
James D. Prendergast	1
Dorothy W. Puccinelli	1

R

Lee F. Randolph	1
Joe Raphael	1
W. F. Rauschnabel	3
Edward A. Reep	2
Charles Reiffel	1
Helen H. Rempel	1
William S Rice	1
John Hubbard Rich	1
Virginia Roberts	1
Margot K. Rocle	1
Marius Rocle	1
Frances Roeding	1
Ethel Rose	1
Worth Ryder	1

S

Helen Salz	1
Geneve R. Sargeant	1
Jack Sarkin	1
Sergey Scherbakoff	1
Paul A. Schmitt	1
Donna Schuster	1
Ben Sears	1
Ralph C. Seigle	1
Millard Sheets	1
Isabel Shepard	1
Elizabeth F. Sherman	1
Leslie Sherman	1
Henrietta Shore	1
Louis B. Siegriest	1
Wilson Silsby	1
Marian Simpson	2
Martha Simpson	1
Burr Singer	2
Nell Sinton	1
A. Katherine Skeele	2

Hassel Smith	1
Dick Snavely	1
Angelo A. Sottosanti	2
Clay Spohn	1
Mary Stanfield	2
Rosamond Stanley	1
Jack Gage Stark	1
Shirley Staschen	3
Ernst Stolz	1
Ina Perham Storey	1
Ray Strong	1
Henry Sugimoto	1
Sharles Surendorf	1
Florence A. Smith	3
Jean Swiggett	2

T

Richard Taggert	1
Edward DeW. Taylor	1
Francis Todhunter	1
Katherine Tooby	1
Florence I. Tufts	2
John Tufts	2
Rupert B. Turnbull	2

U

Tokjo Ueyama	2
B. Ullrich	2
Onestus Uzzell	1

V

| Herman Volz | 1 |

W

Wanda Walden	1
William Wallett	1
Harold E. Warren	1
Emilie S. Weinberg	1
Joseph Weisman	1
Owen Welsh	1
Mathilde L. Weston	1
Harriet Whedon	1
Orrin A. White	1
Jack Wibolt	1
Paul Wildhaber	2
Julian Williams	1
Robert Windrem	1
Hamilton Wolf	1
Stella Wong	1
Philip Wood	1
Norah Woodward	1
James Couper Wright	1
Phyllis Wrightson	1

Y

Thomas Yamamoto	2
Alfred Ybarra	2
George Yphantis	1

Z

Bernard Zakheim	1
William Zeran	1
Milford Zornes	2
Vera Zumsteg	1

CALIFORNIA ART IN RETROSPECT, 1850-1915

A
Olga Ackerman 1
Gertrude P. Albright 1
Henry Alexander 2
Arthur Atkins 2

B
Mathew Barnes 1
Hiram R. Bloomer 1
Cora Boone 1
Ray Boynton 1
William Bradford 1
Anne Bremer 1
Henry Joseph Breuer 1
Belmore Browne 1
Ferdinand Burgdorff 1
Caroline Rixford Byrd 1

C
Guisseppe Cadenasso 1
Emil Carlsen 2
Will Carrigan 1
Alice B. Chittenden 1
William Clapp 1
W. A. Coulter 1
Rinaldo Cuneo 1

D
Edwin Deakin 1
Maurice Del Mue 1
G. J. Denny 1
Maynard Dixon 1

F
William B. Faville 1
E. Charlton Fortune 1

G
John Gamble 1
Charles Henry Grant 1
Percy Grey 1

H
William Hahn 1
H. Hammerstrom 1
Armin Hansen 1
W. H. Hansen 1
Julie Heyneman 1
Thomas Hill 1
Clarence Hinkle 1
Clark Hobart 1
Grace Hudson 1

I
Benoni Irwin 1

J
Louise Janin 1
Amedee Joullin 1
Chapel Judson 1
Chris Jurgensen 1

K
William Keith 3
Anna Klumpkey 1

L
Lorenzo P. Latimer 1

M
Spencer Macky 1
Arthur Mathews 1
Lucia Mathews 1
Francis McComas 1
Evelyn McCormick 1

N
Charles Christian Nahll 1
E. Narjot deFranchville 1
Eugen Neuhaus 1

O
Eliz. C. O'Sullivan 1

P
Jules Pages 1
De Witt Parshall 1
R. F. H. Partington 1
Orrin Peck 1
Charles Rollo Peters 1
Gottardo Piazzoni 1
Bruce Porter 1

R
Joseph Raphael 1
Henry Raschen 1
Mary C. Richardson 1
William Ritschel 1
Julian Rix 1
Charles D. Robinson 1
Guy Rose 1
Toby Rosenthal 1

S
Matteo Sandona 1
Geneve R. Sargent 1
Will Sparks 1
Joe Strong 1

T
Jules Tavernier 1

V
Frank Van Sloan 1

W
Elmer Wachtel 1
Marion K. Wachtel 1
Thad Welch 1
William Wendt 1
Guest Wickson 1
Dora Norton Williams 1
Virgil Williams 1
Theodore Wores 1
Ella K. Wormster 1

Y
Fred Yates 1
Raymond A. Yelland 1

SOCIETY OF WESTERN ARTISTS 10th Annual Exhibition 1949 San Francisco Museum		**40 California Painters** Long Beach & S. F. Art Museums Early 50s
OIL PAINTINGS	Marques E. Reitzel	Ruth Armer
	Robert C. Rishell	Paul Darrow
Katherine H. Allen	Hazel Rittenhouse	Francis De Erderly
Jonathan Batchelor	Bianca Royce	Richard Diebenkorn
Peter Blos	Matteo Sandona	Ralph Du Casse
Rockwell Brank	Paul A. Schmitt	Leonard Edmondson
Leslie Buck	Clyde Scott	Jules Engel
Nedra Carter	George Seideneck	Edgar Ewing
Jean A. Center	Florence M. Senior	Lorser Feitelson
Josephine Capwell	Henrietta Shore	Keith Finch
Cecil Chamberlin	Howard E. Smith	Richard Haines
William H. Clapp	Herman Struck	Leah Rinne Hamilton
Michael Clinton	James Swinnerton	Ynez Johnston
Lucienne A. Collaer	Joan Thoren	John Paul Jones
Brother Cornelius	Francis Todhunter	Karl Kasten
William F. Dabelstein	Helen Van Cleve	Walter Kuhlman
Will Dakin	Maria Von Ridelstein	Roger Kuntz
L. E. DeJoiner	C. Von Schneidau	Irene Lagorio
Denes DeHolesch	H. M. Ward	Frank Lobdell
Earl Don DeLappe	Florence E. Ware	S. MacDonald-Wright
Florence R. Earnest	Ruby Zahn White	Robert Mallary
Gladys Ferguson	Edna B. Wing	Douglas McClellan
Fortunato V. Figone	A. G. Warshawsky	John McLaughlin
J. R. Ford	Mildred Watterworth	Lee Mullican
Eugene M. Frandzen		Alexander Nepote
Will Frates		David Park
Mabelle B. Fulmer	WATERCOLORS	Clayton Pinkerton
Wendall N. Gates	William R. Cameron	George D. Randall
Arthur Hill Gilbert	W. E. Chamberlin	Orrel Reed
Duncan Gleason	Eric Doering	Richard Ruben
Frederic M. Grant	Alfred Eichler	Felix Ruvolo
Leon Grant	Minna Benz Hoffmann	John Saccaro
Grace Hamilton	Eleanor Hughes	Sueo Serisawa
Ernest Handel	Elizabeth Jacobs	Millard Sheets
Carl F. Hobby	James A. Lawrence	Peter Shoemaker
James A. Holden	Nat Levy	Lundy Siegriest
Lawrence F. Hosmer	Stanley M. Long	Howard Warshaw
Emil Hugentobler	Laura Maxwell	June C. Wayne
Alfred Jonniaux	Robert Paplow	Richard A. White
Hans Jorgensen	Max Petersen	Jack Zajac
Albin Kern	Rollin Pickford Jr.	
Claude Kinnoull	Noel Quinn	
Louis Klein	Catherine Seideneck	
Beulah H. Kosty	Carlo Taliabue	
Paul Lauritz	William C. Watts	
Madalyn B. Lener	Rene Weaver	
Maurice Logan	Paul Whitman	
Syvester Mateo		
Thomas A. McGlynn	SCULPTURE	
Joshua Meador	Jonathan Batchelor	
Vida E. Miller	Mary Ann Brown	
Frank H. Myers	Kisa Beeck	
George Demont Otis	Roger N. Burnham	
Alexis Pencovic	John D. Fuller	
Charles Polowetski	Wendall N. Gates	
Ray P. Radliff	G. B. Portanova	
Lee F. Randolph	Carlo Taliabue	

Abowitz, Dorothy — *Santa Monica*
Abrahamson, Victor — *San Francisco*
Aldrin, Anders — *Los Angeles*
Allen, Gene — *Los Angeles*
Ames, Jean Goodwin — *Claremont*
Angelo, Waldo — *Beverly Hills*
Asseln, Roberta — *Los Angeles*

B Babitz, Mae — *Los Angeles*
Barnard, John F., Jr. — *Long Beach*
Barrett, Altina — *Beverly Hills*
Beaman, R. B. — *Redlands*
Bellows, Una Lee — *Santa Ana*
Bender, Robert — *Los Angeles*
Bennett, Lyle Hatcher — *Van Nuys*
Berman, Eugene — *Los Angeles*
Bertoia, Harry — *La Jolla*
Bisno, Barbara — *Beverly Hills*
Bisttram, Emil — *Los Angeles*
Boileau, L. — *Los Angeles*
Borowsky, Marvin — *Los Angeles*
Bowden, H. — *Sausalito*
Bowman, Dorothy — *Los Angeles*
Brandt, Rex — *Corona del Mar*
Brice, William — *Los Angeles*
Buff, Conrad — *Los Angeles*

C Cannon, Dorothy — *North Hollywood*
Carey, Pat Ryan — *Los Angeles*
Carpenter, Donald — *Los Angeles*
Casey, James — *National City*
Cavanna, Elise — *Los Angeles*
Chuey, Robert A. — *Los Angeles*
Cohen, Stanley H. — *Berkeley*
Collins, Kenneth — *El Monte*
Conroy, V. — *Los Angeles*
Cornin, Jon — *Berkeley*
Cornish, John — *Santa Monica*
Coutts, Jeane — *Palm Springs*
Coze, Paul — *Pasadena*
Curlee, Wallace — *Fillmore*

D Darrow, Paul — *Claremont*
de Erdely, Francis — *Los Angeles*
Diebenkorn, Richard — *Sausalito*
Dike, Phil — *Los Angeles*
Dixon, John — *Los Angeles*
Dobrin, Arnold — *Los Angeles*
Doolittle, Marjorie — *Carmel*

E Edel, Maximilian — *West Los Angeles*
Engel, Julius — *Los Angeles*
English, Harold — *Los Angeles*
Ewing, Edgar — *Los Angeles*

F Feitelson, Lorser — *Los Angeles*
Ferber, Louise — *Los Angeles*
Fischinger, Oskar — *West Hollywood*
Flannery, Kay — *Los Angeles*
Flock, Wyatt R., Jr. — *Pasadena*
Florey, V. — *Los Angeles*
Flu, Richard S. — *Los Angeles*
Fordham, Ellwood — *Venice*
Frary, Michael — *Hollywood*
Fry, Mary L. Finley — *Hollywood*
Fulton, Cora-Fair — *Claremont*

G Gebhardt, Harold — *Burbank*
Goldin, Leon — *Los Angeles*
Graham, Ellwood — *Monterey*
Grant, Gene — *Los Angeles*
Grod, Niussia — *Los Angeles*
Greene, Simon — *Hollywood*

H Haines, Richard — *Santa Monica*
Hall, Clem — *Los Angeles*
Harbst, Eleanor — *Alhambra*
Harris, Thomas D. — *Glendale*
Heerman, Catharine — *Los Angeles*
Heller, Jules — *Los Angeles*
Hendel, Meta C. — *San Francisco*
Herbert, Leonard — *Los Angeles*
Hickman, Robert J. — *Los Angeles*
Houdek, Robert E. — *Compton*
Hultberg, John — *Los Angeles*

J Jackson, Robert — *Glendale*
Jarvaise, James — *Los Angeles*
Jensen, Frank A. — *Hermosa Beach*
Johnston, Ynez — *Berkeley*
Jones, Richard K. — *Los Angeles*

K Keller, Robert A. — *Los Angeles*
Kendall, Lillian — *Fairfax*
Kennedy, Simon — *Los Angeles*
Kester, Lenard — *Los Angeles*
Kiechle, Edgar O. — *Studio City*
Kimball, Ward — *San Gabriel*
Kohn, Edmond — *Los Angeles*
Kovatch, Jack — *Los Angeles*
Kreisl, George — *Beverly Hills*

Kuntz, Roger	*Claremont*
Kwok, John J.	*Los Angeles*
L Ladd, James	*San Diego*
LaGatta, John	*Santa Monica*
Lam, Simon	*Los Angeles*
Langford, Ruth	*Los Angeles*
Lawrence, James A.	*San Mateo*
Lebrun, Rico	*Los Angeles*
Leung, Monroe	*Los Angeles*
Leven, Boris R.	*Los Angeles*
LeVinson, Lionel	*West Los Angeles*
Lewis, James Arthur	*Pasadena*
Liefeld, Marian	*West Hollywood*
Locker, Jack	*Los Angeles*
Loran, Erle	*Berkeley*
Lutz, Dan	*Los Angeles*
M Mattox, Charles	*Los Angeles*
McClellan, Douglas	*Claremont*
McCormick, Edward	*Burbank*
McCullough, George	*Wilmington*
McIntosh, Robert J.	*Los Angeles*
McLaughlin, John D.	*Dana Point*
Meek, Martha	*Long Beach*
Merrild, Knud	*Los Angeles*
Mesches, Arnold	*Hollywood*
Montague, Ward	*San Anselmo*
Munger, Martha	*Santa Monica*
Musselman, Darwin	*Oakland*
N Nepote, Alexander	*Oakland*
Nepote, Hanne-Lore	*Oakland*
Nerger, Ethel Pearce	*San Francisco*
Norman, Ruth	*Los Angeles*
O O'Bergh, Carl	*Long Beach*
O'Connell, Michael	*Los Angeles*
O'Malley, J. M.	*Hollywood*
Olds, Marion	*Los Angeles*
Osgood, John	*San Diego*
Owen, Dale	*Santa Monica*
P Pabian, Al	*Los Angeles*
Palansky, Abraham	*Los Angeles*
Park, Anna Elizabeth	*Claremont*
Perez, Manuel	*Encino*
Perrin, Robert	*West Los Angeles*
Phillips, Blanche	*Marin City*
Pinto, James	*Los Angeles*
Pollack, Addison S.	*Los Angeles*
Post, Rudd	*Lancaster*
Pumphry, Bert	*Los Angeles*
R Reep, Edward A.	*Studio City*
Reichman, Frederick	*San Francisco*

Reid, Ken	*Los Angeles*
Rotblatt, Evelyn	*Santa Monica*
S Sarkisian, Armen	*Los Angeles*
Saulter, Leon	*Los Angeles*
Schaller, Edwin S.	*Burbank*
Scott, David	*Claremont*
Scott, Jonathan	*South Pasadena*
Serisawa, Sueo	*Los Angeles*
Sexton, Fred	*Los Angeles*
Sheets, Millard	*Claremont*
Shepherd, Nina	*Claremont*
Shore, Merle	*Hollywood*
Siegel, Jack	*Los Angeles*
Siegriest, Lundy	*Oakland*
Slick, Barbara	*Berkeley*
Smeltzer, Robert H.	*Los Angeles*
Smith, Robert A.	*South Pasadena*
Smith, Walter A.	*Burbank*
Steinlauf, Saul	*Los Angeles*
Stern, Arthur H.	*Los Angeles*
Stewart, Albert	*Claremont*
Stone, Nathalie	*Los Angeles*
Stussy, Jan	*Los Angeles*
Surendorf, Charles	*Columbia*
Syminton, Emily	*Los Angeles*
V Van Leyden, Karin	*Los Angeles*
Van Young, Oscar	*Los Angeles*
Veres	*Los Angeles*
W Wade, Bennett	*Santa Monica*
Wallett, William	*Los Angeles*
Waring, Pegot	*Beverly Hills*
Warshaw, Howard	*Beverly Hills*
Weinstein-Sherak, Jac	*Los Angeles*
Whenham, George B.	*Los Angeles*
Whitaker, Irwin	*Carmel*
Wildhaber, Paul	*Los Angeles*
Wilks, Ben	*Los Angeles*
Willis, Brooks	*Los Angeles*
Wood, Melvin	*Claremont*
Woodruff, James W.	*Los Angeles*
Y Ybarra, Alfred	*Los Angeles*
Yoakum, Delmer	*Inglewood*
Z Zornes, Milford	*Claremont*

Arts of Southern California: Painting

Forty painters are represented in this exhibition. Twenty have been of national importance during the past fifteen years; they are referred to as the "Distinguished". The other twenty, called the "Vanguard", are promising painters of recent discovery. Various schools of expression and trends in contemporary art are represented in this comprehensive exhibit.

A SURVEY EXHIBITION PREPARED BY

LONG BEACH MUSEUM OF ART

JANUARY 5th TO FEBRUARY 2nd, 1958

The selection is based on an objective compilation of nominations and recommendations received from art critics, art editors, art organizations, galleries, painting instructors, art historians, museum personnel, chairmen and directors of art departments of universities, colleges, and art schools in Southern California.

PARTICIPATING PAINTERS

DISTINGUISHED	VANGUARD
William Brice	Sam Amato
Hans Burkhardt	Karl Benjamin
Francis de Erdely	Paul Darrow
Leonard Edmondson	Robert Ellis
Edgar Ewing	Connor Everts
Lorser Feitelson	Robert Frame
Keith Finch	Shirle Goedike
Richard Haines	Leon Goldin
Ejnar Hansen	James Jarvaise
Ynez Johnston	Robert Johnson
John Paul Jones	Irene Koch
Roger Kuntz	Douglas McClellan
Dan Lutz	James McGarrell
S. Macdonald-Wright	John McLaughlin
Lee Mullican	Orrel P. Reed, Jr.
Channing Peake	David Schnabel
Richards Ruben	Vic Smith
Sueo Serisawa	Jan Stussy
Millard Sheets	Don Yacoe
Howard Warshaw	Jack Zajac

OTHER PAINTERS RECOMMENDED

DISTINGUISHED

Oronzo Abbatecola
Arthur Beaumont
Mary Bowling
Rex Brandt
Robert Chuey
Van D. Copeland
Robert Cremean
Leland Curtis
Phil Dike
Jules Engel
Fritz Faiss
George Gibson
Ted Gillen
Duncan Gleason
Martin Green
John Hilton
Clarence Hinkle
Marjorie Hyde
Francis Kelly
Leonard Kester
Emil Kosa, Jr.
Rico Lebrun*
Helen Lundeberg
Elaine Malco
Joshua Meador
Ben Messick
Velma May Messick
William Munson
Agnes Pelton
Polia Pillin
Edward Reep
Henry L. Richter
Stewart Robertson
Benton Scott
Karl Seethaler
Burr Singer
Peter Volkus
June Wayne
Jirayn Zorthian

VANGUARD

Josephine Ain
John Altoon
Webster Anderson
Jeanne Couttes Anguiano
Mele Anguiano
Kalman Aron
Walter Askin
Irma Attridge
Max Bailey
Jack Baker
Edward Betts
Sergei Bongart
Harry Bornstein
Dorothy Bowman
Howard Bradford
Sue Bravender
Bettina Brendel
Donald Brewer
Maurice Broderson
Dorothy Brown
William Brill
Freeman Butts
Gerald Campbell
Elena K. Canavier
Harry Carmecn
Poppy Clark
Robert Clark
Samuel Clayberger
Katherine Conover
Ruth Codman
Harry Cohen
Russell Combs
Carol Cornell
Keith Crown
Leonard Cutrow
Donald Dame
Anita Delano
Orval Dillingham
William Dole
Renate Druks
Douglas Duder
Catherine Fels
Howard Fenton
Milton Gershgoren
James Grant
Lucille Brown Greene
Christian Gronfeldt
Frederick Hammersley
Robert Hansen
Herrica Hartmetz
Wilbur Haynie
Gilbert Henderson
Dale Hennesy
William Hesthal
James Hueter
Robert Irwin
Tony Ivins
George James
Dorothy Jordan
Karl Kanol

Sheldon Kirby
Gerd Koch
Edmund Kohn
Leonard Kaplan
Evelyn Kane
Felicia Kaner
James Knibb
Josephine Y. Kopenhauer
Wayne LaCom
Susan Lautmann
John Leeper
Blessing Le Mohn
Donald Lent
Hilda Levy
Linda Lewis
Albert Londaville
Dorothy Lotts
Marty Lubner
Theo Lukits
John Martin
J. Patrick MacLean
Malcolm McClain
William McEnroe
Geraldine McLaughlin
Arnold Mesches
Jay Meuser
Walter Mix
Martin Mondrus
Joseph Mugnaini
Shirley Murphy
Mary Beich Myers
Stowe Norman
Gordon Nunes
Ruth Osgood
Mary Parker
Aubrey J. R. Penny
Florence Philleo
Marion Pike
Marlyn Prior
Roland Reiss
Shirley Rice
Arthur Richer
Larry Rink
Julian Ritter
Herbert Ryman
Marvin Saltzman
Bently Schaad
Amalia Schulthess
Fred Sexton
R. Sheppard, Mrs.
Marcia Shlaudeman
Jerold Simon
Eva Slater
Fran Soldini
Joseph Stanley
David Stiles
Donald Stocks
James Strombotne
Willie Suzuki
Michio Takayama
Robert Thomas
Charles Thompson
Jean Thompson
Carla Tomaso
Herbert B. Turner

Oscar Van Young
Gordon Wagner
Eugene Wallin
Elsa Warner
Guy Williams
Paul Winslow
Tyrus Wong
Leona Wood
Robert E. Woods
Joseph Young
Curtis Zahn

A
Boyd Allen
Ella Alluisi
Jeremy Anderson
Ruth Armer
Victor Arnautoff
Walter Askin
Richard Ayer

B
Francis Baldwin
George Ball
Katherine Barieau
Joel Barletta
Roger Barr
Mona Beaumont
Robert Bechtle
Elio Benvenuto
Elmer Bischoff
Lucienne Bloch
Adrienne Bonn
Dorr Bothwell
Joseph Brooks
Joe Brotherton
William Brown

C
Louise Boyer Cardeiro
Sandra Carlson
Sung Woo Chun
Marian Clark-Cooch
Gail Cole
Richard Cole
V. Conroy
Lucy Coons
Dorothy P. Cravath
Harry Crotty
Marie G. Cruess

D
Bethel DeBoie
Tony DeLap Jr.
Robert Dhaemers
Richard Diebenkorn
Leola Dixon
Ralph DuCasse
Helen Dunham

E
Mary Erkenbrack
Earl Escher

F
D. Faralla
Charles Griffin Farr
William Faulker
Bella Feldman
Amy Dewing Fleming
Peter Forakis
Syd Fossum
Esther T. Fuller

G
Nancy Genn
Lida Giambastiani
Charles E. Gill
John W. Gill
Art Grant
Ethel Grau

H
Hildegarde Haas
Lez L. Haas
Teresa Caselle Hack
John Haley
Jean Halpert-Ryden
Leah R. Hamilton
Maggie Hazell
Wally Hedrick
Hon-Chew Hee
Meta C. Hendel
Otto G. Hitzberger
Robert L. Holdeman
Arthur S. Holman

J
Edward Johanson
Doris Miller Johnson
Ralph Johnson

K
Evelyn Kane
Felicia Caner
Karl Kasten
Mar Jean Zegart Kett
Adrienne Kraut

L
Irene Lagorio
George Laisner
Maurice Lapp
Hilda Levy
Robert Loberg
Seymour Locks
Erle Loran

M
Henry Marie-Rose
Caroline Martin
Gardiner McCauley
Robert McChesney
Charles E. Modecke
Keith Monaghan
William Morehous
Doris C. Morrison
Jose Moya del Pino
Gertrude Murphy
Darwin Musselman

N
Emiko Nakano
Mary Navratil
Richard E. Nelson
Alexander Nepote
Ethel Nerger

James Nichols
Kiyoo Nobuyuki

O
N. Eric Oback
Otis Oldfield
Samuel Ow

P
David Park
Irene Pattinson
Rose Pauson
Werner Philipp
Clayton Pinkerton
Theodore Polos
Elsie Lower Pomeroy
George Post
Samuel Provenzano
Ralph Putzker

Q
Elizabeth Quandt

R
Sonya Rapoport
Henry Rasmussen
Fred Reichman
Deborah Remington
Richard Reynolds
John E. Richards
Peter Rodriguez
Liesel Rosenthal
Leighton Ross
Avrum Rubenstein

S
John Saccaro
Charles Safford
Helen Salz
Isobel Sanford
Zygmund Sazevich
Peter Shoemaker
Louis Siegriest
Lundy Siegriest
David Simpson
Nell Sinton
Lee Splivalo
Gilbert Steed
Juliette Steele
Helen G. Steinau
Edna Stoddard
Mel Strawn
Florence A. Swift

T
Earl Thollander
David Tolerton
Horst B. Trave
Stavros Trian
Serge Trubach

V
Benjamin Vaganov

Beth Van Hoesen
W
Charles Ward
Jules Wasserstein
James Weeks
Glenn Wessels
Ketherine Westphal
Emil White
Richard A. White
R. Alan Williams
Hamilton Wolf
William F. Wolff
Paul Wonner
Y
Noriko Yamamoto

Treasury of Living Art Desert Art Center

ADAMS, FRANK, Box 668, Sky Forest, Calif., Phone 4702
ALBERT, KARL, 1828 Sierra Vista, Alhambra, Calif., Phone AT 4-5864
ALEXANDER, ANITA, 1011 Cielo Drive, Palm Springs, Calif., Phone 324-9226
ALEJANDRO, NEPOMUCENO, 30-840 Mission Drive, Palm Springs, Calif.
AMIS, TOM, 5255 ½ Meridian Street, Los Angeles 42, Calif.
ANDERS, ALTA M., 1840 Davis Drive, Fallbrook, Calif., Phone 728-2029
ANDERSON, ULA, Box 135, Redlands, Calif.
ARNER, SAMUEL D., Box 687, Cathedral City, Calif., Phone 328-3251
ASH, DALE K., 30-400 San Diego Drive, Palm Springs, Calif.
ANGUIANO, JEANNE COUTS, 654 Cannon Drive, Palm Springs, Calif.
AZZARELLI, SALVATORE, 2599 S. Palm Canyon Drive, Palm Springs, Calif.,
BABIN, AILEEN, P.O. Drawer 758, Desert Hot Springs, Calif., Phone 329-5555
BACON, FLORENCE, 77-900 Michigan, Palm Desert, Calif., Phone FI 6-2235
BAKER, MARCILLE A., 32-299 Shifting Sands Trail, Palm Springs, Calif.,
BAKERSFIELD ART ASSOCIATION, 1930 R Street, Bakersfield, Calif.
BALKINS, ALMON J., 1280 Palos Verde Avenue, Palm Springs, Calif.,
BALLINGER, CATHERINE S., 2160 Laurel Avenue, Pomona, Calif., Phone NA 9-3274
BEAN, WILLIAM, 46-173 Highway 74, Apt. 6, Palm Desert, Calif.
BEARDEN, CLAIRE, Royal Palms 34-851 Date Palm Drive, Palm Springs, Calif.
BECK, PAULINE, 15 Hillside Avenue, Rancho Park, Palm Springs, Calif.
BECKER, FREDERICK W., 38-660 Pel Air Drive, Cathedral City, Calif., Phone 328-1958
BEELER, MARTAIN J., 3532 Madera Avenue, Los Angeles 39, Calif., Phone NO 5-7328
BELMONT, STEVEN, 15-156 Washington Street, Fontana, Calif., Phone 822-6171
BENEDICT, ELIZABETH M., 5140 Harriett Avenue So., Minneapolis, Minn.
BENDER, BILL, Star Route Box 154, Oro Grande, Calif., Phone CHapel 5-5170
BENNETT, ANN M., 322 Onyx, Balboa Island, Calif.
BENNING, CORAL, 2580 Junipero, Palm Springs, Calif., Phone 325-3829
BERG, CHESTER E., 1653 Vista Way, El Cajon, Calif., Phone 442-8483
BERUBE, GAILE, 11 Beverly Hills, Palm Springs, Calif.
BERTRAND, LUCILLE, Box 151, Palm Desert, Calif., Phone FI 6-6289
BIRKES, ALICE L., Sky Ridge Park, Cathedral City, Calif.
BLANE, HAZEL R., 225 So. Grand Street, Orange, Calif.
BODNER, JOSEPH, 15-924 Parthenia Street, Sepulveda, Calif., Phone EX 8-5852
BOHANNAN, TOY, 30-955 San Gabriel Circle, Palm Springs, Calif., Phone 327-2600
BONAR, LESTER, 1562 Munson Avenue, Los Angeles 42, Calif.
BOLLINGER, MARGARET E., 46-171 Highway 74, Palm Desert, Calif., Phone FI 6-8681
BOUCHER, AL, 71-170 Cypress Lane, Cathedral City, Calif.
BORCHARD, THERESA, 19-473 Grand Avenue, Elsinore, Calif.
BOWMAN, LORI, 11-505 Culver Park Drive, Culver City, Calif., Phone EX 8-5852
BORMAN, LEONARD, P.O. Box 533, Joshua Tree, Calif.
BRADY, RUTH, 1234 Catalina Blvd., San Diego 7, Calif.
BOYER, EDA, 5 Ramon Circle, Rancho Trailer Park, Palm Springs, Calif.
BRANDES, LINNEX, 32-132 Rancho Vista Drive, Palm Springs, Calif., Phone 328-2806
BRADY, DONNA, 68-544 2nd St., P.O. Box 518, Cathedral City, Calif.,
BRAY, CARL G., 77-689 Highway 111, Palm Desert, Calif., Phone FI 6-6551
BRICKMAN, EUGENE J., 414 South St. Andrews Place, Los Angeles 5, Calif.,
BROTT, ADELE JOAN, 32-329 Whispering Palms Trail, Palm Springs, Calif.,
BROWN, EDNA M., P.O. Box 698, Desert Hot Springs, Calif., Phone 329-4311
BROWN, MARY ELLA, Sky Ridge Park, Cathedral City, Calif., Phone 328-9007
BROWN, ELIZABETH J., 13-501 E. Tracy Street, Baldwin Park, Calif.,
BROWN, TRACY S., 666 Plaza Amigo, Palm Springs, Calif., Phone 327-2242
BUDD, HARRY K., 507 Larkspur Avenue, Corona Del Mar, Calif., Phone OR 3-6618
BUFF, ETHEL, 81-920 Victoria Street, Indio, Calif., Phone DI 7-1594
CAGE, MABEL, 2965 Waverly Dr., Los Angeles 39, Calif.
CARSON, DON, 22 Alvarado Street, Berkeley, Calif.
CAMPBELL, ANN, 77-334 Missouri Drive, Palm Desert, Calif.
CAMPBELL, CHARLES, P.O. Box 843, Hemet, Calif.

CANEDO, ALEXANDER, 503 N. Robertson Blvd., Los Angeles 48, Calif.,
CASELLA, VIRGINIA L., No. 12 Silver Spur Tr. Pk., Phone FI 6-8881
CHISNALL, FRED R., Box 2.63, Rancho Mirage, Calif.,` Phone 328-2802
CHISNALL, EVELYN, 42470 E. Veldt, Ranch Mirage, Calif., Phone 328-2802
CLEAVES, MARIE L., 66-126 W. Estrella, Desert Hot Springs, Calif.,
CLARKE, ADELINE E., 272 Via Las Palmas, Palm Springs, Calif., Phone 325-5624
COBLENTZ, GEORGE W., 1020 18th Street Apt. C., Santa Monica, Calif.,
CLEEK, LEONARD W., 1540 Sagebrush Rd., Palm Springs, Calif.
COCHEMS, RALPH W., 1943 Tachevah Drive, Palm Springs, Calif.,
CORDREY, EARL S., 274 W. Alejo Road, Palm Springs, Calif.
CORNWALL, VIOLA, 21 N. 100 West, St. George, Utah
CORNWALL, MABLE, 11-790 Peach Tree Road, Yucaipa, Calif.
CROW, ANNA G., P.O. Box 163, Cathedral City, Calif., Phone 328-2823
COVINGTON, SADIE A. 2714 Anza Trail, Palm Springs, Calif., Phone 327-2665
CULBERTSON, NAOMI, Star Route No. 1, Box 624, 29 Palms, Calif.,
CREAMER, MARY, 33-881 Chula Vista, Dana Point, Calif.
CUMMINS, MARJORIE RANSOM, 31-479 Avenue E, Yucaipa, Calif.,
CRAVENS, GIFFORD, 82-248 San Jacinto, Indio
CREESE, MARJORIE REED, Forks of Salmon, Calif.
DALLONS, JOHN, 11-609 Lenox Street, Yucaipa, Calif.
DALLONS, SUZANNE, 587 Vista Oro, Palm Springs, Calif., Phone 324-2775
DANNER, VANCE, 1672 N. Riverside Drive, Palm Springs, Calif., Phone 325-5634
DEAN, WAYNE, 1406 Garden Street, Redlands, Calif.
DE GASTON, VIOLET, 34 Hollywood, Rancho Trailer Park, Palm Springs, Calif.,
DE MILLE, LESLIE B., 929 Duke Place, Anaheim, Calif.
DE PEW, MAURINE, 1011 La Cadena Drive No. 14, Riverside, Calif., Phone 684-4157
DE VOSS, CHARLOTTE, Van B. Ranch Route No. 1, Box 62, Coachella, Calif.
DEXTER, PEGGY, 1915 El Oro Way, Palm Springs, Calif., Phone 325-5618
DOERING, BONNIE, 1831 Old Orchard Road, Los Angeles 49, Calif.,
DONS, ED M., P.O. Box 94, Bermuda Dunes, Calif., Phone DI 7-2016
DOMELA, JAN M., 560 Hanley Avenue, Los Angeles 49, Calif.
DUNCAN, DARWIN, 12-422 Lambert Circle, Garden Grove, Calif., Phone LE 9-4869
ECKLES, MABEL, 5042 Pioneer Blvd., Whittier, Calif.
EICKELAND, PETER, 7306 El Verno Drive, Buena Park, Calif.
ELLIOTT, ELIZABETH M., 564 Ramon, Laguna Beach, Calif.
ELSTAD, BERT, 2012 Leeward Lane, Newport Beach, Calif., Phone MI 6-8235
ESSIG, JEAN GRACE, 39-905 Budd Lane, Apt. 16, Cathedral City, Calif.
FAGERSTAM, WILLY PETERSEN, 34-845 Avenue D, Yucaipa, Calif.,
FENTON, IRENE, 45-999 Verba Santa, Palm Desert, Calif., Phone FI 6-2486
FISHER, JULIUS, 31-382 Avenida La Gaviota, Palm Springs, Calif., Phone 328-2983
FORBES, E. L., 1104 E. Everett Place, Orange, Calif., Phone KE 8-1509
FOSTER, DON, 5541 Ravia Street, Lakewood, Calif.
FRANKS, LEON, 384 N. Coast Blvd., Laguna Beach, Calif., Phone HY 4-4444
FREY, JOSEPH & KATHERINE FREY, 148 Beckley's Circle, Palm Springs, Calif.,
FRIDAY, EVE, 1303 Briger, Las Vegas, Nevada
GARRICK, CAMPBELL, 2014 Howard, Whittier, Calif.
GERAGHTY, BETZ, 1557 S. Riverside Drive, Palm Springs, Calif., Phone 325-5656
GIBBIAN, ERIC H., Desert Braemar Apt. 21, Cathedral City, Calif.
GIBBS, GEORGE S., 1380 Park Row, La Jolla, Calif.
GIESHEN, ELSA, 2025 Crestview Drive, Laguna Beach Calif., Phone 494-3914
GILL, STANLEY H., Sky Ridge Trailer Park, Cathedral City, Calif.
GLASS, HENRY, 505 N. Electric, Alhambra, Calif., Phone 282-7104
GNAGY, JON, 53-530 Country Club Drive, Idyllwild, Calif., Phone 659-2136
GOLTERMANN, FLORENCE, Star Route No. 2, Box 241, Yucca Valley, Calif.,
GOMEZ, M. A., 2905 Bayview Drive, Manhattan Beach, Calif., Phone FR 2-3219
GOODALL, GRACE, 384 N. Coast Blvd., Laguna Beach, Calif.
GRAVES, MARY BETH, 128 Chula Vista, Palm Springs
GRAVES, O. E. L., 1994 Yucca, Palm Springs, Calif., Phone 327-2002
GRIERSON, EVELYNE B., 3206 W. 132nd Street, Hawthorne, Calif.,
HAAK, CRYSTAL, 1429 Riverside Drive, Palm Springs, Calif.
HAFER, HELEN, 1037 W. Chapman, Orange, Calif.
HAGER, BILL, 63-957 Radio Road, Palm Springs, Calif., Phone 324-1835

HARRIS, SAM HYDE, 16 Champion Place, Alhambra, Calif., Phone AT 4-3872
HARTLEY, FRED, Desert Braemer, Apt. C, Cathedral City, Calif.
HARTMAN, HARRY I., Citrus Avenue, Los Angeles 36, Calif.
HEATH, HAZEL, Sky Ridge Park, Cathedral City, Calif., Phone 328-9007
HEAVIN, STELLA P., 26-393 Sun City Blvd., Sun City, Calif., Phone 679-2169
HEINECKE, G. W., 34-794 Avenue E, Yucaipa, Calif.
HEINLEY, PAUL, P.O. Box 335, Palm Desert, Calif., Phone 328-4124
HICKEY, VINCENT, 12-432 Yorba Street, Orange, Calif.
HINCKLEY, LAWRENCE B., P.O. Box 175, Fillmore, Calif.
HILLS, PALMER J., General Delivery, Idyllwild, Calif.
HILTON, JOHN, Box 114, 29 Palms, Calif.
HIRLEMAN, Donald W., P.O. Box 677, Palm Springs, Calif., Phone 324-3351
HIRSCH, OTTO R., General Delivery, Cathedral City, Calif.
HISEY, BILL L., 964 Tuxedo Circle, Palm Springs, Calif., Phone 325-6989
HISEY, THOMAS, 777 E. Union Street, Pasadena, Calif.
HITCHCOCK, ROY, 1153 San Lucas Rd., Palm Springs, Calif., Phone 325-5758
HOEPTNER, LIDA S., 15-115 S. W. Jeffrey Road, Santa Ana, Calif., Phone 544-3018
HOLDITCH, FRANCESKA S., 965 Chino Canyon Road, Palm Springs, Calif.,
HOLDEN, PAMELA and GEORGE, P.O. Box 452, Battle Mountain, Nevada
HOPKINS, WILLIAM, General Delivery, Palm Springs, Calif., Phone 327-2825
HUNSUCKER, EVELYN N., P.O. Box 313, Thermal, Calif.
HUNTER, MARGARET L., P.O. Box 757, Indio, Calif., Phone DI 7-0393
HUSEBY, ARLEEN, 1215 Oakglenn Avenue, Arcadia, Calif., Phone 447-6667
HYDE, PASCAL, 300 E. Ramon Road, Palm Springs, Calif., Phone 325-2505
INCH, HILDA, 1202 Upas Street, San Diego 3, Calif., Phone CY 8-5751
JARRETT, MARY, 450 S. Swall Drive, Beverly Hills, Calif., Phone CR 1-3654
JENKINS, BETTY, 1545 Riviera Drive, Pasadena, Calif., Phone EL 5-2659
JEFFERY, R. L. (DR.), Sand & Shadows, Highway 74, Palm Desert, Calif.,
JOHNSON, GLADYS L., 158 Caravan Sahara Park, Palm Springs, Calif.,
JOHNSON, GRACE W., 236 Poppy Avenue, Monrovia, Calif.
JOHNSON, KATHERINE KING, 13 Sky Ridge Pk., 68-915 H, Cathedral City, Cal.,
JONES, ANITA HASKELL, 1732 Mesa Drive, Palm Springs, Calif., Phone 325-5437
KALER, EDDIE K., P.O. Box 970, Palm Springs, Calif., Phone 327-1571
KALISZ, GENE A., P.O. Box 612, Apple Valley, Calif., Phone CH 7-7031
KELLAR, PHYLLIS A., Lead, South Dakota
KIESTER, RAY, 1855 The Alameda, San Jose, Calif.
KLEINJUNG, LILLIAN S., P.O. Box 292, Desert Hot Springs, Calif., Phone 329-5175
KLINE, SHIRLEY, 134 Palo Verde, Palm Springs, Calif., Phone 325-2744
KLEPPEL, F. CHARLES, 2905 Bayview Drive, Manhattan Beach, Calif.
KLOSS, MARGARET H., 37-152 Ferber Drive, Cathedral City, Calif.,
KREHM, WILLIAM P., 1485 E. Hofer Street, Banning, Calif., Phone 849-2834
LAKE, HARRIETT E., P.O. Box 1121, Palm Desert, Calif., Phone FI 6-8747
LANDRY, ROBERT, 8882 Del Rose Avenue, Springs Valley, Calif., Phone 327-2861
LANGSTON, GILDA E., 896 N. Raymond Avenue, Pasadena, Calif.,
LAU, MRS. PAUL, 7325 N. 14th St., Phoenix 20, Arizona
LAURITZ, PAUL, 3953 Clayton Avenue, Hollywood, Calif.
LAWRENCE, MARION E., 348 Raincloud, Ramon Pk., Palm Springs, Calif.,
LAWTON, W. F., 9421 E. Apache Trail, Mesa, Calif.
LEWIS, MARYLAND, Box 483, Dana Point, Calif., GY 6-5174
LIBBY, CLARICE, 2156 Rural Place, Costa Mesa, Calif.
LINDBERG, OSCAR W., 1640 Montrose Avenue, Hemet, Calif.
LINDROTH, GRELA, 5359 Elmwood Road, San Bernardino, Calif.
LINUS, AXEL, 243 Avenida Ortega, Palm Springs, Calif., Phone 324-2485
LOGAN, KICKAPOO, 1959 Cloverfield Avenue, Santa Monica, Calif.,
LOGAN, LEE, 459 6th Avenue, Twin Falls, Idaho, Phone 733-8650
LOZIER, PHILIP, General Delivery, Cathedral City, Calif.
LOY, HOWARD, 3840 Glenfeliz Boulevard, Los Angeles 39, Calif.,
LOVE, RALPH, P.O. Box 197, Temecula, Calif., Phone 676-2813
LYON, GLADYS S., 355 Mountain View Place, Palm Springs, Calif.,
MacARTHUR, MRS. PETER J., 460 Via Lola, Palm Springs, Calif., Phone 324-1833
MacLEAN, GEORGIA, 1139 Abrigo Road, Palm Springs, Calif., Phone 324-1914
MacPHERSON, EARL, 1905 Araby Drive, Palm Springs, Calif., Phone 327-2021

McCOY, WILTON, 68-415 Treasure Trail, Cathedral City, Calif., Phone 328-2021
McCULLEY, BEATRIZ MAURINE, 74-373 Pepper Grass Street, Palm Desert, Calif.,
McCONKEY, WILLIAM S., 1209 E. Ocean Blvd., Long Beach, Calif.
McCREA, HAZEL H., 1295 Elm Avenue, Beaumont, Calif., Phone 845-2247
MAYERS, ELSA L., 1165 Abrigo Road, Palm Springs, Calif.
McDONALD, O., 260 E. Avenue L, Calimesa, Calif., Phone 797-4631
McGILL, WILLIAM S., 1290 E. Ocean Blvd., Long Beach, Calif.
McGREW, R. BROWNELL, P.O. Box 411, La Quinta, Calif., Phone DI 7-4217
MAXWELL, JAMES E., 4282 Almond Street, Riverside, Calif.
McGUIRE, ESTHER, 300 E. Ramon Road, Palm Springs, Calif.
MAASS, MARIE D., 502 Compadre Road, Palm Springs, Calif.
MARTIN, KIRK, Box 542, Yucca Valley, Calif., Phone 365-7207
MARKS, MACKIE M., 5345 Mountain View Drive, Palm Springs, Calif.,
MEADOR, JOSHUA, Box 117, Caspar, Calif.
MATHEWSON, HAZEL, P.O. Box 97, 29 Palms, Calif., Phone 367-9276
MEEHAN, HAZEL, 153 S. Pepper Street, Orange, Calif., Phone 538-6085
MARSHALL, MRS. ELSIE, 7626 Johnson View, Yucca Valley, Calif.
MEISENBACH, ALBERTUS C., 3705 W. Ramsey, Banning, Calif., Phone 849-9912
MERRITT, MARSHALL, 10 Glen Ridge Avenue, Los Gatos, Calif., Phone 354-3924
METZGER, HILDEGARD, P.O. Box 391, Morongo Valley, Calif., Phone 342-6531
MILLER, GEORGE, P.O. Box 116, Desert Hot Springs, Calif., Phone 329-5694
MILLER, JANE C., The Wooden Latch, 54-500¼ Pinecrest Drive, Idyllwild, Calif.
MILLONIG, HILDEGARD, 683 Indian Trail, Palm Springs, Calif., Phone 324-4017
MITCHELL, LLOYD, 9150 Las Tunas, Temple City, Calif., Phone AT 6-484
MOAK, STERLING, 199 W. Racquet Club Road, Palm Springs, Calif..
MOORTON, PATRICIA, 1701 S. Palm Canyon Drive, Palm Springs, Calif.,
MORGANTHALER, PAT, 11-281 Hermosa Drive, Fullerton, Calif.
MORTON, LUCILLE L., 7492 Hopi Trail, Yucca Valley, Calif., Phone 365-8522
MOYER, VIRGINIA, Silver Spur Trailer Park, Palm Desert, Calif.
MURRAY, MADELYNE, Pinto Mountain Road, P.O. Box 583, 29 Palms, Calif.
NEAL, LAURA, 2937 Madison Avenue, Carlsbad, Calif.
NAYLOR, EVELYN and THOMAS, Beckley's Circle, Hwy. 111, Palm Springs, Cal.,
NEIL, DOTY, 823 Calle Tomas, Palm Springs, Calif., Phone 328-2021
NEILSON, MADELINE, 37-801 Neilson Road, Cathedral City, Calif.,
NILS, DEANA, 1156 Glenneyer, Laguna Beach, Calif.
NOSANOV, HARRY G., 6021 2nd Street, Desert Hot Springs, Calif.,
NUFER, GLENN, P.O. Box 127, Morongo Valley, Calif.
OLAINE, LOLITA A., 1296 Alameda de Las Pulgas, Redwood City, Calif.,
O'NEILL, F. JACK, 347 No. Lima, Burbank, Calif., Phone 846-5682
OSTER, GENEVA, 2916 West 132nd Street, Gardena, Calif., Phone DA 3-2849
OSTRANDER, J. MARVIN, 150 N. Baristo Road, Palm Springs, Calif.,
OWENS, AL, 63-903 Oasis, Palm Springs, Calif.
OWEN, FLORENCE, 3121 Arvia St., Los Angeles, Phone CA 1-5688
PARSONS, CLAUDE, 393 Bonhill Road, Los Angeles 49, Calif.
PACK, RODNEY X., P.O. Box 76, Yucca Valley, Calif., Phone 365-8396
PAUL, A. K., 1620 Indian Trail, Palm Springs, Calif.
PALASKE, BILLIE, 142 Laguna Drive, Sahara Trailer Park, Palm Springs, Calif.,
PENNEY, PAULA MUNSON, 48-149 Silver Spur Trail, Palm Desert, Phone FI 6-1672
PENNEY, FRED, 48-149 Silver Spur Trail, Palm Desert, Calif., Phone FI 6-6355
PENROD, HAROLD, 8 Forest Home Blvd., Forest Falls, Calif., Phone PY 4-2578
PERSONA, W., 950 Glenneyer Street, Laguna Beach, Calif., Phone 494-1977
PETERSON, WILLIAM K., 34-130 Eureka Avenue, Yucaipa, Calif., Phone 797-0553
PIERREL, GILBERT A., 877 Cottonwood Avenue, Palm Springs, Calif.,
PIETSCH, NINA, P.O. Box 2804, Palm Springs, Calif.
PORRI-RUNKLE, ELSIE J., 435 Fairview, Arcadia, Calif.
QUARLES VAN UFFORD, ELIZABETH, 1632 Via Entrada, Palm Springs, Calif.,
RABE, BENJAMIN J., 1421 Cajon Street, Redlands, Calif., Phone 793-5445
RANDALL, REBEL, 32-112 Rancho Vista Drive, Palm Springs, Calif.,
RANDALL, VICKIE, 32-112 Rancho Vista Drive, Palm Springs, Calif.,
REED, ESMERALDA, P.O. Box 152, Whitewater, Calif., Phone 324-5344
RICHMOND, ISABELLE, 1565 E. Mission Road, Fallbrook, Calif.,
ROBERTS, ELIZABETH, F., 68-877 C Street, Cathedral City, Calif.,
ROBERTS, MABEL, General Delivery, Cathedral City, Calif., Phone 328-1545

ROBERTS, MARY W., 300 E. Ramon Road, Palm Springs, Calif., Phone 325-5205
ROPP, J. MARIE, P.O. Box 876, Desert Hot Springs, Calif., Phone 329-3484
ROSENTHAL, ROSE, 4331 4th Avenue, Los Angeles 8, Calif., Phone AX 3-1135
ROSSI, ROBERTO, 1743 E. Maple Street, Pasadena, Calif., Phone SY 5-2986
ROSSBACK, DOROTHY, P.O. Box 312, Kernville, Calif., Phone DR 6-2873
ROTHBART, EDNA, 483 Via Sol, Palm Springs, Calif., Phone 324-9464
RUSK, GERTRUDE, Indio, Calif.
SALMON, MILDRED, 247 Stevens Road, Palm Springs, Calif., Phone 324-2294
SAMUELSON, VAL A., 68-489 Grandview, Cathedral City, Calif., Phone 328-4872
SAWYER, CLIF, 2280 Araby Drive, Palm Springs, Calif., Phone 324-9521
SAURMANN, SALLY S., 9316 S. Figueroa, Los Angeles, Calif.
SCHADE, LELA, 1710 W. Southgate Avenue, Fullerton, Calif., Phone 525-8527
PATTY SCRATCH, 1418 N. Geneseo, Hollywood, Calif. or 32-660 Shifting Sands Tr.
SCHUMACHER, MARGE, 32-603 Desert Vista Rd. P.O. Bx. 638, Palm Spgs., Cal.,
SEAVY, MRS. WALTER, 26-596 Orange Avenue, Redlands, Calif.
SHERER, MARY R., 386 High Drive, Laguna Beach, Calif., Phone HY 4-3246
SEGO, BESSIE M., 13-490 Bryant, Yucaipa, Calif.
SIMMONS, FRANCIS, 505 Trailer Village, Palm Springs, Calif., Phone 324-2591
SHADDIX, B. J., 25-505 Fern Valley Road, Idyllwild, Calif.
SITTER, LARRY, 1450 N. Riverside Drive, Palm Springs, Calif., Phone 325-3529
SIMMICH, MYRNA, 5972 Olive Avenue, Long Beach, Calif.
SMIT, DERK, 23-522 Paseo de Valencia, Laguna Hills, Calif.
SMITH, DORIS DEAN, 359 N. 7th Street, Colton, Calif.
SMITH, DR. EDMUND H., 74 Sky Ridge Park, Cathedral City, Calif.,
SMITH, W. H., 183 Merito Place, Palm Springs, Calif.
SORENSEN, CARL, P.O. Box 602, Cathedral City, Calif., Phone 328-2844
SMITH, RUTH ANN, 82-237 Luce Avenue, Indio, Calif., Phone DI 7-3059
SPENCER, ANGELA & CHESTER, P.O. Box 267, Yucca Valley, Calif.,
SOBEL, FRIEDA, No. 1 Alessandro, Palm Springs, Calif., Phone 324-3843
STEPHENS, AILEEN, 618 Mesquite Avenue, Palm Springs, Calif., Phone 325-3306
SOUTHERN, DOROTHY, 2950 Via Vaguero, Palm Springs, Calif., Phone 325-3384
STOVALL, ARNO, Beckley's Circle Highway 111, Palm Springs, Calif., and
        1771 Monita Drive, Ventura, Calif., Phone 328-9018 or 643-3379
SQUIRE, OLIVE (FAVOR), 92 Santa Paula, Safari Trailer Park, Palm Springs, Calif.
STREMSKI, STELLA, 7963 Lemon Circle, La Mesa, Calif.
SUTHERLAND, JESSIE, 345 W. Lemon Avenue, Arcadia, Calif.
TAYLOR, BESSIE A., 23-832 Placid Lane, Colton, Calif., Phone 825-6508
TAYLOR, DARWIN Y., 31-305 Calle Jessica, 1000 Palms, Calif., Phone EX 0-2585
TEEPLE, OLIVE MAY, 2020 Victoria Drive, Santa Ana, Calif.
TEMPLETON, NANCY, P.O. Box 255, Wrightwood, Calif., Phone CH 9-3637
TEPLER, MRS. BEATRICE, 230 N. Carmelita Avenue, Hemet, Calif.
TITUS, WALTON C., 1327 N. Laurel Ave., Los Angeles 46, Calif.
THOMAS, LOUISE, 1033 Friar Court, Palm Springs, Calif., Phone 325-6783
TOENJES, CAROLYN R., General Delivery, Palm Springs, Calif.
TRACY, MARGUERITE, P.O. Box 63, Riverside, Calif.
TUTTLE, SHERLE, 1341 Park Row, La Jolla, Calif.
TREPAGNIER, LOUIS, 1682 E. Mendocino Street, Altadena, Calif., Phone SY 4-1437
TYREE, RALPH, 2422 Keys Road, Ceres, Calif.
ULLOA, DOMINGO O., 1412 El Centro Avenue, El Centro, Calif., Phone 352-5004
VAN AKEN, F. A. D., 5171 El Verano, Eagle Rock, Calif., Phone 255-2816
VAN AKEN, LAURENT, 5171 El Verano, Eagle Rock, Calif., Phone 255-2816
VAN DEUSEN, LENA, 570 Gale Hill Avenue, Lindsay, Calif., Phone 2-3231
VON SCHNEIDAU, CHRISTIAN, 1023 Emerald Bay, Laguna Beach and Kernville, Cali
VORE, DOROTHY, 417 S. Alte Vista, Monrovia, Calif.
WHITE, CHESTER, 833 W. 14th Street, Ontario, Calif.
WALTON, AMY, 4651 Lemona Avenue, Sherman Oaks, Calif., Phone ST 4-4130
WARD, KEITH, 34-807 Cedar Avenue, Yucaipa, Calif., Phone 797-7561
WARD, MARGARET, 34-807 Cedar Avenue, Yucaipa, Calif., Phone 797-7561
WEBB, FIRNE, 674 Eileen Circle, Beaumont, Calif., Phone 845-4175
WELLS, BYRON, P.O. Box 837, Balboa, Calif.
WHITCOMB, ESTHER & WARD, 819 Sonora Road, Costa Mesa, Calif.,
WHITE, DOLLY (AURORA) 14005 Whiterock Drive, La Mirada, Calif.,

WHITE, RUSSELL, El Adobe Motel, 29 Palms, Calif.
WHITE EAGLE, CARLOS, 30-605 Walker Avenue, Palm Springs, Calif.
WIESE, ROBERT H., P.O. Box 997, Desert Hot Springs, Calif.
WILCOXON, JOAN W. 524 Calle Abronia, Palm Springs, Calif.,
WILKINS, BERNICE, Box 152, Desert Hot Springs, Calif.
WISHY, ZENA WITTENBERG, 2425 Tuscan Road, Palm Springs, Calif.,
WOLSETH, JAMES, 581 B Street, Cathedral City, Calif., Phone 82887
WOOD, BOB, 520 Euclid Avenue, Beaumont, Calif.
WORCHESTER, EVA, 2086 Barona Road, Palm Springs, Calif., Phone 327-2296
WORKMAN, ESTER E., 13-331 Monte Vista, 1,000 Palms, Calif., Phone EX 0-2304
YELLENTI, NICOLAS, P.O. Box 59, Landers, Calif., Phone 364-2309
YOUNGHUSBAND, JOHN, 1015 Buena Vista Drive, Palm Springs, Calif.,
ZINT, WADE, 116 Travelodge Lane, Cathedral City, Calif.
ZUTTO, HARRY J., 3725 Fairway Blvd., Los Angeles 43, Calif., Phone AX 4-6324

MEMBERS TOO LATE TO BE CLASSIFIED

BRATTAINE, STAN, 1200 E. Peck St., Compton, Calif.
CROMWELL, JOANE, 71480 Mirage, Rancho Mirage, Calif., P.O. Box 488
HANAN, HERTA, 450 E. Arenas, Palm Springs, Calif., Phone 325-5555
HIGHBEE, LLOYD L., 2649 Baltic Ave., Long Beach, Calif., Phone GA 7-1988
HOVIS, AUGUSTA B., 74-565 Yucca Tree Dr., Palm Desert, Calif.
LAIRD, FRANCES, D at F St., Cathedral City, Calif.
OMELICH, FELIX L., 29 Sky Ridge, Cathedral City, Calif.
McCLAIN, CAROL, 141 Beckley Circle, Palm Springs, Calif., Telephone 328-9018
McCULLOUGH, KATHERINE, 2053 Brentwood, Palm Springs, Calif.
YANAGA, HARRY Y., 23 Coachella Heights, Coachella, Calif., Phone EX 8-3212
ZAHN, EARL H., 80-870 Highway 111, Indio, Calif., DI 7-6056
WILLIAMSON, MARIAM, 533 E St., Cathedral City, Calif.
PEPPERLING, SHIRLEY, 13802 Linner St., Garden Grove, Calif.

Treasury of Living Art Desert Art Center

1970

Desert Art Center Membership

ARCINIAGA, ALFREDO, 747 N. Claudina St., Anaheim, Calif. 92805
ADAMS, MR. & MRS. DAVID, 142 Beckley Circle, Palm Springs, Calif. 92262
ADAMS, HARVEY C., 738 Maria, Spring Valley, Calif. 92077
ASHLEY, MRS. TOOTIE, 455 S. San Jacinto Ave., Hemet, Calif. 92343
ASMAR, MISS ALICE, P.O. Box 1965, Hollywood, Calif. 90028
ANDERS, ALTA M., 1840 Davis Drive, Fallbrook, Calif. 92028
ANDERSEN, MRS. FLORENCE, 432 Chestnut Ave., Redlands, Calif. 92373
ANDERSON, CAROLYN, 81-291 Alberta Ave., Indio, Calif. 92201
ANDERSON, CLAIRE RUWE, 22 Araby — Sahara Pk., Palm Springs, Calif. 92262
ANGUIANO, MRS. JEANE COUTTS, 654 Canon Drive, Palm Springs, Calif. 92262
ALBRIGHT, CHARLES J., 1424 Gilbert Ave., Fullerton, Calif. 92633
BABIN, AILEEN, P.O. Box Dr. 758, Desert Hot Springs, Calif. 92240
BAILEY, ANNY M. K., 2952 Java Road, Costa Mesa, Calif. 92626
BAKER, ALFRED L., 1845 Princeton, Glendale, Calif. 91204
BAKER, MARCILLE, 32-299 Shifting Sands Tr., Palm Springs, Calif. 92262
BALL, LYLE V., 181 Bret Harte, Reno, Nevada 89502
BALLARD, DOROTHY E., 2001 Haciendo Blvd., Hacienda Heights, Calif. 91745
BARKS, CARL, P.O. Box 818, San Jacinto, Calif. 92383
BARKS, GARE', P.O. Box 818, San Jacinto, Calif. 92383
BARNETT, MARIAN, 572 Manzanita Dr., Los Osos, San Luis Obispo, Calif. 93401
BARTKO, WILLIAM J., 658 Cloudy Moon Dr., Box 205 Borrego Springs, Calif. 92004
BEARDON, CLAIRE, 54-850 Via De Anza, Palm Springs, Calif. 92262
BEAULIEU, JOSEPH P., 68-718 Victoria Dr., Palm Springs, Calif. 92262
BECK, KAY, 240 Via Olivera, Palm Springs, Calif. 92262
BECKER, FREDRICK W., 38-660 Bel Air Dr., Cathedral City, Calif. 92234
BELMONT, STEVEN, 15156 Washington Drive, Fontana, Calif. 92335
BENDER, BILL, Star Rt. Box 154, Oro Grande, Calif.
BERG, CHESTER, 1653 E. Vista Way, El Cajon, Calif. 92022
BERGER, DEAN W., 1011 Ramona Ave., Corona, Calif. 91720
BERNARD, MRS. TROLLY, 450 Chuckwalla, Palm Springs, Calif. 92262
BERUBE, GAILE F., 12 Hollywood, Rancho Park, Palm Springs, Calif. 92262
BETTIS, LAWRENCE M., 3530 Brayton Ave., Long Beach, Calif. 90807
BILLS, MELVA FARWELL, P.O. Box 394, Idyllwild, Calif. 92349
BLACK, SYLVIA, c/o Village Print Shop, 235 S. Indian Ave., Palm Springs, Calif.
BLANK, RUTH, c/o Ben Black Co., 206 N. Indian Ave., Palm Springs, Calif. 92262
BONAR, LESTER M., 1562 Munson Ave., Los Angeles, Calif. 90042
BONDI, LAWRENCE, 29005 Covecrest Dr., Palos Verdes, Calif. 90274
BORMAN, LEONARD, 60001 Onaga Trail, Joshua Tree, Calif. 92252
BOSSICK, THERESA, 44-595 San Jose, Palm Desert, Calif. 92260
BOWMAN, LORI, 4718C La Villa Marina, Marina Del Rey, Calif. 90291
BOYD, SHIRLEY, 2195 E. Alejo Road, Palm Springs, Calif. 92262
BOYER, EDA, 330 Lei Canyon Mobile Court, Palm Springs, Calif. 92262
BRADY, DONNA, 248-B Forbes Lane, Cathedral City, Calif. 92234
BRADY, RUTH K., 1234 Catalina Blvd., San Diego, Calif. 92107
BRAHEME, BERTA, 2151 Belding Dr., Palm Springs, Calif. 92262
BRAINERD, DOROTHY, 1130 Emma St., Ashland, Oregon 97520
BRAUNSCHWEIGER, HELEN, 551 Perugia Way, Los Angeles, Calif. 90024
BRAY, CARL G., 77-689 Highway 111, Palm Desert, Calif. 92260
BRIMER, ORA, 211 Main, Huntington Beach, Calif. 92646
BROTT, ADELE JOAN, 32-329 Whispering Palms, Palm Springs, Calif. 92262
BROWN, LLILABETH, 13501 E. Tracy St., Baldwin Park, Calif. 91706

BROWN, JESSE, 1964 Mayflower Pl., Hemet, Calif. 92343
BUCHHORN, ELLEN, P.O. Box 1052, Palm Desert, Calif. 92260
BUNKER, ZADDIE, 474 Hermosa Pl., Palm Springs, Calif. 92262
BURGESS, JAMES H., 74-405 Goleta, Palm Desert, Calif. 92260
BURNETT, LEE, 77-630 California Dr., Palm Desert, Calif. 92260
BYRNE, JEAN CAROLL, 1355 Catalina Drive, Laguna Beach, Calif. 92651
CAMPBELL, ANN, 77-334 Missouri Dr., Palm Desert, Calif. 92260
CAPPS, TONY, 2715 Junipero Ave., Palm Springs, Calif. 92262
CARTER, MARILYN, 81-348 Alberta Ave., Indio, Calif. 92201
COBLENTZ, GEORGE W., 10415 Canoga Ave., #134, Chatsworth, Calif. 91311
COCKRUM, DR. JAMES C., 622 S. Clara St., Anaheim, Calif. 92804
COLBUS, FRED H., 6800 Empire Grade, Santa Cruz, Calif. 95060
COLETTA, JAMES A., #10-1133 Laguna Canyon Rd., Laguna Beach, Calif. 92651
COOK, PAULINE, 45-420 Abronia Trail, Palm Desert, Calif. 92260
COONS, MRS. ROBBIN, 2309 Pebble Beach Dr., Palm Springs, Calif. 92262
COOPER, JEWEL, 28-940 Olympia Way, Sun City, Calif. 92381
CORY, MARY A., 15 Diamond E Drive, Siulver Spur Trailer Park, Palm Desert, Calif.
COUSINS, MR. & MRS. JOHNNIE, 68-733 Grove St., Cathedral City, Calif. 92234
CRABB, CECILE, 28 Cleveland, Palm Springs, Calif. 92262
CREELMAN, MARY ELLEN, 433 Via Lido Soud, Newport Beach, Calif. 92660
CROWELL, ANDA, 563 Paseo De Anza, Palm Springs, Calif. 92262
CURRY, BETTY N., 970 Guatay Ave., Chula Vista, Calif. 92011
CURRY, W. R., 317 - 13th Street, Sparks, Nevada 89431
CURTIS, BELVA R., 1029 W. 1st, Spokane, Washington 99204
DALLONS, SUZANNE, 587 Vista Oro, Palm Springs, Calif. 92262
DARLING, MARJORIE ADAMS, 1990 Barona Rd., Palm Springs, Calif. 92262
DANNER, VANCE, 1672 No. Riverside Drive, Palm Springs, Calif. 92262
DAYTON, GERTRUDE E., 952-D Springfield St., Upland, Calif. 91786
de HAVEN, MARTEL, P.O. Box 861, Morro Bay, Calif. 93442
DE PEW, MAURINE IRVING, 1011 La Cadena Dr., #24, Riverside, Calif. 92501
DE VAULT, PEARL, 965 W. Nicolet, Banning, Calif. 92220
de VOSS, CHARLOTTE, 2550 Pacific Coast Hwy. 121, Torrance, Calif. 90505
DE WILDE, JOHN, 9164½ Sunset Blvd., Hollywood, Calif.
DE WITT, FRANCES, 203 Malibu Drive, Palm Springs, Calif. 92262
DIBBEN VICTORIA E., 5018 Cahuenga Blvd., North Hollywood, Calif. 91601
DONS, ED. M., 79-282 Eisenhower Way, Indio, Calif. 92201
DONAHUE, ELEANOR L., 68-639 G. St., Cathedral City, Calif. 92234
DOUGLAS, F. C., 12106 S. York Ave., Hawthorne, Calif. 90250
DOWDEN, NOEL, 1684 E. Main, Rt. 2, Brawley, Calif. 92227
DUKES, MARY McRAE, 1916 Manoa Rd., Honolulu, Hawaii 96822
DUNCAN, DARWIN, 12422 Lambert Circle, Garden Grove, Calif. 92641
DUNN, LOUISE, 9 Travelodge Lane, Cathedral City, Calif. 92234
DUSCH, ALICE, 610 Ranger Rd., Fallbrook, Calif. 92028
EDWARD, BURTON P., 4135 Oak Hollow Road, Claremont, Calif. 91711
ELLIOTT, ELIZABETH, 564 Ramona, Laguna Beach, Calif. 92651
ELLIS, MRS. CATHERINE, P.O. Box 686, Cathedral City, Calif. 92234
EMERY, MARGARET, 100 Beckley Circle, Palm Springs, Calif. 92262
EUBANKS, MARJORIE, 29092 Desert Hills Road, Sun City, Calif. 92381
EWING, NANCY I., 2214 W. Ridgewood Santa Ana, Calif. 92701
EVANS, JAMES L., 73-625 Santa Rosa Way, Apt. #14, Palm Desert, Calif. 92260
FARBER, BLANCHE A., 2429 French St., Santa Ana, Calif. 92706
FELTS, LUCE, 48-070 Beverly Drive, Palm Desert, Calif. 92260
FENTON, IRENE, A.I.F.A., Box 573, Palm Desert, Calif. 92260
FILER, PEGGY, 73-845 Highway 111, Palm Desert, Calif. 92260
FLEISCHMAN, SAM, 924 San Lucas, Palm Springs, Calif. 92262
FOLLANDSBEE, GLADYS, 1345 Camino Primrose, Palm Springs, Calif. 92262
FORBES, E. L., 2121 E. Catalina St., Santa Ana, Calif. 92701
FOSTER, C. B., P.O. Box 295, Palm Desert, Calif. 92260
FREY, JOSEPH, 148 Beckley Circle, Palm Springs, Calif. 92262
FRANK, LELA, 81-292 Helen Ave., Indio, Calif. 92201
GENTRY, VIOLET J., P.O. Box 223, Palm Springs, Calif. 92262

GERSHON, ELSIE, 6014 Fairfax Ave., Los Angeles, Calif. 90056
GILBERTSON, GLADYS, 39-430 Del Air, Cathedral City, Calif. 92234
GLADFELTY, GENE, 1600-B E. 4th Street, Ontario, Calif. 91762
GLASGOW, DOROTHY, 42-965 Massachusetts, Palm Desert, Calif. 92260
GLASS, HENRY R., 505 No. Electric Ave., Alhambra, Calif. 91801
GOMEZ, ANTONIO MARCO, 2905 Bayview Drive, Manhattan Beach, Calif. 90266
GOODALL, GRACE, 972 Arapahoe St., Los Angeles, Calif. 90006
GOULD, DOROTHY, P.O. Box 433, Palm Desert, Calif. 92260
GRAVES, MILDRED I., 77-800 Michigan Dr., Apt. K-8, Palm Desert, Calif. 92260
GREGORY, JULIE, 405 Hawaihae St., (Hawaii Kai) Honolulu, Hawaii 96821
GRIMM, HEINER, c/o Al Faber, Box 593, Palm Desert, Calif. 92260
GROVER, NAOMI, Rt. 2, Box 1351, Crescent City, Calif. 95531
GUAY, MR. JEAN, 8210 Gould Ave., Hollywood, Calif. 90046
GUISE, HELEN M., P.O. Box 2705 Palm Springs, Calif. 92262
HAFER, HELEN, 1037 W. Chapman, Orange, Calif. 92668
HAGER, BELL, 175 Radio Road, Palm Springs, Calif. 92262
HALSTEAD, MURIEL, 267 Palos Verdes Dr. W., Apt. #7, Palos Verdes Estates, Calif.
HANDMAN, JO ANN, Star Rt. Box 965A, Lytle Creek, Calif. 92358
HANSEN, NADINE, P.O. Box 399, Yucca Valley, Calif. 92284
HARDY, MARGARET, 2244 Brookside, Orange, Calif. 92667
HAYWOOD, CHARLES L., 1680 La Cresta Drive, Pasadena, Calif.
HELLTHALER, KURT E., 224 Lei Drive, Palm Springs, Calif. 92262
HEMPHILL, ETTA, 5351 La Pasada, Long Beach, Calif. 90815
HERZOG, KAY, 274 Araby, Sahara Trailer Park, Palm Springs, Calif. 92262
HESS, ARTA, 67-751 Highway 111, Palm Springs, Calif. 92262
HIERS, LEE, 3135 Tyrol Drive, Laguna Beach, Calif. 92651
HILTON, JOHN W., P.O. Box 14, Twenty Nine Palms, Calif. 92277
HODGSON, MARGARET, 14439 Anola St., Whittier, Calif. 90604
HOLDEN, RONALD, 1317 Justin Ave., Glendale, Calif. 91201
HOPPER, MRS. BEEBE, 731 Beech Ave., Chula Vista, Calif. 92010
HOUSTON, LUETHEL, 73-651 B Golf Course Lane, Palm Desert, Calif. 92260
HOWELL, VIVIAN, 43 Santa Ana St., Palm Springs, Calif. 92262
HUNSUCKER, EVELYN, P.O. Box 403, Oxnard, Calif. 93030
HUNTER, MARGARET L., P.O. Drawer EEE, Indio, Calif. 92201
HURST, ELEANOR, 4824 Schuyler, La Mesa, Calif. 92041
HUSEBY, ARLEEN, 1215 Oakglen Ave., Arcadia, Calif. 91006
JAGGARS, ROSINE, 68-620 Nightingale St., Cathedral City, Calif. 92234
JAMES, VIRGINIA, P.O. Box 248, South Pasadena, Calif. 91030
JEFFERY, DR. R. L., 46-123 Highway 74, Palm Desert, Calif. 92260
JENKINS, MRS. ROBERT E., 1000 N. Point St., Fontana East No. 1402
    San Francisco, Calif. 94109
JOHNSON, ALICE A., 37-155 Melrose Drive, Palm Springs, Calif. 92262
JOHNSON, F. ERICK, 33-944 Ave. F., Yucaipa, Calif. 92399
JOHNSON, MAE C., P.O. Box 463, Morongo Valley, Calif. 92256
JOHNSON, MRS. MARSH, P.O. Box 2189, Reno, Nevada 89505
JOHNSON, RICHARD V., 440 W. San Antonio Dr., Long Beach, Calif. 90807
JONES, MRS. CLAIR B., P.O. Box 433, Corona Del Mar, Calif. 92625
JOSEPH, VIVIAN, 729 N. Sunrise Way, Palm Springs, Calif. 92262
KELLER, ADRIAN D., 68-481 Grandview Ave., Cathedral City, Calif. 92234
KELLER, MARGARETE, 16-548 Chatsworth St., Granada Hills, Calif. 91344
KELSEY, BETTY, 2167 Carillo Road, Palm Springs, Calif. 92262
KETTLE, KAY, 11 Buckeye, Mt. Herman, Calif.
KIRKER, ARTHUR W., 839 So. Olive St., Anaheim, Calif.
KLINE, SHIRLEY, 134 Palo Verde Ave., Palm Springs, Calif. 92262
KLOSS, MARGO, 37152 Ferber Dr., Cathedral City, Calif. 92234
KRAMER, ALLEN EDGAR, 331 West Point Dr., Claremont, Calif. 91711
KREHM, MRS. WILLIAM P., 1485 E. Hoffer, Banning, Calif. 92220
KUFFNER, FRITZIE, 271 So. Indian Ave., Palm Springs, Calif. 92262
KUMMER, WILLIAM JOSEPH, 772 Indian Ave., Palm Springs, Calif. 92262
LAKE, HARRIETT, P.O. Box 1121, Palm Desert, Calif. 92260
LANDRY, ROBERT, 8125 Lincoln St., Lemon Grove, Calif. 92045

LANGSTON, GILDA E., 896 N. Raymond, Pasadena, Calif. 91103
LAWRITZ, PAUL, 3955 Clayton, Los Angeles, Calif.
LEA, CLARA B., 269 Araby, Sahara Park, Palm Springs, Calif. 92262
LEWIS, MARYLAND, 33762 Chula Vista Ave., Dana Point, Calif. 92629
LIBBEY, CLARICE, 68-539 J. Street, Cathedral City, Calif. 92234
LINGO, GEORGE, Box 172, Palm Desert, Calif. 92260
LINSK, MRS. RITA, 1548 Santa Ana Canyon Rd., Orange, Calif.
LINUS, AXEL, 243 Avenida Ortega, Palm Springs, Calif. 92262
LLYWELYN, LUCY, 1653 W. 122nd St., Los Angeles, Calif. 90047
LOBBEREGT, DOROTHY, 60272 Overture Dr., Palm Springs, Calif. 92262
LOGAN, KICKAPOO, 19 Carmel Dr., Safari Park, Palm Springs, Calif. 92262
LO PORTO, DOROTHY, 1062½ Beaumont Ave., Beaumont, Calif.
LOY, HOWARD, 3840 Glenfeliz Blvd., Los Angeles, Calif. 90039
LUBO, F. BRUCE, SR., 16632 Golden West #2, Huntington Beach, Calif. 92647
LUTHRINGER, M. TOMREN, 35-123 Avenue B, Yucaipa, Calif. 92399
Mc CANDLES, CORAL, 209 Ave. E, Redondo Beach, Calif. 90277
McCREA, HAZEL H., 267 Palos Verdes Dr. West, Apt. 11, Palos Verdes Estates, Calif.
Mc CREA, HELEN, 1295 Elm Ave., Beaumont, Calif. 92223
McFARLAN, MRS. FLORENCE, 80-200 Ave. 50, Indio, Calif. 92201
McGRATH, BRUCE, 1440 Murial, Albuquerque, New Mexico
McKINNON, JOHN M., 81-490 Date Palm, Indio, Calif. 92201
Mc COY, WILTON & MYRTLE, P.O. Box 384, Cathedral City, Calif. 92234
Mc CULLEY, BEATRIX MAURINE, 74-373 Peppergrass St., Palm Desert, Calif. 92260
MAHER, LUCILLE, 1230 Warner Ave., Los Angeles, Calif. 90024
MAIDEN, NORMAN C., 430 So. Patencio Road, Palm Springs, Calif. 92262
MAINS, RUDELLA, 1710 N. Via Miraleste, Palm Springs, Calif. 92262
MALCO, ELAINE, 5441 El Cedral, Long Beach, Calif. 90815
MARGOLIS, DAVID, 572 No. Indian Ave., Palm Springs, Calif. 92262
MARTIN, HAZEL, 44-214 North 2nd St. E, Lancaster, Calif. 93534
MARTIN, VAL, 10826 Locust, Bloomington, Calif. 92316
MASON, DR. RALPH, 3051 Hickok Way, Riverside, Calif. 92506
MATHEWS, BETTY LOU, 715 9th St., Apt. A, Santa Monica, Calif. 90402
MAURER, CARL, 4796 Harmony Lane, Santa Maria, Calif.
MEEHAN, HAZEL, 153 S. Pepper St., Orange, Calif. 92668
MENNE, HARRY, 290 Hillandale Ct., Riverside, Calif. 92507
MERRITT, MARSHALL, #10 Glenridge Ave., Los Gatos, Calif. 95030
MEYERS, HELEN K., 3122 Alta Laguna Blvd., Laguna Beach, Calif. 92651
MILES, DON, 566 W. Palm St., Altadena, Calif. 91002
MINDESS, ZELDA W., 2915 Guadalupe Rd., Araby Estates, Palm Springs, Calif.
MINER, BERYL D., 640 N. Indian Ave., Palm Springs, Calif. 92262
MINOR, MR. H., P.O. Box 745, San Jacinto, Calif. 92383
MITCHELL, LLOYD J., 9150½ Las Tunas Dr., Temple City, Calif. 91780
MOAK, STERLING, 911 W. Racquet Club Road, Palm Springs, Calif. 92262
MOSER, CLARENCE H., 569 E. Brookwood St., Brea, Calif. 92612
MURRAY, MADLYNE, P.O. Box 583, Twenty Nine Palms, Calif. 92277
NAYLOR, EVELYN & THOMAS, 39 Skyridge Park, Cathedral City, Calif. 92234
NIELSON, MADELINE, 37-801 Nielson Rd. Cathedral City, Calif. 92234
OLSON, HAZEL, 947 East Olive St., Colton, Calif.
O'REILLY, RAY, 37-156 Palo Verde Drive, Palm Springs, Calif. 92262
PARKER, HENRIETTA, 1179 May Drive, Palm Springs, Calif. 92262
PARKINSON, LEE K., #3 Parkinson Plaza, 3725 Washington Blvd., Ogden, Utah
PARSONS, CLAUDE P., 393 Bonhill Road, Los Angeles, Calif. 90049
PARSONS, MRS. MARILYN, 14875 Rodeo Dr., Victorville, Calif. 92392
PATRICK, MARIE, 73-561 Feather Trail, Palm Desert, Calif. 92260
PATTON, JACK, 140 Via Lola, Palm Springs, Calif. 92262
PAUL, AUGUST K., 1644 Sagebrush, Palm Springs, Calif. 92262
PAYNE, KEN, 811 Discovery St., Yreka, Calif. 96097
PENNEY, FRED D., 48-149 Silver Spur Trail, Palm Desert, Calif. 92260
PENNEY, PAULA, 168 No. Palm Canyon Drive, Palm Springs, Calif. 92262
PERCIVAL, LOLA V., 38-660 Bel Aire, Cathedral City, Calif. 92234
PERSONA, WM., 952 Glen Neyre St., Laguna Beach, Calif.

PETERSON, WILLIAM K., Gen. Del., Hamer, Idaho 83425
PINE, ANN, 3433 Magnolia Blvd., W., Seattle, Wash. 98199
PLASCJAK, ANTHONY M., 495 Camino Norte, Palm Springs, Calif. 92262
POTTER, FRANK, 812 "P" St., Sanger, Calif. 93657
PRINGLE, MR. & MRS. KEITH, P.O. Box 193, 2683 Roosevelt, Carlsbad, Calif. 92008
PULLEY, JAMES E., 3547 Las Palmas Ave., Glendale, Calif. 91208
RABE, BENJAMIN, 1421 Cajon St., Redlands, Calif. 92373
RANDALL, MARGUERITA D., 611 Dry Falls Road, Palm Springs, Calif. 92262
RAY, JIMMY, P.O. Box 2514, Palm Springs, Calif. 92262
REED, BETTE, 418 Berrian, Claremont, Calif. 91711
REED, JAMES F., 810 South Orange Grove Blvd., Pasadena, Calif. 91105
REID, EULALIE, P.O. Box 422, Morongo Valley, Calif. 92256
RICHMOND, ISABELLE, Richmond Studio, 1565 East Mission Rd., Fallbrook, Calif.
RICHTER, CATHERINE M., 1747 Watson Way, Vista, Calif. 92083
ROGERS, MARION J., 5974 W. 75th St., Los Angeles, Calif. 90045
ROLOFF, JERRI, 249 Verde Vista Dr., Thousand Oaks, Calif. 91360
ROPP, J. MARIE, P.O. Box 876, Desert Hot Springs, Calif. 92240
ROSE, JENNIE, 43-035 Texas Ave., Palm Desert, Calif. 92260
ROSENTHAL, ROSE, 4331 4th Ave., Los Angeles, Calif. 90008
ROSSI, ROBERTO, 2021 Mountain St., Pasadena, Calif. 91104
ROZENBURG, BERTHA OGDEN, 2243 Girasol Ave., Palm Springs, Calif. 92262
RUGE, DR. EDW. C., P.O. Box 1123, Palm Desert, Calif. 92260
RUNKLE, ELSIE JANE, 435 Fairview Ave., Arcadia, Calif. 91006
RUSKIN, SAUL, 180 Prescott Dr., Palm Springs, Calif. 92262
SACKETT, FLORENCE C., 810 Brookside Blvd., Grants Pass, Ore. 97526
SASSE, HELENE H., Clara Bee Lodge, Palm Springs, Calif. 92262
SCHADE, LELA, 1710 W. Southgate, Fullerton, Calif. 92633
SCHMIDT, JAY, 34-925 Dewey Ave., Yucaipa, Calif. 92399
SCHULTZ, CAROLINE REEL, 5361 Balboa Ave., San Diego, Calif. 92117
SCHUMACHER, MARJORIE, P.O. Box 638, Palm Springs, Calif. 92262
SCHUMACHER, STANLEY, P.O. Box 638, Palm Springs, Calif. 92262
SCHWEDLER, RUTH, 1128 #4 Calle Rolph, Palm Springs, Calif. 92262
SCOGGIN, IRENE, 6812 Saddle Pack Rd., Joshua Tree, Calif. 92252
SCOTT, PAULINE, 2930 Eulalia Cir., Palm Springs, Calif. 92262
SHARPE, BEVERLY, 2583 No. Palm Canyon Drive, Palm Springs, Calif. 92262
SHARPE, MARJORIE, 565 Woodland Dr., Los Osos, Calif. 93401
SHERER, MARY, 386 High Dr., Laguna Beach, Calif. 92651
SIMMONS, FRANCIS A. 505 E. Plaza Parkway, Palm Springs, Calif. 92262
SINGER, MRS. MARGARETTE, 2908 Pratt Ave., Chicago, Ill. 60645
SITTER, LARRY, 1450 No. Riverside Dr., Palm Springs, Calif. 92262
SKILLICORN, MRS. W. KEENEN, 2356 Silvertree Road, Claremont, Calif.
SMITH, KATCHIE, 280 Ash Ave., Chula Vista, Calif. 92010
SMITH, MRS. ED. LESTER, 72-835 Homestead Road, Palm Desert, Calif. 92260
SMITH, RUTH ANN, 82-237 Luce Ave., Indio, Calif. 92201
SMITH, WILLA E., 8656 Washington, La Mesa, Calif. 92041
SONNENBERG, BEATRICE, 4203 Ladoga, Lakewood, Calif. 90713
SORENSEN, CARL, P.O. Box 602, Cathedral City, 92234
SOUTHERN, DOROTHY, 2960 Via Vaquero, Palm Springs, Calif. 92262
SOUTHWORTH, LYDIA, 527 Redlands Ave., Newport Beach, Calif. 92660
SPENCER, ANGELA, P.O. Box 267, Yucca Valley, Calif. 92284
STAL, L.D.S.J., P.O. Box 213, Murrieto, Calif. 92362
STARNER, JANE (IONE), 3011 W. 4th St., Los Angeles, Calif. 90005
STARR, MURL, 6117 Valley View, Joshua Tree, Calif. 92252
STEERS, CHARLES R., 1316 W. Colonial Ave., Anaheim, Calif. 92802
STEPHENS, AILEEN, 618 Mesquite, Palm Springs, Calif. 92262
STONE, FERN CUNNINGHAM, 1076 El Alameda, Palm Springs, Calif. 92262
STOVALL, MRS. ARNO H., Beckley Circle, Palm Springs, Calif. 92262
STUART, MARJORIE McNEELEY, P.O. Box 915, Yucca Valley, Calif.
SWINNERTON, JAMES, 72-628 Pitahaya, Palm Desert, Calif. 92260
TAYLOR, BESSIE ADA, 35585 Persimmon St., Yucaipa, Calif. 92399
TAYLOR, DARWIN, 71-305 Halgar Road, Rancho Mirage, Calif. 92270

TAYLOR, MARTIN R., 2949 E. Maple, Apt. A, Orange, Calif. 92667
TAYLOR, NONA, 8437 Tepic Dr., Paramount, Calif. 90723
THOMAS, MILDRED, 2466 So. Palm Canyon Dr., Palm Springs, Calif. 92262
THRONSON, HAZEL, 74-325 Fairway Drive, Palm Desert, Calif. 92260
TICE, FLORÉNCE, 134 Fondulac, Ramon Park, Palm Springs, Calif. 92262
TOAPANTA, MANUEL R., 270 So. Gramercy Place, Los Angeles, Calif. 90004
TOBIAS, MARTIN, 4094 Jones Ave., Riverside, Calif. 92505
TOSH, DE MURL, 30-291 San Louis Rey, Palm Springs, Calif. 92262
TRUE, HESTER ALICE, 11344 E. Taddy St., Norwalk, Calif.
TUCKER, DON, 5026 Via Jacinto, Santa Barbara, Calif. 93105
TURNER, BARBARA PAYNE, 2444 Alhambra Dr., Canyon Country Club,
     Palm Springs, Calif. 92262
TURONETT, MR. & MRS. ARMAND
TYLER, MARGARET, 82-616 Miles Ave., Indio, Calif. 92201
VAIL, MARJORIE M., 2560 Las Lomitas Way, Covina, Calif. 91722
VALERIE, JOAN, 73-563 Homestead, Twenty Nine Palms, Calif.
STEENBERG, JEANNE VAN, 72-579 Beavertail, Palm Desert, Calif. 92260
WAGNER, HARRIET W., #1 Circle A Drive, Palm Desert, Calif. 92260
WAGNER, MARK, 41-323 McDowell St., Hemet, Calif. 92343
WALLACE, WILLIAM A., P.O. Box 294, Mountain Center, Calif. 92361
WALTERS, WILLIAM, 1667 Santa Barbara, Glendale, Calif. 91208
WARD, KEITH, 222 Camino Alturas, Palm Springs, Calif. 92262
WEBB, FIRNE, 385 East Racquet Club Rd., Palm Springs, Calif. 92262
WELLS, BYRON, P.O. Box 837, Balboa Calif. 92661
WESTERFIELD, LT. COL. JAMES P., P.O. Box 595, Mecca, Calif. 92254
WHITE, CHARLES A., Drawer NN, Indio, Calif. 92201
WHITE, WAYNE, 2252 Christina, Stockton, Calif. 95204
WIDDOWSON, CLIFF, 11523 Louise Ave., Lynwood, Calif.
WIESE, ROBERT H., Box 997, Desert Hot Springs, Calif. 92240
WILDER, GARY, P.O. Box 174, Thousand Palms, Calif. 92276
WILKINS, BERNICE, Box 152, Desert Hot Springs, Calif. 92240
WILLIS, MILDRED F., P.O. Box 188, Sedro Woolley, Washington 98284
WISHY, ZENA WITTENBERG, P.O. Box 2763, Palm Springs, Calif. 92262
WOLSETH, MR. & MRS. JAMES, 584 C St., Cathedral City, Calif. 92234
WOOD, CARYL, 2711 Sierra Way, Bishop, Calif.
WOODS, EDMOND F., 465 Second Ave., Chula Vista, Calif. 92010
WOODY, ERMA, 48-230 Birdie Way, Palm Desert, Calif. 92260
WOODY, Z. V., 48-230 Birdie Way, Palm Desert, Calif. 92260
WORCESTER, EVA, 2086 Barona Rd., Palm Springs, Calif. 92262
YATES, LORAYNE, 262-A Via Olivera, Palm Springs, Calif. 92262
YELLENTI, NICHOLAS, P.O. Box 59, Landers, Calif. 92284
ZINT, WADE, 117 E. Wilson, Costa Mesa, Calif. 92627
ZUTTO, HARRY, 25770 Musselburgh Dr., Sun City, Calif. 92381

Rowena Meeks Abdy
Rbt. Ingersoll AitkenNA
Gertrude P. Albright
Herman Oliver Albright
Henry Alexander
Aaron Altman
Fortunato Arriola
Arthur Atkins
John W. Audubon ANA
Amanda P. Austin
Thomas A. Ayres

B

Louis S. Bacon
George H. Baker
Addie L. Ballou
Leonardo Barbieri
Mathew R. Barnes
Peter Baumgras
Chester Beach NA
Arhtur Bechwith
Mary P. Benton
Arthur Wm. Best
Harry Cassie Best
Albert Bierstadt
Ralph A. Blakelock
Hiram Henry Bloomer
John G. Borglum
Lester David Boronda
John D. Borthwick RA
Raymond S. Boynton
William Bradford ANA
Sophie M. Brannan
Anne M. Bremer
Henry J. Breuer
Thomas L. Bromley
Samuel M. Brookes
John Ross Browne
Albertus Browere
Elbridge A. Burbank
Ferdinand Burgdorff
George H. Burgess
Norton Bush
Richard J. Bush
George B. Butler Jr.
Frederick A. Butman

C

Guiseppe Cadenasso
Eugene Camerer
Charles J. Carlson
Emil Soren Carlson
Wm. de la M. Cary
Frederick Catherwood
Alice B. Chittenden
Antoine Claveau
John Cloudman
William F. Cogswell

James T. Colby
Vincent Colyer ANA
Ashley D. M. Cooper
George V. Cooper
John C. Cornell
Wm. Alexander Coulter
Palmer Cox
Charles Math. Crocker
Edward Wilson Currier

D

A. Jerome D'Arcy
Sidney Tilden Dakin
Paul de Longpre
George DeLuce
Gideon J. Denny
Charles John Dickman
Harold L. Doolittle
Emil Dresel
John Henry Dunnel

E

Harrison Eastman
Alexander Edouart
Henry Arthur Elkins

F

Henry F. Farny
Charles Frederick
Augusto Ferran
Mary Hallock Foote
Henry Chapman Ford
Ben Foster NA
Paul Frenzeny
Arthur Burdett Frost
George Albert Frost

G

Charles B. Gifford
Robert S. Gifford
George Henry Goddard
Richard LeB. Goodwin
Charles Graham
Henry Percy Gray
Wm. Wallace V. Gray
Andrew Jackson Grayson
Joseph D. Greenbaum
Henry Dick. Gremke
James Martin Griffin
Trautman Grob
Albert L. Groll NA

H

Karl William Hahn
James Hamilton
Eli Harvey
Armin Hansen
Ejnar Hansen
Herman W. Hansen
Joseph A. Harrington
Birge L. Harrison NA

Thomas A. Harrison
Alfred A. Hart
Martin J. Heade
Frank Heath
Herman Herzog
Andrew Putnam Hill
Edward Rugus Hill
Thomas Hill
Thomas H. Hinckley
Charles J. Hittell
Ransom G. Holdredge
Grace C. Hudson

J

William F. Jackson
William H. Jackson
Albert Jenks
Wm. Smith Jewett ANA
Karl H. Jonnevold
Christian Jorgenson
Amadee Joullin
Wm. Lees Judson
Edward Jump

K

William Keith
John Ross Key
Alfred Kepps
Anna Eliz. Klumpke
John Koch
Eugen M. Krieg
Oscar Kunath

L

Lorenzo P. Latimer
Joseph Leo
Mignard Lewis
Pascal Loomis
Matilda Lotz
Julius Ludovici
Fernard H. Lungren

M

William L. Marple
Francis Sam. Marryat
Xavier Martinez
Lucia K. Mathews
Clara T. McChesney
Francis John McComas
William B. McMurtrie
Jules Carlos Mersfelder
Pietro Mezzara
Thomas Moran
Gilbert D. Munger
Eadweard Muybridge

N

Charles C. Nahl
Hugo W. A. Nahl
Erneste Narjot
David D. Neal

Eugen Neuhaus

O

Mrs. W. H. Oaks
Thomas S. Officer
Samuel S. Osgood ANA

P

Jules Francois Pages
John H. E. Partington
Francis M. Pebbles
Orrin M. Peck
Ernest C. Peixotto NA
Henri H. Penelon
Enoch Wood Perry NA
Charles Rollo Peters
Gottardo Piazzoni
John Pope ANA
H. M. T. Powell

R

Wilbur A. Reaser
J. F. Reichardt
Mary C Richardson
William Ritschel
Julian Warbridge Rix
Charles D. Robinson
Cleveland Rockwell
Alfred C. Rodriguez
Charles A. Rogers
Charles H. Rogers
Toby Edw. Rosenthal
Thomas Ross

S

Geneve R. Sargeant
Frederick F. Schafer
Benjamin W. Sears
Stephen Wm. Shaw
Charles D. Shed
George Henry SmillieNA
James David Smillie NA
Gustayas Sohon
John A, Stanton
Meyer Straus
Elizabeth Strong
Joseph D. Strong Jr.
James Everett Stuart

T

Jules Tavernier
Bernard Taylor
S. Seymour Thomas
Douglas Tilden
Roger Peterson Toft
Domenico Tojetti
Edwardo Tojetti
John M. Tracy

V

Albert R. Valentien
Durbin Van Vleck
JeanJaques Viojet
Edward Vischer
Carl Von Perbandt

W

James Walker
Juan B. Wandseforde
Harry W. Watrous NA
August Fred. Wederoth
Thaddeus Welch
Francis M. Wells
Frederick Whymper
Lemanuel M. Wiles
Virgil M. Williams
Evelyn A. Winthrow
Henry Wolf NA
Theodore Wores

Y

Sidney J. Yard
Frederick Yates
Raymond D. Yellend
Harvey O. Young

Z

Rufus F. Zogbaum

A SURVEY OF ART WORK

in the City and County of
SAN FRANCISCO

Published by the Office of Mayor Joseph L. Alioto
in 1975 as a San Francisco Bicentennial project.

Mark Adams
Rbt. Ingersoll Aitken
Maxine Albro
Victor Arnautoff
David Arnold
Ruth Asawa
F. Asborjornsen

B
Milton Bancroft
Fletcher Benton
Elio Benvenuto
Victor Bergeron
Franz Bergman
Ray Bertrand
Jane Berlandina
Lucien Bloch
Patti Bowler
Ray Boynton
Frank Brangwyn
Helen Bruton
Beniamino Bufano
Jagoda Buic
George Bullock

C
Dudley C. Carter
Lynn Chadwick
Ralph Chesse
Howard Chandler Christy
Don Clever
Gerome Connor
Carl H. Conrads
Lisa Cook
Miguel Covarrubias
Ruth Wakefield Cravath
Henri Crenier
Dewey Crumpler
M. Earl Cummings
Rinaldo Cuneo
Ben F. Cunningham

D
Tony De Lap
Aristedes Demetrios
Stephen De Staebler
Vittorio DiColvertaldo
Stephen Dimitroff
Maynard Dixon
Paul Gustave Dore
Frank Vincent Dumond
Alfred DuPont

E
David Edstrom
Mary E. Erckenbrack
Frederick John Eversley

F
Duane Faralia

Helen Forbes
Daniel Chester French

G
William Gaskin
Guillaume Geefs
Adolph Gottleib
Charles Grafly
Josep Grau-Garriga
Henri Leon Greber
Francoise Grossen
Orazio Grossoni
Jules Guerin
Willi Gutman

H
Parker Hall
Edith Hamlin
Emile Hannaux
Frank Happersberger
George Harris
William Hesthal
Hilaire Hiler
James Holden
John L. Howard
Robert B. Howard
Clara Huntington

J
Sargent Johnson

K
Aleksandra Kasuba
Lee Kelley
Dong Kingman
Freda Koblick

L
Lucien Labaudt
Gordon Langdon
Leo Lentelli
James Leong
Jean Leslie
Alvin Light
Gwen Lux

M
Ursula Malbin
Dean Mallette
Henri Marie-Rose
Marino Marini
Julian Martinez
Marcello Mascherini
Arthur F. Mathews
J. McQuarrie
Emily J. Michels
H. M. Michelson
Angelina Minutoli
William Mitchell
Henry Moore
Jo Mora

Jack Moxom
Jose Moya Del Pino

N
Masayuki Nagare
Emile Norman
Stefan Novak
Win Ng

O
Otis Oldfield
Fred Olmsted
Jacques Overhoff

P
David Park
Haig Patigan
Charles O. Perry
R. Hinton Perry
Gottardo Piazzoni
Nelson Pool
Bruce Porter
John Baptiste Portonova
James Pradier
Mary Gardner Preminger
Dorothy W. Pucinelli
Raymond Pucinelli
Arthur Putnam

R
Anton Refregier
Ernst Reitschel
Harry S. Richardson
Diego Rivera
Auguste Rodin
Hal Bayard Runyon
David Russo

S
Zygmund Sazevich
Rupert Schmid
Jacques Schnier
Suzanne Scheuer
Frederick Schweigardt
Raymond Sells
Jacob Sheinbach
Thomas Sheilds-Clarke
Marion Simpson
Antonio Sotomayor
Ralph Stackpole
Francois Stahley
Jan Peter Stern
John Stoll
Wm. Wetmore Story

T
Carlos Taliabue
Douglas Tilden
David Tolerton
Edward Terada
Armand Trahan

V
Armand Vaillancourt
Peter Van Der Berge
Frank Van Sloun
Frede Vidar
Herman Volz
Michael Von Meyer
Peter Voulkos

W
George Wilson Walker
Edgar Walter
Adolph A. Weinman
F. Marion Wells
Glen Wessels
Bruce Wolfe
Robert Woodward
Clifford Wight

Z
Bernard Zakheim

THE SAN FRANCISCO GE-
NERAL HOSPITAL MEDICAL
COLLECTION 1978

Gloria Cozzo Adams
Sister Adele
William Aiken
John Almond
Lawrence Andrews
Ruth Asawa

B
Dennis Beall
Bruce Beasley
Cleveland Bellow
Pauline Blanc
Todor Bodurov
David Bradford
Frederick Brayman
Don Brodeur
Joan Brown
Kathan Brown
Selma Brown
Beniamino Bufano

C
Francisco X. Camplis
Arthur Carraway
Rolando Castellon
Philip Chan
Richard Allen Clarke
Frederick Comendant
Gerald Concha
Gordon Cook

D
Oscar de Leon
Angel del Valle
Eleanor Dickinson
James Dong

E
Yasuhiro Esaki
Melvyn Ettrick

F
Charles Griffin Farr

Alan Che Mah Fong
Howard Reed Foote
Patricia T. Forrester
William Frej
Gustl French
Sekio Fuapopo
Mary Fuller
Gale Fulton-Ross

G
Aparicio Gil
James Gorman
Maria Goya
Richard Graf
Stanley Greene

H
Patrick Hansen
Theresa Harned
Rob Harper
Walt Hartlage
Sachi Tsutsumi Hayward
Wally Hedrick
Carol Heineman
Hisako Hibi
Ivars Hirss
Sam Horn
Blanche Phillips Howard
John Langley Howard
Sandria Ann Hu
Margo Humphrey
Jean Hyson

I
John Ihle

J
Beverly Jaeger
Randy James
Bill Jefferson
Marie Johnson

K
Karl Kasten
David Kessler
Robert Kingsbury
Dale Kistemaker
Toby Judith Klayman
Freda Koblick
Lawrence C. Kolawole

L
Ray Lauzzana
James Thomas Lawrence
Elisa Leptich
Carlos Loarca
Donald Longanecker

M
Ralph Maradiaga
Masachi Matsumoto
Robert McManus
Alex McMath
John Douglas Mercer
Mansaku Minashima
Arthur Monroe
Robert Moon
David Moore
Victor Moscoso
Luis Alonso Munez

N
Junko Nakamura
Kenjilo Nanao
Eileen Frances Nelson
Ruby Newman

O
Arthur Okamura
Tomiko Okamura
Hajime Okuba

P
Emily Lou Packard
Leroy Wheeler Parker
Gary Paterson
Robbie Plays
George Post
Gilbert Precival
Raimondo Puccinelli

Q
Elizabeth Quandt

R
Eleanor Rappe
Barbara Rees
Fred Reichman
James Edward Reid
Harry Richardson
Michael Rios
Peter Rodriguez

S
Takami Sakurai
Dean Santner
Jacques Schnier
Stephanie I. Scott
Raymond Sells
Louis Siegriest
Angelo Sottosanti
James Bruce Southard

T
Calvin Tondre
Paul Tracy
Kazuhiro Tsuruta

V
Beth Van Hoesen
Carlos Villa
Manuel Villamor
Kim Kieu Vuong

W
Gerald Walberg
Charles Ware
Stan Washburn
Marvin Wax
Tony Williams
Susan Elizabeth Willson
John Winkler
William Wolff
Louvina Wong

Y
Rene Yanez

California Painters & Sculptors
The Modern Era Exhibition at the

San Francisco Art Museum and at the Smithsonian during 1977

Arlo Acton
Tom Akawie
Peter Alexander
Robert Alexander
William Allen
Terry Allen
John Altoon
Jeremy Anderson
Ruth Armer
Robert Arneson
Charles Arnoldi
Ruth Asawa
Michael Asher
B
John Baldessari
Matthew Barnes
John Baxter
Paul Beattie
Robert Bechtle
Larry Bell
Billy Al Bengston
Karl Benjamin
Fletcher Benton
Ed Bereal
Tony Berlant
Ben Berlin
Eugene Berman
Wallace Berman
Elmer Bischoff
William Brice
Nick Brigante
Ernest Briggs
Richard Brodney
Joan Brown
Beniamino Bufano
Chris Burden
Hans Burkhardt
C
Vija Celmins
Judy Chicago
William Clapp
Grace Clements
Robert Colescott
Bruce Conner
Edward Corbett
Robert Cremean
D
Ronald Davis
Jay DeFeo
Roy DeForest
Tony DeLap
Richard Diebenkorn
Laddie John Dill
James Budd Dixon

Maynard Dixon
William Dole
Edward Dugmore
E
Leonard Edmondson
James Eller
Frederick Eversley
F
Clair Falkenstein
Faralla
Lorser Feitelson
Oskar Fischinger
Llyn Foulkes
Terry Fox
Sam Francis
Howard Fried
G
Charles Garabedian
August Gay
Sonia Gechtoff
William Geis
Selden Gile
David Gilhooly
Ralph Goings
Joe Goode
Robert Graham
H
Howard Hack
Lloyd Hamrol
Newton Harrison
Julius Hatofsky
Wally Hedrick
Phillip Hefferton
Gilbert Henderson
Maxwell Hendler
George Herms
Tom Holland
Arthur Holman
Charles Howard
Robert Howard
Robert Hudson
John Hultberg
Nick Hyde
I
Robert Irwin
J
Richard Jackson
Jack Jefferson
Jess
Daniel LaRue Johnson
Sargent Johnson
Ynez Johnston
David Jones

K
Craig Kauffman
James Kelly
Adaline Kent
Edward Kienholz
Robert Kinmont
Peter Krasnow
Walter Kuhlman
L
Lucien Labaudt
Rico Lebrun
Alvin Light
Frank Lobdell
Seymour Locks
Maurice Logan
Helen Lundeberg
M
Stanton MacDonald-Wright
Tom Marioni
Bill Martin
Fred Martin
Xavier Martinez
Fred Mason
John Mason
Arthur Mathews
Lucia Mathews
Robert McChesney
John McCracken
James McCray
John McLaughlin
Richard McLean
Jerry McMillan
Cliff McReynolds
Jim Melchert
Knut Merrild
Edward Moses
Lee Mullican
N
Bruce Nauman
Manuel Neri
Maria Nordman
O
Nathan Oliveira
Gordon Onslow-Ford
P
Harold Paris
David Park
Agnes Pelton
Richard Pettibone
Gottardo Piazzoni
Peter Plagens
Don Potts
Clayton S. Price
Kenneth Price
R
Joseph Raffael
Mel Ramos
Roland Reiss
Deborah Remington

Gregg Renfrow
Sam Richardson
Arthur Richter
Philip Roeber
Richards Ruben
Allen Ruppersberg
Edward Ruscha

S
Betye Saar
John Saccaro
Darryl Sapien
Paul Sarkisian
Peter Saul
Ursula Schneider
Richard Shaw
Millard Sheets
Louis Siegriest
David Simpson
Nell Sinton
Rex Slinkard
Hassel Smith
Clay Spohn
Ralph Stackpole
Norman Stiegelmeyer
Clyfford Still
James Strombotne

T
Ben Talbert
Gage Taylor
Sam Tchakalian
Wayne Thiebaud
Michael Todd
Charls Tracy
Jim Turrell

V
DeWain Valentine
James Valerio
Carlos Villa
Bernard Von Eichman
Stephan Von Huene
Peter Voulkos

W
Howard Warshaw
Julius Wasserstein
James Weeks
William Wegman
Douglas Wheeler
William T. Wiley
Guy Williams
Paul Wonner
Tom Wudl

Y
Richard Yokomi

Z
Jack Zajac

A CENTURY OF CALIFORNIA PAINTING 1870-1970

AN EXHIBITION SPONSORED BY

CROCKER-CITIZENS NATIONAL BANK

Separate exhibitions held in 1970 at Los Angeles, Fresno, Santa Barbara, San Francisco, Santa Clara, Sacramento, and Oakland.

1870 - 1880
Albert Bierstadt (1830-1902)
Samuel Marsden Brookes (1816-1892)
Gideon Jacques Denny (1830-1886)
Karl Wilhelm Hahn (1835-1887)
Jules Tavernier (1844-1889)

1880 - 1890
Henry Alexander (1862-1895)
Thomas Hill (1829-1908)
William Keith (1839-1911)
Julian Rix (1850-1903)
Raymond D. Yelland (1848-1900)

1890 - 1900
Emil Carlsen (1853-1932)
Edwin Deakin (1838-1923)
Christian Jorgenson (1860-1935)
Thaddeus Welch (1844-1919)
Theodore Wores (1858-1939)

1900 - 1910
Xavier Martinez (1869-1943)
Arthur Mathews (1860-1945)
Eugen Neuhaus (1879-1963)
Charles Rollo Peters (1862-1928)
Gottardo Piazzoni (1872-1945)

1910 - 1920
E. Charlton Fortune (1885-1969)
Armin Hansen (1886-1957)
Clarence Hinkle (1880-1960)
Francis McComas (1874-1938)
Joseph Raphael (1872-1950)

1920 - 1930
Maynard Dixon (1875-1946)
Selden Gile (1877-1947)
Clayton S. Price (1874-1950)
William Ritschel (1864-1949)
Frank Van Sloun (1879-1938)

1930 - 1940
Otis Oldfield (1890-1969)
Dorr Bothwell (1902-
William Gaw (1891-
Matthew Barnes (1880-1951)
Emmy Lou Packard (1914-

1940 - 1950
Edward Corbett (1919-
James Budd Dixon (1902-1967)
Lorser Feitelson (1898-
David Park (1911-
Clay Spohn (1900-

1950 - 1960
Elmer Bischoff (1916-
Jess Collins (1923-
Richard Diebenkorn (1922-
Rico Lebrun (1900-1964)
Hassel Smith (1915-

1960 - 1970
Keith Boyle (1930-
Joan Brown (1938-
Nathan Oliveira (1928-
Wayne Thiebaud (1920-
William Wiley (1937-

A

Rowena Meeks Abdy
William Adam
Ansel Easton Adams
Cassily Adams
Charles P. Adams
John Wolcott Adams
Kenneth Miller Adams
Mark Adams
Alfred Thomas Agate
Kate Ahrens (Ahrins)
Ben Aiken
Robert Ingersoll Aitken
Karl Albert
Gertrude Part. Albright
Hermann Oliver Albright
Maxine Albro
James Madison Alden
C. Alexander
Henry Alexander
Katherine Allan
Albert Arthur Allen
Boyd Allen
Glen Allen
C. Harry Allis
Vera Allison
Marcelino Almeida
Albert Ames
F. James Anderson
Gunnar Anderson
Jeremy Anderson
Ralph Anderson
William Anderson
Valenti Michael Angelo
Sibyl Anikeef
George Applegarth
Laura Adams Armer
Sidney Armer
Thomas Armstrong
William W. Armstrong
Victor M. Arnautoff
Fortunato Arriola
Gus Arriola
A. Asti
John Atherton
Wm. Arthur Atkins
Barry Atwater
John Woodhouse Audubon
Edward J. Austen
Alexander Austin
Amanda P. Austin
Charles Percy Austin
Isabel More Austin
Kenneth Newell Avery

John C. Ayres
Thomas A. Ayers

B

Seth Babson
Standish Backus Jr.
Henry Bacon
Mrs. W. G. Badger
Martin Baer
Henry Baerer
Theodore Baggelmann
W. B. Baird
George Holbrook Baker
Jack Baker
C. A. Baldwin
Helen Johnston Balfour
F. Carlton Ball
Katherine M. Ball
Ruth Norton Ball
Addie L. Ballou
E. Geoffery Bangs
Edmond Lorenzo Barber
Maria Barber
Mary Dunkin Barber
Leonardo Barbieri
Henry Barkhaus
Carroll Barnew
Matthew Rackman Barnes
Earl D. Barnett
William Barr
Benny Barrios
Lionel Barrymore
Herman Barth
Wm. Newton Bartholomew
Dana Bartlett
Mrs. Dana Bartlett
Gray Bartlett
Frances G. Barnett
Loren Roberts Barton
Ernest Batchelder
Perez Batchelder
Frederick Bauer
John Jay Baumgartner
Peter Baumgras
Martha Wheeler Baxter
Chester Beach
Dennis Beall
Donald Jeffries Bear
Arthur Edwaine Beaumont
Mona Beaumont
C. A. Beck
Dunbar Beck
Charles Joseph Becker
Frederick W. Becker
Joseph E. Becker

Francis A. Beckett
Arthur Beckwith
Frederick Wm. Beechey
Richard B. Beechey
Cecil C. Bell
Ida Bell
Bill Bender
Billy Al Bengston
Charles H. Benjamin
F. R. Bennet
Mrs. Joseph A. Benton
Mary P. S. Benton
May Benton
Frank (Franz) Bergman
John Alfred Bergner
Jane Berlandia
Eugene Berman
A. Bernard du Hautcilly
Fanny Berry
Adolph Berson
Alice M. L. Best
Arthur William Best
Harry Cassie Best
Ray Bethers
Hoyland B Bettinger
Sarkis Beulan
Kuhne Beveridg
Albert Bierstadt
Frederick Bigland
Henry Bill
Frederick Wm. Billing
Nella F. Binckley
Theo Binner
Geraldine Rose Birch
Reginald B. Birch
Elmer Bischoff
Franz Albert Bischoff
Reuben L. Blake
Ralph Albert Blakelock
Duncan Geo. Blakiston
Arnold Blanch
Hiram Reynolds Bloomer
Peter Blos
Robert Fred. Blum
Ernest L. Blumenschein
Karl Bodmer
Homer H. Boelter
Chesley Bonestell
Leon Durand Bonnet
Cora Boone
J. Boot
John Edward Borein
Carl Oscar Borg
John Gutzon Borglum

Solon Borglum
Lester David Boronda
Randal Wm. Borough
John David Borthwick
Edward Bosqui
Hobart Van Z. Bosworth
Dorr Hodgson Bothwell
Cornelis Botke
Jessie Arms Botke
Jean De Botton
Burton S. Boundey
Firmin Bouvy
George Bowman
H. Boyd
Ray Scepter Boynton
J. T. Boysen
William Bradford
Henry Wm. Bradley
Alexandra C. Bradshaw
Amy Brainard
John Alex. Brandon Jr.
Sophie Marston Brannan
Maurice Braun
Helen Braunschweiger
Carl G. Bray
Hugh H. Breckenridge
Anne Milly Bremer
Carl C. Brenner
Henry Joseph Breuer
Ada Agusta Brewster
Hester Briggs
Anne W. Brigman
W. Henry Bringhurst
Joseph Britton
Howard Joseph Brodie
Helen A. Tanner Brodt
Thomas Bromley
Samuel Marsden Brookes
B. V. Brooks
Gertrude Stone Brooks
Mildred Bryant Brooks
Charles Broughton
Alburtis dO. Browere
A. Page Brown
Arthur Brown Jr.
Benjamin CHambers Brown
Bolton Coit Brown
David W. Brown
Dorothy Brown
Eliphalet Brown Jr.
Mrs. Enos Brown
Florinne Brown
Grafton Tyler Brown
Howell Chambers Brown
Belmore Browne
Carl Albert Browne
Hablot Knight Browne
J. Ross Browne
Kenneth Browne
C. A./W. Brubaker

Edward Bruce
Joseph G. Bruff
Al Brule
George DeForest Brush
Esther Bruton
Helen Bruton
Margaret Bruton
Mary Katherine Bryan
Ella Buchanan
Claude Buck
Margaret Warriner Buck
Jean Buckley
Beniamino B. Bufano
Conrad Buff
C. L. Bugbee
F. Buhler
Arthur V. Bull
Charles Livingston Bull
William H. Bull
Sidney Bunce
Elbridge Ayer Burbank
Ferdinand Burgdorff
George Henry Burgess
Hubert F. Burgess
Wm. Hubert Burgess
Alfred Ray Burrell
Elizabeth Eaton Burton
W. Busch
Norton Bush
Richard J. Bush
Robert Bush
Benjamin F. Butler
Edward A. Butler
Miner Frederic Butler
Frederick A. Butman

C
Alexandre Cabanel
Dick Cabral
Michel Cabera
Giuseppe Cadenasso
Ettore Cadorin
Corrado Cagli
Arthur James Cahill
Wm. Vincent Cahill
Alexander S. Calder
Caroline E. Callahan
Eugene Camerer
Malcolm Paul Cameron
Blendon Reed Campbell
Charles Campbell
Isabella Frowe Campbell
Albert Campbell-Shields
Sarah M. Campion
Milton Caniff
Jennie V. Cannon
Robert Coles Caples
Josephine E. Capwell
L. Cardini
Soren Emil Carlsen
Brents Carlton

Dudley Carpenter
William Louis Carrigan
Pruett Carter
Solomon Nunes Carvalho
John Joseph Casey
Ira D. G. Cassidy
Castleman
A. D. Castro
George Catlin
Chadwick
Cham
Cecil F. Chamberlin
Frank T. Chamberlin
Winnie E. Chamberlin
H. Chancellor
Sarah Eliz. Chandler
Shu-Chi Chang
George Chann
Will Emerson Chapin
Herman Cherry
Alice Whipple Chesley
Minnie Calista Childs
Frederick R. Chisnall
Alice Brown Chittenden
Louis Choris
Katherine Choy
Wm. Henry Clapp
M. Clareau
Alson Skinner Clark
Claude Clark
Galen Clark
Robert Clark
Claveau
John Willard Clawson
Henry Cleenewerck
Paul Lewis Clemens
Grace Clements
John D./G. Cloudman
Oscar Regan Coast
Cobb
William F. Cogswell
Sam Colburn
Joseph Foxcroft Cole
Edmund Thomas Coleman
Michael Coleman
George B. Collins
Herbert A. Collins
Roi Clarkson Colman
Samuel Colman
Vincent Colyer
Anna Botsford Comstock
Albert Clinton Conner
Barnaby Conrad Jr.
Charles R. Cook
Gordon Cook
Mary Cook
William B. Cooke
Baldwin Coolidge
Fred Combs
Astley D. M. Cooper

Colin Campbell Cooper
Geo. Victor Cooper
James Graham Cooper
Ron Cooper
Mrs. Newton Cope
William Copeland
A. Coquardon
Mario Corbett
Virginia M. Corcoran
Jose Cordero
Sister Mary Corita
Francisco Cornejo
Dean Cornwell
John O'Hara Cosgrave
Tito Costa
John Wesley Cotton
Mary J. Coulter
Wm. Alexander Coulter
Irving Couse
Alice Hobbs Coutts
Gordon Coutts
Miguel Covarrubias
Chas. Brinton Cox
Kenyon Cox
Louise H. K. Cox
Walter L. Cox
Ernest Coxhead
Ray Frederick Coyle
Charlotte M. Crabtree
Charles Craig
Thomas Theodore Craig
Allan Gilbert Cram
Virginia Sims Cranston
Junius Cravan
Dorothy W. P. Cravath
Ruth Barrows Cravath
Josiah P. Cressy
Charles Mathew Crocker
Mrs. James Crocker
Thomas Crocker
Joane Cromwell
Mary Crete Crouch
Edward Cucuel
H. L. A. Culmer
Emil Cummings
Melvin Earl Cummings
Rinaldo Cuneo
Cornelia E. Cunningham
John Cunningham
Marion Cunningham
Patricia Cunningham
Frank Wm. Cuprien
Gordon Currie
Edw. Wilson Currier
Elizabeth Curtis
Ida Maynard Curtis
Leland S. Curtis
Frank E. Cutter
Francis Harvey Cutting

D

Wm. F. Dabelstein
Maude Daggett
Carl C. Dahlgren
Marius Dahlgren
Zahad Dake
Samuel T. Dake(i)n
J. B. Dale
Robert W. Daley
Salvador Dali
Cyrus Edwin Dallin
Fred Dangerfield
Wm. Swift Daniell
Russell H. Daniels
Felix O. C. Darley
Honore Daumier
Homer C. Davenport
Don David
Arthur Bowen Davies
John A. Davies
Donna F. Davis
Goode Davis
John C. Davis
Lewis E. Davis
Willis E. Davis
Oriana Day
Vera Fera Dayton
Edwin Deakin
Mallette Dean
Ilona De Barkow
C. De Berghes
John Decker
Fortune De Conte
Roy De Forest
Cornelia De Gavere
Betty De Jong
Henri G. De Kruif
John Delafield
Richard Delafield
Edouard De Lessert
Maurice Del Mue
Paul De Longpre
Jose Moya Del Pino
Valere De Mari
Gideon Jacques Denny
Geo. Horatio Derby
Louis De Rome
Isadore Laurent De Roy
Theophilus D'Estrella
Tomas De Suria
Richard P. De Treville
Gaspard D. De Vancy
Patrick James Devine
Victor De Wilde
Alfred Dewitt
Sarah B. Dr Wolfe
Joe De Yong
Cristobal Diaz
John Reed Dickinson

Charles John Dickman
Richard Diebenkorn
Ferdinand Dieppe
Philip Latimer Dike
Lucienne B. Dimitroff
L. Maynard Dixon
Otto Dobbertin
Wm. de Leftwich Dodge
Allen B. Doggett
Misha Dolnikoff
Elaine B. Dooley
Thomas J. Donnelly
Marjorie H. Doolittle
Thomas A. Dorgan
William H. Dougal
Arthur W. Dowe
Michael Jos. Doyle
Joseph Drayton
Emil Dresel
Horace Duesbury
Frederick M. Du Mond
Charles S. Duncan
Darwin W. Duncan
Geraldine B. Duncan
Gregor Duncan
Raymond Duncan
Mary Stewart Dunlap
Julia E. Dunn
J. Henry Dunnel
Nicholas R. Dunphy
Alfred Du Pont
Kedma Du Pont
Darrow P. Durham
Peter S. Duval
Clarkson Dye

E

Eagan
Sybil Unis Easterday
Thomas M. Easterly
Harrison Eastman
Seth Eastman
Charles Fred. Eaton
W. Edgar
Alexander Edouart
Peter David Edstrom
James Edwards
Florence Elliott
Clarence A. Ellsworth
Peter Henry Emerson
William Otto Emerson
Bertha Luce Emery
Englehardt
Amber Eustas
Mary Orwig Everett
Carl A. Eytel

F

Gus Fagenstein/Fager-
    steen/Fagosteen
B. A. Fagioni

Edward Fairman
Claire Falkenstein
Carl Fallberg
Annie Fallon
G. R. Fardon
Edward McN. Farmer
Alfred V. Farnsworth
Henry F. Farny
William B. Faville
Nicolai I. Fechin
Lyonel Feininger
Lorser Feitelson
Diovole Fenala
Charles Fenderich
Harry Fenn
Nora H. Fennell
Augusto Ferran
Oscar Lewis Fest
Minerva Figg
Alexander Finta
Henry Firks
Nelle Fischer
Harry "Bud" Fisher
Harrison Fisher
Hugo Antoine Fisher
Hugo Melville Fisher
Mark Fisher
Frank Morley Fletcher
Frederick Flohr
Harry Stuart Fonda
Alexander Forbes
Helen Kath. Forbes
Henry Chapman Ford
Joseph Forenza
Victor Clyde Forsythe
E. Charlton Fortune
Forest Don. Foth
Fowzer
Gene Frances
G. M. Francis
John Bond Francisco
Eugene C. Frank
Dwight Franklin
James Earle Fraser
William Frates
Fredericks
William R. Freeman
Paul Frenzeny
Emil Frick
William Friedriksen
Washington F. Friend
Charles Arthur Fries
Lyman Parsons Frisbie
Maren M. Froelich
Finn Haakon Frolich
Anna S. Root Frost
Geo. Albert Frost
Jack/John Frost
John D. Fuller

Lola Fuller
Thomas Fuller
Mabelle B. Fulmer
Karoly Fulop
Dorothy Furuya

G

George Gaethke
Robert Merrell Gage
Gagliardi
Goddard Fred. Gale
Oscar Galgiani
Alexander Galt
John M. Gamble
Leona Garibaldi
G. G. Gariboldi
J. H. Garrigan
John Garth
William A. Gaw
Auguste Francois Gay
J. P. Gaynor
May E. Gearhart
Yun Gee
Lillian Mathilde Genth
Arnold Genthe
Frank/Franz Geritz
John Emmett Gerrity
William Lewis Gerstle
Lida M. Giambastiani
Louis Gianoli
George Gibbs
Luke Edmond Gibney
G(George?) Gibson
Chas. Braddock Gifford
W. B. Gifford
Robert Gilberg
Arthur Hill Gilbert
Robert Gilbert
Seldon Connor Gile
James Gill
Wm. Chas. Fred. Gillam
Ronald Debs Ginther
Lee Girvin
Louis M. Glackens
Gleason
Joseph Duncan Gleason
Edwin S. Glover
Grigory Gluckmann
Geo. Henry Goddard
Fred Fredden Goldberg
Reuben L. Goldberg
Franz M. Goldstein
Elling Wm. Gollings
Nathaniel D. Goodell
Nellie Stearns Goodloe
Warren Goodrich
George Goodwin
Richard L. Goodwin
Dolph Gotelli
John Gott

Galen Gough
Richard Graf
Charles Grafly
Cecilia B. Graham
Charles S. Graham
F. Grain
Eugene Grandin
Charles Henry Grant
Ethel Grau
O. E. L. Graves
Henry Percy Gray
Wm./Wallace V. Gray
Andrew Jackson Grayson
Joseph David Greenbaum
Charles S. Greene
Henry Mather Greene
Henry "Dick" Gremke
Elmer Grey
James Martin Griffin
Wm. Alexander Griffith
John Grillo
Paul Grimm
A. W. Grippen
Ernest Henry Griset
Casimir C. Griswold
Trautman Grob
Dan Sayre Groesbeck
Carl Ewald Grunsky
Pearl Harder Guenther
Jules Guerin
Norman Guerke
Charles F. B. Guillou
Victor Gulielmo
Richard Gwartney

H

Dagmar Haarbauer
W. H. Hackett
Harriet C. M. Hackwood
Elmer S. Hader
Mrs. Ballard Hadman
Johan Hagemeyer
Nels Hagerup
William Hahn
Kenneth Alden Haines
D. J. Hall
Jean Gates Hall
Kate Montague Hall
Mrs. Olin C. Halstead
F. F. Hamilton
James Hamilton
Leah Rinne Hamilton
Minerva Bart. Hamilton
Edith Anne Hamlin
Heliodor Hammarstrom
Ada Hanifan
Adelaide Hanscom
Armin Carl Hansen
Hermann W. Hansen
James Lee Hansen

Jo Hanson
Frank Happersberger
Thornton Harby
J. F. Harley
Fidelia F. Harlow
Alexander F. Harmer
Charles H. Harmon
Sophie Harpe
Joseph A. Harrington
Harris
George Harris
Sam Hyde Harris
Birge Harrison
Thomas Alex. Harrison
Alfred A. Hart
Margery Stocking Hart
Marsden Hartley
Russell Hartley
Ernest Haskell
Charles I. Havens
Thomas Hayes
William Jacob Hayes
William C. Hayes
Frank Lucien Heath
Lillian J. Dake Heath
Carl A. Hedstrom
Harry Heinie
George D. Heisley
C. Henckel
Meta C. Hendel
Ernest Martin Hennings
Herman Gus. Herkomer
Edith Harvey Heron
Lucy D. Herr
E. S. Herrick
Kate Powers Herrick
George J. Herriman
Albert Herter
Herman Herzog
William J. Hesthal
Julie Helen Heyneman
Edouard Hildebrandt
Hilaire Hiler
Andrew Putnam Hill
Edward Rufus Hill
Ellen Hill
John Henry Hill
Thomas Hill
William Hayes Hill
W. H. Hilliard
John Wm. Hilton
William Hayes Hilton
Lawrence Hinckley
Clarence Keiser Hinkle
David Howard Hitchcock
Joseph Hitchins
Charles Hittell
Clark Hobart
Lewis Hobart

Carl Hoerman
Charles Hoffbauer
Victor Hoffman
O. Hoffman
Mrs. Roy A. Hohberger
Ransom G. Holdredge
Tom Holland
Ralph Wm. Holmes
L. Holst
Kenneth Gordon Hook
Carl Hopfer
Nellie Hopps
Donal Hord
Laurence Hosmer
Alfred Hossack
Houghton
Thomas Houseworth
John Hovey
Charles Howard
John Galen Howard
John Langley Howard
Julie Kaye Howard
Robert B. Howard
Henry Martin Hoyt
Mrs. M. T. Hubbard
Henry Salem Hubbel
Charles Brad. Hudson
Gary Hudson
Grace Carpenter Hudson
Lillian Mae Huebner
Wm. Gordon Huff
John Hultberg
William Humphreys
Esther Anna Hunt
Gertrude Hunt
Mrs. Archer Huntington
James Mason Hutchings
William Rich Hutton
Helen Hyde

I

John L. Ihle
Gleb Alexander Ilyin
Peter Alexander Ilyin
Marie Imhof
Stanley Inchbold
George Inness
Linna V. Irelan
Mrs. M. K. Irving
Benoni Irwin
Ben Isham
Eugene Ivanoff
John Ivey

J

Everett Gee Jackson
Jessie Glen Jackson
M. Jackson
Martin Jacob Jackson
W. C. Jackson
Wm. Franklin Jackson

Wm. Henry Jackson
Jacobs
Dinah James
Carl Jameson
Emil Janel
Louise Janin(e)
Dorothy Jeakins
Jenke
George R. Jenkins
Louisa Jenkins
Albert Col Jenks
Wm. Dunbar Jewett
Wm. Smith Jewett
Caroline R. Johnson
Frank Tenney Johnson
G. H. Johnson
Mrs. Gardiner Johnson
Ralph Johnson
Sargent C. Johnson
John Wesley Jones
Seth C. Jones
Walter Jones
William Henry Jones
Carl Henrik Jonnewold
Alfred Jonniaux
Christian A. Jorgensen
Hans F. Jorgenson
Sydney Joseph
Amedee Joullin
Charles Chapel Judson
William Lees Judson
Edward Jump
Captain R. Jump
Kenneth Jung

K

Reuben Kadish
Carl Kahler
J. Kaler
Oscar Kaltschmidt
Paul Kane
Gertrude F. B. Kanno
Todd Karns
Karl Kasten
Sarkis Katchadourian
Leo Katz
Carl Kauba
Ferdinand Kaufmann
Charles Keck
Charles Keeler
Louise Mapes Keeler
Maud Russell Keever
William Keith
George Fred. Keller
Jean Kellogg
John Kelly
Ruth Kelsey
Edward Windsor Kemble
Minnie Eliz. Kemper
Rodney Kendrick

Marjorie R. Kennard
Norman M. Kennedy
Adaline Kent
Edward Meyer Kern
R. H. Kern
Victor Kerney
Lenard Kester
Myrtle Kester
John Ross Key
Margaret Kidder
B. W. Kilburn
Charles P. Kimball
Dong Moy Shu Kingman
Elbridge Kingsley
Gordon Neale Kinzer
Glo Kirby
Glad Marke Kistmer
Addie L. Kleist
Orpha Mae Klinker
Gene Kloss
Anna Eliz. Klumpke
Joseph Knowles
Squire Knowles
Augustus Koch
John Koch
W. H. D. Koerner
Isidore Konti
Ben Koontz
Charles Koppel
Ivan Petrovich Korukin
Emil Jean Kosa Jr.
Joseph M. Kratina
Wm. Victor Krausz
Mrs. Henry Krebese
Joseph Kreling Jr.
Joseph Kriss
Florence M. Kromer
Louis Krupp
Max H. Kruse
Chas. Conrad Kuchel
Walter Kuhn
Julius Kummer
Oscar A. Kunath
Geo. Albrecht F. Kuner

L

Lucien A. Labaudt
Alfred Lambourne
Joseph Lamson
Paul H. Landacre
Chauncey Langdon
Theodore Langgreth
Cyrille P. T. LaPlace
Vincenzo Larosa
Lee Lash
Bessie Mona Lasky
Lorenzo P. Latimer
Laura Louise Laurie
Paul Lauritz
Dillon Lauritzen
John Lavalle

Augustus Laver
Herbert M. Lawrence
Ernest Lawson
Louis Lebreton
Rico Lebrun
Lechard
Chee Chin S. C. Lee
Joseph Lee
Robert J. Lee
Edward Lehman(n)
Kathryn W. Leighton
Thomas C. Leighton
Alfred L. Lemercier
Arthur Lemmon
Pedro Joseph Lemos
Alfred Lenz
Margaret N. Levick
Levy
Nat Levy
Edmonia Lewis
H. Emerson Lewis
Herbert T. Lewis
Jeanette M. Lewis
Thomas E. Lewis
Dorothy Wright Liebes
Andrew J. Lindsay
Axel Linus
Henry Lion
Howard Little
John T. Little
Ted Littlefield
Caroline Alma Lloyd
Florence Lockwood
Richard Lofton
Maurice Geo. Logan
Stephen Longstreet
Pascal Loomis
John Lopes
Lorenzo Lorain
Eric Loran
Matilda Lotz
Boris Lovet-Lorsky
Aimee Annette Lozier
Fred Ludekens
Wright S. Ludington
Alice Emilie Ludovici
Julius Ludovici
Glen Lukens
Eleanore M. Lukits
Florence Lundborg
Fernand H. Lungren
Louis O. Lussier
Dan S. Lutz

MC

Clara Tag. McChesney
Alberta B. McCloskey
Wm. Joseph McCloskey
Francis John McComas
Geo. Herbert McCord

M. Evelyn McCormick
James McCourtney
J. Wilbur McCutchan
William T. McDermitt
Bernard McDonagh
Julie McDonald
Blanche E. B. McGaw
Nonette McGlashan
Thomas A. McGlynn
R. B. McGrew
Buckley MacGurrin
Wm. F. McIllwraith
Wm. A. McIlvaine Jr.
S. S. McIntyre
Grace E. McKinstry
Marcelle McKusick
Gerald W. McLaughlin
John McLaughlin
Louise MacLeod-Thorp
George McManus
Wm. Birch McMurtrie
John A. McQuarrie
Paul McReynolds

M

Constance Macky
Donald Macky
Eric Spencer Macky
Mrs. William Maillard
Robert Mallary
Michael Malloy
Olof C. Malmquist
Erwin Mannheim
Jean Mannheim
Florence Manor
Irving Marcus
William Lewis Marple
Frederick M. Marriott
Francis Samuel Marryat
Freda Marshall
Martin
Antone Martin
Caroline L. Martin
E. Hall Martin
Fletcher Martin
Thomas Mower Martin
Giovanni Martinelli
Micaela Martinez
Xavier Martinez
Joyce Massey
Jean Masson
Arthur Frank Mathews
Lucia K. Mathews
J. Muir Mathieson
Johanna Mathieson
Marianne Mathieu
George Mathis
Clarence Mattei
John B. Matthew
Laura M. Maxwell

Florence Land May
Bernard Ralph Maybeck
Paul Kirkland Mays
Lewis Henry Meakin
Paul Meltsner
George W. Melville
Mary Teresa Menton
William Merchant
Charles Merck
Warren Chase Merritt
Jules J. C. Mersfelder
Antoinette deF. Merwin
Charles Meryon
Ivan Messenger
Benjamin N. Messick
Richard Max Meyer
Hans Meyer-Kassell
Wm. Henry Meyers
Pietro Mezzara
Hildreth Miere
P. V. Mighels
Gertrude W. Mihsfeldt
Hannah Millard
Alec Miller
Alfred Jacob Miller
Barse Miller
Henry Miller
Hugh Blight Miller
Lillian May Miller
Lorraine Miller
Neva Miller
Ralph Davison Miller
Arthur H. T. Millier
Jessie Lincoln Mitchell
George Miyasaki
Ralph Fullerton Mocine
Hilda Mohle
Alfred Montgomery
Edwin Moody
Edwin S. Moore
Frank Monyague Moore
H. Humphrey Moore
Joseph Jacinto Mora
Edward Moran
Peter Moran
Thomas Moran
Rosa C. Moretti
Charlotte Eliz. Morgan
Julia Morgan
Mary DeN. Morgan
Richard Allen Morris
Morrison
Robert Motherwell
Matilda F. Mott
John Mottram
Louis C. Mullgardt
Gilbert Davis Munger
Frank H. Myers

N

Louis Nagel
Chas. Christian Nahl
Hugo A. W. Nahl
Margery Nahl
Perham Wilhelm Nahl
Virgil T. Nahl
Frank A. Nankivell
George Napier
Heinrich Nappenbach
E. Narjot deFranchville
Thomas Nash
Daniel W. Nason
David Dalhoff Neal
Charles Austin Needham
Dominic Needham
C. P. Neilson
Bruce Nelson
John Peter Nelson
Vladimir Nemkoff
Alexander Nepote
Carl Eugen Neuhaus
Alfred Neumeyer
Kate W. Newhall
Joseph Cather Newsom
Samuel Newsom
Emrich Nicholson
John Wm. Nicoll
Louise Everett Nimmo
Thomas Noble
B. J. O. Nordfeldt
Charles W. Nystrom

O

Mrs. A. T. Oakes
Mrs. W. H. Oakes
Chiura Obata
Frank Morgan O'Brien
O'Connell
Jean B. O'Connor
Thomas Story Officer
Robert E. Ogilby
John C. Oglesby
William H. O'Grady
Ann O'Hanlon
Richard E. O'Hanlon
Arthur Okamura
Mine Okubo
Otis Wm. Oldfield
Nathan Oliveira
Myron Angelo Oliver
Frederick Olmstead
Helen A. O'Malley
Alexander Orloffsky
Doris Ormsby
Lillie V. O'Ryan
Sam. Stillman Osgood
John O'Shea
Mrs. Denis O'Sullivan
Fessenden Nott Otis
George Demont Otis

Margaret O'Toole
Geo. Martin Ottinger
Jacques Overhoff
Charles Hamilton Owens

P

Jules Eugene Pages Jr.
Jules Francis Pages Sr.
Jos. Paget-Fredericks
Robert Treat Paine
Anna Palmer
Frances Flora Palmer
Frederick L. M. Pape
Phil Paradise
Charles Louis Parish
David Park
Thomas S. Parkhurst
De Witt Parshall
Douglas E. Parshall
C. R. Parsons
Marion Randall Parsons
Virgil F. Partch II
Gertrude Partington
John H. E. Partington
Richard L. Partington
Roi Partridge
Tarmo A. Pasto
Haig Patigian
Martha Patterson
Philip Kran Paval
Edgar Samuel Paxson
Edgar Alwin Payne
Henry Payot
Titian Ramsey Peale
Felix Achilles Peano
Lucius C. Pease
Francis Marion Pebbles
Orrin Peck
Joshua H. Peirce
Ernest Cliff. Peixotto
Ralph Dubose Pekor
Simeon Pelenc
Agnes Pelton
Henri Penelon
Gaetano Pennachio
Leonora N. Penniman
Albert S. Pennoyer
Victor Seman Perard
Don Louis Perceval
George W. Percy
Eva Green Perine
Lilita Perine
Enoch Wood Perry Jr.
Lois Jean Perry
Fritiof Persson
Charles Rollo Peters
Dewitt Peters
Mrs. Robert B? Peters
Roland Petersen
Sidonie Petetin

M. Fancher Pettis
Timothy L. Pfleuger
Edith Catlin Phelps
Werner Philipp
C. B. Phillips
Helen Eliz. Phillips
Gottardo F. Piazzoni
B. W. Pierce
Minerva Pierce
Frederick Piercy
Emile M. Pissis
Emma C. O. Pixley
Edmundo Pizzella
Corene Bain Place
George Taylor Plowman
Alexis M. Podchernikoff
Willis J. Polk
Max Pollak
Theodore C. Polos
Julius Pommer
Eugene A. Poole
Horatio Nelson Poole
Marion Holden Pope
Bruce Porter
James Tank Porter
George Booth Post
Zenas Potter
Hiram Powers
John Prendergast
Victor Prevost
Clayton S. Price
Irene Price
William Henry Price
Vicki Prioste
Alexander Phim. Proctor
Burt Proctor
Raymond Puccinelli
Hanson Duvall Puthuff
Arthur Putnam

Q

Henry Quinan
Cornelia B. S. Quinton

R

Saul Rabino
Benjamin O. Raborg
Ellen G. Emmet Rand
Lee F. Randolph
William Ranney
Joseph Raphael
Henry Raschen
Marion C. M. Raulston
Louis Edward Rea
Alice Matilda Reading
Edward W. Redfield
Granville S. Redmond
Allen C. Redwood
Marjorie Reed
Henry Reeks
Jos. Mason Reeves Jr.

Anton Refregier
Manuel Rivera Regalado
Alver Regli
Jesse Reichek
Helen Reichle
James W. Reid
Merritt J. Reid
Robert Reid
Charles Reiffel
Maria A. Reimers
Frederic Remington
Arthur Remsen
Joseph Warren Revere
Andria Rexroth
Jacques Joseph Rey
Louis Martin Rey
Paul M. Reynolds
Richard Reynolds
William S. Rice
Frances Rich
John Hubbard Rich
Edward Richardson
Mary Curtis Richardson
Theodore Richardson
Joachim F. Richardt
Alice Rideout
Winifred Rieber
Riegart
C. Riehn
Sidney H. Riesenberg
Lutah Maria Riggs
Thomas Emerson Ripley
Robert C. Rishell
Caroline Evelyn Risque
William Ritschel
Hazel Rittenhouse
Candelario Rivas
Diego Rivera
Laura G. Rivol
Julian Walbridge Rix
Fred. Goodrich Robbins
Betty Repine Roberts
J. P. Robertson
Alfred Robinson
Boardman Robinson
Charles D. Robinson
Charles H. Robinson
Cleveland Rockwell
Elizabeth A. Rockwell
Norman Rockwell
Alfred C. Rodriguez
L. H. Roethe
Paulus Roetter
Charles A. Rogers
E. A. Rogers
Margaret E. Rogers
Warren E. Rollins
Frederick Rondel
Eloise Roorbach

Julius J. Rorphuro
Guy Rose
Herman Rose
A. Rosenthal
Bernard J. Rosenthal
Kenneth Ross
Marion Ross
Mary Herrick Ross
Thomas Ross
Adolphe Rouarque
P. Roullier
Charles S. Rouse
Ann Roy
Mrs. Edna B. Roys
Mrs. Christopher Ruess
William H. Rulofson
Jules Rupalley
Bruce Alex. Russell
Charles Marion Russell
Felix Ruvolo
Charles James Ryan

S

Charles W. Saalburg
John Saccard
G. Fabricio Sala
Helen Arnstein Salz
George E. Samerjan
Detlef Samman(n)
Fred E. Samuels
Frank Samuelson
William Sanderson
Henry Sandham
Matteo Sandona
Edward Field Sanford
Ross Santeo
Geneve R. Sargeant
Henry Sargent
Frank P. Sauerwe(i)n
Wallace B. Sawyer
Frederick Grayson Sayre
Zygmund Sazevich
Frederick Ferd. Schafer
Sergey J. Scherbakoff
Rupert Schmid(t)
Julius Schmidt
Paul A. Schmitt
Jacques Schnier
Dorner T. Schueler
Maude W. Schumacher
Herman Schuyler
David Francis Schwartz
Robert Schwartz
Albert C. Schweinfurth
Fred. Wm. Schweigardt
Father L. Sciocchetti
Benton Francis Scott
Clyde Eugene Scott
Nellie Burrell Scott
Victor Seamon

Benj. Willard Sears
Geo. Joseph Seideneck
Yoshida Sekido
Olaf Carl Seltzer
Ettore Serbaroli
Fulgenzio Seregni
Helen Moore Sewell
Fred Sexton
Dan Shapiro
Frank Henry Shapleigh
Joseph Henry Sharp
Louis Hovey Sharp
William A. Sharp
Stephen Wm. Shaw
Ada Romer Shawhan
Charles D. Shed
Millard Sheets
Edwin Allen Sherman
William J. Shew
Walter Shirlaw
May Bradford Shockley
Henrietta M. Shore
Mrs. Ward Shultz
Waldemar E. Sichelkow
Lundy Siegreist
Wilson Silsby
William Posey Silva
David Simpson
Marian Simpson
William Simpson
Chas. James Dindelar
Virginia Singer
Lola MacDon. Sleeth
Rex Slinkard
David Slivka
Blanding Sloan
Louis Sloan
Clark Ashton Smith
Cornelius Cole Smith
Mrs. E. Tanner Smith
Elmer Boyd Smith
Ernest Browning Smith
Frank Edwin D. Smith
George Washington Smith
Howard E. Smith
Jack Wilkinson Smith
Jerome Howard Smith
Thomas A/H. Smith
Eda StJohn Smitten
Eugen Leslie Smyth
William Smythe
Alphonse Sondag
Al Sontag
Antonio Sotomayor
Jacquewin Soule
Frederick Spang
Clay Edgar Spann
Will Sparks
Fanny J. Spaulding

George Spiel
Peter Stackpole
Ralph Stackpole
Elmer Stanhop
George M. Stanley
John Mix Stanley
John A. Stanton
Jack Gage Stark
Rama D. Stearns
Aaron Stein
Henry Steinegger
Maurice Sterne
Barbara Stevenson
Arthur Stewart
Bernice Stewart
Alison Stilwell
Don Stine
John Ward Stinson
Charles S. Stobie
B. Stocqueler
Gjura Stojana
John T. E. Stoll
Frank Fred. Stone
William Wetmore Story
Hubert Stowitts
Meyer Straus
Mel Strawn
Elizabeth Strong
Jos. Dwight Strong Jr.
Ray Strong
Dorothy Stuart
James Everett Stuart
Alfred Sully
Thomas Sully
Chas. Fred. Surendorf
Leland Susman
Kate Sutherland
Samuel Sutter
W. S. Sutton
Edward Howard Suydam
Edward Robinson Swain
James Gilchrist Swan
William F. Swasey
Lloyd Sweigert
James Guil. Swinnerton
John Sykes
George Gardner Symons

T

W. Taber
Phebe T. M. C. Taber
Chas. Alfred Taliferro
Reuben Tam
Fausto Tasca
Clarence Taubenheim
Jules Tavernier
Bayard Taylor
Edgar Dorsey Taylor
Edward Dewitt Taylor
Henry Fitch Taylor

Will L. Taylor
Prince Zourab Tchkotova
Flora Telschow
Sibyl S S. Terry
Newton J. Tharp
John William Theiss
Wayne Thiebaud
Burt Randolph Thomas
John Hudson Thomas
Stephen Seymour Thomas
Frank Wildes Thompson
Joan Thoren
Douglas Tilden
W. Tileseus Von Tilenau
George Tirrell
Frederic Tobin
Peter Petersen Toffts
P. Tognelli
Domenico Tojetti
Edward Tojetti
Virgil Tojetti
Manuel J. Tolegian
Joaquin Torres
John Martin Tracy
Stella Gert. Trask
Emily Travis
Numa S. Trivas
Leon Trousset
Theodore T'Scharner
John Burnside Tufts
Warren Tufts
Luther Turton

U

Kathryn L. Uhl
Beatrice Ullrich
Gladys Unger

V

A. A. Vaillancourt
Manuel Valencia
Albert Valentien
Napoleon P. Vallejo
Robert H. Vance
Charles Vanderhoff
Les Vandre
Ernesr Van Harlington
Beth Van Hoesen
Frank J. Van Sloun
Durbin Van Vleck
Carrie Van Wie
Emma F. Van Winkle
Oscar Van Young
Jean Varda
Vasquez
Florence Veach
Godfrey Fran. Veseley
Hernando Gonzallo Villa
David V. Villasenor
Jean Jacques Vioget
Edward Vischer

Calthea Campbell Vivian
Clara Augusta Vivian
William Voegtlin
Charles Von Berg
Carl E. Von Eichendorf
Bernard J. Von Eichman
Hermann Von Friederici
Georg H. Von Langsdorff
Michael Von Meyer
Carl Von Perbandt
Maria Von Ridelstein
Harold Von Schmidt
Adam Clark Vroman
Edouard Antonin Vysekal

W

W.W. W.
Elmer Wachtel
Marion Kavanagh Wachtel
Vitus Wackenreuder
Blanche Collet Wagner
J Edward Walker
James Walker
Samuel Walker
Marion G. Wallace
Moira Wallace
Katherine E. Wallis
Edgar Walter
Solly H. Walter
Henry Gordon Walton
Juan B. Wandesforde
Harold M. Ward
Florence E. Ware
Pegot Waring
Abel G. Warshawsky
Carleton E. Watkins
Susan Watkins
Robert Watson
Wm. Clothier Watts
June Wayne
George A. Weaver
Nonna Owings Webb
P. Weber
Hutton Webster Jr.
William Weeks
William H. Weeks
Emilie S. Weinberg
Albert Weinert
Bonnie Welch
Ludmilla Pilat Welch
Thaddeus Welch
Larry Welden
Winfield S. Wellington
Anna M. Wells
Cady Wells
F. Marion Wells
August Wenderoth
Julia M. B. Wendt
William Wendt
Albert Beck Wenzell

Fritz Werner
Glenn Anthony Wessels
Benjamin Franklin West
Isabelle C. P. West
Virgil West
Tulita Westfall y de
          Boronda
Edward Weston
Otheto Weston
S. Wetteland
Albertine R. Wheelan
White
Edith White
Paul Whitman
Sarah S. Whitney
Joseph Whittle
Frederick Whymper
Neil C. Whyte
Ethel Marian Wickes
Guest Wickson
Gunnar M. Widforss
Max Wieczorek
Olaf S. Wieghorst
Fritz Wikersheim
Charles Wilcomb
Lemuel Maynard Wiles
William Wiley
William Hancock Wilke
James F. Wilkins
Williams
Elizabeth Williams
Ella Williams
Frederick B. Williams
Gluyas Williams
Virgil Williams
J(James?) R. Willis
George Wilner
Bryan Wilson
Charles Theller Wilson
John Wilson
Oregon Wilson
W. F. Wilson
Carl Wimar
John W. J. Winkler
Emily?Emilie W. Winn
Charles Allan Winter
Daniel Winter
George Winter
William Winter
Phyllis Winterburn
Denny Winters
Jack Wisby
Grace N. Wishaar
Evelyn Almond Withrow
Otto Wix
Galen Wolf
Hamilton Achille Wolf
Paul Wonner
Mrs. E. Shotwell Wood

Leonard Sutton Wood
Stanley H. Wood
Selden J. Woodman
Richard Caton Woodville
Ellamarie Woolley
Joseph Worchester
Willard E. Worden
Lucia Wores
Theodore Wores
Katherine Swan Works
George Alex. Wright
Lloyd Wright
Stanton McDonald Wright
Phyllis Wrightson
William Wrigley Jr.
Carl Wuttke
Emanuel Wyttenbach

Y

Sydney Jones Yard
Frederick Yates
Walter R. Yeager
Jimmie Yee
Raymond Dabb Yelland
William Ray. Yelland
Karl J. Heinrich Yens
Cabot Yerxa
Richard Yip
Charles H. Young
George J. Young
Harvey Otis Young

Z

Jack Zajac
Bernard Baruch Zakheim
Matthew Zakheim
Nathan Zakheim
Alex Zeller
Fred. Almond Zimmerman
James Milford Zornes

Sacramento Valley Landscapes A multi-gallery exhibition of historical and contemporary works. --1979 Sponsored by Univ. of Calif., Davis		**IMPRESSIONISM—THE CALIFORNIA VIEW 1890 — 1930** Exhibition at Oakland & L. A. County Art Museums. --1981

A
Alfred I. Agate

B
Henry Bainbridge
George H. Baker
Albert Bierstadt

C
John Cameron
George Casilear
George V. Cooper
Thomas L. Cox
Richard Crozier

D
Fred Dalkey
David Dangelo
Frank Day
Joe Draegert

E
Robert Else

F
Darrell Forney

G
Ralph Goings

H
Richard W. Hackett
Carl William Hahn
Marilyn Halevi
Thomas Hill
Harvey Himelfarb

I
George Inness Jr.

J
William F. Jackson

K
William Keith
Dennis Kellett
Gregory Kondos
Margie Kopp

L
James Lamson
Horst G. Leissl
George W. Lewis
Mary A. Lewis

M
Margery Mann
Joseph Mannino
William Lewis Marple
Philip Menard
Barse Miller
Edward Norton Moore

N
Charles Christian Nahl
Erneste Narjot

Eugen Neuhaus
Maurine Morse Nelson

P
Roland Petersen

R
Ed Ramos
Don Reich
Natalie Robb
Charles D. Robinson

S
Benjamin W. Sears
Daniel Shapiro
Rupert Snyder
James W. Steel
James E. Stuart
Mary Swisher

T
C. A. M. Taber
Bayard Taylor
Wayne Thiebaud
Harry Troughton

V
Roger Vail
Manuel Valencia Jr.
Carl Von Perbandt

W
Juan B. Wandesforde
Larry Welden
Morrell F. Wise
Paul Wonner

Y
Harvey O. Young

Franz Arthur Bischoff
Maurice Braun
Anne Millay Bremer
William Vincent Cahill
S. Emile Carlsen
William Merritt Chase
William Henry Clapp
Alson Skinner Clark
Colin Campbell Cooper
E. Charlton Fortune
August Francois Gay
Selden Connor Gile
Armin Carl Hansen
Sam Hyde Harris
E. Childe Hassam
Clarence Keiser Hinkle
Clark Hobart
Paul Lauritz
Mary Amanda Lewis
Maurice Logan
Jean Mannheim
Arthur Frank Mathews
Richard Emil Miller
E. Bruce Nelson
Eugen Neuhaus
Lillie May Nicholson
Jules Eugene Pages
Edgar Allwyn Payne
Charles Rollo Peters
Clayton S. Price
Hanson Duvall Puthuff
Lee Fritz Randolph
Joseph Raphael
Granville Redmond
Robert Reid
Wm. Frederick Ritschel
Guy Rose
Donna Norine Schuster
Louis Bassi Siegriest
William Wendt
Theodore Wores

PLEIN AIR PAINTERS OF CALIFORNIA—THE SOUTHLAND Book by Ruth Westphal-1982 (Most beautiful book on California art--in-depth coverage)	**Virginia Steele Scott Memorial Collection** and Examples from the Permanent Collection Laguna Beach Art Museum - 1980	

LOS ANGELES
  Dana Bartlett
  Franz Arthur Bischoff
  Benjamin C. Brown
  Frank T. Chamberlin
  Alson Skinner Clark
  John Bond Francisco
  Sam Hyde Harris
  Clarence K. Hinkle
  Paul Lauritz
  Jean Mannheim
  Hanson Duvall Puthuff
  Granville S. Redmond
  Guy Rose
  Donna Norine Schuster
  Jack Wilkinson Smith
  Elmer Wachtel
  Marion K. Wachtel
 	
LAGUNA BEACH
  George Ken. Brandriff
  Frank Cuprien
  William A. Griffith
  Anna Althea Hills
  Thomas L. Hunt
  Joseph Kleitsch
  Edgar Alwin Payne
  George Gardner Symons
  William Wendt
 	
SAN DIEGO
  Maurice Braun
  Charles Arthur Fries
  Alfred R. Mitchell
  Charles Reiffel
	Walter Askin
	Misha Askenazy
	B
	McClelland Barclay
	Dana Bartlett
	Arthur Beaumont
	Frederick W. Becker
	Edward Betts
	Louis Betts
	Barbara Blair
	Carl Oscar Borg
	George Kennedy Brandriff
	Rex Brandt
	Conrad Buff
	C
	Frank T. Chamberlin
	Howard Clapp
	Elanor Colburn
	D
	John Decker
	Francis de Erdely
	Phil Dike
	E
	Leonard Edmondson
	F
	Michael Frary
	Betty Davenport Ford
	James Fuller
	G
	Joe Duncan Gleason
	Grigory Gluckman
	H
	Richard Haines
	Ejnar Hansen
	Anna Althea Hills
	John Herbert Hinchman
	Clarence K. Hinkle
	J
	James Jarvaise
	K
	Leonard Kester
	Dong Kingman
	Joseph Kleitsch
	Katherine Knox
	Emil J. Kosa Jr.
	Roger Kuntz
	L
	Paul Lauritz
	Dan Lutz
	M
	Jean Mannheim
	Elizabeth McNaughton
	Lola M. S. Miller
	N
	Crandall Norton
	O
	Ruth Osgood
	P
	Edgar Alwyn Payne
	Ruth Eaton Peabody
		R
		Granville S. Redmond
		Arthur G. Rider
		Guy Rose
		S
		Donna N. Schuster
		Frederick Schwankovsky
		Jonathan Scott
		Sueo Serisawa
		Millard Sheets
		Jack Wilkinson Smith
		James G. Swinnerton
		George Gardner Symons
		W
		Elmer Wachtel
		Shirley Weeks
		William Wendt
		Frederic Whitaker
		Robert E. Wood
		Virginia Woolley
		V
		Oscar Van Young
		Frede Vidar
		Z
		Jack Zajac

Peggy and Harold Samuel's <u>Artists of the American West</u> is a well-researched, thoroughly-competent reference for the collector of Western art. Apart from the usual biographical data, the authors have attempted to specify where a signature sample can be located, and often provide indication of painting value. Also, the book includes over 300 illustrations of paintings by the more important artists.

Abdy, Rowena Meeks
Abert, James W.
Abeyta, Narcisco P.
Achey, Mary E
Acosta, Manuel G.
Adam, William
Adams, Cassidy
Adams, Charles P.
Adams, Kenneth M.
Adams, Willis
Adney, Edwin T.
Agate, Alfred T.
Akin, Louis B.
Albright, Floyd T.
Albright, Herman O.
Alden, James M
Allen, John D.
Allen, Thomas
Allison, William M.
Ames, Ezra
Amick, Robert W
Anderson, Clarence W.
Andres, Charles J.
Andrews, George H.
Applegate, Frank G.
Armin, Emil
Armstrong, M. K.
Armstrong, William W.
Arpa, y Perea
Arriola, Fortunato
Arthurs, Stanley M.
Asah, Spencer
Asmar, Alice
Atencio, Gilbert B.
Atwood, Robert
Auchiah, James
Audubon, John J.
Audubon, John W.
Ault, George C
Austin, Charles P.
(Awa Tsireh)
Ayres, Thomas A

B

Babcock, Dean
Babcock, Ida D.
Bachmann, Max
Back, Joseph W
Bacon, Frank
Bacon, Irving R.
Bagg, Henry H.
Bagley, James M.
Baker, George H.
Baker, H. Roy
Baker, William H.
Bakos, Jozef G.
Baldridge, Cyrus L.
Baldwin, Clifford P.
Balink, Henry C.
Ballou, Bertha
Bancroft, Albert S.
Bancroft, William H.
Banvard, John
Barchus, Eliza R.
Barker, Charles F.
Barker, George

Barker, Olive R.
Barnes, Matthew R.
Barnett, Isa
Barnouw, Adriaan J
Barr, Paul E.
Barr, William
Barrett, Lawrence L
Barse, George R.
Bartholomew, William M.
Bartlett, Dana
Bartlett, Gray
Bartlett, John R.
Bartlett, Paul W
Bartoli, J
Barton, Loren R
Bassett, Reveau M.
Battese, Stanley
Baumann, Gustave
Baumhofer, Walter M.
Baur, Theodore
Beament, Thomas H.
Beard, Daniel C.
Beard, George
Beard, James C
Beard, James H
Beard, Thomas F.
Beard, William H.
Beardsley, Jefferson
(Beatien Yazz)
Beatty, John W.
Beaugureau, Francis H.
Beaulaurier, Leo J
Beauregard, Donald
Beaver, Fred
Becker, Arthur E.
Becker, August H
Becker, F Otto
Becker, Frederick W
Becker, Joseph
Beckmann, Max
Beckwith, Arthur
Beeler, Joe
Begay, Arpie
Begay, Harrison
Beil, Charles A.
Bell, Thomas S.
Bell, William A
Bellows, George W.
Bell-Smith, Frederick M.
Bemis, William O.
Benda, Wladyslaw T.
Bender, William
Benjamin, Lucile J
Benrimo, Thomas D.
Bensell, George E.
Benton, James C
Benton, Thomas Hart
Berghaus, Albert
Berke, Ernest
Berkley, Stanley
Berninghaus, Julius C.
Berninghaus, Oscar E.
Berry, Noah
Best, Arthur W
Best, Harry C.

Betts, Edwin C.
Betts, Harold H
Biddle, George
Bierhals, Otto
Bierstadt, Albert
Big Bow, Woodrow W.
Bingham, George C.
Birchim, Dorcas
Bisbing, Henry S.
Bischoff, Eugene H.
Bisttram, Emil Jr.
Bjorklund, Lorence F.
Bjurman, Andrew
Blackowl, Archie
Blair, John
Blake, William P.
Blakelock, Ralph A.
Blue Eagle, Acee
Blum, Jerome S.
Blumenschein, Ernest L.
Blumenschein, Helen G.
Blumenschein, Mary S.
Bodfish, William P
Bodmer, Karl
Bofill, Antoine
Boisseau, Alfred
Boles, David
Bolton, Hale W
Bonheur, Marie R.
Bonner, Mary A.
Bonwell, E.
Borein, John E.
Borg, Carl Oscar
Borglum, James L.
Borglum, John Gutzon
Borglum, Solon H.
Borthwick, John D.
Bosin, Francis B.
Boss, Homer
Botke, Cornelius
Botke, Jessie Arms
Boundrey, Burton S.
Boutelle, De Witt C.
Bovee, I.
Boyle, Ferdinand T. L.
Boyle, John J.
Boynton, Ray S.
Bramlett, James E
Brandriff, George K.
Brandt, Carl L.
Bransom, John P
Braun, Maurice
Breneiser, Stanley G.
Brenner, Carl C .
Brett, Dorothy E.
Breuer, Henry J
Brewer, Nicholas R.
Brewerton, George D.
Brinley, Daniel P.
Bromley, Valentine W.
Bromwell, Elizabeth H
Brookes, Samuel M.
Broome, B. C.
Browere, Albertis dO.
Brown, Benjamin C.

Brown, Donald
Brown, Dorothy W.
Brown, Grafton T
Brown, H. Harris
Brown, Henry B
Brown, Howell C.
Brown, Paul
Brown(e), Charles F.
Browne, Charles F.
Browne, John R
Bruff, Joseph G.
Brush, George dF.
Bruton, Margaret
Bryan, William E.
Bryant, Harold E.
Bryant, Will
Buchser, Frank
Buff, Conrad
Bugbee, Harold D.
Buhler, F.
Bull, Charles L.
Bunnell, Charles R.
Burbank, Elbridge A.
Burgdorff, Ferdinand
Burgess, George H.
Burr, George E.
Burt, Marie Haines
Bush, Norton
Bush-Brown, Henry K.
Butler, Howard R.
Butman, Frederick A.
Bywaters, Jerry

C

Cabot, Hugh
Cadenasso, Guiseppe
Cahill, Arthur J.
Calhoun, A. R.
Calyor, Nicolino V
Camerer, Eugene
Cames, Vina
Camfferman, Margaret G.
Camfferman, Peter M
Campbell, Albert H
Campbell, Orson D.
Caples, Robert C
Carpenter, Earl
Carpenter, Ellen M.
Carr, M. Emily
Carter, Charles M.
Carvalho, Solomon N.
Casilear, John W.
Casnelli, Victor
Cassidy, Ira Diamond
Castaigne, J. Andre
Catherwood, Frederick
Catlin, George
Caylor, Harvey W.
Ce-Komo-Pyn
Chain(m), Mrs. James A.
Chalee, Pop
Chamberlain, Norman S.
Champney, James W.
Chandler, Floyd C.
Chapin, John R.
Chapman, Charles S

Chapman, Frederick A
Chapman, Frederick T.
Chapman, John G.
Chapman, Kenneth M.
Chappel, Alonzo
Chappell, Bill
Charlton, John
Chee, Robert
Cheney, Russell
Cherry, Emma R
Chiriacka, Ernest
Chittenden, Larry
Choh
Choris, Louis
Christadoro, Charlie
Christensen, Carl C
Christy, Howard C
Cisneros, Jose
Clark, Allen
Clark, Alson S.
Clark, Benton H.
Clark, Eliot C.
Clark, James L.
Clark, Matt
Clarke, John L.
Claveau, Antoine
Clawson, John W.
Cleenewerck, Henry
Clunie, Robert
Clymer, John
Coast, Oscar R.
Coe, Ethel L.
Colby, Vincent V.
Cole, Joseph F.
Cole, Thomas
Coleman, Arthur P.
Coleman, Edmund
Coleman, Mary Darter
Collings, Charles J.
Col(e)man, Samuel
Colton, Mary R
Colton, Walter
Colyer, Vincent
Compera, Alexis
Comstock, Enos B
Constantine
Cook, Harold
Cook, Howard W
Cooke, George
Cooper, Astley D M.
Cooper, Colin C.
Cooper, Emma L.
Cooper, George V.
Cooper, James G.
Cooper, J
Cope, Gordon N.
Cordero, Jose
Cornwell, Dean
Corwin, Charles A.
Cory, Kate T.
Cotton, John W
Couse, E. Irving
Coutts, Alice
Coutts, Gordon
Cowles, Russell

Cox, Charles B.
Cox, Charles H.
Cox, Clark
Cox, Jacob
Cox(e), W. M H.
Coze, Paul
Craig, Charles
Cram, Allan G.
Crane, G. W.
Crawford, Thomas
Crawford, Will
Creutzfeldt, Benjamin
Crews, Seth F.
Critcher, Catherine C
Cross, Frederick G.
Cross, Henry H.
Crumbo, Woodrow W
Cue, Henry J.
Culmer, Henry L.
Cummings, Charles A.
Cuneo, Cyrus C
Cuneo, Rinaldo
Cuprien, Frank W.
Currier, Edward W.
Curry, John S.
Curtis, Leland
Curtis, Philip C
Cushing, Howard G

D

Dabich, George
Dahlgren, Carl C.
Dahlgren, Marius
Daingerfield, Elliott
Dale, John B
Dallin, Cyrus E
Dalton, John J.
Damrow, Charles
Dann, Frode
Darge, Fred
Darley, Felix O. C.
Dasburg, Andrew M.
Datus, Jay
Daugherty, James H.
Davey, Randall
Davies, Arthur B.
Davis, Cornelia C.
Davis, Floyd M.
Davis, Georgina A.
Davis, Jessie F. S.
Davis, Leonard M.
Davis, Lew E.
Davis, Richard
Davis, Theodore R
Davis, Wayne L.
Day, Benjamin H
Deakin, Edwin
Deas, Charles
DeBatz, Alexander
DeBeaumont, Charles E.
DeCamp, Ralph E.
DeForest, Henry J.
DeForest, Lockwood
DeGrandmaison, Nicolas
DeGrazia, Ettore
DeHaan, Chuck

DeHaven, Franklin
Dehn, Adolph A
Delano, Gerard C
Delessard, Auguste
Dellenbaugh, Frederick S
DelMue, Maurice A.
DelPino, Jose M
Deming, Edwin W
Denny, J. G.
DeRyke, Emma
DeSmet, Pierre J.
DeTobriand, Regis D.
DeVaudricourt, A.
DeVere, J.
DeWolf, Wallace L.
DeYong, Joe
DeYoung, Harry A.
Diaz, Cristobal
Dibble, George S.
Dick, George
Dickeson, Montroville W.
Dickinson, Darol
Dickman, Charles J.
Diederick, Wilhelm H
Dixon, L. Maynard
Dodge, Aydee
Dodge, William dL.
Donahue, Vic
Donshea, Clement
Dougal, William H
Dougherty, Paul
Dow, Arthur W.
Dozier, Otis
Drayton, Joseph
Dresel, Emil
Dube, Louis T
Dudley, Jack
Duer, Douglas
Dufault, Joseph
Dumas, Jack
Dumond, Frederick M
Dumond, Frank V.
Duncanson, Robert S.
Dunn, Harvey T.
Dunnell, John H.
Dunton, William H.
Durkin, John
DuTant, Charles
Dyck, Paul
Dye, Charlie

E

Eakins, Thomas
Earle, Eyvind
Earle, Lawrence C.
East, Pattie R.
Eastman, Harrison
Eastman, Seth
Eastmond, Elbert H
Eaton, Charles H.
Eber, Elk
Echohawk, Brummeth
Eckford, Jessiejo
Edouart, Alexander
Edwards, Harry C.
Edwards, Lonnie C

Egan, John J
Eggenhofer, Nick
Eilshemius, Louis M.
Eisenlohr, Edward G
Elder, John A.
Elkins, Henry A.
Elliott, Henry W.
Ellis, Fremont F.
Ellsworth, Clarence A.
Elwell, Robert F
Emmerlee, Berla I.
Emerson, Robert E.
Enderson, S B
Ensor, Arthur J
Ernesti, Richard
Ertz, Edward F.
Evans, Edwin
Evans, Jessie Benton
Evans, Richard
Everett, Joseph A F.
Everett, Raymond
Eytel, Carl
Eyth, Louis
Eytinge, Soloman Jr.

F

Fairbanks, Avard T.
Fairbanks, John B
Fairbanks, John L.
Fairchild, Hurlstone
Falter, John P.
Fanshaw, Hubert
Farnham, Sally J.
Farny, Henry F.
Faulkner, Barry
Fausett, Lynn
Fell, Olive
Fellows, Frederick
Fenn, Harry
Ferran, Augusto
Ferris, Jean L. G
Fery, John
Field, Lawrence B
Firfires, Nicholas S.
Firks, Henry
Fischer, Anton O.
Fish, C. B
Fisher, Alvan
Fisher, Hugo A
Fisher, Philip D
Fisk, Harry T.
Fisk, W.
Fitzgerald, Lionel L.
Fitzgerald, Pitt L
Fleck, Joseph A.
Fleming, John
Fletcher, Calvin
Fletcher, Clara T.
Fletcher, Sydney
Fleury, Albert F.
Foote, Mary Hallock
Forbes, Edwin
Forbes, Helen K.
Ford, Henry C.
Forsythe, Victor C.
Foster, Benjamin

Fox, Charles L.
Fox, R. Atkinson
Francisco, John Bond
Fraser, James E.
Fraser, John A.
Fraser, T. Douglas
Frazer, Mabel P.
Frazier, Esther Y.
Frederiksen, Mary M.
Free, John D.
Freeman, W E.
Frenzeny, Paul
Friberg, Arnold
Friend, Washington F.
Fripp, Charles C.
Fripp, Thomas W.
Frost, Arthur B.
Frost, John
Fuchs, Feodor
Furlong, Charles W.

G

Gage, George W.
Galli, Stanley W.
Galpins, Cromwell
Gambee, Martin
Gannam. John
Garel, Leo
Gaspard, Leon
Gaul, William G.
Gibberd, Eric W.
Gibbs, George
Gideon, Samuel E
Gifford, Charles B.
Gifford, Robert S.
Gifford, Sanford R.
Girder, Robert F.
Gillen, Denver L.
Gissing, Roland
Glover, Edwin S.
Goddard, George H.
Gollings, Elling W.
Gomez, Marco A.
Gonzales, Boyer
Gonzalez, Xavier
Goodwin, Philip R
Goodwin, Richard L. B.
Gookins, James F.
Gordon-Cummings, Connie
Gotzsche, Kai G
Graham, Charles
Grandee, Joe Ruiz
Grant, Blanche C.
Gray, U
Grayson, J H. Lee
Greatorex, Eliza P.
Green, Hiram H.
Greene, Hamilton
Greene, Leroy E
Greer, James E
Greer, Jefferson E
Gremke, Henry D
Grenet, Edward L.
Griffith, Louis O.
Grigware, Edward T.
Grimm, Paul

Griset, Ernest H.
Griswold, Casimir C.
Grob, Ttautman
Groll, Albert L.
Gropper, William
Grose, D C.
Groth, John A.
Grotz, William
Grover, Oliver D.
Guillaume, Louis M.

H

Haag, Herman H.
Haddock, Arthur E.
Hadra, Ida W.
Hafen, John
Hahn, William
Haines, Marie B.
Hall, Cyrenius
Hall, Sydney P.
Hall, William
Hambridge, Edward J.
Hamilton, James
Hammock, Earl G.
Hammond, Arthur J
Hammond, John
Hamp, Francis
Hampton, Bill
Hampton, John W.
Hanna, Thomas K.
Hansen, Armin C
Hansen, Herman W.
Hansen, Oscar J. W
Happel, Carl
Harding, Chester
Harman, Fred Jr.
Harmer, Alexander F.
Harmon, Charles H
Harrington, Joseph
Harris, Lawren S.
Harris, Robert G.
Harrison, Lovell B.
Hart, Alfred
Hartley, Marsden
Hartung, F.
Harvey, Eli
Harvey, George
Harvey, Gerald
Harwood, Burt S.
Haskell, Ernest
Hassam, F Childe
Haughey, James M.
Hauser, John
Hawthorn, Edith G
Hayes, William J
Heaney, Charles E.
Health, Frank L.
Heger, Joseph
Heikka, Earle E.
Heilge, George
Heinrich, Roy F.
Heinze, Adolph
Helbig, Bud
Heming, Arthur H H
Henckel, Carl
Henderson, James

Henderson, John R.
Henderson, William P.
Hendricks, Emma S.
Henning, Albin
Hennings, Ernest M.
Henri, Robert
Herbst, Frank C.
Herman, Mr.
Herrera, Joe H.
Herrera, Velino S.
Herrick, Henry W.
Herzog, Hermann
Hess, Sara M.
Hesselius, Gustavus
Hicks, Bobby
Hicks, Edward
Higgens, Eugene
Higgens, William V.
Higham, Sydney
Hill, Abby W.
Hill, Alice S.
Hill, Edward R.
Hill, Evelyn, C.
Hill, John H.
Hill, Robert J.
Hill, Thomas
Hilton, John W.
Hinckley, Thomas H.
Hind, Henry Y.
Hind, William G. R.
Hine, Henry G.
Hinkle, Clarence K.
Hitchens, Joseph
Hittell, Charles J
Hockaday, Hugh
Hoeffler, Adolph J.
Hoffman, Frank B
Hoffman, Malvina C.
Hogan, Thomas
Hogner, Nils
Hogue, Alexandre
Hokeah, Jack
Holdredge, Ransom G.
Holgate, Edwin H.
Hollings, Holling C.
Holme, John F.
Holmes, William H.
Holt, Percy W.
Hood, Harry
Hooper, Will P.
Hopkins, Arthur
Hopkins, Frances A. B.
Hopkinson, Harold
Hopper, Edward
Hoppin, Agustus
Hord, Donal
Horn, Trader
Horsfall, Robert B.
Hoskins, Gayle P.
Houghton, Arthur B.
Houghton, Merritt D.
Houser, Allan C.
Howard, Robert B.
Howe, Oscar
Howland, John Dare

Hoxie, Vinnie R.
Huddle, William H.
Hudson, Grace C.
Hughes, Edward J.
Hulings, Clark
Humphrey, Elizabeth B.
Humphriss, Charles H.
Hunt, Wayne
Hunter, Russell V.
Hunter, Warren
Hurd, L. P.
Hurd, Peter
Hurley, Wilson
Hutchison, D. C.
Hutton, William R.

I

Imhof, Joseph A.
Inman, Henry
Innes, John
Inness, George Jr.
Inness, George Sr.
Ireland, Leroy
Irwin, Col DeLaCherois
Issacs, Andrew

J

Jackson, Alexander Y.
Jackson, Everett G.
Jackson, Harry A.
Jackson, William H.
Jacobs, Ned
Jacobson, Oscar B.
James, Rebecca S.
James, William R.
Jarvis, Miss M.
Jarvis, W. Frederick
Jefferys, Charles W.
Jepperson, Samuel H.
Jewett, William S.
John, Grace S.
Johnson, Frank T.
Johnson, Garrison
Johnson, Harvey
Johnson, Jonathan E.
Johnston, Francis H.
Johnston, Walt
Jonson, Raymond
Jorgenson, Christian
Joullin, Lucile
Judson, William L.
Jump, Edward

K

Kabolie, Fred
Kahler, Carl
Kane, Paul
Kauba, Carl
Kaufmann, Theodore
Keith, William
Keller, Arthur J.
Keller, Clyde L.
Kelley, Ramon
Kemble, Edward W.
Kemeys, Edward
Kenderdine, Augustus F.
Kensett, John F.
Kern, Benjamin J.

Kern, Edward M.
Kern, Richard H.
Kerswil, Roy
Key, John Ross
Kidd, Steven R.
Kihn, William L.
Kimmel, Lu
King, Charles Bird
Kingsley, Rose
Kirkham, Reuben
Kirkland, Forrest
Kissel, Elonora
Kittleson, John H.
Kleiber, Hans
Klepper, Frank E.
Klinker, Orpha
Kloss, Gene
Knapp, Martha S.
Knaths, Otto K.
Knee, Gina
Knox, Susan R.
Koerner, William H.
Koppel, Charles
Korb, Robert P.
Krans, Olaf
Krieghoff, Cornelius D.
Kroll, Leon
Kuchel, Charles C.
Kuhler, Otto
Kuhn, Robert F.
Kuhn, Walt
Kummer, Julius H.
Kuniyoshi, Yasuo
Kunstler, Morton
Kurz, Rudolph F.

L

Lackey, Vinson
Lambdin, Robert L.
Lambourne, Alfred
Lamson, J.
Lane, Remington W.
Laning, Edward
Lapham, J. M.
Laplace, Cyrille P. T.
Large, Virginia
Larson, Bent F.
LaRue, Walt
Lasalle, Charles
Latham, Barbara
Latimer, Lorenzo P.
Latoix, Gaspard
Lauderdale, Ursula
Lauritz, Paul
Lavender, Eugenie A.
Lawrence, Sydney M.
Lawson, Ernest
Lawson, Robert
Lea, Tom
Leaming, Charlotte
Learned, Harry
Lee, Charlie
Lee, Joseph
Lee, Robert M.
LeFrank, Margaret
Leftovich, Bill

Leggett, Lucille
Lehnert, F.
Leigh, William R.
Leighton, Alfred C.
Leighton, Kathryn W.
Leitch, Robert P.
LeMoyne, Jacques dM.
Lenders, Emil W.
Lent, Frank T.
Leutze, Emanuel G.
Lewis, Edmonia
Lewis, Henry
Lewis, James Otto
Lewis, Minard
Lewis, Thomas L.
Lillywhite, Raphael
Lindeberg, Carl
Lindneux, Robert O.
Lindsay, Andrew J.
Lindsay, T. C.
Lion, Henry
Lithgow, David C.
Lochrie, Elizabeth D.
Lockwood, John W.
Loeffler, Gisella
Loemans, Alexander F.
Loft, P.
Lone Wolf
Long, Stanley M.
Loomis, Chester
Loomis, Pascal
Lopp, Harry L.
Lorenz, Richard
Lotave, Carl G.
Lougheed, Robert E.
Lovell, Tom
Lowell, Orson B.
Ludekens, Fred
Lundborg, Florence
Lungkwitz, Carl H. F.
Lungren, Fernand H.
Lynch, Brandon

M

Mabry, Jane
MacDonald, James E. H.
MacDonald, James W.
MacDonald, L. W.
Mack, Leal
MacLeod, Pegi N.
MacMonnies, Fred W.
MacNeil, Hermon A.
Madan, Frederic C.
Magafan, Ethel
Mahier, Edith
Mails, Thomas E.
Major, William W.
Mandelman, Beatrice
Marchand, John N.
Marcou, Jules
Marcy, John
Marks, George B.
Marlatt, H. Irving
Marple, William L.
Marryat, Francis S.
Martin, Fletcher

Martin, John B.
Martin, Kirk
Martin, Thomas M.
Martinez, Julian
Martinez, Maria
Martinez, Pete
Martinez, Xavier
Masterson, James W.
Mathews, Alfred
Mathews, Arthur F.
Mathies, J. L. D
Matthews, Marmaduke
Matulka, Jan
Matzen, Herman N.
Maurer, Louis
Mauzey, Merritt
May, Philip W.
Mayer, Frank B.
Mays, Paul K.
McArdle, Henry A.
McCall, Robert T.
McCarthy, Frank C.
McClung, Trevor
McClymont, John I.
McComas, Francis J.
McCombs, Soloman
McCormick, Howard
McCouch, Gordon M
McEwen, Katherine
McGrew, Ralph B.
McIlroy, Carol
McIlvaine, William Jr.
McIlwraith, William F.
McLeary, M.
McMurry, Leonard
McMurtrie, William B.
Mead, Ben C.
Meakin, Louis H
Means, Elliott A
Mechau, Frank A. Jr.
Meeker, Joseph R.
Megargee, Alonzo
Megilp,
Meigs, John L.
Melrose, Andrew W.
Merrick, William M.
Merrild, Knud
Messenger, Ivan
Metcalf, Willard L.
Meuttman, W.
Mewhinney, Ella K.
Meyer, Richard M.
Meyerheim, Paul F.
Meyers, Robert W.
Meyers, William H.
Miller, Alfred J.
Miller, Ralph D.
Millet, Francis D.
Miner, Frederick R.
Mirabel, Vincente
Mitchell, Alfred
Mitchell, Alfred R.
Mitchell, Arthur
Mitchell, George B.
Mitchell, Thomas J.

Mizen, Frederick K.
Mollhausen, Heinrich B.
Momaday, Alfred M.
Monaghan, Eileen
Montoya, Alfredo
Montoya, Geronimo C.
Moody, Edwin
Moon, Carl
Moore, John W.
Moore, Tom J.
Mopope, Stephen
Mora, Francis Luis
Moran, Edward
Moran, Peter
Moran, Thomas
Morang, Alfred G.
Morang, Dorothy
Morgan, Robert F.
Morris, Edmund M.
Morris, Ernest
Morris, Florence A.
Morris, George L. K.
Moser, John H.
Mosler, Henry
Moyers, William
Moylan, Lloyd
Mozley, Loren N.
Mruk, Walter
Mueller, Michael
Mulford, Stockton
Mullen, F E.
Muller, Dan
Mulvany, John
Munger, Gilbert D.
Murdock, John
Murphy, Hermann D.
Mutzel, Gustave
Myers, Frank H.
Myers, William H.

N

Naha, Raymond
Nahl, Charles C.
Nahl, Hogo W. A.
Nailor, Gerald A.
Nappenbach, Henry
Narjot, Erneste E. dF.
Nash, Willard A.
Nason, Daniel W.
Nast, Thomas
Neagle, John
Neal, David D.
Nehlig, Victor
Nepote, Alexander
Neseman, Enno
Nestler, Al
Neuhaus, Eugen
Newberry, John S.
Newsam, Albert
Ney, Elisabet
Nichols, Henry H.
Nicols, Audley D.
Noble, John
Nonnast, Paul E.
Nordfeldt, Bror J. O.
Numkena, Lewis Jr.

O

Oberhardt, William
O'Brien, Lucius R.
Oertel, Johannes A. S.
Ogden, Henry A.
O'Hara, James F.
O'Keefe, Georgia
Olson, J. Olaf
Olson, Merle
Olstad, Einar H.
Onderdonk, Julian
Onderdonk, Robert J.
O'Neil, John
Oqwa Pi
Ormes, Mrs. Manley D.
Osgood, Samuel S.
Otis, Fessenden N.
Otnes, Fred
Otter, Thomas P.
Ottinger, George M.
Owen, Bill

P

Paap, Hans
Palenske, Reinhold H.
Paley, Robert L.
Palmer, Frances F.
Panabaker, Frank S.
Paradise, Philip H.
Paris, Walter
Parish, Charles L.
Parker, James K.
Parkinson, William J.
Parrish, Ann
Parrish, Charles L.
Parrish, Joan
Parrish, Maxfield
Parrish, Thomas
Parrott, William S.
Parshall, DeWitt
Parshall, Douglas E.
Parsons, Charles H.
Parsons, Ernestine
Parsons, Orrin S.
Paxton, Edgar S.
Payne, Edgar A.
Peabody, Ruth E.
Peale, Charles W.
Peale, Titan R.
Pearce, Helen S.
Pease, Lucius C.
Pease, Nell C. Mc.
Peck, Henry J.
Peck, Orin
Peirce, Gerry
Peirce, Joshua H.
Peixotto, Ernest C.
Pena, Tonita
Penelon, Henri
Penfield, Edward
Perceval, Don L.
Perillo, Gregory
Perkins, Granville
Perry, Enoch W.
Pescheret, Leon R.
Petet, Poko

Peters, Charles R.
Peters, Leslie H.
Peticolas, Edward F.
Petri, Frederick R.
Pettrick, Ferdinand F. A.
Philbrick, Stacey
Phillips, Bert G.
Phillips, Clair D.
Pierce, Martha
Piercy, Frederick
Pillsbury, Thomas G.
Pitman, Theodore B.
Pleissner, Ogden M.
Pogzeba, Wolfgang
Pohl, Hugo D.
Point, Father Nicolas S.J.
Polelonema, Otis
Politi, Leo
Polk, Frank
Pomarede, Leon
Poor, Henry V.
Poore, Henry R.
Pop Chalee
Poray, Stan P.
Potter, William J.
Potthast, Edward H.
Powell, Arthur J. E.
Powell, Asa L.
Powell, H. M. T.
Powell, Lucien W.
Powers, Hiram
Pranishnikoff, Ivan P.
Pratt, Henry C.
Prendergast, John
Preuss, Charles
Price, Clayton S.
Price, Julius M.
Price, Norman M.
Prior, Melton
Proctor, Burt
Proctor, A. Phimister
Prowse, Robert
Pruitt, A. Kelly
Putthuff, Hanson D.
Putman, Donald
Putnam, Arthur
Pyle, Howard

Q

Quigley, Edward B.
Quintana, Ben
Quintana, Joe A.
Quirt, Walter W.

R

Raborg, Benjamin
Rabut, Paul
Racine, Albert
Rae, John
Ralston, James K.
Ramsey, Lewis A.
Ranney, William T.
Raschen, Henry
Ravlin, Grace
Ray, Joseph J.
Ray, Robert D.
Read, Thomas B.

Reaney, Thomas A.
Reaugh, Charles F.
Redwood, Allen C.
Reed, Doel
Reed, Earl M.
Reed, Majorie
Reedy, Leonard H.
Regamey, Felix E.
Reid, Robert
Reiffel, Charles
Reinhart, Benjamin
Reiss, Fritz W.
Remington, Frederic S.
Remington, S. J.
Rettig, John
Reusswig, William
Revere, Joseph W.
Reynolds, James E
Rhees, N.
Rhind, John M.
Ribak, Louis L
Rice, William S
Richards, Frederick dB.
Richards, Lee G.
Richardt, Ferdinand J.
Richmond, Leonard
Richter, Albert B.
Riddles, Leonard
Riesenberg, Sidney H.
Riger, Robert
Riley, Kenneth P.
Riley, Mary G.
Rindisbacher, Peter
Rishell, Robert
Ritschel, William
Rix, Julian W.
Robbins, Charles D.
Roberts, Jack
Robinson, Alfred
Robinson, Boardman
Robinson, Charles D.
Rockwell, Norman
Rodewald, Fred C.
Roerich, Nicholas K.
Roetter, Paulis
Rogers, Charles A.
Rogers, Randolph
Rogers, William A.
Rohland, Paul
Rollins, Warren E.
Rolshoven, Julius
Rook, Edward F.
Roper, Edward
Rose, Guy
Rosenbaum, David H.
Rosenthal, Doris
Rossi, Paul A.
Rossiter, Thomas P.
Rouland, Orlando
Rowe, Clarence H.
Rungius, Carl C. M.
Rush, Olive
Russell, Charles M
Russin, Robert I
Ryan, Thomas

Ryder, Albert Pinkham

S

Sabo, Betty
Saintin, Jules E.
Saint-Memin, Charles B.
Salinas, Porfirio
Salisbury, Cornelius
Salisbury, Paul
Salisbury, Rosine H.
Sample, Paul S.
Samuel, William M. G.
Sanchez y Tapia, Lino
Sanderson, William
Sandham, J. Henry
Sandor, Mathias
Sandusky, William H.
Sandy, Percy T.
Sandzen, Sven B.
Santee, Ross
Sauerwein, Frank P.
Saul, Chief Terry
Savage, Annie D.
Savitt, Samuel
Sawyer, Edward W.
Sawyer, Philip A.
Schaare, Harry J.
Schaefer, Mathilde
Schaefer, Frederick
Schaldach, William J.
Schatzlein, Charles
Schell, Francis H.
Scheuerle, Joseph
Schimmell, William B.
Schimonsky, Stanislas
Schiwetz, Edward M.
Schleeter, Howard B.
Schmidt, Albert H.
Schmidt, Alwin E.
Scholder, Fritz
Schonborn, Anton
Schoolcraft, Harry R.
Schoonover, Frank E.
Schott, Arthur
Schreiber, Georges
Schrech, Horst
Schreyvogel, Charles
Schuchard, Carl
Schultz, Hart M.
Schumann, Paul R.
Schuyler, Remington
Schwiering, Conrad
Scott, Charles H.
Scott, Harold W.
Scott, James P.
Scott, Jessie
Scott, John
Scott, Julian
Scriver, Robert M.
Sears, Philip S.
Seavey, Julian R.
Sedgwick, Francis M.
Seffel, E. A Jr.
Sells, C. H.
Seltzer, Olaf C.
Seton, Ernest T.

Seward, Coy A.
Sewell, Amos
Seymour, Samuel
Shadbolt, Jack L.
Shapleigh, Frank H.
Sharer, William E.
Sharp, Joseph H.
Sharp, Louis H.
Shaw, Joshua
Shaw, Stephes W.
Shaw, Sydney D.
Shebl, Joseph J.
Sheets, Nan J.
Sheldon-Williams, Inglis
Shepherd, J. Clinton
Sheppard, William L.
Sherman, Lenora W.
Shirlaw, Walter
Shonnard, Eugenie F.
Shope, Irwin
Shrader, Edwin R.
Shrady, Henry M.
Shurtleff, Roswell M.
Shuster, William H.
Sibell, Murcel V.
Sickles, Noel D.
Simons, George
Simpson, Wallace
Simpson, William
Skeele, Anna K.
Skelton, Leslie J.
Skinner, Charlotte B.
Skirving, John
Sloane, Eric
Sloan, John
Smalley, Katherine
Smedley, William T.
Smellie, Robert
Smillie, James D.
Smith, Alfred A.
Smith, Cecil A.
Smith, Charles L.
Smith, Dan
Smith, DeCost
Smith, Elmer B.
Smith, Erwin E.
Smith, Francis D.
Smith, Gean
Smith, Jack Wilkinson
Smith, Jerome H.
Smith, John R.
Smith, Lillian W.
Smith, Paul K.
Smith, Sidney P.
Smith, William A.
Smith, Xanthus R.
Smoky, Lois
Smythe, Eugene L.
Snyder, W. L.
Sohon, Gustavius
Soldwedel, Frederic
Sommer, Otto
Sonnichsen, Yngvar
Spalding, Elizabeth
Spampinato, Clemente

Sparks, Arthur W.
Sparks, Wil
Sparks, William F.
Speed, U. Grant
Spens, Nathanaie
Sprague, Isaac
Spruce, Everett F.
Sprunger, Elmer
Squires, C. Clyde
Squires, Henry
Squires, Lawrence
Stahley, Joseph
Stahr, Paul
Stanley, Charles StG.
Stanley, John Mix
Stansfield, John H.
Stanson, George C.
Starkley, Jo-Anita
Stearns, Junius B.
Steele, Sandra
Stefan, Ross
Steffen, Randy
Steider, Doris
Steinegger, Henry
Steinke, Bettina
Stella, Joseph
Stephens, Charles H.
Stephens, Henry L.
Sterne, Maurice
Stevens, John
Stevens, Kelly H.
Stevens, Lawrence T.
Stevenson, Branson G.
Stevenson, Edna B.
Stewart, LeConte
Stieffel, Hermann
Stiha, Vladin
Stitt, Hobart D.
Stobie, Charles S.
Stockwell, Samuel B.
Stojana, Gjura
Stone, Willard
Stoops, Herbert M.
Storelli, Felix M. F.
Strahalm, Franz S.
Strang, Ray C.
Strathearn, Robert P.
Strayer, Paul
Street, Frank
Strobel, Max
Strobel, Oscar A.
Strong, Joseph
Stuart, Frederick D.
Stuart, Gilbert C.
Stuart, James E.
Styka, Adam
Sully, Alfred
Suydam, Edward H.
Swanson, Jack N.
Sweeney, Dan
Swing, David C.
Swinnerton, James G.
Symons, George G.

T

Taber, W.

Tafaga, Joseph
Taft, Lorado Z.
Tahome, Quincy
Tait, Agnes
Tait, Arthur F.
Tallant, Richard H.
Talmage, Algernon M.
Tappan, William H.
Tavernier, Jules
Taylor, Baynard
Taylor, James E.
Taylor, Rolla S.
Taylor, William L.
Teasdel, Mary
Teel, Lewis W.
Teichert, Minerva K.
Terry, W. Eliphalet
Thayer, Emma H.
Thomas, Bernard P.
Thomas, Marjorie H.
Thomas, S. Seymour
Thomason, John W.
Thompson, Jerome B
Thomson, Tom
Thornton, Mildred V.
Thorpe, Everett C.
Thurston, Jack L.
Thwaits
Tibbles, Yosette
Tidball, John C.
Timeche, Bruce
Tindall, N.
Toddy, Jimmy
Toft, Peter P.
Toledo, Jose R.
Tommey, Bob
Tonk, Ernest
Torneman, Axel
Toschik, Larry
Tousey, T. Sanford
Travis, Olin H.
Triggs, James M.
Trotter, Newbold H.
True, Allen T.
Tsatoke, M.
Tschudi, Rudolf
Tsinajenie, Andrew V.
Tucker, Allen
Tuckerman, Lilia M.
Tullidge, John
Turner, Charles Y.
Turner, Elmer
Twachtman, John H.
Tyler, Gerald H.

U

Ufer, Walter
Ulreich, Eduard B.

V

Valencia, Manuel
Vanderhoof, Charles A.
Vanderlyn, John
Vanderveer, Miss M. H.
Van Ryder, Jack
Van Soelen, Theodore
Van Wart, Ames

Varian, George E.
Varley, Frederick H.
Vavia, Frank J.
Vebell, Edward T.
Velarde, Pubita
Ventres, M. P.
Verelst, John
Verner, Frederick A.
Vierra, Carlos
Villa, Hernando G.
Villiers, Frederick
Vioget, Jean J.
Vischer, Edward
Vivian, Calthea C.
Volk, Stephen A. D.
Von Beckh, H. V. A.
Von Berg, Charles L.
Von Egloffstein, F. W.
Von Iwonski, Charles G.
Von Langdorff, Georg H.
Von Perbandt, Carl A. R.

W

Waano-Gano, Joseph T. N.
Wachtel, Elmer
Wachtel, Marion K.
Wagoner, Harry B.
Wagoner, Robert
Walker, Gilbert M.
Walker, James
Wall, Bernhardt T.
Wallace, Lewis
Walls, Stanley K.
Walters, Emil
Walton, Henry
Wandesforde, James
Wanker, Maude W.
Wapah, Nayah
Ward, Charles C.
Ward, Edmund F.
Ward, John Q. A.
Ward, Florence E.
Warner, Olin L.
Warre, Henry J.
Warren, Constance W.
Warren, Melvin C.
Watchetaker, George S.
Watson, Dawson
Waud, Alfred R.
Waud, William
Waugh, Alfred S.
Waugh, Sidney
Weavey, W. H.
Webb, Vonna O.
Webber, Charles T.
Webber, John
Weeks, Edwin L.
Weggeland, Danquart A.
Wein, Adolph A.
Weir, Robert W.
Welch, Thaddeus
Welliver, Les
Wells, Cady
Wells, William L.
Wenck, Paul
Wendt, William L.

West, Benjamin	Wyeth, Newell C.	
West, Helen	Wyle, Florence	
West, Levon	Wyttenbach, E.	
West, Lowren	**Y**	
West, Walter R.	Yazzie, James W.	
Weston, William P.	Yeager, Walter R.	
Weygold, Frederick P.	Yelland, Raymond D.	
Wheeler, Hughlette Tex	Yena, Donald	
Whitaker, Eileen	Yohn, Frederick C.	
Whitaker, Frederic	Young, Harvey O.	
White, Fritz	Young, John J.	
White, George G.	Young, Mahonri M.	
White, George H.	Young, Phineas H.	
White, John	Young-Hunter, John	
White, Orrin A.	Yves	
White, Thomas G.	**Z**	
White Bear	Zang, John J.	
White Bear	Ziegler, Eustace P.	
Whitefield, Edwin	Ziegler, Samuel P.	
Whiteside, Frank R.	Zimbeaux, Frank I. S.	
Whittredge, Thomas W.	Zogbaum, Rufus F.	
Wiboltt, Aage C.	Zorach, Margarente T.	
Widforss, Gunnar M.	Zorach, William	
Wieghorst, Olaf		
Wiggins, Myra A.		
Wilcox, Frank N.		
Wild, John C.		
Wiles, Lemuel M.		
Wilgus, William J.		
Wilkins, James F.		
Williams, Frederick B.		
Williams, James R.		
Williams, Virgil		
Williamson, John		
Wilson, Charles B.		
Wilson, Jeremiah,		
Wilson, Thomas H.		
Wilwerding, Walter J.		
Wimar, Charles		
Winan, Walter		
Wingate, Curtis		
Winter, George		
Withrow, Eva A.		
Wittmack, Edgar F.		
Wolf, Joseph		
Wolf, Pegot		
Wolfe, Byron B.		
Woole, Muriel S.		
Wood, Robert		
Wood, Robert E.		
Wood, Stanley		
Wood, Stanley L.		
Woodside, John A.		
Woodville, Richard C.		
Woodward, John D.		
Wores, Theodore		
Worlds, Clint		
Worrall, Henry		
Wright, Alma B.		
Wright, Henry C. S.		
Wright, Rufus		
Wright, Thomas J.		
Wueste, Louise H.		
Wyeth, Andrew N.		
Wyeth, Henriette Z.		

WESTERN - DAWDY

The initial volume on Western art by Dawdy
was recently supplemented by a second volume (referred as Dawdy 1 and Dawdy 2 herein). The supplement covers many additional
artists, and provides more complete data
on some of the Dawdy 1 artists. Generally,
the biographical sketches are not as complete as in Samuels, but, with the addition
of Dawdy 2, many artists not covered by
Samuels are picked up.

Abdy, Rowena M.
Abert, James W.
Achey, Mary E
Achleitner, Otto
Adair, Ruby
Adam, William
Adams, Cassilly
Adams, Charles P
Adams, Corrine D.
Adams, Kenneth M.
Adams, Wayman
Adams, Willis A.
Agate, Alfred T.
Ahrens, Carl H.
Akin, Louis B.
Albright, Gertrude P.
Albright, Hermann O.
Alden, James
Alden, James M.
Alexander, Henry
Allen, John D.
Allen, Marion B
Allen, Thomas
Altmann, Aaron
Alvarez, Mabel
Ames, Albert
Amick, Robert W
Anderson, Carl
Anderson, Clarence W
Anderson, George
Anderson, Gunda J. E
Applegate, Frank G
Armann, Kristinn P
Armstrong, Thomas
Armstrong, William W.
Arpa, Jose
Arriola, Fortunato
Askenazy, Mischa
Atkins, Arthur
Attridge, Irma G.
Atwood, Robert
Audubon, John J.
Audubon, John W.
Austin, Amanda P.
Austin, Charles P
Ayres, Thomas A

B

Babcock, Dean
Babcock, Ida D.
Bacon, Irving R.
Bagdapoulis, William S.
Bagg, Henry H.
Bagley, James M.
Bailey, Minnie M
Bailey, Vernon H.
Baker, George H.
Bakos, James G.
Baldridge, Cyrus L.
Baldwin, Clifford P.
Balink, Henry C.
Ballin, Hugo
Ballou, Addie L.
Ballou, Bertha
Bancroft, Albert S
Bancroft, William H.

Banta, Mattie E.
Banvard, John
Barber, Edmund L.
Barbieri, Leonardo
Barile, Xavier J.
Barker, George
Barker, Olive R.
Barnes, Mathew R.
Barr, Paul E.
Barr, William
Barrett, Lawrence
Barrington, George
Bartholemew, W. N.
Bartlett, Dana
Bartlett, Gray
Bartlett, John R.
Barton, Loren R.
Bassett, Reveau
Bauer, Frederick
Baumann, Gustave
Baumgras, Peter
Baxter, Martha W.
Beard, Daniel
Beard, George
Beard, James C.
Beard, James H.
Beard, William H
Beaumont, Arthur E.
Beauregard, Donald
Becker, Frederick
Becker, Otto
Beckwith, Arthur
Beecher, Genevieve T.
Beechey, Richard B.
Beek, Alice D. E.
Belden, George
Bellows, George W.
Benda, Wladyslaw
Berninghaus, Oscar E
Bennett, Bertha
Bennett, Gertrude
Bennett, Joseph H.
Benton, Mary P. S.
Benton, Thomas H.
Berg, George L.
Bergmann, Frank W.
Berlander, Jean L
Berlandina, Jane
Best, Arthur W.
Best, Harry C.
Bettinger, Hoyland B.
Betts, E. C.
Beznics, George
Biddle, George
Bierstadt, Albert
Bigot, Toussaint F.
Bingham, George C.
Birch, Geraldine R.
Birch, Reginald B.
Birren, Joseph P.
Bischoff, Eugene H
Bischoff, Franz Albert
Bistram, Emil
Black, LaVerne N.
Blake, William P.

Blakelock, Ralph A.
Blanch, Arnold
Blanch, Lucille
Block, Albert
Bloomer, Hiram R.
Blumenschein, Ernest L.
Blumenschein, Mary S G.
Bodmer, Karl
Bogert, George H.
Bolton, Hale W.
Bonner, Mary
Borein, Edward
Borg, Carl Oscar
Borglum, Elizabeth
Borglum, Gutzon
Borglum, Solon H.
Boronda, Lester D
Borthwick, John D.
Bosque, Edward
Boss, Homer
Botke, Cornelius
Botke, Jessie A.
Boundey, Burton S.
Boynton, Ray
Bradford, William
Bradley, H. W.
Brandon, John A.
Brandriff, George K.
Brannan, Sophie M.
Braun, Maurice
Bremer, Anne
Breneiser, Elizabeth D.
Breneiser, Stanley G.
Brenner, Carl C.
Brett, Dorothy E.
Breuer, Henry J.
Brewer, Nicholas R.
Brewerton, George D.
Britton, Joseph
Brockman, Ann
Brodt, Helen T.
Bromley, Thomas L.
Bromley, Valentine W.
Bromwell, Henrietta
Brooks, Samuel M.
Browere, Alburtis D. O.
Brown, Benjamin C.
Brown, Dorothy W.
Brown, Grafton T
Brown, Henry B.
Brown, Howell C.
Browne, Belmore
Browne, J. Ross
Browning, J. Wesley
Bruff, Joseph G.
Brush, George dF.
Bruton, Esther
Bruton, Helen
Bruton, Margaret
Bryant, Harold E.
Buchser, Frank
Buff, Conrad
Buisson, Daniel S.
Bull, Charles L.
Bullock, Mary J. M.

Bunnell, Charles R.
Burbank, Elbridge A.
Burgdorff, Ferdinand
Burgess, George H.
Burgess, Henrietta
Burlin, H. Paul
Burr, George E.
Burrell, Alfred R.
Bush, Ella S.
Bush, Norton
Bush, Richard J.
Butler, George B.
Butman, Frederick A.
Byxbe, Lyman

C

Cadenasso, Guiseppe
Cahill, Arthur J.
Cahill, William V.
Caldwell, George W.
Calyo, Nicolino
Camerer, Eugene
Cameron, Anna F.
Camfferman, Peter M.
Campbell, Albert H.
Campbell, Blendon R.
Campbell, Orson D.
Capps, Charles M.
Carlsen, Emil
Carlson, John F.
Carpenter, Ellen M.
Carter, Charles M.
Carter, Pruett A.
Carvalho, Solomon N.
Casilear, John W.
Casy, William M.
Cassidy, Gerald
Casterton, Eda N.
Catherwood, Frederick
Catlin, George
Caylor, H. Wallace
Chadwick
Chain, Helen
Chalmers, Helen A.
Chamberlain, Norman S.
Chamberlin, Frank T.
Chapman, Kenneth M.
Charlot, Jean
Cheney, Russell K.
Chin, Chee
Chittenden, Alice B.
Choris, Ludovic
Christensen, C. C. A.
Clark, Allan
Clark, Alson S.
Clark, Benton
Clark, Emelia M. G.
Claveau, Antoine
Clawson, John W.
Clements, Edith S.
Cloudman, J. D.
Clunie, Robert
Coast, Oscar R.
Cockcroft, Edythe
Coe, Ethel L.
Cogswell, William F.

Colbert, F. Overton
Colburn, Eleanor
Colby, James
Cole, George T.
Coleman, Edmund T.
Colman, R. Clarkson
Colman, Samuel
Colton, Mary R.
Colton, Walter
Colyer, Vincent
Comparet, Alexis
Coolidge, John E.
Cooper, Astley D. M.
Cooper, Colin C.
Cooper, Frederick G.
Cooper, George V.
Cooper, James G.
Cordero, Jose
Cornell, John V.
Cornwell, Dean
Corwin, Charles A.
Cory, Kate T.
Cotton, John W
Coulter, Mary J.
Coulter, William A.
Couse, Irving
Couthouy, J. P.
Coutts, Alice
Coutts, Gordon
Cowles, Russell
Cox, Charles B.
Cox, Kenyon
Cox, Louise H. K.
Cox, Palmer
Cox, W. H. M.
Coxe, R. Cleveland
Craig, Charles
Craig, Thomas B.
Cram, Alan G.
Crawford, Will
Critcher, Catherine C.
Crocker, Charles M.
Cross, Henry H.
Culmer, Henry L. A.
Cummings, Charles A.
Cuneo, Rinaldo
Cuprien, Frank W.
Currier, Cyrus B.
Currier, Edward W.
Currier, Walter B.
Curry, John S.
Curtis, Leland
Cutting, Francis H.

D

Dahlgren, Carl
Dahlgren, Marius
Dakin, Sidney T.
Dale, John B.
Dann, Frode N.
Danner, Sara K.
Dasburg, Andrew M.
Davenport, Homer C.
Davey, Randall
David, Lorene
Davies, Arthur B.

Davis, Cecil C.
Davis, Cornelia C.
Davis, Jessie F. S.
Davis, Leonard M.
Davis, Theodore R.
Dawes, Edwin M.
Dawson-Watson, Dawson
Deakin, Edwin
Deas, Charles
DeCamp, Ralph
DeCora, Angel
DeForest, Lockwood
DeGavere, Cornelia
Degen, Ida D.
DeHaven, Franklin B.
Dehn, Adolf
DeJong, Betty
DeKruif, Henry G.
DeLamater, Edgar
Delano, Gerard C.
Dellenbaugh, Frederick S.
DelMue, Maurice A.
DeLongpre, Paul
DelPino, Jose M.
Deming, Edwin W.
Dennison, George A.
Denny, Gideon J.
Deppe, Ferdinand
DeSuria, Tomas
DeVol, Pauline H.
Dewey, Alfred J.
DeWolf, Wallace L.
DeYong, Joe
DeYoung, Harry A.
Diaz, Cristobal
Dickey, S.
Dickman, Charles J.
Dillingham, John E.
Dinning, Robert J.
Dixon, Maynard
Dobson, Margaret A.
Dolan, Elizabeth H.
Donnelly, T. J.
Doolittle, Harold L.
Doolittle, Marjorie H.
Dorgan, Thomas A.
Dougal, William H.
Dougherty, Paul
Dow, Arthur W.
Drayton, Joseph
Dressel, Emil
Dripps, Clara R.
DuBois, Patterson
Ducasse, Mabel L.
Duhaut-Cilly, Bernard A.
DuMond, Helen S.
Dunbier, Augustus W.
Duncan, Charles S.
Duncan, Johnson K.
Dunlap, Helena
Dunlap, James B.
Dunlap, Harvey T.
Dunn, Marjorie C.
Dunnell, John H.
Dunphy, Nicholas

Dunton, W. Herbert
Duval, Ella M.
Duvall, Fannie E.
Dye, Clarkson
Dye, Olive B.
Dyer, Agnes S.

E

Eakins, Thomas
East, Pattie R.
Eastman, Harrison
Eastman, Seth
Eastmond, E. H.
Eaton, Charles F.
Eaton, Charles H.
Eaton, W. R.
Edmonston, William D.
Edouart, Alexander
Eggenhofer, Nick
Egloffstein, F. W.
Eilshemius, Louis M.
Eisenlohr, Edward G.
Elkins, Henry A.
Elliott, Florence
Elliott, Henry W.
Elliott, Ruth C.
Ellis, Fremont F.
Ellsworth, Clarence A.
Elwell, R. Farrington
Emeree, Berla I.
Englehart, Joseph E.
English, Harold M.
Ertz, Edward F.
Euwer, Anthony H.
Evans, Edwin
Evans, Jessie B.
Everett, Joseph A. F.
Everett, Mary
Everett, Raymond
Eytel, Carl

F

Fairbanks, J. Leo
Fairbanks, John B.
Fairchild, Hurlstone
Farnsworth, Alfred V.
Farny, Henry F.
Fauseth, Lynn
Fechin, Nicolai
Fenderich, Charles
Fenn, Harry
Ferran, Augusto
Fery, John
Fiene, Ernest
Fisher, Harrison
Fisher, Hugh A.
Fiske, Frank B.
Fleck, Joseph A.
Fletcher, Calvin
Fletcher, Frank M.
Fletcher, Godfrey
Fonda, Harry S.
Foote, Mary H.
Forbes, Helen K.
Ford, Helen L.
Ford, Henry C.
Forsythe, Clyde

Fortune, E. Charlton
Foster, Ben
Foster, Will
Francisco, J. Bond
Franklin, Dwight
Fraser, Douglass
Fraser, John A.
Frazer, Mabel P.
Federiksen, Mary
Freeman, W. R.
Fremont, John
Frenzeny, Paul
Fries, Charles A.
Fripp, Charles E.
Froelich, Maren M.
Fromont-Delormel, Jacques
Frost, Arthur B.
Frost, George A.
Frost, John
Fulton, Fitch

G

Gale, Edmund W.
Gamble, John M.
Gaspard, Leon
Gaul, William G.
Gaw, William A.
Gearhart, May
Gellert, Emery
Gentilz, Theodore
Geritz, Franz
Gerste, William L.
Gibberd, Eric W.
Gibbs, George
Gifford, Charles B.
Gifford, Robert S.
Gifford, Sanford R.
Gilbert, Arthur H.
Gilder, Robert F.
Gile, Selden C.
Gilliam, Marguerite H.
Gilstrap, W. H.
Glass, Bertha
Gleason, Duncan
Gloe, Olive
Goddard, George H.
Golden, Charles O.
Gollings, Elling W.
Goodwin, Richard L. B.
Gookins, James F.
Gordon-Cumming, Constance
Gotzsche, Kai G.
Gourley, Bess E.
Grafstrom, Olaf
Graham, Charles
Graham, Robert A.
Graham, William
Grandmaison, Nickoli de
Grant, Blanche C.
Grant, Charles H.
Graves, Martha P.
Gray, Percy
Greatorex, Eliza P.
Green, Rena
Greenbaum, Joseph
Green, LeRoy E.

Gregg, Paul
Gremke, Henry D.
Grenet, Edward L.
Griffin, James M.
Griffith, William A.
Grigware, Edward T.
Griset, Ernest H.
Grob, Trautman
Groll, Albert L.
Grumsky, Carl E.
Guenther, Pearl H.
Guislane, J. M.
Gullickson, Gustave I.
Gustin, Paul

H

Haag, Herman H.
Hadra, Ida W.
Hafen, John
Hafen, Virgil O.
Hager, Luther G.
Hagerman, Percy
Hagerup, Nels
Hahn, Carl W.
Haig, Mabel G.
Hall, Arthur W.
Hall, Cyrenius
Hall, Norma B.
Hall, Sydney P.
Hamilton, Hamilton
Hamilton, James
Hamilton, Minerva B.
Hammock, Earl G.
Hamp, Margaret
Handforth, Thomas S.
Hanscom, Trude
Hansen, Armin C.
Hansen, Ejnar
Hanson, Herman W.
Harding, Goldie P.
Harley, Steven W.
Harmer, Alexander F.
Harmon, Charles H.
Harpold, Gertrude M.
Harrington, Joseph A.
Harris, Grace G.
Harrison, Lowell B.
Harrison, Thomas A.
Hart, Alfred A.
Hart, Cornelia
Hartley, Masden
Hartman, C. Bertram
Hartnett, Eva V.
Harvey, Eli
Harwood, Burt
Harwood, James T.
Haskell, Ernest
Haswell, Robert
Hauser, John
Hauswirth, Frieda
Hayden, Sara S.
Hayes, William J.
Heade, Martin J.
Heaney, Charles E.
Heap, Gwinn H.
Heath, Frank L.

McClung, Florence W.
McClusky, Grace D.
McClymont, John I.
McComas, Francis J.
McCord, George Herbert
McCormick, Howard
McCormick, M. Evelyn
MacDonald-Wright, Stanton
McEwen, Katherine
McGlynn, Thomas A.
McIllwraith, William F.
McIlvaine, William Jr.
Mack, Leal
MacLaren, T.
MacLennan, Eunice C.
MacLeod, Alexander
McMicken, Helen P.
McMurtrie, William B.
McNeely, Perry
MacNeil, Hermon A.
Mahier, Edith
Major, William W.
Mangravite, Pepino
Mannheim, Jean
Marchand, John N.
Marlatt, H. Irving
Marple, William L.
Marriott, Fred M.
Marryat, Samuel F.
Martin, John A. L.
Martin, John B.
Martin, Thomas M.
Martinez, Pete
Martinez, Xavier
Mason, Elizabeth
Mason, Roy M.
Masterson, James W.
Mathews, Alfred E.
Mathews, Arthur F.
Mathews, Felix A.
Mathews, Lucia K.
Mattern, Karl
Mauer, Louis
Mauzey, Merritt
Maxwell, Laura
Mays, Paul K.
Meakin, Louis H.
Megargee, Lon
Melcher, Bertha C.
Melrose, Andrew
Merrild, Knud
Merrill, Arthur
Mersfelder, Jules
Metcalf, Willard L.
Mewhinney, Ella K.
Meyer, Richard M.
Meyers, Ralph
Meyers, William H.
Mezzerer, Peter
Miller, Alfred J.
Miller, Evylena N.
Miller, Marie C.
Miller, Mildred B.
Miller, Ralph D.
Millier, Arthur

Mills, John H.
Mitchell, Alfred R.
Mitchell, Laura M. D.
Mitchell, Minnie B. H.
Mizen, Frederic K.
Mollhausen, Heinrich B.
Moerenhout, Jacques A.
Moody, Edwin
Moon, Carl
Moore, Edwin S.
Moore, Frank M.
Moore, Tom J.
Mora, Francis Luis
Mora, Joseph J.
Moran, Edward
Moran, Peter
Moran, Thomas
Morey, Anna R.
Morgan, Mary D.
Morris, Florence A.
Morris, William C.
Morris, William H.
Morris, William V.
Moser, John H.
Mosler, Henry
Moss, Charles E.
Mount, William S.
Moylan, Lloyd
Mudge, Zachariah
Mulford, Laura L.
Muller, Dan
Mulvany, John
Mundy, Louise E.
Munger, Gilbert
Murie, Olaus J.
Murray, Frederick S.
Musgrave, Arthur F.
Myers, Frank H.

N

Nahl, Charles C.
Nahl, H. W. Arthur
Nahl, Perham W.
Nahl, Virgil T.
Nappenbach, Henry
Narjot, Erneste
Nash, Willard A.
Nason, Daniel W.
Neal, David D.
Nedwill, Rose
Nelson, Bruce
Nesemann, Enno
Neuhaus, Eugen
Newberry, John S.
Newcombe, Warren
Newell, George G.
Newsom, Archie T.
Nicholl, Thomas J.
Nicols, Harley DW.
Nimmo, Louise E.
Noble, John
Noble, Mamie J.
Nordfeldt, Bror J. O.
Norton, Elizabeth
Norton, Helen G.
Norton, John W.

O

Oakes, M.
Obata, Chiura
Officer, Thomas S.
Ogden, Henry A.
Ogilby, Robert E.
O'Keefe, Georgia
Oldfield, Otis
Olds, Elizabeth
Olson, Albert Byron
Olstad, Einar H.
Onderdonk, Julian
Onderdonk, Robert J.
O'Neill, James K.
Osgood, Samuel S.
Osthaus, Edmund H.
Ostner, Charles L.
Otis, Fessenden N.
Otis, George D.
Ottinger, George M.
Owens, Charles H.

P

Pages, J. F.
Pages, Jules
Palenske, Reinhold H.
Palmer, Jessie A.
Pape, Hans
Paris, Francois E.
Paris, Walter
Park, Hazel A. H.
Parrish, Anne L.
Parrish, Charles L.
Parrish, Maxfield
Parrish, Thomas
Parrott, William S.
Parshall, DeWitt
Parshall, Douglass E.
Parsons, Charles
Parsons, Ernestine
Parsons, Orin S.
Partington, J. H. E.
Partridge, Roi
Patterson, Viola
Paxson, Edgar S.
Payne, Edgar A.
Payne, Elsie P.
Peale, Titian R.
Pearce, Helen S.
Pearson, Edwin
Pearson, Ralph M.
Pease, Lucius C.
Pebbles, Francis M.
Peck, Orrin
Peirce, Joshua H.
Peixotto, Ernest C.
Pelton, Agnes
Penelon, Henri
Penniman, Leonora N.
Pennoyer, A. Sheldon
Pentenrieder, Erhard
Percy, Isabelle C.
Perry, Enoch W.
Peters, Charles R.
Peters, Constance E.
Petri, Richard

Phelps, Edith C.
Phillips, Bert C.
Phillips, Clair D.
Piazzoni, Gottardo
Pickett, James T.
Pierce, Martha
Pierce, Minerva
Piercy, Frederick
Platt, George W.
Podchernikoff, A.
Point, Nicolas
Pommer, Mildred N.
Poole, H. Nelson
Poor, Henry V.
Poore, Henry R.
Pope, John
Pope, Marion H.
Porter, Bruce
Potter, William J.
Potthast, Edward H.
Powell, H. M. T.
Powell, Lucien W.
Powell, Pauline
Pratt, Henry C.
Pratt, Lorus
Prendergast, John
Preuss, Charles
Price, Clayton S.
Price, Eugenia
Price, Mimmie
Prior, Melton
Proctor, Alexander P.
Puthuff, Hanson D.

Q

Quigley, E. B.
Quinton, Cornelius B. S.

R

Raborg, Benjamin
Ralston, J. K.
Ramsey, Lewis A.
Randolph, Lee F.
Rankin, Mary K.
Rankin, Myra W.
Ranney, William
Ransonnette, Charles
Raphael, Joseph
Raschen, Henry
Rathbone, Augusta P.
Ratliff, Blanche C.
Ravalli, Antonio
Rea, Lewis E.
Read, Henry
Reade, Roma
Reaser, Wilber A.
Reaugh, Frank
Redmond, Granville
Redwood, Allen C.
Reed, Doel
Reedy, Leonard
Regamey, Felix E.
Reid, Albert T.
Reid, Robert
Reiffel, Charles
Reimer, Cornelia
Reiss, F. Winold

Remington, Frederic
Revere, Joseph W.
Rey, Jacques J.
Reynard, Grant T.
Reynolds, Harry R.
Rhodes, Helen N.
Rich, John Hubbard
Richards, Lee G.
Richardson, Mary C.
Richardt, Joachim F.
Richter, Albert B.
Richter, Henry L.
Rieber, Winifred
Riesenberg, Sidney H.
Rising, Dorothy M.
Ritschel, William
Ritter, Anne G.
Rix, Julian W.
Robbins, Frederick G.
Robinson, Adah M.
Robinson, Alfred
Robinson, Boardman
Robinson, Charles D.
Rockwell, Cleveland
Rodriguez, Alfred C.
Roethe, L. H.
Rogers, C. A.
Rogers, Charles H.
Rogers, Margaret E.
Rogers, William A.
Rollins, Helen J.
Rollins, Warren E.
Rolshoven, Julius C.
Rorphuro, Julius J.
Rose, Guy
Rosenthal, Doris
Rosenthal, Toby E.
Ross, Thomas
Rothery, Albert
Rudolph, Alfred
Rungius, Carl
Rush, Olive
Ressell, Charles M.
Rutland, Emily
Ruxton, George A. F.
Ryder, Chauncey F.
Ryder, Worth

S

Saint-Clair, Norman
Sample, Paul S.
Sandham, J. Henry
Sandona, Matteo
Sandor, Mathias
Sandusky, William
Sandzen, Sven B.
Santee, Ross
Sargeant, Geneve R.
Sauerwen, Frank P.
Sawyer, Myra L.
Sawyer, Philip A.
Sayre, F. Grayson
Schafer, Frederick F.
Scherbakoff, Sergey J.
Scheuerle, Joe
Schimonsky, Stanislaus W.

Schiwetz, Edward M.
Schonbrun, Anton
Schott, Arthur
Schreck, Horst
Schreyvogel, Charles
Schuchard, Carl
Schultz, Hart M.
Schwartz, Davis F.
Scott, Clyde E.
Scott, Julian
Seltzer, Olaf C.
Seton, Ernest C.
Seward, Coy A.
Seyffert, Leopold
Seymour, Samuel
Shapleigh, Frank H.
Sharp, Joseph H.
Shaw, Harriet M. J.
Shaw, Stephen W.
Shaw, Sydney D.
Shed, Charles D.
Sheets, Nan
Shepard, William E.
Sherman, John
Shettle, William M.
Shindler, A. Zeno
Shirlaw, Walter
Shonnard, Eugenie F.
Shrader, Edwin R.
Shuster, Will
Siegriest, Louis
Silva, William P.
Simons, George
Simpson, William
Skeele, Anna K.
Skelton, Leslie
Skinner, Charlotte B.
Skinner, Mary D.
Sloan, John
Smalley, Katherine
Smart, Emma
Smedley, William T.
Smet, Pierre-Jean
Smillie, George H.
Smillie, James D.
Smith, Dan
Smith, David H.
Smith, DeCost
Smith, Dorman H.
Smith, F. Carl
Smith, Francis D.
Smith, Francis H.
Smith, Gean
Smith, Helen S.
Smith, Isabel E.
Smith, J. H.
Smith, Jack W.
Smith, Ralph W.
Smith, Russell
Smythe, William
Sohon, Gustavus
Sonnichsen, Yngvar
Soutter, Louis J.
Spalding, Eliza H.
Sparks, Arthur W.

Sparks, Will
Spencer, Robert
Spens, Nathaniel
Spivak, H. David
Sprague, Issac
Sprague, Julia F.
Springer, Eva
Squires, Harry
Squires, Lawrence
Squires, Warren
Stackpole, Ralph
Stanley, Charles S. G.
Stanley, John M.
Stansfield, John H.
Staples, Clayton H.
Stark, Jack G.
Stegall, Irma M.
Stein, Aaron
Steinegger, Henry
Sterling, Dave
Sterne, Maurice
Stevenson, Edna B.
Stewart, LeConte
Stieffel, Hermann
Stobie, Charles S.
Stockfleth, Julius
Stonier, Lucille H.
Stoll, John T. E.
Stoops, Herbert M.
Storm, Alfrida A.
Story, Julian
Strang, Ray
Strater, Henry
Straus, Meyer
Strobel, Oscar
Strong, Elizabeth
Strong, Joseph D. Jr.
Struck, Herman
Stuart, Frederick D.
Stuart, James E.
Sturges, Lee
Sully, Alfred
Suydam, Edward H.
Swain, Francis W.
Swan, James G.
Swan, Walter B.
Swasey, William F.
Sweeney, Dan
Swing, David C.
Swinnerton, James G.
Sykes, John
Symons, George G.

T

Tabor, Robert B.
Tallant, Richard D.
Tappan, William H.
Tavernier, Jules
Taylor, Bayard
Taylor, Frederick T.
Taylor, James E.
Teague, Donald
Teasdale, Mary
Teichmueller, Minette T.
Thayer, Emma H.
Thomas, S. Seymour

Thomason, John W. Jr.
Thompson, John E.
Tibbles, Yosette L. F.
Tidball, John C.
Tindall, N.
Todhunter, Francis
Tofft, Peter
Tojetti, Domenico
Tojetti, Edwardo
Tompkins, Florence W.
Tonk, Ernest
Torrey, Elliot B.
Tracey, John M.
Travis, Olin H.
Trobriand, Phillippe R.
Trotter, Newbold H.
Truax, Sarah E.
True, Allen T.
Truesdell, Edith P.
Truitt, Uni B.
Tucker, Alan
Tuckerman, Lilia
Tullidge, John
Turner, Elmer

U

Ufer, Walter
Utley, Tabor

V

Valencia, Manuel
VanBriggle, Artus
VanCleve, Helen
VanRyder, Jack
VanSloun, Frank
VanSoelen, Theodore
VanVeen, Pieter
VanVleck, Durbin
Varian, Lester E.
Vaudicourt, Augustus
Varva, Frank J.
Vierra, Carlos
Villa, Hernando G.
Villers, Frederick
Viojet, Jean Jacques
Visher, Edward
Vitousek, Juanita J.
Vollmer, Grace L.
VonPerbandt, Carl
VonSchmidt, Harold

W

Wachtel, Elmer
Wachtel, Marion
Wadsworth, W.
Wagner, Robert L.
Waldo, Eugene L.
Walker, James
Walker, William A.
Wallace, Lewis
Walters, Emily
Walton, Henry
Wandesforde, Ivan B.
Wanker, Maude W.
Ware, Florence E.
Warner, Nell W.
Warre, Henry J.
Warshawsky, Abel G.

Watrous, Harry W.
Waud, Alfred R.
Weaver, Buck
Webb, Vonna
Webber, John E.
Weggeland, Daniel
Weisser, Leonie O.
Welch, Ludmilla
Welch, Thaddeus
Wells, Lucy D.
Wenck, Paul
Wenderoth, August F.
Wendt, Julia B.
Wendt, William
Werntz, Carl N.
West, Virgil W.
Weggold, Frederick P.
Weyss, John E.
White, Nona L.
White, Orrin A.
Whiteside, Frank R.
Whittredge, Worthington
Whymper, Frederick
Widforss, Gunnar M.
Wieczorek, Max
Wieghorst, Olaf
Wiggins, Myra A.
Wiles, Lemanuel M.
Wilke, William H.
Wilkins, James F.
Williams, James R.
Williams, Virgil
Wilwerding, Walter J.
Wimar, Charles
Winkler, John W.
Wisby, J.
Withrow, Eva A.
Wolle, Muriel S.
Wood, A. M.
Wood, Stanley
Wood, Stanley L.
Woodville, Richard C.
Wores, Theodore
Worrall, Henry
Wostry, Carlo
Wray, Henry R.
Wright, Alma B.
Wright, Thomas J.
Wueste, Louise H.
Wyant, Alexander H.
Wyeth, N. C.

Y

Yard, Sydney
Yates, Frederick
Yeager, Walter
Yelland, Raymond D.
Yens, Carl
Young, Aretta
Young, Florence
Young, Harvey B.
Young, John J.
Young, Mahonri
Young-Hunter, John
Young, Phineas

Z

Ziegler, Eustace P. Ziegler, Henry Zimbeaux, Frank I. Zimmerman, Ella A. Zogbaum, Rufus F.		

Abbot, Hazel N.
Abbott, Edward R.
Abbott, Marguerite E.
Abrams, Lucien
Acher, Herbert VanB.
Ackerman, Olga M.
Ackerman, Virginia
Adams, Grace A. R.
Adlon, Emma
Albinson, E. Dewey
Albright, Lloyd L.
Aldrich, Clarence N.
Aldrin, Anders
Alexander, Dora B.
Allen, Gregory S.
Allen, Marion B.
Allen, Mary C.
Allen, Mary G. S.
Allen, Pearl W.
Allis, C. Harry
Anderson, Alice S.
Anderson, Dorothy V.
Anderson, Louise C. V.
Andrews, Willard H.
Angelo, Valenti
Ankeney, John S.
Antlers, Max H.
Applegate, Frank G.
Appleton, Norman R.
Armer, Laura A.
Armer, Ruth
Armer, Sidney
Arms, John T.
Armstrong, Samuel J.
Armstrong, Voyle N.
Arnautoff, Victor M.
Arnstein, Helen
Arpa, Jose
Ashford, Frank C.
Atkins, Florence E.
Atkinson, Leo F.
Atkinson, William S.
Atwater, G. Barry
Atwood, Mary H.
Aunspaugh, Vivian L.
Austen, Edward J.
Austin, Ella M.
Avery, Kenneth N.
Avey, Martha

B

Babcock, Dean
Babcock, Roscoe L.
Bacharach, Herman I.
Bacon, Henry
Bailey, Walter A.
Bailache, Anne D.
Bain, Lilian P.
Bainbridge, Henry
Baker, Grace M.
Baker, William H.
Baldaugh, Anni
Baldridge, Cyrus L.
Balfour, Helen J.
Balfour, Roberta
Ballinger, Harry R.

Ballow, Addie L.
Bankson, Glen P.
Barber, Mary D.
Barchus, Eliza R.
Barfoot, Dorothy
Barnett, Jay W.
Barney, Alice P.
Barney, Esther S.
Barnouw, Adriaan J.
Barns, Cornelia
Barrows, Albert
Barnett, Frances G.
Basinet, Victor Hugo
Bateman, Talbot
Baumgartner, John J.
Baxley, Ellen C.
Baze, Willi
Beach, D. Antoinette
Beall, Cecil C.
Beecher, Harriet F.
Beggs, Thomas M.
Behman, Frederick
Beiler, Ida Zoe
Bell, Blanche B.
Bell, Thomas S.
Belmont, Steven
Bemus, Mary B.
Bendle, Robert
Benedict, Frank M.
Benedict, J. B.
Benjamin, Charles H.
Bennett, Joseph H.
Bennett, Ruth M.
Benolken, Lenore E.
Benrimo, Thomas D.
Bensco, Charles J.
Bentley, Rachel
Benton, Thomas Hart
Bergquist, F. O.
Berlin, Harry
Berman, Eugene
Berson, Adolph
Bessel, Evelyn B.
Bessinger, Frederic H.
Best, Mrs. A. W.
Best, Arthur W.
Best, Harry C.
Best, Margaret C.
Betts, Grace M.
Bewley, Murray P.
Bierach, S. E.
Billing, Frederick W.
Bintliff, Martha B.
Bishop, Katherine B.
Black, Mary C. W.
Black, Oswald R.
Blackburn, Josephine E.
Blackshear, Kathleen
Blackstone, Harriet
Blaine, Mahlon
Blakeman, Thomas G.
Blakeston, Duncan G.
Blashfield, Edwin H.
Bleil, Charles G.
Blesch, Rudolph

Bloser, Florence P.
Blumenstiel, Helen A.
Boak, Milvia W.
Bock, Charles P.
Boething, Marjory A.
Bohlman, Herman T.
Bolmar, Carl P.
Bolton, Hale W.
Bonestall, Chesley
Bonner, Mary
Bonnet, Leon D.
Bontecou, Helen
Boone, Cora M.
Booth, Eunice E.
Borghi, Lillian L.
Born, Ernest A.
Borzo, Karel
Boswell, Leslie A.
Boswell, Norman G.
Bosworth, Hobart VanZ.
Bouzek, Cathryn
Bower, Frances
Bowers, Beulah S.
Bowles, Caroline H.
Bowling, Charles T.
Boyd, Byron B.
Boyd, W. J.
Boynton, Anne F.
Braddock, Katherine
Brady, Mary C.
Brasher, Rex
Breckenridge, Dorothy
Breeze, Louisa
Brewster, Ada A.
Breyman, William
Brigante, Nicholas P.
Briggs, Annie F.
Brisac, Edith Mae
Brochaud, Joseph F.
Brooks, Mabel H.
Broughton, Charles
Brougier, Rudolphe W.
Brown, Bess L.
Brown, Bolton C.
Brown, Dayton R. E.
Brown, Frances S. N.
Brown, Grafton T.
Brown, John W.
Brown, Thomas A.
Browne, Carl A.
Browne, Lewis
Browning, Amzie D.
Bruce, Edward
Brumback, Louise U.
Brunet, Adele L.
Bryan, William E.
Bryant, Everett, Lloyd
Bryson, Hope M.
Buchanan, Ella
Buck, Margaret W.
Bufano, Benjamino B.
Bull, W. H.
Burdett, Dorothy M.
Burks, Garnett
Burrell, Louise H.

Burt, Marie B. H.
Butler, Andrew R.
Butler, Bessie S.
Butler, Courtland
Butler, Edward B.
Butler, Howard R.
Butler, Mary
Butler, Rozel O.
Butterfield, M.

C

Cahill, Katherine K.
Caldwell, Ada B.
Calkins, Bertis H.
Callahan, Caroline
Cameron, Edgar Spier
Cameron, William R.
Campbell, Fannie S.
Cakpbell, Isabella F.
Campbell, Myrtle H.
Cannon, Jennie V.
Capwell, Josephine E.
Carew, Berta
Carey, Rockwell W.
Carlson, Charles J.
Carlson, Zena P.
Carpenter, Miss A. M.
Carpenter, Dudley S.
Carpenter, Louise
Carr, Emily
Carrothers, Grace N.
Casey, John J. C.
Cashin, Nora
Chadwick, Grace W.
Chafee, Olive H.
Chain, Helen
Chamberlain, Samuel V.
Champlin, Ada B.
Chandler, Helen C.
Chaplin, Prescott
Chapman, John G.
Chapman, Josephine E.
Chapman, Minerva J.
Cheever, Walter L.
Chenoweth, J. A.
Chepourkoff, Michael G.
Cherry, Emma R.
Chesney, Letita
Chesney, Mary
Chiapella, Edouard E.
Chillman, James Jr.
Chouinard, Nelbert M.
Christensen, Ethel L.
Christensen, Florence
Christie, Mae Allyn
Church, Grace
Ciprico, Marguerite F.
Clack, Clyde Clifton
Clapp, William H.
Clark, Arthur B.
Clark, Helen B. M.
Clarke, Frank
Claxton, Virgie
Cleaver, Alice
Cleaves, Muriel M.
Cleenewerck, Henry

Clement, Catherine
Clopath, Henriette
Clover-Bew, May
Clute, Beulah M.
Coan, Helen E.
Coburn, Frank
Cocking, Mar G.
Cockrell, Dura B.
Colburn, Laura R.
Colby, George E.
Colby, Madolin
Colby, Vincent V.
Cole, Blanche D.
Collier, Estelle E.
Colton, Mary-Russell F.
Conant, Homer B.
Condit, Mrs. C. L.
Connell, Mary K.
Connelly, Lillian B.
Conner, Albert C.
Conner, Paul
Conway, John S.
Cook, E. F.
Cook, Paul R.
Cooney, Fanny Y. C.
Coover, Nell B.
Cope, George
Corder, Elene M.
Cordero, Jose
Corson, Stanley
Cory, Fanny Y.
Cosgrove, Earle M.
Costello, Val
Coughlin, Mildred M.
Courtney, Leo
Cox, Charles H.
Crabb, Robert J.
Crapuchettes, Emile J.
Crawford, Esther Mabel
Cressy, Birl
Cressy, Josiah P.
Cressy, Meta
Crew, Katherin
Criley, Theodore
Crittenden, Ethel S.
Cronau, Rudolf D. L.
Cronin, Marie
Cross, Ernest
Crow, Louise
Crowder, William
Crowell, Margaret
Cruess, Marie G.
Culbertson, Josephine M.
Cundell, Nora L. M.
Cunningham, Theodore S-A.
Curjel, E.
Curry, John S.
Curtis, Elizabeth
Curtis, Ida M.
Curtis, Rosa M.
Cutler, Frank E.

D

Dailey Anne E.
Daingerfield, Elliott
Dana, Gladys E.

Dando, Susie M.
Daniell, William S.
Daroux, Leonora
Dasberg, Andrew M.
Davenport, McHarg
Davey, Randall
Davidson, John
Davis, Cornelia C.
Davis, Willis E.
Dawes, Pansy
Day, Richard W.
Dean, Eva E.
Deane, Keith R.
Deane, Lillian R.
Dearborn, Annie F.
de Boronda, Tulita
Debouzek, J. A.
DeConte, Fortune
DeFrasse, Louise
DeJoiner, Luther E.
DeLaHarpe, Joseph
Delano, Annita
Deming, Mabel R.
DeSaisett, Ernest P.
Dethloff, Peter H.
Deutsch, Boris
DeVille, E. George
Dewey, Alfred J.
DeWolfe, Sarah B.
DeYoung, Harry A.
Dixon, Ethel
Dodge, Arthur B.
Dodge, William L.
Doke, Sallie G. F.
Dolan, Nellie H.
Dolecheck, Christine A.
Doran, Robert C.
Dorgeloh, Marguerite R.
Dorney, Genevieve
Dosch, Roswell
Douglas, Aaron
Douglas, Haldane
Douglass, Ralph W.
Downes, John I. H.
Drake, Will H.
Dudley, Katherine
DuMond, Frank V.
Dunlap, Helena
Dunlap, Mary S.
Dustin, Silas S.

E

East, Pattie R.
Easterday, Sybil U.
Easton, Frank L.
Eastwood, Raymond J.
Eckford, Jessiejo
Edens, Annette
Edgerly, Beatrice
Edie, Fern E.
Edmiston, Alice R.
Eisele, Cristian C.
Eisenlohr, Edward G.
Elder, Inez S.
Ellis, Clyde G.
Elms, Willard F.

Elshin, Jacob A.
Enser, John F.
Eresch, Josie
Ernst, Max
Escherich, Elsa F.
Euler, Edwin Reeves
Evans, Anne
Evans, Jessie B.
Everett, Elizabeth R.
Everett, Raymond

F

Fabian, Lydia D.
Failing, Ida C.
Faille, Carl A.
Fallis, Belle S.
Farrington, Walter Moses
Fay, Nellie
Fazel, John W.
Feitelson, I. Lorser
Fenyes, Eva S.
Ferguson, Elizabeth F.
Ferguson, Lillian P.
Finta, Alexander S.
Firebaugh, Nettie K.
Firks, Henry
Fisher, Howard
Fisher, H. Melville
Fisken, Jessie
Fitzgerald, James
Fjellboe, Paul
Folawn, Thomas J.
Foltz, Lloyd C.
Force, Clara G.
Foresman Alice C.
Forkner, Edgar
Forman, Kerr S.
Forster, Washburne
Foster, Bertha K.
Foster, Grace
Foster, Willet S.
Fowler, Eva
Francis, Muriel W.
Frank, Eugene C.
Frantz, Alice M.
Frazee, Issac J.
Frazier, John R.
Free, Mary Arnold
French, Grace A.
Frey, Charles D.
Friend, Washington F.
Fritz, Eleanor V.
Frost, Francis S.
Fuertes, Louis A.
Fuller, Adella R.
Fuller, Alfred
Fulop, Karoly
Fulton, Cyrus J.
Furlong, Charles W.

G

Gale, Goddard
Gale, Jane G.
Garbett, Cornelia B.
Garden-Macleod, Louise E.
Garland, Marie T.
Garnsey, Julian E.

Garrison, Martha H.
Garth, John
Gaskin, William
Gaw, Hugh
Gay, Mary
Gearhart, Frances H.
Geise, Rose M.
Geiser, Bernard
Gellenbeck, Anna P.
Gelwicks, Frances Slater
Genter, Paul H.
George, Margaret
Gere, Nelle H.
Gerlach, Albert A.
Gerrer, Robert G.
Gerrity, John E.
Gerstle, Miriam A.
Ghirardelli, Alida
Gibson, Mestre L.
Gideon, Samuel E.
Gilbert, Robert
Gilchrist, Meda
Gildersleeve, Beatrice
Gill, De Lancey
Gilliam, William C. F.
Gillette, Frances W.
Gilliam, Marguerite
Gimeno, Harold
Gimeno, Patricio
Girardin, Frank J.
Gjonovich, Miles
Goddard, Florence M.
Goeller, Miss E. Shotwell
Goldberg, Reuben L.
Goldstein, Louise M.
Golton, Glenn
Gonzalez, Boyer
Gonzales, Xavier
Goodan, Tillman P.
Goodwin, Philip R.
Goss, Louise H.
Graf, Gladys H.
Grain, Frederick
Grandstaff, Harriet P.
Gray, Kathryn
Gray, Mary C.
Gray, Percy
Gray, Una
Green, Emma E.
Green, Hiram H.
Greener, Charles T.
Gregg, Paul
Grell, Louis F.
Griffin, Worth D.
Griffith, Conway
Griffith, Lillian
Griffith, Louis O.
Grigg, Joanna
Groesbeck, Dan S.
Grosse, Garnet D.
Grosser, Eleanor M.
Grothjean, Francesca C. R.
Grubb, Ethel Mc.
Gruenfeld, John Casper
Guillot, Ann

Gundlach, Max E. H.
Gunn, Florence

H

Habeger, Ruth
Haddock, Arthus
Hader, Berta H.
Hader, Elmer S.
Haffner, F. J.
Hagendorn, Max
Haines, Marie B.
Hall, Florence S.
Hall, Leola
Hall, Parker L.
Halseth, Edna S.
Haltom, Minnie H.
Hamilton, Edgar S.
Hannon, Olga R.
Harding, Neva W.
Hardwick, Lily N.
Harland, Mary
Harmer, Thomas C.
Harper, William A.
Harris, Georgia M.
Harris, Greta
Harris, Samuel H.
Harshe, Robert B.
Hartmann, Sadakishi
Hartwell, Nina R.
Harvey, Paul
Hastings, Marion K.
Hatfield, Dalzell
Hatfield, Karl L.
Hawkins, Grace M.
Hayden, Harriet C. W.
Hayes, Lee
Haynes, Elsie H.
Hazard, Arthur M.
Hazen, Bessie E.
Hazen, Fannie W.
Heath, Edda M.
Heath, Lillian J. D.
Hebert, Marian
Heil, Elizabeth
Heinze, Adolph
Hekking, William M.
Heller, Bessie P.
Henderson, Evelyn
Hendricks, Emma S.
Henning, Virginia
Henri, Robert
Heron, Edith H.
Herrick, Hugh M.
Herrington, Florence E.
Herrmann, Fernande L.
Herter, Albert
Hessova, Bess
Hiatt, Maurine
Hiler, Hilaire
Hill, Alice S.
Hill, John H.
Hill, Robert J.
Hill, Stephen G.
Hilliard, William H.
Hilton, William H.
Hinchman, John H.

Letcher, Blanche
Levings, Mark M.
Levy, Nat
Lewis, Alonzo V.
Lewis, Han
Lewis, H. Emerson
Lindhardt, Dagmar B.
Lindsay, Ruth A.
Lingen, Penelope
Litchfield, Donald
Little, Gertrude L.
Littlejohn, Hugh W.
Littlejohn, Margaret M.
Loemans, Alexander F.
Loft, P.
Logan, Maurice G.
Loomis, Chester
Loomis, William A.
Lorie, Hortense P.
Lorraine, Alma R.
Lovins, Henry
Lowdon, Elsie M.
Lukits, Theodore N.
Lundmark, Leon
Lussier, Louis O.

M

McAllister, E. P.
McArdle, Henry A.
McBride, Eva A.
McBurney, James E.
McCague, Lydia S.
McCann, James F.
McClelland, Cyranius B.
McCormick, Donald
McCormick, M. Evelyn
McCoun, Alice L. T.
McCrea, Samuel H.
McCreery, Mrs. Franc R.
McCrossen, Preston
McCulloch, Maxie T.
McDermitt, William T.
MacDonald, Katharine H.
McDuffie, Jane L.
McElroy, Jane
McEwen, Katherine
McGaw, Blanche E. B.
McGee, Will T.
McGill, Eloise P.
McGill, Leona L.
MacGilvary, Norwood H.
McGrath, Lenore K.
McGraw, Hazel F.
MacGurrin, Buckley
Machefert, Florence L. B.
McKinstry, Grace E.
MacKnight, Dodge
Macky, Eric Spencer
MacLean, Christina
McLean, Grace
McLendon, Louise
Macleod, Louisa E. G.
McManus, George
McMillan, Mary L.
McMurdo, James T.
Maines, J. R.

Maison, Mary E.
Mako, B.
Manbert, Barton
Mann, Virginia
Manoir, Irving K.
Many, Alexis
Maratta, Hardesty G.
Marble, John N.
Mari, Valere de
Marin, John
Marsh, Charles Howard
Marsh, Harold D.
Marsh, Mary E.
Marshall, Frank H.
Martin, E. Hall
Martin, J. H.
Martin, John B.
Martin, Sue P.
Martinet, Marjorie D.
Martinez, Alfredo R.
Mattei, Clarence R.
Matthew, John B.
Mattocks, Muriel
Matzinger, Philip F.
Maybelle, Claude S.
Mayer, Louis
Mayhew, Nell D. B.
Meadows, Dell
Means, Mary M.
Meeker, Joseph R.
Meeks, Constance A.
Melvill, Antonia M.
Menager, Pierre
Menzler-Peyton, Bertha S.
Merck, Charles
Merrill, Arthur
Merritt, Ingeborg J.
Merritt, Warren C.
Mersfelder, Lou
Merwin, Antoinette dF. P.
Mesic, Miss Julian C.
Messenger, Ivan
Metcalf, Augusta I. C.
Mettlen, Franke W.
Meyer-Kassel, Hans
Meyers, Ralph
Milam, Annie N.
Milburn, Oliver
Miles, Emily H.
Miles, Harold W.
Miles, Maud M.
Miller, Anna H.
Miller, Delle
Miller, Edith M.
Miller, Henry
Miller, Maude A.
Miller, Myra
Miller, Richard E.
Millier, Arthur
Milsk, Mark
Miner, Frederick R.
Mitchell, Arthur R.
Mitchell, Eleanor B.
Mitchell, Gladys V.
Mocine, Ralph F.

Modjeska, Marylka H.
Modra, Theodore B.
Mohling, Fred H.
Molina Campos, Florencio
Monges, Henry B.
Monhoff, Frederick
Monkvold, Oscar E.
Monroe, Laura P.
Monserud, Wilma
Montalboddi, Raffaelo
Montgomery, Alfred
Montrichard, Raymond D.
Moon, Grace
Moore, Harry H.
Moore, John M.
Moran, Mary N.
Moran, Paul N.
Morgan, Charles L.
Morgan, Charlotte E. B.
Morris, Ada
Morris, James S.
Morris, Louise
Morrow, Julie M.
Morse, Vernon J.
Mott-Smith, May
Mountfort, Arnold G.
Mowbray, Harry S.
Mueller, Alexander
Mueller, Lola P.
Mueller, Michael J.
Muench, Agnes L.
Mukoyama, K.
Muller, Dan
Mullgardt, Louis C.
Munras, Esteban
Munsell, William A. O.
Murphy, Harry D.
Murphy, James E. Jr.
Murphy, Lawrence M.
Murphy, Minnie B. H. P.
Myers, Datus E.
Myers, Lloyd B.

N

Nankivell, Frank A.
Nau, Carl W.
Nave, Royston
Neilson, Charles P.
Neilson, Kay
Newby, Ruby W.
Newton, Helen F.
Neyland, Watson
Nice, Blanche H.
Nichols, Audley D.
Nichols, Pegus M.
Nicholson, Isabel L.
Nielson, Charles P.
Noble, John
Nomura, Kenjiro
Nordberg, C. A.
Norling, Ernest R.
Noyes, George L.
Nugent, Meredith
Nuttall, Thomas
Nye, Elmer L.
Nye, Myra

O

O'Brien, Smith
O'Donnell, Julian E.
Oestermann, Mildred C.
O'Hara, Eliot
O'Kane, Regina
O'Keeffe, Georgia
Oliver, Myron A.
Olson, Callie W.
Olson, J. Olaf
O'Malley, Power
Onderdonk, Julian
Orchardson, Charles M. Q.
Orr, Alfred E.
O'Ryan, Lillie V.
O'Shea, John
O'Sullivan, Elizabeth C.
Oswald, Emilie L.
Otis, George D.
Otte, William L.
Owles, Alfred

P

Packard, Alton
Packard, Mabel
Paice, Philip S.
Palmer, Jessie A.
Palmerton, Don F.
Parish, Annabelle H.
Parker, Cora
Parker, William G.
Parkhurst, Thomas S.
Parkinson, William J.
Parslow, Evalyn A.
Parsons, George F.
Partington, Richard L.
Partridge, Imogene
Partridge, Roi G.
Patrick, John D.
Patterson, Ambrose
Patterson, Howard A.
Patterson, Martha
Paulus, Christoph D.
Paval, Philip K.
Pawla, Frederick A.
Peabody, Ruth E.
Pearson, Nils Anton
Pearson, Ralph M.
Peers, Marion
Perkins, Katherine L.
Perl, Margaret A.
Perret, Ferdinand
Peters, Charles R. III
Petetin, Sidonia
Phister, Jean Jaques
Phoenix, Frank
Pickering, Hal
Pierce, Lucy V.
Pierce, William H. C.
Pinnington, Jane
Piper, Natt
Pitts, Lendall
Pizzella, Edmundo
Plotner, Rosa H.
Plowman, George T.
Pneuman, Mildred Y.

Pogany, Willy A.
Pogson, Annie L.
Pohl, Hugo D.
Polkinghorn, George
Pollak, Max
Polowetski, Charles E.
Pomeroy, Elsie L.
Pommer, Julius
Poock, Fritz
Poole, Eugene A.
Poray, Stan P.
Potter, Louis Mc.
Potter, Zenas L.
Powell, Arthur J. E.
Powell, J. S.
Powell, Jennette M.
Price, William H.
Pries, Lionel H.
Probst, Thorwald A.
Proper, Ida S.
Pushman, Hovsep T.
Pyle, Clifford C.

Q

Quinan, Henry B.

R

Rabino, Saul
Rahtjen, Fitzhugh
Randall, George A.
Raschen, Henry
Raulston, Marion C.
Rauschnabel, W. F.
Ravagli, Angelino
Ravlin, Grace
Raymond, Grace R.
Reckless, Stanley L.
Rederer, Franz
Reed, Earl M.
Reeser, Lillian
Reeves, Joseph M. Jr.
Regalado, Manuel R.
Reid, Aurelia W.
Reitzel, Marques E.
Renner, Otto H.
Renshawe, John H.
Reynolds, Alice M.
Reynolds, George
Rezac, Henry
Rice, Lucy W.
Rice, William S.
Richardson, Theodore J.
Richardson, Volney A.
Richmond, Evelyn K.
Rickard, Marjorie R.
Riddell, William W.
Rider, Arthur G.
Rider, Charles J.
Riess, William J.
Rife, Dwight W.
Righter, Alice L.
Righter, Mary
Rindisbacher, Peter
Rindlaud, Mrs. M. Bruce D
Ring, Alice B.
Ripley, Thomas E.
Risher, Anna P.

Rivera, Diego
Roberts, Hermine M.
Roberts, Maurine H.
Robertson, Jane P.
Ribinson, Charles H.
Robinson, Irene B.
Robinson, Virginia Isabel
Rochard, Pierre
Rockwell, Bertha
Rocle, Margaret K.
Rocle, Marius R.
Roerich, Nicholas K.
Rogers, Eleanor G.
Romero de Romero, Esquip.
Roney, Harold A.
Ronnebeck, Arnold
Ropp, Roy M.
Rose, Ethel B.
Rosenberg, Louis C.
Rosenthal, Mildred
Ross, Mary H.
Rothstein, Theresa
Rozaire, Arthur D.
Ruderdorf, Lillian C.
Rudhyar, Dane
Rudy, James F.
Runquist, Albert C.
Runquist, Arthur
Russell, Morgan
Ruthrauff, Frederick G.
Rutledge, Ann
Rutledge, Bertha V.
Rutt, Anna H.
Ryan, William R.

S

Saalburg, Allen R.
Saisett, Ernest P de
Salazar, Maria
Salz, Helen A.
Salzbrenner, Albert
Sammann, Detlef
Samuels, W. G. M.
Sandefur, John C.
Sands, Gertrude L.
Sandzen, Sven B.
Sargent, Paul T.
Sawyer, Edmund J.
Sayer, Edmund S.
Scammon, Laurence N.
Schaffer, L. Dorr
Schevill, William V.
Schiwetz, Edward M.
Schlaikjer, Jes W.
Schmidt, Albert H.
Schmidt, Karl
Schmidt, Otto
Schmitt, Paul A.
Schneider, Isobel
Schneider, Otto H.
Schoonover, Frank E.
Schouler, Willard C.
Schroder, Arnold
Schroeder, George E.
Schroff, Alfred H.
Schulman, Abraham G.

Schultz, George F.
Schumann, Paul R.
Schupbach, Mae Allyn
Schuster, Donna N.
Schuyler, Remington
Schwankovsky, Frederic J.
Schwarz, Frank H.
Schwentker, Hazel F.
Scofield, Edna M.
Scott, Anna P.
Scott, Carlotta B.
Scott, Nellie B.
Scott, Quincy
Scruggs, Margaret A.
Scudder, Alice R.
Scutt, Winifred
Sears, Benjamin W.
Seavey, Julian R.
Seavey, Lilla B.
Seawell, Henry W.
See, Imogene
Seeberger, Pauline B.
Seely, Walter F.
Seewald, Margaret
Seideneck, George J.
Sekido, Yoshida
Senat, Prosper L.
Sepeshy, Zoltan L.
Serbaroli, Hector
Sewall, Blanche H.
Sewall, Howard S.
Sexton, Frederick L.
Seymour, Ralph F.
Shannon, Ailleen P.
Sharp, Louis Hovey
Sharp, William
Sharp, William A.
Shaw, Lois Hogue
Shead, Ralph
Shear, Fera W.
Sheckell, T. O.
Sheeler, Charles
Sheffers, Peter W.
Shepard, Clare
Shepherd, Nellie
Sheridan, Joseph M.
Sherman, Elizabeth E.
Sherrer, Sabrina D.
Shields, Emma B.
Shiras, George E.
Shisler, Clare S.
Shiva, Ramon N.
Shively, Douglas
Shockley, May B.
Shorb, Mrs. D. L.
Shore, Henrietta M.
Shoven, Hazel B.
Shupp, Alice C.
Shurtliff, Wilfred H.
Siboni, Emma B.
Sichel, Harold M.
Silsby, Clifford F.
Silsby, Wilson
Silvius, Paul T.
Simkins, Martha

Simmang, Charles
Simpson, E. V.
Simpson, Marian
Singerman, Gertrude S.
Skeats, Miall
Skelly, Alta L.
Skelton, Phillis H.
Skene, Harold V.
Sleeth, L. MacDonald
Sloan, Edna
Sloan, J. Blanding
Sloan, John
Slutz, Helen B.
Small, Hazel
Smart, Edmund H.
Smellie, Robert
Smith, Annie
Smith, Camille
Smith, Charles L. A.
Smith, E. Bert
Smith, Edwin J.
Smith, Elmer B.
Smith, Ernest B.
Smith, George W.
Smith, Howard E.
Smith, Irwin E.
Smith, John F.
Smith, Katharine E.
Smith, Lillian B.
Smith, Lillian W.
Smith, Linus B.
Smith, Margery H.
Smith, Marietta R.
Smith, Paul K.
Snow, E. E.
Somervell W. Marbury
Sooy, Louise P.
Sorkner, E.
Souder, Mary R.
Southworth, Frederick W.
Spafard, Myra B.
Spalding, Elisabeth
Spaulding, Grace
Spencer, Guy R.
Spencer, Margaret F.
Spohn, Clay Edgar
Sprague, Elizabeth
Spratt, Alberti
Sprenkle, Arthur G.
Stacey, Anna L.
Stacey, John F.
Stair, Ida M.
Staley, Willie Anna
Stanley, George
Stanton, Lucy May
Starkey, Jo-Anita
Starr, Katharine
Stedman, Wilfred H.
Steele, Albert W.
Stensen, Matthew C.
Stephens, Clara J.
Sterba, Antonin
Sterchi, Eda E.
Sternfield, Edith A.
Stetson, Katherine B.

Stevens, Esther
Stevens, Helen B.
Stevens, Kelly H.
Stevens, Lawrence T.
Stevens, Ruth T.
Stevens, Stanford
Stevens, Will H.
Stewart, Dorothy N.
Stewart, Worth
Stimson, John W.
Stinchfield, Estelle
Stinson, Lucile S.
Stockton, Pansy
Stojana, Gjura
Stone, George M.
Stone, Viola P.
Stover, Allen J.
Stowitts, Hubert J.
Strahalm, Frank S.
Strater, Henry
Streator, Harold A.
Streight, Howard A.
Stringfield, Vivian F.
Stuber, Dedrick B.
Sutter, Samuel
Svoboda, Josef C.
Swartz, Harold C.
Swift, Florence A. W.

T

Tadama, Fokko
Tait, Agnes G.
Talberg, Carl H.
Talbot, Catherine
Tamotzu, Chuzo
Tanaka, Yasushi
Tanberg, Ella H.
Tapp, Marjorie D.
Tatum, Edward H.
Tauozky, David A.
Taylor, Edward DeW.
Taylor, Minnie C.
Taylor, Rolla S.
Taylor, Will L.
Teesdale, Christopher H.
Teichert, Minerva K.
Temple, C. M.
Terry, Eliphalet
Terry, John C.
Theiss, John W.
Theobald, R. C.
Thoma, Eva
Thomas, Alice B.
Thomas, D. F.
Thomas, Helen H.
Thomas, Marian
Thomas, Marjorie H.
Thomas, Stephen Seymour
Thompson, Hannah
Thompson, Thomas H.
Thomson, Adele U.
Thorndike, Willis H.
Thurston, Jane McD.
Tietjens, Marjoeie H. R.
Tillotson, Alexander
Timmerman, Walter

Timmons, Edward J. F.
Tingley, Blanche
Tirrell, John
Titus, Mrs. Aime B.
Tobriner, Haidee
Toeplitz, Charlotte V.
Tokita, Kamekichi
Tolman, Ruel P.
Towner, Miss Xaripa
Townsley, Channel P.
Tranquillitsky, Vasily G.
Traver, Charles Warde
Travis, Diane
Travis, Kathryne H.
Travis, Olin H.
Trease, Sherman
Treidler, Adolph
Triebel, Frederic E.
Trousset, Leon
Trucksess, F. Clement
Trucksess, Frances H.
Truesdell, Edith P.
Truesworthy, Jessie
T'Scharner, Theodore
Tschudy, Herbert B.
Turnbull, D. Gale
Turney, Ester

U

Ueyama, Tokio
Uhler, Ruth P.
Ulber, Althea
Underwood, Addie
Underwood, J. A.
Unsworth, Edna G.

V

Valentien, Albert R.
Valentien, Anna M.
Valle, Maude R. F.
Vallombrosa, Medora H.
Vanderhoff, Charles A.
Vanderhule, Lavina
Vann, Esse B.
VanPelt, Ellen W.
VanSweringen, Norma
VanWestrum, Anni
VanZandr, Hilda
Vik, Della B.
Vinatieri, Frank V.
Vincent, Andrew McD.
Vivian, Calthea C.
Vogel, Elmer H.
Volck, Fannie
Von der Lancken, Frank
VonHassler, Carl
VonSchneidau, Christian C.
Voss, Nellie C.
Vreeland, Francis W.
Vysekal, Edouard A.
Vysekal, Luvena B.

W

Wagenhals, Katherine
Waggoner, Elizabeth
Wagner, Blanche C.
Wagoner, Harry B.
Walker, John Law

Wall, Bernhardt
Wall, Gertrude R.
Wallace, John L.
Walter, Solly H.
Walter, Valyne G.
Walters, Carl A.
Ward, Harold M.
Ward, J. Stephen
Ward, Jean S.
Wardin, Frances M.
Warhanik, Elizabeth C.
Warner, William R.
Warshawsky, Alexander
Washburn, Max M.
Waterbury, Laura P.
Waterman, Myron A.
Watkins, Catherine W.
Watkins, Susan
Watrous, Mary E.
Watson, Adele
Watson, Jesse N.
Watts, Eva A.
Watts, William C.
Webb, Edith B.
Webb, Margaret E.
Weedell, Hazel E.
Weeks, Isabelle M. L.
Weinberg, Emilie S.
Wentz, Henry F.
Werner, Fritz
Wesselhoeft, Mary F.
Wessels, Glenn A.
West, Benjamin F.
Westfall, Tulita B.
Weston, Mrs. Otheto
Westrum, Anni von
Wheelan, Albertine R.
Wheeler, Janet D.
Wheelock, Warren F.
Wheete, Glenn
Wheete, Treeva
Whetsel, Gertrude P.
Whitaker, Frederic
Whitcraft, Dorothea F.
White, Edith
White, Inez M. P.
White, Jessie A.
Whitehan, Edna May
Whiteley, Rose
Whitlock, Frances J.
Whitlock, Mary Ursula
Whitman, Paul
Whittemore, Frances D.
Whittemore, Margaret E.
Wiberg, Fritjof
Wiboltt, Jack Aage C.
Wideman, Florence P.
Wilcocks, Edna M.
Wilcox, Frank N.
Wildhack, Robert J.
Wilford, Loran F.
Wilkin, Mildred P.
Wilkinson, Edward
Willard, Frank H.
Willard, Howard W.

Willard, Miss L. L.
Willey, Edith M.
Williams, Clifton
Williams, Florence A.
Williams, John C.
Williams, John L. S.
Williams, Lawrence P.
Williams, Louise H.
Williamson, Clara McD.
Williamson, Shirley
Willis, J. R.
Willis, Katherine
Willis, Ralph T.
Willits, Alice
Willmarth, William A.
Wilson, Charles T.
Wilson, Donna A.
Wilson, Floyd
Wilson, Hazel M.
Wilson, Helen
Wilson, Jeremy
Wilson, William J.
Winchell, Ward
Winebrenner, Harry F.
Winterburn, George T.
Winterburn, Phyllis
Wintermote, Mamie W.
Wirth, Anna M. B.
Wiser, Guy B.
Wolf, Hamilton A.
Wood, Annie A.
Wood, Charles E. S.
Wood, Katheryn L.
Wood, Madge McA.
Woodson, Marie L.
Woollett, William L.
Woolley, Virginia
Woolsey, Wood W.
Works, Katherine S.
Worthington, Mary E.
Woy, Leota
Wragg, Eleanor T.
Wright, James G.
Wright, Jennie E.
Wulff, Timothy M.
Wyatt, A. C.
Wyttenbach, Emanuel

Y

Yardley, Ralph O.
Young, Frank H.
Young, Myrtle M.
Younkin, William LeF.
Yphantis, George

Z

Zakheim, Bernard B.
Zetterlund, John
Ziegler, Samuel P.
Zilverberg, Jake
Zim, Marco
Zimmerman, Frederick A.
Zorach, Marguerite T.

WESTERN - OTHER

Included in this section are some of the
books with less artist coverage than Samuels and Dawdy, and a number of major or
special purpose exhibitions.

The two Harmsen books emphasize paintings
which are a part of the very important
Harmsen collection, but include a biographical sketch. The Cowboy in Art provides
a picture of the artist and one of his
paintings, along with a very folksy biographical sketch. The sketch has often
been derived from personal interview.

Another important source included here is
the 10 year cumulative index of the maga-
zine Southwest Art. This index lists approximately 750 artists for which articles
have been written in the 120 issues between
May 1971 and May 1981. Most of the traditional artists are included, but coverage
is especially strong on the emerging artists.

HARMSEN'S (WESTERN AMERICANA)&(AMERICAN WESTERN ART)

A COMBINED LISTING OF INCLUDED ARTISTS

A
Manuel Acosta
Cassilly Adams
Charles Partridge Adams
Kenneth Adams
Louis Akin
Stanley Arthurs

B
H. Ray Baker
Jozef Bakos
Henry Balink
Gray Bartlett
Gustave Baumann
Theodore Baur
Donald Beauregard
August Becker
Joe Beeler
Tom Benrimo
Charles Berninghaus
Oscar Berninghaus
Albert Bierstadt
Emil Bisttram
LaVerne Nelson Black
Ralph Blakelock
Ernest Blumenschein
Edward Borein
James Boren
Carl Oscar Borg
Homer Boss
George DeForest Brush
Harold Bryant
Conrad Buff
Elbridge A. Burbank
Paul Burlin
George Elbert Burr

C
Pruett Carter
Wm. de la M. Cary
John Casilear
Gerald Cassidy
George Catlin
Charles S. Chapman
Benton Clark
Samuel Colman
Howard Cook
A. D. M. Cooper
Dean Cornwell
E. Irving Couse
Charles Craig
Henry H. Cross

D
Elliott Daingerfield
Cyrus Dallin
Felix Darley
Andrew Dasburg

Randall Davey
Herndon Davis
Gerald Curtis Delano
Edwin Deming
Maynard Dixon
Harvey Dunn
Herbert Dunton
Charles du Tant
Charlie Dye

E
Nick Eggenhofer
Henry Elkins
Fremont Ellis
Clarence Ellsworth
R. Farrington Elwell

F
Henry Farny
Nicolai Fechin
Nicholas Firfires
Harrison Fisher
Joseph Fleck
Clyde Forsythe
Charles A. Fries

G
Leon Gaspard
Gilbert Gaul
William Gollings
Glenna Goodacre
Philip Goodwin
Olaf Grafstrom
Joe Grandee
Francis Greenman
Paul Gregg
Albert Groll

H
John Hampton
H. W. Hansen
Fred Harman
Marsden Hartley
John Hauser
Earle Heikka
William P. Henderson
E. Martin Hennings
Robert Henri
Victor Higgins
Thomas Hill
Thomas Hinckley
Joseph Hitchins
Charles Hittell
Frank Hoffman
Ransom Holdredge
William H. Holmes
John D. Howland
Grace Hudson
Russell Hunter

Peter Hurd

I
Joseph Imhoff

J
William Henry Jackson
Ned Jacob
Will James
Frank Tenney Johnson
Raymond Jonson
Amedee Joullin

K
Karl Kauba
William Keith
Henry Keller
Ramon Kelley
Edward Kemeys
Charles Bird King
W. H. D. Koerner
Pawel Kontny

L
Charles Lanman
Harry Learned
William Leigh
Thomas L. Lewis
Raphael Lillywhite
Robert Lindneux
Ward Lockwood
Lone Wolf
Richard Lorenz
Robert Lougheed
Waldo Love
Fernand Lungren

M
Leal Mack
John Marchand
John Marin
Roy Mason
Clarence McGrath
R. Brownell McGrew
Alfred Jacob Miller
Arthur Mitchell
Frederic Mizen
F. Luis Mora
Thomas Moran
Alfred Morang
William Moyers
Walter Mruk
Dan Muller

N
Ernest Narjot
Willard Nash
Victor Nehlig
B. J. O. Nordfeldt

O
Georgia O'Keeffe

P
Sheldon Parsons
Edgar S. Paxson
Edgar Alwin Payne
Burt Phillips
Wolfgang Pogzeba
R
J. K. Ralston
Henry Raschen
Robert D. Ray
Doel Reed
Marjorie Reed
Leonard Reedy
Frederic Remington
Louis Ribak
A. L. Ripley
Julian Rix
Warren E. Rollins
Julius Rolshoven
Carl Rungius
Charles M. Russell
Tom Ryan
Chauncey Ryder
S
Mathias Sandor
Frank Sauerwein
F. Grayson Sayre
Frank Schoonover
Charles Schreyvogel
Conrad Schwiering
Julian Scott
Olaf Seltzer
James Sessions
Bill Sharer
Joseph Sharp
Will Shuster
John Sloan
George Smillie
DeCost Smith
Will Sparks
John Mix Stanley
Ross Stefan
Maurice Sterne
Vladan Stiha
Charles Stobie
Howard Steight
James E. Stuart
Jimmie Swinnerton
T
Arthur Tait
Richard Tallant
Jules Tavernier
Donald Teague
Paul Troubetskoy
Allen True
James Turpen Jr.
U
Walter Ufer
V

Manuel Valencia
Dirk van Driest
Theodore Van Soelen
Carlos Vierra
Adrien Voisin
Harold Von Schmidt
W
James Walker
Thad Welch
Cady Wells
Frederick Weygold
Fritz White
Frank Whiteside
Worthington Whittredge
Olaf Wieghorst
Irving Wiles
Lemuel Wiles
Charles Wimar
Byron B. Wolfe
N. C. Wyeth
Y
Harvey Young
Mahonri Young
John Young-Hunter

The West Remembered
Artists & Images 1837-
1973   The Earl Adams
Collection Santa Bar-
bara & SF. 1973

Charles P. Adams
Kenneth M. Adams

George Barrington
Joe Beeler
Oscar E. Berninghaus
LaVerne N. Black
Ralph A. Blakelock
Ernest L. Blumenschein
Edward Borein
Carl Oscar Borg
George K. Brandriff
Dorothy E. Brett

William M Cary
Gerald Cassidy
George Catlin
Vincent Colyer
George A. Corwin
Eanger Irving Couse
Alan G. Cram

Edwin W. Deming
Maynard Dixon
Joseph E. N. Dufault
    (Will James)

Harvey Dunn

Nicolai Fechin
Clyde Forsythe

Leon Gaspard
J. B. Girard

E. Martin Henning
Hermann Herzog
Frank Hoffman
John S. A. Houser

Joseph Imhof

"Will James" See Dufault

William Keith

Henry Lion
Fernand Lungren

John N. Marchand
Alfred J. Miller
Jo Mora

Edgar Paxson
Don Perceval
Charles R. Peters
Burt Procter
Arthur Putnam

A. C. Redwood
Leonard H. Reedy
Frederic Remington
Charles M. Russell

Frank P. Saurwein
    (Sauerwen)
Joseph H. Sharp

Jules Tavernier

Olaf Weighorst
Charles Wimar

Rufus F. Zogbaum

CUMULATIVE INDEX "SOUTHWEST ART"

Covers magazines from May 1971 to May 1981   The May 1981 issue provides details as to issue, author, title, page #, etc.

Andrew Dasburg
Robert Daughters
Diane David
Donald Davis
Lew Davis
Richard Davis
Douglas Dawson
John Dawson
Edgar Degas
Juan Dell
Louis DeMartino
Louis DeMayo
Mike Desatnick
Paul Detlefsen
Austin Deuel
Jim Deutsch
Lisette DeWinne
Paul DiBert
Tom Dickson
John Diehl
James Disney
Maynard Dixon
Gene Dobos
Gene Dodge
Douglas Downs
Don Doxey
John Doyle
Dirk Van Driest
Lee Dubin
Jesse DuBois
Terry Dunlap
Marcel Duchamp
Ed Dwight
Charlie Dye
Larry Dyke
Alex Dzigurski

E

Luis Eades
Valoy Eaton
Ken Eberts
Ted Egri
Yasu Eguchi
Peter Ellenshaw
Fremont Ellis
R. C. Ellis
Carl Embrey
Wayne Eustice
Don Esley
Dave Ewart

F

Burr Fairlamb
John Falter
Gerald Farm
Nicholai Fechin
James Fetherolf
Mel Fillerup
Donny Finley
Nicholas Firfires
Arthur Fitzsimmons
Alan Flattmann

Joseph A. Fleck
Wayne Floeck
John Flores
Dale Ford
Pat Ford
Jill Fogelson
Paul Forsters
Will Foster
Lincoln Fox
Cliff Frague
Robert Frame
Harold Frank
Robert Freimark
Loren Fry

G

Bernard Garbutt
Michael Garman
David Garrison
Cal Gaspard
Frank Gauna
Lathrop Gay
Lorenzo Ghiglieri
Len Gibbs
Carol Gibson-Sayle
Laura Gilpin
Andre Gisson
Kathy Glidden
Carol B. Giltsch
Rod Goebel
Chaim Goldberg
Rolland Golden
Arnold Goldstein
Glynn Gomez
Marco A. Gomez
Walt Gonske
Glenna Goodacre
Veryl Goodnight
R. C. Gorman
Joe Grandee
Martin Green
Bette Greenberg
A. D. Greer
R. V. Greeves
Robert Grieves
Walter Griffin
Ken Grissom
John Grossman
Gary Grotey
Robert Gunn
Alma Gunter
Raul Guterrez
Woody Gwyn

H

Jan Hagara
Frank Hagel
David Halback
Bettie Haller
Jim Hamilton
Lee Hamilton

Frederick Hammersley
Bill Hampton
Lucille C. Hampton
John W. Hampton
Una Hanbury
Enoch K. Haney
Adrian Hansen
Ken Harbaugh
Helen Hardin
Jerry Harp
Pamela Harr
Alan Harrill
Andre Harvey
G. Harvey
Maurice Harvey
Paul Hathaway
Larry Hayden
Elle Hazak
Donald M. Hedin
Earle Heikka
Orlin Helgoe
C. M. Henderson
E. Martin Hennings
Paul Henry
Gary Herbert
Ed Herbes
Herman Herzog
Terrence Hick
Bill Hill
G. S. Hill
Jim Hill
Tom Hill
Jack Hines
Armando Hinojosa
William Hoey
Helen Hoffman
Del Holt
Winslow Homer
Dick van den Hoogen
Harold Hopkinson
Kris Hotvedt
Frank Howell
Peter Hsu
Bill Hughes
Clark Hullings
John Humphrey-Henninger
David Humphreys
Helen Hunter
Warren Hunter
Peter Hurd
Allan Husberg
Doug Hyde

I

Sandy Ingersoll
Wayne Ingram

J

Harry Jackson
Ned Jacob
Norma Jay
Lee Jayred

Paul Jenkins
P. G. Jensen
Luis Jimenez
Mamie Joe
Donal C. Jolley
Douglas Johnson
Frank Tenney Johnson
Harvey Johnson
James Harvey Johnson
R. Bradford Johnson
Clair Jones
Covelle Jones
Holmes Ed Jones
Lee Jones
Nathan Jones
Jack Jordan
Stephen Juharos

K

Buffalo Kaplinski
Martin Katon
Robert Katona
Margaret Keane
Don Keller
Ramon Kelley
Gib Kendrick
Rockwell Kent
Roy Kerswill
Charles Kinghan
Tom Kirby
John Kittelson
Sybil Klein
Gene Kloss
Ray Knaub
Kay Knapp-Witherspoon
Grace Knox
William L Ko
Jeanne Koch
Martin Koch
Ben Konis
Janusz Kozikowski
Stefan Kramer
Jack Kroehnke
Janet Kruskamp
Otto Kuhler
Robert Kuhn
Susan Kulbacki
Mort Kuntsler

L

Paul Lantz
Mario Larrinaga
Carol Latta
D H Lawrence
Alois Lecoque
Gary D Leddy
Bob Lee
David Lee
Lawrence Lee
Ann Leggett
Mary Lehman

William R Leigh
Jerry Lemon
August Lenox
Marie Lesher
Phillip Lewandowski
Thomas L Lewis
Bonny Lhotka
Jon Lightfoot
Gustav Likan
Keith Lindberg
Robert Lindneux
Bart Lindstrom
Janet Lippincott
Elizabeth Lochrie
Gisella Loeffler
Joseph Lonewolf
Bernique Longley
Patricia R Loree
Robert Lougheed
Ronald Louque
Frank Lyon
Shirley Lee Lyon

M

Thomas Maciaone
Grant MacDonald
Stanton Macdonald-Wright
Daniel MacMorris
Merrill Mahaffey
Rosemary Maloney
Thomas E Mails
Americo Makk
Eva Makk
A B Makk
Frank J Malina
Beatrice Mandelman
Bart Mann
Anthony Manzo
Doug Marcy
Lajos Markos
John Marsh
Frank H Marshall
Alfredo Ramos Martinez
Maria Martinez
Ramos Martir
Edith Maskey
Pat Mathiesen
Buck McCain
Robert McCall
Frank McCarthy
D Michael McCarthy
Donald G McCauley
Maxine McClendon
Roger McCoy
Dave McGary
Clay McGaughy
R Brownell McGrew
Hilary McGuire
Molly McGuire
Pat McGuffin

Carol McKellroy
Ted McKinney
Nancy McLaughlin
George McMahan
Stanley Meltzoff
Armand Merizon
Gerry Metz
Alberto Meza
Gary Michael
Albert Michini
Dan Mieduch
Gary P Miller
Vel Miller
Wendell Minor
Robert Montanucci
Audrey Montgomery
R J Moore
Wayland Moore
William A Moore
Thomas Moran
Maher Morcos
Alfred Morang
Guy Morrow
Tom Morrow
Forrest Moses
Grandma Moses
Gary Moss
Tom Moss
Sid Mountain
William Moyers
Robert Mosk
William Muller-Lux
Charles E Murphy
Richard A Myer
Gary Myers

N

Dan Namingha
Michael Naranjo
John Naylor
David J Negron
Charles Nelson
William Nelson
Doc Tate Nevaguaya
Louise Nevelson
Susan Newcomb
Bo Newell
Jerry Newman
Gary Niblett
Del Nichols
Leonardo Nierman
John Nieto
Patricia Nix
David Nordahl
Ancel Nunn
Geraldine Nunn

O

Jose Garcia Ocejo
Georgia O Keeffe
Janet O'Leary
Kermit Oliver

Marcia Oliver
John O'Neill
Ken Ottinger
David Outhwaite

P

Gita Packer
Peter Paona
Diana Parker
Robert Miles Parker
Wilma Parker
Lee K. Parkinson
Peter Parnall
Terry Pardue
Violet Parkhurst
Maxfield Parrish
Asterio Pascolini
Edgar S. Paxson
Louise Pearson
Charles Pebworth
Dale Peche
James Pedersen
Armado Pena Jr.
Les Perhacs
Gregory Perillo
Robert Perine
Tom Perkinson
Roger Tory Peterson
Mack Petty
Harold A. Phenix
George Phippen
Dick Phillips
Byron Pickering
Hilda Pierce
Judith Pierce
Jeanette Pincus
John Pitre
Paul Pletka
Hugo Daniel Pohl
Don Polland
Gordon Pond
Theresa Potter
Ace Powell
John Prazen
Phil Prentice
Alexander Proctor
Roy Purcell

Q

Howard Quam

R

Al Radomski
Joseph Raffael
Bob Ragland
Bill Rains
Don Ray
Dale Rayburn
Genevieve Reckling
Miksel Redman
Herman Rednick
Kevin Red-Star

Maynard Reece
Doel Reed
Jacques Regar
Mary Regat
Peter Reginato
Winold Reiss
Frederic Remington
Jim Reno
Jim Rey
James Reynolds
Chang Reynolds
Theda Rhea
Louis Riback
Noble Richardson
Hank Richter
Mark Rickerson
Douglas Ricks
Cynthia Rigden
Morris Rippel
Robert Rishell
J. Bernard Rivard
Edith Robertson
Bruce Roberts
Julian Robles
Jacqueline Rochester
Rocky Rodgers
Auguste Rodin
George Rodrique
Dorothy Rohner
Lee Rommel
Rosamond
Bonnie Rose
Peg Rosenlund
Nagasawa Rosetsu
Percival Rosseau
Carl Roters
David Grant Roth
Melva Rue
Charles M. Russell
Andrew Rush
Ford Rushing
Tom Ryan

S

Betty Sabo
David Sanders
Santiago de Santiago
Allen Sapp
Robert Sarsony
Marco Sassone
Bill Schenck
Robert Schilling
William Schimmel
Mary Jane Schmidt
Fritz Scholder
Elmer Schooley
S. C. Schoneberg
Robert Schuhsler
Conrad Schwiering
R. Scott

Sandy Scott
Mike Scovel
Drake Seaman   Gus
J. L. Searle   Shafer
Naida Seibel
O. C. Seltzer
Bud Shackleford
William E. Sharer
Joseph Henry Sharp
Don Shaw
A. J. Sheznayder
Robert Shufelt
Dennis Silvertooth
Cleda M. Simmons
Lee Simpson
Anthony Sinclair
Raymond Sipos
Gary Slater
Eric Sloane
W. A. Slaughter
Dick Sloviaczek
Bruce Smith
Carl J. Smith
Cecil Smith
Craig Smith
Jaune Smith
Jerry Smith
Linda K. Smith
Pat Smoot
Mort Solberg
Paolo Soleri
David Soloman
Elke Sommer
H. J. Soulen
Teryl Speers
James Stafford
David Stark
Ross Stefan
Ben Stahl
Harry Sternberg
Bettina Steinke
Bill Stevenson
Hannah Stewart
Vladan Stiha
M. Stinson
Shannon Stirnweis
Don Stivers
Stan Stokes
Nancy Stonington
Tim Stortz
Paul Strisik
Earl Stroh
Charles Sultan
Gregory Sumida
Robert Summers
Arthur Sussman
Wally Swank
Gary Swanson
Mark Swanson

Paul Swain
Trudy Sween
Edward Szmyd

T
Paul Tadlock
Masary Takiguchi
Chuzo Tamotzu
Ann Taylor
Loretta Taylor
Lyle Tayson
Howard Terpning
Emmitt Thames
Jim Thomas
Richard D Thomas
Ronald Tomason
Mark Thompson
Richard Thompson
Torger Thompson
Brent Thomson
Ray Tidd
Jonny Tiger
Bob Timberlake
Doris Tischler
Jacqueline G Tolg
Dennis Torzeski
Dee Toscano
Emile Rainbow Touraine
Olin Travis
Raul Trejo
Jesse Trevino
Jean Pierre Trevor
Dick Turner
James Turner

U
Agnese Udinotti
Walter Ufer

V
Tony Van Hasselt
Arie Van Selm
Oscar Van Young
Pablita Velarde
Joe Velazquez
Russ Vickers
Veloy Vigil
Jose Vives-Atzara
Adrien Voisin
Harold Von Schmidt

W
John Waddell
John Phillip Wagner
Gordon Wagner
Lee Waisler
George Walbye
Edward D Walker
Jim Walsten
Melvin Warren
Doug Wassom
Robert Watson
Robert Wee

Justin Wells
Ronnie Wells
William Wendt
Uwe Werner
Eileen M Whitaker
Frederic Whitaker
Elizabeth White
Fritz White
Travis Whitfield
Olaf Wieghorst
Jim Wilcox
Katheryn Williams
Jason Williamson
Hollis Williford
Douglas F Wilson
Nock Wilson
Rubye Wilson
Dalhart Windberg
Lawrence Wing
Geoff Winningham
Helen Winslow
Bob Wolf
Francis Woodahl
Beatrice Wood
Robert E Wood
Jack Woods
David Wright
Joan Wright
Stanton Macdonald-
Wright
N C Wyeth
Henrietta Wyeth
Jamie Wyeth
Bruce Wynne

Y
Tom Yanosky
Frank Yantorno
Nathan Youngblood
Nancy Youngblood
Meia Youngblood
Dave Youngdahl
Ruby Yount
Glenda G Youritzin

Z
Frank Zamora
Bill Zaner
Jessica Zemsky
Billy Zimmatore
Clyde Zulch

THE COWBOY IN ART BY ED AINSWORTH

World Publishing 1968

Ramon Adams
Kenneth M. Adams
Stella Akana
Charlie Aldrich
Clay Allison
Ernesto Alvarez
Anthony Amaral
Robert Amick
Andy Anderson
Bronco Billy Anderson
Charlie Andreas
Spencer Asah
Gilbert Atencio
Ted Austin

B

Spencer Bagdatopolis
Paul Bailey
George C. Bales
Henry Balink
Grey Bartlett
Revcan Basset
Stanley Battese
Edward F. Beale
Thomas Beard
Arthur Beaumont
Joe Beeler
Sharon Beeler
Harrison Begay
Bill Bender
Helen Bender
Thomas Hart Benton
Ernest Berke
Oscar F. Berninghaus
Alfred Bierstadt
Earl Derr Biggers
Dorcas Birchim
James Birchim
Laverne Black
Ernest L. Blumenschein
Richard Bock
Karl Bodmer
Eugene Bolton
Rosa Bonheur
Ed Borein
Lucille Borein
Carl Oscar Borg
Gutzon Borglum
Lincoln Borglum
Solon Borglum
F Blackbear Bosin
Cyrus Boutwell
L H Brague
James E. Bramlett

George Bridgman
Robert E. Brislawn
Robert E. Brislawn Jr.
Homer Britzman
George deForest Bush
Howard Bryan
Harold Bugbee
Robert F. Burgess
Paul Burlin

C

G. Raymond Campbell
Yakima Canute
Mrs. Archie Carothers
Pruitt Carter
William d. Cary
Gerald Cassidy
George Catlin
Pop Chalee
Charles S. Chapman
Kenneth Chapman
Bill Chappell
Faye Martin Chappell
Larry Chittenden
Rene A. Chouteau
Howard Chandler Christy
Iron Eyes Cody
Philip G. Cole
Alice Cinradt
Harold Cook
James S. Copley
James B. Cornette
Dean Cornwell
E. Irving Couse
Will Crawford
Henry H. Cross
Nelson Crow
John S. Curry
Ken Curtis

D

Emmett Dalton
Felix O. C. Darley
Randall Davey
Harold D. Davidson
Jo Davidson
Theodore R. Davis
William Heath Davis
Charles Deas
Chuck De Haan
Joe De Yong
George Dick
Darol Dickinson
Rudolph Dirks
L. Maynard Dixon

J. Frank Dobie
Adee Dodge
Brian Donahue
Eileen Donahue
Kelly Donahue
Vic Donahue
Fred Downer
Ernest Dufault
Josephine Dufault
Jean Dufault
Edward Dufner
Frank V. Du Mond
Charley Duncan
Harvey Dunn
Herbert Dunton
Thomas A. Dwyer
Paul Dyck
Charlie Dye

E

Seth Eastman
Bob Edgren
Nick Eggenhofer
Edward G. Eisenlohr
Verne Elliott
Clarence Ellsworth
R. Farrington Ellwell
Carl Eytel

F

Glenn W. Faris
Henry Farney
Sally James Farnham
Dave Farr
George Farr
Nicolai Fechin
A. G. Feers
Fred Fellows
Jackie Fellows
Nicholas Firfires
Anton Otto Fisher
William A. Fisher
Curley Fletcher
Clyde Forsythe
Cotta Owen Forsythe
Leon Franks
James Earle Fraser
Laura Gordon Fraser
John D. Free
Jackie Freeman
W. E. Freeman

G

Leon Gaspard
Gilbert Gaul
Daisy Margaret Gero
Charles Dana Gibson

Thomas Gilcrease
Cal Godshall
Joie Godshall
Bill Gollings
Oliver Gollings
Marco Antonio Gomez
Marge Gomez
Charlie Goodnight
Trail Goodnight
Philip Goodwin
St. George Gore
Robert A. Grahame
Joe Grandee
John Gray
L. Frank Green
Paul Gregg
Juan de Grivala

H

J. Evetts Haley
William Hall
Stuart Hamblen
Alice Hampton
Bill Hampton
John Hampton
Ejnar Hansen
Herman W. Hansen
Oscar J. W. Hansen
John Wesley Hardin
Fred Harman Jr.
Fred Harman III
Lola Andrews Harmon
Phil Harris
Paul Harvey
Phoebe A. Hearst
Earl Heikka
Wm. Penhallow Henderson
Joseph Hergesheimer
Shelia A. Herron
Ben Hibbs
Victor Higgins
John W. Hilton
Frank B. Hoffman
Tom Holland
Winslow Homer
Charles Honey
Emerson Hough
Allan Houser
W. H. Huddle
Wayne Hunt
Warren Hunter
Henrietta Wysth Hurd
Peter Hurd
Jane Hyatt

I

Ernesto Icaza

J.

Andrew Jackson
C. W. Jackson
Harry Jackson
Jim Bob Jackson

George Wharton James
Harry James
Frank Tenney Johnson
Harvey W. Johnson
Velma Johnson
Bud Jones
Gerald Harvey Jones
Pat Jones
Frank Jordan

K

Archie Cleghorn Kaaua
Willie Kaniho
William Keith
Clarence B. Kelland
John Henry Kittleson
Lillian Lusk Koerner
Wm. Henry D. Koerner
Dean Krakel
Albert D. Kurtz
Friederich Kurz

L

M. J. Lamb
Paul Landacre
Philippe de Lannoy
Walt La Rue
Tom Lea
Arley Leck
O. M. Lee
Robert M. Lee
V. M. Lee
Bill Leftowich
William R. Leigh
John D. Lewis
Thomas Lewis
Raphael Lillywhite
Robert Lindneux
Lone Wolf
Stanley Long
Stephen H. Long
Richard Lorenz
Flora H. Loughead
Robert Loughead
Jack Low
Fred Ludekens
Charles F. Lummis

M

Billy Magee
Louis Magee
Dona Marina
George Marks
George Lewis Marks
Gordon Marks
Don Marquis
Frank Martinez
Pete Martinez
Xavier Martinez
Fletcher Martin
Kirk Martin
Bill Mauldin
Fred Maxwell

Henry McBride
Lea Franklin McCarty
John McClure
R. L. McCollister
Frank McCoy
Harold McCracken
Clay McGaughy
R. Brownell McGrew
John McMillan
Jim McNab
Lefty McPeters
Ben Carlton Mead
Lon Megaree
John Meigs
Johnnie Mennick
Carolyn Meyers
Frederick Meyers
Helen Meyers
Robert W. Meyers
Tom Meyers
Alfred Jacob Miller
Cactus George Miller
Albert K. Mitchell
Mike Monroney
James Monteith
Grove Mooney
Frank Moore
Richard Moore
Domingo Mora
Joe Mora
Luis Mora
G. Morales
Edward Moran
Thomas Moran
Tom Morgan
Emil Aim Morhardt
Ernest Morris
Joanne Moyers
William Moyers

N

Charles Christian Nahl
Ernest Narjot
Van Kirke Nelson
Major North

O

Ruth Koerner Oliver
Julian Onderdonk
William Owen O'Neill
John O'Shea
Richard F. Outcault

P

James Parker
James Palmer Parker
John Palmer Parker
Arthur Parkhouse
Lew Parrish
Sheldon Parsons
Edgar Samuel Paxson
Edgar Payne
Charles Payzant

Titian R. Peale
Henri Penelon
Fred Penney
Paula Penney
Alejandro Peters
Bert Geer Phillips
Darrell Phippen
Ernie Phippen
George Phippen
Loren Phippen
Winola Phippen
Eben Pilow
Ace Powell
C. S. Price
Burt Procter
Katherine Procter
Gifford MacG. Proctor
A. Phimister Proctor
A. Kelly Pruitt
Anna Marie Pruitt
Ikna Purdy
Howard Pyle

Q

E. B. Quihley

R

J. Ken Ralston
William Ranney
Boyd L. Rasmussen
Leonard J. Reach
Frank Reaugh
Marjorie Reed
Walter Reed
Frederic Remington
Frederic Renner
Chester A. Reynolds
Cora Hicks Reynolds
James Reynolds
J. Wellington Reynolds
Eugene Manlove Rhodes
Lawrence P. Richards
Peter Rindisbacher
Dorothy Olsen Rishell
Lynn Rishell
Robert Rishell
Dwight Roberts
Jack Roberts
Norman Rockwell
Astrea Rogers
Jim Rogers
Roland Rollins
Paul Rossi
Carl Runguis
Charles M. Russell
Rusty Rawlings
Tom Ryan

S

Sacajawea
Porfiro Salinas
Paul Salisbury

Ross Santee
John Singer Sargent
C. Terry Saul
William Schimmel
Felix G. Schmidt
Frank Schoonover
Charles Schreyvogel
Auguste Schwabe II
Conrad Schwiering
O. C. Schwiering
Robert Macfie Scriver
Frances Sedgwick
Olaf Seltzer
Samuel Seymour
Joseph Henry Sharp
Frank Shaw
Joseph J. Shebl
Millard Sheets
Lenore Sherman
Irvin Shorty Shope
Stephen Slesinger
Richard Smart
Spencer Smith
Gordon Snidow
Sue Snidow
Earl Snook
Eleanor Snook
Phil Spear
Grant Speed
Ray J. Spaulding
Ed Springer
Joe Stahley
George Stanley
John Mix Stanley
Debbie Steele
George Steele
Sandra Steele
Olive Stokes
Fred Stone
Ray Strang
George M. Straszer
Robert P. Strathearn
Jack Swanson
A. M. G. Swede Swenson
Jimmie Swinnerton

T

Joseph Tafoga
Quincy Tahoma
Arthur F. Tait
Donald Teague
Bernard P. Thomas
Dan Thornton
B. D. Titsworth
Ilia Tolstoy
Bob Tommey
Ernest Tonk
Ed Trumball
Andy Tsinaginie
Joseph M. W. Turner

U

Walter Ufer

V

Ed Vail
James K. Van Brunt
Jack Van Ryder
Theodore Van Soelen
Hayward Veal
Carlos Vierra
Gregorio de Villalobos
Harold Von Schmidt

W

Norajean Wagoner
Robert Wagoner
James Walker
Charles Warner
Lucille Warren
Melvin C. Warren
Hughlette Tex Wheeler
Stewart Edward White
Harold Whitley
T. F. Whitley
R. H. Whitley
Karl Wieghorst
Mabel Wieghorst
Olaf Wieghorst
Roy Wieghorst
Jesse Wilkinson
Ben Ames Williams
Hank Williams
J. R. Williams
Irving Nat Wills
Charles Wilmar
Charles Banks Wilson
Curtis Wingate
Owen Wister
George Woolf
Clint Worlds
Andrew Wyeth
N. C. Wyeth

Y

Beatien Yazz
James Wayne Yazzie
Donald Yena

Z

Rufus Zogbaum

THE WEST AS ART

MAJOR EXHIBITION, SPRING 1982, PALM SPRINGS DESERT MUSEUM

Lita Albuquerque	Robert Hudson	Wayne Thiebaud
James Madison Alden	George Inness	Joyce Treiman
William Allan	Luis Jimenez Jr.	Walter Ufer
Henry C Balink	Frank Tenney Johnson	Marion K. Wachtel
Thomas Hart Benton	William Keith	James Walker
Oscar E. Berninghaus	William R. Leigh	Andy Warhol
Albert Bierstadt	Marilyn Levine	Cady Wells
George Caleb Bingham	Roy Lichtenstein	William Wendt
Ernest L. Blumenschein	Helen Lundeberg	Thomas W. Whittredge
John Edward Borein	Stanton MacDon.-Wright	Frederick S. Wight
Carl Oscar Borg	Michael Maglich	William T. Wiley
Jack Boynton	Xavier Martinez	Jim Youngerman
Alburtus Browere	Arthur F. Mathews	Connie Zehr
Joan Brown	Francis McComas	Marguerite T. Zorach
John Buck	Richard McLean	William Zorach
Conrad Buff II	Michael McMillen	James Milford Zornes
David Bungay	Alfred Jacob Miller	
Elbridge Ayer Burbank	Thomas Moran	
Deborah Butterfield	Charles Christian Nahl	
George Catlin	Ernest Narjot	
Norman S. Chamberlain	Don Nice	
Elanor Colburn	Georgia O'Keeffe	
Robert Colescott	Maxine Olson	
Eanger Irving Couse	Tom Palmore	
Andrew Dasburg	Edgar A. Payne	
Edwin Deakin	Charles Rollo Peters	
Roy De Forest	Bert Geer Phillips	
Richard Diebenkorn	Henry Cheever Pratt	
L. Maynard Dixon	Arthur Putnam	
W. Herbert Dunton	Joseph Raffarl	
Max Ernst	Wm. Tyler Ranney	
Henry F. Farny	Henry Raschen	
Nicolai Fechin	Frederic Remington	
Lorser Feitelson	Sam Richardson	
Joseph Fleck	Julian Rix	
Victor C. Forsythe	Warren E. Rollins	
Llyn Foulkes	Julius C. Rolshoven	
James Earle Fraser	Edward Ruscha	
John Marshall Gamble	Charles Marion Russell	
Leon Gaspard	Peter Saul	
Arshile Gorky	Olaf C. Seltzer	
Adolph Gottleib	Joseph Henry Sharp	
William Hahn	Joshua Shaw	
Marsden Hartley	Millard Sheets	
E. Martin Hennings	John Sloan	
Robert Henri	Hassel Smith	
George Herms	Otto Sommer	
Victor Higgins	James Everett Stuart	
Thomas Hill	James Surls	
Ransom G. Holdredge	Jimmy Swinnerton	
Grace Carp. Hudson	Jules Tavernier	

<u>ARTISTS OF THE CANYONS AND CAMINOS-SANTA FE, THE EARLY YEARS</u> by Edna Robertson & Sarah Nestor

Kenneth Adams
Frank Applegate
Mary Austin

B
Jozef Bakos
Teresa Bakos
Henry C. Balink
Charles Barrows
Gustave Baumann
Jane Baumann
Donald Beauregard
Harry Behn
Yolanda Belloli
George Bellows
Oscar F. Berninghaus
Betty Binkley
Emil Bistram
George W. Blodgett
E. Boyd
Ernest L. Blumenschein
Wesley Bradfield
H. Paul Burlin
Witter Bynner

C
Edgar S. Cameron
Lorraine Carr
Mary Cassatt
Gerald Cassidy
Ida Sizer Cassidy
Kenneth Chapman
Howard Coluzzi
May Connell
Aaron Copeland
E. Irving Couse
Russell Cowles
Catherine C. Critcher
Louise Crow
Fayette Curtis
Natalie Curtis

D
Alfred Dasburg
Andrew Dasburg
Ida Dasburg
Randall Davey
Arthur B. Davies
Elizabeth DeHuff
Claire Dieman
Allison S. Dodge
John Dorman
Katherine Dudley
Dorothy Dunn
W. Herbert Dunton
Frank Duvenek

E
Fremont F. Ellis
O. S. Emblem
Louis Ewing

F
Arthur Davidson Ficke
Reginald Fisher
Robert Frost

G
Ed Garman
William Glackens

H
Marsden Hartley
Bert Harwood
Calla Hay
E. Martin Hennings
Alice Corbin Henderson
William P. Henderson
Robert Henri
Edgar I. Hewett
Victor Higgins
Edward Hopper
Russell Vernon Hunter
Peter Hurd

J
E. Dana Johnson
Raymond Jonson

K
Dorothy Kent
Alice Klauber
Ernest Knee
Leon Kroll
Yasua Kunioshi

L
Jean Baptiste Lamy
Paul Lantz
Ernest Lawson
Vachel Lindsey
Mabel Dodge Luhan
George Luks
William Lumpkins

M
Henry McBride
Sara Parsons Mack
Maria Martinez
John Gaw Meem
Willard L. Metcalf
Gladys Milligan
Fred Monhoff
Peter Moran
Alfred Morang
James Morris
Walter Mruk
Arthur F. Musgrave
Alice Clark Myers
Evaline Myers
Datus Myers
Ralph Myers

N
Willard Nash

Helen Needham
Guyrah Newkirk
B. J. O. Nordfeldt
Jesse Nusbaum

O
Georgia O'Keeffe

P
Sheldon Parsons
Howard A. Patterson
Bert G. Phillips
Maurice B. Prendergast

R
Grace Ravelin
Charles S. Rawles
Lynn Riggs
Eliseo Rodriguez
Warren Rollins
Julius Rolshoven
Doris Rosenthal
Alice Oliver Rossin
Alfonso Roybal
Olive Rush

S
Carl Sandburg
John S. Sargent
Frank Sauerwein
Cartaino Scarpitta
Albert H. Schmidt
Cyril Kay Scott
Joseph Henry Sharp
Eugenie Shonnard
Will Shuster
John Sloan
Eva Springer
George Stanley
G. C. Stanson
Myrtle Stedman
Maurice Sterne
Beulah Stevenson
Dorothy Stewart
Beulah Sutherland

T
Chuzo Tamotzu
Edmund Tarbel

U
Walter Ufer

Theodore Van Soelen
Mary R. Van Stone
Norma Van Swearington
Carlos Vierra

W
Cady Wells
Harold West
James A. M. Whistler
Amelia Eliz. White
Martha White
Brooks Willis
Etna Wiswall
Wilbur Wiswall

FIFTY GREAT WESTERN ILLUSTRATORS By JEFF DYKES	THE WOMAN ARTIST IN THE AMERICAN WEST 1860-1960 by PHIL KOVINICK Muckenthaler Cult. Ctr.	SEVENTH ANNUAL EXHIBITION, COWBOY ARTISTS OF AMERICA -1972
Joe Beeler	Mary E. Michael Achey	Joe Beeler
Lorence F. Bjorklund	Helen Hoff Aupperle	James Boren
Ernest L. Blumenschein	Eliza Rosanna Barchus	John Clymer
Edward Borein	Harriet Foster Beecher	Darol Dickinson
Harold Dow Bugbee	Zoe Ida Beiler	Charlie Dye
Jose Cisneros	Dorothy E. Betts	Nick Eggenhofer
Will Crawford	Grace May Betts	Fred Fellows
Harold James Cue	Eliz. Keefer Boatright	Nicholas Firfires
Edwin Willard Demming	Mary Anita Bonner	John Hampton
Joe De Yong	Helen Tanner Brod	Fred Harman
L. Maynard Dixon	Ada Bertha Caldwell	Harry Jackson
E. N. DufaultWill James	Helen Henderson Chain	Ned Jacob
Harvey Thomas Dunn	Sally Harfield Clark	Harvey Johnson
W. Herbert Buck Dunton	Mary R. Ferrel Colton	John Kittelson
Nick Eggenhofer	Catherine C. Critcher	Robert Lougheed
Clarence A. Ellsworth	Cornelia Cassidy Davis	Brownell McGrew
Rbt. Farrington Elwell	Cornelia de Gavere	George Marks
Anton Otto Fischer	Jessie Benton Evans	William Moyers
Thomas Fogarty	Eva Scott Fenges	Frank Polk
Philip Goodwin	Mary Hallock Foote	James Reynolds
Peter Hurd	Helen Katherine Forbes	Tom Ryan
D. C. Hutchison	E. Charlton Fortune	Robert Scriver
Frank Tenney Johnson	Const. Gordon-Cummings	Irvin Shope
Arthur Ignatus Keller	Norma Bassett Hall	Gordon Snidow
William H. D. Koerner	Edith Hamlin	Grant Speed
Tom Lea	Cyria Allen Henderson	J. N. Swanson
William R. Leigh	Abby R. Williams Hill	James Teague
Fernand H. Lungren	Marvina Hoffman	Melvin Warren
John N. Marchand	Grace Carpenter Hudson	Byron Wolfe
Ben Carlton Mead	Anna Hyatt Huntington	
Alfred Jacob Miller	Alice Glasier Kloss	
Carl Moon	Nell Augusta Knopf	
Joseph J. Jo Mora	Katherine W. Leighton	
Don Louis Perceval	Eliz. Davey Lochiel	
Frederic S. Remington	Matilda Lotz	
Clarence Rowe	Jane Robonson Mabry	
Charles Russell	Augusta I. C. Metcalfe	
Ross Santee	Maud Maple Miles	
Edward Buck Schiwetz	Mary DeNeale Morgan	
Frank E. Schoonover	Georgia T. O'Keeffe	
Charles Schreyvogel	Madeline Fish Park	
Elmer Boyd Smith	Agnes Pelton	
Herbert M. Stoops	Bertha Menzler Peyton	
Edward H. Suydam	Grace Ravlin	
John Wm. Thomason Jr.	Marjorie Reed	
George E. Varian	Imogene See	
Harold Von Schmidt	Nan Jane Sheets	
Stanley L. Wood	Lillian Wilhelm Smith	
Newell Convers Wyeth	Bettina Steinke	
Mahonri M. Young	Mary H. Teasdale	
Rufus F. Zogbaum	Olive F. Vandruff	
	Calthea Camp. Vivian	
	Marion Kav. Wachtel	
	Edith White	
	Muriel Sibell Wolle	

Gifford, R. Swain
Gifford, S. R.
Gignoux, Regis F.
Gilbert, Arthur Hill
Giles, Howard E.
Gillespie, Gregorie
Glackens, William J.
Gonzales, Xavier
Gorsline, Douglas
Grabach, John R.
Grain, Frederick
Gramatky, Hardie
Grant, Gordon
Granville-Smith, W.
Graves, Abbott
Gray, Henry P.
Gray, Mary
Greacen, Edmund
Greacen, Nan
Greatorex, Eliza
Green, Frank R.
Greene, Balcomb
Greene, Daniel E.
Greene, E. D. E.
Greenwood, Marion
Griffin, Walter
Griswold, C. C.
Groll, Albert L.
Gropper, William
Groshans, Werner
Grosz, George
Groth, John
Grover, Oliver D.
Guerin, John
Guerin, Jules
Gumpel, Hugh
Gute, Herbert
Gwathey, Robert

H

Haggin, Ben Ali
Hale, Lilian W.
Hale, Philip L.
Hall, Ann
Hall, Fred G.
Hall, George Henry
Hamilton, H.
Hamilton, W. R.
Hansen, Armin
Harding, Chester
Harding, George
Harmon, Lily
Harper, W. St John
Harris, J. T.
Harrison, Alex
Harrison, Birge
Hart, James M.
Hart, William
Harvey, George
Haseltine, W. S.

Hassam. Childe
Havens, James D
Hawthorn, C. W.
Hays, William Jacob
Hayes, William J.
Healey, Geo. P. A.
Hechenbleikner, Louis
Heintleman, A
Heitland, W. T.
Helck, Peter
Heller, Helen West
Henderson, J.
Hennessy, W. J.
Henri, Robert
Henry, Edward L.
Herter, Albert
Hibbard, Aldro T.
Hicks, Thomas
Higgens, Eugene
Hildebrandt, H.
Hill, John W.
Hill, Tom
Hills, Laura
Hirsch, Joseph
Hitchcock, George
Hoeber, Arthur
Hoffman, Henry
Hook, Walter
Hollerbach, Serge
Homer, Winslow
Hope, James
Hopkins, James R.
Hopkinson, Charles
Hoppin, Thomas F.
Hovenden, Thomas
Howe, William H.
Howland, Alf C.
Hows, John A.
Hoyle, Raphael
Hubbard, R. W.
Hubbell, Henry S.
Hudson, Eric
Huntington, Daniel
Huntley, Victor H.
Hurd, Peter
Hurley, E. T.
Hutchison, F. W.
Hyde, William H.

I

Ingham, Charles C.
Inman, Henry
Inman, J. O'Brien
Inness, George
Inness, George Jr.
Ipsen, Ernest L.
Irvine, Wilson
Irving, J. B.
Irwin, Benoni
Isenburger, Eric

Isham, Samuel

J

Jamison, Philip
Jelinek, Hans
Jewett, William
Jocelyn, N.
Johansen, John C.
Johnson, Avery
Johnson, David
Johnson, Eastman
Johnson, F. T.
Jones, Alfred
Jones, Carol Pyle
Jones, Francis C.
Jones, H. Bolton
Jongers, Alfred
Jonynas, Vytautask

K

Kaep, Louis J.
Kamihara, Ben
Kappel, Philip
Kappes, Alfred
Kautzky, T.
Kayn, Hilde
Keith, Dora W.
Keller, Henry
Kendall, Sergeant
Kensett, J. F.
Kent, Rockwell
Kepes, Gyorgy
Kester, Lenard
Keyes, Bernard
Keyser, Nicaise
King, Paul
Kinghan, Charles
Kingman, Dong
Kinney, Troy
Kinsler, E. Raymond
Kirk, Frank C.
Kirschenbaum, Jules
Klebe, Gene
Kline, William F.
Kloss, Gene
Knaths, Karl
Koch, John
Koerner, Henry
Kohn, Misch
Konrad, Adolf
Kosa, Emil Jr.
Kost, F. W.
Kroll, Leom
Kronberg, Louis
Kufferman, Lawrence
Kyle, Joseph

L

Laessig, Robert H.
LaFarge, John
Lambdin, James
Lamdin, G. C.

The National Academy of Design (NAD) is
the ultimate elective honorary society
for American artists. It is a direct
American counterpart to the British
Royal Academy. There are four degrees
of membership (in order of increasing
importance): Elects, Associates, Aca-
demicians, and Honoraries. Additionally,
membership is categorized as to artistic
speciality such as Painting, Watercolor,
Graphic Arts, Sculpture, and Architecture.
Membership is also devided as to Living
and Dead. All of these are shown on separate lists such as Painting, Associate,
Living. I combined all of the names from
the 1976 roster into a single list, but
eliminating the Sculptor and Architect
categories. My rationale was that if a
particuliar artist were listed, I could
later check into the type membership.

National Academy of Design

Abbey, Edwin A.
Adams, Joseph A.
Adams, Kenneth M.
Adams, Wayman
Agate, Alfred
Agate, Fred S.
Aiken, Charles
Albee, Grace
Albee, Percy
Albert, Ernest
Albright, Ivan
Albright, Malvin
Alexander, Francis
Alexander, J. W.
Allen, Charles C.
Allen, Junius
Allen, Thomas
Allston, Washington
Ames, Joseph
Anderson, Alex
Anderson, Harry
Anderson, Karl
Anshutz, .Thomas
Apt, Charles
Arms, J. T.
Aronson, David
Asplund, Tore
Audubon, J. J.
Audubon, J. W.
Audubon, V. G.
Auerbach-Levy, Wm.
Avery, Ralph

B

Bacher, Otto
Bacon, Peggy
Baer, William J.
Baker, George A.
Ballin, Hugo
Ballinger, Harry R.
Barnet, Will
Barse, G. R. Jr.
Bates, Kenneth
Baum, Walter E.
Baumgartner, W.
Beal, Gifford
Beal, Reynolds
Beard, James H.
Beard, Wm. H.
Beaux, Cecilia
Beck, Margit
Beckwith, J. C.
Belcher, Hilda
Bell, E. A.
Bellows, A. F.
Bellows, George W.
Bendiner, Alfred
Bennett, William J.
Benson, Frank W.
Benton, Thomas Hart

Berman, Eugene
Berneker, L. F.
Berninghaus, O. E.
Betts, Edward
Betts, Louis
Bicknell, F. A.
Bierstadt, Albert
Biggs, Walter
Birch, Thomas
Birney, Wm. V.
Bischoff, Elmer
Bishop, Isabel
Bittinger, Charles
Blakelock, R. A.
Blashfield, E. H.
Blauvelt, Chas. F.
Blondell, J. De.
Blum, Robert E.
Blume, Peter
Blumenschein, Ernest
Blumenschein, M. G.
Bogardus, Mrs. M.
Bogert, Geo. H.
Bogle, James
Bohm, Max
Bohrod, Aaron
Bolton, Wm. Jay
Bongart, Sergei
Borg, Carl Oscar
Borie, Adolphe
Bosa, Louis
Bosley, Fred A.
Boston, J. H.
Botts, Hugh
Bouche, Louis
Boughton, G. H.
Boutelle, De Witt C.
Bower, Alexander
Bowes, Betty M.
Boyd, Fiske
Brackman, Robert
Bradford, F. S.
Bradford, William
Brandegee, R. B.
Brandt, Carl L.
Brandt, Rexford
Breckenridge, H. H.
Bredin, R. Sloan
Breinin, Raymond
Brevoort, James R.
Bricher, Alf. T.
Bridges, Fidelia
Bridgman, F. A.
Brinley, D. P.
Bristol, John B.
Brockhurst, Gerald
Brook, Alexander
Brown, John A.
Brown, John Geo.

Brown, Roy
Browne, Belmore
Browne, Charles F.
Browne, George E.
Browne, Syd
Browning, Colleen
Bruce, Edward
Bruestle, George M.
Brush, Geo. DeF.
Brussel-Smith, Bern.
Bryant, Henry
Buehr, K. A.
Buller, Cecil
Bunce, William G.
Bunner, A. F.
Burchfield, Charles
Burroughs, B
Butler, George B.
Butler, H. R.
Bye, Ranulph DeB.

C

Cafferty, J. H.
Callahan, Kenneth
Carlsen, Cines
Carlsen, Emil
Carlson, John F.
Carpenter, F. B.
Carrigan, William L.
Carroll, John
Carter, Clarence
Caser, Ettore
Casilear, John W.
Castellon, Federico
Chadbourn, Alfred C.
Chamberlain, Samuel
Champney, J. W.
Chapin, Francis
Chapman, Charles S.
Chapman, C. T.
Chapman, J. G.
Chase, Adelaide C.
Chase, Harry
Chase, Wm. M.
Chavez, Edward
Cheffetz, Asa
Chen, Chi
Cheney, John
Cheney, S. W.
Chiara, Alan R.
Church, Fred E.
Church, F. S.
Ciampaglia, Carlo
Cikovsky, Nicolai
Clark, Eliot
Clark, Walter
Clarkson, Ralph
Clemens, Paul Lewis
Clinedinst, B. W.
Clooney, James C.

Clover, L. P. Jr.
Cobb, Ruth
Coes, Kent Day
Coffin, William A.
Cohen, Lewis
Coiner, Charles
Cole, Alphqeus P.
Cole, Thomas
Cole, Timothy
Coleman, C. C.
Colman, Samuel
Colyer, Vincent
Coman, C. B.
Connaway, Jay
Cook, Howard
Cook, Peter
Cooper, Colin C.
Cooper, Mario
Cornelius, Peter Von
Cornoyer, Paul
Cornwell, Dean
Costigan, John E.
Cotten, William
Coughlin, Jack
Couse, E. I.
Covey, Arthur S.
Cox, Allyn
Cox, Gardner
Cox, Kenyon
Cox, Louise
Coyle, James
Craig, Thomas B.
Cranch, C. P.
Cranch, John
Crane, Bruce
Crisp, Arthur
Cropsey, J. F.
Crowninshield, F
Csoka, Stephen
Cummings, T. A.
Cummings, T. S.
Cummings, Willard
Curran, Charles C.
Curry, John C.
Currie, Bruce
Curry, John S.
Cushing, H. G.

D

Dabo, Leon
Daguerre, Louis J. M.
Dahlberg, Edwin L.
Daingerfield, E
Dallas, Jacob A.
Dana, W. P. W.
Danforth, M. I.
Daniel, Lewis C.
Darley, F. O. C.
Davey, Randall
Davidson, George
Davis, Charles H.

Davis, Gladys R.
Day, J. Francis
Dearth, H. G.
Deas, Charles
DeForest, L.
DeHaas, M. F. H.
DeHaven, B. F.
Dehn, Adolph
Deines, E. Hubert
DeKnight, Avel
Delbros, Julius
De La Roche, Paul H.
DeLuce, Percival
DeMaine, Harry
DeMartini, Joseph
DePol, John
DeRose, A. L.
Derrick, William R.
Dessar, Louis P.
Detwiller, F. K.
Dewey, Charles M.
Dewing, T. W.
Dickinson, Edwin
Dickinson, Sidney
Dielman, Fred
Dike, Philip, L.
Dinnerstein, Harvey
Dix, Charles T.
Dobbs, Charles T.
Dobkins, Alexander
Dodd, Lamar
Dodge, John W.
Dodghty, Thomas
Dolph, J. H.
Domjan, Joseph
Dougherty, Paul
Drake, William H.
DuBois, Guy Pene
Dufner, Edward
Duggan, Peter P.
Dumond, Frank V.
Dunlap, William
Dunn, Harvey
Dunsmore, J. W.
Durand, Asher B.
Duveneck, Frank

E

Eakins, Thomas
Eames, John Heagan
Earle, L. C.
Eastlake, Charles L.
Eaton, Charles H.
Eby, Kerr
Edmonds, F. W.
Edwards, G. W.
Ehninger, J. W.
Eichenberg, Fritz
Elliott, Charles L.
Emmet, Lydia F.

Estes, Richard
Etnier, Stephen
Evergood, Philip
Evers, John

F

Fabri, Ralph
Fanshaw, S. R.
Farndon, Walter
Farnsworth, Jerry
Faulkner, Barry
Fawcett, Robert
Faxon, Wm. B.
Ferguson, H. A.
Fiene, Ernest
Fisher, Alanson
Fisher, Alvan
Fisher, Anna
Fiske, Gertrude
Fitch, John Lee
Fitzgerald, Edmund
Flagg, Charles M.
Flagg, George W.
Flagg, Jared
Flagg, Montague
Flock, Joseph
Florsheim, Richard
Folinsbee, John F.
Foote, Will H.
Fortess, Karl E.
Foster, Ben
Fowler, Frank
Franzen, August
Frasconi, Antonio
Frazier, Kenneth
Freeman, James E.
Freer, Fred W.
Frieseke, Fred K.
French, Frank
Fromkes, Maurice
Frothingham, James
Frothingham, S.
Fuller, George
Fuller, Henry B.
Fuller, Lucia F.

G

Gaertner, C. F.
Gahman, Floyd
Gannam, John
Gannet, Ruth
Garber, Daniel
Gasser, Henry
Gaugengigl, I. M.
Gaul, Gilbert
Gay, Edward
Genth, L. M.
Gervasi, Frank
Geyer, Harold C.
Gibson, George
Gibson, Chas. Dana

Gifford, R. Swain
Gifford, S. R.
Gignoux, Regis F.
Gilbert, Arthur Hill
Giles, Howard E.
Gillespie, Gregorie
Glackens, William J.
Gonzales, Xavier
Gorsline, Douglas
Grabach, John R.
Grain, Frederick
Gramatky, Hardie
Grant, Gordon
Granville-Smith, W.
Graves, Abbott
Gray, Henry P.
Gray, Mary
Greacen, Edmund
Greacen, Nan
Greatorex, Eliza
Green, Frank R.
Greene, Balcomb
Greene, Daniel E.
Greene, E. D. E.
Greenwood, Marion
Griffin, Walter
Griswold, C. C.
Groll, Albert L.
Gropper, William
Groshans, Werner
Grosz, George
Groth, John
Grover, Oliver D.
Guerin, John
Guerin, Jules
Gumpel, Hugh
Gute, Herbert
Gwathey, Robert

H

Haggin, Ben Ali
Hale, Lilian W.
Hale, Philip L.
Hall, Ann
Hall, Fred G.
Hall, George Henry
Hamilton, H.
Hamilton, W. R.
Hansen, ,Armin
Harding, Chester
Harding, George
Harmon, Lily
Harper, W. St John
Harris, J. T.
Harrison, Alex
Harrison, Birge
Hart, James M.
Hart, William
Harvey, George
Haseltine, W. S.

Hassam. Childe
Havens, James D
Hawthorn, C. W.
Hays, William Jacob
Hayes, William J.
Healey, Geo. P. A.
Hechenbleikner, Louis
Heintleman, A
Heitland, W. T.
Helck, Peter
Heller, Helen West
Henderson, J.
Hennessy, W. J.
Henri, Robert
Henry, Edward L.
Herter, Albert
Hibbard, Aldro T.
Hicks, Thomas
Higgens, Eugene
Hildebrandt, H.
Hill, John W.
Hill, Tom
Hills, Laura
Hirsch, Joseph
Hitchcock, George
Hoeber, Arthur
Hoffman, Henry
Hook, Walter
Hollerbach, Serge
Homer, Winslow
Hope, James
Hopkins, James R.
Hopkinson, Charles
Hoppin, Thomas F.
Hovenden, Thomas
Howe, William H.
Howland, Alf C.
Hows, John A.
Hoyle, Raphael
Hubbard, R. W.
Hubbell, Henry S.
Hudson, Eric
Huntington, Daniel
Huntley, Victor H.
Hurd, Peter
Hurley, E. T.
Hutchison, F. W.
Hyde, William H.

I

Ingham, Charles C.
Inman, Henry
Inman, J. O'Brien
Inness, George
Inness, George Jr.
Ipsen, Ernest L.
Irvine, Wilson
Irving, J. B.
Irwin, Benoni
Isenburger, Eric

Isham, Samuel

J

Jamison, Philip
Jelinek, Hans
Jewett, William
Jocelyn, N.
Johansen, John C.
Johnson, Avery
Johnson, David
Johnson, Eastman
Johnson, F. T.
Jones, Alfred
Jones, Carol Pyle
Jones, Francis C.
Jones, H. Bolton
Jongers, Alfred
Jonynas, Vytautask

K

Kaep, Louis J.
Kamihara, Ben
Kappel, Philip
Kappes, Alfred
Kautzky, T.
Kayn, Hilde
Keith, Dora W.
Keller, Henry
Kendall, Sergeant
Kensett, J. F.
Kent, Rockwell
Kepes, Gyorgy
Kester, Lenard
Keyes, Bernard
Keyser, Nicaise
King, Paul
Kinghan, Charles
Kingman, Dong
Kinney, Troy
Kinsler, E. Raymond
Kirk, Frank C.
Kirschenbaum, Jules
Klebe, Gene
Kline, William F.
Kloss, Gene
Knaths, Karl
Koch, John
Koerner, Henry
Kohn, Misch
Konrad, Adolf
Kosa, Emil Jr.
Kost, F. W.
Kroll, Leon
Kronberg, Louis
Kufferman, Lawrence
Kyle, Joseph

L

Laessig, Robert H.
LaFarge, John
Lambdin, James
Lamdin, G. C.

Story, Julian R.
Strisik, Paul
Strosahl, William
Stuart, Gilbert
Stuempfig, Walter
Sully, Jane
Sully, Thomas
Suydam, James A.
Swain, William
Symons, G. G.

T

Tait, Arthur
Talbot, Jesse
Tam, Reuben
Tanner, Henry O.
Tarbell, E. C.
Taylor, John
Taylor, Prentiss
Teague, Donald
Thayer, Abbott H.
Thompson, A. W.
Thompson, C. G.
Thompson, J.
Thompson, L. P.
Thompson, Thomas
Thon, William
Thorndike, G. Q.
Thorne, William
Tiffany, Louis C.
Tobey, Mark
Toney, Anthony
Tooker, George
Torrey, M. C.
Townsend, Ernest
Trebilcock, Paul
Turner, Charles Y.
Turner, Helen M.
Turner, Janette
Twibill, George W.
Tyler, G. W.
Tyson, Carroll S.

U

Ufer, Walter
Ulrich, Charles F.
Unwin, Nora S.

V

V. Boskerck, R. W.
Vanderlyn, J.
Van Elten, K.
Van Laer, A. T.
Van Soelen, Theo.
Vedder, Elihu
Ver Bryk, C.
Vernet, Emilie J.
Vickrey, Robert
Vincent, H. A.
Vinton, Fred P.
Volk, Douglas
Volkert, Edw. C.

Vollmering, Joseph
Von Neumann, Robert
Vonnoh, Robert W.

W

Waldo, S. L.
Walker, H. O.
Walker, Horatio
Wall, William G.
Wallcott, H. M.
Walleen, Hans Axel
Waltman, Harry F.
Wappers, E. C. Gus
Ward, Edgar M.
Ward, Lynd
Warner, Everett
Warren, A. W.
Warren, Ferdinand E.
Washburn, C.
Waters, Herbert
Watkins, Franklin
Watrous, H. W.
Watson, Stuart
Watt, William G.
Waugh, Fred J.
Waugh, Samuel B.
Webb, J. Louis
Webster, Larry
Weidenaar, Reyn. H.
Weinedel, Carl
Weir, J. Alden
Weir, John F.
Weir, Robert W.
Weldon, Charles D.
Wendt, William
Wengenroth, Stow
Wentworth, Murray
Wenzler, H. A.
Wescott, Paul
Wetherill, E. K. K.
Wheat, John Potter
Whitaker, Eileen M.
Whitaker, Frederic
White, Charles
White, Doris
White, Edwin
Whitehorne, James
Whitney, Edgar A.
Whittemore, Wm. J.
Whittredge, W.
Whorf, John
Wickey, Harry
Wickwire, Jere
Wiggins, Guy
Wiggins, J. C.
Wightman, Thomas
Wiles, Gladys
Wiles, Irving R.
Williams, F. B.
Williams, J. Scott

Williams, John A.
Williams, K. S.
Williamson, John
Wilmarth, L. E.
Wilson, D. W.
Wilson, Edward A.
Wilson, Jane
Wilson, Matthew
Wilson, Sol
Winkler, John W.
Winter, Andrew
Winter, Ezra
Witt, John
Woelfle, A. W.
Wolf, Henry
Wood, Robert E.
Wood, Thomas W.
Woodbury, C. H.
Wortman, Denys
Wotherspoon, W. W.
Wright, Catherine
Wright, Charles C.
Wright, George
Wust, Alexander
Wyant, Alex. H.
Wyeth, Andrew
Wyeth, Henriette
Wyeth, James
Wyeth, N. C.

Y

Yates, Cullen
Yewell, George H.
Young, Charles M.

Z

Zimmerman, Paul
Zornes, Milford

USA - MODERN

Although my primary interest has been in
the early California artists, I have oc-
casionally encountered modern art that
has stirred my soul. Not wanting to miss
valuable paintings, I wanted references in
my handbook that would give me a handle on
the emerging artists, and the modernists.

Therefore, in this section, you have a cut
of the '60s (a combined list of the 7 volume set of <u>Prize-Winning Painters</u>), a cut
of the '70s (a combined list of 3 volumes
of the <u>Artist-USA</u> series), and a cut of
the modern, in style, painters through inclusion of the index from Cummings' <u>A Dictionary of Contemporary American Art</u>.

AMERICAN WATERCOLOR SOCIETY—PAST MEMBERS
From 1966 roster

A

Agnes D. Abbott..................1881-1917
Edwin A. Abbey, N.A..........1877-1911
Margaret Adams 1944-1965
Wayman Adams, N.A. 1925-1959
Charles A. Aiken, A.N.A..........1938-1964
Ernest Albert 1918-1946
Adam Emory Albright.............1916-1960
Ivan Le Lorraine Albright..........1945-1960
Charles Curtis Allen, N.A..........1945-1950
Frank L. Allen....................1926-1966
Frank D. Allison 1934-1951
Abraham A. Anderson 1873-1942
Edward Anderson 1955-1962
Nicholas Angelo 1957-1961
A. V. S. Anthony..................1874-1907
A. Arinoff 1942-1951
William F. Armstrong...........1933-1936
Gladys Atwood 1930-1932
William J. Aylward.............1915-1956

B

LaForce Bailey 1936-1955
A. H. Baldwin....................1875-1895
Henry A. Bancel..................1937-1961
Marion D. Harris Barton..........1947-1960
Charles Basing 1917-1933
Rutledge Bate 1945-1960
Warren Baumgartner, N.A........1941-1963
Bertha Baxter 1922-1967
Gifford Beal, N.A................1910-1955
Reynolds Beal 1908-1951
Arthur Beaumont 1922-1963
J. Carroll Beckwith.............1882-1918
James Beckwith 1954-1960
Hilda Belcher, N.A..............1921-1963
A. F. Bellows, N.A..............1867-1893
Rainey Bennett 1955-1966
Frank W. Benson, N.A..........1927-1951
Sandor Bernath 1923-1945
Louis F. Berneker 1918-1937
Leonard Besser 1958-1966
E. M. Bicknell 1909-1932
Walter Biggs, N.A...............1939-1968
Sally Cross Bill 1942-1951
Emil J. Bistran..................1930-1932
Robert Blair 1944-1960
E. H. Blashfield, P.N.A..........1884-1936
Walton Blodgett 1931-1963
Robert Blum, N.A................1883-1903
E. L. Blumenschein, N.A..........1913-1944
D. Jeanne Boardman 1957-1960
Albert Bobbett 1874-1892
Theodore Bolton 1942-1946
George H. Boughton, N.A........1874-1905
Gertrude B. Bourne..............1922-1957
Minerva Brooks Bourne..........1946-1954
Harriette Bowdoin 1942-1946
Alexander Bower, N.A..........1946-1952
John Rutherford Boyd..........1933-1951
Carolyn G. Bradley.............1929-1954
Sophie M. Brannan..............1942-1957
Gladys Brannigan 1942-1944

Harold Breul 1944-1967
Anna Richard Brewster...........1942-1946
Alf. T. Bricher..................1873-1908
Fidelia Bridges, A.N.A. 1875-1923
James Brockway 1942-1949
Carl Broemel 1944-1946
Frank A. Brown..................1957-1960
J. G. Brown, N.A., P.A.W.S.......1867-1914
Gertrude G. Brown 1942-1958
Roy Brown, N.A., P.A.W.S.........1917-1956
Walter Brown 1867-1893
Syd Browne, A.N.A..............1939-1960
George Elmer Browne, N.A........1916-1946
Matilda Browne 1921-1942
Colleen Browning 1954-1959
Mary Bryant 1955
A. F. Bunner....................1881-1898
Charles Burchfield, N.A............1952-1966
Sydney R. Burleigh..............1916-1931
Gilbert Burling 1867-1892
Cameron Burnside 1945-1954

C

E. C. Cabot.....................1874-1902
Katherine Calvin 1942-1951
Vincent D. Campanella...........1939-1955
Edmund S. Campbell..............1942-1950
Pati Stiles Carlock..............1942-1946
John F. Carlson, N.A. 1916-1945
Caroline Carson 1867-1874
Clarence Carter, A.N.A............1957-1966
J. Wells Champney...............1873-1903
Francis Chapin, N.A..............1957-1964
Carleton T. Chapman, N.A........1880-1925
Harry Chase, A.N.A..............1884-1889
Sidney M. Chase.................1949-1958
William Chase, N.A...............1880-1916
Edward Christiana 1950-1960
John W. Chumley.................. 1966
F. S. Church, N.A................1875-1924
George M. Clark.................1883-1904
B. West Clinedinst, N.A..........1901-1931
LeRoy Clinker 1947-1961
Constance Cochrane 1939-1963
Robert H. Coen..................1945-1951
C. Myles Collier.................1908-1909
Samuel Colman, N.A., P.A.W.S.....1867-1920
Gordon W. Colton 1929-1955
Mary Russel F. Colton............1922-1962
Nicolas U. Comito................1952-1960
Lorraine Conant 1950-1959
Colin Campbell Cooper, N.A.......1904-1937
Edgar Corbridge 1944-1954
Betty Corter 1937-1938
Staats Cotsworth 1959-1967
E. Irving Couse, N.A.............1901-1936
Arthur Covey, N.A. 1945-1960
J. W. S. Cox....................1948-1967
William Craig 1867-1893
Christopher P. Cranch, N.A........1867-1892
Bruce Crane, N.A................1882-1937
Jasper F. Cropsey, N.A...........1867-1900
Leslie Crump 1942-1962

Stephen Csoka, N.A. 1959-1960
Charles C. Curran, N.A. 1894-1942
Bruce Currie .1959-1961
Eleanor Park Curtis. 1932-1960

D
F. O. C. Darley. 1868-1888
Liz Dauber 1948-1962
Carson S. Davenport. 1942-1946
Gladys Rockmore Davis, N.A. 1959-1960
M. G. DeBonnet 1940-1946
Mabel Mason deBra 1933-1946
Francis DeEderly 1954-1959
M. F. H. DeHaas. 1867-1895
Adolph Dehn, N.A. 1951-1968
Elena DeHellebranth 1963
Percival DeLuce 1877-1914
Harry DeMaine, A.N.A. 1923-1952
Robert E. Dodds 1967
Adelaide Deming 1939-1957
Thure De Thulstrup. 1883-1933
Frederick K. Detwiller, A.N.A. 1939-1953
Frederick Dielman, N.A. 1883-1935
Frederic Dondel 1867-1892
Walter Douglas 1913-1948
Mary F. Doux 1942-1945
W. H. Drake. 1890-1926
Paul Dubaniewicz 1955-1962
Edward Dufner, N.A. 1909-1948
Harold C. Dunbar. 1922-1942
Alan C. Dunn. 1942-1945
Alex G. Dunn 1867-1882
Harvey Dunn, N.A. 1950-1952
John Ward Dunsmore, A.N.A.,
  P.A.W.S. .1914-1945
Frederick F. Durand. 1867-1874
Hazard Durfee 1955-1960
James Dwyer 1942-1946

E
L. C. Earle, A.N.A. 1891-1921
Charles Harry Eaton, A.N.A. 1888-1901
Charles Warren Eaton. 1895-1939
J. O. Eaton, A.N.A. 1869-1875
Charles Ebert 1942-1962
Mary Roberts Ebert. 1921-1958
Ethel Edwards 1954-1960
George Wharton Edwards, N.A. 1886-1950
Eliz. Shippen Green Elliot. 1942-1946
Gladys Atwood Ennis 1937-1954
George Pearce Ennis, P.A.W.S. 1921-1936
K. Everett 1868-1872

F
J. M. Falconer. 1867-1903
Walter Farndon, N.A. 1922-1964
Henry Farrer 1867-1903
T. C. Farrer. 1867-1892
George Feldman 1942-1955-1957-1960
Harry Fenn .1867-1911
Edythe Ferris 1931-1954
Bob Fink 1940-1960
Anna Fisher 1921-1942
William Forsyth 1922-1942
Ben Foster, N.A. 1909-1926
Antonio Frasconi, A.N.A. 1958-1960

John A. Fraser. 1868-1898
Alfred Fredericks 1867-1907
Robert Freeman 1963
Fred W. Freer. 1883-1908
Robert Freiman 1956-1963

G
John Gannam, A.N.A. 1950-1964
Ramon Garcia 1949-1957
Robert David Gauley 1922-1943
Robert Geissman 1957-1961
Chas. D. Gibson, N.A., H.M. 1944-1962
W. Hamilton Gibson. 1886-1897
R. Swain Gifford. 1867-1905
Paul L. Gill. 1930-1940
Lorraine C. Gillette. 1960-1966
Raphael Gleitsmann 1955
Xavier Gonzalez, N.A. 1948-1960
John Goss .1926-1963
Frank Gosstyla 1957-1960
Robert A. Graham 1942-1948
David H. Granno 1957-1960
Gordon Grant, N.A. 1908-1962
Ralph W. Gray 1942-1945
Edmund Greacen, N.A. 1922-1949
Frank Russell Green 1892-1940
Barton B. Griffin. 1942-1950
Walter Griffin, N.A. 1919-1935
Lloyd C. Griscom. 1926-1960
Carrie C. Griswold, N.A. 1867-1918
Charles P. Gruppe 1910-1941
Joseph Guerin 1939-1954
Jules Guerin, N.A. 1900-1946
Frida Gugler 1942-1960
J. M. Guislain 1922-1944
Leland R. Gustavson. 1962-1966
Seymour J. Guy, N.A. 1867-1910

H
Grace E. Hackett 1942-1950
Gertrude Hadenfeldt 1942-1945
Mabel B. Hall 1942-1946
John Halpin 1867-1867
Hamilton Hamilton, N.A. 1883-1928
Ejnar Hansen 1955-1966
Lily Harmon 1957-1960
George-Pop-Hart 1921-1933
William Hart, N.A., P.A.W.S. 1867-1894
Childe W. Hassam, N.A. 1891-1935
Anna Hasselman 1936-1966
James D. Havens, A.N.A. 1957-1960
Charles W. Hawthorne, N.A. 1921-1930
C. C. Haynes. 1939-1953
Ethel C. Haythe. 1942-1950
Frank Hazell 1926-1957
Lucille Hobbie Heimrod 1957-1967
Michael Heiter 1951-1963
Z. Vanessa Helder 1947-1948
William J. Hennessy, N.A. 1875-1917
Edward L. Henry, N.A. 1888-1919
Harry Hering 1933-1967
Prudence C. Herrick. 1942-1948
Albert Herter, N.A. 1898-1950
Eugene Higgins, N.A. 1922-1957
James F. Hind. 1872-1903
Arnold Hoffman 1930-1966

Harry L. Hoffman, A.N.A............1919-1964
William Hofmann, Jr...............1959-1967
A. L. Hofmeister.................1954-1960
J. Lars Hoftrup.................1925-1954
Ruth Holberg 1942-1946
Marian Freeman Holland.........1960-1961
Winslow Homer 1877-1910
Hiroshi Honda 1965-1967
Edward Hooper 1867-1870
Charles Hopkinson, N.A. 1926-1960
Edward Hopper   1957
Winfield Hoskins 1944-1961
Harriet E. House................1955-1960
Thomas Hovenden 1882-1895
Kenneth G. How...............1926-1950
Lucile Howard 1942-1950
Ralph Hulet 1951-1960
James S. Hulme...............1942-1948
John Young Hunter.............1938-1955
L. C. Hunter 1942-1948
Lucy Hurry 1942-1950
Frank T. Hutchens.............1922-1939
Alfred Hutty 1926-1954

I

Ernest L. Ipsen, N.A.............1926-1946
Hildegard Iskraut 1956-1960

J

Leonebel Jacobs 1930-1967
Louis Jambor 1944-1954
Sandra James 1944-1961
Frank Tenney Johnson, N.A........1926-1939
Alfred Jones 1869-1900
H. Bolton Jones...............1883-1927
Francis C. Jones, N.A............1888-1932
Lena E. Jordan................1942-1951
I. A. Josephi.................1909-1936
Isaac Josephi 1921-1954
Oscar Julius 1922-1966
Victor Julius 1923-1950

K

C. S. Kaelin...................1922-1936
Jeannette Kann 1955-1962
Alfred Kappes 1881-1894
William J. Kaula...............1939-1954
Theodore Kautzky, N.A..........1939-1953
Hilde B. Kayn, A.N.A............1942-1950
George C. Keegan 1963-1965
Arthur L. Keller................1900-1925
Helen Keller, H.M. 1949-1968
Alfred Khouri 1961-1962
B. Cory Kilvert................1938-1946
Edward Klauck 1948-1960
Alonzo Klaw 1918-1942
William Fair Kline.............1920-1931
Bernard Klonis 1948-1957
Alvin Koehler 1942-1946
John R. Koopman..............1926-1951
Arthur M. Kraft...............1948-1955
Louis Kronberg, N.A. 1922-1960

L

John La Farge, N.A..............1868-1910
Eric A. Lakes..................1954-1958

F. M. Lamb....................1919-1942
Mary B. Lane..................1942-1946
Karl Larsson 1942-1948
Frank J. Lathrop...............1871-1909
William L. Lathrop, N.A..........1897-1938
Henri Laussucz 1937-1960
John Lear 1955-1962
Charles LeClair 1959-1967
Mong Q. Lee..................1957-1960
Thelma Lehmann 1955-1967
E. Leutze, N.A.................1867-1868
Martin Lewis 1926-1960
Arthur Lidov 1960-1967
Gaell Lindstrom 1958-1961
William J. Linton..............1868-1897
William H. Lippincott, N.A........1884-1920
Georg Lober, N.A., H.M..........1947-1961
Sanford Low 1942-1946
C. A. Luce....................1959-1963
Arthur Lumley 1867-1874

M

Clara T. MacChesney............1921-1929
Mary Nicholena MacCord 1921-1955
Norwood Norman MacGilvary......1918-1951
William Magrath 1868-1918
Thomas R. Manley..............1944-1946
Edith F. Marsden...............1942-1947
Basil E. Martin..................   1962
Maude M. Mason, A.N.A..........1922-1957
Harry Mathes 1960-1961
Sascha Maurer 1949-1960
Constart Mayer, A.N.A...........1867-1868
George W. Maynard, N.A..........1881-1923
Richard F. Maynard 1944-1961
George H. McCord..............1883-1909
David McCosh 1955-1966
S. G. McCutcheon..............1881-1892
M. J. McDonald 1873-1892
C. Morgan McIlhenny............1885-1904
E. Ormond McMullen 1939-1963
J. Jay McVicker................1948-1960
Roderick F. Mead...............1933-1941
Emma Mendenhall 1921-1964
Charles Mente 1889-1936
H. C. Merrill..................1944-1961
Willard L. Metcalf..............1894-1925
Herbert Meyer 1926-1932
John F. Meyer.................1942-1946
William O. Meyer...............1942-1945
Charles H. Miller, N.A...........1881-1922
Charles F. W. Mielatz............1908-1919
Francis D. Millet 1886-1912
Victor Millonzi 1944-1947
Bruce Mitchell 1960-1963
G. B. Mitchell 1930-1966
Kevin Monaghan 1954-1960
Charles H. Moore..............1867-1871
Philip Moose 1944-1960
F. Luis Mora, N.A...............1904-1940
Edward Moran 1872-1903
Leon Moran 1886-1939
E. Percy Moran................1886-1932
Thomas Moran, N.A..............1872-1926
Vesta Morehouse 1932-1966
Matt. Morgan 1875-1893
James Henry Moser..............1900-1914

Frank H. Moser.................1949-1957
Alphonse M. Mucha.............1909-1939
Henry Muhrman................1874-1918
Helen Chance Muller............1937-1964
Dora L. Murdock................1922-1932
J. Francis Murphy, N.A..........1881-1921
Nellie Littlehale Murphy.........1938-1946
E. Murray.....................1867-1868
Stowe C. Myers................1936-1961
M. Myerson...................1944-1946

N

Charles Austin Needham.........1908-1925
Antonio Nell..................1942-1961
Donald Nester......................1954
G. Glenn Newell, N.A...........1908-1947
Hugh Newell...................1880-1916
H. R. Newman.................1867-1873
J. C. Nicoll, N.A., P.A.W.S........1867-1918
Hobart Nichols, P.N.A., H.M.,
    P.A.W.S....................1925-1962
Spencer Baird Nichols, N.A.......1922-1950
Rhoda Holmes Nicholls..........1922-1930
Robert Nisbet, N.A.............1942-1961
E. Parker Nordell...............1926-1958
Margaret F. Norris..............1939-1957
Irving Nurick..................1959-1963
Leonard Ochtman, N.A...........1892-1934
Mina Fonda Ochtman...........1921-1926
Ivan Olinsky, N.A..............1944-1961
Henry Olsen...................1932-1962
J. Olaf Olson..................1921-1950
William Church Osborne, H.M......1944-1953
John O'Shea...................1922-1941

P

Josephine Paddock.............1946-1963
Allen I. Palmer................1942-1950
Walter L. Palmer, N.A...........1891-1932
Phil Paradise, A.N.A............1955-1960
James Wingate Parr.............1949-1960
Clara Weaver Parrish............1921-1925
Charles Parsons, A.N.A..........1872-1910
Arthur Parton, N.A.............1883-1914
Charles Robert Patterson........1922-1958
Henry S. Patterson.............1939-1959
Helen L. Peabody...............1942-1948
Clara Elsene Peck..............1931-1967
James E. Peck.................1948-1960
Edward Penfield...............1907-1927
A. Sheldon Pennoyer...........1942-1957
Charles H. Pepper.............1942-1950
Granville Perkins..............1877-1896
Harley Perkins................1942-1944
E. Wood Perry, N.A............1877-1915
Raymond Perry................1922-1946
Martin Petersen...............1942-1947
A. Conway Peyton.............1919-1932
Bertha Menzler Peyton..........1921-1947
Jane Peterson Philipp..........1921-1966
Gerry Pierce..................1957-1961
Donald Pierce.................1956-1962
Marion L. Pierce...............1942-1946
Althea Hill Platt..............1921-1932
Charles A. Platt...............1889-1933
Charles E. Pont...............1942-1946
W. Merritt Post, A.N.A..........1898-1935

Edward H. Potthast, N.A.........1900-1927
Arthur J. E. Powell, N.A.........1937-1954
Ivan P. Pranishnikoff...........1878-1912
Gregorio Prestopino............1959-1960
A. Phimister Proctor...........1896-1946
Edward A. Psolka..............1965-1967

Q

Larry Quackenbush, A.N.A.......1966-1967
Arthur Quartley, N.A............1881-1886
Noel Quinn...................1953-1961

R

H. W. Ranger, N.A.............1888-1916
Will Rannells.................1942-1946
Saul Raskin..................1925-1966
Seward Hume Rathbun..........1937-1966
A. Sherman Raveson...............1964
A. L. Rawson.................1867-1867
George Recca.................1942-1960
McIvor Reddie................1964-1967
Edward A. Reep...............1954-1966
F. K. M. Rehn, N.A............1891-1914
Charles S. Reinhart, A.N.A.......1877-1896
Winold Reiss.................1944-1954
Paul Remmy..................1955-1957
Henry Reuterdahl..............1909-1912
M. R. Rhoades................1962-1967
W. T. Richards, N.A............1874-1905
Charles H. Richert.............1942-1947
Victor W. Ritchie..............1959-1966
William Ritschel, N.A...........1909-1949
Ilse Ritter...................1959-1962
Morton Roberts, A.N.A..........1951-1963
Lucille H. Roberts.............1951-1952
H. W. Robbins, N.A............1873-1904
Alex Charles Robinson..........1908-1941
Florence Robinson.............1921-1937
Theodore Robinson............1891-1897
Will S. Robinson, N.A., P.A.W.S....1898-1945
Jay Roland...................1945-1960
Ogden N. Rood................1867-1877
Ernest Roth, N.A..............1919-1960
Peter Rotier..................1937-1963
Chauncey Ryder, N.A...........1912-1949

S

Dorothy Salisbury..............1936-1960
Birger Sandzen................1939-1954
Charles Nicholas Sarka..........1928-1963
N. Sarony....................1867-1871
Charles Nicolas Sarua, L.M.........1960
Walter Satterlee...............1873-1908
Wells M. Sawyer...............1942-1960
Herbert Scheffel..............1951-1962
Alice Schile..................1921-1960
Alexander Schilling............1894-1939
Albert Felix Schmit............1907-1950
Arthur Schneider..............1907-1942
Theophile Schneider.....1942-1955, 1958-1960
W. G. Schneider...............1904-1917
Zoltan Sepeshy, N.A...........1957-1966
Grant M. Simon...............1947-1960
Barbara Simons...............1953-1960
Jas. D. Smillie, N.A., P.A.W.S......1867-1909

W. Granville-Smith 1900-1938
Jacob Getlar Smith.............1939-1958
Minna Walker Smith.............1942-1959
Syd Solomon   1963
W. E. Spader...................1925-1954
Leontine G. Spencer............1936-1965
William McK. Spierer...........1947-1965
Lee Splivalo 1957-1963
Caroline Stern 1936-1967
Arno Sternglass 1952-1960
W. Lester Stevens, N.A. 1955-1961
Robert Sutton   1963
William Swanberg 1954-1960
Valerie Swenson 1950-1964

T
Anthony Thieme 1930-1954
Louis C. Tiffany, N.A...........1866-1933
Armand Trivilini 1954-1964
Edward L. Turner 1952-1960
Winthrop Turney 1949-1957

V
Alex. T. Van Laer, N.A., P.A.W.S....1880-1920
Oscar Van Young................1954-1960
James Villani 1939-1967
Patricia A. Villemain 1947-1955

W
Anne A. Waldron...............1934-1954
Everett Warner 1912-1963
Ferdinand Warren, N.A. 1944-1960
Kenneth Washburn 1944-1960
Jay Weaver 1942-1960
Walter L. White 1939-1963
Helen S. Whittemore...........1939-1954
William J. Whittemore, A.N.A......1891-1955
John Whorf, N.A................1948-1959
Max Wieczorek 1939-1958
Lawrence Nelson Wilbur 1942-1960
Frank N. Wilcox................1956-1964
Roy E. Wilhelm................1948-1954
John Alonzo Williams, N.A........1888-1951
Peggy Dodds Williams...........1942-1960
Andrew Winter, N.A.............1939-1958
Elizabeth Withington 1942-1962
Milton L. Wolsky...............1948-1962
Thomas W. Wood, N.A., P.A.W.S...1868-1903

Y
Mahonri Young, N.A.............1942-1957

Z
George A. Zabriskie, H.M.........1944-1951

AWS— ACTIVE MEMBERS   1966

A

Agnes A. Abbot
Ben Abril
Perry Acker
Telka Ackley
Helen Douglas Alexander
Cathy Altvater
Harry Anderson
John M. Angelini
Joseph Arcier
Winifred Lefferts Arms
Howard Arnold
Tore Asplund
Irene Aunio
Philip Austin
Ralph Avery
Gordon Aymar

B

Standish Backus, Jr.
Merrill A. Bailey
H. R. Ballinger
Arthur J. Barbour
Sara Bard
Robert Barrett
A. Charles Barton
Loren Barton
C. C. Beall
Francis H. Beaugureau
Antimo Beneduce
Frank C. Bensing
Harriet Berenson
Sylvia Bernstein
Dante Bertoni
Donald Bester
Edward Betts
Carroll Bill (L.M.)
John I. Bindrum
Morris Blackburn
Warren C. Blackwell
Lee E. Blair
Preston Blair
Arnold Blanch (H.M.)
Carolyn Blish
Robert W. Bode
Bogomir Bogdanovic
Harry Bonath
Sergei Bongart
Yetta Bornstein
Jack Bookbinder
Jessie Arms Botke
Betty Miller Bowes
Robert Brackman
Constance C. Bradshaw
Glenn R. Bradshaw
Joan Irving Brandt
Rex Brandt
Paul Bransom
Frederic S. Briggs
Walter Brightwell
Wallace E. Brodeur
Carl Broemel (L.M.)

Alden Bryan
Mary Bryan
Richard Brzozowski
Emily Goldsmith Buck
Rudolf Bundas
Arnold Burchess
Lola Burns
Ranulph Bye

C

Harrison Cady
Elizabeth Callan
Edmund J. Canelli
Victor Capellupo
James Carlin
S. Ohrvel Carlson
Jae Carmichael
James Carr
B. Shirley Carter
Betty M. Carter
Jess Dan Cauthorn
Ada Rasario Cecere
Robert Censoni
Montague Charman
David M. Checkley
Chen Chi
Alan R. Chiara
Betty Christensen
John W. Chumley
Caesar A. Cirigliano
Eliot Clark (H.P.)
Rene Clarke
Shirley Clement
Ruth Cobb
Kent Day Coes
Hy Cohen (L.M.)
Loring Coleman
Charles Colombo
Robert Conlan
Howard Connolly
Mildred D. Conte
Mario Cooper
John E. Costigan
Robert C. Craig (L.M.)
Alfred D. Crimi
Arthur Crisp (L.M.)
Dick Crocker
Roger L. Crossgrove
Dorothy W. Crumb
B. L. Cuming (L.M.)

D

Edwin L. Dahlberg
Robert Daley
Priscilla Dalmas
George C. Dangman
Allan A. Davidson
Robert P. Davis
Charles De Feo
Didi Deglin
Avel De Knight
Julius Delbos (L.M.)

Maxwell Desser
John E. DeTore
Phil Dike
Sallie B. Dillard
Stevan Dohanos
Felicie Howell Downs
J. Everett Draper
Arthur A. Drummond
Cal Dunn

E

William H. Earle
Ben Eisenstadt
Paula Eliasoph
Richard Ely

F

Ralph Fabri
James Fallier
Paul Feinman
Hilda Feldman
Mac S. Fisher
Edmond J. FitzGerald
Raymond Fitzgerald, Jr.
Serene Flax
Sir Wm. Russell Flint (H.M.)
Jade Fon
Ruth Van Sickle Ford
Greta Frank
Ruth E. Frost

G

William Gale
John Gallucci
Martin Gambee
Marjorie S. Garfield
Stuart G. Garrett
Jack Garver
Henry Gasser
Robert M. Gatrell
Robert F. Gault
Alice H. Geary
Marjorie Gehner
Edith R. Geiger
Lucile R. Geiser
Frank Gervasi
Ann Gibb
George Gibson
Frederick Gill
Henry S. Gillette
Ellinor Gilly
Morris Gluckman
Albert Gold
Fay Gold
Lawrence Goldsmith
Minerva Walker Goldsmith
Joseph W. Golinkin
Robert E. Goodier
Gilberta D. Goodwin
Douglas Gorsline
Gerald Grace

Angelo John Grado
Hardie Gramatky
Carol Grant
Douglas Grant
Ed. Graves
N. Beveridge Gray
Irwin Greenberg
F. Douglas Greenbowe
Daniel Greene
Irwin Greenwood
Harold Gretzner
Sherman A. Groenke
Emily P. Groom
Earl Gross
John Groth
Ron S. Gulick
Hugh Gumpel
Herbert J. Gute
Frank Guttridge

H

Clem Hall
Robert T. Handville
William A. Hanley
Louise B. Hansen
Howard Hardy
Marian D. Harris
Emily Harte
Vincent A. Hartgen
James Haughey
Charles Hawes
Robert T. Hayes
Arthur K. D. Healy
Donald M. Hedin
W. Emerton Heitland
Peter Helck
Vanessa Helder
Dale Hennesy
E. Adele Hepbron
Christine Herter
Tom Hill
Henry Hintermeister, Jr.
Claus Hoie
Serge Hollerbach
H. E. Holly
Samuel E. Homsey
Stephen E. Horvath
John S. Howell
Ardis Hughes
Ralph Hulett
Marie A. Hull
Nicholas Hupalo
Peter Hurd
Miriam Story Hurford
Jean Hutchinson

I

James Drake Iams
Salvatore Indiviglia
Victor Ing
Shinji Ishikawa

J

Lee Jackson
Leslie Jackson (L.M.)

Frederic James
Philip Jamison
Elsie Ject-key
Rixford Jennings
Lawrence N. Jensen
Paul Jepsen
William Jewell
Marion Jochimsen
Avery Johnson
Cecile Johnson
Homer W. Johnson
Amy Jones
Muriel B. Judd

K

Louis J. Kaep
Robert E. Kaiser
Samuel Kamen
Janet R. Kellogg
Richard Kelsey
Norman Kent
Norman Kenyon
Lenard Kester
Atushi Kikuchi
King B. King
Charles R. Kinghan
Dong Kingman
E. Raymond Kinstler
Gene Klebe
Arnold W. Knauth
A. H. Knighton-Hammond (L.M.)
Ruth Kobler
Mina Kocherthaler
Alexander Kortner
Emil J. Kosa, Jr.
Ann Kovach
Florian G. Kraner
Frederick P. Krause
Morrie Kuramoto

L

Robert H. Laessig
Waihang Lai
B. F. Larsen (L.M.)
Sal La Susa
John Lavalle
Robert Lavin
Fred Leach
Ruth Lee
Hilton Leech
Marilyn Lehmann
Harry Leith-Ross
Samuel Leitman
Jack A. Leonard
Irving Levinson
James Lewicki
Cyril A. Lewis
Manes Lichtenberg
Arne Lindmark
James W. Link
Mary Litt
Luis Llorente
Maurice Logan
W. R. Lohse
Charles E. Luffman
Lawrence Lustig

Dan Lutz
John F. Lynch

M

Glenn MacNutt
John Manship
Joseph Margulies
Louise E. Marianetti
Judy Marken
Fred B. Marshall
May Marshall
Antonio P. Martino
Giovanni Martino
Milton R. Marx
Roy Mason
Greta Matson
Sadie Mattson
E. Ingersoll Maurice
Tran Mawicke
John R. Maxwell
Robert H. Meltzer
John Menihan
Fred Messersmith
Dale Meyers
Noel G. Miles
Barse Miller
Gerhard Miller
Carl N. Molno
Eileen Monaghan
Claude Montgomery
Paul Montgomery
Marc Moon
Robert Eric Moore
Fritzie Morrison
Malcolm L. Murley
Darwin Musselman

Mc

Charles P. McCartney
John W. McCoy
Charles R. McCurry
Dorothy McEntec
John McIver

N

Irving Nachtigal
Edith E. Nagler
Leif Neandross
George Laurence Nelson
Joseph Newman
Tom Nicholas
Edmund E. Niemann
A. Henry Nordhausen
Crandall Norton
Vernon Nye

O

N. Eric Oback
Helen G. Oehler
Eliot O'Hara (L.M.)
Rudolph Ohrning
Tosca Olinsky
Jane Oliver
Olaf Oloffson
Herb Olsen

J. M. O'Malley
Edwin L. Oman
J. O'Melia
Zenowij Onyshkewych
Forrest W. Orr

P

Horace S. Page
Tseng-Ying Pang
Albert Parella
Douglass E. Parshall
Charles Patterson (L.M.)
Liang Peiling
Gerry Peirce
John C. Pellew
Rudolph Pen
C. Robt. Perrin
Carl W. Peters
Gordon Peters
Norton Peterson
John Pike
Henry C. Pitz
Ogden M. Pleissner
Robert Plumb
Alfred Easton Poor
J. Erwin Porter
Katherine P. Porter
George Post
Maurice Potter
Carol Dudley Prichett
Grace Huntley Pugh
Earl Purdy

R

Ethel Rabin
Paul Rahilly
Lois Rapp
H. Sherman Raveson
Nicholas Reale
J. George Recca
Renee Reddy
Lionel S. Reiss
Peter G. Reuter
Grant Reynard
Jerri Ricci
J. Phillip Richards
Walter D. Richards
Raymond Ridabock
Art Riley
A. Lassell Ripley
Marie MacDonnell Roberts
Ethel C. Robertson
Robert Roche
John Rogers
Mary Ronin
Alex Ross
Joseph Rossi
Michael Rossi
Rubi Roth
Norman Guthrie Rudolph
Elizabeth Ryan
Margery A. Ryerson
Rusell Rypsam

S

Saraga P. Saffer

Ruth Perkins Safford
Carl Folke Sahlin
Everett Sahrbeck
George Samerjan
Paul Sample
Joseph Santoro
Lily Saportas
Martha Sawyers
Betty-Lou Schlemm
Bruce Martin Scott
Peggy Scott
William Schimmel
Charles Schorre
Viktor Schreckengost
Lloyd Schulz
George Schuyler
Edwin Schwartz
Gertrude Schweitzer
Arthur Seiden
Alice Seipp
Rhoda Low Seoane
Carl Setterberg
Thomas Sgouros
Irving Shapiro
Millard Sheets
Arthur Shilstone
Paul Shively (L.M.)
Harriet H. Shoup
Pearl Shulver
Marion Simmons
Lawrence Sisson
Wong Siuling
Flora Smith
Howard P. Smith
Walter H. Smith
William Arthur Smith (H.P.)
Vita P. Solomon
Ben Solowey
Frank Soltesz
Paul Souza
D. Alanson Spencer
Enid Spidell
Mrs. Mac Squires
Walt Stan
Clayton Henry Staples
William Starkweather (L.M.)
Roslyn Starr
Harve Stein
Marjorie Stevens
Lionel Stevenson
Ruth Rolston Stevenson
Don Stone
Nell Storer
Edward R. Strawbridge
Paul Strisik
William Strosahl
Clara Stroud
Jean Stull
Harriet Sturtevant
Arthur Sudler
Gene Sullivan
Sandy Sutherland
Robert Swanson
Byron W. Sweet

T

Charles Taylor

Cyrene Taylor
Donald Teague
Allen Terrell
Ernest Thorne Thompson
Kenneth W. Thompson
William Thomson
William Thon
Ethel Hore Townsend
Margy Trauerman
Richard Treaster
Dagmar Haggstrom Tribble (H.M.)
George Tschamber
Earl Tyler
Mary Tyson

V

Anthony J. Vaikfnoras
Jack Vallee
Clara D. Van Benschoten
James Vance
Stuyvesant Van Veen
Carl W. Verburgt
Roger Vernam
Robert Vickrey
Margaret Van Pelt Vilass
Tom Vincent
Kathleen Voute

W

S. Peter Wagner (L.M.)
Jean L. Walker
Hans Axel Walleen (H.P.)
Albert T. Warsaw
Howard N. Watson
Eileen Vanderbilt Webb
Norman Webb
Larry Webster
Reynold Weidenaar
Lee Weiss
John Wenger
John Wenrich
Murray Wentworth
John Wheat
Frederic Whitaker (H.P.)
Doris White
Edgar Whitney
Lawrence Nelson Wilbur (L.M.)
Loran Wilford
J. Scott Williams (L.M.)
Merton Willmore
Florence Dunn Wilmer
Harriet B. Wilson
Lumen Martin Winter
Frederick Wong
Tyrus Wong
Robert E. Wood
Stanley W. Woodward (L.M.)
Howard L. Worner
Catharine Morris Wright
James Couper Wright
Andrew Wyeth

Y

Alex F. Yaworski
Elmer E. Young

Z

Nicola Ziroli
Milford Zornes

USA - AWS

For reasons unknown to me, the American
Watercolor Society has established its
own elective membership. (Perhaps because NAD was not nominating sufficient
watercolorists.) I have herein included
the Past and Active membership directly
from the 1966 roster. Most major city
libraries should have AWS roster data
available, should you desire further in-
formation.

PRIZE-WINNING PAINTERS 1960-1967

Compiled from a 7 volume series (yearly) by Margaret Harold called variously <u>Prize Winning Art</u>, <u>Prize Winning Paintings</u>, Award Winning Art, <u>Prize Winning Artists</u>, etc. (Tieing up all name combinations?) Volumes covered all major USA shows during the year. First Prize winners only. Number = Awards.

Dorothy Abbott	2	Marge Berchin		Edmund Brucker	
Keith Achepohl	2	Dorothy Bergamo		Mary Bryan	
John T. Acorn		Henrietta Berk	2	Glen Bryant	
Marjorie Adams		Anthony Berlant		Sidney Buchanan	
Robert Addison		Jerry D. Berneche		Marien Buchfink	
Donald Adkins		John Bernhardt		James A. Bumgardner	
Samuel M. Adler		Edna M. Berry		Frederick Bunce	
Dongkuk Ahn		Mae Bertoni	2	Helen Van Buren	
Fred Albert		Edward Betts		James Burke	
Robert D. Almquist		Watson Bidwell		Hans Burkhardt	
Herb Altman		Jack Bilander	4	Vincent Burns	
La Monte Anderson		George Bireline		Henry Bursztynowicz	
Robert Angeloch		Carl R. Blair		Larry D. Butcher	
Kero Antoyan		Susan E. Blair	2	**C**	
Garo Antreasian	3	Arnold Blanch		Maxine Roth Cable	
Charles Apt		Larry Blizard		James A. Cain	
Arly Arlon		Frances G. Bloch		Nancy R. Camden	
Gigi Aramesco		Rochelle Blumenfeld		John E. Carlson	3
T. D. Argyropoulos		Sandor Bodo		Matthew Carone	
Bill H. Armstrong		Amelia Bogert		Frank Cassara	
James D. Armstrong		Ronni Bogaev		Merrill Cason	
Bob Arneson	2	Mimi Bolton	2	Kay Cassill	
Russell W. Arnold		Sergei Bongart		Catchi	2
Walter Askin		Eliz. Calvin Bonner		Tom Cavanaugh	2
Mildred Tommy Atkin		Emery Bopp		Tony Cetone	
Barbara Aubin		Harry M. Borgman		Robert O. Chadeayne	
Roxie Hunt Aud		Yetta Bornstein		Walter H. Chapman	
Robert E. Ault		Leverett Boruszak		Berkley Chappell	
Anthony M. Autorino		Louis Bosa		Doris Chase	
B		Roy A. Bostrom		Edward Chavez	
Norman Baasch		Dean Bowman		Lee Chesney	
Jay Backstrand		Robert E. Boyer		Chen Chi	
Clark Bailey		Robert Brackman	2	Dale Chihuly	
Max Bailey		Don Bradley		Thomas Chimes	
David C. Baker	2	Thomas Brady		Tom Chouteau	
Keefe Baker		David Brann		Betty Christensen	
Walter Baldwin Jr.		George Breckner		Barbara Cisek	
John C. Balsey		Fred Brian		Minna Citron	
J. Bardin	4	Lamar Briggs		Jean Clad	
Will Barnet		Bill Bristow		Nancy Kissel Clark	
David Barr		Morris Broderson		Van Clemenson	2
Robert W. Bartlett	2	Robert Broderson		Ruth Cobb	
Edward Basker		Gerald E. Brommer		Bruce Cody	
William Bauer		Robert Broner		Marie Cole	
Eugene Bavinger	3	Harry Brorby		Max Cole	
Herbert Bayer		Nancy Hardin Brorby		Thomas Coleman	
George Beattie		Darrell Brothers		Warrington Colescott	2
Rosemary Browne Beck		Richard Brough	2	Janice Colker	
John J. Bednar		James Beown		John N. Colt	
Wayne Begley		Robert J. Brown		George Constant	2
Evelyn Behan Bell		William T. Brown		Francis P. Cook	
Ture Bengtz		Tom Martin Browne		William S. Cordiner	
Thelma Bennett		Edward M. Brownlee		Jack Coughlin	
Claude Bentley				Jerry Coulter	

Harrison Covington
Richard C. Cramer
E. B. Crocker 3
Robert Cronauer 2
Donald E. Crouch
Herbert P. Cummings
Charles Culver
Earl M. Cunningham 2
Bruce Currie
Samuel L. Curtis

D

Sylvester Damianos
Ignatus J. D'Aquila
Jerry A. Darnell
Jean Paul Darriau
Stefan Davidek
Ronald W. Davis
Stuart Davis
Horace Day
Avel DeKnight
Dante DeMars
Ron Dembosky 3
Gleb Derujinsky
Stephen DeStaebler
John E. DeTore
Orval Dillingham
Edward Dobson
Antonio P. Doctor
David F. Driesbach 2
Paul Arthur Dufour
Charlotte Dunwiddie 2
George Dureau
Joan Dyett

E

John Earnest
Loyce Easley
Charles Anthony Eck
Robert Ecker 2
Leonard Edmundson
Ethel Edwards
Laimons Eglitis
Ted Egri
Fred Eilers
James A. Eisentrager
Jacob Elshin
Paul England
Ruth Ensign
Marjorie Erbes
Helen M. Erickson
James Estley
Frank Ettenberg
Barbara Evans
Grete Holst Evans 2
Edgar Ewing

F

D. Horace Fahey
Gerald Fairclough
Horace L. Farlowe
Charles Faust
Marilyn O. Feighner

Baila Feldman
June Felter
Marie H. Ferneau 2
Clare Ferriter 2
Robert R. Fiedler
Lois Fine
Perle Fine
Max Finkelstein
Morton Fishman
Jack Foote
Wendell Fore Jr.
Charles Forrester
Robert Frame
William L. Freeman
Robert Freimark 3
Ernest Frombach
Shirley Fuerst
Fumiaki Fukita
Steven D. Fuller
Marjorie Furrer

G

George Gach
R. Galant
William Gale
Gustave Galian
Milton Gardener
Ada Garfinkel
Jack Garver
Jan Gary
Lee E. Gaskins
Henry Gasser
H. Irving Gates
T. Gay Jr.
Robert W. Galinas
George Gemanis
Raymond George
Helen Gerardia 2
James Gerwin
Hugh Gibbons
Robert Gibson
Sandra Jean Gierke
Dorothy Gillespie
Harald P. Glass
Larry Godwin
Richard Goetz
Rolland Golden
Leopoldo Gonzales Jr.
Gerald Gooch 2
Sherri Goodall
John Gordon
Richard Gorman
William D. Gorman 2
Marie Goth
Adam Grant
Carol M. Grant
Harold Greaver
George Grecco
Edward Green
Michael Green
Russel B. Green

Ryland W. Greene
Werner Groshans 2
Edward R. Grove
Aaronel DeR. Gruber 3
Leo Grucza
Gennaro Gullini
Frank Gunter
Lena Gurr
Sue Ferguson Gussow

H

Howard Hack 2
Vida B. Hackman
John R. Hadley
Judith Hahn 2
Richard Haines
Eleanor Van Haitsma
Theodore Halkin
Warren Hall
Phyl. Halperin-Bramson
William M. Halsey
Alfred E. Hammer
Raymond Han
Hisao Hanafusa
John Hannah
Judy Hanshu
William W. Harris
Forrest Harrisberger
Robert Harvey
Maury Haseltine
Harold Hasselschwert
Alvin Hatorf
Bits Hayden
Glen R. Heath
Richard Heidsiek
Anna Kolb Henry
Samuel Herman
Joan Dobbs Henry
Marvin T. Herard
Joanna Higgs
Bob Hill
Peter Hill
William J. Hixson
Joe Ferrel Hobbs
David Hodge
William Hoey
Edward F. Hoffman 2
Marvin Hoffman
Hollis Holbrook 2
Alice Holcomb
Tom Holland
Ruth Atkinson Holmes
Merle Holt
Mervin Honig
Peter Hooven
James F. Hopfensperger
Jack Hopkins
Floyd D. Hopper
Lawrence Hosmer
Barbara Housekeeper
Jim Houser 2

Dan Howard 2
Conroy Hudlow
Victor Huggins
Marie Hull
Robert D. Hunter
Robert Hurdelbrink
Sarah Hurt
Grace Hutchings

J

A. B. Jackson
Beatrice Jackson
Billy M. Jackson 2
Hazel Brill Jackson
Ralph Jacobs 3
Arthur Jacobson
Harriet Jacobus
Roland Jahn
Philip Jamison 2
May Janko
Etta Jansen
Ceslovas Janusas
Janet Jenkins
Paul Jenkins
Lawrence N. Jensen
Richard Jerianian
Cecile Ryden Johnson
Lester R. Johnson
Ralph M. Johnson
Marjorie D. Johnston
Carol Pyle Jones 2
Lynn R. Jones
James E. Judd 3

K

Susan Kahn
Ben Kamihira
Arthur L. Kanak 2
Morris Kaplan
Lucien Kapp
Chapman Kelley 2
Charles Kello
Judith Kelly
Viona Ann Kendall
W. Kendrick
Doris W. Kennedy
Robert F. Kennedy
Edna Kessler 3
David F. King
Thomas S. Kinsey
Maurice Kish
Earl Kittleson
M. J. Kitzman
Fred Kline 3
Karl Knaths 3
Tony Ko
Gerd Koch
John Koch 2
Ida Kohlmeyer 10
Edmond Kohn
George Kokines
Darell Koons 3

Chaim Koppelman
George Koras
William Kortlander 2
Richard Kozlow
Sigmund Kozlow
Stephen Kramar
LaVerne Krause
Phyllis Kresnoff
R. J. Kreznar
June Kroll
Leon Kroll
Adolph Kronengold
Naomi Kronengold
Jeffrey Kronsnoble
James K. Y. Kuo

L

Robert Laessig
Joyce King LaForce
Eleanor V. Lakin
Jeanne Lamphere-Beesley
Lillian Lamden
Donald Lanham
William Lasansky
John Laska
Gertrude Lathrop
Paul Lauritz
Pietro Lazzari
Fred Leach
Hilton Leech 2
Rita Leff 2
Gerson Leiber
Leo Leibsohn
Thomas C. Leighton 2
Blessing LeMohn
Arnold Leondar
Ruth Lerman
Dorothy Seain Lewis
Peter Liashkov
Manes Lichtenberg
Evan Lindquist
Janet Lippincott 2
Charles Littler 2
Frank Litto
K. C. Lochhead
Maurice Logan
Keith Long
Ralph Love
Marian Lucas
Jane S. Lyon
Gregory Lysun

MC

William C. MacArthur
James S, McBeth
Clifford T. McCarthy
Robert McChesney
Arthur Maclean
Joan McConnell
Betty McCoon 2
Robert A. McDonald
Jean McEwen

Jean W. McFarland
John W. McIror
Jack McLarty
Jim McLean
Paula McNamara
Raymond McNamara 3
Thomas McPeak
Wendell McPherson
Jean McWhorter

M

Robert Mack
Katy Madsen
Stephen Magada
Georgette Magner
Robert R. Malone
Ben Mahmoud 2
Gordon Mahy
Thal Maitland
Joseph Manning
Nancy Manning
Boris Margo
Herman Maril 3
Molly Marsh
Orr Marshall
Chester Martin
Homer Ray Martin
Antonio Martino 3
Robert E. Marx
Anne L. Maser
Greta Matson
Gene Matthews 2
John D. Maziarz
Dean Meeker
Leo Meissner
Edward Melcarth
Haim Mendelson
Michael Merlucci
Richard L. Merrick
Alan Miller
Dan Miller
Donald Richard Miller
Jane Else Miller
Peter Milton 2
Sue Mitchell
Don Moldroski
Guido Molinari 3
Betty Moncure
Donald Montano
Claude Montgomery
Marc Moon
Don Moore
Loraine Moore 2
Martha Moore 3
William Lee Moreland
George L. K. Morris
Fritzi Morrison 2
Hannah Moscon
Karla Moss
Edward Movitz

Amos H. Mumford
Freddy Munoz
Peter L. Myer 2

N

Jon Naberezny
Thomas Nawrocki
Sally Neberman
Leroy Neiman
Robert A. Nelson 3
Willis W. Nelson 2
Nancy Nemec
Alexander Nepote
Ben Newman
Tom Nicholas
Edward R. Nicholson
Emile Nizet
Haig Norundzaian

O

Howard D. Oagley
N. Eric Oback
Walter J. Obman
Thom O'Connor
Theodore Odza
Ramon E. Oeschgar
Rudolph Ohrning
William Oldaker
Gordon L. Olsen
Herb Olsen
Meridith Olson
J. O'Meilia
Ann Opgenorth
Elsie Orfuss
Janet Orr
Roy L. Owens

P

William Pachner
Guy Palazzola 3
Fred Pallini
David B. Parrish 2
Robert Partin
Ambrose Patterson
Josephine Paul
Ethel Parsons Paulin
Dennis Pearson
Judith Sobel Peck
Jeanne Pellegrino
Donna Perkins
Jack Perlmutter
Nell Perret
Samuel I. Peters
Daniel W. Petersen
Elmer P. Perersen
Roland C. Petersen
Blanche Phillips
Leon N. Phillips
Lorraine D. Pierson
Louise Pike
Walter Plate
Carolyn Plochmann
Linda Plotkin

Ann Carter Pollard
Michael PonceDeLeon 2
William A. Poppe
Charles W. Porter
George Post
Alfred J Pounders 2
William Prevetti
Marilyn Prior
Bill Prokopiof
Donald R. Purdy 2
Ronald Pusich

R

Norman Rabinowitz
Jack W. Ragland
Ted Ramsay
Robert D. Ray
Nicholas Reale
Jo Rebert
Doel Reed
Ann Reichner
Betti Richard
Anna Chuse Richardson
Gregory Ridley Jr.
Harry R. Rittenberg
Marie MacD. Roberts
Mary Ann Robertson
Michael Rocco 2
Mae Rockland
L. Jerome Roldan
Umberto Romano
Marjorie Von Rosenberg
Alan I. Rosiene
Dennis M. Rowan 2
Craig Rubadoux
Nick Ruggieri
Nell H. Russell
Felix Ruvolo

S

Betye Saar
Frank Sampson 3
Belle Sanford
Joseph L. Santoro
Angelo Savelli
Alice P. Schafer
H. Bella Schaeffer
Armin Scheler
Betty Lou Schlemm 2
Ivan Schlieferdecker
Berthold Schmutzhart
David Schnabel
Fritz Schoulder
Elmer Schooley
George Schwacha
Tony Scornavacca 2
Marjorie Scott
John Reid Scudder
Denys Seguin
Alvin Sella
Whitney Sevin
Donald R. Sexauer

Claude E. Seward
Shelby Shackelford
Ronald S. Shap
Vladami Shatalow 2
Maxine Shattuck 2
Elsie Shaw
Romer Shawhan
Sigmund Shawkey
Barclay Sheaks
Russ Shears
Joseph Sheppard
Clair Shoniker
Richard Shorten
Harry Shoulberg
Lily Shuff
Alex Siburny
Carol Sideman
Jean M. Sieben
Maxwell S. Simpson
Clyde Singer 2
Nikolas Skarlis
B. J. Smith
Dolph Smith
Douglas Campbell Smith
Ernest W. Smith
James E. Smith
Norbert Smith
Roger Smith
William A. Smith
William Robert Smith
Walter H. Snelgrove
E. Wesley Soderberg
Syd Solomon
Jack Sonenberg
Harris Sorrelle
James L. Stag
Julius Stanczak 2
Andrew Stasik
Raymond Statlander
Jane Stauffer
J. L. Steg
Marjorie Stevens
William Stilson 2
Done Stone
Elizabeth Stouder
John H. Stritch 3
Eugenia Summer
James B. Swetlick

T

Chester A. Tallant
Ruth Tears
Michael Tekirian
Anthony Terenzio
Joseph Testa-Secca
Thea Tewi
Valfred Thelin 3
Howard Thomas
William Radford Thomas
Gene Thompson
J. B. Thompson 2

William J. Thompson	Jean Woodham	
Arthur Thall 2	Jan Wunderman	
Walter Thrift 2	**Y**	
Harold Thurman	James Yarbrough	
Doris Santo Tourganeau	Fred Yost	
Harold Town	Diane A. Young	
Louis Trakis	Nat Youngblood	
Richard Treaster	**Z**	
Pat Trivigno	John M. Zeilman	
Robert Trotter	Richard C. Ziemann 2	
Harry Troughton	Daniel L. Ziembo	
Janet E. Turner	Rita Zimmerman	
Louis Tytell	Nicola V. Ziroli	
U		
E. E. Ulman		
V		
Richard Vandall		
Alfred Van Loen		
Stuyvesant Van Veen		
Henry Van Wolf		
Nina Ruth Vaughn		
E. J. Velardi Jr.		
Robert Vickers		
Romas Viesulas		
Alex Vilumsons		
Lenore E. Vogt		
W		
Robert S. Wade		
Gordon Wagner		
James A. Walker		
Lee Wallas		
Beverly R. Waltner		
Lyle E. Ward		
Lynd Ward		
Elsa Warner		
Betty Warren 2		
Peggy Watson		
Edna M. Way		
Larry Webster		
Reynold Weidenaar		
Leo Weiss 2		
Roger Welchans		
Dorothy Saxon Wenger		
John Wheat 2		
Charlotte Whinston		
Frederic Whitaker		
Bruce White		
Trude Wiesen		
Fred Wiesener		
Mary S. Williams		
William Wilson		
Richard Wilt		
Don Wink		
Arden Witherwax		
Mildred Wohl 2		
Helen Wolf		
Charles Wollowitz		
Frederick Wong		
Robert E. Wood 2		

#= number of volumes artist is listed in.

A

Albert C Albany
Alice Acheson
Perry Acker
Alma C. Adams 3
Carleton A. Adams
Lillie R. Adkins
Roy Ahlgren
Alta Alberga
Josef Albers 2
Julie D. Albert
Robert T. Alexander
Aljaman
Stephen S. Allwell
Joan B. Altabe 2
Gloria Altorfer 2
Catherine Altwater
Ruth Anaya
David P. Anderson 2
Lucia Anderson
Chappie Angulo
Dorothy Archer 2
Georgio Arciniega
Carl H. Arend 2
Jacob V. Arnautoff 2
Hilda Arp
William Artis 2
Mary Ascher 2
Pearl Ashford
Alice Asmar
Robert R. Auth 3
John Avakian
Rico Averso 2
Norio Azuma

B

Sudad J. Baban
Kathryn H. Bachmann 3
Florence J. Backstrom 3
Maria Bablio
Richard H. Bailey
Meta Bains
Grace Baker
Larry Bakke
Angeles Ballester
Emily J. Baran
Joseph M. Barber
Raymond Barger
Bebe Barkan
Faye Barnette 2
Carmelo S. Barone 3
Marguerite E. Barrow
Richard H. Bartlett 2
John A. Bartok 2

George Reed Barton
Barbara Ross Baumwell
Anne M. Beach 3
Art Beery 3
Giselia Beker
Richard R. Benda 2
Marilyn Bendell
Eugenio P. Benini 2
Harriet Bennett 2
Robert L. Benney
Bruce Benton
Lee R. Benz
Henry Berkowitz 2
Mariette Bevington
Marjorie E. Bevlin
A. Earle Bilcher 2
Jack E. Billet 2
Connie M. Bishop
Edward D. Bisone
Step. H. Bittenbender
Nell Blain
Carl R. Blair
Marjorie Blake
Joyce Carol Blakely 3
Fleurette Blameuser 3
Roy Blankenship 2
Lawrence E. Blazey
Joyce Block 3
Robert M. Bloeser
Carolyn M. Bloomer
Sara Metzner Boal
Sandor Bodo 2
Beverly Bogen 2
Joseph A. Bolinsky 3
Bill Bomar 2
Oriel E. Bond 2
Bette J. Bonde 2
Sergei Bongart
Eliz. V. Booraem 3
Sloan Borochoff 3
Gerry Bosch
Edythe H. Bossert
H. J. Bott
D. Boutin
Donald E. Boyd
Giac Bozzi
Margaret M. Brace
Warren E. Brandon 3
Rex Brandt
Albert H. Braun 2
Bettina Brendel 2
Beverly Brigandi
Michael J. Brodman

Minerva Broh 2
Albert L. Bross
James E. Brotherton 2
Al Brouillette
Bruce Brown 2
Huntley Brown 2
Robert V. Bruckshaw
Ruth T. Brunstetter
George R. Bucher
Harold R. Buckner
Bill Bufano
Miriam G. Burdsall
Joseph Buresch 2
Zdenka Buresch 2
Nicholas Burliuk
Daniel V. Burke
Robert Butterbaugh
E. Anderson Bynum
Elizabeth Byram 2
Mary Byrum 3

C

Robert F. Cage 2
Gloria Calamar 3
Alexander Calder 3
Faust Califano
Lydia Califano
Marilyn Califf
Mary E. Callahan
Jacque Joe Camins
Cosmo Campoli 2
Chas. Gregory Cannon
Vic Capellupo
Jerry L. Caplan
Anthony A. Cardosa 3
Robert J. Cariola
Donald Carmichael 2
M. Antonette Carollo
J. Gordan Carr 2
Richard Carter Clyde
Max Carter
Jeanne Cashin 2
Catchi
Ferdinando Caturani
William Caver
Allen S. Chase
Maxwell M. Chavat
Charlotte W. Chester 3
Theo M. Chunn
Arland Christ-Janer
Lewis Cisle
Biagio A. Civale
Stewart Clare 2
John DeWitt Clark

Richard Clive
Chuck Close
Robert R. Cobb 2
Bette Lee Coburn
Virginia Cocker 2
Sherna Cockrill
Morris Cohen
Maynard R. Coiner
Eleanor F. Colosi 2
Joseph Como
Ina W. Connaway 2
Dee M. Connett
Nancy Conrad
Dennis Consalvi
Charles B. Cooke
David Coolidge 2
Mark Coomer
Joanne B. Cooper
Wayne Cooper
Leslie Cope
Joseph R. Corish 2
Sophie Corwin
Robert Coty
Rae Coulter
Henry Coupe
Sue-Jean Covacevich
Abbe Rose Cox
Ruth R. Craig
Betty J. Craigie 2
Ruth Crawford
Mary E. Crenshaw
Luigi A. Crispino 2
C. Maria Cross
Robert A. Crossetti 2
Craig Crosson
Sharon M. Cullnan 2
M. Angelica Cummings

D

Walter N. Daby
Vincent J. D'Agostino
Oris Dahlen
Chuck A. Dailey 2
Mario DalFabbro
Virginia Dan
Danamark
Roxanne Daniel
Lawrence A. Darrow
Ted Davies
Bertha G. Davis
Jean de Botton 3
Patricia de Haan
Ada Deihi
Willem de Kooning 2
Tauni de Lesseps
Ralph Della-Volpe
Jack C. DeLoney
Helen C. Del Valle
Oscar De Mejo
Joanna de Nassau

Michael N. DeNike
Dorothy Dennison
Caryl Maria DePaoli
Teresa M. DeVito
Robert A. Dhaemers
Helen Dickey
Joseph P. di Gemma
Homer Diman 2
Jim Dine 2
Carolyn A. Dixon
Madeline N. Dixon 3
Marguerite Doernbach
Blanche Dombek
Lorraine J. Douglas
Arthur J. Dowling
Martha Downing
Brandi E. Downs
Clarence I. Dreisbach
Jeanet S. Dreskin
Margaret Webb Dreyer
Jack Drummand
Walter Dubrow
Rita Duis
Jeffery B. Dunn
Lucille M. Durand

E

Nathaniel S. East
Bret Eddy
Jeanne Ehinger
El Cartereto
Bruce R. Elliott
Kosso Eloul
Richard Ely
Betty L. Embrey
Lillian L. Emery 2
Paul G. England 2
Eugenia Eres
Susan K. Ericson
Degen Evans
Edward Evans
Niel Everest
Dick Eyres, Marie Eyres

F

Alexander Farnham 2
Raymond M. Farrell
Harriet FeBland
Terry A. Fecho
Marion Federe 2
Doris Feigl
Frederica H. Fields 2
Alfred Figures
Art File
Josefa Filkosky 2
Harriet Fitzgerald 3
Betty Flanagan
Robert M. Fletcher 2
Walter D. Folger
Mary V. Follett 2
Ruth VanS. Ford 3
Mary C. Fortinash

Inez G. Fourcard 3
Roy Fox 2
Sam Francis
Richard Frank
Helen Frankenthaler 2
Charlotte W. Franklin
Michael Frary
Roslyn Freeborn
Stanley Frey
Richard Freely
Marian L. Freeman
Stephen Fritsch
Sheldon Freund
Laetitia B. Frye 2
Ruth E. Frye
Esther Fuhrman
Ruth M. Fulton

G

Maureen Gallagher
Juanita L. Gammon 2
Eve Garrison 2
Walter R. Garver
Henry M. Gasser
Michael C. Gast
Eric Gay
A. C. Gentry
Warren Gentry
Geo
Boots George
Sylvia James George
Rose Anne Giannini
Louise Gibala 2
Flora B. Giffuni 2
Clyde L. Gilbert
Joan M. Giordano
Ralph V. Gironda
Ted Glover
Hopr Drury Goddard 2
Lawrence R. Godwin
Chaim Goldberg
Edith Dvorah Goldstein
Milton Goldstein
Grace M. Goodrich
Alice Reis Gordon
Mitchell S. Gordon
Ruth Gordon
Stephen Gould 2
Lorrie Goulet
Clem Gouveia
Paul Graban 3
Marlene Graeber-Peters
Dorothy Graham 2
Josephine Graham
Joe Ruiz Grandee
Edith Lorena Gray 3
Florence Graziano
Grebe(P. Grebe Rimmel)
Morris B. Green
Fern Greene 2
Marie Greene-Mercier 3

Michael L. Gressel	2	
Patricia D. Grey		
Cornelius Griffin		
Alice Gripman		
Alice Gross		
Irene Gross		
Lili Gross		
James R. F. Gross		
Dorothy R. Grotz		
Laurine V. Grover	3	
Shirley S. Gruen	3	
Ethel D. Guest		
Johannes S. Guidotti	3	
Ruth L. Guinzberg		
Ruth Gunshor		
Cynthia Guzevich		
Francis J. Gyra		

H

Cynthia R. Haack	3	
George Habergritz		
Gunillia Haglund		
Mildred Sherman Haight		
Violet H. Hain	2	
Frank M. Hamilton	2	
Thomas E. Hanlon		
Cliff Harmon		
Eleanor Harper		
Muriel Harris		
Lawrence V. Harrison		
Norman Henry Harrison		
Jay A. C. Hart		
Vincent A. Hartgen		
Jule F. Hartwick		
Burt Hasen		
Donold G. Hatfield	2	
Gene Hatfield		
James Hawkins	2	
Thomas W. Hawkins	3	
George Austin Hay	3	
Tua Hayes	2	
Zelda Hedden-Sellman	3	
Tincie Hughs Heddins		
Tom Heflin		
Philip Held		
Shirley Hendrick		
Alice C. Henderson		
Connie Sue Hendrix		
Marvin W. Hill	3	
Douglas P. Hinkle		
Theo Hios		
Sunao Hironaka		
Ellen S. Hirsch		
Charles N. Hitchens	3	
David K. Hockensmith		
R. Garey Hodge	2	
Steve Hodges		
Frederick A. Hoffman		
Harry Z. Hoffman	2	
Richard P. Hoffman		
Donald C. Holcombe		
Gino Hollander		
James W. Holmbom		

G. Fred Holschuh		
Margaret McC. Holt	2	
Samuel B. Holvey		
Jan Hoowij		
Kris Hotvedt		
Richard Hough		
Dan Howard		
L. Jeffrey Howard		
James Howell		
Chin Hsiao		
Jacqueline Hudson		
Sophie Hughes		
Rbt. Douglas Hunter		
Lubo Hutsaliuk		
Gladys Huyghe	2	

I

James Drake Iams		
Keith Imus		
Robert Indiana	2	
Lucille Ireland		
Xavier Ironside		
Shelia Isham		
Scott Ittner	2	
Joseph Izzo		

J

Beatrice H. Jackson		
Earlene L. Jackson	3	
James W. Jackson		
Nigel Jackson		
Albert Jacobson		
Demetrios Jameson		
Fritz Janschke		
Loren D. Janzen		
Natalie Jasiukynaite		
Al E. Jericoff		
Mira J. Jesse		
Randy Jeter		
George M. Jewell	2	
Jo Johnsen		
May A. Johnson		
Nellie B. Johnson		
Geraldine H. Jolley	2	
Arthur W. Jones		
E. R. Jones		
L. T. Jones		
Alfred Jonniaux	2	
Philip H. Jordan		
I-Hsiung Ju	2	
Allan G. Junier		

K

Marlene Kaar		
George J. Kafka		
Marty Kalb		
Dimitri Kaligos		
Salahattin Kanidinc		
Muriel S. Kaplan		
Morris Katz		
William C. Kautz		
Esther Kee		
Anna Keener		

Daniel Kelleher		
Wm. Muir Kelley	2	
Thomas Henry Kenny		
Robert E. Kerby	2	
Constantine Kermes		
Kenneth A. Kerr		
Roy Kerswill	2	
Edna L. Kessler		
Susan M. Kester		
Marilyn Kettler		
Gaylord B. Kimble		
Nicolas I. King		
Eugene Kingman		
Ken Knutson		
David Klass		
June H. Kleeman		
Oscar Klein		
Gertrude I. Kleinfeld		
Rudolph H. Klemke		
Ann Kocsis	2	
Kathe S. Koelkebeck	3	
Ronald Kolker		
Gerda Kominick		
Nicolaus Koni	2	
Darell Koons		
George Koras		
Nicholas Koren		
Barbara Korman		
Elinore M. Korow	2	
Theo Kortekaas		
Denis Kowal Jr.		
Philip Kraczkowsky		
William H. Kratka		
Mildred Sands Kratz		
Elaine B. Krause		
Barbara M. Kritzler		
Louis Krupp	2	
Van Kuntz		
Rose Kuper		

L

Rose Labrie	3	
Marilyn LaCroix		
Nina Lacy		
Lenore Laine	2	
Patricia Lambert	2	
J. Lois Lampe	3	
James F. Landenberger		
William Landregan		
Leslie Lang		
Joan S. Lang		
Margo Terzian Lang		
Larian		
Mickey C. Lavy		
David Lax		
Anne Lebkicher		
Carol Lee		
C. Ford LeFevre		
Richard D. Lem	2	
Domenic J. Leo		
Phyllis Leon		

Bernard LePoris
Harold M. Le Roy 3
Steve W. Lesnick 3
Rita Letendre
Menahem Lewin
Dick C. Lewis
Roy Lichtenstein 2
Miriam Lieberman
Paul Lightman
Raeford B. Liles
Mary Lindenberg 2
Nancy E. Lindstrom 2
Lipchitz
Janet Lippincott 2
Sidnee L. Livingstone 2
Biganess Livingstone
Richard E. Loehle
Juan L. Logan
Stefan Lokos
Gwen Long
Sandra Long
Bernique Longley 2
Maurice Loriaux
Kristin Lothrop
Kathlyn M. Love 3
Georgetta M. Lucas 2
Ljuba Lukic
Ella Pine Lungren

MC
Lawrence R. Macaray 2
Jere Macaulay 3
James J. McBride
Jeanne C. McClelland 2
Eunice M. McCloskey 2
Valyne McCready
Edward A. McDaniel
Sybill M. McFadden 2
Jim McGrath
Douglas L. McIlvain 2
Janet B. Mackaig
Allison Macomber
Miriam T. McVeigh 2
J. Jay McVicker

M
Carville V. Mace Jr. 3
Fred Machetanz
Stephen B. Mack
Viggo H. Madsen
Maera
M. Magnus-Henderson
Domenico Maida
Florence K. Maisel
Josef B. Majer 2
Zachary Makarenko
Thomas A. Malloy
Robert R. Malone
Michael D. Mandziuk 2
William Mangum 3
Stephen G. Maniatty
Esther S. Manoque 2

Doris Wmson. Mapes 3
Lucille K. Margosian
Andrew J. Marhefka 2
Herman Maril 2
Pearl B. Marsh
Barbara Martell
Eva Martino
William P. Martmer
Bette Mason
Frank Mason
Robert J. Massey
William W. Massey Jr.
George E. Mathesen
Ron Matros 2
Samizu S. Matsuki 2
Ernest Mauthe
Gabriel H. Mayorga 2
Domenico M. Z. Mazzone
Raymond Mazzone
Edward Mazzucchi 2
Chrystella Meador
Libby E. Medrich 3
Barbara Meeker
Mary L. Meixner 2
Carmine Melito
Gerald L. Merfeld 2
James Merlin 3
Cyril Miles
Barbara D. Miller 3
Eva-Hamlin Miller 3
Frank L. Miller 2
George W. Miller 2
Richard Guy Miller
Rock Miller
Winifred C. Miller
John Mitchell
Jo Anne Mix 2
Chiara Moerschel
Cheri Mohn 3
Nanae Momiyama 2
Marc Moon
R. Albert Moore 3
Robert Eric Moore
Talmadge Moose
Nicolas Mordvinoff 2
Darlene Morgan 3
Helen Bosert Morgan
Fritzi M. Morrison
Jimmie Mosely
Robert Motherwell 2
Eugenie Muelhauser
Buell Mullen
Yvonne Muller 2
Willette M. Munz
Richard D. Murray 2
Margaret L. Muth
Richard A. Myer
Sheldon F. Myers

N
Louis E. Nadalini

Connie Naiman
Mary Spencer Nay
LeRoy Neiman
Thesis Newer
Henry Newman
Doris M. Newson
Margery Niblock
Jeannettie D.Nichols 3
Ward H. Nichols 3
Thaddeus Nie 2
Lloyd T. Nightingale 2
Kenneth Noland
Emily Norman
Kenneth E. Norton 2
Anthony Norwood
Anthony Notaro 2
Kazmiera Novak
Gladys S. Novick
Walter Novoshielski
Fred W. Noyes Jr.

O
James O'Brien
Jerzy F. Ochocki
Bruce A. O'Hara
Susan R. Olah
Claes Oldenberg 2
Donald Olsen
Merle Olson 2
Maury Oren
Leila Brashear Orr 2
Paul Ortlip
John Ottiano
Eva V. Owen 3
Vera H. Owen

P
Andrew Palencar
Wasyl Palijczuk
Frank Palmieri
William Panchak
Maria Pangalos
Christopher Parks
Charles C. Parks
Rod Parkinson
Douglas Parshall
Mary F. Passailaigue 3
Patric
Rowena Pattee
E. Terry Patterson
Jehu D. Paulson
Elizabeth W. Pavlansky
John Payne
Ruth M. Payne
Paul J. Penczner 2
Mary Pennington-Walker
Francisco Perez
Ruz Perlman
Larry D. Peterson
Bela Petheo
J. Petty
Carolyn H. Pfluger

Name	
Nan D. Phelps	3
Margaret Philbrick	2
Vinton L. Pickens	2
Anatol Piejko	2
Delilah W. Pierce	
Marcus H. Pini	
James Pinto	
Sera B. Piromalli	
Gerry Pletcher	2
Carolyn Plochmann	
Naomi Policoff	
Anne B. Post	
Georgette S. Powell	
Leslie I. Powell	
Douglas F. Powers	
Roger Preuss	2
William C. Pribble	
Martin Pribil	2
Ray Prohaska	
Puccini	
Ella Rex Price	
Filomena F. Puglisi	
Erna Purrier	

R

Name	
Jack A. Ragland	
Nicolaus Raicevic	
William J. Rakocy	
Paula Randall	
Lois Rapp	
Hildegard Rath	2
Robert Rauschenberg	2
Karine E. Real	
Junius Redwood	2
Jesse F. Reed	2
Rochelle R. Relis	3
James N. Renfro	2
Carolyn C.Reynard	2
Nancy duPont Reynolds	2
Christine Richards	
Suzanne Richards	
Teo Richet	2
Peter Mark Richman	2
Mary L. Rickman	2
Margaret Rigg	
Ronald G. Rigli	3
P. "Grebe" Rimmei	
Dorothea R. Rinehart	2
R. Charles Ringsmuth	3
Clayton Rippey	2
Ruth G. Roberts	
D. Hall Robertson	3
Robert Robinson	
Ron Roesch	
Charles B. Rogers	
Frank Rogers	
James Rogers	2
Miriam Rogers	
Phyllis J. Rogers	3
Ross J. Rohrer	

Name	
Arthur Rose	
James Rosenquist	
Bernard Rosenquit	
Lawrence Rothbart	
Samuel Rothbart	
Trygve A. Rovalstad	3
Ronald L. Ruble	
Rosalie B. Rudolph	
Sallie Snyder Rusinko	

S

Name	
Yasue Sakaoka	3
Gladys L. Salamone	
Antonio Salemme	
Martha Salamme	
Baruj Salinas	
Rick Salzman	
Betty Sammis	2
Emilio Sanchez	
John Sanders	
Izhak Sankowsky	
William Sapp	
J. Thomas Sarvay	3
Marco M. Sassone	
Betty Schabacker	
Susan Schary	3
Linda Schele	
Fred K. Scheibe	
Scheibe-Stucki	
Elizabeth Y Schesch	
Willi Schiener	
Adele M. Schiff	
Fred L. Schmidt	2
Berthold Schmutzhart	
Richard D. Schneider	
Fritz Scholder	
Michael Schreck	
Charles Schucker	
Ilse Schutz	
John Schultze	
Robert Schuman	
Eloisa Schwab	
William Schwartz	
C. Robert Schwieger	
Harold Sclar	
James H. Scorse	
Mary Cooper Scott	
William H. Scott	
Clark T. Scoville	
Mary Scruggs-Spencer	2
Bonnie C. Seaman	
Stephen Searles	
Paul B. Seckel	2
Alice P. Segall	
Ellen J. Selden	
Irene A. Selonke	2
Dorothy E. Senior	2
Rhoda L. Seoane	2
Benson Seto	
Louise Seymour	

Name	
Clifford D. Shank	
Madeleine E. Sharrer	
Vladimir Shatalow	
Mark Shecter	
Chase Shepard	
Lenore Sherman	
Max Shertz	
A. Sherwood	3
Bette W. Sherwood	3
Sheya	
Georg E. Shook	3
Clover V Shore	3
Ben E. Shute	
Keenan W. Shute	
Charles Sibley	
Dennis V. Siville	
Everett H. Simoneau	2
Marilyn J. Simpson	2
Attilio Sinagra	
Hal Singer	2
Sirena	
Elsa K. Skinner	2
James F. Skinner	
Nolan Skipper	
Andrew D. Skolnick	
Oskars Skuskis	3
Thomas Slettehaugh	
James B. Slusser	
Ingeborg Smedresman	
Gay Smith	3
Harry W. Smith	
James Snyder	
Wilb Snyder	2
Joseph Solman	
Sondheimer	
Sydney R. Sonneborn	
Aaron Sopher	
Douglas M. Spaulding	
Barbara S. Spitz	
Elmer G. Sprunger	
Jerry G. Squier	2
John B. Squillace	
Donna Stanley	
John K. Stanley	
George K. Stark	2
Doris Steider	
Maurice J. Stein	2
Norma R. Stein	
Waneita K. Steinert	
Frank Stella	
Bronka Stern	
Lawrence T. Stevens	
Alice Moren Stolpe	
William R. Stolpin	3
Thomas J. Strickland	
Don Stroud	
Margaret E. Stucki	
George R. Stum	3

Carl C. Sublett 3
Esther Sullivan
Robert T. Summers 2
Anne Tunis Summy 2
Kitty L. Sutton
Harriet Sutton
John E. Swenson 3
Henry A. Swierczynski
Walter Swyrydenko 2
Lenore R. Szesko 2
Konstantyn Szonk-Rusych
June Alaine Szueber 2
Steve E. Szueber

T

Cornelia Damian Tait 3
Rodulfo R. Tardo
C. Fred Taylor
John T. L. Tcheng 3
Marj Teague
Marjorie B. Teller
Jan Ten-Broeke
Virginia A. Terpening 3
Emalita N. Terry
Gary L. Tevis
Valfred Thelin
Elaine Thomas
Reynolds Thomas
Steffen Thomas
Thalia Ann Thomas 2
Louise B. Thomas
Alan F. Thurlow
Mary Keim Tietze
Joyce Timberlake 3
Alton S. Tobey 2
Marjorie Tomchuk 3
Richard Tomlinson
Lois B. Tracy
Helen Treadwell
Olive M. Troemper 2
Helene Trosky
Elma G. Troutman
Leroy Troyer
Virginia True
Hsiao-Hsia Tsai 2
Charles Tucker
Julia G. Turchuk
John E. Turley Jr.
Arthur Turner
Janet E. Turner 3
Ann Turri
Cy Twombly 2
Leo F. Twiggs

U

Evelyn N. Underwood 3
William E. Unger 2
Arthur Upelnieks
Mychajlo R. Urban 2
Richard Carl Urso
A. A. Ushenko 3

V

Florestee Vance
George W. Vance 2
Gloria I. Vachon
Amanda VanDerVoort 2
Mary Van Meter
Rose Van Vranken
Henry Van Wolf 3
Mario A. Vara 2
Ken Vares 2
John Vargo
"Vincent"
JohnVoelker
Elizabeth Veslock 2
Tom Vincent
Peter R. Violante
Ernest Von-Neschke
Von Szitanyi-Walewska 2

W

Eugene Waddell 2
Noble G. Wagner
Herbert B. Walker
Roscoe E. Wallace
Pauline Wallen
Chi-Chien Wang
Andy Warhol 2
Warren P. Whitson
Stella Warwick
Frances M. Watford 2
Bob Watts
June C. Wayne
Joseph C. Webb
Martha Rhea Webb
Emil Weddige 2
Shirley M. Weeks
Roswell Weidner
Jerome H. Weinberger
Anita K. Weiner
Anna Weintraub
David Weisberg
Anton Weiss
Liningston Welch
Duke Wellington 2
Val Welman
Tom Wesselmann
Michael West
Charles M. Wetzel 3
Jay. G. Weynn
Barbara Whipple 2
Ruth McKitrick White 2
Eugene Whitlow
M. Grace Wible 3
Robert M. Wick
Aba Wielhorski
Bill Wiggins 3
Gordon C. Wilcox
John Wilkison
Gerry Williams
Jean T. Williams 3

Robert A. Williams
Tommy Williams
William T. Williams
Dorothy Willingham
Marie S. Wilner 3
Glenn L. Wilson
Joseph P. Wilson 2
Marjorie Wilson
Arthur H. Winer
John Wisinski
St. Regina Wojinski
Ching Wong
Robert E. Wood
Charles E. Wright
Frank E. Wurster
Alfred J. Wyatt 2
Andrew Wyeth 2

X

Xantn

Y

Angela A. Yates (MIA)
Marvin C. Yates
Clifford Yerks
Matsugoro Yoshida
Marlene Yu

Z

Olafs Zeidenbergs
Mildred Zindler
William T. Zivic
Frank Zuccarelli
Ruth V. Zuckerman

(A) Painter; (A₁) Watercolorist; (B) Sculptor; (C) Printmaker; (D) Assemblagist;
(E) Teacher; (F) Happenings; (G) Mosaicist; (H) Draftsman

1. Aach, Herb (A)
2. Acton, Arlo C. (B)
3. Adams, Clinton (A,C)
4. Adams, Pat (A)
5. Adler, Samuel M. (A)
6. Agostini, Peter (B)
7. Albers, Josef (A,C,E)
8. Albert, Calvin (B)
9. Albright, Ivan Le Lorraine (A
10. Alcalay, Albert (A)
11. Alston, Charles Henry (A)
12. Altman, Harold (C,A)
13. Altoon, John (A)
14. Amen, Irving (C)
15. Anderson, Guy Irving (A)
16. Anderson, Jeremy R. (B)
17. Anderson, John S. (B)
18. Anderson, Lennart (A)
19. Andre, Carl (B)
20. Andrejevic, Milet (A)
    An **dre** avic, Millet
21. Andrews, Oliver (B)
22. Antonakos, Stephen (B)
23. Antreasian, Garo (C)
    An **tray** sian
24. Anuszkiewicz, Richard (A)
    Anu **skay** vitch
25. Archipenko, Alexander (B,E)
26. Arman (B,D)
27. Aronson, David (A)
28. Artschwager, Richard (A,B)
29. Atherton, John C. (A)
30. Ault, George C. (A)
31. Austin, Darrel (A)
32. Avedisian, Edward (A)
33. Avery, Milton (A)
34. Azuma, Norio (C)
35. Baber, Alice (A)
36. Baizerman, Saul (B)
37. Bannard, Darby (A)
38. Baringer, Richard E. (A)
39. Barnes, Robert (A)
40. Barnet, Will (A,C,E)
41. Baskin, Leonard (B,C,E)
42. Bauermeister, Mary (A,D)
43. Bayer, Herbert (A)
44. Baylinson, A.S. (A)
45. Baziotes, William A. (A,E)
46. Beal, Gifford (A)
47. Beal, Jack (A)
48. Bearden, Romare (A)
    Roh **mayr**
49. Beattie, George (A)
50. Beauchamp, Robert (A)
    Beecham
51. Bechtle, Robert (A)
    Beck tle
52. Beck, Rosemarie (A)
53. Behl, Wolfgang (B)
54. Bell, Larry (B)
55. Bengston, Billy Al (A)
56. Benjamin, Karl (A)
57. Benton, Fletcher (B)
58. Benton, Thomas Hart (A,E)
59. Ben-Zion (A)

60. Berger, Jason (A)
61. Berman, Eugene (A)
62. Bertoia, Harry (B)
    Ber **toy** a
63. Bess, Forrest Clemenger (A)
64. Biddle, George (A,C)
65. Biederman, Charles (Karel)
    Joseph (B)
    Bee derman
66. Bireline, George (A)
    Beer e line
67. Bischoff, Elmer (A)
    Bish off
68. Bishop, Isabel (A)
69. Bisttram, Emil (A,E)
70. Blackburn, Morris (C)
71. Blaine, Nell (A)
72. Blanch, Arnold (A)
73. Blaustein, Al (A)
74. Bleifeld, Stanley (A)
75. Bloch, Albert (A)
76. Bloom, Hyman (A)
77. Bluemner, Oscar (A)
    Bloom ner
78. Bluhm, Norman (A)
    Bloom
79. Blume, Peter (A)
80. Boardman, Seymour (A)
81. Bodin, Paul (A)
82. Boghosian, Varujan (B,D)
83. Bohrod, Aaron (A,E)
84. Bolomey, Roger (B)
    Bolo **may**
85. Bolotowsky, Ilya (A,B,E)
86. Bontecou, Lee (B)
87. Booth, Cameron (A,E)
88. Bosa, Louis (A)
89. Bothwell, Dorr (C,A)
90. Botkin, Henry (A)
91. Bouché, Louis (A,E)
    Boo **shay**
92. Bourgeois, Louise (B)
    Boo **zwah**
93. Bowman, Geoffrey (A)
94. Bowman, Richard (A)
95. Boyce, Richard (B,E)
96. Boyle, Keith (A)
97. Boynton, James W. (A)
98. Brach, Paul (A)
    Brock
99. Brackman, Robert (A)
100. Brandt, Warren (A)
101. Brecht, George (A,B,D,F)
102. Breer, Robert C. (B)
103. Breinin, Raymond (A,E)
    Brennan
104. Brice, William (A)
105. Briggs, Ernest (A)
106. Broderson, Morris (Gaylord
107. Broderson, Robert M. (A)
108. Brodie, Gandy (A)
109. Broner, Robert (A,C)
    Brauner
110. Brook, Alexander (A)
111. Brooks, James (A)

112. Brown, Carlyle (A)
113. Brown, Joan (A)
114. Brown, William Theo (A)
115. Browne, Byron (A,E)
116. Browning, Colleen (A)
117. Bruce, Patrick Henry (A)
118. Bultman, Fritz (A,B)
119. Bunce, Louis (A)
120. Burchfield, Charles (A₁)
121. Burkhardt, Hans Gustav (A)
122. Burlin, Paul (A)
123. Burliuk, David (A)
124. Cadmus, Paul (A)
125. Caesar, Doris (B)
126. Cajori, Charles (A)
127. Calcagno, Lawrence (A)
    Cal **cahn** yo
128. Calder, Alexander (B)
129. Callahan, Kenneth (A)
130. Callery, Mary (B)
131. Campoli, Cosmo (B)
132. Candell, Victor (A,E)
133. Caparn, Rhys (B)
    Ca **parn**, Reese
134. Carewe, Sylvia (A)
135. Carles, Arthur B. (A,E)
    Carls
136. Casarella, Edmond (C)
137. Castellon, Federico (C,A)
138. Cavallon, Giorgio (A)
139. Chaet, Bernard (A)
    Chate
140. Chamberlain, Elwin (A)
141. Chamberlain, John (B)
142. Cherney, Marvin (A)
143. Chesney, Lee R., Jr. (A)
144. Chinni, Peter (B)
    Keeny
145. Christopher, William (A)
146. Chryssa (B)
    Kree sa
147. Cicero, Carmen Louis (A)
148. Cikovsky, Nicolai (A,E)
    Sih **kahv** ski
149. Cloar, Carroll (A)
    Clore
150. Clutz, William (A)
151. Coates, Ross (A)
152. Congdon, William (A)
153. Conner, Bruce (D,A)
154. Conover, Robert (A)
155. Constant, George (A)
156. Cook, Howard (A)
157. Corbett, Edward (A)
158. Corbino, Jon (A)
159. Cornell, Joseph (D)
160. Covert, John (A)
161. Cowles, Russell (A)
    Coles
162. Cramer, Konrad (A)
163. Crampton, Rollin McNeil
164. Crawford, Ralston (A)
165. Cremean, Robert (B)
    Cre **mee** an
166. Criss, Francis H. (A)

167. Cronbach, Robert M. (B)
168. Curry, John Steuart (A)
169. Cusumano, Stefano (A)
170. Daphnis, Nassos (A,B)
171. D'Arcangelo, Allan (A)
172. D'Arista, Robert (A)
173. Darrow, Paul Gardner (A)
174. Dasburg, Andrew (A)
175. Dash, Robert (A)
176. Davey, Randall (A)
177. Davis, Gene (A)
178. Davis, Jerrold (A)
179. Davis, Ronald (A)
180. Davis, Stuart (A)
181. Day, Worden (A)
182. Decker, Lindsey (B)
183. de Creeft, Jose (B)
184. Deem, George (A)
185. De Erdely, Francis (A,E)
186. De Forest, Roy Dean (A)
187. Dehn, Adolf Arthur (A,C)
188. Dehner, Dorothy (B)
189. de Kooning, Elaine (A)
190. de Kooning, Willem (A)
191. DeLap, Tony (B)
192. Della-Volpe, Ralph (A)
193. De Maria, Walter (B)
194. De Martini, Joseph (A)
195. de Moulpied, Deborah (B)
196. Demuth, Charles (A)
197. De Niro, Robert (A)
198. de Rivera, Jose (B)
199. Deshaies, Arthur (C)
    Da shay
200. Dickinson, Edwin (A,E)
201. Diebenkorn, Richard (A)
    Dee ben korn
202. Diller, Burgoyne (A,E)
203. Dine, Jim (A,F)
204. di Suvero, Mark (B)
205. Dobkin, Alexander (A)
206. Dodd, Lamar (A,E)
207. Dodd, Lois (A)
208. Dole, William (A)
209. Donati, Enrico (A)
210. Dove, Arthur G. (A)
211. Downing, Thomas (A)
212. Doyle, Tom (B)
213. Drewes, Werner (A,E)
214. Drummond, Sally Hazelet
215. Du Bois, Guy Pene (A)
    Du Bwah
216. Duchamp, Marcel (A)
217. Dugmore, Edward (A)
218. Dzubas, Friedel (A)
219. Edie, Stuart (A,E)
220. Edmondson, Leonard (A)
221. Elliott, Ronnie (A)
222. Engel, Jules (A)
223. Engman, Robert (B)
224. Ernst, Jimmy (A)
225. Etting, Emlen (A)
226. Evergood, Philip Howard F
    Dixon (A)
227. Farr, Fred W. (B)
228. Feeley, Paul (A,E)
229. Feininger, Lyonel (A)
230. Feitelson, Lorser (A)
231. Fenton, Alan (A)
232. Ferber, Herbert (B)
233. Ferren, John (A,E)

234. Fiene, Ernest (A)
    Fine
235. Flannagan, John (B)
236. Flavin, Dan (B)
237. Fleischmann, Adolf R. (A)
238. Floch, Joseph (A)
    Flack
239. Follett, Jean F. (A,D)
240. Forakis, Peter (A,B)
    For ah kis
241. Forst, Miles (A)
242. Fortess, Karl E. (A)
    For tess
243. Foulkes, Llyn (A)
    Folks
244. Francis, Sam (A,C)
245. Frank, Mary (B)
246. Frankenthaler, Helen (A)
247. Frasconi, Antonio (C)
248. Freilicher, Jane (A)
    Fry likker
249. French, Jared (A)
    Jard
250. Friedensohn, Elias (A,B)
251. Fuller, Sue (B)
252. Gabo, Naum Neemia
253. Gallatin, Albert E. (A)
    Gal atin
254. Gallo, Frank (B)
255. Ganso, Emil (A)
256. Gatch, Lee (A)
257. Gechtoff, Sonia (A)
    Getch toff
258. Gelb, Jan (A)
259. George, Thomas (A)
260. Georges, Paul (A)
    George's
261. Giambruni, Tio (B)
    Jam bru ni
262. Gibran, Kahlil (A)
263. Gikow, Ruth (A)
    Geeko
264. Gill, James (A)
265. Giobbi, Edward (A)
266. Girona, Julio (B)
    Ji ro na
267. Glackens, William (A)
268. Glarner, Fritz (A)
269. Glasco, Joseph (A)
270. Goldberg, Michael (A)
271. Goldin, Leon (A)
272. Golub, Leon (A)
273. Gonzalez, Xavier (A)
274. Goodman, Sidney (A)
275. Goodnough, Robert (A)
    Good know
276. Goodyear, John (B)
277. Gorchov, Ron (A)
278. Gordin, Sidney (B)
279. Gorky, Arshile (A)
280. Goto, Joseph (B)
281. Gottlieb, Adolph (A)
282. Goulet, Lorrie (B)
    Goo lay
283. Graham, John D. (A)
284. Graham, Robert (B)
285. Granlund, Paul (B)
286. Grant, James (A)
287. Graves, Morris Cole (A)
288. Gray, Cleve (A)

289. Greene, Balcomb (A,E)
290. Greene, Stephen (A)
291. Greenly, Colin (B)
292. Grillo, John (A)
293. Grippe, Peter (B)
    Grippy
294. Grooms, Red (A,F)
295. Gropper, William (A,C)
296. Gross, Chaim (B)
297. Grosser, Maurice (A)
298. Grosvenor, Robert (B)
299. Grosz, George (A,C)
300. Guerrero, José (A)
301. Guglielmi, O. Louis (A)
302. Gussow, Alan (A)
303. Gussow, Roy (B)
304. Guston, Philip (A)
305. Guy, James (B,A)
    G'eye
306. Gwathmey, Robert (A)
307. Hadzi, Dimitri (B)
308. Haines, Richard (A)
309. Hale, Nathan Cabot (B)
310. Hale, Robert Beverly (A,E)
311. Haley, John Charles (A)
312. Hammersley, Frederick (A)
313. Hansen, James Lee (B)
314. Hansen, Robert (A)
315. Hare, David (A,B)
316. Harris, Paul (B)
317. Hartell, John (A)
318. Hartigan, Grace (A)
319. Hartl, Leon (A)
320. Hartley, Marsden (A)
321. Hartman, Robert (A)
322. Harvey, James (A)
323. Harvey, Robert (A)
324. Hatchett, Duayne (B)
325. Hayes, David V. (B)
326. Hebald, Milton (B)
    Hee bald
327. Held, Al (A)
328. Heliker, John Edward (A)
329. Hendler, Raymond (A)
330. Henry, Charles T. (A)
331. Higgins, Edward (B)
332. Hillsmith, Fannie (A)
333. Hinman, Charles (A,B)
334. Hirsch, Joseph (A)
335. Hofmann, Hans (A,E)
336. Holty, Carl Robert (A)
337. Hopkins, Budd (A)
338. Hopper, Edward (A)
339. Horiuchi, Paul (A)
340. Hovannes, John (A)
341. Howard, Charles (A)
342. Howard, Robert A. (B)
343. Hudson, Robert H. (B)
344. Hueter, James W. (A)
    Hooter
345. Hultberg, John (A)
346. Humphrey, Ralph (A)
347. Hunt, Richard (B)
348. Huot, Robert (B)
    Hew itt
349. Indiana, Robert (A)
350. Insley, Will (B)
351. Ippolito, Angelo (A)
352. Irwin, Robert (A,B)
353. Jacobs, David (B)

354. Jarvaise, James (A)
       Zhar **vez**
355. Jenkins, Paul (A)
356. Jensen, Alfred (A)
357. Johns, Jasper (A)
358. Johnson, Ben (A)
359. Johnson, Buffie (A)
360. Johnson, Lester (A)
361. Johnson, Ray (D)
362. Johnston, Ynez (A)
       Eye nez
363. Jones, Howard W. (B)
364. Jones, John Paul (A,C)
365. Judd, Don (B)
366. Kabak, Robert (A)
367. Kacere, John (A)
       Ka **sear** ee
368. Kahn, Wolf (A)
369. Kaish, Luise (B)
370. Kamihira, Ben (A)
371. Kamrowski, Gerome (A,E)
372. Kamys, Walter (A,E)
       Came case
373. Kanemitsu, Matsumi (A)
374. Kantor, Morris (A,E)
375. Kaprow, Allan (A,D,F)
376. Karfiol, Bernard (A)
377. Kasten, Karl (A)
378. Katz, Alex (A)
379. Katzman, Herbert (A)
380. Kauffman, Craig (B)
381. Kearl, Stanley Brandon (B)
       Curl
382. Kearns, James (A)
       Carns
383. Kelly, Ellsworth (A)
384. Kelly, James (A)
385. Kelly, León (León Kelly *y*
       Corrons) (A)
386. Kent, Rockwell (A)
387. Kepes, Gyorgy (A,E)
       Kep ish
388. Keyser, Robert (A)
389. Kienbusch, William (A)
       Keen bush
390. Kienholz, Edward (B,D)
391. Kiesler, Frederick J. (B,A)
       Kees ler
392. King, William Dickey (B)
393. Kipniss, Robert (A)
394. Kipp, Lyman (B)
395. Kirschenbaum, Jules (A)
396. Kline, Franz (A)
397. Knaths, Karl (A)
       (*pron.* K)
398. Koch, Gerd (A)
       Coke
399. Koch, John (A)
       Coke
400. Koenig, John Franklin (A)
       Kay nig
401. Kohn, Gabriel (B)
402. Kohn, Misch (C)
403. Konzal, Joseph (B)
404. Kopman, Benjamin (A)
405. Koppelman, Chaim (C,A)
406. Kortlander, William Clark
407. Krasner, Lee (A)
408. Kriesberg, Irving (A)
       Crize berg

409. Kroll, Leon (A)
410. Krushenick, Nicholas (A)
       Croosh nick
411. Kuhn, Walt (A)
412. Kulicke, Robert (A)
       Cue lick
413. Kuniyoshi, Yasuo (A,E)
414. Kuntz, Roger (A)
415. Kupferman, Lawrence (A,E)
416. Labaudt, Lucien (A)
       Lah **bowe**
417. Lachaise, Gaston (B)
       La **shey**
418. Lamis, Leroy (B)
419. Landau, Jacob (A,C)
420. Landon, Edward (A)
421. Landsman, Stanley (B)
422. Langlais, Bernard (B,A)
       Langley
423. Laning, Edward (A)
       Lanning
424. Lansner, Fay (A)
425. Lanyon, Ellen (A)
426. Lasansky, Mauricio (C,E)
427. Lassaw, Ibram (B)
428. Laufman, Sidney (A)
429. Laurent, John (A)
430. Laurent, Robert (B,E)
431. Lawrence, Jacob (A)
432. Lawson, Ernest (A)
433. Lebrun, Rico (A,E)
434. Lechay, James (A,E)
       Le **shey**
435. Leiber, Gerson (C)
436. Lekakis, Michael (B)
437. Leong, James C. (A)
       Lee ong
438. Leslie, Alfred (A)
439. Levee, John (A)
440. Levi, Josef (B)
441. Levi, Julian (A)
442. Levine, Jack (A)
443. Levinson, Mon (A)
444. Levitan, Israel (B)
445. Lewandowski, Edmund D.
       Lew and ow ski
446. Lewis, Norman (A)
447. LeWitt, Sol (B)
448. Liberman, Alexander (A,B)
449. Lichtenstein, Roy (A)
       Lick ten stine
450. Lindner, Richard (A)
451. Lipchitz, Jacques (B)
       (*pron.* sch)
452. Lippold, Richard (B)
453. Lipton, Seymour (B)
454. Lobdell, Frank (A)
455. Loberg, Robert W. (A)
456. Loew, Michael (A)
       Lowe
457. Loran, Erle (A,E)
458. Louis, Morris (A)
       Lewis
459. Lozowick, Louis (A)
460. Lukin, Sven (B)
461. Lund, David (A)
462. Lundeberg, Helen (A)
463. Lye, Len (B)
464. Lytle, Richard (A)
       Littell
465. Macdonald-Wright, Stanton

466. Machlin, Sheldon (B)
467. MacIver, Loren (A)
       Mac Eye ver
468. Maldarelli, Oronzio (B)
469. Mallary, Robert (B)
470. Mallory, Ronald (B)
471. Man Ray (A)
472. Manship, Paul (B)
473. Manso, Leo (A)
474. Marca-Relli, Conrad (A)
475. Marcus, Marcia (A)
476. Margo, Boris (A,C)
477. Marin, John (A₁)
478. Marisol (Escobar) (B)
479. Markman, Ronald (A)
480. Marsh, Reginald (A,E)
481. Marsicano, Nicholas (A)
482. Martin, Fletcher (A)
483. Martin, Fred (A,H)
484. Martin, Knox (A)
485. Martinelli, Ezio (B)
486. Maryan (A,C)
487. Mason, Alice Trumbull (A)
488. Matulka, Jan (A,E)
489. Mayhew, Richard (A)
490. Mazur, Michael B. (A)
491. McChesney, Robert P. (A)
492. McClellan, Douglas Eugene
493. McFee, Henry Lee (A)
494. McGarrell, James (A)
495. McLaughlin, John (A)
496. McNeil, George (A)
497. Meeker, Dean Jackson (C)
498. Mehring, Howard (A)
       May ring
499. Meigs, Walter (A)
       Megs
500. Menkes, Sigmund (A)
       Menkeys
501. Mesibov, Hugh (B)
502. Mestrovic, Ivan (B)
503. Metcalf, James (B)
504. Miller, Kenneth Hayes (A,E)
505. Miller, Richard McDermott
506. Millman, Edward (A)
507. Mitchell, Fred (A)
508. Mitchell, Joan (A)
509. Mitchell, Wallace (A)
510. Moholy-Nagy, Lazlo (B)
511. Moller, Hans (A)
512. Morin, Thomas (B)
513. Morris, Carl (A)
514. Morris, George L. K. (A)
515. Morris, Kyle R. (A)
516. Morris, Robert (A,B,F)
517. Motherwell, Robert (A)
518. Moy, Seong (A)
519. Moyer, Roy (A)
520. Muller, Jan (A)
521. Mullican, Lee (A)
522. Murch, Walter Tandy (A)
523. Murray, Robert (B)
524. Nadelman, Elie (B)
525. Nakian, Reuben (B)
526. Natkin, Robert (A)
527. Neal, Reginald (A,C)
528. Nepote, Alexander (A)
       Ne **po** ty
529. Nesbitt, Lowell (A)

530. Neuman, Robert S. (A)
        Newman
531. Nevelson, Louise (B)
532. Nevelson, Mike (B)
533. Newbill, Al (A)
534. Newman, Barnett (A)
535. Nivola, Constantino (B)
536. Noguchi, Isamu (B)
537. Noland, Kenneth (A)
538. Nordfeldt, B. J. O. (A)
539. Nowack, Wayne K. (A)
540. O'Hanlon, Richard (B)
541. Ohashi, Yutaka (A)
542. Okada, Kenzo (A)
543. Okamura, Arthur (A)
544. O'Keeffe, Georgia (A)
545. Oldenburg, Claes Thure (A
        Klaus
546. Olitski, Jules (A)
547. Oliveira, Nathan (A)
548. Onslow-Ford, Gordon (A)
549. Opper, John (A,E)
550. Ortman, George (A)
551. Ossorio, Alfonso (A)
552. Osver, Arthur (A)
553. Pace, Stephen (A)
554. Pachner, William (A)
        Pack ner
555. Packard, David (B)
556. Padovano, Anthony (B)
557. Palmer, William C. (A)
558. Paone, Peter (A,C)
        Pay oh ni
559. Paris, Harold P. (B)
560. Park, David (A)
561. Parker, Raymond (A)
562. Parker, Robert Andrew (A)
563. Pasilis, Felix (A)
564. Pattison, Abbott (B)
565. Peake, Channing (A)
566. Pearlstein, Philip (A)
567. Pearson, Henry Charles (A)
568. Peirce, Waldo (A)
569. Penney, James (A)
570. Pereira, I. Rice (A)
        Per err a
571. Perlin, Bernard (A)
572. Peterdi, Gabor (C,A)
        Pet erdi
573. Petersen, Roland Conrad (A
574. Pfriem, Bernard (A)
        Freem
575. Pineda, Marianna (B)
        (pron. ñ)
576. Pittman, Hobson L. (A)
577. Pollack, Reginald (A)
578. Pollock, Jackson (A)
579. Ponce de León, Michael (C)
580. Pond, Clayton (A,C)
581. Poons, Larry (A)
582. Poor, Henry Varnum (A)
583. Porter, David (A)
584. Porter, Fairfield (A)
585. Pousette-Dart, Nathaniel (A
586. Pousette-Dart, Richard (A)
587. Pozzatti, Rudy (C)
588. Prestopino, Gregorio (A)
589. Price, Clayton S. (A)
590. Price, Kenneth (A)
591. Quirt, Walter (A,E)

592. Quisgard, Liz Whitney (A)
593. Rabkin, Leo (A)
594. Racz, Andre (A,C)
        Racks
595. Raffael, Joseph (A)
596. Ramos, Mel (A)
597. Randell, Richard K. (B)
598. Rattner, Abraham (A)
599. Rauschenberg, Robert (A)
600. Reder, Bernard (B)
601. Reichek, Jesse (A,H)
602. Reinhardt, Ad (A,E)
603. Reinhardt, Seigfried Gerhard
604. Remington, Deborah (A)
605. Resika, Paul (A)
        Res i ka
606. Resnick, Milton (A)
607. Reynal, Jeanne (G)
608. Rice, Dan (A)
609. Richenburg, Robert B. (A)
610. Rickey, George (B)
611. Rivers, Larry (A,B)
612. Robinson, Boardman (A,E)
613. Robus, Hugo (B)
614. Rocklin, Raymond (B)
615. Roesch, Kurt (A,E)
        Resh
616. Rogalski, Walter (C)
617. Rohm, Robert (B)
618. Ronald, William (A)
619. Rood, John (B,E)
620. Rosati, James (B)
621. Rosenborg, Ralph M. (A)
622. Rosenquist, James (A)
623. Rosenthal, Bernard (B)
624. Ross, Charles (B)
625. Roszak, Theodore (B)
626. Roth, Frank (A)
627. Rothko, Mark (A)
628. Ruben, Richards (A)
629. Ruscha, Edward (A,H)
        Roo shay
630. Russell, Morgan (A)
631. Ruvolo, Felix (A,E)
632. Sage, Kay (A)
633. Salemme, Attilio (A)
634. Samaras, Lucas (D)
635. Sander, Ludwig (A)
636. Sandol, Maynard (A)
637. Sato, Tadashi (A)
638. Saul, Peter (A)
639. Saunders, Raymond (A)
640. Savelli, Angelo (A,C)
641. Scarpitta, Salvatore (A)
642. Schanker, Louis (A,C,B)
643. Schapiro, Miriam (A)
644. Schlemowitz, Abram (B)
645. Schmidt, Julius (B)
646. Schnakenberg, Henry (A)
647. Schrag, Karl (A,C)
648. Schucker, Charles (A)
649. Schueler, Jon (A)
        Shooler
650. Schwabacher, Ethel (A)
651. Schwartz, Manfred (A,E)
652. Segal, George (B)
653. Seley, Jason (B)
654. Seliger, Charles (A)
655. Seligmann, Kurt (A,C)
656. Sennhauser, John (A)

657. Serisawa, Sueo (A)
658. Shahn, Ben (A)
659. Shaw, Charles (A)
660. Sheeler, Charles (A)
661. Sheets, Millard (A)
662. Shinn, Everett (A)
663. Simon, Sidney (B)
664. Simpson, David (A)
665. Sinton, Nell (A)
666. Siporin, Mitchell (A)
667. Sloan, John (A,E)
668. Smith, David (B)
669. Smith, Hassel W., Jr. (A)
670. Smith, Leon Polk (A)
671. Smithson, Robert (B)
672. Snelgrove, Walter (A)
673. Snelson, Kenneth (B)
674. Solomon, Hyde (A)
675. Solomon, Syd (A)
676. Sonenberg, Jack (A)
677. Soyer, Moses (A)
678. Soyer, Raphael (A)
679. Speicher, Eugene (A)
        Spiker
680. Spencer, Niles (A)
681. Spohn, Clay E. (A,E)
682. Sprinchorn, Carl (A)
        Sprin corn
683. Spruance, Benton (A,C)
684. Spruce, Everett (A)
685. Squier, Jack (B)
686. Stamos, Theodoros (A)
687. Stanczak, Julian (A,E)
        Stan zak
688. Stankiewicz, Richard P. (B)
        Stan kyay vitch
689. Stanley, Robert (A,C)
690. Stasik, Andrew (C)
691. Stefanelli, Joseph (A)
692. Steg, J. L. (C)
693. Stein, Ronald (A)
694. Steinberg, Saul (H)
695. Stella, Frank (A)
696. Stella, Joseph (A)
697. Stern, Gerd (B)
698. Sternberg, Harry (C,E)
699. Sterne, Hedda (A)
700. Sterne, Maurice (A)
701. Stevenson, Harold (A)
702. Still, Clyfford (A,E)
703. Stout, Myron S. (A)
704. Stuempfig, Walter (A)
        Stum fig
705. Sugarman, George (B)
706. Summers, Carol (C)
707. Suttman, Paul (B)
708. Suzuki, James Hiroshi (A)
709. Takai, Teiji (A)
710. Takal, Peter (C)
711. Talbot, William H. M. (B)
712. Tam, Reuben (A,E)
713. Tanguy, Yves (A,C)
        Tan ghee, Eve
714. Tania (Schreiber) (B)
715. Taubes, Frederic (A,E)
        Taubs
716. Tchelitchew, Pavel (A)
        Chel itcheff
717. Thek, Paul (B)

718. Thiebaud, Wayne (A,E)
        Tee bowe
719. Thomas, Robert C. (B)
720. Thompson, Bob (A)
721. Tobey, Mark (A)
722. Tomlin, Bradley Walker (A)
723. Tooker, George (A)
724. Tovish, Harold (B,E)
725. Townley, Hugh (B)
726. Treiman, Joyce (A,B)
        Tree man
727. Trova, Ernest (B,D)
728. Tsutakawa, George (A,E)
729. Twardowicz, Stanley (A)
        Twardo witz
730. Twombly, Cy (A)
731. Tworkov, Jack (A,E)
732. Vander Sluis, George (B,E)
        Sluice
733. Vasilieff, Nicholas (A,E)
734. Vass, Gene (A)
735. Vicente, Esteban (A)
736. Vollmer, Ruth (B)
737. Von Schlegell, David (B)
738. Von Weigand, Charmion (A
        Wee gand, Sharmion
739. von Wicht, John (A)
        Vicht
740. Voulkos, Peter (B,E)
        Vole kos
741. Vytlacil, Vaclav (A,E)
        Vitt la sill
742. Wald, Sylvia (A,C)
743. Waldman, Paul (A)
744. Walkowitz, Abraham (A)
745. Warhol, Andy (A)
746. Warshaw, Howard (A)
747. Washington, James W., Jr.
748. Watkins, Franklin C. (A)
749. Watts, Robert M. (D,F)
750. Wayne, June (A,C)
751. Weber, Hugo (A)
752. Weber, Max (A)
753. Weeks, James (A)
754. Weinberg, Elbert (B)
755. Weinrib, David (B)
756. Welliver, Neil (A)
        Williver
757. Wesselmann, Tom (A)
758. Westermann, H. C. (B)
759. Whitman, Robert (A,F)
760. Wieghardt, Paul (A,E)
        Wig hart
761. Wilde, John (A,E)
        Will dee
762. Wiley, William T. (A)
763. Wilfred, Thomas (Richard E
        Løvstrøm) (B)
764. Wilke, Ulfert S. (A)
        Will ka
765. Willenbecher, John (B)
        beck
766. Williams, Hiram (A)
767. Williams, Neil (A)
768. Wilson, Jane (A)
769. Wines, James (B)
770. Woelffer, Emerson (A)
771. Wolff, Robert Jay (A,E)

772. Wolfson, Sidney (A)
773. Wonner, Paul John (A)
774. Wood, Grant (A)
775. Wyeth, Andrew (A)
776. Xceron, Jean (A)
        Zeron
777. Yektai, Manoucher (A)
        Manu shay
778. Youngerman, Jack (A)
779. Yunkers, Adja (A,C)
        Odd ya
780. Zacharias, Athos (A)
        Zacka rye as
781. Zajac, Jack (B)
782. Zammitt, Norman (B)
783. Zerbe, Karl (A)
784. Zogbaum, Wilfrid (B)
785. Zorach, Marguerite (A)
786. Zorach, William (B)
787. Zox, Larry (A)